FOUNDATIONS OF

International Migration Law

International migration law is an important field of international law, which has attracted exceptional interest in recent years. This book has been written from a wide variety of perspectives for those wanting to understand the legal framework that regulates migration. It is intended for those who are new to this field of study who seek an overview of its many components. It will also appeal to those who have focussed on a particular branch of international migration law but require an understanding of how their specialisation fits with other branches of the discipline – students in international law, migration policy officers, diplomatic and consular stuff, as well as international organisations. Written by migration law specialists and led by respected international experts, this volume draws upon the combined knowledge of international migration law and policy from academia, international, intergovernmental, regional and non-governmental organisations, and national governments. Additional features include case studies, maps, break-out boxes and references to resources, which allow for a full understanding of the law in context.

Brian Opeskin is Professor of Legal Governance at Macquarie University, Sydney. He researches in the broad field of public law, including international migration law and human rights, and has a special interest in interdisciplinary study that examines the intersection between public law and population processes. He previously held positions as Deputy President of the Australian Law Reform Commission, as Head of the Law School at the University of the South Pacific in Vanuatu, and as Associate Professor at Sydney University. He is a Fellow of the Australian Academy of Law.

Richard Perruchoud was, until 2011, Director of the International Migration Law and Legal Affairs Department at the International Organization for Migration ('IOM') in Geneva. Before joining IOM in 1982 he was Adjunct Professor of International Law at the Graduate Institute of International Studies in Geneva and a visiting scholar at Harvard Law School. He has published widely on migration law, human rights and international humanitarian law.

Jillyanne Redpath-Cross has worked for a number of years as a Senior Legal Officer in the Department of International Migration Law and Legal Affairs at the International Organization for Migration in Geneva. During her time at IOM she has worked on issues such as the human rights of migrants, comparative immigration law and policies, migration and security, and smuggling and trafficking in human beings. Prior to joining IOM, she worked as a university lecturer and as an attorney in Australia.

International Organization for Migration (IOM)

FOUNDATIONS OF
International Migration Law

EDITED BY

Brian Opeskin
Richard Perruchoud
Jillyanne Redpath-Cross

CAMBRIDGE
UNIVERSITY PRESS

CAMBRIDGE
UNIVERSITY PRESS

University Printing House, Cambridge CB2 8BS, United Kingdom

Cambridge University Press is part of the University of Cambridge.

It furthers the University's mission by disseminating knowledge in the pursuit of
education, learning and research at the highest international levels of excellence.

www.cambridge.org
Information on this title: www.cambridge.org/9781107608368

© Cambridge University Press 2012

First published 2012

A catalogue record for this publication is available from the British Library

Library of Congress Cataloguing in Publication data
Foundations of international migration law / Edited by Brian Opeskin . . . [et al.].
    p. cm.
Includes bibliographical references and index.
ISBN 978-1-107-01771-9
1. Emigration and immigration law.   2. Refugees – Legal status, laws, etc.
3. Freedom of movement (International law)   I. Opeskin, Brian R.
K3275.F68   2012
342.08′2–dc23

                                                                    2012015493

ISBN 978-1-107-01771-9 Hardback
ISBN 978-1-107-60836-8 Paperback

SUMMARY CONTENTS

DETAILED CONTENTS

PREFACE

International migration has been a topic on the lips of policy makers for a very long time. The policy interests of States vary widely. Some seek to promote immigration to meet local labour shortages, or facilitate emigration to generate a stream of remittances and foster local development. Others take a more cautious approach because of concerns about irregular migration or national security, or because their societies historically have not welcomed foreigners. These different policy stances are reflected in a vast and complex array of national migration laws that span issues of nationality, entry, exit, deportation, detention, visa classes, status determination, migration-related crime and access to social services. These laws are generally well known within States because they are applied on a daily basis by immigration officials, consular officers, border patrols and crime investigators.

By contrast, the framework of international law governing migration is fragmented and unfamiliar. While some pockets are well recognised – refugee law being the principal example – many dimensions of the international legal framework remain unknown to all but a small coterie of specialists. Many individuals who formulate national migration laws, policies and practices, or are required to implement them, are thus unaware of the rich lode of international agreements, customary law, resolutions, recommendations and guidelines informing developments at the national level.

Scholars, too, have not given international migration law the attention it deserves. While most international lawyers happily acknowledge the existence of discrete fields, such as international human rights law, law of the sea, international environmental law, international criminal law and international trade law, mention of 'international migration law' typically draws a long and puzzled silence. To a degree, this is understandable – there is no overarching international migration treaty that embodies the key legal principles, nor is there a global migration institution that monitors State compliance and promotes enforcement. As one measure of this, a recent compilation of international migration law instruments identified over 120 separate treaties, declarations, principles and guidelines, tallying 850 pages. Instead of singularity, there is multiplicity; instead of harmony, there is dissonance or even cacophony.

In recent years, those who are interested in international migration law have had the benefit of a number of valuable publications. These include two edited collections that have examined selected topics in a manner suited to the needs of specialist lawyers in the field; and the publication, by the International Organization for Migration ('IOM'), of a glossary explaining hundreds of migration terms in multiple languages. Yet, there has been no comprehensive book that explains the key elements of the large but fragmented body of contemporary international migration law.

We conceived of this book to fill the gap by producing a foundational text that would be broad in scope but remain accessible in style and format. Thus, while this volume provides a comprehensive account of the major legal themes in international migration law, it is not intended to be exhaustive. We have also sought to explain the practical context of the legal principles by including real-world case studies, maps and break-out boxes that offer additional information about important historical or contemporary migration issues. Curious readers are directed to further reading and resources at the conclusion of each chapter.

Foundations of International Migration Law has been written for people in a wide variety of contexts who wish to gain an understanding of the international legal framework that regulates migration. It is intended for those who are new to international migration law and seek an overview of its many components, as well as those who may have specialised knowledge of a particular branch of international migration law but need to understand how their specialisation interlocks with other branches of the field. We hope it will be useful to students of international law and migration studies, migration policy officers, diplomatic and consular staff, international and regional organisations, as well as non-government and civil society organisations. In keeping with this aim, we have included a chapter on contemporary patterns of international migration – to provide the contextual basis for subsequent discussion – and a chapter on the sources of international migration law for those who are unfamiliar with public international law.

We have been very fortunate in securing a great many talented authors to contribute to this volume. They include international lawyers, migration policy specialists and a human geographer, and their diverse experience spans work in the legal academy; in international, intergovernmental, regional and non-governmental organisations; in national governments; and in consulting work on a wide range of migration assignments. We extend our thanks to each of them for the gusto with which they embraced this project, the high quality of their work and their willingness to meet sometimes pressing deadlines.

The structure and content of the book was significantly shaped by a workshop held in Geneva in May 2011, which was attended by nearly all contributors. There we discussed draft chapters, considered which case studies would best illustrate the legal issues, and canvassed ideas about the location of material and chapters. This spirited, but always constructive, discussion significantly improved the presentation of the material and enhanced the integrity of the final text. In this dynamic field, we have tried to state the law accurately to 30 June 2011, but have taken into account selective developments since that date, where possible.

Our thanks are also due to the Australian Government for generously funding this project and to the New Zealand Government for a smaller financial contribution. Together, these donors made the Geneva workshop possible and contributed to meeting the cost of research assistance, editing and cartography.

No publication of this magnitude is possible without accumulating debts to many people who have assisted in different capacities. We would like to thank Hasmig Schaeffer at IOM for organising the travel and other arrangements for the Geneva workshop and for providing invaluable administrative support throughout the course of the project; Judy Davis for her skilled and careful work in producing the maps to accompany the case studies; Christine Brickenstein, Rebecca Kang and Bronwyn Lo for their assistance with legal research and referencing; and Sarah Hullah for her meticulous editing of a draft of the book. Sinéad Moloney at Cambridge University Press commissioned the book with an enthusiasm that did not wane, despite missed deadlines, while Helen Francis took delivery of the manuscript and turned it into a book that met the high standards of the Press.

Finally, we extend our special thanks to IOM, which embraced the project as part of its international migration law programme and hosted the workshop at its headquarters. More than this, however, IOM has nurtured a significant number of contributors to this volume, including two of the editors, and has provided useful experience in working with international migration law and policy in the field. We are grateful for their continuing support.

BRIAN OPESKIN
RICHARD PERRUCHOUD
JILLYANNE REDPATH-CROSS

Geneva and Sydney

CASE STUDIES

BOXES

FIGURES

MAPS

TABLES

CONTRIBUTORS

GERVAIS APPAVE is the Special Policy Adviser to the Director General of the International Organization for Migration ('IOM') and co-editor of the *World Migration Report 2011*. His professional itinerary and responsibilities have revolved around the analysis of trends in international migration, and the search for effective strategies and policies for the management of migratory flows. He was the founding Director of the Migration Policy, Research and Communication Department at IOM between 2001 and 2006. Between 1997 and 2001 he was the Head and Coordinator of the Intergovernmental Consultations on Asylum, Refugees and Migration. Prior to that he was a public servant with the Australian Department of Immigration.

RICHARD BEDFORD QSO, FRSNZ is Pro Vice-Chancellor (Research) at Auckland University of Technology and Professor of Population Geography in the National Institute of Demographic and Economic Analysis ('NIDEA') at the University of Waikato. He is a specialist in migration research and since the mid-1960s he has been researching processes of population movement in the Asia-Pacific region. He was elected to Fellowship of the Royal Society of New Zealand in 2000 and made a Companion of the Queen's Service Order ('QSO'). In 2010 he was awarded the Royal Society's Dame Joan Metge Medal in the Social Sciences for his contributions to research on migration and to building research capability in the social sciences.

JACQUELINE BHABHA is the Jeremiah Smith Jr Lecturer at Harvard Law School, Research Director at Harvard's François-Xavier Bagnoud Center for Health and Human Rights, Adjunct Lecturer on Public Policy at Harvard Kennedy School, and Harvard University's Adviser on Human Rights Education. She publishes extensively on migration, refugee protection, children's rights and citizenship, including *Moving Children: Child Migration in the 21st Century* (forthcoming), *Children without a State: A Global Human Rights Challenge* (2011) and *Seeking Asylum Alone: Unaccompanied and Separated Children and Refugee Protection* (2006). She is co-founder of the Alba Collective, a non-governmental organisation enhancing the financial security and rights of rural women and girls in developing countries.

VINCENT CHETAIL is Professor of International Law at the Graduate Institute of International and Development Studies, Geneva. He is also Director of the Programme for the Study of Global Migration, and Research Director at the Geneva Academy of International Humanitarian Law and Human Rights. He has published numerous books and articles on international migration law, international refugee law, human rights law and humanitarian law. He is Editor-in-Chief of *Refugee Survey Quarterly*. He also serves regularly as a consultant to governments, non-governmental organisations and international organisations, including the United Nations High Commissioner for Refugees, the International Labour Organization and IOM.

RYSZARD CHOLEWINSKI is Migration Policy Specialist in the International Migration Branch of the International Labour Office. He works on policy, research and training activities with a view to advancing a rights-based approach to labour migration with the International Labour Organization's (ILO) tripartite constituents. Prior to joining the ILO, he was Senior Migration Policy and Research Specialist at IOM in Geneva (2005–10) and Reader in Law at the University of Leicester in the United Kingdom (1992–2005). He has written extensively on the laws and policies relating to international labour migration, the rights of migrant workers, and various aspects of the emerging European Union law and policy on migration.

MICHAEL DIVINE received his BA in Global Studies, summa cum laude, from the University of Minnesota in 2008 and is currently completing his JD. He has worked on behalf of non-nationals through the Asylum Law Project and with the International Institute of Minnesota. In 2011 he received an Upper Midwest Human Rights Fellowship for his work supporting human rights in the Middle East.

JAMES C. HATHAWAY is the James E. and Sarah A. Degan Professor of Law and Director of the Program in Refugee and Asylum Law at the University of Michigan. He is also Distinguished Visiting Professor of International Refugee Law at the University of Amsterdam, Professorial Fellow of the University of Melbourne, and Senior Visiting Research Associate at Oxford University's Refugee Studies Programme. Hathaway serves as Counsel on International Protection to the US Committee for Refugees and Immigrants, and as Founding Patron and Honorary Director of Asylum Access, a non-profit organisation committed to delivering innovative legal aid to refugees in the Global South.

NATALIE KLEIN is Professor and Dean at Macquarie Law School, Macquarie University, Sydney, Australia, where she teaches and researches in different areas of international law. She is the author of *Maritime Security and the Law of the Sea* (2011) and *Dispute Settlement and the UN Convention on the Law of the Sea* (Cambridge University Press, 2005). Prior to joining Macquarie, she worked in the international litigation and arbitration practice of Debevoise & Plimpton LLP, served as counsel to the Government of Eritrea and was a consultant in the Office of Legal Affairs at the United Nations. Her masters and doctorate were earned at Yale Law School.

SOPHIE NONNENMACHER has been working for the International Organization for Migration (IOM) since 2000 on labour migration issues at its headquarters in Geneva, Switzerland. At the end of 2009 she moved to the IOM Bangkok Regional Office to take up the position of Head of the Regional Counter-Trafficking Unit for South East Asia. In 2011, Ms. Nonnenmacher assumed the position of Regional Policy and Liaison Officer for Asia and Pacific. She specialises in all aspects of international labour migration, developing additional expertise on workers' mobility as manifested in GATS Mode 4 and other regional free trade arrangements. In her present capacity, she is developing regional strategies and supporting the development of migration policy in the region.

IRENA OMELANIUK is Senior Migration Adviser to the Global Forum on Migration and Development, a position she has held since the Forum's inception in 2007. She has worked in the Australian Department of Immigration, including as a diplomat in Mexico and Washington DC. She has also worked at IOM, including as Director of Migration Management Services, and more recently as Migration Adviser to the World Bank. She was Editor-in-Chief of the *World Migration Report 2005*, and has published and led discussions at United Nations and other international conferences on migration, gender and development. Irena is a German-born Australian citizen, currently living in Washington DC.

BRIAN OPESKIN is Professor of Legal Governance at Macquarie University, Sydney. He researches in the broad field of public law, including international migration law and human rights, and has a special interest in interdisciplinary study that examines the intersection between principles of public law and population processes. He previously held positions as Head of the Law School at the University of the South Pacific in Vanuatu, as Commissioner and Deputy President of the Australian Law Reform Commission, and as Associate Professor at Sydney University. In 2010 he was elected a Fellow of the Australian Academy of Law.

RICHARD PERRUCHOUD was, until 2011, Director of the International Migration Law and Legal Affairs Department at IOM in Geneva. Before joining IOM in 1982 he was Adjunct Professor of International Law at the Graduate Institute of International Studies in Geneva and a visiting scholar at Harvard Law School. He has published widely on migration law, human rights and international humanitarian law. He holds degrees in law (LLB, LLM, LLD) from the University of Geneva.

RYSZARD PIOTROWICZ is Professor of Law at Aberystwyth University. He has also taught at the Universities of Tasmania, Durham and Glasgow. He is an Alexander-von-Humboldt Research Fellow. He works mostly in migration law, especially on trafficking of human beings. He has been a member of the European Commission's Group of Experts on Trafficking in Human Beings since 2008 and has advised several international organisations on the legal aspects of people trafficking. He is the Book Reviews Editor for the *International Journal of Refugee Law*. He has also worked with the International Committee of the Red Cross and national Red Cross societies throughout Europe in the dissemination of international humanitarian law, and is co-author and co-editor of *International Military Missions and International Law* (2011).

KAROLINE POPP is a Migration Policy Officer at IOM in Geneva, where she focusses on migration policy and policy dialogue, in particular questions of global and regional migration governance, integration, and the linkages between migration and climate change. She has also conducted extensive research on issues related to regional consultative processes on migration. She holds a Bachelor's degree in Geography from Oxford University and a Master's degree in Dispute and Conflict Resolution from the School of Oriental and African Studies, University of London.

JILLYANNE REDPATH-CROSS has worked for a number of years as a Senior Legal Officer in the International Migration Law and Legal Affairs Department at IOM in Geneva. During her time at IOM she has worked on issues such as the human rights of migrants, comparative immigration law and policies, migration and security, and smuggling and trafficking in human beings. Prior to joining IOM, she worked as a university lecturer and as an attorney in Australia. She completed her LLM at the University of Cambridge, United Kingdom, and her BA/LLB at Monash University, Australia.

IVAN SHEARER is Emeritus Professor of Law at the University of Sydney and an Adjunct Professor in the School of Law, University of South Australia. He has broad teaching and research interests in international law. He has served as an elected member of the United Nations Human Rights Committee (2001–8) and as a Senior Member of the Australian Administrative Appeals Tribunal (2004–8). He is a member of the Panel of Arbitrators of the Permanent Court of Arbitration, The Hague, and served in two recent international arbitrations and in two cases before the International Tribunal for the Law of the Sea, Hamburg. In 1995 he was appointed a Member of the Order of Australia (AM).

DAVID WEISSBRODT is the Regents Professor and Fredrikson & Byron Professor at the University of Minnesota Law School. He teaches international human rights law and immigration law, and established both the University of Minnesota Human Rights Center and the University of Minnesota Human Rights Library (www.umn.edu/humanrts). He served as a member and Chairperson of the United Nations Sub-Commission on the Promotion and Protection of Human Rights. In 2000–3 he was designated the United Nations Special Rapporteur on the Rights of Non-Citizens. He is the author of more than 200 articles and books, including *The Human Rights of Non-Citizens* (2008).

ABBREVIATIONS

APC Asia-Pacific Consultations on Refugees, Displaced Persons and Migrants

APEC Asia-Pacific Economic Cooperation

ASEAN Association of Southeast Asian Nations

AU African Union

BV business visitors

CAN Andean Community of Nations (*Comunidad Andina*)

CARICOM Caribbean Community and Common Market

CEDAW *Convention on the Elimination of All Forms of Discrimination against Women* (1979)

CIREFCA International Conference on Central American Refugees

CPA Comprehensive Plan of Action for Indochinese Refugees

CRC *Convention on the Rights of the Child* (1989)

CRPD *Convention on the Rights of Persons with Disabilities* (2007)

CSME Caribbean Single Market Economy

CSS contractual service suppliers

DPRK Democratic People's Republic of Korea

ECOWAS Economic Community of West African States

EEA European Economic Area

EEZ exclusive economic zone

EMS executives, managers and specialists

EU European Union

EU-LAC European Union–Latin America and the Caribbean Summit

GATS *General Agreement on Trade in Services* (1994)

GATT *General Agreement on Tariffs and Trade* (1947)

GCC Gulf Co-operation Council

GCIM Global Commission on International Migration

GDP gross domestic product

GFMD Global Forum on Migration and Development

GMG Global Migration Group

ICCPR *International Covenant on Civil and Political Rights* (1966)

ICERD *International Convention on the Elimination of All Forms of Racial Discrimination* (1965)

ICESCR	*International Covenant on Economic, Social and Cultural Rights* (1966)
ICJ	International Court of Justice
ICMC	International Catholic Migration Commission
ICPD	International Conference on Population and Development
ICRMW	*International Convention on the Protection of the Rights of All Migrant Workers and Members of their Families* (1990)
ICT	intra-corporate transferee
IDP	internally displaced person
IGAD-RCP	Intergovernmental Authority on Development – Regional Consultative Process on Migration
IGC	Inter-governmental Consultations on Asylum, Refugee and Migration Policies in Europe, North America and Australia
ILC	International Law Commission
ILO	International Labour Organization
IMO	International Maritime Organization
IOM	International Organization for Migration
IRF	inter-regional fora
IRP	inter-regional process
LDC	least developed country
LNTS	League of Nations Treaty Series
MERCOSUR	Common Market of the South (*Mercado Común del Sur*)
MFN	most favoured nation
MIDSA	Migration Dialogue for Southern Africa
MIDWA	Migration Dialogue for West Africa
MOST	Management of Societal Transformation
MOUs	Memoranda of Understanding
NGO	non-governmental organisation
OAS	Organization of American States
OECD	Organisation for Economic Co-operation and Development
OHCHR	Office of the High Commissioner for Human Rights
OSCE	Organization for Security and Co-operation in Europe
RCP	regional consultative process on migration
SACM	South American Conference on Migration
SARRED	International Conference on the Plight of Refugees, Returnees and Displaced Persons in Southern Africa
SICA	Central American Integration System (*Sistema de la Integración Centroamericana*)
SOLAS	*International Convention for the Safety of Life at Sea* (1974)
SOPEMI	OECD's Continuous Reporting System on Migration (Système d'Observation Permanente sur les Migrations)
UAE	United Arab Emirates
UDHR	*Universal Declaration of Human Rights* (1948)
UN	United Nations
UNCLOS	*United Nations Convention on the Law of the Sea* (1982)

UNCTAD	United Nations Conference on Trade and Development
UNCTOC	*United Nations Convention against Transnational Organized Crime* (2000)
UNDESA	United Nations Department of Economic and Social Affairs
UNDP	United Nations Development Programme
UNESCO	United Nations Educational, Scientific and Cultural Organization
UNFCCC	*United Nations Framework Convention on Climate Change* (1992)
UNHCR	United Nations High Commissioner for Refugees
UNICEF	United Nations Children's Fund
UNITAR	United Nations Institute for Training and Research
UNODC	United Nations Office on Drugs and Crime
UNRWA	United Nations Relief and Works Agency
UNTS	United Nations Treaty Series
UNWTO	United Nations World Tourism Organization
WHO	World Health Organization
WTO	World Trade Organization

1 Conceptualising international migration law

BRIAN OPESKIN, RICHARD PERRUCHOUD AND JILLYANNE REDPATH-CROSS

1.1. THE EVOLUTION OF INTERNATIONAL MIGRATION LAW

Migration has been an integral part of human activity for as long as people have inhabited the earth. Whether moving as individuals, families or tribes, migration is an age-old response to the physical need for food, shelter and security, and the psychological need for adventure and exploration. However, while migration has marked all periods of human history, the phenomenon of 'international migration' had to await the reordering of the geopolitical landscape as a collection of territorial States in which governments had authority over settled populations residing within defined geographic boundaries.[1]

The *Treaty of Westphalia* (1648) was a critical turning point in establishing that new landscape, but for the next two centuries individuals still enjoyed substantial freedom in traversing the boundaries of the State. This reflected an attitude of hospitality to strangers that was inherited from ancient cultures and expressed through cosmopolitanism. This attitude can be seen in the scholarly works of the great writers of international law of the eighteenth and nineteenth centuries, who, with few exceptions, took a liberal attitude to the movement of people across borders for trade, commerce and other purposes.[2] If law in this early period paid scant attention to regulating migration, it was partly for the practical reason that the number of people involved was modest because modes of transport were confined to land crossings by foot or horse, and sea crossings by wind-powered sailing vessels. There were some notable exceptions to this *laissez-faire* approach, but the circumstances in which law was invoked to regulate international migration were few.

---

1 Friedrich Kratochwil, 'Of Systems, Boundaries, and Territoriality: An Inquiry into the Formation of the State System' (1986) **39**(1) *World Politics* 27.
2 James Nafziger, 'The General Admission of Aliens under International Law' (1983) **77** *American Journal of International Law* 804.

Change came with the Industrial Revolution, which generated great interest in the New World and provided new means for getting there. There was substantial migration to the New World from Europe and Asia,[3] but it was the latter, particularly, that drew the attention of national laws. Fuelled by racist concerns about hordes of Asian immigrants, many States began to erect legal barriers to entry through legislative enactments, supported by sympathetic national courts. Famously, in 1891, the Supreme Court of the United States upheld the right of the legislature to exclude foreigners if they were considered dangerous to the peace of the country. Selectively invoking one of the great writers of international law, Emmerich de Vattel, the Court proclaimed:

> It is an accepted maxim of international law, that every sovereign nation has the power, as inherent in sovereignty, and essential to self-preservation, to forbid the entrance of foreigners within its dominions, or to admit them only in such cases and upon such conditions as it may see fit to prescribe.[4]

Notwithstanding the invocation of Vattel to support the stance taken under national law, the development of international migration law in this period remained rudimentary. Its potential was nevertheless recognised by some scholars. As early as 1927, Louis Varlez delivered a course of lectures at the newly established Hague Academy of International Law on international migration law, which he defined as the body of international norms applicable to migration.[5] Varlez summarised all elements of international law applicable to emigration and immigration at the bilateral, regional and multilateral levels, and highlighted areas that remained within the national jurisdiction of States. He suggested that migrants were more 'international' than 'national' in character and that they should be protected as such under international law, free from intervention by their own State.[6] Presciently, he concluded that 'we are witnessing extremely lively and fertile legislative activity that makes it possible, better perhaps than for any other phenomenon, to follow the ever evolving life of the law'.[7] This conclusion is still valid today.

The corpus of international migration law developed in a slow and piecemeal fashion in the interwar period. Studies on international migration law were limited in scope to areas of specific concern. One topic of considerable interest was nationality, leading to the *Convention on Certain Questions relating to the Conflict of Nationality Law* (1930) and the *Protocol relating to Military Obligations in Certain Cases of Double Nationality* (1935).[8] The distinction between nationals and foreigners was, and remains, central to the international law governing migration. States had a strong interest in clear rules on nationality, which

---

3 Wilbur Zelinsky, 'The Hypothesis of the Mobility Transition' (1971) 61(2) *Geographical Review* 219.
4 *Nishimura Ekiu* v. *United States* 142 US 651 (1891), 659.
5 Louis Varlez, 'Les migrations internationales et leur réglementation' (1927) 20(V) *Recueil des cours* 165.
6 Ibid. 333–4.   7 Ibid. 343 (Editors' translation).
8 *Convention on Certain Questions relating to the Conflict of Nationality Law*, opened for signature 13 April 1930, 179 LNTS 89 (entered into force 1 July 1937); *Protocol relating to Military Obligations in Certain Cases of Double Nationality*, opened for signature 12 April 1935, 178 UNTS 227 (entered into force 25 May 1937).

affected, for instance, their duty to admit members of their own community upon entry or return.

Another topic of concern was the plight of millions of European refugees who had been dislocated by the First World War or had fled the Russian Revolution of 1917.[9] Many had no nationality, or no means of proving nationality, and thus no capacity to access basic rights in the States in which they found themselves. The League of Nations sought to address the problem by establishing High Commissioners to provide substitute documentation (Nansen passports) and over-see their resettlement. Conventions concluded under the auspices of the League of Nations, such as those of 1933 and 1938,[10] became the forerunners of the legal regime for refugee protection necessitated by the Second World War.

A third topic of international interest in this period was the elimination of exploitation through forced labour, human trafficking and slave trading. These concerns were not confined to cross-border movement, but the international dimensions of these practices made them ripe for global action. The first steps to abolish slave trading had in fact come through national law much earlier, com-mencing with the United Kingdom in 1807,[11] and continuing through national abolitionist movements throughout the nineteenth century.[12] On the international plane, in 1924 the League of Nations established the Temporary Slavery Commission to review slavery in all its forms, which led to the *Slavery Convention* (1926).[13] Within a few years, the International Labour Organization ('ILO') had concluded a convention to tackle exploitation of forced labour, which has now been ratified by nearly all States.[14]

The depravities of the Second World War, with its orchestration of human misery on an unparalleled scale, ushered in a new order of laws and institutions, which had a dramatic impact on the evolution of international migration law. The *Universal Declaration of Human Rights* (1948) ('Universal Declaration'), while not a binding legal instrument, proclaimed itself as a 'common standard of achievement for all peoples and all nations' and became the kernel around which customary interna-tional law would later crystallise.[15] Several provisions of the Universal Declaration addressed the phenomenon of international migration, which was burgeoning in the post-war period – the entitlement to rights and freedoms without distinction based on national or social origin or other status (art. 1); the prohibition of the slave

9 James Hathaway, 'The Evolution of Refugee Status in International Law: 1920–1950' (1984) 33(2) *International and Comparative Law Quarterly* 348.
10 *Convention relating to the International Status of Refugees*, opened for signature 28 October 1933, 159 LNTS 3663 (entered into force 13 June 1935); *Convention concerning the Status of Refugees coming from Germany*, opened for signature 10 February 1938, 192 LNTS 4461 (entered into force 25 October 1938).
11 *Abolition of the Slave Trade Act 1807* (UK) (47 Geo III Sess. 1 c. 36), abolishing slave trading, followed by the *Slavery Abolition Act 1833* (UK) (3 & 4 Will. IV c. 73), abolishing slavery.
12 Mike Kaye, '1807–2007: Over 200 Years of Campaigning against Slavery' (Anti-Slavery International, 2005).
13 *Slavery Convention*, opened for signature 25 September 1926, 60 LNTS 254 (entered into force 9 March 1927).
14 *Convention concerning Forced or Compulsory Labour* (ILO Convention No 29), opened for signature 10 June 1930, 39 UNTS 55 (entered into force 1 May 1932). In mid 2012 there were 175 States parties.
15 *Universal Declaration of Human Rights*, GA Res 217A (III), UN Doc A/810 (10 December 1948).

trade (art. 4); equality before the law without discrimination (art. 7); the right to leave any country and to return to one's own country (art. 13); the right to seek asylum from persecution in other countries (art. 14); the right to a nationality and not to be arbitrarily deprived of one's nationality (art. 15); the right to protection of the family (art. 16); and more generally the right of everyone (including migrants) to social security, work, a reasonable standard of living and education (arts. 22–26).

The primary goal of the Universal Declaration was educative – to 'strive by teaching and education to promote respect for these rights and freedoms'[16] – yet the massive social dislocations of the Second World War generated problems that required immediate legal solutions. In the post-war years, under the auspices of the United Nations, the international community concluded a raft of treaties addressing migration-related problems, including the plight of refugees (at first in Europe, but later more generally),[17] the situation of persons who had no nationality and were therefore stateless,[18] and measures to reduce statelessness.[19]

A range of international human rights instruments also emerged, addressing rights and freedoms to be enjoyed by 'everyone', including migrants. These included two international covenants that gave legal effect to the hortatory statements of the Universal Declaration.[20] Specific human rights treaties followed, directing attention to the problems encountered by particular classes of vulnerable persons (e.g., women, children, migrants) or arising from particular repugnant practices (e.g., racial discrimination, torture). Many of these specialised instruments reformulated norms that had evolved elsewhere – for example, the *Convention on the Rights of the Child* (1989) proclaims the right of every child to registration at birth, a name and a nationality (art. 7),[21] restating principles articulated in the Universal Declaration. Significantly, the United Nations General Assembly adopted the *International Convention on the Protection of the Rights of All Migrant Workers and Members of their Families* (1990), which sets out a comprehensive framework for protecting migrant workers across all migratory stages – from pre-departure, to transit, settlement and return.[22] However, this convention has not been widely ratified, especially by migrant-receiving States.

---

16 See also Mary Ann Glendon, *A World Made New: Eleanor Roosevelt and the Universal Declaration of Human Rights* (Random House, 2001).

17 *Convention relating to the Status of Refugees*, opened for signature 28 July 1951, 189 UNTS 150 (entered into force 22 April 1954); *Protocol relating to the Status of Refugees*, opened for accession 31 January 1967, 606 UNTS 267 (entered into force 4 October 1967).

18 *Convention relating to the Status of Stateless Persons*, opened for signature 28 September 1954, 360 UNTS 117 (entered into force 6 June 1960).

19 *Convention on the Reduction of Statelessness*, opened for signature 30 August 1961, 989 UNTS 175 (entered into force 13 December 1975).

20 *International Covenant on Civil and Political Rights*, opened for signature 16 December 1966, 999 UNTS 171 (entered into force 23 March 1976); *International Covenant on Economic, Social and Cultural Rights*, opened for signature 16 December 1966, 993 UNTS 3 (entered into force 3 January 1976).

21 *Convention on the Rights of the Child*, opened for signature 20 November 1989, 1577 UNTS 3 (entered into force 2 September 1990).

22 *International Convention on the Protection of the Rights of All Migrant Workers and Members of their Families*, opened for signature 18 December 1990, 2220 UNTS 3 (entered into force 1 July 2003).

1.2. THE EVOLUTION OF INTERNATIONAL MIGRATION INSTITUTIONS

Despite realisation of the 'fertile legislative activity' anticipated by Varlez, new international law was not adequate in itself to meet the challenges posed by flourishing international migration. New international institutions were developed with diverse functions, ranging from operational support for migrants, to monitoring compliance with, and encouraging enforcement of, the new legal instruments. One of the first – the ILO – was established long before, by the *Peace Treaty of Versailles* (1919), and specifically included in its mandate the 'protection of the interests of workers when employed in countries other than their own' because exploitative labour conditions were thought to constitute a threat to world peace.

The challenges of refugees and displaced persons in the wake of the Second World War led to the establishment of two new bodies that remain the world's principal migration agencies today. The United Nations High Commissioner for Refugees ('UNHCR') was established by the General Assembly in 1950 to provide international protection for refugees, with the optimistic goal of completing its three-year mandate and then disbanding. In practice, its mandate has been progressively extended to cover not only refugees, but also internally displaced persons, stateless persons and other groups in analogous circumstances, and today it operates with a staff of more than 7,685 people working in 125 States. The International Organization for Migration ('IOM') was established in 1951 in similar circumstances but with a different mandate, namely, to help European governments identify resettlement countries for 11 million people uprooted by the war, and other migrants, and arrange their transportation and integration in new homelands. As with UNHCR, IOM's scope of activities has broadened significantly, making it the leading international agency to advance the understanding of migration issues, encourage social and economic development through migration, and uphold the human rights and wellbeing of migrants. It is an intergovernmental organisation outside the United Nations system, has a membership of 146 States, and operates with some 7,800 staff working in some 140 States.

The evolution of the international human rights framework has added many other bodies to the suite of those concerned with the different facets of international migration, which are described in detail elsewhere in this book. Bodies established under the various human rights treaties, such as the Human Rights Committee and the Migrant Workers Committee, play a role in scrutinising state action, considering individual complaints about alleged breaches of the treaties, and providing interpretive guidance through 'General Comments'. The Human Rights Council – an organ of the United Nations General Assembly – has its own processes for strengthening the promotion and protection of human rights around the globe. These include universal periodic reviews of State compliance, and a number of thematic mandates (i.e., Special Rapporteurs) on migration, trafficking in persons, contemporary forms of slavery, and racism and xenophobia.

1.3. INTERNATIONAL MIGRATION LAW TODAY

As the foregoing discussion indicates, international migration law has evolved markedly over the past decades. The literature highlights the substantial increase in the number of treaties relating to specific aspects of migration at the global, regional and bilateral levels, illustrating the growing importance of international law in this field.[23] International migration law has thus been transformed into a body of law whose richness and diversity are probably unmatched. From counter-trafficking to rescue at sea, from stranded migrants to regional consultative processes, there is a wealth of new migration norms which call for a restatement or compilation of the law.

International law contains a fairly detailed set of norms, principles and rules relating to migration: a recent compendium of international migration law instruments, both hard and soft law but limited to universal instruments, spanned over nine hundred pages.[24] Included were instruments on human rights, labour law, nationality, statelessness, trafficking, smuggling, international maritime law, state security, detention, international humanitarian law, refugee law, migration and development, diplomatic and consular protection, minorities and international trade law.

This extensive list raises the question of the scope of international migration law. The editors of the compendium described the subject matter in these terms:

> Currently, 'international migration law' is an umbrella term for the complex web of legal relationships among persons, groups and States that together regulate the movements of individuals. It is a branch of law that has developed over time and, indeed, continues to develop with the ever-increasing need for international cooperation and regulation involving States, migrants and international civil society in general.[25]

The main pillars of international migration law are, first, the human rights and duties of persons involved in migration, as defined in a variety of international instruments; and second, the principles and standards deriving from State sovereignty, among which are the right to protect borders, confer nationality, safeguard national security, admit and expel non-nationals and combat smuggling and trafficking. To this, a third pillar may now be added, namely, the law promoting cooperation among States to manage the international movement of people.

---

23 Richard Plender, *International Migration Law* (Martinus Nijhoff, 2nd edn, 1988) xiv.
24 Richard Perruchoud and Katarína Tömölová (eds.), *Compendium of International Migration Law Instruments* (TMC Asser Press, 2007).
25 Ibid. v.

The evolution of international migration law in the past few decades has been extraordinary. Looking at the first pillar (human rights), historically migrants looked to their State of nationality for diplomatic or consular protection; now, while this type of protection remains important, human rights treaties have instituted protection mechanisms open to all, including migrants, at the universal and regional levels. The consequences of this development are not yet fully used by migrants and their representatives. Some aspects of the second pillar (State sovereignty) have been developed as well, particularly in the field of detention and exclusion, and the need to balance protection of human rights with security. The third pillar has witnessed important changes requiring States to cooperate more closely in almost every aspect of migration.

1.4. A SEARCH FOR ORDER

International migration law today is at a juncture that prompts reflection, if not introspection. On the one hand, the tremendous growth in the number and range of legal norms regulating international migration is undeniable; on the other hand, those norms do not present themselves in a coherent and integrated form. The tension has been reflected in colourful metaphors. Lillich once described the rights of non-nationals in international law as resembling 'a giant unassembled juridical jigsaw puzzle', albeit one in which 'the number of pieces is uncertain and the grand design is still emerging',[26] while Aleinikoff has labelled the field as one of 'substance without architecture', forming no coherent regime.[27]

To state that there is today both more and less international migration law than might be supposed,[28] that international migration law is an unassembled jigsaw, or that there are areas where international migration law could be better developed, does not affect its existence. In an irreducibly pluralistic world, international law develops in different directions, and so-called gaps are mere fields left to the authority and responsibility of States under national law. For the future, one may call for a more comprehensive and better-regulated framework for managing international migration, but existing international law already provides a good starting point for the development of a well-regulated system. The rubric 'international migration law' thus serves the function of piecing together various aspects of international law governing all facets of migration, ensuring internal coherence of

---

26 Richard Lillich, *The Human Rights of Aliens in Contemporary International Law* (Manchester University Press, 1984) 122.
27 Alexander Aleinikoff, 'International Legal Norms on Migration: Substance without Architecture' in Ryszard Cholewinski, Richard Perruchoud and Euan Macdonald (eds.), *International Migration Law* (TMC Asser Press, 2007) 467, 479.
28 Alexander Aleinikoff, 'International Legal Norms and Migration: A Report' in Alexander Aleinikoff and Vincent Chetail (eds.), *Migration and International Legal Norms* (TMC Asser Press, 2003) 1, 2.

norms rooted in, and borrowed from, branches of law as diverse as human rights, criminal law, humanitarian law, and so on.

New types of law, or legal regimes, do emerge in response to new needs. Sometimes this occurs quite rapidly, as happened with the emergence of space law once space flight became a technological reality with the launch of the world's first artificial satellite in 1957.[29] More commonly, legal regimes emerge from the gradual accretion of law and practice over substantial periods of time. Since the Second World War – the most formative period of international migration law – international law has witnessed the rise of international economic law, international environmental law, international criminal law, the law of the sea, and many other areas that are now considered to be discrete and specialised domains. To ask at what point a set of legal norms becomes a special legal regime is much like asking an oyster when a grain of sand becomes a pearl: not only is there no defining moment, but the descriptive failure does nothing to diminish what has been created.

The questions may be asked: can international migration law be properly regarded as a *self-contained* legal regime or a *special* legal regime? The first question is easier to answer and draws a clear negative response. In a strict sense, the notion of a self-contained regime defines a system with special rules, quite distinct from general rules of international law, which includes mechanisms for countering breaches. Examples are the dispute settlement system under the World Trade Organization or the operation of diplomatic law, with its reciprocal privileges and immunities.[30] International migration law manifestly does not correspond to this notion. A broader notion of a self-contained regime was considered by the Permanent Court of International Justice in the *Case of the S. S. Wimbledon*, where the Court held that the regime regulating the passage of vessels through the Kiel Canal was fully governed by specific treaty provisions, without the need to resort to other sources of law or general public international law, which may have different rules.[31] International migration law would hardly fit into this enlarged concept either. In sum, international migration law does not have the characteristics of a self-contained regime within the meaning identified by international courts in these cases.

The question whether international migration law constitutes a special legal regime is more contested. An initial difficulty is that opinions vary as to the meaning of 'regime' in this context, and how it differs from the notion of a 'branch' or 'field' of international law.[32] Some consider the terms interchangeable; others

---

29 In 1959 the United Nations established the Committee on the Peaceful Uses of Outer Space (COPUOS), which negotiated five international treaties that now form the core of space law.

30 *United States Diplomatic and Consular Staff in Tehran (United States of America v. Iran) (Judgment)* [1980] ICJ Rep 3, [86].

31 *Case of the SS Wimbledon (United Kingdom v. Germany) (Judgment)* [1923] PCIJ (ser A) No 1, 3, 23–4.

32 Vincent Chetail, 'Migration, droits de l'homme et souveraineté: le droit international dans tous ses états' in Vincent Chetail (ed.), *Mondialisation, migration et droits de l'homme: le droit international en question, Volume II* (Bruylant, 2007) 13, 21.

opt for a restrictive definition that would confine a regime to a well-defined set of rules governing a field of activity, with its own enforcement mechanisms, generally based on a treaty. In this regard, there is merit in Koskenniemi's view that the solution should be functional rather than doctrinaire:

> the widest of special regimes – denominations such as 'international criminal law', 'humanitarian law', 'trade law', 'environmental law' and so on – emerge from the informal activity of lawyers, diplomats, pressure groups, more through shifts in legal culture and in response to practical needs of specialization than a conscious act of regime-creation. Such notions mirror the functional diversification of the international society or, more prosaically, the activities of particular caucuses seeking to articulate or strengthen preferences and orientations that seem not to have received sufficient attention under the general law.[33]

We prefer to avoid the terminological debate and to regard international migration law as a distinct *field* of international law that deals with a specific but diverse subject matter. Its content encompasses all the norms, principles and rules that regulate international migration and the rights and duties of persons involved in migration. It is not autonomous in the sense that it sits outside the discipline of public international law. Rather, it has a reflexive relationship with public international law – absorbing the latter's sources, structures and methodology, and reflecting back new developments through which the discipline of public international law continues its organic growth.

The search for order in international migration law also raises the larger question of global migration governance. Calls for better governance have often stemmed from the view that current arrangements reflect a chaotic web of international laws, institutions and processes, and that these tangled networks produce sub-optimal outcomes for sending and receiving States, and for migrants themselves. International laws comprise legally binding instruments ('hard' law) and non-binding declarations and principles ('soft' law), and even within the former there are layers of multilateral, regional and bilateral treaties in force for different States, on diverse topics, and qualified by different reservations. International institutions have diverse and sometimes overlapping mandates, different operational capacities, and span the full gamut of international, intergovernmental, non-governmental and civil society organisations. International migration processes have expanded exponentially, revealing major differences in their effectiveness, in addition to their disparate geographical, temporal and material scope.

The calls for better global migration governance are based on familiar arguments: globalisation has generated new problems that cannot be solved within national borders, and effective regulation requires an international response. Two potential solutions have come to dominate discussions about the way forward; both rely on more formal architecture to give greater coherence to international

---

33 Martii Koskenniemi, *Fragmentation of International Law: Difficulties Arising from the Diversification and Expansion of International Law*, International Law Commission, 58th sess, UN Doc A/CN.4/L.682 (13 April 2006), 84–5.

migration law. The first calls for a new supranational organisation – a World Migration Organization – to make effective, generous and humane global migration policy, free from the narrow political interests that typically motivate individual States.[34] Needless to say, supranational governance in the field of migration is, and will remain, resisted by States – even 'soft' governance limited to well-defined topics is difficult to put in motion at the global level. As a result, many now consider discussions on the architecture of supranational migration governance to be unproductive.

A second solution calls for an overarching instrument on international migration that would consolidate, in a single place, the substantial volume of extant principles that are currently dispersed across different instruments and different branches of international law. Such a treaty would set out a comprehensive framework of rights and duties of States and individuals, and provide supervisory mechanisms for monitoring and enforcement. It is probably unrealistic to expect such a treaty to encompass all three pillars of international migration law – human rights, state sovereignty and international cooperation – since the last, especially, is too diverse. There is merit, however, in codifying the human rights principles under the first pillar, notwithstanding the criticism that efforts would be better spent improving the implementation of existing norms.[35] Indeed, scholars have already begun the task of drafting an 'International Migrants Bill of Rights' as a 'dynamic blueprint for the protection of the rights of migrants, drawing from all areas of international law, including treaty law, customary international law, areas of State practice and best practices'.[36]

1.5. STRUCTURE OF THIS BOOK

The variety of topics that fall within the rubric of international migration law presents an organisational challenge for a book that seeks to cover the foundations of the field. Scholarly books typically demand a linear treatment of their subject matter whereas, in reality, international migration law is a web of interrelated norms. It follows that many alternative orderings of the material may be justified, and we experimented with several of them before settling on the present structure.

This book seeks to lay down the foundations of the subject through central concepts and principles, before examining higher-order problems. Readers who do not wish to read the chapters sequentially should make liberal use of the tools provided to find a quick entry point to the material that interests them – the detailed table of contents, the index, the glossary, the appendices of cases and international

---

34 See Arthur Helton, 'Unpleasant Surprises Await' (2002) 58(6) *Bulletin of the Atomic Scientists* 94.
35 Aleinikoff, above n. 27, 478.
36 Georgetown University Law Center, 'International Migrants Bill of Rights' (2010) 24 *Georgetown Immigration Law Journal* 395.

instruments, and the cross-referencing within each chapter to relevant discussion elsewhere in the book. What follows is a quick guide to the succeeding chapters.

Chapter 2 sets the scene by examining contemporary patterns of international migration – a matter too often neglected in accounts of the legal framework. International migration is a complex phenomenon and understanding it is made harder by the paucity of reliable data and the diversity of definitions used by the States collecting it. Migration in the twenty-first century is much more complicated than in previous periods of history, for while globalisation has made borders more porous to the movement of goods, capital, services and information, the movement of people across borders has become increasingly regulated. The chapter examines the resultant patterns of migration from different perspectives – stocks and flows, global and regional, regular and irregular, temporary and long-term, voluntary and forced – and speculates about the migration pressures that will come from projected demographic changes over the next forty years.

Chapter 3 asks the fundamental question, 'Where does international migration law come from?' and discusses the diversity and dynamism of sources of law in this field. Two sources of 'hard law' are treaties and customary international law – the former arising from binding legal commitments voluntarily undertaken by States and the latter from widespread State practice, when coupled with a belief that the practice is obligatory. The legal principles derived from hard sources have been supplemented by a rich fabric of 'soft law', namely the non-binding instruments (declarations, resolutions and guidelines) adopted by States and international organisations. In a field where States are often reluctant to constrain their sovereign power to regulate the cross-border movement of people, soft law has been a fertile ground for generating new international norms.

Chapter 4 explores two legal concepts that are fundamental to understanding the rights of individuals to migrate from one State to another, namely, nationality and statelessness. Nationality is the legal bond that exists between an individual and a State, signalling formal membership of that community and entailing obligations of allegiance by the individual and protection by the State. Nationality can be acquired by birth or naturalisation, and may be lost by renunciation by the individual, revocation by the State or extinction of the State. Statelessness arises when a person is not considered to be a national by any State. Stateless persons – thought to number around 12 million globally in 2010 – are some of the most vulnerable and oppressed people in the world, but legal measures to reduce statelessness have met with only modest success.

Chapter 5 examines the power of the State to control its external borders as an attribute of its sovereignty. This key principle underpins the modern framework of international migration law and finds expression in the State's power to admit persons into its territory and to expel non-nationals from its territory. However, the exercise of these powers is constrained by international law, including human rights norms. In relation to entry, States are required to admit their own nationals, must not return refugees to a territory where their life or freedom would be threatened, and must not discriminate on certain grounds (e.g., race) in the admission of non-nationals. In relation to exit, States must allow any person to leave the country (subject to limited exceptions), but they can expel non-nationals so long as international procedural safeguards are met. Today, the authority of States to regulate entry and exit is not disputed: the exceptions to the discretionary power of States are well defined, if not always respected in practice.

Chapter 6 turns to the human rights of migrants, which is a leitmotif that resurfaces throughout the book. International law gave protection to foreigners long before the dawn of the United Nations era (such as a State's right to exercise 'diplomatic protection' in respect of a national injured abroad by a foreign State), but it is since the founding of the United Nations that there has been the most remarkable growth. The norms of equality and non-discrimination are directly relevant to migrants, but all international human rights norms are significant because they apply to every human being, and therefore include migrants. The chapter surveys the major rights and freedoms in their application to migrants, including the specialised instruments that apply to migrant workers. It is clear that there is no shortage of beneficent legal principles, but many migrants continue to suffer discrimination, exploitation and persecution, revealing a significant gap between rights and reality.

Chapter 7 addresses one type of forced migration – the situation of refugees and asylum seekers. Born out of the massive dislocations in Europe from two world wars, the *Convention relating to the Status of Refugees* (1951) ('Refugee Convention')[37] establishes a legal framework for providing international protection to persons who cannot seek the protection of the State of their nationality because they have a 'well-founded fear of being persecuted for reasons of race, religion, nationality, political opinion, or membership of a particular social group'. The chapter considers the criteria for refugee status and the rights afforded to those who qualify. The most fundamental right arises from the duty of States not to return a refugee to the frontier of a territory where his or her life or freedom would be threatened – the duty of *non-refoulement*. Despite the strength of the legal structure, the refugee system is a system under strain. The number of refugees is large – nearly 10 million globally in 2010. One-quarter of all States have not ratified the Refugee Convention; implementation is atomised under a State-based system of compliance; and the burden of offering protection to refugees falls very disproportionately on the developing world.

Chapter 8 examines the legal protections afforded to women, children and other marginalised migrant groups, such as those with disabilities. Numerically, these groups are well represented today in migrant stocks and flows, but historically

---

37 *Convention relating to the Status of Refugees*, opened for signature 28 July 1951, 189 UNTS 150 (entered into force 22 April 1954).

they have been largely invisible because the paradigmatic migrant was considered to be an able-bodied, adult male who leaves home to seek his fortune or save his life. Addressing these marginalised groups within a single chapter should not be taken to imply, however, that they are similarly and invariably vulnerable or disempowered. Individuals within each of these groups enjoy rights and freedoms under general human rights norms, but specialised instruments expand upon those rights in particular contexts. Thus, there are separate treaties addressing the rights of children, discrimination against women, and the rights of persons with disabilities, as well as overlapping instruments addressing migrant workers and other matters. The critical problem facing these groups of migrants is not a normative vacuum, but a failure of political will to implement existing laws.

Chapter 9 examines the legal regimes that address human trafficking and smuggling. Although legal regulation of these practices has older roots, current efforts centre around two protocols that were concluded in 2000 as part of an international effort to combat transnational organised crime.[38] Trafficking and smuggling sometimes possess common features, but they are conceptually distinct. Trafficking is a criminal activity that typically involves the recruitment of persons by deceptive or other means for the purpose of their exploitation – whether for sexual purposes, sweatshops, agricultural or domestic labour, forced marriage or organ harvesting. The victim's participation is non-consensual. Smuggling is a criminal activity that involves procuring the irregular entry of a person into a State of which he or she is not a national for material benefit. This may be a consensual commercial transaction, but in practice the social and economic disadvantage that encourages people to participate in smuggling is similar to that which makes them vulnerable to trafficking. The clandestine nature of both practices makes it difficult to quantify the effectiveness of the protocols, but they provide a helpful legal framework in the fight against these practices.

Chapter 10 considers a topic that has been largely sidelined in the migration literature, namely, how the legal regimes that regulate air and sea transport intersect with the web of norms that comprise international migration law. Difficulties arise because the regulatory regimes governing civil aviation and maritime transportation focus on delimiting rights and obligations in respect of commercial activities that have frequent contact with multiple States. In this environment, the human rights of the migrants who make those journeys are sometimes obscured. The chapter examines the mechanisms employed by States to intercept migrants before they reach the State's frontier; the co-opting of commercial carriers in screening out irregular migrants through penalty regimes known as carrier sanctions; interdiction at sea;

---

38 *Protocol to Prevent, Suppress and Punish Trafficking in Persons, Especially Women and Children, Supplementing the United Nations Convention against Transnational Organized Crime*, opened for signature 15 November 2000, 2237 UNTS 319 (entered into force 25 December 2003); *Protocol against the Smuggling of Migrants by Land, Sea and Air, Supplementing the United Nations Convention against Transnational Organized Crime*, opened for signature 15 November 2000, 2241 UNTS 507 (entered into force 28 January 2004).

stowaways; smuggling by sea; and the rescue of persons in distress at sea. Although the relevant legal instruments are occasionally punctuated by humanitarian concerns, they also underpin the State's sovereign authority to control its borders by deterring irregular migration by sea or air.

Chapter 11, and the following chapter, examine the theme of labour migration from different perspectives. A very large part of international migration is bound up with the world of work, and the area has spawned a large number of specialised legal instruments. Since 1919, the ILO has played a key role in drawing up international minimum labour standards aimed at safeguarding the rights of migrant workers, including conventions, recommendations, principles and guidelines. The United Nations has also responded with a core human rights document, the *International Convention on the Protection of the Rights of All Migrant Workers and Members of their Families* (1990).[39] Despite shortcomings in ratification and implementation of these instruments, an international rule of law framework exists for protecting the rights of migrant workers. This is much needed, given the increasing integration of the global economy and the rise of precarious forms of employment.

Chapter 12 continues the theme of labour migration in the specific context of temporary labour mobility under the regime of international trade law. Although it is infrequently discussed within the mainstream of international migration law, the topic is significant because it is the only multilateral legal framework that seeks to *liberalise* the international movement of persons. The mechanism for doing so is the *General Agreement on Trade in Services* (1994) ('GATS'), which promotes different modes of trade in services between member States of the World Trade Organization. One such mode (Mode 4) is where labour crosses an international border to provide a service in another State. The potential of GATS Mode 4 to facilitate labour mobility is significant, but is far from fully realised. International migration is enabled by GATS only to the extent that member States make mutual commitments to allow entry of particular classes of persons in specific sectors of the economy. To date, these commitments have been limited and favour high-skilled employment, to the disadvantage of developing States. The prospects of further trade liberalisation under the current round of multilateral negotiations appear to be bleak, but regional trade frameworks provide a more optimistic outlook.

Chapter 13 marks an important shift from the substantive content of international migration law to the global institutions and processes that facilitate the progressive development of migration norms. A complex array of international institutions and processes has emerged in recent decades in response to increasing globalisation, greater awareness of the need for coordinated international efforts to manage migration, and heightened attention by governments. Of the

---

39 See above n. 22.

intergovernmental organisations, IOM is the only one whose mandate relates exclusively to migration, but bodies such as the Organisation for Economic Co-operation and Development have done much to advocate for greater global governance from the perspective of their members. Within the United Nations, there is a plethora of agencies whose work impacts on international migration at an operational, policy or strategic level. The work of UNHCR and the ILO has already been mentioned. The involvement of so many agencies provides opportunities to focus on different attributes of migration, but at the potential cost of gaps and overlaps, inefficiencies and conflicting agendas. Beyond the United Nations, a range of global fora has emerged in recent years and spurred further dialogue among States, but whether they will result in real institutional change remains an open question.

Chapter 14 is the counterpart of Chapter 13 and addresses the growing number and range of regional institutions and processes that deal with international migration. A large proportion of international migration in fact takes place between States within confined geographic regions (e.g., Europe, Africa, Asia, Latin America, Oceania), making regional arrangements especially relevant in finding solutions to shared challenges. The regional arrangements vary widely, from the highly developed free movement regime under the Schengen agreement in Europe, to the non-binding fora that comprise the regional consultative processes, to the wider groupings that straddle geographical regions and are known as inter-regional fora. Many of these arrangements are of relatively recent origin and their contribution to fostering international cooperation on migration remains to be seen.

Chapter 15 closes the book with an examination of emerging legal issues in international migration. In a field that is fragmented and dynamic, construction sites abound, but three areas are selected for special attention – internally displaced persons, environmentally induced migration and stranded migrants. The first of these is instructive for the way in which guiding principles have become accepted as the appropriate legal framework for addressing a situation of forced migration that falls outside the refugee system because the persons affected have not crossed an international border. Although not formally applicable to international migration, it can provide lessons for this domain. The second area, environmentally induced migration, has become a topic of hot debate because of the anticipated impacts of climate change on human displacement and resettlement. There is broad consensus that the Refugee Convention does not cover so-called 'climate refugees', but commentators are divided on whether it should be amended to give it that coverage, or a new instrument created to address the protection and assistance needs of these persons. Another option is to adopt non-binding principles akin to those adopted for internal displacement. The third area, stranded migrants, covers those caught between removal from the State in which they are present and their inability to gain entry to any other State. More research is needed before it can be confidently asserted that the category of stranded migrants has sufficient empirical coherence and validity to justify the development of a new framework of law and policy.

This précis of the subject matter of this book indicates that the foundations of international migration law have evolved rapidly and drawn inspiration from diverse areas of international law. As one of the present authors has stated, 'international migration law is perhaps the branch of law most resembling public international law – a dynamic law, in constant evolution, with occasionally blurred boundaries; a law as yet unfinished but necessary for understanding and managing one of the most pressing problems of our times.'[40]

40 Richard Perruchoud, 'Droit international et migration' (2005) 24(4) *Refugee Survey Quarterly* 81, 87 (Editors' translation).

2 Contemporary patterns of international migration

RICHARD BEDFORD

2.1. INTRODUCTION

Migration is challenging in many different ways: conceptually, methodologically and as a process that is fundamental to the lives of everyone. Of the three demographic processes that change populations (fertility, mortality and migration), migration is the least amenable to definition and analysis. Yet despite considerable debate among researchers and policy makers about what sorts of spatial mobility are encompassed by the term 'migration', it is often the only demographic process that governments attempt to manage or regulate through specific policies. As a result, migration frequently assumes greater visibility in the media and public consciousness than the process that usually underpins growth and structural change in most populations – the balance of births over deaths, or what is termed 'net natural increase'. It is natural increase, not net migration (the balance of immigrants over emigrants), that generally makes the major contribution to population growth.

In the eyes of some demographers, migration is the tail that wags the population dog.[1] This metaphor seems appropriate when one considers that the total estimated net migration loss of 92 million from the less developed regions to the more developed regions between 1960 and 2010 is equivalent to just 2 per cent of the 3.85 billion growth in the estimated population of the less developed regions over the same fifty-year period. In the developed regions, the 92 million net migration gain from the less developed regions is equivalent to 28 per cent of the 324.5 million increase in their estimated population over that period.[2]

Unlike births and deaths, which are mostly unambiguous events, migration requires some arbitrary definition because it is not a single event in a lifetime,

---

1 Ian Pool, 'Searching for Demography's Missing Link: Momentum' (2005) 31(2) *New Zealand Population Review* 1.
2 United Nations Department of Economic and Social Affairs, 'World Population Prospects: The 2010 Revision' (United Nations, 2011) Tables F01, F19.

nor is it necessarily the same from one occurrence to the next. As Skeldon observed, '[a]ll people move during their lifetime and it is incumbent upon the analyst and policy maker to decide which of these moves are significant'.[3] He went on to remind us that '[i]t is worth remembering that in virtually all societies a basic punishment is the withdrawal of freedom of movement through imprisonment'.

A basic human right that is guaranteed in most democracies is freedom of movement within the boundaries of one's State of nationality. There is also a human right to leave any country, including one's own, but there is no corresponding right to enter another country, unless you are a national. Issues relating to the rights of nationals and others crossing international boundaries are explored in Chapter 5.

This chapter has six substantive sections. Section 2.2 reviews the distinction between international migration and internal migration, and introduces the wide range of types of movement of people across national boundaries. Section 2.3 outlines some inherent contradictions in contemporary international migration in the wider context of globalisation. In Section 2.4 an important distinction between 'stocks' and 'flows' of migrants is introduced, along with the use of visa categories to define groups of migrants. Section 2.5 summarises some of the distinguishing features of contemporary international population movement at a global scale. This is followed in Section 2.6 by a more detailed examination of several types of movement, with reference to the major continental regions. A number of these types are the subject of separate chapters elsewhere in this book. The chapter concludes with an overview in Section 2.7 of the latest projections of population growth, urbanisation and net migration that have been produced by the United Nations Population Division.

2.2. WHAT IS INTERNATIONAL MIGRATION?

Human spatial mobility is best conceptualised as a complex system of short-term, long-term, short-distance and long-distance movements. Just what these terms mean depends on the units of analysis used by statisticians in their censuses, surveys and published statistics on those people who cross boundaries between places and regions within States and between States. *Internal migration* refers to the movement of people within States, and *international migration* refers to the movement of people across State boundaries.

The division between internal and international migration does not mean very much in some situations, such as the movement of European Union ('EU') nationals within the EU. Germans, for example, have freedom to move within Germany

---

3 Ronald Skeldon, *Migration and Development: A Global Perspective* (Addison Wesley Longman, 1997) 2.

(internal migration) as well as freedom to move into any other State within the EU (international migration). However, in most other regional groupings of States a defining characteristic of international migration is the requirement to produce a passport at the border, along with some evidence – usually a visa – that you have a right to enter another State.

Approval to move into a town or rural community within one's State is not normally a requirement faced by nationals, although in most European States it is necessary to produce a passport or an equivalent identity document when registering for accommodation. In China, rights to reside in particular parts of the country, and to obtain particular socio-economic entitlements, have been defined by *hukou* status.[4] China has a very large 'floating' population of internal migrants who do not have the legal right to settle in the places to which they have moved.

There is far more mobility within States than across national boundaries, especially in large countries, such as Australia, Brazil, Canada, China, the Russian Federation and the United States. There are also strong linkages between internal and international migration, especially with regard to migration from rural to urban areas. The exodus from Europe to the 'New World' in the nineteenth and twentieth centuries, for example, was closely linked with what Zelinsky has termed the 'great shaking loose of migrants from the countryside' that accompanied the breakdown of feudal peasant agricultural systems with the onset of the Industrial Revolution.[5]

The transition from what are essentially rural societies and economies, dominated by production of foods and commodities for local consumption, to societies where populations are increasingly concentrated in towns and cities, dependent for their livelihoods on production of goods and services for local, national and international markets, has been a universal trend since the nineteenth century. This urbanisation transition has been accompanied by unprecedented flows of people within and between States.

By 2009 the United Nations estimated that 50 per cent of the world's 6.8 billion people were living in urban areas.[6] By 2050 it is estimated that the world's urban population might be close to 6.5 billion (not far from the total population in 2009) or the equivalent of 70 per cent of the projected 9.3 billion people under the medium growth variant scenario.[7] Saunders suggests that '[w]hat will be remembered about the twenty-first century, more than anything else except perhaps the effects of a changing climate, is the great and final shift of human populations out

---

4 The Chinese *hukou* or family registration system essentially ties people to a residency registration in their hometown, largely preventing them from accessing a range of public services (such as health insurance and free schooling for children) once they migrate to other places. The system has attracted a great deal of critical comment: see, e.g., Kam Chan and Will Buckingham, 'Is China Abolishing the Hukou System?' (2008) 195 *China Quarterly* 582.
5 Wilbur Zelinsky, 'The Hypothesis of the Mobility Transition' (1971) 61(2) *Geographical Review* 219, 236.
6 United Nations Department of Economic and Social Affairs, 'World Urbanization Prospects: The 2009 Revision – Highlights' (United Nations, 2010).
7 United Nations Department of Economic and Social Affairs, above n. 2.

of agricultural life and into cities'.[8] Much of the movement from rural to urban areas will be internal migration, but there will also be extensive international movements. A critical issue will be the ability of cities to provide a successful transition to an urban livelihood for people arriving in unprecedented numbers and at unprecedented rates within and between States in most parts of the world.

There are numerous classifications and typologies of international migration that cover the wide range of short-term and long-term movements across international borders, ranging from tourist visits, seasonal labour flows, movement associated with education, through to permanent settlement. The United Nations has prepared a series of definitions and classifications of different types of spatial mobility, with a view to seeking standardisation in the collection of data on population movement.[9] However, as the International Organization for Migration ('IOM') points out, 'countries collecting data on migration do so to support their own national legislation, administrative and policy needs and are therefore often reluctant to adopt concepts and definitions that would allow for regional and international coherence at the expense of their own specific use of the data collected'.[10]

The typologies of population movements that have been developed by researchers cover the complex mix of regular flows (e.g., labour migration, family reunion and humanitarian migration) and irregular flows (e.g., voluntary undocumented movement across international borders, people smuggling and human trafficking).[11] A common distinction made within regular international migration flows is between the short-term tourist and visitor movements on the one hand, and longer-term temporary work, business and residential migration on the other. Within the irregular flows, voluntary undocumented migration (both short-term and long-term movement without appropriate documentation) and people smuggling are usually distinguished from involuntary movements associated with human trafficking.

The irregular flows, along with those humanitarian movements associated with refugee migration, have captured considerable attention from lawyers with an interest in international migration, especially regarding the human rights of those who move from one State to another. Several chapters in this book address these flows and the issues that have challenged lawyers specialising in the regulatory frameworks governing international flows of people.

There is also a rapidly expanding industry, which includes increasing numbers of law firms, providing professional assistance to clients who wish to satisfy the

---

8 Doug Saunders, *Arrival City. How the Largest Migration in History Is Reshaping Our World* (William Heinemann, 2010) 1.

9 United Nations Department of Economic and Social Affairs, 'Recommendations on Statistics of International Migration: Revision 1' (United Nations, 1998).

10 International Organization for Migration, *World Migration Report 2010: The Future of Migration: Building Capacities for Change* (IOM, 2010) 237.

11 See, e.g., Skeldon, above n. 3, 57–9; Zelinsky, above n. 5.

regulations governing entry to another State, especially entry that allows migrants to work and reside at their chosen destination. In countries like Australia, Canada, New Zealand, the United Kingdom and the United States there are vibrant immigration consultancy industries, which have been subject to increasing regulation in recent years to ensure good practice and fair treatment of clients. Australia, Canada and New Zealand have legislation governing the registration and behaviour of immigration consultants.

International migration in the late twentieth and early twenty-first centuries is thus a major business as well as a very significant demographic process. It is important to keep both of these dimensions in mind when examining international migration. The reasons given by people for crossing international borders are very much affected by the regulatory frameworks they need to negotiate to gain the right to stay in another State.

In several States that favour immigration, such as Australia and New Zealand, priority is placed on migrants with skills that can meet particular needs in the internal labour market. Migration to join family members or for humanitarian reasons is accorded much less priority under contemporary immigration policy. Yet recent longitudinal surveys of immigrants in both countries have demonstrated that the great majority of highly skilled migrants have chosen to move to these States for lifestyle reasons, especially for their families, rather than for economic reasons.[12]

The reverse situation applies in the United States. The biggest flow of regular permanent migrants into that country has been admitted through the 'family reunion' avenue. Yet the main motive for migrants from all over the world seeking access to residence in the United States is economic, namely, to obtain wage employment, to obtain greater skills to improve their chances of getting wage employment, or to become a business operator in the world's richest and most advanced capitalist economy.

The migration industry also has a thriving, highly exploitative criminal dimension that is exemplified by people smuggling and human trafficking. Such is the desperation of increasing numbers of people to escape living in places experiencing violent internal conflict, repressive political regimes or severe economic hardship that some seek entry to other States through irregular channels. There are many unscrupulous 'entrepreneurs' who take advantage of this desperation and extort significant sums of money or other forms of wealth in return for what is often a highly risky passage to a State of choice. Chapter 9 addresses the processes of trafficking and smuggling in detail.

---

12 Lesleyanne Hawthorne, 'Competing for Skills: Migration Policies and Trends in New Zealand and Australia' (New Zealand Department of Labour, 2011); Anne-Marie Masgoret, Paul Merwood and Manuila Tausi, 'New Faces, New Futures: New Zealand – Findings from the Longitudinal Immigration Survey' (New Zealand Department of Labour, 2009).

Papademetriou's claim that irregular migration 'has been by far the fastest rising single form of migration during the past 10 years' may well be valid if one restricts the definition of migration to people who intend staying in the State to which they move.[13] If one extends the definition to include temporary moves for work, study, family-related reasons, business activity or extended holidays, then irregular migration may not be the fastest-growing form of population movement across international borders. The 2011 report of the United Nations World Tourism Organization ('UNWTO') documents over 1 billion moves into countries by non-resident tourists around 2010.[14] This compares with 168 million international tourists forty years earlier in 1968, and 14 million sixty years earlier in 1948.[15]

Legal flows of people across international borders have been increasing at an exponential rate, especially in the more developed countries. These short-term visits are often precursors to longer visits, some of which lead on to study, work and eventual residence. Indeed, transitioning to residence via several different types of permits has long been common in Europe and the United States, and has become much more prominent in States like Australia, Canada and New Zealand, which have deliberately sought new settlers in a more open and aggressive way than most States.

Irregular migration, and an associated anti-immigrant rhetoric from right-wing political parties, dominates much of the media commentary on immigration as we enter the second decade of the twenty-first century. Yet the contemporary global context within which international migration is situated is anything but negative. Population movement between States is an integral part of globalisation and an essential driver of future economic growth and security in States where there is currently a backlash against immigration.

2.3. MIGRATION AND GLOBALISATION

It is a fundamental contradiction of contemporary globalisation that regulation of population movement across national boundaries has increased during an era characterised by increasingly porous borders for movement of raw materials, goods, capital, services and information. As Massey and Taylor observed: 'Whether this contradiction can be sustained is one of the fundamental questions of the twenty-first century, and how it is resolved – through the termination of global trade or the opening of countries to freer immigration – will determine

---

13 Demetrios Papademetriou (ed.), *Europe and its Immigrants in the 21st Century: A New Deal or a Continuing Dialogue of the Deaf?* (Migration Policy Institute and Luso-American Foundation, 2006) xviii.
14 United Nations World Tourism Organization, 'UNWTO Tourism Highlights' (UNWTO, 2011).
15 Zelinsky, above n. 5, 246–7.

much about population size, composition and structure of the world's developed nations.'[16]

International migration in the twenty-first century is much more complicated than it was during a previous phase of globalisation between the 1880s and the outbreak of the First World War. During this era of expansion in the international economy, based on free trade and mobile capital, there were virtually no controls on the movement of people across national boundaries. It is estimated that during the nineteenth century and the first two decades of the twentieth century more than 50 million people left Europe for destinations in the Americas, Oceania and elsewhere.[17] There were no border controls that inhibited the movement of Europeans, even if their presence was generally not welcomed by indigenous peoples living in the countries they went to. Indeed, European settlers in many parts of the world could be characterised as 'boat people' – strangers arriving by sea and staying to seek a new life in lands that belonged to others, rather than immigrants who sought approval in advance for permission to enter the State and stay short-term or as permanent residents.

Having taken control of their new 'homes', the settlers did not take long to begin restricting entry of strangers arriving from other parts of the world, especially countries in Asia. From the 1880s, the European populations of Australia, Canada, New Zealand and the United States began restricting entry. The modern era of immigration policy began with attempts to regulate entry of Chinese and Indians, and it was much more targeted and selective than has been characteristic of the contemporary phase of globalisation. Restrictions on entry of people from particular parts of the world were removed in Canada and the United States during the 1960s, in Australia in 1972 and in New Zealand in 1986.

From the middle of the twentieth century, after the disruption caused by two world wars, the recession of the 1930s, and the Cold War in the 1950s and 1960s, a new phase of globalisation emerged, associated with rapid increases in cross-border movements of raw materials, manufactured goods, services, information (greatly enhanced by the evolution of computer technology) and people. The 1970s is usually taken to be the beginning of this latest phase of globalisation, and, once again, the rapid growth in volume of population movements within and between States is rooted in structural transformations that are linked with the incorporation of States into the global market economy.

The latest phase of globalisation is characterised by another apparent contradiction: a freeing up of eligibility to seek work and residence in many developed countries while at the same time tightening up control of cross-border movements

---

16 Douglas Massey and Edward Taylor, 'Back to the Future: Immigration Research, Immigration Policy and Globalization in the Twenty-First Century' in Douglas Massey and Edward Taylor (eds.), *International Migration. Prospects and Policies in a Global Market* (Oxford University Press, 2004) 373.

17 Imre Ferenczi, 'International Migration Statistics' in Walter Willcox (ed.), *International Migrations, Volume I: Statistics* (National Bureau of Economic Research, 1929) 47 cited in Massey and Taylor, above n. 16, 374.

through visa requirements, electronic monitoring of approvals for entry and screening of arrivals based increasingly on international cooperation between security intelligence agencies. There has been a return to a form of border control that was widely condemned during the Cold War between Western and Eastern Europe – the construction of walls to stem the flow of people across national boundaries. The challenge for the twenty-first-century wall-builders is that migrant populations are many times greater than they have ever been in the past and they are travelling much longer distances, often through several States, to reach their intended destinations.

2.4. MIGRANT STOCKS, FLOWS AND VISA CATEGORIES

One of the few relatively consistent sets of data relating to international migration is the numbers of people in a State who were born in another State – the migrant stocks. While these statistics give an indication of the extent to which a State's population has been impacted by immigration, by themselves the sizes and birth-place compositions of migrant stocks tell us nothing about when the migrants arrived, whether they moved directly to the places where they were living at the time of the census or survey and whether they have moved within the State or to other States in the past.

The United Nations Population Division has estimated that the stock of people living outside their State of birth for a minimum of one year (its definition of an immigrant) was around 214 million in 2010, or 3.1 per cent of world population (Table 2.1).[18] Approximately 70 million of these immigrants were living in Europe, which now includes many of the States that emerged following the collapse of the former Soviet Union. These 70 million immigrants include 30 million ethnic Russians, who had been internal migrants until the early 1990s but were reclassified as international migrants when the Soviet Union broke up into a large number of independent States.[19] Once adjustments are made for political changes like these, which can have a profound impact on the classification of migrant stocks, Europe's share of the world's immigrant stock falls to well below the stock for Asia.

Migrant stocks, defined by birthplace, are just one indicator of migration, and not necessarily a very useful one if the intention is to indicate the magnitude and relative importance of contemporary population flows between countries. Migrant flow data are even harder to estimate than information on stocks because the

18 Data sources for Table 2.1: United Nations Development Programme, *Human Development Report 2009. Overcoming Barriers: Human Mobility and Development* (UNDP, 2009) 146; United Nations Department of Economic and Social Affairs, above n. 2.
19 Papademetriou, above n. 13, xvii.

Table 2.1 Populations, immigrant stocks and percentages of populations who are immigrants by major region, 2010

Region	Population (millions)	Migrant stock (millions)	Migrant stock (%)
Africa	1,022.2	19.3	1.89
Asia	4,164.3	61.3	1.47
Europe	738.2	69.8	9.46
Latin America and Caribbean	590.1	7.5	1.27
Northern America	344.5	50.0	14.51
Oceania	36.6	6.0	16.39
All regions	6,895.9	213.9	3.10

resultant numbers are determined by who is counted as a migrant and how the count is made. Some States, such as Australia and New Zealand, which do not have land borders with neighbouring States, have very good systems for recording continuously almost everyone who crosses their international borders.

Most of the world's people live in States that have land borders with neighbouring States, and statistics collected at the border or at major airports cannot capture everyone crossing their borders. Residents in twenty-five European States (many within the EU, plus some like Switzerland and Norway that are not in the EU) have the right under the Schengen agreement to 'roam freely'. There are very incomplete border crossing statistics in Europe; information on people entering and leaving States is collected through registration systems at the places where they stay.

The other major type of migration data relates to the visa categories used to regulate the flows of short-term and long-term migrants into States. Most developed countries have broadly similar streams of migrants covered by their visas: skilled workers, investors and entrepreneurs, students, temporary workers at all skill levels, tourists and short-term visitors, family members and some humanitarian categories including refugees and asylum seekers. Who is classified as being a 'migrant', and what information is collected on them, depends on 'political determinations about what to collect or not to collect and, more importantly, what to report and not to report'.[20] Measurement of migration thus remains a critical and contested area in migration research simply because statistics on the volume and types of migrants depend on definitions adopted in censuses (migrant stocks and flows), at the border (flow statistics) and by immigration authorities (visa category statistics).

20 Ibid.

2.5. A GLOBAL PERSPECTIVE ON MIGRANT STOCKS AND FLOWS

It has become fashionable to refer to the contemporary era as 'the age of migration'.[21] Yet it is difficult to identify a time when migration was unimportant. Skeldon has suggested that:

> Our era is certainly *an* age of migration, but it is not *the* age of migration. There have been many times in the past when migration has been just as significant. Although more people may be moving over longer distances today than ever before, this is due primarily to the fact that there are more people alive in the world today and that modern technological development in transport has facilitated the conquest of distance.[22]

The United Nations Population Division has estimated the world's population mid-2010 to be 6.89 billion (Table 2.2).[23] The great majority (82 per cent) were living in countries classified by the United Nations as 'less developed' (70 per cent) or 'least developed' (12 per cent). There are currently forty-nine countries in the

Table 2.2 Populations, international migrant stocks, tourist/visitor arrivals and refugees by major country groups around 2010 (millions)

Population and migrant groups	Country groups[a] More developed	Less developed	Least developed	World
Population (2010)	1,235.9	4,827.7	832.3	6,895.9
% total	17.9	70.0	12.1	100
International migrant stocks (2010)	127.7	74.7	11.5	213.9
% total	59.7	34.9	5.4	100
Tourist/visitor arrivals (2007)	629.6	416.5	14.5	1,060.6
Refugees (2010)	2.4	11.9	2.1	16.4
% total	14.6	72.6	12.8	100
Migrant stock as % of total population	10.3	1.5	1.3	3.1
Tourist/visitor arrivals as % of total population	50.9	8.6	1.7	15.4
Refugees as % of total population	0.2	0.2	0.3	0.2

[a] More developed countries are found in Europe and North America and include Australia, Japan and New Zealand. There are currently forty-nine least developed countries in Africa, Asia, the Caribbean and the Pacific. The less developed countries comprise the other countries in Africa, Asia (excluding Japan), Latin America and the Caribbean, and the Pacific Islands.

21 Stephen Castles and Mark Miller, *The Age of Migration: International Population Movements in the Modern World* (Guilford Press, 4th edn, 2009).
22 Skeldon, above n. 3, 194.
23 Data sources for Table 2.2: populations, migrant stocks and refugees: United Nations Department of Economic and Social Affairs, above n. 2; tourist visitors and arrivals: United Nations Statistics Division, 'Statistical Yearbook 53rd Issue' (United Nations, 2010) 625–81.

'least developed' category with an aggregate population of around 832 million. Sixty per cent of the world's international migrant stock was in the developed countries, with 35 per cent in the less developed and 5 per cent in the least developed countries.

Stocks of international migrants are heavily concentrated in the more developed world, and this pattern is replicated in the flows of tourist and visitor arrivals. UNWTO has estimated that just over half of the 1 billion tourists in 2010 crossing international borders travelled to countries in Europe (527 million, 52 per cent).[24] In Table 2.2 data on tourist flows have been drawn from estimates for 2007 published by the United Nations Statistics Division because its data can be aggregated for the three groups of countries shown in the table. Just less than 60 per cent of the arrivals recorded in 2007 crossed the national boundaries of countries in Europe and North America, as well as the international borders of Japan, Australia and New Zealand.[25]

At this very high level of aggregation, the distribution of short-term flows mirrors reasonably closely the distribution of migrant stocks. The distribution of the estimated 16.4 million refugees, on the other hand, is much closer to the distribution of the global population: 73 per cent are to be found in the less developed countries, 13 per cent in the least developed countries and only 15 per cent in the more developed group (Table 2.2). There are thus quite different distribution patterns for the destinations of short-term and long-term voluntary migrants and those forced by persecution to leave their home States. Most refugees end up living for many years in temporary camps in neighbouring States to the ones they have fled. Refugee flows have a very different set of drivers and patterns from those that are linked with voluntary short-term and long-term migration.

In 2010, the numbers of refugees in each of the three broad country groups were equivalent to around one-fifth of 1 per cent of their respective estimated populations. These are very small percentages and the summary statistics disguise a highly uneven pattern in the distribution of refugees across specific States. In the case of migrant stocks the percentages are much higher, reaching the equivalent of 10 per cent of the 1.24 billion population in the more developed countries, while hovering around the 1 per cent mark for the less and least developed countries. In the more developed countries the 629.6 million tourist/visitor arrivals in 2007 were the equivalent of 50 per cent of the population in these countries – five times the size of the migrant stock numbers. A similar situation was found in the less developed

---

24 United Nations World Tourism Organization, above n. 14.
25 The aggregate figures for visitor numbers need to be treated with caution as there is no consistent method for collecting statistics on short-term visitors at the border. The United Nations Statistics Division, above n. 23, 640, lists eight different data series used in the compilation of their tourist/visitor arrivals, all of which exclude residents from the figures. Some include same-day visitors who cross the State's border; some record tourists by registration in hotels rather than at the border (common in Europe). Notwithstanding these limitations, the data in Table 2.2 are useful for indicating the broad magnitude and distribution pattern of short-term arrivals at a global scale.

countries, where the 416.5 million short-term arrivals were more than five times the 74.7 million migrants who had been born in other States.

IOM has estimated that the global stock of international migrants by 2050 could be as high as 405 million, based on rates of increase in migrant stocks since 1990.[26] If the global population reaches 9.3 billion by 2050 (the medium variant projection by the United Nations Population Division in 2011), the estimated international migrant stock could be equivalent to 4.4 per cent of world population. If, over the next forty years, short-term visitor flows were to grow at just half the average annual rate (2.3 per cent) that they did between 1967 and 2007 (4.6 per cent per annum) then by 2050 there might be over 2.7 billion tourists/visitors crossing international borders – the equivalent of 29 per cent of the estimated 9.3 billion population by mid-century. This is double the 15 per cent that 1.06 billion tourist arrivals equates to when compared with the 2010 global population estimate (Table 2.2).

International population mobility will increase substantially over the next forty years, partly because of the changing sizes and age structures of populations in the more and less developed countries, partly because of the ongoing urbanisation of the world's population and, linked to the latter, partly because of the increasing wealth and material aspirations of populations in Asia, especially China and India. Increasing flows of workers from low-income to high-income countries will be necessary as the search for work by people from the former coincides with the need for the latter to maintain the sizes of their workforces as their populations age as a result of low fertility.

Even though the current global economic crisis has resulted in a reduction in the volume of population movement between States,[27] an increasing flow of labour from less developed to more developed countries will remain an important structural feature of the global economy in the twenty-first century. The key drivers of contemporary international migration are likely to strengthen over the next few decades, resulting in an increase in volumes of short-term and long-term movements between States.[28] Environmental changes linked with global warming and ongoing urbanisation, especially in coastal locations, will become an increasingly important driver of internal as well as international migration, adding further stimulus to the intensifying mobility of the world's population (see Chapter 15). Some of these issues are discussed further in Section 2.7 below.

---

26 International Organization for Migration, above n. 10, 3.
27 Ibid.; Bimal Ghosh, 'The Global Economic Crisis and Migration. Where Do We Go From Here?' (International Organization for Migration, 2011).
28 Global Commission on International Migration, 'Migration in an Interconnected World: New Directions for Action' (GCIM, 2005); World Bank, 'Global Economic Prospects 2006: Economic Implications of Remittances and Migration' (World Bank, 2006); Organisation for Economic Co-operation and Development, 'International Migration Outlook: SOPEMI 2010' (OECD, 2010); United Nations Development Programme, above n. 18; International Organization for Migration, above n. 10.

2.6. REGIONAL PERSPECTIVES ON MIGRANT STOCKS AND FLOWS

One of the most basic and heavily tested propositions about human spatial mobility relates to the distances that migrants travel – the great majority of migrants go only a short distance because of the constraints of cost and effort on long-distance movement. This may seem contradictory in light of concerns in some parts of the world about large numbers of people seeking to enter their States, especially from States at some distance from them. Yet the great bulk of short-term and long-term international migration is between States that are geographically close rather than between those that are distant. There are exceptions, such as the extensive temporary labour migration from parts of South and Southeast Asia to the Middle East oil-producing countries, and the flows of skilled migrants from Asia and Africa into Europe and the United States. But the latter are comparatively small flows by comparison with the volume of movements within and between States in Africa and Asia.

The University of Sussex's Development Research Centre on Migration, Globalisation and Poverty ('DRC'), in association with the United Nations Population Division, has produced a matrix of migrant stocks relating to 2000–2, the period when many of the 200 countries listed held their last national population census.[29] On the basis of the relationship between country of birth and country of residence at the time of the census, it is possible to identify the immigrant populations living in each major continental region as well as the numbers who had been born in each region but were living in another region (the emigrants) (Table 2.3).[30] The immigrants and emigrants for the six 'continental' regions are the same people being assessed in two ways – where they came from and where they went. They sum to the same total of 175.8 million, which was the estimated total global stock of migrants living outside their States of birth in 2000–2.

In four of the six regions shown in Table 2.3 more than 50 per cent of their immigrant stocks came from States within the region (the numbers along the diagonal in Table 2.3 refer to movements within each region).[31] In the cases of Africa (57 countries and territories) and Asia (50 countries and territories) almost three-quarters of the people born outside their country of residence in 2000–2 were estimated to have come from other countries within the region (82.4 per cent in Africa, 72.4 per cent in

29 Development Research Centre on Migration, Globalisation and Poverty, *Global Migrant Origin Database* (2007) University of Sussex, www.migrationdrc.org; United Nations Department of Economic and Social Affairs, 'Trends in International Migrant Stock: The 2008 Revision' (POP/DB/MIG/Stock/Rev.2008, United Nations, 2009).

30 Data sources for Table 2.3: percentage distributions: United Nations Development Programme, above n. 18, 150; immigrant and emigrant stocks 2000–2: Development Research Centre on Migration, Globalisation and Poverty, above n. 29.

31 The patterns for *emigrants* from particular regions are rather different. For a discussion of emigration within Oceania, see: Richard Bedford, 'International Migration in the South Pacific Region' in Mary Kritz, Lin Lim and Hania Zlotnik (eds.), *International Migration Systems: A Global Approach* (Clarendon Press, 1992) 41; Richard Bedford, 'International Migration, Identity and Development in Oceania: A Synthesis of Ideas' in Douglas Massey and Edward Taylor (eds.), *International Migration: Prospects and Policies in a Global Market* (Oxford University Press, 2004) 230.

Table 2.3 Regional patterns of migration: percentages of immigrant and emigrant stocks by source or destination, and estimated immigrant stocks (millions), 2000–2

Region	Continent/region (percentages)					
	Africa	Asia	Euro	LA/Car.	Nth Am.	Oceania
(a) Immigrant source (%)						
Africa	82.4	6.3	12.3	1.0	3.1	4.4
Asia	6.8	72.4	27.3	5.6	26.6	28.7
Europe	8.4	17.3	53.7	21.8	20.4	48.2
LA/Caribbean	1.8	2.7	4.7	59.1	46.0	1.7
Northern America	0.5	1.1	1.4	12.5	3.1	2.6
Oceania	0.1	0.3	0.5	0.2	0.9	14.4
Total	100.0	100.0	100.0	100.0	100.0	100.0
Immigrant stocks (millions)	14.8	59.3	50.1	5.6	40.9	5.1
(b) Emigrant destinations (%)						
Africa	52.6	1.7	2.5	1.1	2.2	1.4
Asia	12.5	54.7	16.0	5.1	14.7	8.7
Europe	28.9	24.5	59.0	10.3	23.6	20.1
LA/Caribbean	0.2	0.5	2.5	13.4	21.0	0.6
Northern America	4.9	16.4	15.4	69.8	34.9	22.5
Oceania	0.9	2.2	4.6	0.3	3.7	46.7
Total	100.0	100.0	100.0	100.0	100.0	100.0
Emigrant stocks (millions)	25.1	73.6	45.2	16.5	13.7	1.6

Asia). In terms of total numbers of immigrants, intra-regional migration accounted for approximately 55 million of a total estimated immigrant stock of 74 million in the two regions (14.8 million in Africa, 59.3 million in Asia). In Europe (48 countries and territories) and Latin America and the Caribbean (46 countries and territories) the percentages of intra-regional immigrants were lower – 53.7 per cent and 59.1 per cent respectively. Countries in Asia, especially former colonies of Britain and France, accounted for prominent shares of the immigrant stock in Europe, while countries in Europe accounted for 21.8 per cent of the immigrant stock in Latin America (Spain and Portugal) and the Caribbean (Britain and France).

In the remaining two regions, Northern America (5 countries and territories) and Oceania (24 countries and territories), the shares of immigrant stock born in States in the region were much lower (3.1 per cent in Northern America, 14.4 per cent in

Oceania). These small shares are partly a function of the much smaller numbers of States that could be sources of immigrants, but perhaps more importantly these are the regions containing four of the traditional countries of immigration: Australia, Canada, New Zealand and the United States. Immigrants from countries in Asia (26.6 per cent) outnumber immigrants from Europe (20.4 per cent) in the case of Northern America's migrant stock, while the reverse is found in Oceania, where 48.2 per cent of the immigrant stock came from States in Europe and 28.7 per cent from States in Asia.

2.6.1. Regional migration systems

Within and overlapping the continental regions are regional systems of migration that are manifested in strong cultural, economic, social and political links between particular groups of States – systems that contain the major sources and destinations of migrants from the region. Kritz *et al.* and Skeldon have examined several enduring regional migration systems in different parts of the world where international population movements complement other flows and exchanges taking place between States.[32] Kritz and Zlotnik note that 'international migrations do not occur randomly but usually take place between countries that have close historical, cultural, or economic ties. Moreover, migrants are increasingly assisted in their moves by networks of earlier migrants, labour recruiters, corporations, travel agents, or even development agencies'.[33]

The networks in different parts of the world that assist with the mobilisation and recruitment of migrants, and with the organisation of migration, link the various States into coherent migration systems. Well-established ones have been identified in West Africa,[34] the southern cone of Latin America,[35] the Caribbean[36] and the South Pacific region.[37] There are several others, especially in Asia, Europe and North America, and the boundaries of these systems are fluid, not fixed. A critical component of all migration systems, and a key process responsible for the fluidity of their boundaries, is the international mobility of workers, students, tourists and visitors who have permission to stay at their destination for a specified period of time. The mobility behaviour of different types of temporary migrants has been increasingly gaining the attention of policy makers and researchers in recent years.

---

32 Mary Kritz, Lin Lim and Hania Zlotnik (eds.), *International Migration Systems: A Global Approach* (Clarendon Press, 1992); Skeldon, above n. 3.

33 Mary Kritz and Hania Zlotnik, 'Global Interactions: Migration Systems, Processes and Policies' in Mary Kritz, Lin Lim and Hania Zlotnik (eds.), *International Migration Systems: A Global Approach* (Clarendon Press, 1992) 1.

34 Paulina Makinwa-Adebusoye, 'The West African Migration System' in Mary Kritz, Lin Lim and Hania Zlotnik (eds.), *International Migration Systems: A Global Approach* (Clarendon Press, 1992) 63.

35 Jorge Balan, 'The Role of Migration Policies and Social Networks in the Development of a Migration System in the Southern Cone' in Mary Kritz, Lin Lim and Hania Zlotnik (eds.), *International Migration Systems: A Global Approach* (Clarendon Press, 1992) 115.

36 Alan Simmons and Jean Guengant, 'Caribbean Exodus and the World System' in Mary Kritz, Lin Lim and Hania Zlotnik (eds.), *International Migration Systems: A Global Approach* (Clarendon Press, 1992) 94.

37 Bedford, above n. 31.

CASE STUDY 2.1 The West African migration system

The West African migration system links the fifteen States shown in Map 2.1, which comprise the Economic Community of West African States ('ECOWAS').[38] ECOWAS was set up in 1975 with the primary objective of 'promoting cooperation and development in all fields of economic activity . . . and social and cultural matters for the purpose of raising the standard of living of its peoples'. The migration system predates ECOWAS by several centuries, and the Economic Community simply gave contemporary reinforcement to a series of trading and labour exchanges that have linked societies in this part of Africa for a very long time. A distinctive set of political, ethno-cultural, geographical (climatic) and economic factors created what has been termed 'a loosely integrated organic region where major inter-territorial and international migrations have occurred historically'.[39]

There were major African kingdoms in West Africa long before the advent of the infamous Atlantic slave trade that caused absolute decline in the region's population.[40] The creation of colonies for Britain and France in the nineteenth century introduced a series of artificial political boundaries that paid scant attention to the indigenous ethnic groups and their traditional patterns of agriculture and population movement. Notwithstanding attempts to regulate migration, considerable movement between colonies persisted. This was often seasonal and in response to changing labour demands on commercial plantations and in the evolving coastal towns.[41]

By 2010 the region's population totalled around 304.3 million – more than four times what it had been in 1950 towards the end of the colonial era (Table CS 2.1A).[42] In 2010 there were an estimated 8.4 million people living in the ECOWAS member States who had been born in other States. This migrant stock comprised only 2.8 per cent of the total population in 2010 – a very small share by comparison with some other regions. West Africa is a region of fast population growth, with numbers expected to more than double again between 2010 and 2050. Nigeria dominates strongly in demographic and economic terms, with more than half the region's population in 2010, and a projected population for 2050 (389.6 million) that will alone exceed the whole region's 2010 population (304.3 million).

Evidence of the enduring importance of population movement between States in the West African migration system can be found in the origins and destinations of

---

38 The treaty was signed on 28 May 1975 in Lagos by fifteen States. Cape Verde became the sixteenth member in 1976 following its independence, while Mauritania withdrew in 2000, reducing membership to fifteen. The tables include Mauritania in the tallies for historical purposes.

39 Makinwa-Adebusoye, above n. 34, 63.   40 Skeldon, above n. 3, 70.

41 For discussions of colonial and post-colonial mobility in West Africa, see Makinwa-Adebusoye, above n. 34, 6379; Skeldon, above n. 3, 1746; Kenneth Swindell, 'People on the Move in West Africa: From Pre-Colonial Polities to Post-Independence States' in Robin Cohen (ed.), *The Cambridge Survey of World Migration* (Cambridge University Press, 1995) 196; Aderanti Adepoju, 'The Politics of International Migration in Post-Colonial Africa' in Robin Cohen (ed.), *The Cambridge Survey of World Migration* (Cambridge University Press, 1995) 166.

42 Data sources for Table CS 2.1A: population estimates, United Nations Department of Economic and Social Affairs, above n. 2; migrant stock estimates, United Nations Department of Economic and Social Affairs, above n. 6.

migrants in 2002–3 (Table CS 2.1B).[43] Around 83 per cent of the migrant stock in West African States had been born in States within the region, with a further 5 per cent from States of birth elsewhere in Africa. Just less than 12 per cent came from other parts of the world. The major exceptions were the islands that comprise Cape Verde, where 30 per cent of its immigrants were from outside of Africa, and Ghana, with its links to other parts of Africa and the United Kingdom (its former colonial power). In the case of West Africans living outside their countries of birth, there is greater variability across the region in the importance of the three destination areas shown in Table CS 2.1B. However just less than 70 per cent of the West African migrant stock was still living within their region in 2002–3, with 10 per cent in other countries in Africa, and 21 per cent living outside the continent, mainly in Europe. The migration system remains strong and now has a new dimension that builds on an old practice of undocumented movement into Europe, via Cape Verde and the Canary Islands.[44]

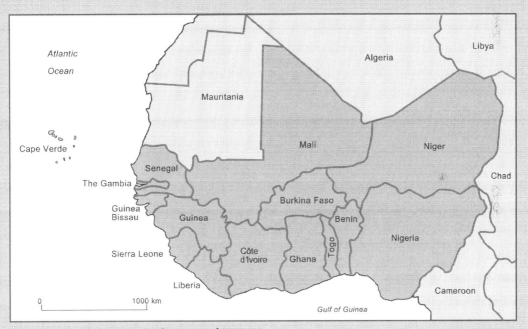

Map 2.1 Member States of ECOWAS

43 Data source for Table CS 2.1B: Development Research Centre on Migration, Globalisation and Poverty, above n. 29.

44 For further discussion of irregular migration between West Africa and Europe, see Organisation for Economic Co-operation and Development, *Regional Challenges of West African Migration: African and European Perspectives* (OECD, 2009); Michael Samers, *Migration* (Routledge, 2010) 14.

Table CS 2.1A West African population growth, 1950–2050, and migrant stock, 2010 (thousands)

State	Population			Migrant stocks 2010		
	1950	2010	2050	No.	% total pop.	% female
Benin	2,255	8,850	21,734	232	2.5	45.5
Burkina Faso	4,284	16,469	46,721	1,043	6.4	50.8
Cape Verde	178	496	632	12	2.4	50.4
Côte d'Ivoire	2,630	19,738	40,674	2,407	11.2	45.1
Gambia	271	1,728	4,036	290	16.6	50.5
Ghana	4,981	24,392	49,107	1,852	7.6	41.8
Guinea	3,094	9,982	23,006	395	3.8	53.1
Guinea–Bissau	518	1,515	3,185	19	1.2	50.0
Liberia	911	3,994	9,660	96	2.3	45.1
Mali	4,638	15,370	42,130	163	1.2	47.6
Mauritania[a]	657	3,460	7,085	99	2.9	42.2
Niger	2,462	15,512	55,435	202	1.3	53.9
Nigeria	37,860	158,423	389,615	1,128	0.7	47.4
Senegal	2,416	12,434	28,607	211	1.6	51.2
Sierra Leone	1,895	5,868	11,088	107	1.8	45.7
Togo	1,395	6,028	11,130	185	2.7	50.2
Total West Africa[b]	70,451	304,261	743,850	8,441	2.8	46.5
Total Africa	229,895	856,327	1,960,102	19,263	1.9	46.8
% West Africa	30.6	35.5	37.9	43.8	–	–

[a] Mauritania withdrew from ECOWAS in 2000, but is included here for historical purposes.
[b] Including St Helena with an estimated population of 4,000 in 2010.

Table CS 2.1B West African migrant stock: sources and destinations, 2002–3 (percentages)

State	Birthplaces of migrants to West Africa			Destinations of West Africa-born		
	Within West Africa	Other Africa	Other States	Other West Africa	Other Africa	Other States
Benin	97.1	1.1	1.8	81.3	10.3	8.4
Burkina Faso	83.0	6.2	10.7	91.4	2.6	6.0
Cape Verde	10.2	59.2	30.7	18.6	15.2	66.2
Côte d'Ivoire	90.7	6.0	3.2	44.8	2.9	52.3
Gambia	94.6	1.3	4.1	42.1	2.6	55.3
Ghana	58.9	22.9	18.1	72.0	2.8	25.2

Table CS 2.1B (cont.)

State	Birthplaces of migrants to West Africa			Destinations of West Africa-born		
	Within West Africa	Other Africa	Other States	Other West Africa	Other Africa	Other States
Guinea	81.5	8.8	9.7	86.8	3.5	9.7
Guinea–Bissau	88.4	5.5	6.0	60.7	4.3	35.0
Liberia	78.9	1.6	19.5	32.1	2.8	65.1
Mali	78.6	10.2	11.2	85.5	5.5	8.9
Mauritania	87.8	6.3	5.9	67.4	8.5	24.1
Niger	89.7	2.3	6.0	89.4	3.8	6.7
Nigeria	75.8	9.8	14.4	20.6	41.7	37.7
Senegal	83.6	5.4	11.1	44.0	11.7	44.3
Sierra Leone	88.8	6.0	5.2	38.1	2.9	59.1
Togo	83.5	4.9	11.6	73.3	10.5	16.2
Total West Africa	83.5	4.9	11.6	69.3	10.1	20.6

2.6.2. Temporary migration

It has already been noted that the migrant stock data do not include the much larger populations of temporary residents and visitors, and these temporary flows can include large shares from outside the region. Table 2.4 contains a summary of international tourist arrivals by broad region of destination.[45] UNWTO has observed that the global financial crisis has caused numbers of arrivals in Europe to fall below levels of the mid-2000s, but in all other regions the 2010 data represent the largest numbers of international tourist arrivals ever recorded. The fastest growth in the past decade has been in Africa and Asia, and UNWTO expects this to continue, especially in Northeast Asia and the Middle East. Much of this movement is intra-regional, between neighbouring States.

Similar patterns can be found with reference to the movement of contract labour, although it is difficult to quantify the scale of temporary forms of movement in many parts of the world because of poor migration data collection systems and the substantial undocumented flows.

Hugo has shown that the main destinations of migrant workers from countries in Asia are in fact States in the Middle East (which are included in Asia as this region is

45 Data source for Table 2.4: United Nations World Tourism Organization, above n. 14, 4.

Table 2.4 International tourist arrivals, 2010

Region of destination	Arrivals (millions)			Change (%)	
	1990	2000	2010	1990–2000	2000–10
Africa	14.8	26.5	49.4	79.1	86.4
Asia[a]	60.2	124.6	252.5	107.0	102.6
Europe	261.5	385.6	476.6	47.5	23.6
LA and Caribbean	21.1	36.7	51.6	73.9	40.6
Northern America	71.7	91.5	98.2	27.6	7.3
Oceania	5.2	9.6	10.9	84.6	13.5
All regions	434.5	674.5	939.2	55.2	39.2

[a] Includes the Middle East.

Table 2.5 Stocks of Asian migrant workers from selected States in Asia, main destination, various years

Origin country	Number	Destination	Year
Myanmar	1,840,000	Thailand	2006
Thailand	340,000	Saudi Arabia, Republic of China (Taiwan), Myanmar, Brunei, Singapore, Malaysia	2002
Laos[a]	173,000	Thailand	2004
Cambodia	183,500	Thailand, Malaysia, Republic of China (Taiwan)	2006
Philippines	8,233,200	Middle East, Malaysia, Japan	2006
Malaysia	250,000	Japan, Republic of China (Taiwan)	1995
Indonesia	2,700,000	Malaysia, Republic of China (Taiwan), Saudi Arabia, UAE, Singapore, Republic of Korea	2007
China	530,000	Middle East, Asia, Pacific	2004

[a] Undocumented. All the other stocks are estimates of documented workers.

defined by the United Nations) (Table 2.5).[46] Flows of low-skilled contract workers tend to be between States in relatively close proximity, although this is changing with the increasing demand for labour at all skill levels in many States. There is a stronger distance decay effect applying to temporary migration than is the case with long-term or permanent movement.

46 Graeme Hugo, 'Best Practice in Temporary Migration for Development: A Perspective from Asia and the Pacific' (2009) 47(5) *International Migration* 23.

CASE STUDY 2.2 Migration to the Gulf States

Since the mid-1970s the six Gulf States that comprise the Gulf Co-operation Council ('GCC') – Saudi Arabia, United Arab Emirates ('UAE'), Kuwait, Qatar, Oman and Bahrain – have become one of the major destinations for temporary labour migrants in the world. This cluster of one large desert country (Saudi Arabia) and five very small countries is third after Europe and North America as the destination for labour migrants in the early twenty-first century. Included in the GCC's estimated population of 43.5 million in 2010 are 15.1 million people born in other countries – the equivalent of just less than 35 per cent of the total (Table CS 2.2A).[47] With around three-quarters of their population born elsewhere, the small oil-producing States of Kuwait and Qatar have the highest proportions of immigrants of any State in the world.

The heavy gender bias towards males in the labour migration flows is reflected in the sex ratios for the Gulf States (Table CS 2.2A). All have ratios of men to women that favour males, with Qatar (three males to every female) and UAE (2.3 males to every female) having the most extreme gender imbalances (the global average is 1.07 males per female). The male-dominated sex ratios in the population at large tend to disguise a significant migration of female labour into these States as well, usually via a sponsorship system (*kafala*) whereby households recruit domestic support directly.[48] Much of this female labour migration is not recorded officially – it is largely unregulated – and the *kafala* system has been the subject of criticism on the grounds of lack of protection of workers from exploitation by unscrupulous employers.[49]

Table CS 2.2A Gulf State populations and migrant stocks, 2010 (thousands)

State	Population			Sex ratio	Migrant stocks	
	Males	Females	Total	(M/F)	No.	% total pop.
Bahrain	788	494	1,282	1.595	315	24.6
Kuwait	1,633	1,104	2,737	1.479	2,098	76.7
Oman	1,634	1,148	2,782	1.423	826	29.7
Qatar	1,331	438	1,769	3.039	1,305	73.8
Saudi Arabia	15,196	12,252	27,448	1.240	7,289	26.6
UAE	5,224	2,288	7,512	2.283	3,293	43.8
Total	25,806	17,724	43,530	1.456	15,126	34.7
World	3,477,830	3,418,059	6,895,889	1.017	214,000	3.1

47 Data sources for Table CS 2.2A: population data, United Nations Department of Economic and Social Affairs, above n. 2; International Organization for Migration, above n. 10, 209.

48 International Organization for Migration, above n. 10, 247.

49 See, e.g., Nicola Piper, *New Perspectives on Gender and Migration: Livelihood, Rights and Entitlements* (Routledge, 2008), and various papers in *Middle East Institute Viewpoints: Migration and the Gulf* (Middle East Institute, February 2010).

Drawing on the University of Sussex's global migration database,[50] the sources of the immigrant stocks in the Gulf States around 2002 can be seen to vary quite markedly by State, but in all of them, countries in South Asia, especially India, are very important sources (Table CS 2.2B). In Oman, Qatar and UAE, migrants born in South Asian countries accounted for more than 75 per cent of the overseas-born, and in four Gulf States, Indian-born immigrants accounted for 75 per cent or more of the South Asian migrants. The other main source areas were States in the Middle East and North Africa, the Philippines and Indonesia in Southeast Asia, and, for Kuwait especially, States in Europe and Latin America. Saudi Arabia differed somewhat from the others, with large shares of their immigrants coming from neighbouring States and Muslim countries in North Africa.

The dominance of labour markets by migrant workers in all the Gulf States (non-nationals comprised just over 50 per cent of Saudi Arabia's workforce in 2008)[51] has created tensions between locals and immigrants. While it is common to point to the marginalisation of immigrant workers in these States, many nationals feel they are being excluded from their own labour markets due to their mismatched skills and a reluctance of both public and private sector employers to employ them. As Colton has observed, 'Consequently we see the Gulf States entering a new phase in their role as one of the largest employers of labor migrants in the world confronting the challenge of how to preserve jobs for their nationals'.[52]

Table CS 2.2B Sources of immigrants, Gulf States, around 2002–3 (percentages)[a]

Region	Bahrain	Kuwait	Oman	Saudi Arabia	UAE	Total
South Asia	64.6	26.0	82.9	42.5	74.9	50.8
Other Asia	15.4	14.1	2.3	13.3	3.3	10.6
North Africa/ME	12.1	7.9	10.6	37.5	11.1	25.7
Other Africa	2.1	7.9	2.0	5.7	1.5	4.7
Europe	4.3	27.8	2.1	0.5	7.3	5.5
North America	0.2	1.8	0.01	0.5	0.4	0.6
Latin Am. and Caribbean	1.1	13.7	0.03	0.01	1.5	2
Oceania	0.2	0.8	0.0	0.0	0.02	0.1
% Indian in South Asian migrant population	89.2	76.1	60.4	46.9	90.3	73.9
Total overseas-born	254,300	1,107,700	681,700	5,254,800	1,922,000	9,220,500

[a] Qatar is not shown separately because in the DRC database all of its 409,400 migrant stock is shown as being born in India. It is unlikely there were only Qatar-born and India-born living in Qatar with none in residence who had been born in other Gulf or Middle East countries or other parts of the world.

50 Development Research Centre on Migration, Globalisation and Poverty, above n. 29.
51 Onn Winckler, 'Labor Migration to the GCC States: Patterns, Scale and Policies' (2010) (February) *Middle East Institute Viewpoints* 9, 12.
52 Nora Colton, 'The International Political Economy of Gulf Migration' (2010) (February) *Middle East Institute Viewpoints* 34, 36.

There is also great diversity within the temporary flows of contract labour in terms of types of workers and the visa conditions under which they are permitted to be in the State where they are employed. An example of this diversity is given in the top five rows of Table 2.6,[53] which lists temporary worker migration into member States of the Organisation for Economic Co-operation and Development ('OECD') by category of entry in the years 2005–8.

There is considerable variability across OECD countries in the extent to which temporary foreign workers are used in their labour markets, with Australia, Germany and the United States having in excess of 300,000 such workers in 2008, and Canada, Japan, Spain and the United Kingdom having over 100,000. The main seasonal worker flows are into Germany (over 300,000 per annum), Spain and Italy, while the countries making extensive use of working holidaymakers in their horticulture, viticulture and tourism industries include Australia, New Zealand and the United Kingdom.

The OECD notes that temporary workers 'numbered approximately 2.3 million in 2008, significantly higher than the number of permanent labour migrants, which stood at roughly 1.5 million. A significant proportion of this migration occurs between OECD countries.'[54] They go on to observe that the statistics are incomplete in their coverage of countries and categories, and that the definitions of workers who are 'temporary' are not consistent across all countries. Notwithstanding the caveats, the OECD suggests that 'the statistics shown [in Table 2.6] provide a reasonably complete view of temporary worker movements which are consistent over time and provide an indication of developments in this area'.[55]

The impacts of the 2008 global economic crisis on employer demand for temporary workers were becoming visible in the statistics for 2008: several countries experienced declines in excess of 10 per cent over the 2007 worker totals, with France, Italy and the Netherlands experiencing much larger falls in numbers. However, in other countries there was growth in numbers, especially in Australia, Belgium, Canada, Spain and Sweden. Some of these increases are likely to turn to decreases, especially in Belgium and Spain, as the recession continues to dampen economic growth in Europe.

The economic crisis has also had an impact on the very sizeable flows of international students into OECD countries. There has been a reduction in these flows into Australia and New Zealand since 2008, resulting in considerable pressure on private training organisations and tertiary institutions that had developed significant budget dependency on revenue generated by international enrolments. There is also increasing competition from institutions in Asia for international students and these are capturing a growing share of students seeking advanced

53 Data source for Table 2.6: Organisation for Economic Co-operation and Development, above n. 28, 31.
54 Ibid. 30.   55 Ibid. 31–2.

Table 2.6 Temporary worker migration in OECD countries by category and State, 2005–8

Category/State	Temporary workers (000s)				Change (%) 2007–8
	2005	2006	2007	2008	
Category					
Trainees	105	121	138	136	−1.4
Working holidaymakers	221	225	245	274	11.8
Intra-company transfers	85	98	116	118	1.7
Seasonal workers	615	606	619	642	3.7
Other temporary workers	1,136	1,313	1,303	1,148	−11.9
All categories	2,163	2,362	2,421	2,319	−4.2
Europe					
Austria	18	15	15	16	6.7
Belgium	5	16	30	34	13.3
Denmark	5	5	7	7	0.0
Finland	19	22	24	25	4.2
France	27	29	30	22	−26.7
Germany	390	353	349	332	−4.9
Italy	85	96	66	40	−39.4
Netherlands	47	75	52	17	−67.3
Norway	51	73	86	74	−14.0
Portugal	8	7	5	5	0.0
Spain	97	167	164	183	11.6
Sweden	5	5	9	14	55.6
Switzerland	104	117	109	99	−9.2
United Kingdom	275	266	225	184	−18.2
Northern America					
Canada	123	139	165	193	17.0
USA	367	426	484	443	−8.5
Mexico	46	40	28	23	−17.9
Oceania					
Australia	183	219	258	300	16.3
New Zealand	78	87	99	99	0.0
Asia					
Republic of Korea	29	39	53	47	−11.3
Japan	202	164	165	161	−2.4
All States	2,163	2,362	2,421	2,319	−4.2

qualifications within the region. In 2007 it was estimated that around 2.5 million international students were enrolled in OECD countries, and this accounted for 86 per cent of the global total for that year. The largest numbers were in the United States (596,000), the United Kingdom (352,000), Australia (212,000), Germany (207,000), France (200,000) and Japan (115,000).[56] The numbers of international students often exceed those of temporary workers.

Drawing on a concept developed by Hawthorne in her analysis of international student migration in Australia,[57] the OECD noted that the temporary movement of students 'is taking place largely in the context of so-called "two-step migration" by which migrants are first attracted as international students and then retained as highly skilled long-term workers in a second step'.[58] As the OECD goes on to explain:

> Most OECD countries now allow international students the opportunity to search for work for a specified period following the completion of study. The time period varies from six months in France, New Zealand or Finland to up to one year in Germany or Norway, and has been extended in recent years in some countries, for example in the Netherlands, from three months to one year. In Canada [as well as Australia and New Zealand] permanent residence has been also facilitated for international graduates.[59]

The boundaries between migration for study and work, and between short-term and long-term migration are becoming increasingly blurred. This is resulting in the old distinctions between 'permanent' and 'temporary' migration, and between labour migration and migration for other reasons, becoming much less useful as analytical categories in the contemporary global migration system.[60]

2.6.3. Permanent-type migration

It is difficult to get consistent data on migration that results in permanent settlement because only a small number of States have visa categories specifically for people who intend to settle. The OECD points out that the term 'permanent' in its statistics does not generally mean that the immigrants enter the State with the right of permanent residence except in Australia, Canada, New Zealand and the United States – States that were largely settled by immigrants within historical memory.[61] In almost all other States, immigrants receive a temporary permit on arrival. They observe that: 'The holding of temporary permits does not necessarily imply that immigrants with such permits are always viewed as temporary by the destination country. The temporary permits which some migrants receive can be renewed until a more stable permit is granted or the nationality of the destination country is acquired.'[62] The designation 'permanent' does not mean that the migrants intend to

---

56 Ibid. 43.
57 Lesleyanne Hawthorne, 'How Valuable Is "Two-Step Migration"? Labour Market Outcomes for International Students Migrating to Australia' (2010) 19(1) *Asian Pacific Migration Journal* 5.
58 Organisation for Economic Co-operation and Development, above n. 28, 41.   59 Ibid. 44.
60 Samers, above n. 44.   61 Organisation for Economic Co-operation and Development, above n. 28, 28.
62 Ibid.

reside at the destination either – it implies that they are on an entry pathway that could lead to the right to reside in that State.

The statistics in Table 2.7[63] on what the OECD terms 'permanent-type migration' have been standardised according to a common definition of 'permanent', except for those States in brackets. In the case of the latter, national statistics have not been standardised due to insufficient information. Excluded from the permanent flows in Table 2.7 are international students (even if they might be engaged in 'two-step migration'), trainees, persons on exchange programmes, seasonal or contract workers, service providers, installers, artists entering the State to perform or exhibit, or persons engaged in sporting events. The OECD notes that where migrants have the right of free entry to another State, such as within the EU, the determination of 'permanent' migration is problematic. In some States these people may not be identified in national statistics at all; in others they may receive a nominal permit that indicates whether the movement is likely to be permanent or not. Where information is available, the OECD defines 'permanent' in the context of free movement as entry to another State with the intention of staying twelve months or more, which is also the 'long-term' residence category in countries like Australia and New Zealand.

Two things stand out in the statistics presented in Table 2.7. The first is the sizeable increases in numbers of permanent-type migrants in some countries in 2007, especially in southern Europe. The OECD points out that this is due, in large measure, to the entry of Bulgaria and Romania into the EU in that year. Large numbers of Bulgarians and Romanians who had been entering other EU countries irregularly in earlier years thus became part of the official national statistics after 2007. In the case of Portugal, the large increase between 2007 and 2008 is the result of a regularisation programme for long-term resident Brazilians, thus allowing them to enter the official statistics on immigration for the first time.

The second prominent feature is the reductions in permanent-type migration following the onset of the global financial crisis, especially in Spain, the Czech Republic, Ireland and Italy. According to the OECD this was due mainly to reductions in free movement migration for lower-skilled migrants who would have been attracted to industries such as construction and hospitality, which experienced rapid contractions in labour demand following the onset of the crisis. The OECD estimates that around 44 per cent of all migration in the European Economic Area ('EEA') is free movement migration, 'where it now significantly exceeds family migration of persons from outside the EEA (28% of the total), as well as labour migration from other countries'.[64]

---

63 Data source for Table 2.7: Organisation for Economic Co-operation and Development, above n. 28, 27.
64 Ibid. 29.

Table 2.7 Permanent-type migration in OECD countries, 2005–8

State	Permanent-type migration (000s)				Change (%) 2007–8
	2005	2006	2007	2008	
Europe					
Austria	–	32.9	50.2	52.9	5.4
Belgium	35.0	35.6	40.3	43.9	8.9
Czech Republic	55.9	63.0	98.8	71.8	−27.3
Denmark	16.9	20.2	25.4	37.5	47.6
Finland	12.7	13.9	17.5	19.9	13.7
France	167.8	168.1	160.7	167.5	4.2
Germany	196.1	166.4	282.8	228.3	−19.3
(Hungary)	25.6	19.4	22.6	–	–
Ireland	66.1	88.9	89.5	67.6	−24.5
Italy	193.5	171.3	571.5	424.7	−25.7
(Luxembourg)	13.8	13.7	15.8	16.8	6.3
Netherlands	60.3	61.3	69.8	82.5	18.2
Norway	25.7	28.0	43.8	51.0	16.4
(Poland)	38.5	34.2	40.6	41.8	3.0
Portugal	11.5	25.1	42.9	65.9	53.6
(Slovak Republic)	7.7	11.3	14.8	16.5	11.5
Spain	–	–	682.3	391.9	−42.6
Sweden	53.7	74.4	74.4	71.3	−4.2
Switzerland	78.8	86.3	122.2	139.3	14.0
United Kingdom	369.4	354.2	364.4	347.4	−4.7
Middle East					
(Turkey)	169.7	191.0	174.9	175.0	0.1
Northern America					
Canada	262.2	251.6	236.8	247.2	4.4
USA	1,122.4	1,266.3	1,052.4	1,107.1	5.2
Mexico	11.5	25.1	42.9	65.9	53.6
Oceania					
Australia	167.3	179.8	191.9	205.9	7.3
New Zealand	59.4	54.8	52.2	51.7	−1.0
Asia					
Republic of Korea	153.6	189.4	184.2	194.7	5.7
Japan	98.7	104.1	106.5	97.7	−8.3
All States	3,474	3,730	4,872	4,484	−8.0

In the OECD member States that are not in Europe the fluctuations in permanent-type migration over the period 2005–8 have been less severe, except in the case of Mexico, which experienced a 44 per cent increase between 2007 and 2008. It is not clear whether this has been caused by a significant influx from other Latin American countries following the onset of the economic crisis. IOM reported that Central American countries had been hurt more than South American countries by the economic crisis due to their strong ties to the economies of the United States and Canada.[65] IOM went on to report that 'the recent steep drop in the flows from Mexico (from 1 million in 2006 to 600,000 in 2009) is largely due to potential irregular Mexican migrants deciding to stay at home, as legal immigration levels have remained largely unchanged'.[66]

2.6.4. Persons of concern to UNHCR

At the end of 2010 there were 34 million 'persons of concern' to the United Nations High Commissioner for Refugees ('UNHCR').[67] Over three-quarters (77 per cent) of these people were in the African and Asian regions (including the Middle East) as these are defined by the United Nations, and 74 per cent were either internally displaced persons ('IDPs') (14.7 million) or refugees (10.5 million) (Table 2.8).[68] The other major groups were stateless persons (3.5 million),[69] returned IDPs (2.9 million), asylum seekers (0.8 million) and others of concern because of their severely compromised humanitarian situation (1.3 million). Included in the refugee and IPD statistics are people living in like situations – in camps outside their regions or States of origin after fleeing deteriorating economic, social or environmental conditions at home. Those in refugee-like situations have not sought asylum at their destination and many are either hoping to move on to other States or to return to their homes when conditions improve in the future.

Several chapters in this book address the situations of persons of concern: Chapter 4 covers nationality and statelessness; Chapter 7 addresses refugees and asylum; Chapter 9 examines trafficking and smuggling; Chapter 8 reviews women, children and people living with disabilities; and Chapter 15 explores the growing incidence of internal displacement as an emerging migration issue. In this section and the next, summary statistics are provided to set the scene for the more considered assessments of these migrant groups in later chapters.

---

65 International Organization for Migration, above n. 10, 158.   66 Ibid. 160.
67 United Nations High Commissioner for Refugees, '60 Years and Still Counting: Global Trends 2010' (UNHCR, 2011) 2. UNHCR refers collectively to refugees, internally displaced persons, returnees, stateless persons and a broad group of people whose humanitarian situations are considered to be seriously compromised, as 'persons of concern'.
68 Data source for Table 2.8: United Nations High Commissioner for Refugees, above n. 67.
69 UNHCR estimates there are at least 12 million stateless persons, most of whom are not reported in official statistics.

As UNHCR approached the sixtieth anniversary of the *Convention relating to the Status of Refugees* (1951)[70] and the fiftieth anniversary of the *Convention on the Reduction of Statelessness* (1961),[71] it reported that around 800,000 resettlement places would be needed in 2011, but the annual quotas offered by the small number of States that accept 'Convention' refugees on a regular basis remained at only 80,000 – just one-tenth of the number required. During 2010, 98,000 refugees (73,000 assisted by UNHCR) were admitted for resettlement by twenty-two countries. The United States (71,400), Canada (12,100) and Australia (8,500) received 94 per cent of these. Overall, this represented 13,600 fewer resettled refugees than in 2009, mainly because of new security clearance requirements in the countries of settlement. On a more positive note, UNHCR reported that Japan, Paraguay and Romania accepted refugees for resettlement for the first time.[72]

In 2010, 70 per cent of refugees were stuck in what UNHCR terms 'protracted situations', where 25,000 or more refugees of the same nationality have been in exile for five years or more in any given asylum State.[73] Just under half the refugees (49 per cent) were women and girls, and 40 per cent were hosted by just three States: Pakistan (1.9 million), Iran (1.1 million) and Syria (1 million). Fifty per cent of the refugees under UNHCR responsibility were Afghani (3 million), Iraqi (1.7 million) or Somali (0.8 million) in origin. Other major sources reported by UNHCR in 2010 were the Democratic Republic of the Congo (476,700), Myanmar (415,700), Colombia (395,600), Sudan (387,200), Vietnam (338,700 refugees in China who are now settled there) and China (184,600). In the case of IDPs the following countries had more than 1 million displaced persons at the end of 2010: Colombia (3.7 million), Democratic Republic of the Congo (1.7 million), Sudan (1.6 million), Somalia (1.5 million), Iraq (1.3 million) and Pakistan (1 million).[74]

UNHCR reported that during 2010 at least 837,500 individual applications for asylum or refugee status were submitted to governments or UNHCR offices in 166 States or territories (Table 2.8). Just over three-quarters of these applications were made in States in Africa (39 per cent) and Europe (36 per cent). Europe's share of asylum seekers is double its share of the world's refugees (15 per cent), and while the numbers of asylum seekers each year are much smaller than the stocks of refugees in most European countries, concern about numbers seeking asylum has been increasing for some time. The United Nations Development Programme ('UNDP') points out that 'Only a minority of asylum seekers succeed in obtaining either refugee status or residency, and those whose request is denied can face

---

70 *Convention relating to the Status of Refugees*, opened for signature 28 July 1951, 189 UNTS 150 (entered into force 22 April 1954).
71 *Convention on the Reduction of Statelessness*, opened for signature 30 August 1961, 989 UNTS 175 (entered into force 13 December 1975).
72 United Nations High Commissioner for Refugees, above n. 67, 19.   73 Ibid. 14.
74 Ibid. Statistical Appendix, Table 1.

Table 2.8 Persons of concern to UNHCR, 2009

(A) Refugees, IDPs, asylum seekers and stateless persons (000s)

Region	Refugees	IDPs	Asylum seekers	Stateless persons	Subtotal 4 groups	% Subtotal
Africa	2,408.7	6,230.1	329.6	21.1	8,989.5	30.4
Asia[a]	5,715.8	4,376.4	72.4	2,853.2	13,017.8	44.1
Europe	1,587.4	419.3	302.8	588.7	2,898.2	9.8
LA and Caribbean	373.9	3,672.1	71.4	–	4,117.4	13.9
Northern America	430.1	–	57.3	–	487.4	1.6
Oceania	33.8	–	4.0	–	37.8	0.1
All regions	10,549.7	14,697.9	837.5	3,463.0	29,548.1	100.0

(B) Returned refugees, returned IDPs and others of concern (000s)

Region	Return refugees	Return IDPs	Others of concern	Subtotal 3 groups	Total all groups[b]	% total
Africa	43.5	979.4	164.1	1,187.0	10,176.5	30.0
Asia[a]	152.3	1,940.9	1,001.7	3,094.9	16,112.7	47.5
Europe	1.8	3.0	89.8	94.6	2,992.8	8.8
LA and Caribbean	0.1	–	–	0.1	4,117.5	12.1
Northern America	–	–	–	–	487.4	1.4
Oceania	–	–	–	–	37.8	0.1
All regions	197.7	2,923.3	1,255.6	4,376.6	33,924.7	100.0

[a] Includes the Middle East.
[b] Includes the groups covered in Part A of the table.

precarious situations. Their experience depends on the policies of the destination country.'[75] Most of the more developed countries provide asylum seekers some access to emergency public health services, but more restricted access to preventive care. In the less developed countries, access by asylum seekers to public health services is often much more restricted.

In its 2010 SOPEMI report, the OECD recorded 355,400 asylum seekers across twenty-nine member States in 2008 – slightly down on the 357,700 reported for 2007.[76] Five States received between 30,000 and 40,000 requests (Canada, France, Italy, United Kingdom, United States), although it was Norway, Sweden and Switzerland that received the highest per capita requests (Table 2.9).[77] States with

75 United Nations Development Programme, above n. 18, 64.
76 Organisation for Economic Co-operation and Development, above n. 28, 40.
77 Data source for Table 2.9: ibid. 40.

fewer than 500 asylum seekers requesting refugee or residence status were Iceland, Republic of Korea, New Zealand and Portugal. The main sources of asylum seekers in Europe are States in Eastern Europe, the Middle East and Africa, while in North America it is States in Latin America and the Caribbean that feature as leading sources. States in east and southern Asia are the main sources for Australia and New Zealand.

The distances travelled by asylum seekers have been increasing and now reach to the opposite side of the world for States in Europe. The success rate for asylum seekers in gaining refugee status or being granted temporary protection is not high, especially given the increases in residence approvals and legal temporary worker flows into most OECD countries since 2005. In the absence of opportunities to gain legal residence status at their destinations, the OECD considers that asylum seekers will be a significant source of irregular migration if they are refused refugee status and then decide to stay on in Europe.[78]

2.6.5. Irregular migration, smuggling and trafficking

IOM has suggested that somewhere between 10 and 15 per cent of the estimated 214 million international migrant stock might be in 'an irregular situation'.[79] If this is the case, then the number of migrants without a valid visa for their presence or activities in the country of residence could be anywhere between 20 and 30 million – well above the estimated numbers of refugees and asylum seekers. IOM emphasises, however, that the great majority of these people would have entered their countries of residence legally and either overstayed their authorised period of approved residence, or engaged in economic activity, including employment, while on a visitor's visa.

Irregular migration is complex and it is difficult to measure and control. There are a variety of routes to irregularity. Migrants can wilfully enter a State unlawfully by crossing the border without appropriate documentation and thus gain their irregular status through the way they arrive as undocumented migrants. For migrants already in a State legally, their situation can change in-country either because of their activities (especially gaining employment when on a visitor's visa) or because they have stayed on despite the expiry of their temporary residence or work visa. Both routes to irregular status are of concern to governments, especially in the more developed States.

Smuggling is a variant of irregular migration that involves payment for assistance in making a clandestine border crossing. Criminal gangs are often involved in providing this service, and as Chapter 9 notes, the two largest flows of smuggled persons are from Latin America (especially Mexico) to the United States, and from sub-Saharan Africa to Europe. Drawing on data from the

78 Ibid. 41.   79 International Organization for Migration, above n. 10, 29.

Table 2.9 Inflows of asylum seekers in OECD countries, levels and main States of origin, 2008

State	Asylum seekers 2008		
	Number	Per 000 pop.	Top 3 sources
Europe			
Austria	12,800	1.54	Russia, Afghanistan, Serbia
Belgium	12,300	1.16	Russia, Iraq, Serbia
Czech Republic	1,700	0.16	Ukraine, Turkey, Mongolia
Denmark	2,400	0.44	Iraq, Afghanistan, Iran
Finland	4,000	0.75	Iraq, Somalia, Afghanistan
France	35,400	0.57	Russia, Serbia, Mali
Germany	22,100	0.27	Iraq, Serbia, Turkey
Greece	19,900	1.78	Pakistan, Afghanistan, Georgia
Hungary	3,100	0.31	Serbia, Pakistan, Somalia
Iceland	100	0.31	Serbia, Afghanistan, Nigeria
Ireland	3,900	0.88	Nigeria, Pakistan, Iraq
Italy	30,300	0.51	Nigeria, Somalia, Eritrea
Luxembourg	500	1.03	Serbia, Bosnia/Herzegovina, Iraq
Netherlands	13,400	0.82	Iraq, Somalia, China
Norway	14,400	3.02	Iraq, Eritrea, Afghanistan
Poland	7,200	0.19	Russia, Iraq, Vietnam
Portugal	200	0.02	Sri Lanka, Colombia, Congo DR
Slovakia	900	0.17	Georgia, Moldova, Pakistan
Spain	4,500	0.10	Nigeria, Colombia, Côte d'Ivoire
Sweden	24,400	2.65	Iraq, Somalia, Serbia
Switzerland	16,600	2.17	Eritrea, Somalia, Iraq
Turkey	13,000	0.18	Iraq, Afghanistan, Iran
United Kingdom	31,300	0.51	Zimbabwe, Afghanistan, Iran
North America			
Canada	34,800	1.05	Mexico, Haiti, Colombia
USA	39,400	0.13	China, El Salvador, Mexico
Oceania			
Australia	4,800	0.22	China, Sri Lanka, India
New Zealand	300	0.07	Iraq, Iran, Sri Lanka
Asia			
South Korea	400	0.01	Sri Lanka, Pakistan, Myanmar
Japan	1,600	0.01	Myanmar, Turkey, Sri Lanka
All States	355,400	0.33	Iraq, Serbia, Afghanistan

United Nations Office on Drugs and Crime, in 2010 there were approximately 3 million attempted irregular crossings of the southern border of the United States, most of which were facilitated by smugglers. In the case of irregular crossings from Africa to Europe, the numbers are much smaller (around 150,000 per annum) and, again, it is estimated that a significant proportion are assisted by smugglers. Data on smuggling are difficult to obtain, but it is now widely recognised that it is a very large and profitable business in most parts of the world, which takes advantage of a desire by increasing numbers of people to escape human rights abuses, armed conflict, civil unrest, environmental degradation and economic want by moving to another State where opportunities for a safe and better life are perceived to exist.

The most problematic dimension to irregular migration is human trafficking because it involves the violation of basic human rights and is commonly identified with sexual exploitation. Unlike smuggling, trafficking involves women, men and children essentially being 'sold' for sexual services, bonded labour, domestic servitude, forced marriage, organ removal, begging, illicit adoption and conscription, among other forms of exploitation.[80] UNDP captured the essence of the migrants' vulnerability when it observed:

Once caught in a trafficking network people may be stripped of their travel documents and isolated, so as to make escape difficult if not impossible. Many end up in debt bondage in places where language, social and physical barriers frustrate their efforts to seek help. In addition, they may be reluctant to identify themselves, since they risk legal sanctions or criminal prosecution.[81]

Trafficking is very difficult to combat – it thrives in environments of labour market exclusion and disempowerment in the country of origin; demand for illegal labour in the destination country; and a naïve belief among potential migrants in the promise of well-paid jobs abroad. IOM has observed that:

When destination countries tolerate high levels of irregular migration, they undermine their own legal immigration systems. There is little credibility for immigration law if migrants and migrant smugglers and human traffickers are allowed to circumvent the policies in place to determine who enters, for what purposes, and for what period of time.[82]

Irregular migration is a feature of the migration systems in all continents and regions; it is perceived to be increasing and becoming more complex, not just because of the variety of routes to irregularity, but also because of the difficulties in distinguishing the particular needs and rights of various types of migrants, including asylum seekers and unaccompanied minors, who are part of the wider system of irregular migration flows.[83] It is generally agreed that irregular migration will further increase as a result of the effects of the global economic crisis. As restrictions on legal entry become tighter, more people seeking opportunities for work in one of the more

80 United Nations Development Programme, above n. 18, 65.   81 Ibid. 66.
82 International Organization for Migration, above n. 10, 30.   83 Ibid.

developed or emerging economies will choose to put themselves in an irregular situation with regard to their entry status. It is in such situations that exploitation can thrive in the burgeoning service industry that facilitates international migration.

Different forms of irregular migration, especially trafficking and smuggling, regularly attract media attention as States attempt to monitor flows across land boundaries more effectively due to their preoccupation with security and border protection. Notwithstanding these global security concerns, IOM points out: 'it is important not to fuel fear and negative perceptions of the North being overrun by poor migrants from the South, while of course not ignoring the vexing incidence of irregular migration today'.[84] As has been emphasised already, the great majority of people who enter other States do so legally. International migration is largely driven by voluntary decisions to spend variable lengths of time in other States, ranging from short visits to long-term residence.

2.7. LOOKING AHEAD

The world's population passed 7 billion in October 2011, twelve years after the 6 billion mark was reached in 1999.[85] According to the United Nations Population Division's 2010 medium variant projection, world population is projected to increase another billion by 2025, after a further fourteen years, and the 9 billion mark is projected for 2043, eighteen years later. Between 2010 and 2050 nearly 2.5 billion people (the equivalent of total world population in 1950) could be added to the 2010 total (Table 2.10).[86] Eighty-nine per cent of this increase will be in Africa (1.17 billion) and Asia (978 million), with the remaining 11 per cent (262.9 million) spread over Europe, the Americas and Oceania. The only region that will see a significant increase in its share of the total is Africa (up from 14.8 to 23.6 per cent). All other regions will have a decline in their share of the total except Oceania, which is projected to increase its share from 0.5 to 0.6 per cent. The greatest growth will be in the least developed countries, where the population is projected to more than double over the next forty years. Europe's population is projected to be smaller in 2050 than it was in 2010, despite significant immigration. Low levels of fertility and a rising number of deaths within populations that are getting progressively older because of low fertility will keep population growth very low in Europe.

Accompanying this significant global population growth will be accelerating urbanisation, especially in the least developed and less developed parts of the world (Table 2.11).[87] The United Nations Population Division's urban population

---

84 Ibid. 29.   85 United Nations Department of Economic and Social Affairs, above n. 2.
86 Data source for Table 2.10: ibid.
87 Data source for Table 2.11: United Nations Department of Economic and Social Affairs, above n. 6.

Table 2.10 Projected population change, 2010–50

Region	Population (millions)		% of total pop.		% growth
	2010	2050	2010	2050	2010–50
Africa	1,022.2	2,191.6	14.8	23.6	114.4
Asia	4,164.3	5,142.2	60.4	55.3	23.5
Europe	738.2	719.3	10.7	7.7	−2.6
LA and Caribbean	590.1	750.9	8.6	8.1	27.2
Northern America	344.5	446.9	5.0	4.8	29.7
Oceania	36.6	55.2	0.5	0.6	50.8
More developed	1,235.9	1,311.7	17.9	14.1	6.1
Less developed	4,827.7	6,267.9	70.0	67.4	29.8
Least developed	832.3	1,726.5	12.1	18.6	107.4
All regions	6,895.9	9,306.1	100.0	100.0	35.0

Table 2.11 Projected urban population change, 2010–50

Region	Urban pop. (millions)		% total pop. urban[a]		% growth
	2010	2050	2010	2050	2010–50
Africa	413.0	1,230.9	40.4	56.2	198.0
Asia	1,757.3	3,382.4	42.2	65.8	82.4
Europe	533.3	582.3	72.2	81.0	9.2
LA and Caribbean	468.8	647.7	79.4	86.3	38.2
Northern America	288.8	404.3	83.8	90.5	40.0
Oceania	25.1	38.4	68.9	69.6	52.4
More developed	929.9	1,099.8	75.2	83.8	18.2
Less developed	2,307.0	4,271.8	47.8	68.2	85.2
Least developed	249.4	914.4	30.0	53.0	266.6
All regions	3,486.3	6,286.0	50.1	67.5	80.3

[a] Percentage of the region's total population (see Table 2.10) that is urban.

projections suggest that the numbers living in towns and cities could increase by as much as 2.8 billion over the period 2010–50.[88] This is more than the total projected

88 Ibid.

population growth of 2.4 billion over the same period. Just under two-thirds of this urban growth will occur in Africa (194 per cent increase) and Asia (72 per cent increase), and while most of it will be associated with internal migration from rural areas to local towns and cities, there will also be considerable international migration between urban areas within Africa and Asia.

The United Nations' projections suggest that over two-thirds of the world's population could be living in urban areas by 2050. The projected 2.8 million increase in town and city dwellers is equivalent to 80 per cent of the global urban population in 2010. Natural increase within urban populations will be the main driver of population growth in most of the more advanced countries, but in the less and least developed world it will be migration that drives the growth of what Saunders describes as 'arrival cities' – 'places where the next great economic and cultural boom will be born, or where the next great explosion of violence will occur'.[89] These arrival cities are found in all regions, but will be especially prominent in Africa, Asia and parts of Oceania, where urbanisation will be most rapid over the coming decades.

'South–South' migration, or migration between developing countries, will become much more prominent than 'South–North' migration, or movement into the more developed countries. Indeed, the United Nations Population Division's estimates of net migration gains and losses at the broad regional level suggest that there will be smaller aggregate net migration gains to more developed countries over the next forty years than there were over a comparable period between 1960 and 2010 (Table 2.12).[90] This is despite the substantial population growth in less and least developed countries and the increasing demand for labour within more developed countries as their populations age. The United Nations Population Division's projections indicate that from around 2010 the numbers of people of working age (15–64 years) in the more developed countries will begin to decline in absolute terms, while those in the less and least developed countries will continue to increase. The great bulk of the latter increase will be absorbed within the less and least developed countries, especially within their burgeoning urban areas.

The 2010 projections suggest that net migration losses from Asia to other parts of the world will be larger between 2010 and 2050 than they were over the previous forty years (Table 2.12). It is these flows that will play a major role in meeting the labour needs of the more developed countries as their labour forces shrink. In the African and Latin American regions the overall net migration losses are projected to fall. Indeed, in the least developed countries, which are projected to experience the most rapid urbanisation, the net migration losses to other regions could have the largest percentage decline.

89 Saunders, above n. 8, 3.
90 Data source for Table 2.12: United Nations Department of Economic and Social Affairs, above n. 2.

Table 2.12 Projected net migration gains and losses, 1960–2010 and 2010–50 (millions)

Region	Net migration		Change in net gain/loss	% change in net gain/loss
	1960–2010	2010–50		
Africa	−19.4	−18.3	1.1	−5.7
Asia	−36.2	−44.9	−8.7	24.0
Europe	37.2	36.3	−0.9	−2.4
LA and Caribbean	−34.0	−21.4	12.6	−37.1
Northern America	47.1	44.3	−2.8	−5.9
Oceania	5.3	4.0	−1.3	−24.5
More developed	92.1	87.0	−5.1	−5.5
Less developed	−62.7	−68.9	−6.2	9.9
Least developed	−29.4	−18.1	11.3	−38.4
All regions[a]	0.0	0.0	0.0	0.0

[a] There is zero net migration at the global level – the gains and losses at the regional level are cancelled out when flows are aggregated for all States.

The final trend that merits mention in the context of prospective developments in migration patterns is related to the gender and family composition of contemporary flows. The feminisation of international migration has attracted considerable attention in recent years from the International Labour Organization as well as migration researchers, especially in the context of the transnational flows of domestic workers.[91] There has been a progressive shift from male-dominated international migration towards flows with a much greater gender balance, especially since the 1990s. The largest of these flows occurs within the Asian region, especially from South and Southeast Asia to the Middle East and to countries in Northeast Asia (Japan, Hong Kong, the Republic of Korea).

A major challenge with all the flows, whether dominated by males or females of younger working age, is the impact their absence has on the families left behind. The considerable research on remittance flows from overseas workers tends to highlight the positive contribution opportunities to work offshore make to family livelihoods in communities where there are limited opportunities for earning cash incomes.[92] The social costs of such movement have tended to be downplayed in a discourse that emphasises economic returns.

91 A useful synthesis can be found in Piper, above n. 49. See also Nicola Piper and Margaret Satterthwaite, 'Migrant Women' in Ryszard Cholewinski, Richard Perruchoud and Euan Macdonald (eds.), *International Migration Law: Developing Paradigms and Key Challenges* (TMC Asser Press, 2007) 237 and Chapter 8 in this book.
92 There is an extensive literature on remittances and migration. Useful overviews can be found in World Bank, above n. 28, and International Organization for Migration, above n. 10.

Increasing interest in the flows of domestic workers, however, is only one component of the growing attention being given to family dimensions of migration. Chapter 8 discusses the situation relating to child migrants, and the widespread incidence of child trafficking, especially of young girls. A group that receives less attention is the elderly parents who, almost universally, are denied the opportunity to move as freely as their children or younger siblings. Except for the United States, where family migration has been prioritised, nearly all governments have placed restrictions on the entry of older people in their immigration policies. In States like Australia and New Zealand there are age limits on migrants in the skilled migration categories and quotas for family migration streams. Policies that include specific age and family relationship selection criteria will become increasingly difficult to manage in the future as populations age and as competition for migrant labour increases.

IOM has provided a fitting conclusion for this chapter and a useful migration context for the chapters that follow, when it stated in the opening paragraphs of its *World Migration Report 2010*:

Over the next few decades, international migration is likely to transform in scale, reach and complexity, due to growing demographic disparities, the effects of environmental change, new global political and economic dynamics, technological revolutions and social networks. These transformations will be associated with increasing opportunities – from economic growth and poverty reduction, to social and cultural innovation. However, they will also exacerbate existing problems and generate new challenges – from irregular migration, to protecting the human rights of migrants . . .

International migration involves a wider diversity of ethnic and cultural groups than ever before; significantly more women are migrating today on their own or as heads of households . . . the number of people living and working abroad with irregular status continues to rise; and there has been a significant growth in temporary migration and circulation.[93]

The latest 'age of migration' has certainly not yet run its course. An ongoing challenge for researchers and professionals addressing dimensions of international migration is to avoid a tendency to perpetuate old stereotypes, such as 'permanent' and 'temporary', in their analyses by always acknowledging that there are complex interdependencies between different types of movement across national boundaries. Typologies of movement can be useful starting points, but, as was stressed in the introduction to this chapter, migration is a complex phenomenon and the boundaries between specific categories have become increasingly blurred. Research that focusses on analysis of systems of movements of various overlapping types, rather than focussing on defining more precisely specific types of movements, is more likely to capture the complexity of contemporary international migration.

---

93 International Organization for Migration, ibid. 3.

KEY REFERENCES

Castles, Stephen and Miller, Mark, *The Age of Migration: International Population Movements in the Modern World* (Guilford Press, 4th edn, 2009)

Cohen, Robin (ed.), *The Cambridge Survey of World Migration* (Cambridge University Press, 1995)

International Organization for Migration, *World Migration Report 2010: The Future of Migration: Building Capacities for Change* (IOM, 2010)

Kritz, Mary, Lim, Lin and Zlotnik, Hania (eds.), *International Migration Systems: A Global Approach* (Clarendon Press, 1992)

Massey, Douglas and Taylor, Edward (eds.), *International Migration: Prospects and Policies in a Global Market* (Oxford University Press, 2004)

Massey, Douglas S., Arango, Joaquín, Hugo, Graeme, Kouaouci, Ali, Pellegrino, Adela and Taylor, Edward J., *Worlds in Motion: Understanding International Migration at the End of the Millennium* (Oxford University Press, 1998)

Organisation for Economic Co-operation and Development, *International Migration Outlook: SOPEMI 2010* (OECD, 2010)

Samers, Michael, *Migration* (Routledge, 2010)

Segal, Uma, Elliott, Doreen and Mayadas, Nazneen (eds.), *Immigration Worldwide: Policies, Practices and Trends* (Oxford University Press, 2010)

Skeldon, Ronald, *Migration and Development: A Global Perspective* (Addison Wesley Longman, 1997)

United Nations Development Programme, *Human Development Report 2009. Overcoming Barriers: Human Mobility and Development* (UNDP, 2009)

KEY RESOURCES

Global Commission on International Migration: www.gcim.org

International Organization for Migration: www.iom.int

Organisation for Economic Co-operation and Development: www.oecd.org

United Nations Department of Economic and Social Affairs, Population Division: www.un.org/esa/population

United Nations Development Programme, Human Development Reports: http://hdr.undp.org

United Nations High Commissioner for Refugees: www.unhcr.org

United Nations Office on Drugs and Crime: www.unodc.org

United Nations Statistics Division: http://unstats.un.org/unsd

United Nations World Tourism Organization: www.unwto.org

University of Sussex, Development Research Centre on Migration, Globalisation and Poverty: www.migrationdrc.org

World Bank: www.worldbank.org

Sources of international migration law

VINCENT CHETAIL

International law has been defined as consisting of 'rules and principles of general application dealing with the conduct of states and of international organizations and with their relations *inter se*, as well as with some of their relations with persons, whether natural or juridical'.[1] As underlined by this definition, international law is no longer exclusively limited to the relations between States. The twentieth century witnessed a dramatic evolution of the international legal system, characterised by two major developments. First, a quantitative change has taken place through the unprecedented growth of international rules, which now cover virtually all human activities. Second, this metamorphosis has been accompanied by a qualitative change, with the emergence of new subjects of international law, such as individuals, international organisations and multinational corporations.

However, States remain the primary subjects of international law. In a sensitive area such as international migration, it has become conventional to underline the centrality of sovereignty. According to the famous statement of the Supreme Court of the United States in 1892, '[i]t is an accepted maxim of international law, that every sovereign nation has the power, as inherent in sovereignty, and essential to its self-preservation, to forbid the entrance of foreigners within its dominions, or to admit them only in such cases and upon such conditions as it may see fit to prescribe'.[2]

This reflects a basic assumption of classical international law: a State possesses primary authority over its territory and population and, by virtue of its sovereignty, may therefore decide if and how it permits non-nationals to enter its territory. The elusive concept of sovereignty, however, is misleading for assessing the role of international law in the field of migration.[3]

The authority of States, and their correlative responsibilities, are better appraised by reference to the concept of domestic jurisdiction enshrined in art. 2(7) of the

---

1 American Law Institute, *Restatement (Third) of Foreign Relations Law of the United States* (1987) [101].
2 *Nishimura Ekiu* v. *United States* 142 US 651 (1892) 659.
3 See Vincent Chetail, 'Migration, droits de l'homme et souveraineté: le droit international dans tous ses états' in Vincent Chetail (ed.), *Mondialisation, migration et droits de l'homme: le droit international en question, Volume II* (Bruylant, 2007) 13.

Charter of the United Nations (1945). Domestic jurisdiction is traditionally understood as the domain of activities in which the State is not bound by international law. But it is not a monolithic notion; it has evolved along with developments in international law. As early as 1923, the Permanent Court of International Justice explained in the *Nationality Decrees Case* that '[t]he question whether a certain matter is or is not solely within the [domestic] jurisdiction of a State is an essentially relative question; it depends upon the development of international relations'.[4]

From this angle, the movement of persons – although in principle a domestic issue – has been internationalised by a complex and heteroclite set of norms. The main sources of international law listed in art. 38 of the *Statute of the International Court of Justice* (1945) ('ICJ Statute') reveal a relatively dense picture. This chapter reviews the sources of international legal norms that govern international migration by examining treaty law (Section 3.1), customary law (Section 3.2) and subsidiary sources of law, namely, general principles of law and judicial decisions (Section 3.3). Section 3.4 concludes by assessing the role of 'soft law' on the traditional sources of international migration law.

3.1. TREATY LAW

3.1.1. Definition

A treaty is defined in the *Vienna Convention on the Law of Treaties* (1969) ('Vienna Convention') as 'an international agreement concluded between States in written form and governed by international law, whether embodied in a single instrument or two or more related instruments and whatever its particular designation'.[5]

This authoritative definition calls for two remarks. First, treaties are primarily concluded between States. However, the fact that the Vienna Convention only regulates treaties between States does not affect the legality of other kinds of agreements, such as those between States and other subjects of international law. For example, treaties can be concluded between States and international organisations, or between international organisations themselves. This type of treaty is governed by a distinct legal regime set out in the *Vienna Convention on the Law of Treaties between States and International Organizations or between International Organizations* (1986).[6]

Second, the 1969 Vienna Convention does not require a treaty to take a particular form or to have a specific designation. The term 'treaty' is a generic one that embraces all kinds of international agreements in a written form. It can have a

---

4 *Nationality Decrees Issued in Tunis and Morocco (Advisory Opinion)* [1923] PCIJ (ser B) No 4, 24.
5 *Vienna Convention on the Law of Treaties*, opened for signature 23 May 1969, 1155 UNTS 331 (entered into force 27 January 1980) art. 2(1)(a).
6 *Vienna Convention on the Law of Treaties between States and International Organizations or between International Organizations*, opened for signature 21 March 1986, UN Doc A/CONF.129/15 (not yet in force).

great variety of names, such as 'Protocol', 'Charter', 'Covenant', 'Pact', 'Statute', 'Arrangement'. Although some denominations may be more solemn than others, the terms used by States have no legal significance. As the International Court of Justice ('ICJ') has acknowledged, 'terminology is not a determinant factor as to the character of an international agreement'.[7] Hence, 'international agreements may take a number of forms and be given a diversity of names'.[8] For instance, a joint communiqué issued by Prime Ministers,[9] or even the minutes of a meeting signed by Foreign Ministers,[10] have been considered as international agreements binding on those States. In sum, 'just as one should never judge a book by its cover, one should never assume that the name given to an international instrument automatically indicates its status ... as a treaty'.[11]

The decisive criterion for determining the existence of a treaty is the intention of the parties to create obligations under international law. If that intention is lacking, the instrument is not a treaty. Although it is by nature difficult to prove intention, it is commonly inferred from the terms of the instrument and the circumstances in which it was drawn up.[12] In other words, both the text and the context of the instrument should establish that parties have agreed to enumerate commitments creating rights and obligations in international law. In practice, this is easily presumed from the use of prescriptive expressions, such as 'shall', 'agree', 'obligation' or 'right'. However, the intention to create obligations under international law may be more difficult to assert in a 'memorandum of understanding'. Although their political and practical effect may be considerable, such instruments are generally not binding, for they simply express an agreed course of action without creating specific legal commitments. An increasing number of such memoranda have been adopted for enhancing bilateral cooperation on migration issues (see Chapter 11). Typical examples are the memoranda of understanding establishing bilateral migration partnerships in 2009–10 between Switzerland and, respectively, Bosnia-Herzegovina, Kosovo and Serbia, whose provisions state that they 'do not create any legal rights and obligations between the Signatories'.[13] By contrast, the memoranda of understanding on bilateral labour cooperation, signed in 2002–3 by Thailand with Laos, Cambodia and Myanmar, constitute bilateral treaties, since they spell out detailed obligations agreed on by States parties.[14]

---

7 *South West Africa Cases (Ethiopia* v. *South Africa; Liberia* v. *South Africa) (Preliminary Objections)* [1962] ICJ Rep 319, 331.

8 *Maritime Delimitation and Territorial Questions between Qatar and Bahrain (Qatar* v. *Bahrain) (Jurisdiction and Admissibility)* [1994] ICJ Rep 112, 120.

9 *Aegean Sea Continental Shelf (Greece* v. *Turkey) (Judgment)* [1978] ICJ Rep 3, 39–40.

10 *Maritime Delimitation and Territorial Questions between Qatar and Bahrain (Qatar* v. *Bahrain) (Jurisdiction and Admissibility)* [1994] ICJ Rep 112, 121–2.

11 Anthony Aust, *Modern Treaty Law and Practice* (Cambridge University Press, 2000) 23–4.

12 *Aegean Sea Continental Shelf (Greece* v. *Turkey) (Judgment)* [1978] ICJ Rep 3, 40.

13 See, e.g., *Memorandum of Understanding between the Swiss Federal Council and the Government of the Republic of Serbia Establishing a Migration Partnership*, signed 30 June 2009.

14 See, e.g., *MOU between the Government of Lao People's Democratic Republic and the Government of the Kingdom of Thailand on Labour Co-operation*, signed 18 October 2002.

3.1.2. Typology

Given the great variety of designations, classifying treaties can be a perilous exercise. The International Law Commission has observed that 'there is no exclusive or systematic use of nomenclature for particular types of transactions' and, as a result, 'an extraordinarily varied nomenclature has developed which serves to confuse the question of classifying international agreements'.[15]

Although treaties can be categorised in a number of ways, the two most common classifications are based on the number of parties and their geographical scope. With regard to the first classification, treaties are *bilateral* when they are concluded between only two parties, and *multilateral* if there are more than two. This may overlap with the second classification. With regard to their geographical scope, multilateral treaties may be subdivided into *universal* conventions when ratification is open to all States of the world, and *regional* conventions when ratification is limited to States from a particular geographic area.

This classical, albeit rudimentary, taxonomy provides an instructive mapping of the conventional norms governing international migration. International migration law is constituted by three normative layers at the universal, regional and bilateral levels. At the universal level, there is no comprehensive treaty governing all aspects of international migration. The relevant conventional norms are dispersed among a variety of instruments. Multilateral treaties devoted exclusively to international migration are limited in number and specific in scope. The four main multilateral instruments are the *Convention relating to the Status of Refugees* (1951) ('Refugee Convention'), as amended by its 1967 Protocol;[16] the *International Convention on the Protection of the Rights of All Migrant Workers and Members of their Families* (1990) ('ICRMW');[17] the *Protocol against the Smuggling of Migrants by Land, Sea and Air, Supplementing the United Nations Convention against Transnational Organized Crime* (2000) ('Smuggling Protocol');[18] and the *Protocol to Prevent, Suppress and Punish Trafficking in Persons, Especially Women and Children, Supplementing the United Nations Convention against Transnational Organized Crime* (2000) ('Trafficking Protocol').[19]

This eclectic set of multilateral treaties captures only one parcel of the broader migration picture. The Refugee Convention is exclusively focussed on forced

---

15 United Nations, *Yearbook of the International Law Commission 1964* (United Nations, 1965) 188.

16 *Convention relating to the Status of Refugees*, opened for signature 28 July 1951, 189 UNTS 150 (entered into force 22 April 1954); *Protocol relating to the Status of Refugees*, opened for accession 31 January 1967, 606 UNTS 267 (entered into force 4 October 1967).

17 *International Convention on the Protection of the Rights of All Migrant Workers and Members of their Families*, opened for signature 18 December 1990, 2220 UNTS 3 (entered into force 1 July 2003).

18 *Protocol against the Smuggling of Migrants by Land, Sea and Air, Supplementing the United Nations Convention against Transnational Organized Crime*, opened for signature 15 November 2000, 2241 UNTS 507 (entered into force 28 January 2004).

19 *Protocol to Prevent, Suppress and Punish Trafficking in Persons, Especially Women and Children, Supplementing the United Nations Convention against Transnational Organized Crime*, opened for signature 15 November 2000, 2237 UNTS 319 (entered into force 25 December 2003).

migration and establishes for this purpose a comprehensive legal regime based on three components: (a) the definition of a refugee identifies persons in need of international protection through the notion of a 'well-founded fear of persecution'; (b) the principle of *non-refoulement* prohibits States from sending refugees back to territories where their life or freedom would be threatened; and (c) refugee status attracts minimum standards of treatment and basic rights of those admitted into the territory of the asylum State (see Chapter 7). As regards so-called voluntary migration, the ICRMW focusses on the human rights of migrant workers and their families during the whole migration cycle, from pre-departure to post-arrival. One set of fundamental rights applies to all migrant workers (including undocumented migrants) and restates basic rights already enshrined in general human rights instruments. A broader set of rights and guarantees is accorded to migrant workers in a regular situation (see Chapter 11). By contrast to the human rights approach promoted by the ICRMW, the Smuggling Protocol is primarily concerned with fighting transnational criminality. It obliges States parties to establish smuggling of migrants as a criminal offence in their national legislation and encourages them to collaborate in preventing and combating such practices, while offering some protection to smuggled migrants (see Chapter 9).

The limited number of treaties devoted specifically to migration does not fairly reflect the weight of international legal norms in this area. Many other multilateral agreements – though drafted for a more general purpose – are relevant to migration. The major human rights treaties, such as the *International Covenant on Civil and Political Rights* (1966) ('ICCPR')[20] and the *International Covenant on Economic, Social and Cultural Rights* (1966) ('ICESCR')[21] are generally applicable to everyone, irrespective of nationality or statelessness (see Chapter 6). The ICCPR also enshrines tailored provisions that are particularly crucial for migrants, such as the right to leave any country and return to one's own country (art. 12) and due process guarantees on expulsion (art. 13). Among the specific human rights treaties, the *International Convention on the Elimination of All Forms of Racial Discrimination* (1965) is relevant to the highly passionate and xenophobic atmosphere that often surrounds migration.[22] The *Convention on the Rights of the Child* (1989)[23] provides guidelines for facilitating family reunification (art. 10) and ensuring protection of refugee children (art. 22), while the *Convention against Torture and Other Cruel, Inhuman or Degrading Treatment or Punishment* (1984)[24] and the *International*

---

20 *International Covenant on Civil and Political Rights*, opened for signature 16 December 1966, 999 UNTS 171 (entered into force 23 March 1976).

21 *International Covenant on Economic, Social and Cultural Rights*, opened for signature 16 December 1966, 993 UNTS 3 (entered into force 3 January 1976).

22 *International Convention on the Elimination of All Forms of Racial Discrimination*, opened for signature 21 December 1965, 660 UNTS 195 (entered into force 4 January 1969).

23 *Convention on the Rights of the Child*, opened for signature 20 November 1989, 1577 UNTS 3 (entered into force 2 September 1990).

24 *Convention against Torture and Other Cruel, Inhuman or Degrading Treatment or Punishment*, opened for signature 10 December 1984, 1465 UNTS 85 (entered into force 26 June 1987) art. 3.

Convention for the Protection of All Persons from Enforced Disappearance (2006)[25] prohibit States parties from returning a person to another State if there is a substantial risk of torture or enforced disappearance.

Beyond the confines of international human rights law, Mode 4 of the *General Agreement on Trade in Services* (1994) ('GATS') is devoted to the movement of persons for supplying services (see Chapter 12).[26] This is the only universal instrument specifically addressing the sensitive issue of admission for labour purposes, although its scope remains circumscribed to the provision of services. There are many other multilateral treaties that have a direct or indirect impact on migration, covering topics as diverse as international transportation, extradition, slave trading, child adoption and child abduction. The universal legal framework governing migration thus consists of a wide range of multilateral treaties belonging to numerous branches of international law, including human rights law, refugee law, labour law, trade law, maritime and air law, criminal law, nationality law and consular law. Although not exhaustive, Box 3.1 lists the main universal treaties constituting the fabric of international migration law.

These universal treaties have been supplemented by regional agreements, whether for the purpose of protecting human rights or facilitating free movement. An increasing number of economic integration schemes have been concluded in Africa, the Americas and the Caribbean (see Chapter 14). The most accomplished free movement regime has been established within the European Union. The creation of an 'area without borders' has also initiated the harmonisation of national legislation through the adoption of myriad European Union directives and regulations governing asylum, family reunification, admission of highly qualified workers, students and researchers, the status of long-term third-country nationals and other related measures on migration controls.

Finally, bilateral treaties have been a traditional vehicle for regulating the movement of persons. Although their importance has declined as a consequence of the development of regional integration schemes, bilateral treaties are still prominent. They cover a variety of fields, such as labour mobility, readmission and extradition. Bilateral treaties probably represent the most promising avenue for enhancing inter-State cooperation on migration.

3.1.3. Ratification and entry into force

A treaty does not create obligations for States unless two conditions are fulfilled. First, the State must have given its consent to be bound, and second, the treaty must have entered into force, both generally and for the State in question. Article 11 of

---

25 *International Convention for the Protection of All Persons from Enforced Disappearance*, opened for signature 20 December 2006, UN Doc A/RES/61/177 (entered into force 23 December 2010) art. 16.

26 *Marrakesh Agreement Establishing the World Trade Organization*, opened for signature 15 April 1994, 1867 UNTS 3 (entered into force 1 January 1995) annex 1B ('*General Agreement on Trade in Services*').

BOX 3.1 Principal international treaties relating to migration

Subject matter	Treaties	Entry into force	States parties
Human Rights Law	International Convention on the Elimination of All Forms of Racial Discrimination	1969	174
	International Covenant on Economic, Social and Cultural Rights	1976	160
	International Covenant on Civil and Political Rights	1976	167
	Convention on the Elimination of All Forms of Discrimination against Women	1981	187
	Convention against Torture and Other Cruel, Inhuman or Degrading Treatment or Punishment	1987	149
	Convention on the Rights of the Child	1990	193
	International Convention on the Protection of the Rights of All Migrant Workers and Members of their Families	2003	44
	Convention on the Rights of Persons with Disabilities	2008	103
	International Convention for the Protection of All Persons from Enforced Disappearance	2010	29
Refugee Law	Convention relating to the Status of Refugees (as amended by the Protocol relating to the Status of Refugees)	1954/1967	147
	Agreement relating to Refugee Seamen	1961	21
	Protocol to the Agreement relating to Refugee Seamen	1975	16
Labour Law	ILO Convention No 29 concerning Forced Labour	1932	175
	ILO Convention No 87 concerning Freedom of Association and Protection of the Right to Organise	1950	150
	Convention for the Suppression of the Traffic in Persons and of the Exploitation of the Prostitution of Others	1951	82
	ILO Convention No 97 concerning Migration for Employment	1952	49

Subject matter	Treaties	Entry into force	States parties
	Convention on the Abolition of Slavery, the Slave Trade and Institutions and Practices Similar to Slavery	1957	123
	ILO Convention No 105 concerning the Abolition of Forced Labour	1959	169
	ILO Convention No 111 concerning Discrimination in Respect of Employment and Occupation	1960	169
	ILO Convention No 118 concerning Equality of Treatment of Nationals and Non-Nationals in Social Security	1964	37
	ILO Convention No 143 concerning Migrations in Abusive Conditions and the Promotion of Equality of Opportunity and Treatment of Migrant Workers	1978	23
	ILO Convention No 182 concerning the Prohibition and Immediate Action for the Elimination of the Worst Forms of Child Labour	2000	174
Trade Law	General Agreement on Trade in Services	1995	153
Maritime and Air Law	Convention on International Civil Aviation	1947	190
	Convention on Facilitation of International Maritime Traffic	1967	114
	International Convention for the Safety of Life at Sea	1980	159
	International Convention on Maritime Search and Rescue	1985	98
	Convention on the Law of the Sea	1994	162
	International Convention on Salvage	1996	59
Criminal Law	Convention against Transnational Organized Crime	2003	163
	Protocol to Prevent, Suppress and Punish Trafficking in Persons, Especially Women and Children	2003	146
	Protocol against Smuggling of Migrants by Land, Sea and Air	2004	129
Consular and Diplomatic Law	Vienna Convention on Diplomatic Relations	1964	187
	Vienna Convention on Consular Relations	1967	173

Subject matter	Treaties	Entry into force	States parties
Nationality Law	Protocol relating to a Certain Case of Statelessness	1937	24
	Convention on Certain Questions relating to the Conflict of Nationality Laws	1937	21
	Protocol relating to Military Obligations in Certain Cases of Double Nationality	1937	26
	Convention on the Nationality of Married Women	1958	74
	Convention relating to the Status of Stateless Persons	1960	66
	Convention on the Reduction of Statelessness	1975	38

Sources: Texts and ratification status are available from the UN, ILO and IMO databases listed at the conclusion of this chapter. Ratification status shown is as at mid-2011.

the Vienna Convention stipulates that a State's consent may be expressed through a variety of means – 'by signature, exchange of instruments constituting a treaty, ratification, acceptance, approval or accession, or by any other means if so agreed'. The main ambiguity in this area relates to the difference between 'signature' and 'ratification'. The confusion comes from the fact that signature may have two different legal meanings. On the one hand, signature occurs at the end of the treaty negotiation process for the single purpose of adopting and authenticating the final text of the treaty, without creating any binding effect. On the other hand, signature can also express the consent of a State to be bound by the treaty in a similar way to ratification. Generally, the treaty itself indicates whether signature or ratification expresses the consent to be bound. Where the treaty is silent, the Vienna Convention privileges an empirical method: the consent to be bound is expressed by signature when the negotiating States agreed that signature should have that effect (art. 12).

In practice, ratification remains the most common mode of expression used by States because their national constitutions usually require parliamentary approval of treaties. Adoption of the final text of the treaty (by signature) is accordingly distinguished from consent to be bound (by ratification) in order to give governments time to submit the treaty to parliament. In any event, a State that signs a treaty for the purpose of authenticating the final text is never obliged to ratify it. However, a treaty that has been signed but not ratified still has some legal effects. Although the treaty is not binding as such, a signatory State is obliged to refrain from acts that would defeat the 'object and purpose' of the treaty until it has made clear its intention not to become a party to the treaty (art. 18). In addition to signature and ratification, 'accession' is another term for expressing consent to be bound to a multilateral treaty when the State did not participate in negotiations leading to the adoption of the treaty.

The expression of consent to be bound by ratification, signature or accession does not mean that the treaty is automatically binding. It will be binding only if the treaty has entered into force. Multilateral treaties generally suspend their entry into force until a specified number of ratifications has been reached, the number varying from one convention to another. For instance, the Refugee Convention required only six ratifications (art. 43) and rapidly came into force in 1954, three years after its adoption, whereas the ICRMW required twenty ratifications (art. 87) and finally came into force in 2003, thirteen years after its adoption. Besides the technical question of entry into force, the number of States parties to a multilateral treaty is indicative of its degree of acceptance within the international community, and therefore affects both the universality of the treaty and its impact on customary international law (discussed below). Here again the comparison between the Refugee Convention and the ICRMW is telling: in mid-2011 the former had been ratified by 147 States, the latter by only 44.

The low awareness of the ICRMW as well as recurring misperceptions about its exact content are the most immediate reasons for this situation. It is commonly believed that its ratification implies a loss of sovereignty on admission policies. However, this assertion is clearly contradicted by the text of the ICRMW, which provides in art. 79 that 'Nothing in the present Convention shall affect the right of each State Party to establish the criteria governing admission of migrant workers and members of their families.' In the same vein, art. 35 restates that the ICRMW shall not be interpreted as implying the regularisation of migrant workers or members of their families in an irregular situation. Beyond the misunderstandings about its content, two contradictory lines of legal argument are commonly advanced by States for refusing to ratify it. On the one hand, notably in Asia and South Africa, national law is not always compatible with the ICRMW and would therefore need to be amended in the event of ratification. On the other hand, in Western countries, it is the very fact that national law is generally in line with the ICRMW that is invoked as a reason for non-ratification. This emphasises that the most significant obstacle to ratification is political (see Chapter 11).

3.1.4. Observance and enforcement of treaties

Once a treaty has entered into force, it is binding for all States parties. The most fundamental principle of treaty law is encapsulated in the Latin maxim *pacta sunt servanda*, which is codified in art. 26 of the Vienna Convention. It means that parties to a treaty must honour their obligations and perform them in good faith. Treaties create rights and obligations only for those who are party to them. They have no effect on third States which have not expressed their consent to be bound, except on very rare occasions (arts. 35–37). For States parties, the treaty is binding in respect of their entire territory unless a different intention appears from the treaty itself or is otherwise established (art. 29). Moreover, the binding nature of a treaty covers all its provisions as well as any annex, such as the 'Annex on Movement of Natural Persons Supplying Services', which forms an integral part of the commitments under GATS. By contrast, the preamble of a treaty and any other final declaration – such as the *Final Act of the United Nations Conference of Plenipotentiaries on the Status of Refugees and Stateless Persons* (1951)[27] – are not binding, even if they remain useful for interpreting the treaty.

As a result of the principle *pacta sunt servanda*, and as stated in art. 27 of the Vienna Convention, a State party cannot invoke its own national law as justification for its failure to perform the treaty. The ICJ has reaffirmed 'the fundamental principle of international law that international law prevails over domestic law'.[28] National legislation on migration control must thus conform to all the relevant treaties ratified by a State. If new legislation is necessary in order to comply with a treaty, the State must modify its national law before the treaty enters into force for that State. Failure to do so will result in a breach of the treaty and entail the international responsibility of the State.

Although treaties take precedence over national law at the international level, the picture is more nuanced within the domestic legal order. From the latter perspective, the impact of international law on national law depends on which of two constitutional models applies. According to the monist theory, international law is part of national law. In countries such as France, Germany and the Russian Federation, treaties duly ratified are binding within the domestic legal order and prevail over legislative enactments. By contrast, according to the dualist theory, international law and national law are distinct legal orders. A treaty has no binding force in national law unless and until it is specifically incorporated by a legislative act. This is the case in the United Kingdom, Australia and many other common law jurisdictions, although many such States adopt a monist approach regarding customary international law. Furthermore, in such countries treaties can be used as an aid to interpret national law even if they have not been incorporated into national law by legislation.

The constitutional practice governing the relationship between international law and national law thus varies considerably from one State to another. Even in a monist country, such as the United States, treaties have the status of federal law and prevail over State law, but they can be superseded by a subsequent federal law. Moreover, treaties apply directly within the domestic legal order only when they are self-executing. Generally speaking, a treaty is self-executing where its

---

27 *Final Act of the United Nations Conference of Plenipotentiaries on the Status of Refugees and Stateless Persons*, UN Doc A/CONF.2/108/Rev.1 (25 July 1951).

28 *Applicability of the Obligation to Arbitrate under Section 21 of the United Nations Headquarters Agreement of 26 June 1947 (Advisory Opinion)* [1988] ICJ Rep 12, 26.

terms determine the rights or duties of individuals without requiring any further national legislation. In such a case, the relevant treaty can be invoked before a domestic tribunal. The self-executing character of a treaty is crucial since, in the absence of an international court with compulsory jurisdiction binding all States, international law is primarily applied by national tribunals. Domestic judicial review accordingly remains the most effective way of enforcing international law.

However, the dependence of international law vis-à-vis national law should not be overestimated. Both sources of law are often intermingled and frequently coincide in substance. Indeed, national constitutions generally reiterate fundamental human rights and freedoms, including the right to leave any country and to return to one's own country. Similarly, nationality laws often reflect the treaty-law obligation to reduce statelessness (see Chapter 4), while immigration laws also recognise family reunification. Moreover, at the inter-State level, any violation of a treaty entails the international responsibility of the State under the conditions codified in the *Draft Articles on Responsibility of States for Internationally Wrongful Acts* adopted by the International Law Commission in 2001.[29] As stated in art. 3 of the Draft Articles, the existence of an internationally wrongful act is independent of its characterisation as a lawful act under national law.

The central principles governing the law of state responsibility have been developed in the context of injuries committed against aliens by the host State. The most traditional mechanism relies on diplomatic protection exercised by the national State of the injured alien (see Chapter 6). However, this mechanism suffers from two limitations. Diplomatic protection is not a right of the national concerned, but a right of the State, which the State can refuse to exercise. Moreover, even if the national State decides to exercise its diplomatic protection, it is equally free to choose a course of action it considers the most opportune for invoking the responsibility of the host State. This can include a wide range of peaceful means, such as consular consultation, negotiation, mediation, judicial and arbitral proceedings, and (more exceptionally) counter-measures or severance of diplomatic relations.

The enforcement scheme of international law thus remains a highly decentralised and State-centric one. As with any international tribunal, the ICJ can exercise its jurisdiction only if the States involved in a dispute have consented. State consent to the ICJ's jurisdiction can be expressed in advance in the final clauses of a treaty for any future dispute regarding the application of that convention. Such a 'compromissory clause' can be found in the Refugee Convention and in the *International Convention on the Elimination of All Forms of Racial Discrimination* (1965).

---

29 International Law Commission, 'Draft Articles on Responsibility of States for Internationally Wrongful Acts' (UN Doc Supplement No 10 (A/56/10), United Nations, 2001).

In practice, this possibility has never been used for the former and only once for the latter.[30]

Because of the limits inherent in the traditional inter-State settlements of disputes, human rights treaty bodies are an important alternative for defending the rights of migrants. Except for the Committee on the Rights of the Child, all eight United Nations treaty bodies are competent to examine complaints submitted by individuals with regard to alleged violations by States parties, where States have accepted that jurisdiction. Although these bodies are not necessarily a panacea for ensuring respect for the basic rights of migrants, they are bound to play an increasing role in this field. For instance, 80–90 per cent of all individual complaints submitted to the Committee against Torture concern alleged violations of art. 3 on the principle of *non-refoulement*.[31] The Migrant Workers Committee will have competence to examine individual complaints of alleged breaches of the ICRMW once ten States parties have accepted the Committee's jurisdiction (art. 77). Although a Committee's final observations are not formally binding, they retain a particularly persuasive authority. Moreover, regional human rights courts established in Europe, the Americas and Africa can deliver binding judgments for any violation of their respective instruments.

The violation of a multilateral treaty by one State cannot justify its termination or suspension by the other States parties with regard to the 'provisions relating to the protection of the human person contained in treaties of a humanitarian character' (art. 60(5) Vienna Convention). Such treaties include all the general human rights treaties, the Refugee Convention and the ICRMW. In extreme cases, a State can nevertheless decide to denounce a treaty. While unilateral denunciation of general human rights treaties is not permitted, the Refugee Convention envisages such a possibility provided that two conditions are fulfilled: a denouncing State must notify its decision to the United Nations Secretary-General, and the denunciation becomes effective after a one-year period. A similar procedure is provided by the ICRMW with an additional temporal restriction: denunciation is only possible if undertaken five years after the Convention's entry into force for the State concerned (art. 89).

3.1.5.   Reservations

Besides the radical option of denouncing a treaty, States may formulate reservations at the time of ratification. While a State may agree to be bound by most of the

---

30 *Case concerning Application of the International Convention on the Elimination of All Forms of Racial Discrimination (Georgia* v. *Russian Federation) (Preliminary Objections)* [2011] ICJ Rep.

31 Vincent Chetail, 'Le Comité des Nations Unies contre la Torture et l'Expulsion des Étrangers: dix ans de jurisprudence (1994–2004)' (2006) **16**(1) *Revue Suisse de Droit International et Européen* 63, 66.

provisions of a treaty, it may object to others. In such a case, reservations affect the scope of the State's legal obligations by excluding or modifying some treaty provisions. Article 2(1)(d) of the Vienna Convention defines a reservation as 'a unilateral statement, however phrased or named, made by a State, when signing, ratifying, accepting, approving or acceding to a treaty, whereby it purports to exclude or to modify the legal effect of certain provisions of the treaty in their application to that State'.

While a reservation cannot in principle be made to a bilateral treaty, States are generally free to ratify a multilateral treaty with reservations. This possibility acts as an incentive for them to ratify multilateral treaties, thereby encouraging universal participation. However the proliferation of reservations can in turn jeopardise the very purpose of the treaty and undermine its provisions. The dilemma between the universality of a treaty and the integrity of its provisions is graphically illustrated by the *Convention on the Rights of the Child* (1989): of the 193 States parties (which notably excludes the United States and Somalia), 75 have formulated substantial reservations.

The need to strike a balance between the objectives of universality and integrity justifies three exceptions to the right to enter reservations (art. 19). First, a treaty can prohibit any reservation in general. For example, an absolute prohibition can be found in all the treaties concluded under the auspices of the International Labour Organization ('ILO'), including those adopted on migrant workers.

Second, a treaty can provide that only specified reservations may be made by States parties. For example, the Smuggling Protocol only permits reservations to art. 15(2) (settlement of disputes). Conversely, other treaties – such as the Refugee Convention – may prohibit reservations on the most fundamental provisions of the treaty for the purpose of preserving the core content of primary legal norms. Article 42 accordingly prohibits any reservation to art. 1 (refugee definition), art. 3 (non-discrimination), art. 4 (freedom of religion), art. 16(1) (access to courts), art. 33 (*non-refoulement*) and arts. 36–46 (including the compulsory jurisdiction of the ICJ).

Third, when the two previous exceptions are not explicitly envisaged by a treaty, any reservation incompatible with the object and purpose of the treaty is prohibited (see Case Study 3.1). This general principle is notably restated in the ICRMW (art. 91(2)). Compatibility with the object and purpose of a treaty is an arguably vague criterion for assessing the legality of a reservation and can raise controversies. As a way to mitigate the subjectivity inherent in the criterion, reservations can be formulated only to specific provisions. Article 88 of the ICRMW underlines that a ratifying State is not allowed to exclude the application of any part of the Convention, or to exclude any particular category of migrant workers from its application. More generally, as is the case for the other human rights treaty bodies, the Migrant Workers Committee can examine and assess reservations formulated by States parties, even if it is not formally empowered to give binding decisions.

CASE STUDY 3.1 Reservations to the ICCPR and ICESCR in the field of migration

States may make reservations to general human rights treaties for many purposes, including the preservation of national legislation with respect to non-nationals. However, this type of reservation remains the exception rather than the rule under both the ICESCR and the ICCPR. Of the forty-one States parties that have formulated and maintained a reservation to the ICESCR, only seven reservations relate to non-nationals (Bahamas, Belgium, China, France, India, Kuwait and Monaco). Likewise, among the sixty-two reserving States parties to the ICCPR, only thirteen reservations relate to non-nationals (Austria, Belize, France, India, Liechtenstein, Malta, Mexico, Monaco, Netherlands, Pakistan, Switzerland, Trinidad and Tobago, and the United Kingdom).

Such reservations are frequently labelled 'interpretative declarations'. However, as stated in art. 2(1)(d) of the Vienna Convention, the name given to a statement does not affect its legal status as a reservation. One must look to the substance of the statement to assess whether it purports to exclude or modify the legal effect of certain provisions of the treaty. An illustration of disguised reservations may be found in France's declaration when it ratified the ICESCR in November 1980:

> The Government of the Republic declares that arts. 6 [right to work], 9 [right to social security], 11 [right to adequate standard of living] and 13 [right to education] are not to be interpreted as derogating from provisions governing the access of aliens to employment or as establishing residence requirements for the allocation of certain social benefits.

Though presented as a declaration, this statement is a reservation because it purports to modify the legal effect of the relevant articles to the extent provided by national legislation on the access of aliens to employment and social benefits.

The same observation can be made with regard to the general declaration to the ICESCR formulated by Kuwait in 1996: 'The Government of Kuwait declares that while Kuwaiti legislation safeguards the rights of all Kuwaiti and non-Kuwaiti workers, social security provisions apply only to Kuwaitis.' In contrast to the French declaration, the Kuwaiti declaration has prompted objections from several European countries. Finland, Germany, Italy, Norway and Sweden regarded the broad exclusion of aliens from the right to social security as incompatible with the object and purpose of the treaty. The generality of a reservation remains the most common ground of objection. Similar examples can be found in reservations to the ICCPR. In particular, Pakistan 'reserves its right to apply its law relating to foreigners' with regard to art. 13 governing expulsion. This broad reference to national law has elicited objections from nineteen Western States because of its vague and indeterminate nature. Curiously, India has formulated exactly the same reservation without raising any objection.

Besides art. 13 of the ICCPR, most reservations aimed at preserving national immigration legislation relate to art. 12, which concerns the right to leave any country and to enter one's own country. Such reservations have been made by Austria, Belize, the Netherlands, Switzerland, Trinidad and Tobago, and the United Kingdom. Although it prompted no objection, the United Kingdom reservation is probably the most problematic with regard to the object and purpose of the ICCPR. It asserts in general terms that:

> The Government of the United Kingdom reserves the right to continue to apply such immigration legislation governing entry into, stay in and departure from the United Kingdom as they may deem necessary from time to time and, accordingly, their acceptance of article 12(4) and of the other provisions of the Covenant is subject to the provisions of any such legislation as regards persons not at the time having the right under the law of the United Kingdom to enter and remain in the United Kingdom.

This overview calls for two general remarks. First, human rights law applies to non-nationals and nationals alike, except as otherwise provided in the terms of the Covenants and in the reservations formulated by States parties. Second, when carried out by States, assessment of the compatibility of a reservation with the object and purpose of the Covenants is affected by political expediency, to the detriment of cogent legal considerations. Treaty bodies are accordingly more apt to fulfil this task in an independent manner.

3.1.6. Interpretation

Because any treaty is the result of negotiated compromises reconciling contradictory claims, it is bound to formulate rights and obligations in general and abstract terms. This inevitably produces some ambiguity regarding the concrete meaning of its provisions. Interpreting a treaty is thus a critical operation that conditions its very application in the real world. However, it is generally at the stage of interpretation that controversies between States parties are the most difficult to reconcile. The situation may become intractable in the absence of an international tribunal duly authorised to settle the dispute.

Although international law provides authoritative rules of interpretation, they should not be overestimated because 'the interpretation of documents is to some extent an art, not an exact science'.[32] There are three main doctrines of interpretation: the subjective approach (intention of the parties), the objective approach (text of the treaty) and the teleological approach (purpose of the treaty). These doctrines are not mutually exclusive but form a single interpretative continuum (see Case Study 3.2). Article 31 of the Vienna Convention accordingly encapsulates all three doctrines in the following general rules of interpretation:

---

32 United Nations, above n. 15, 54.

CASE STUDY 3.2 The meaning of persecution under the Refugee Convention

Although persecution constitutes the cornerstone of the refugee definition, the term is not defined by the Refugee Convention. Article 31 of the Vienna Convention has been instrumental in interpreting persecution as a serious violation of human rights. Three steps may be distinguished.

First, interpretation must be based, above all, on the text of the treaty according to the ordinary meaning of its terms. Some national courts have resorted to the *Shorter Oxford English Dictionary*, which provides the following definition of persecution: 'to pursue with malignancy or injurious action, especially to oppress for holding a heretical opinion or belief'.[33] This first step is clearly insufficient for the task at hand and requires further inquiry into the broader context of the concept of 'persecution'.

Second, a treaty must be interpreted as a whole, having regard to all of its provisions. Hence, the meaning of persecution can be appraised by reference to arts. 31 and 33 of the Refugee Convention, which both advert to threats to life or freedom. Subsequent State practice has confirmed this contextual interpretation. Defining persecution by reference to human rights has been acknowledged in national case law and regional instruments.[34] This understanding has undoubtedly mirrored the development of international human rights law since the adoption of the Refugee Convention in 1951. Similarly, the *Rome Statute of the International Criminal Court* (1998) defines persecution for the purpose of crimes against humanity as the 'intentional and severe deprivation of fundamental rights contrary to international law'.[35] While the rationales of international criminal law and refugee law differ, this understanding of persecution remains a 'relevant [rule] of international law applicable in the relations between the parties' under art. 31(3)(c) of the Vienna Convention.

Third, any interpretation must also take into consideration the object and purpose of the treaty. The human rights understanding of persecution is reinforced by the very objective of the Refugee Convention. The first words of its Preamble refer to the *Universal Declaration of Human Rights* (1948) and reaffirm that 'human beings shall enjoy fundamental rights and freedoms without discrimination'. In sum, the combination of different rules mentioned in art. 31 of the Vienna Convention converge in interpreting 'persecution' as a serious violation of human rights.

---

33 *R* v. *Immigration Appeal Tribunal; Ex parte Jonah* (1985) Imm AR 7, 13.

34 See, e.g., *Council Directive 2004/83/EC of 29 April 2004 on Minimum Standards for the Qualification and Status of Third Country Nationals or Stateless Persons as Refugees or as Persons who Otherwise Need International Protection and the Content of the Protection Granted* [2004] OJ L 304/12, art. 9(1)(a), (b).

35 *Rome Statute of the International Criminal Court*, opened for signature 17 July 1998, 2187 UNTS 3 (entered into force 1 July 2002) art. 7(2)(g).

1 A treaty shall be interpreted in good faith in accordance with the ordinary meaning to be given to the terms of the treaty in their context and in the light of its object and purpose.

2 The context for the purpose of the interpretation of a treaty shall comprise, in addition to the text, including its preamble and annexes:

   (a) any agreement relating to the treaty which was made between all the parties in connection with the conclusion of the treaty;

   (b) any instrument which was made by one or more parties in connection with the conclusion of the treaty and accepted by the other parties as an instrument related to the treaty.

3 There shall be taken into account, together with the context:

   (a) any subsequent agreement between the parties regarding the interpretation of the treaty or the application of its provisions;

   (b) any subsequent practice in the application of the treaty which establishes the agreement of the parties regarding its interpretation;

   (c) any relevant rules of international law applicable in the relations between the parties.

4 A special meaning shall be given to a term if it is established that the parties so intended.

The preparatory work of a treaty and the circumstances of its conclusions may be used as 'supplementary means of interpretation' (art. 32). Recourse to such auxiliary means is confined to two circumstances: (a) to confirm the meaning resulting from the primary rules of interpretation mentioned in art. 31; or (b) to determine the meaning of a provision which is otherwise ambiguous or obscure, or leads to a result that is manifestly absurd or unreasonable. Apart from these two circumstances, preparatory works are not considered an authoritative means of interpretation. The secondary role attributed to the drafting history is justified by the fact that preparatory works are frequently confusing and partial because, by definition, the final text of the treaty has not yet been adopted by the negotiating parties. Moreover, while the *travaux préparatoires* may be instructive in understanding the historical environment surrounding the conclusion of a treaty, the risk inherent in their use lies in a backward-looking interpretation that no longer reflects the current understanding and is divorced from the subsequent evolution of international law.

While arts. 31 and 32 of the Vienna Convention codify customary international law, other methods of interpretation not mentioned there retain validity. In particular, the principle of evolutive interpretation – though implicit in art. 31(3)(c) – is a well-established method frequently used in the fields of human rights law, trade law and refugee law. According to this principle, treaties must be interpreted as living instruments in light of present-day conditions, with due regard to subsequent developments of international law.

3.2. CUSTOMARY INTERNATIONAL LAW

Despite the unprecedented development of treaties since the second half of the twentieth century, customary international law remains a vital source of the contemporary international legal system. International customs are indeed the only vehicle for creating truly universal norms binding all States without exception. However, this dynamic process of law creation is sometimes difficult to grasp with certainty. Its unwritten form immediately raises the question of how to identify it, which can lead to controversy among States. Article 38(1)(b) of the ICJ Statute defines international custom as 'a general practice accepted as law'. A custom accordingly results from the combination of two components: an objective element (State practice) and a subjective one (conviction to be bound, or *opinio juris*).

3.2.1. State practice

The relevant practice that constitutes customary law emanates chiefly from the conduct of States and, more occasionally, from that of other subjects of international law. At the national level, the State practice may be found in a great variety of forms, such as constitutions, legislation, administrative regulations, government policies and the case law of national tribunals. At the international level, the relevant practice includes treaties (especially multilateral ones), resolutions of international organisations (including those of the United Nations General Assembly), diplomatic correspondence, official statements at international conferences or organisations, and positions taken by governments before international courts.

Whatever its sources, the practice must have two characteristics to be able to support the formation of a rule of customary law. First, the practice should amount to a 'constant and uniform usage' as stated by the ICJ in the *Asylum Case*. This case concerned a Peruvian national who was granted asylum by Colombia at the Colombian Embassy in Lima, Peru, after an unsuccessful military rebellion in Peru. Peru refused to issue a 'safe conduct' to permit him to leave the country on the ground that he was not charged with a political offence. The ICJ found that Colombia was not entitled to unilaterally qualify the nature of the offence and that Peru was accordingly not bound to give the necessary safe conduct.

The facts brought to the knowledge of the Court disclose so much uncertainty and contradiction, so much fluctuation and discrepancy in the exercise of diplomatic asylum and in the official views expressed on various occasions, there has been so much inconsistency in the rapid succession of conventions on asylum, ratified by some States and rejected by others, and the practice has been so much influenced by considerations of political expediency in the various cases, that it is not possible to discern in all this any constant and uniform usage, accepted as law, with regard to the alleged rule of unilateral and definitive qualification of the offence.[36]

---

36 *Asylum Case (Colombia v. Peru) (Judgment)* [1950] ICJ Rep 266, 277.

Although this case concerned a regional custom in Latin America, a constant and uniform usage is also required for establishing a universal custom. The consistency of the relevant practice must nonetheless be assessed with a degree of flexibility. In a later case, the ICJ explained that State practice need not be in absolute conformity with the purported customary norm:

> In order to deduce the existence of customary rules, the Court deems it sufficient that the conduct of States should, in general, be consistent with such rules, and that instances of State conduct inconsistent with a given rule should generally have been treated as breaches of that rule, not as indications of the recognition of a new rule.[37]

The duration of the relevant practice is no longer a decisive criterion for the purpose of creating a customary norm. This is the direct consequence of the intensification of international relations and the development of means of communication. As acknowledged by the ICJ, the passage of only a short time period is not a bar to the formation of a new rule of customary law provided that State practice is extensive enough.[38] This last qualification underlines the second key requirement: the generality of the practice.

Although there is no magic number of States for determining how general a practice must be, international jurisprudence has developed two complementary criteria of assessment: a general practice must be both *widespread* and *representative*, including States whose interests are specially affected. The generality of the practice is accordingly inferred from a qualitative test rather than a quantitative test based on the number of States that adhere to the practice. This qualitative test calls for two remarks. The notion of 'specially affected States' is of limited value in matters of common interest, such as human rights or international migration: in the latter case, every State is affected by the movement of persons, whether as a country of emigration, transit or immigration. Moreover, the representative character of a general practice is traditionally understood as including States from different regions of the world, as well as all major political and socio-economic systems. Beyond these general guidelines, it is not possible to be more specific. Nevertheless, the apparent difficulty of demonstrating the generality of a practice should not be overestimated: in the vast majority of cases, it is inferred from broad participation in universal treaties concluded under the auspices of the United Nations.

3.2.2.   *Opinio juris*

A consistent and general practice is not sufficient in itself to create an international custom. The most decisive constitutive element is not material but

---

37 *Military and Paramilitary Activities in and against Nicaragua (Nicaragua* v. *United States) (Merits)* [1986] ICJ Rep 14, 98.
38 *North Sea Continental Shelf (Federal Republic of Germany* v. *Denmark)* [1969] ICJ Rep 3, 44.

psychological – it relies on the conviction to be bound by such a norm (also known by the Latin maxim, *opinio juris sive necessitatis*). In other words, the practice must be accompanied by the belief of States that their conduct is obligatory as law.[39] The tautology inherent in this formulation has given rise to some vexed theoretical questions because it relies on the postulate that a custom is binding because it is considered as binding. But how can a practice develop into a norm of customary law if States must be convinced that the rule in question is already binding? Moreover, this element of customary law refers to a state of mind and thus artificially suggests that collective entities, such as States, may have a psychology.

Besides the difficulties in grasping this elusive concept, *opinio juris* remains essential for distinguishing a legal rule from a social usage. The conduct of States may be prompted by humanitarian considerations, political convenience or tradition, without any sense of legal duty. An archetypal example is the tradition of granting asylum to victims of persecution. This long-standing practice did not give rise to an individual right to be granted asylum. Article 14 of the *Universal Declaration of Human Rights* (1948) refers instead to 'the right to seek and to enjoy asylum'.[40] This euphemism was carefully worded to avoid any sense of obligation on the part of States to grant asylum.

However, this does not mean that States have a discretionary power to refuse admission of refugees. The main binding norm in the field is the principle of *non-refoulement* (see Chapter 7). Its customary character raises an additional difficulty because of the nature of the obligation. The prohibition of *refoulement* is an obligation of abstention (not to return), rather than an obligation of conduct (to admit). As acknowledged by the Permanent Court of International Justice, it is possible to speak of an international custom only if an abstention is motivated by the conviction of States that they have a duty to abstain.[41] The difficulty of proving the binding nature of an abstention may explain why some authors are still reticent to acknowledge *non-refoulement* as a principle of customary international law.

Although a detailed study is beyond the scope of this chapter, the main arguments invoked in favour of such a customary norm may be summarised in the following observations. First, the relevant practice is widespread and representative; more than 90 per cent of member States of the United Nations are party to one or several treaties endorsing the principle of *non-refoulement*, whether the Refugee Convention or other universal or regional human rights treaties. Second, of the few States that have not ratified one of these instruments, none claims to possess an unconditional right to return a refugee to a country of persecution. Instead they attempt to justify such conduct by invoking exceptions or by alleging that

39 Ibid.   40 *Universal Declaration of Human Rights*, GA Res 217A (III), UN Doc A/810 (10 December 1948).
41 *Lotus Case (France* v. *Turkey)* [1927] PCIJ (ser A) No 10, 28.

returnees are not refugees.[42] Third, the customary nature of *non-refoulement* is asserted in a large amount of material, including national legislation, case law and resolutions of international and regional organisations. Notably, in 2001, a declaration of States parties to the Refugee Convention and its Protocol acknowledged 'the principle of *non-refoulement*, whose applicability is embedded in customary international law'.[43]

This brief recital of the arguments in favour of a customary rule highlights the methodology generally used for asserting the existence of *opinio juris*. While *opinio juris* is non-material by nature, it can only be deduced from material acts. The conviction to be bound is revealed through and by State practice. *Opinio juris* and State practice are thus two faces of the same coin. Both elements of the customary law process are intertwined to such an extent that it may be difficult to distinguish them. This is further confirmed by the use of treaties as a proof of customary international law.

3.2.3. Relationships between customary and treaty law

A treaty may interact with international custom in three ways. First, a treaty can codify customary international law by recasting an existing custom in written form. Rarely are treaties pure restatements of customary norms, but many of their provisions can have a declaratory nature. In such cases, both conventional and customary norms have the same content, with two distinct legal bases. Treaty provisions codifying customary rules may be found in various areas related to migration. An illustration is art. 1 of the *Convention on Certain Questions relating to the Conflict of Nationality Laws* (1930), which restates that 'It is for each State to determine under its own law who are its nationals. This law shall be recognised by other States in so far as it is consistent with international conventions, international custom, and the principles of law generally recognised with regard to nationality.'[44]

Similar restatements of customary international norms may be found in specific treaty provisions, such as the duty to rescue persons in distress at sea[45] or the right of consular officers to visit a national detained in a foreign country.[46]

Second, a treaty can crystallise an emerging custom. When a customary rule is in the process of development, its incorporation into a multilateral treaty may

---

42 State reliance on exceptions strengthens a rule rather than weakens it: *Military and Paramilitary Activities in and against Nicaragua (Nicaragua v. United States) (Merits)* [1986] ICJ Rep 14, 98.

43 *Declaration of States Parties to the 1951 Convention and/or Its 1967 Protocol relating to the Status of Refugees*, UN Doc HCR/MMSP/2001/09 (16 January 2002) [4].

44 *Convention on Certain Questions relating to the Conflict of Nationality Law*, opened for signature 13 April 1930, 179 LNTS 89 (entered into force 1 July 1937).

45 *United Nations Convention on the Law of the Sea*, opened for signature 10 December 1982, 1833 UNTS 3 (entered into force 14 November 1994) art. 98.

46 *Vienna Convention on Consular Relations*, opened for signature 24 April 1963, 596 UNTS 261 (entered into force 19 March 1967) art. 36(1)(c).

have the effect of fixing the nascent custom. The very adoption of a treaty, though it has not yet entered into force, may give birth to a custom. The ICJ acknowledged this possibility in relation to the law of the sea and the concept of the 'exclusive economic zone': even before the *United Nations Convention on the Law of the Sea* (1982) entered into force in 1994, the ICJ accepted that the exclusive economic zone had become part of customary law.[47] This zone was established principally for the purpose of exploring and exploiting natural resources within 200 nautical miles of the baselines of the territorial sea, but it retains relevance in the field of migration because coastal States have exclusive jurisdiction over artificial islands, installations and structures in the zone, including jurisdiction with regard to 'immigration laws and regulations' (art. 60(2)).

Third, a treaty can provide the impetus for the formation of a new custom. In such a case, the multilateral treaty constitutes the starting point of a customary law process that will eventually become binding even for States that did not ratify the convention. According to the ICJ, three prerequisites must be fulfilled for a provision of a treaty to generate a customary rule: (a) the provision should potentially be of 'a fundamentally norm-creating character such as could be regarded as forming the basis of a general rule of law'; (b) 'even without the passage of any considerable period of time, a very widespread and representative participation in the convention might suffice of itself'; and (c) 'State practice ... should have been both extensive and virtually uniform in the sense of the provision invoked; – and should moreover have occurred in such a way as to show a general recognition that a rule of law or legal obligation is involved'.[48]

Besides the principle of *non-refoulement*, an obvious candidate for this generative process is the right to leave any country, endorsed in art. 12(2) of the ICCPR. A rule of customary international law can be inferred from the widespread and representative participation of States in six United Nations treaties and four regional treaties on human rights, which all acknowledge this right. Among the plethora of other relevant materials, freedom to leave has been restated in resolutions of the United Nations General Assembly, the Human Rights Council and other regional bodies; in a substantial number of bilateral agreements; and in national constitutions, legislation and case law. The *Final Act of the Conference on Security and Cooperation in Europe* (1975) was a turning point in this customary law process, as the traditional opponents to the right to leave – the Soviet Union and other Communist States – acknowledged this right. Although the right to leave does not ensure a correlative right to enter a foreign country, it guarantees a critical right for migrants – the freedom to emigrate. It includes a twofold obligation for States: a negative obligation not to impede departure from its territory and a positive obligation to issue travel documents. Restrictions are

---

47 *Continental Shelf (Libyan Arab Jamahiriya v. Malta) (Judgment)* [1985] ICJ Rep 13, 29–34.
48 *North Sea Continental Shelf (Federal Republic of Germany v. Denmark)* [1969] ICJ Rep 3, 41–3.

nevertheless possible provided they have a legal basis and are necessary to protect national security or public order (see Chapter 5).

A similar customary law process has been acknowledged with regard to a core content of fundamental rights embodied in several ILO treaties. Besides widespread participation in the relevant treaties, the customary nature of the rules was endorsed by the *ILO Declaration on Fundamental Principles and Rights at Work* (1998):

> All Members, even if they have not ratified the Conventions in question, have an obligation arising from the very fact of membership in the Organization to respect, to promote and to realize, in good faith and in accordance with the Constitution, the principles concerning the fundamental rights which are the subject of those Conventions, namely:

(a) freedom of association and the effective recognition of the right to collective bargaining;
(b) the elimination of all forms of forced or compulsory labour;
(c) the effective abolition of child labour; and
(d) the elimination of discrimination in respect of employment and occupation.[49]

The applicability of these fundamental guarantees to migrants was further confirmed in 2004 at the 92nd International Labour Conference:

> The fundamental principles and rights at work are universal and applicable to all people in all States, regardless of the level of economic development. They thus apply to all migrant workers without distinction, whether they are temporary or permanent migrant workers, or whether they are regular migrants or migrants in an irregular situation.[50]

The relationship between treaty law and customary law may prove to be relatively dense and dynamic in a field such as migration. They interact in a mutually supportive way, although they remain distinct sources of international law. Whether a treaty codifies, crystallises or generates a custom, the former does not supersede the latter, nor vice versa. As acknowledged by the ICJ, conventional and customary rules retain 'a separate existence', and 'customary international law continues to exist and to apply, separately from international treaty law, even where the two categories of law have an identical content'.[51] The autonomous existence of these two sources of law has practical importance. Although identical in content, the two rules are subject to different regimes regarding their respective application: States parties to a convention will be monitored by treaty bodies, such as those established by human rights instruments.

On a theoretical plane, the parallel existence of conventional and customary rules is reinforced by the absence of hierarchy between a treaty and a custom. Both have the same binding nature. When their content diverges, the conflict of norms has to be resolved in one of two ways: either the later rule overrides the earlier one

---

49 *ILO Declaration on Fundamental Principles and Rights at Work*, adopted by the International Labour Conference, 86th sess (18 June 1998).
50 International Labour Conference, 'Report VI: Towards a Fair Deal for Migrant Workers in the Global Economy' (International Labour Office, 2004) 82.
51 *Military and Paramilitary Activities in and against Nicaragua (Nicaragua v. United States) (Merits)* [1986] ICJ Rep 14, 95–6.

(*lex posterior derogat legi priori*) or the special rule takes precedence over the general rule (*lex specialis derogat legi generali*). These two maxims may nonetheless raise more problems than solutions. The *lex posterior* supposes to determine the precise moment of the formation of a custom (which can be an impossible mission), while the *lex specialis* says nothing about what should be 'general' or 'special' and how to interpret these vague terms. The limits inherent in these rudimentary principles reveal the difficulty in reconciling diverging norms in an international legal system grounded on the absence of hierarchy.

3.2.4. Peremptory norms of general international law

The only exception to the consensual basis of the international legal system arises in the context of peremptory norms of general international law, also known as *jus cogens*. Traditionally linked to the notion of international public order, the concept of *jus cogens* presupposes that some rules are so fundamental to the international community that States cannot derogate from them in any manner whatsoever. Because of the importance of peremptory norms, no treaty can controvert them without becoming void. Article 53 of the Vienna Convention defines *jus cogens* as 'a norm accepted and recognized by the international community of States as a whole as a norm from which no derogation is permitted'. Peremptory norms are thus by nature limited to a core content of fundamental principles. Identification of such norms has raised long-standing debates among academics, but international jurisprudence provides some examples. The landmark *Barcelona Traction Case* has been particularly influential in asserting the existence of such norms in the field of migration. The ICJ stated that:

> When a State admits into its territory ... foreign nationals ... it is bound to extend to them the protection of the law and assumes obligations concerning the treatment to be afforded them. These obligations, however, are neither absolute nor unqualified. In particular, an essential distinction should be drawn between the obligations of a State towards the international community as a whole, and those arising vis-à-vis another State in the field of diplomatic protection. By their very nature the former are the concern of all States ... Such obligations derive, for example, in contemporary international law, from the outlawing of acts of aggression, and of genocide, as also from the principles and rules concerning the basic rights of the human person, including protection from slavery and racial discrimination.[52]

As this statement implies, human rights norms are particularly relevant in the field of migration. Among other 'basic rights of the human person', the prohibition of torture is acknowledged as a norm of *jus cogens*.[53] Although the prohibition of

---

52 *Barcelona Traction, Light and Power Company Limited (Belgium v. Spain), (Second Phase)* [1970] ICJ Rep 3, 32.
53 See *Filártiga* v. *Peña-Irala*, 630 F 2d 876 (2nd Cir, 1980), 884, 890; *Prosecutor* v. *Furundzija (Judgment)* (International Criminal Tribunal for the Former Yugoslavia, Trial Chamber II, Case No IT-95–17/1-T, 10 December 1998) [153]; *Al-Adsani* v. *United Kingdom* (2002) 34 Eur Court HR 273, [61]; *Caesar* v. *Trinidad and Tobago*, Inter-Am Ct HR (Ser C) No 123 (11 March 2005) [70].

torture is interpreted as encompassing a prohibition on removing a person to a State where there is a real risk of torture, the peremptory nature of *non-refoulement* remains more controversial.

In line with the prohibition of racial discrimination, the Inter-American Court of Human Rights affirmed that 'the principle of equality before the law, equal protection before the law and non-discrimination belongs to *jus cogens*, because the whole legal structure of national and international public order rests on it'.[54] From that premise, it deduced some far-reaching assertions regarding labour rights of migrant workers:

A person who enters a State and assumes an employment relationship, acquires his labor human rights in the State of employment, irrespective of his migratory status, because respect and guarantee of the enjoyment and exercise of those rights must be made without any discrimination. In this way, the migratory status of a person can never be a justification for depriving him of the enjoyment and exercise of his human rights, including those related to employment.[55]

The rights in question notably include the prohibition of forced labour and child labour, freedom of association, freedom to organise and join a trade union, and the right to fair wages and social security. However, a difference of treatment does not constitute discrimination if the criteria for differentiation are 'reasonable and objective'. In other words, the differentiation between nationals and non-nationals must be proportionate to the aims pursued by States in their immigration policy. This requires a subtle case-by-case assessment, which remains difficult to systematise in the absence of principled guidance from treaty bodies. States accordingly retain a broad margin of appreciation in assessing proportionality.

In sum, while the fundamental principle of non-discrimination is not contested as such, its implications for non-nationals are still difficult to grasp with certainty. This highlights the schizophrenic nature of international law, which is grounded on two contradictory forces. On the one hand, 'universal respect for, and observance of, human rights and fundamental freedoms for all without distinction' is acknowledged by the *Charter of the United Nations* (1945) (art. 55) as one of the founding principles of the international legal order. On the other hand, respect for the principle of non-discrimination is largely left to a decentralised scheme entrusted to States. Much more remains to be done in elucidating the normative and practical consequences of the non-discrimination principle in its application to nationals and non-nationals.

---

54 *Juridical Condition and Rights of the Undocumented Migrants (Advisory Opinion)* OC-18/03, Inter-Am Ct HR (Ser A) No 18 (17 September 2003) [101].
55 Ibid. [133]–[134].

3.3.   SUBSIDIARY SOURCES OF INTERNATIONAL LAW

While treaties and international customs constitute the primary sources of international law, the ICJ Statute envisages additional sources, namely, general principles of law and judicial decisions, the latter as a subsidiary means for determining rules of law.

3.3.1.   General principles of law

Article 38(1)(c) of the ICJ Statute lists among the sources of international law 'the general principles of law recognized by civilized nations'. Because of its colonial connotation, the term 'civilized nations' is no longer acceptable and must be understood as referring to the main national legal systems. This provision was initially drafted in 1920 and, since then, international law has evolved from a European-centric regime to a truly universal one. Today, general principles of international law accordingly encompass the principles common to the major legal systems of the world. They nonetheless constitute a subsidiary source of international law because they can only be resorted to where there is no applicable norm in treaty law or customary law. Their function is thus to fill gaps in the international legal system. Although they have played an important role in the past, they have been marginalised in more recent times by the expansion of treaties and customs.

In the field of migration, general principles of law were instrumental in developing minimum standards of treatment of aliens during the nineteenth century and the first half of the twentieth century (see Chapter 6). These principles required that aliens not be treated below a common standard of conduct recognised by most nations. Although the content of this standard has raised long-standing controversies among States, it has been progressively refined in international jurisprudence. This incremental process has been crystallised in a core content of basic guarantees, most notably including the right to life, respect for physical integrity, freedom of conscience, prohibition of arbitrary detention, the right to a fair trial in civil and criminal matters, and the right to property (save for public expropriation with fair compensation).

As is apparent from this enumeration, the minimum standard of treatment has been the forerunner of human rights law at the international level. It has been critical for infusing the rule of law into the field of migration, which was traditionally considered a matter of exclusive state discretion. Nowadays, while it still retains some residual value, the minimum standard is absorbed to a large extent by human rights treaties and customary law.

3.3.2. Judicial decisions

Article 38(1)(d) of the ICJ Statute describes judicial decisions as 'subsidiary means for the determination of rules of law'. They are not a source of law, but evidence as to whether some rules have become part of international law. Judicial decisions include judgments of international, regional and national courts and tribunals. National decisions are particularly relevant in areas related to migration – such as extradition, readmission and refugee determination – but their value and merits vary considerably.

Much more weight attaches to decisions of international courts. While their function is to apply international law rather than make international law, the border between the two is frequently blurred. For instance, in the landmark *Soering Case*, the European Court of Human Rights construed the general prohibition of torture, degrading and inhuman treatment as encompassing an additional obligation not to remove persons to a State where there is substantial risk of such mistreatment.[56] This dynamic interpretation has since been confirmed by many other treaty bodies and accordingly constitutes a key norm in the field of forced migration.

Among the great diversity of international tribunals, the ICJ retains a preeminent position as the principal judicial organ of the United Nations. Its judgments are formally binding only between the parties to a particular dispute, but they have considerable authority beyond that. Indeed, the ICJ's decisions have been instrumental in determining whether an international custom or a norm of *jus cogens* exists. This crucial function is exemplified in *Asylum Case* and *Barcelona Traction Case* discussed above. Similarly, the *Nottebohm Case* has had a significant influence on the customary law regime governing nationality. The ICJ provided an authoritative definition of nationality and restated the primary competence of States to determine nationality (see Chapter 4).[57]

Furthermore, the ICJ plays a decisive role in interpreting international rules and, in particular, multilateral treaties. In such cases, the interpretation given by the Court is not confined to the States involved in the dispute, but extends to all States parties to the treaty. A typical example is found in the *Avena Case*, which concerned the interpretation of art. 36(1)(b) of the *Vienna Convention on Consular Relations* (1963) governing the rights of foreign detainees to communicate with consular officers.[58] The ICJ observed that this provision:

> contains three separate but interrelated elements: the right of the individual concerned to be informed without delay of his rights under Article 36, paragraph 1(b); the right of the consular post to be notified without delay of the individual's detention, if he so requests; and the

---

56 *Soering* v. *United Kingdom* (1989) 11 EHRR 439, [87]–[88].
57 *Nottebohm Case (Liechtenstein* v. *Guatemala) (Second Phase)* [1955] ICJ Rep 4, 20, 23.
58 *Vienna Convention on Consular Relations*, opened for signature 24 April 1963, 596 UNTS 261 (entered into force 19 March 1967).

obligation of the receiving State to forward without delay any communication addressed to the consular post by the detained person.[59]

The Court made two important clarifications to the scope and content of the obligations under this provision. First, it is for the authorities of the arresting State, on their own initiative, to inform the arrested person of his or her right to ask that the consulate be notified. The fact that the person does not make such a request or that the consular authorities learn of the arrest through other channels does not remove the obligation to inform the arrested person of his or her rights. Second, the Court explained that the duty to inform 'without delay' does not necessarily mean immediately upon arrest. However, 'there is ... a duty upon the arresting authorities to give that information to an arrested person as soon as it is realized that the person is a foreign national, or once there are grounds to think that the person is probably a foreign national'.[60]

The ICJ further refined the meaning of art. 36(1)(b) in the *Diallo Case* in 2010. It held that the obligations under this provision are applicable 'to any deprivation of liberty of whatever kind, even outside the context of pursuing perpetrators of criminal offences',[61] thus including detention for the purpose of carrying out expulsion. The *Diallo Case* was also the occasion to settle the interpretation of two provisions of the ICCPR in the context of expulsion. In line with the Human Rights Committee, the Court stated that the prohibition of arbitrary detention and the related procedural guarantees in art. 9 are not limited to criminal proceedings; they apply equally to administrative detention to effect the forcible removal of an alien from a State's territory.[62] Moreover, the requirement under art. 13 of the ICCPR and art. 12(4) of the *African Charter on Human and Peoples' Rights* (1981)[63] that any expulsion must be decided 'in accordance with law' was construed by the ICJ as requiring compliance with both national and international law.[64]

3.4. SOFT LAW

Apart from the traditional sources listed in art. 38 of the ICJ Statute, international migration law has also been framed by the development of 'soft law', which refers to non-binding instruments adopted by States and international organisations.

---

59 *Avena and Other Mexican Nationals (Mexico v. United States)* [2004] ICJ Rep 12, 43.   60 Ibid. 49.

61 *Case concerning Ahmadou Sadio Diallo (Republic of Guinea v. Democratic Republic of the Congo)* [2010] ICJ Rep 1, [91].

62 Ibid. [77].

63 *African Charter on Human and Peoples' Rights*, opened for signature 27 June 1981, 1520 UNTS 217 (entered into force 21 October 1986).

64 *Case concerning Ahmadou Sadio Diallo (Republic of Guinea v. Democratic Republic of the Congo)* [2010] ICJ Rep 1, [65].

Soft law is not a source of international law as such, but it has been instrumental in three different ways: it provides evidence of customary law; it gives guidance in the application of a treaty; and it can be used as a privileged avenue for facilitating inter-State cooperation.

3.4.1.   Soft law and customary law

Soft law may interact with customary law in a similar way to treaties: it can codify, crystallise or generate a custom. Resolutions of international organisations and, in particular, those of the United Nations General Assembly are influential in demonstrating the existence of *opinio juris*. The ICJ acknowledged that '[t]he effect of consent to the text of such resolutions . . . may be understood as an acceptance of the validity of the rule or set of rules declared by the resolution by themselves'.[65] It further explained that:

> General Assembly resolutions, even if they are not binding, may sometimes have normative value. They can, in certain circumstances, provide evidence important for establishing the existence of a rule or the emergence of an *opinio juris*. To establish whether this is true of a given General Assembly resolution, it is necessary to look at its content and the conditions of its adoption.[66]

Two conditions should be fulfilled in assessing whether a resolution reflects an *opinio juris*. The content of the resolution should be written in prescriptive terms for the purpose of highlighting the existence of an obligation. Additionally, the conditions of its adoption must reflect a high degree of acceptance by States: it should be adopted by consensus or at least by a broad and representative majority.

General Assembly resolutions capable of reaching this twofold threshold are relatively rare in the field of migration. Two declarations of special interest are the *Declaration on Territorial Asylum* (1967) and the *Declaration on the Human Rights of Individuals Who Are Not Nationals of the Country in which They Live* (1985).[67] Both restate existing norms endorsed in multilateral treaties and were unanimously adopted by the General Assembly. By contrast, the annual resolutions on international migration and development, though adopted without vote, are generally worded in recommendatory terms for '[encouraging] efforts by Member States and the international community to continue to promote a balanced, coherent and comprehensive approach to international migration and development, in

---

65 *Military and Paramilitary Activities in and against Nicaragua (Nicaragua* v. *United States) (Merits)* [1986] ICJ Rep 14, 100.

66 *Legality of the Threat or Use of Nuclear Weapons (Advisory Opinion)* [1996] ICJ Rep 226, 254–5.

67 *Declaration on Territorial Asylum*, GA Res 2312, UN GAOR 22nd sess, 1631st plen mtg, Supp No 16, UN Doc A/RES/ 2312(XXII) (14 December 1967); *Declaration on the Human Rights of Individuals Who Are Not Nationals of the Country in which They Live*, GA Res 40/144, UN GAOR, 40th sess, 116th plen mtg, Supp No 53, UN Doc. A/RES/40/ 144 (13 December 1985).

particular by building partnerships and ensuring coordinated action to develop capacities, including for the management of migration'.[68]

3.4.2. Soft law and treaty law

Soft law interacts with treaties in two main ways: it can complement a treaty by detailing its general provisions and it can provide a persuasive tool for interpreting treaty norms.

Soft law as a complement to treaties

Non-binding instruments may complement a treaty by filling in gaps or detailing specific issues arising from its application. This kind of instrument has been concluded under the auspices of the International Maritime Organization for tackling the difficulties arising in implementing the obligation to provide assistance to migrants in distress at sea (see Chapter 10).[69] A comprehensive framework has been detailed for this purpose in three instruments: *Guidelines on the Allocation of Responsibilities to Seek the Successful Resolution of Stowaways Cases* (1997);[70] *Interim Measures for Combating Unsafe Practices Associated with the Trafficking or Transport of Migrants by Sea* (1998, as revised);[71] and *Guidelines on the Treatment of Persons Rescued at Sea* (2004).[72] The latter Guidelines 'are intended to help Governments and masters better understand their obligations under international law and provide helpful guidance with regard to carrying out these obligations'. The duty of the master to render assistance is accordingly complemented by a set of operational standards for reinforcing coordination between States in the application of their obligations.

A similar use of soft law may be found in ILO conventions, which are usually supplemented by recommendations. In particular, both the *Convention concerning Migration for Employment (Revised)* (1949) ('ILO Convention No 97') and the *Convention concerning Migrations in Abusive Conditions and the Promotion of Equality of Opportunity and Treatment of Migrant Workers* (1975) ('ILO Convention No 143') are complemented by recommendations.[73] Though not binding, the

---

68 *International Migration and Development*, GA Res 65/170, UN GAOR 65th sess, UN Doc A/RES/65/170 (17 March 2011) [2].

69 The relevant treaties are: *International Convention for the Safety of Life at Sea*, opened for signature 1 November 1974, 1184 UNTS 3 (entered into force 25 May 1980); *International Convention on Maritime Search and Rescue*, opened for signature 27 April 1979, 1405 UNTS 119 (entered into force 22 June 1985); *United Nations Convention on the Law of the Sea*, opened for signature 10 December 1982, 1833 UNTS 3 (entered into force 14 November 1994).

70 International Maritime Organization, *Guidelines on the Allocation of Responsibilities to Seek the Successful Resolution of Stowaway Cases*, Res A.871(20), (adopted on 27 November 1997).

71 International Maritime Organization, *Interim Measures for Combating Unsafe Practices Associated with the Trafficking or Transport of Migrants by Sea*, IMO Doc MSC/Circ.896/Rev.1 (adopted 1998, revised 2001).

72 International Maritime Organization, *Guidelines on the Treatment of Persons Rescued at Sea*, IMO Doc MSC 78/26/Add.2, Annex 34 (adopted 20 May 2004).

73 *Convention concerning Migration for Employment (Revised)* (ILO Convention No 97), opened for signature 1 July 1949 (entered into force 22 January 1952); *Convention concerning Migrations in Abusive Conditions and the Promotion of*

recommendations provide a common line of action for States parties on several substantial issues. They are also much more detailed than the text of the treaty itself. For instance, whereas ILO Convention No 143 envisages family reunification and social welfare in rather vague and permissive terms, Recommendation No 151 spells out the conditions for their benefit. The degree of precision of the norm is thus inversely proportional to its binding nature. Although the rationale of this method is debatable, its implicit objective is to promote more favourable standards in the implementation of the conventions. Each State party can accordingly choose between maximal application of the conventions by reference to the recommendations and minimal application by reference to the conventions alone.

Soft law as a tool of interpretation

Soft law also plays a significant role in promoting a common interpretation of a treaty. Non-binding instruments may be concluded with this aim at the time the treaty is adopted, but more frequently they are adopted by States after the treaty's conclusion. In such cases, soft law instruments can be considered as a means of interpretation for asserting the subsequent State practice under art. 31(3)(b) of the Vienna Convention.

This kind of instrument is relatively common in migration matters. One example is the 'Conclusions on the International Protection of Refugees' adopted by the Executive Committee of the United Nations High Commissioner for Refugees ('UNHCR'). Although not formally binding, Conclusions have persuasive authority in so far as the agency's governing body comprises seventy-nine representative States parties to the Refugee Convention. Its Conclusions accordingly contribute to an authoritative interpretation on a broad range of provisions, including the principle of *non-refoulement* (art. 33), exemption from penalties for illegal entry and conditions of detention (art. 31), expulsion (art. 32), identification documents (art. 28), right to education (art. 22) and employment (arts. 17–19).

By contrast, the 'Handbook on Procedures and Criteria for Determining Refugee Status',[74] and other related guidelines, are less authoritative because they have been adopted by UNHCR itself and not by States parties. Notwithstanding this, these documents are frequently based on State practice and provide persuasive guidance by virtue of art. 35 of the Refugee Convention, which obliges States parties to cooperate with UNHCR. Several national courts have inferred from this general obligation that 'such Guidelines should be accorded considerable weight'.[75] UNHCR has also adopted guiding principles on a wide array of other key issues,

Equality of Opportunity and Treatment of Migrant Workers (ILO Convention No 143), opened for signature 24 June 1975 (entered into force 9 December 1978). *Migration for Employment Recommendation (Revised)* (ILO Convention No R86), (1 July 1949); *Recommendation concerning Migrant Workers* (ILO Convention No R151), (28 June 1975).

74 United Nations High Commissioner for Refugees, *Handbook on Procedures and Criteria for Determining Refugee Status* (UNHCR, 1992).

75 *R* v. *Uxbridge Magistrates Court; Ex parte Adimi* [1999] EWHC Admin 765 (29 July 1999).

such as the protection of refugee women and children, and standards for the detention of asylum seekers.[76]

The supervisory role of human rights treaty bodies also enables them to interpret their respective instruments. Although States are not bound by these interpretations, the 'general comments' of treaty bodies have gained considerable influence in promoting a common understanding of treaty obligations. This is particularly important for restating the applicability of human rights norms to non-nationals and in supporting a contextual interpretation in the field of migration. The most significant comments include those of the Human Rights Committee on freedom of movement and the position of aliens under the ICCPR,[77] and those of the Committee on the Elimination of Racial Discrimination on refugees, displaced persons and discrimination against non-citizens.[78]

3.4.3. Soft law and global governance

Soft law can have virtue on its own without any particular connection to the sources of international law. It has become the privileged avenue for facilitating inter-State cooperation and international dialogue. Migration is the most emblematic, and perhaps the most promising, area for the instrumental use of soft law.

Although this phenomenon has experienced unprecedented acceleration during the past decade, its origin dates back to the United Nations International Conference on Population and Development, which took place in 1994. The *Cairo Declaration on Population and Development*, and the accompanying Programme of Action, provided the first comprehensive approach to migration-related cooperation at the multilateral level and paid particular attention to the migration-development nexus.[79] While the long-term priority is 'to make the option of remaining in one's country viable for all people', the Programme of Action stressed the 'positive impacts [of migration] on both the communities of origin and the communities of destination, providing the former with remittances and

---

76 United Nations High Commissioner for Refugees, 'Guidelines on the Protection of Refugee Women' (UNHCR, 1991); United Nations High Commissioner for Refugees, 'Guidelines on Protection and Care of Refugee Children' (UNHCR, 1994); United Nations High Commissioner for Refugees, 'Revised Guidelines on Applicable Criteria and Standards relating to the Detention of Asylum-Seekers' (UNHCR, 1999).

77 Human Rights Committee, 'General Comment No 15: The Position of Aliens under the Covenant' (UN Doc HRI/GEN/1/Rev.1, 11 April 1986); Human Rights Committee, *General Comment No 27: Freedom of Movement* (Article 12), 67th sess, UN Doc CCPR/C/21/Rev.1/Add.9 (2 November 1999).

78 Committee on the Elimination of Racial Discrimination, 'General Recommendation No 22: Article 5 and Refugees and Displaced Persons' (UN Doc A/54/18, 24 August 1996); Committee on the Elimination of Racial Discrimination, *General Recommendation No 30: Discrimination Against Non Citizens*, UN Doc 10/01/2004 (1 October 2004). See also Committee on the Rights of the Child, *General Comment No 6: Treatment of Unaccompanied and Separated Children outside their Country of Origin*, 39th sess, UN Doc CRC/GC/2005/6 (1 September 2005).

79 *Cairo Declaration on Population and Development*, International Conference of Parliamentarians on Population and Development (4 September 1994).

the latter with needed human resources'.[80] This balanced approach to the migra-tion–development nexus was intended to be based on three complementary objectives:

a To address the root causes of migration, especially those related to poverty;
b To encourage more cooperation and dialogue between countries of origin and countries of destination in order to maximize the benefits of migration to those concerned and increase the likelihood that migration has positive consequences for the development of both sending and receiving countries;
c To facilitate the reintegration process of returning migrants.[81]

However, the twenty-year Programme of Action largely remained a dead letter in the absence of real cooperation between countries of emigration and countries of immigration. Furthermore, the proposal to convene a United Nations conference on migration and development was regularly postponed because of the reluctance of the European Union, the United States and Canada. The two following decades were dominated by security-focussed unilateralism, which patently failed to meet its objective of eliminating irregular migration. The need for a new approach suddenly resurfaced at the turn of the millennium.

Since 2003, the United Nations has attempted to play a leading role in pro-moting a mutually beneficial approach to the migration–development nexus between developed and developing States. In 2006 the General Assembly con-vened the High-Level Dialogue on International Migration and Development.[82] As a result of this meeting, the Global Forum on Migration and Development ('GFMD') was established for the purpose of strengthening multilateral coopera-tion. Contrary to the initial proposal, the GFMD is a state-driven process outside the United Nations. Moreover, it is not intended to be a decision-making process. Despite the lack of consensus in favour of a norm-setting negotiation, inter-governmental consultations are held on a regular basis: the GFMD is convened every year, which is unusual for this kind of worldwide consultation (see Chapter 13).

In parallel to the GFMD, many other multilateral initiatives have been under-taken during the past decade. The most notable is the *Multilateral Framework on Labour Migration* adopted by the ILO in 2005.[83] As is apparent from its subtitle, this framework spells out 'non-binding principles and guidelines for a rights-based approach to labour migration'. It accordingly identifies a compre-hensive set of guiding principles for facilitating the management of labour

---

80 United Nations Population Information Network, 'Programme of Action' (International Conference on Population and Development, 1994) ch. X, [10.1].

81 Ibid. [10.2].

82 United Nations General Assembly, 'High-Level Dialogue on International Migration and Development' (United Nations, 14–15 September 2006).

83 International Labour Organization, 'Multilateral Framework on Labour Migration: Non-Binding Principles and Guidelines for a Rights-Based Approach to Labour Migration' (ILO, 2006).

migration with due respect for migrants' rights. The effervescence surrounding migration within intergovernmental circles also prompted the International Organization for Migration to launch the International Dialogue on Migration in 2001 and to promote the International Agenda for Migration Management, which was adopted in 2004 as a result of a state-owned consultative process.[84] Among many other (somewhat repetitive) initiatives, this new area of dialogue has been accompanied by further informal regional consultative processes.

As a result of this exceptional mobilisation, migration has become one of the highest priorities on the international agenda. The credibility test for the managing migration approach hinges on its ability to legalise labour migration.[85] If States fail to legalise labour migration properly, the managing migration rhetoric will be remembered as another missed opportunity in the long and turbulent history of North–South relations.

3.5. CONCLUSION

Like many human activities, leaving one country for another is not outside the realm of international law. This overview of the main sources of international law makes clear that international migration is regulated by a fairly detailed but heteroclite set of norms. As observed by Aleinikoff, 'there is both more and less international law than might be supposed'.[86] There is more international law than decision makers presume, but there is less international law than activists may desire.

From a dispassionate perspective, the increasing role of international law in a field traditionally considered as falling within the domestic jurisdiction of States is not surprising. Migration is, in essence, a question of international law. It relies on a triangular relationship between a migrant, a State of origin and a State of destination. In both normative and political terms, this relationship has nonetheless remained a partial and unbalanced one. Typically, it has been viewed through the myopic lens of States of destination to the detriment of migrants and their States of origin.

This chapter reveals a more subtle picture. The normative framework governing migration is firmly anchored in treaty law, customary law, general principles of law

---

84 International Organization for Migration, *International Dialogue on Migration* (IOM, 2011) www.iom.int/jahia/Jahia/international-dialogue-migration; Berne Initiative, 'International Agenda for Migration Management' (International Organization for Migration, Swiss Federal Office for Migration, 2005).

85 Vincent Chetail, 'Paradigm and Paradox of the Migration–Development Nexus: The New Border for North–South Dialogue' (2008) 52 *German Yearbook of International Law* 183.

86 Alexander Aleinikoff, 'International Legal Norms and Migration: A Report' in Alexander Aleinikoff and Vincent Chetail (eds.), *Migration and International Legal Norms* (TMC Asser Press, 2003) 1, 2.

and *jus cogens*. Its content is nevertheless dispersed among a wide variety of areas, such as human rights, asylum, nationality, human trafficking, labour, extradition, and consular and diplomatic protection, to mention some of the most emblematic ones. International migration law comprises an amalgam of these norms, but it is still far from constituting a clear-cut regime. International migration law is the result of a compartmentalised construction that undermines its understanding and coherent application. From that perspective, it resembles 'a giant unassembled juridical jigsaw puzzle', for which 'the number of pieces is uncertain and the grand design is still emerging'.[87]

The fragmentation of the legal regime governing migration is exacerbated by the prominent role of territorial sovereignty and the absence of a world migration organisation. However, the past decade has witnessed a growing awareness of the need for inter-State cooperation. The key challenge of this new area of dialogue is its ability to promote a balanced and comprehensive approach with due regard to the interests of all stakeholders. States are more aware than ever that migration is a matter of common interest that cannot be managed on a unilateral basis. But they still have to learn to collaborate on an issue that has been regarded traditionally as a core component of their sovereignty.

KEY REFERENCES

Aleinikoff, Alexander and Chetail, Vincent (eds.), *Migration and International Legal Norms* (TMC Asser Press, 2003)

Boeles, Pieter and Den Heijer, Maarten, *European Migration Law* (Intersentia, 2009)

Bogusz, Barbara, Cholewinski, Ryszard, Cygan, Adam and Szyszczak, Erika (eds.), *Irregular Migration and Human Rights: Theoretical, European and International Perspectives* (Martinus Nijhoff, 2004)

Chetail, Vincent, *Code de Droit International des Migrations* (Bruylant, 2008)

Chetail, Vincent (ed.), *Research Handbook on Migration and International Law* (Edward Elgar, 2012)

Chetail, Vincent (ed.), *Mondialisation, migration et droits de l'homme: le droit international en question* (Bruylant, 2007)

Cholewinski, Ryszard, *Migrant Workers in International Human Rights Law: Their Protection in Countries of Employment* (Clarendon Press, 1997)

Cholewinski, Ryszard, Perruchoud, Richard and Macdonald, Euan (eds.), *International Migration Law: Developing Paradigms and Key Challenges* (TMC Asser Press, 2007)

Goodwin-Gill, Guy and McAdam, Jane, *The Refugee in International Law* (Oxford University Press, 3rd edn, 2007)

Hathaway, James, *The Rights of Refugees under International Law* (Cambridge University Press, 2005)

Lillich, Richard, *The Human Rights of Aliens in Contemporary International Law* (Manchester University Press, 1984)

Perruchoud, Richard and Tömölová, Katarina (eds.), *Compendium of International Migration Law Instruments* (TMC Asser Press, 2007)

Weissbrodt, David, *The Human Rights of Non-Citizens* (Oxford University Press, 2008)

87 Richard Lillich, *The Human Rights of Aliens in Contemporary International Law* (Manchester University Press, 1984) 122.

KEY RESOURCES

European Journal of Migration and Law: www.brill.nl/
european-journal-migration-and-law

Georgetown Immigration Law Journal: www.law.
georgetown.edu/journals/gilj

International Court of Justice: www.icj-cij.org

International Journal of Refugee Law: http://ijrl.
oxfordjournals.org

International Labour Organization, Database on
International Labour Standards: www.ilo.org/ilolex/

International Law Commission: www.un.org/law/ilc

International Organization for Migration, Migration Law
database: www.imldb.iom.int

Refugee Survey Quarterly: http://rsq.oxfordjournals.org

United Nations High Commissioner for Refugees, Refworld:
www.refworld.org

United Nations Treaty Collection: http://treaties.un.org

4 Nationality and statelessness

IVAN SHEARER AND BRIAN OPESKIN

4.1. PRINCIPLES OF NATIONALITY

4.1.1. The concept of nationality

Nationality is essentially an institution of domestic law, but it has consequences in international law. Under domestic law, a national owes a duty of allegiance to the State, and may be obliged to pay taxes and render military service to that State. A national has the right of permanent residence and the right to participate in public life and, in most States, enjoys social benefits available only to nationals. Under the laws of some States, criminal jurisdiction may be exercised over a national even in respect of crimes committed abroad.

Nationality is a key concept in international migration law. The ability of individuals to change their residence to another State, or even to travel abroad temporarily for business or pleasure, is constrained by questions of nationality. Nationality is also important in international law generally. Until the emergence of human rights law in the era of the United Nations, how a State treated its own nationals was regarded as a matter of exclusive domestic jurisdiction and not subject to international law. However, States did have international obligations towards foreign nationals in their territory, and a foreign State could defend the interests of its nationals if they were breached by the host State. Thus, the rights of individuals were mediated through the bond of nationality. The foreign State could act on behalf of its nationals by exercising the right of 'diplomatic protection', since an injury to a national was regarded as an injury also to the State of which he or she is a national.[1]

Historical background

The modern concept of nationality developed only after the emergence of an international community of separate sovereign States following the Peace of

---

1 *Panevezys-Saldutiskis Railway Case (Estonia v. Lithuania)* [1939] PCIJ (ser A/B) No 76.

Westphalia in 1648. Before that time, people were the subjects of local rulers or city entities, which in turn were often subject to superior authorities such as the Pope, the Holy Roman Emperor or the Emperor of China. During the periods of the Roman Republic and the Roman Empire, Roman citizenship was a proud boast (*civis romanus sum* – 'I am a Roman citizen') and brought with it both privileges and responsibilities, while the peoples of the outlying parts of the Empire were merely subjects not enjoying the full rights of Roman citizens. Beyond the borders of the Empire lived the barbarians whose forms of community were not considered to be of any significance. Within the borders of the Empire, the place of origin of a non-Roman citizen was merely a matter of geographical curiosity rather than having legal consequences.[2] Apart from these considerations, concepts of citizenship or nationality hardly arose in the periods before travel became a real possibility for larger numbers of people. Foreigners, other than merchants on established trade routes, were often treated with suspicion and even hostility.

Allegiance and protection

The modern concept of nationality embodies the reciprocal notions of allegiance and protection. The idea of allegiance has old roots: it was a duty owed by individuals to their local ruler, such as a king, a prince or a lord. Duties of allegiance were strengthened during the Middle Ages by the feudal system in Europe and elsewhere. Under English law, personal status and land tenure depended upon one's relationship to the local lord, to whom duties of military service and the payment of produce were owed. Notions of allegiance persist in legal systems today, such as in the oaths of allegiance that many States require as a precondition to acquiring nationality by naturalisation; and in the crime of treason, which can be committed only by nationals who owe a duty of allegiance to the State.

In continental Europe, where laws descended from Roman law, duties of allegiance were balanced by the lords' duty to protect their subjects. This notion of protection is echoed in contemporary international law and practice, where States may exercise a right of protection of their nationals where they have suffered injury by another State – such as by expropriation of property without adequate compensation, breach of a concession or other agreement, denial of justice by the courts or police brutality. The topic has received extensive consideration by international courts and, more recently, by the United Nations International Law Commission ('ILC'),[3] which formulated *Draft Articles on Diplomatic Protection* in 2006.[4]

---

2 An exception was that, under Roman law, the law to be applied among non-Roman citizens in their civil affairs, and between citizens and non-citizens, was *jus gentium* – 'the law of peoples'.

3 The International Law Commission was established by the United Nations in 1947 to work for the 'progressive development of international law and its codification'. Sometimes its draft articles are submitted to international conferences for adoption as Conventions. In other cases, the draft articles are not submitted for adoption but constitute valuable evidence of State practice, and are influential in guiding the future practice of States and the jurisprudence of international courts and tribunals.

4 International Law Commission, *Draft Articles on Diplomatic Protection* (UN GAOR, 61st sess, Supp No 10, UN Doc A/61/10, 2006).

Diplomatic protection may begin by way of representations through diplomatic channels, proceed to the stage of formal protest and end with the invocation of available remedies before international judicial or arbitral tribunals. Diplomatic protection gives access to the highest levels of government in the host State, but a State may also act on behalf of its nationals abroad by offering a lower level of consular assistance, such as providing replacement travel documents, registering nationals born abroad and providing help and advice during crises. International law may regulate the circumstances in which a State may espouse a claim on behalf of a national where there is no more than a tenuous link between that individual and the State, as illustrated by the *Nottebohm Case* (see Case Study 4.1).[5]

Most States regard the extension of diplomatic protection to its nationals as something lying within the State's discretion, having regard to all the circumstances and the nature of relations between themselves and the offending State. Although the State has the right to refuse to espouse the claim of one of its nationals, it should give serious consideration to such a request.[6] The *Draft Articles on Diplomatic Protection* extend a State's right of diplomatic protection to persons whom it recognises to be refugees if they are lawfully and habitually resident in the State's territory at the time of the injury – but the right cannot be asserted against the State of the refugees' nationality.

Citizenship contrasted

The terms 'citizen', 'national' and 'subject' are often used interchangeably today. Yet there was a time when differences between the terms had greater significance. The term 'subject' came to be disfavoured and was replaced by the term 'citizen' when former monarchies became republics, such as the United States in 1776 (previously a collection of colonies under the British Crown) and France in 1789. When European colonial empires were extended to Africa, Asia and other places, it became necessary to distinguish between different categories of nationals. 'Nationals', 'subjects' and 'protected persons' were terms used to describe the inhabitants of the colonial territories, while the term 'citizen' was often reserved for those inhabitants of the metropolitan territory of the colonial power. Commonly, the latter alone had the right to reside in the metropolitan territory or exercise political rights, such as voting.

The distinction became of increasing importance with the phenomenon of large numbers of people from poorer States fleeing persecution, or seeking a better life, in more affluent States, especially the metropolitan territory of colonial powers. Racial considerations played an important role in this distinction, as well as the ability of often relatively small European States possessing large colonial territories to absorb any sizeable influx.[7] The United Kingdom has faced particular difficulties in this

---

5 *Nottebohm Case (Liechtenstein* v. *Guatemala) (Second Phase)* [1955] ICJ Rep 4.

6 See, e.g., *Van Zyl* v. *Government of the Republic of South Africa* [2007] SCA 109 (RSA) 109.

7 See the example of British Protected Persons expelled from Uganda in 1972 by President Idi Amin, considered by the English Court of Appeal in *R* v. *Secretary of State for the Home Department; Ex parte Thakrar* [1974] QB 684.

regard. *Protocol 4 to the European Convention for the Protection of Human Rights and Fundamental Freedoms* (1963) provides that 'No one shall be deprived of the right to enter the territory of the State of which he is a national' (art. 3(2)).[8] Because of the complexities of British nationality legislation, whereby some categories of overseas British nationals were excluded from the right of abode in the United Kingdom, the United Kingdom has been obliged to refrain from ratifying that Protocol.[9]

Today, the term 'national' is still commonly used in discussions of public international law, while the term 'citizen' is more frequently used in constitutions and national legislation. However, there is no fixed rule and the meaning of the terms will depend on the context in which they are used. The terms may also coexist – for example, a person may be both a national of France and a citizen of the European Union, entitling him or her to vote in European elections.[10]

Sources of law on nationality

Nationality is, in principle, regulated by domestic law.[11] As stated in art. 1 of the *Convention on Certain Questions relating to the Conflict of Nationality Law* (1930): 'It is for each State to determine under its own law who are its nationals. This law shall be recognised by other States in so far as it is consistent with international conventions, international custom, and the principles of law generally recognised with regard to nationality.'[12] In practice, States were relatively slow to establish conditions of nationality by legislation. France was the first, in 1791; others followed in the nineteenth century, such as Great Britain in 1844.

In more recent times, international law has restricted the freedom of States to regulate questions of nationality. Some international conventions prescribe criteria by which a conferring State must be guided, especially for the avoidance of statelessness (discussed below). Mainly, however, international law deals only with the *consequences* of nationality as conferred by domestic law by nullifying or limiting the effects of an attribution of nationality contrary to international conventions, international custom or general principles of law. An example is the injunction against extending nationality to persons who are totally unconnected to the territory of the national State against their will.[13] Regional instruments have been at the forefront of new developments in the international regulation of nationality, and these are discussed in Chapter 14.

---

8   *Protocol 4 to the European Convention for the Protection of Human Rights and Fundamental Freedoms*, opened for signature 16 September 1963, ETS 46 (entered into force 2 May 1968).

9   Ian Hendry and Susan Dickson, *British Overseas Territories Law* (Hart, 2011) 151–74, 197–209.

10 The *Maastricht Treaty* (art. 20(1)) created European citizenship in 1992, but expressly provided that it 'shall be additional to and not replace national citizenship': *Treaty on European Union*, opened for signature 7 February 1992, 1757 UNTS 3 (entered into force 1 November 1993).

11 *Nationality Decrees Issued in Tunis and Morocco* (*Advisory Opinion*) [1923] PCIJ (ser B) No 4.

12 *Convention on Certain Questions relating to the Conflict of Nationality Law*, opened for signature 13 April 1930, 179 LNTS 89 (entered into force 1 July 1937).

13 Harvard Law School, *Draft Convention on Nationality* (1929) 23 AJIL, Special Supplement, art. 15.

CASE STUDY 4.1 The *Nottebohm Case*

Nottebohm Case (Liechtenstein v. Guatemala) (Second Phase) [1955] ICJ Rep 4

In this case the International Court of Justice ('ICJ') discussed the nature of nationality and saw it as based on 'the social fact of attachment'.

Mr Friedrich Nottebohm was a German national who emigrated from Germany to Guatemala, in Central America, in 1905. He established prosperous business interests there and, although making some visits to Germany, made Guatemala his home. On the approach of the Second World War he feared that he might be disadvantaged due to his German nationality. With the help of his brother, who lived in Liechtenstein, he succeeded in obtaining the nationality of that country in 1939 through the payment of substantial sums of money and dispensation from the normal residence requirements. By this act of naturalisation he lost his German nationality by operation of German law. He returned to Guatemala on the basis of a residence visa for Guatemala stamped in his Liechtenstein passport and resumed his life there. Following the entry of the United States into the war against Germany in December 1941, Guatemala also declared war against Germany. Despite his protestation of neutral (Liechtenstein) nationality, Mr Nottebohm was declared an enemy alien, arrested and deported to the United States, where he was interned. After the war he was denied re-entry to Guatemala. All his property was confiscated in accordance with a Guatemalan decree applicable to enemy aliens.

In proceedings before the ICJ, Liechtenstein sought to assert its right of diplomatic protection in respect of its national, Mr Nottebohm. However, the Court rejected Liechtenstein's right to espouse the claim of Mr Nottebohm. It did not deny the right of States to determine who are their nationals, but on the basis of the facts the Court decided that Mr Nottebohm lacked a 'genuine connection' with Liechtenstein sufficient to justify Liechtenstein's espousal of his claim against Guatemala. In other words, the Court was not declaring that Liechtenstein's conferral of nationality on Mr Nottebohm was contrary to international law; rather, that its right of diplomatic protection in respect of this national could not be invoked against Guatemala. Although not expressly stated in the judgment, the crucial factor appears to have been that the case was brought against the State with which Mr Nottebohm was most closely connected, albeit not a national.

The notions of 'real and effective nationality' and 'genuine link', as expressed by the Court, have not escaped criticism by commentators. Although these notions have been applied in treaties in determining the nationality of ships,[14] the reference to a 'genuine link' in the maritime context is not intended to disentitle recognition of a 'flag of convenience' by other States, but to ensure that the flag State implements effectively its duties with respect to vessels under its control.[15] A further move away from the persuasive force of the decision in the *Nottebohm Case* is marked by the ILC's *Draft Articles on Diplomatic Protection* (2006),

---

14 *Convention on the High Seas*, opened for signature 29 April 1958, 450 UNTS 11 (entered into force 30 September 1962) art. 5(1); *United Nations Convention on the Law of the Sea*, opened for signature 10 December 1982, 1833 UNTS 3 (entered into force 14 November 1994) art. 91.

15 *The M/V Saiga (No 2) Case* (1999) 120 ILR 143 (International Tribunal for the Law of the Sea).

which omit any qualification by way of a 'genuine link' of the right of a State to exercise diplomatic protection of a person who has acquired that nationality 'in accordance with the law of that State, by birth, descent, naturalisation, succession of States, or in any other manner not inconsistent with international law'.

Thus the *Nottebohm Case*, although well known to international lawyers, is to be seen now as having limited value as an authority. However, if understood in light of the assertion of the Court that it was considering only the particular facts of the case, then the Court may have upheld the right of Liechtenstein to protect Mr Nottebohm as against other States, but not as against the State with which he was most closely connected and, in a sense, of which he was a *de facto* national. That was the view of the Italian–United States Conciliation Commission in the *Flegenheimer Case*.[16]

16 *Flegenheimer Case*, Decision No 182, 14 Reports of International Arbitral Awards 327 (20 September 1958).

4.1.2. Acquisition of nationality

Article 15 of the *Universal Declaration of Human* Rights (1948) states that 'Everyone has the right to a nationality.'[17] Nationality can be acquired either by birth or by later naturalisation.

Nationality by birth

There are two alternative criteria applied by States in attributing their nationality to persons upon birth. One is to apply *jus soli* ('law of the soil'), so that any child, regardless of the status of the parents, acquires the nationality of the State in whose territory it is born. This has traditionally been the approach of countries of the English common law inheritance. It has been extended by some of those States to births occurring on board ships flying the flag of that State or on aircraft registered in that State, and hence regarded as a notional extension of the territory.

A well-known example of *jus soli* is the Fourteenth Amendment to the *United States Constitution*, which has provided, since 1868, that all persons born in the United States are 'citizens of the United States'. There has been ongoing debate about whether 'birthright citizenship' should be granted to the children of undocumented migrants,[18] and particular controversy about the commodification of nationality through 'birth tourism' – a practice whereby agents facilitate the travel of pregnant women from foreign States to the United States for the purpose of giving birth on United States soil.

The other criterion is *jus sanguinis* ('law of the blood'), which determines nationality of a child by descent from that of its parents. This was the general approach of

17 *Universal Declaration of Human Rights*, GA Res 217A (III), UN Doc A/810 (10 December 1948).
18 Peter Schuck and Rogers Smith, *Citizenship Without Consent: Illegal Aliens in the American Polity* (Yale University Press, 1985); Peter Spiro, *Beyond Citizenship: American Identity after Globalization* (Oxford University Press, 2008) 9–32.

countries of Roman (civil) law inheritance. However, there are now considerable variations in the law and practice of States of both legal traditions. For example, in a study of the nationality laws of twenty-five (mostly developed) States in 2001, over half recognised nationality on the basis of both *jus soli* and *jus sanguinis*.[19]

Consistent with the principle that nationality is regulated by domestic law, international law does not prescribe one approach or the other, but nor is it entirely silent. For example, art. 1 of the *Convention on the Reduction of Statelessness* (1961) obliges States parties to apply the principle of *jus soli* where the person would otherwise become stateless.[20] Conversely, a well-established exception in customary international law is that a child born to parents who are foreign diplomats does not automatically acquire the nationality of a host State that applies *jus soli*.[21]

Legislation in a number of countries has employed both approaches or made exceptions, depending upon the circumstances. In recent years, faced with the possibility of large inflows of refugees, States hitherto applying *jus soli* have limited attribution of nationality by birth to children born in the territory to parents who are nationals or permanent residents. For example, a child of asylum seekers who arrive in a common law country before the birth will not necessarily obtain the nationality of the State in which asylum is sought.[22]

In States applying *jus sanguinis*, the issue arises whether descent depends on the nationality of the mother or the father. State practice has tended to prefer the nationality of the father, but where the father is unknown or the birth occurs outside marriage, the legislation of some States then confers nationality by descent from the mother. Modern legislation tends to avoid discrimination on gender grounds; hence it may be possible in some countries for a child to have three nationalities at birth: that of the place of birth (*jus soli*), that of the mother (*jus sanguinis*) and that of the father (*jus sanguinis*). Gender equality has been promoted by the *Convention on the Elimination of All Forms of Discrimination against Women* (1979) ('CEDAW'), which in art. 9 requires States parties to grant women equal rights with men with respect to the nationality of their children.[23] However, principles of equality are not always upheld in national courts.[24]

---

19 Patrick Weil, 'Access to Citizenship: A Comparison of Twenty-Five Nationality Laws' in Alexander Aleinikoff and Douglas Klusmeyer (eds.), *Citizenship Today: Global Perspectives and Practices* (Carnegie Endowment for International Peace, 2001) 17, 20.

20 *Convention on the Reduction of Statelessness*, opened for signature 30 August 1961, 989 UNTS 175 (entered into force 13 December 1975).

21 Confirmed by the *Convention on Certain Questions relating to the Conflict of Nationality Law*, opened for signature 13 April 1930, 179 LNTS 89 (entered into force 1 July 1937) art. 12; *Optional Protocol concerning the Acquisition of Nationality to the Vienna Convention on Diplomatic Relations*, opened for signature 18 April 1961, 500 UNTS 223 (entered into force 24 April 1964) art. II; and *Optional Protocol concerning Acquisition of Nationality to the Vienna Convention on Consular Relations*, opened for signature 24 April 1963, 596 UNTS 469 (entered into force 19 March 1967) art. II.

22 For example, a child born in Australia to non-citizen parents can obtain citizenship only after ten years of residence: *Australian Citizenship Act 2007* (Cth) s 12. In the United States, by contrast, *jus soli* gives such a child immediate citizenship by birth: *United States Constitution* amend XIV.

23 *Convention on the Elimination of All Forms of Discrimination against Women*, opened for signature 18 December 1979, 1249 UNTS 13 (entered into force 3 September 1981).

24 For example, in 2011 the United States Supreme Court upheld a citizenship law that made it more difficult for fathers to transmit their US citizenship to their children born abroad and out of wedlock than for mothers to do so: *Flores-Villar* v. *United States* 131 S. Ct. 2312 (2011).

Nationality by naturalisation

Naturalisation is a voluntary act by which a person already possessing a nationality, or a person with no nationality, seeks and is granted the nationality of another State. Legislation frequently requires, as preconditions for the grant of nationality, a prolonged residence in the State, good character, knowledge of the language and customs, and ability to be self-supporting. International law does not prescribe particular conditions for naturalisation, but it sometimes imposes limitations. For example, in relation to residence, the *European Convention on Nationality* (1997) provides that a State shall not require a period of residence of more than ten years as a precondition for applying for naturalisation.[25] In relation to competence in the national language, the *Council of Europe Convention on the Avoidance of Statelessness in relation to State Succession* (2006) obliges parties, in the case of State succession, not to discriminate in granting naturalisation on the basis of language.[26] Considerations of national security may, however, be a valid ground for denying an application for naturalisation.[27]

The grant of nationality by naturalisation does not require the consent of the State of original nationality, nor is that State obliged to recognise the change. Cases have occurred, for example, where naturalised persons or their descendants have visited the State of original nationality and have found themselves subject to military call-up or other public duties. It is also a general principle that individuals may not be forced to change their nationality against their will. For example, under the law of armed conflict, it is unlawful for an occupying power to decree that all persons in the occupied territory shall henceforth be nationals of the occupying power.[28]

State practice in the past discouraged the acquisition of more than one nationality. As a consequence, legislation often provided that the State's nationality was automatically lost upon voluntary acquisition of another nationality. Similarly, legislation often provided that the grant of nationality by naturalisation required the renunciation of the former nationality by way of a formal declaration. Recent practice, however, has tended to allow a naturalised person to opt to retain the former nationality, thus becoming a dual national (see below).

Particular issues arise in respect of marriage and adoption. Under international conventions, naturalisation of the husband during marriage does not automatically involve a change of nationality of the wife, except with her

---

25 *European Convention on Nationality*, opened for signature 6 November 1997, ETS No 166 (entered into force 1 March 2000) art. 6(3).

26 *Council of Europe Convention on the Avoidance of Statelessness in relation to State Succession*, opened for signature 19 May 2006, CETS No 200 (entered into force 1 May 2009) arts. 4–5.

27 *Borzov* v. *Estonia*, Human Rights Committee, UN Doc CCPR/C/81/D/1136/2002 (25 August 2004).

28 *Hague Convention (IV) respecting the Laws and Customs of War on Land and its Annex: Regulations concerning the Laws and Customs of War on Land*, opened for signature 18 October 1907 (entered into force 26 January 1910) arts. 42–56.

consent.[29] Some States impose stringent requirements on the naturalisation of persons who marry nationals of that State. This is to avoid 'marriages of convenience', or 'sham marriages', in which there is no genuine marital relationship between the parties because the marriage is used merely as a vehicle for acquiring nationality. Many States also confer nationality on an adopted child of a national, although practices vary depending on whether the adoption was completed overseas or locally. The grant of nationality is one way of satisfying the requirement in art. 5 of the *Convention on Protection of Children and Cooperation in respect of Intercountry Adoption* (1993) that a child adopted under the Convention 'be authorised to enter and reside permanently' in the receiving State.[30]

4.1.3.   Loss of nationality

Article 15 of the *Universal Declaration of Human Rights* (1948) states that 'No one shall be arbitrarily deprived of his nationality nor denied the right to change his nationality.' In practice, nationality can be lost:

- by a voluntary act of the national;
- by an act of the State of nationality; or, more rarely
- by extinction of the State, or acquisition of part of the State by another State.

The most important example of the first class is voluntary renunciation of nationality, which is permitted under the law of many States as a corollary of the right to change one's nationality. The third class is considered below under 'State succession'.

The second class encompasses a wide variety of circumstances in which a State may revoke a person's nationality automatically by operation of law or in the exercise of executive discretion. Loss of nationality may occur automatically as a result of the actions of a national in obtaining another nationality, or serving in the armed forces or civil service of another State. Nationality might be lost under the laws of some States by a woman who marries a national of a foreign State, the laws of which provide for the automatic attribution of the husband's nationality to the wife. Such automatic attribution, however, is contrary to art. 9 of CEDAW. Nationality may also be revoked in the case of naturalised persons who have obtained naturalisation by fraud, or abused their status by committing serious criminal offences or giving aid to an enemy power in time of armed conflict.

Nationals by birth are not subject to denationalisation under modern international law, thus making nationality a more robust legal status when acquired by birth than by naturalisation. One example from the past – Nazi Germany's denationalisation of

---

29 *Convention on Certain Questions relating to the Conflict of Nationality Law*, opened for signature 13 April 1930, 179 LNTS 89 (entered into force 1 July 1937) art. 10; *Convention on the Nationality of Married Women*, opened for signature 29 January 1957, 309 UNTS 65 (entered into force 11 August 1958) art. 1; *European Convention on Nationality*, opened for signature 6 November 1997, ETS No 166 (entered into force 1 March 2000) art. 4(d).

30 *Convention on Protection of Children and Cooperation in respect of Intercountry Adoption*, opened for signature 29 May 1993, 1870 UNTS 167 (entered into force 1 May 1995). There were eighty-eight States parties in mid-2012.

German Jews in 1941[31] – would now be contrary to international law, since denationalisations based on ethnic, racial or religious discrimination are forbidden by art. 5 of the *International Convention on the Elimination of All Forms of Racial Discrimination* (1965) and by art. 26 of the *International Covenant on Civil and Political Rights* (1966) ('ICCPR').[32] The latter provision also prohibits discrimination on the ground of 'political or other opinion' – a proscription that would have been breached by the past practice of the Soviet Union and some other Eastern European States of denationalising political dissidents or nationals who had sought asylum abroad.

International law qualifies the competence of a State to revoke an individual's nationality by the requirement that the deprivation must not be arbitrary. Arbitrariness may take many forms.[33] A discretionary executive action not sanctioned by law is likely to be arbitrary, but so too are certain actions that are formally authorised by law. Deprivations of nationality that are discriminatory (e.g., on grounds of race, colour, sex, or religion) constitute a violation of human rights and are *prima facie* arbitrary. So too are deprivations of nationality that do not serve a legitimate State purpose, or lack proportionality because they do not adopt the least intrusive means of achieving the desired goal. Deprivations of nationality may be arbitrary if they are procedurally unfair (e.g., denying the national an opportunity to oppose the proposed action), or if the action is substantively unreasonable in the circumstances. Loss of nationality resulting in statelessness is also generally prohibited: this is expressly provided for in the *Convention on the Reduction of Statelessness* (1961) subject only to limited exceptions (art. 8), and arguably it is also an instance of unreasonableness that may make the deprivation arbitrary.

4.2. PRINCIPLES OF STATELESSNESS

4.2.1. The concept of statelessness

A person is stateless if he or she is not considered to be a national by any State. This definition of statelessness is known as *de jure* statelessness because it arises from the absence of the formal bond of nationality, where nationality is determined according to the laws of each State. While clearly undesirable, *de jure* statelessness is not inconsistent with customary international law, which recognises the general competence of States to confer or withdraw their nationality.[34] The operation of a

---

31 The first step was taken in 1935 when a distinction was drawn between 'citizens' and 'nationals' of the German Reich. The former were persons of 'German or kindred blood' and alone possessed full political rights. Jews thus remained nationals until even this was taken away in 1941.

32 *International Convention on the Elimination of All Forms of Racial Discrimination*, opened for signature 21 December 1965, 660 UNTS 195 (entered into force 4 January 1969); *International Covenant on Civil and Political Rights*, opened for signature 16 December 1966, 999 UNTS 171 (entered into force 23 March 1976).

33 Human Rights Council, 'Human Rights and Arbitrary Deprivation of Nationality' (UN Doc A/HRC/13/34, United Nations, 2009) 5–8.

34 Paul Weis, *Nationality and Statelessness in International Law* (Sijthoff and Noordhoff, 2nd edn, 1979) 162.

State's laws may thus leave a person without any nationality, subject only to important treaty obligations that modify this situation for States parties.

Statelessness, like nationality, is a key concept in international migration law because the absence of nationality can have a significant impact on an individual's ability to cross international borders and on the treatment of such persons if they do so. The international mobility of stateless persons is adversely affected by the difficulties they face in obtaining identity and travel documents, and by the reluctance of States to admit such persons into their territory when no other State is required to accept their return in the event that the stateless person wishes to leave or is required to do so.

The concept of *de jure* statelessness has been criticised as being too narrow. Some individuals technically possess a nationality but are unable to enjoy its benefits because they cannot prove their nationality or because the State of their nationality is not able or willing to offer them protection. This lack of effective nationality has been described as a situation of *de facto* statelessness. An example of *de facto* statelessness is the situation of women and children who have been subjected to human trafficking and are held in a foreign State in conditions akin to slavery, with no access to their passports and no practical possibility of seeking the protection of their national State.

The concept of *de facto* statelessness provides a useful tool for considering the ways in which nationality, or its absence, affects the legal rights of individuals. It may also have operational significance in so far as it affects which international agency has responsibility for affording protection. Yet, if viewed as a legal concept, *de facto* statelessness is a broad and imprecise notion that generates discord with established legal regimes for protecting refugees and human rights more generally. For this reason, international instruments that address issues of statelessness are generally confined to *de jure* statelessness. Thus, the *Convention relating to the Status of Stateless Persons* (1954) defines a stateless person as 'a person who is not considered as a national by any State under the operation of its law'.[35]

The number of stateless persons in the world today is very large. At the end of 2010, the United Nations High Commissioner for Refugees ('UNHCR') had *identified* 3.46 million stateless persons in sixty-five countries, and *estimated* the global population of stateless persons to be around 12 million.[36] These figures may be compared with the 9.95 million refugees whose plight is generally much better known. Information on the magnitude of stateless populations is incomplete, however, because the majority of States do not register stateless persons and cannot provide reliable data. Of those States for which reliable data are available, Nepal has the largest stateless population (800,000), followed by Myanmar

---

35 *Convention relating to the Status of Stateless Persons*, opened for signature 28 September 1954, 360 UNTS 117 (entered into force 6 June 1960) art. 1.

36 United Nations High Commissioner for Refugees, '60 Years and Still Counting: Global Trends 2010' (UNHCR, 2011). In 2009, 6.6 million persons were identified as stateless. The reduction to 3.46 million in 2010 reflects changes in the method of counting stateless persons rather than an actual reduction in statelessness.

(797,000) and Thailand (543,000), while stateless populations of more than 100,000 are also found in Latvia, Syria, Iraq and Estonia.[37]

Difficulties of estimation are compounded by the nexus between statelessness and status as a refugee or internally displaced person. Statelessness, and the lack of State protection that this implies, may be a primary reason why individuals decide to flee their place of origin, but such persons cannot strictly become refugees until they are outside the State of their habitual residence (see Chapter 7).[38] Many stateless persons do not cross international borders and are unable to access the benefits of the international regime of refugee protection.

UNHCR is the principal United Nations agency that addresses the challenges of statelessness. Since its inception, UNHCR has had responsibility for stateless refugees, but this mandate was extended beyond refugees by the United Nations General Assembly in 1974 – when the *Convention on the Reduction of Statelessness* (1961) came into force – and extended again in 1994 and 1995.[39] The mandate is universal in that it is not restricted to States parties to the relevant international instruments. There is a degree of similarity, and sometimes overlap, between the agency's functions with respect to stateless persons and refugees, both of whom lack national protection. UNHCR seeks to collect reliable data on stateless persons for the purpose of discharging its functions; actively promotes wider ratification of the relevant treaties; and has acknowledged the need to 'redouble its efforts' to address statelessness in coordination with other agencies, organisations and civil society.[40]

4.2.2. Paths to statelessness

De jure statelessness may arise either at birth, because a child does not acquire an original nationality according to the law of any State, or it may arise subsequently if a person loses his or her nationality without acquiring another nationality. *De facto* statelessness usually arises in situations of State repression and is addressed below in relation to the human rights of stateless persons.

Statelessness at birth results from the circumstance that nationality is determined by the law of each State, and States adopt different bases for granting their nationality. If all States adopted the *jus soli* principle, statelessness at birth would not arise because all children are born in the territory of one State or another (once the principle is extended to ships and aircraft). However, application of the *jus sanguinis* principle can lead to statelessness at birth in various ways, which are illustrated by the following examples.

The first is where a child is born in a State that applies the *jus sanguinis* principle to parents who are themselves stateless. With no nationality to receive from its parents

---

37 Ibid. Annex Table 7.

38 *Convention relating to the Status of Refugees*, opened for signature 28 July 1951, 189 UNTS 150 (entered into force 22 April 1954) art. 1A.

39 GA Res 3274 (XXIX) (10 December 1974); GA Res 49/169 (23 December 1994); GA Res 50/152 (21 December 1995).

40 United Nations High Commissioner for Refugees, 'UNHCR Action to Address Statelessness: A Strategy Note' (2010) 22(2) *International Journal of Refugee Law* 297.

by descent, the child inherits the parents' statelessness, thus perpetuating social and economic disadvantage from one generation to another. This is the experience of many Bidun children born in Kuwait.[41] A second example is where a child is born in State A (which applies the *jus sanguinis* principle based only on paternal descent) to a mother who is a national of State A and a father who is stateless. The child is unable to acquire the mother's nationality because of State A's gendered nationality laws, while the father has no nationality to confer. A third example is where a child is born in State A (which applies the *jus sanguinis* principle based only on paternal descent) to a mother who is a national of State A and a father who is a national of State B (which applies the *jus soli* principle). The mother is unable to confer her nationality on her child because of State A's gendered nationality laws, while the father's nationality is unavailable because it is not conferred by descent and the child is not born in State B. As discussed below, a number of human rights treaties address the problem of statelessness at birth by imposing obligations on States to grant nationality to children who would otherwise be stateless.

Statelessness can also arise subsequent to birth if a person loses his or her nationality without acquiring another nationality. There are many ways this can occur, reflecting the variety of circumstances in which nationality may be lost through renunciation, revocation or State succession, as discussed above. For example, a person may become stateless, even if temporarily, by renouncing an existing nationality in anticipation of acquiring a new one. A person may become stateless if a State revokes its nationality upon discovering that the person obtained it by misstatement or fraud. The United States has done this in respect of naturalised immigrants who were later found to have concealed their Nazi involvement during the Second World War. Large groups of people may become stateless when States fragment or recombine. The complex effects of State succession on nationality are illustrated by the Bihari people of Bangladesh, many of whom have remained stateless since Bangladesh won its war of independence from Pakistan in 1971 (see Case Study 4.2).

Special problems of statelessness arise where a woman's nationality is dependent on that of her husband. Upon marriage, she may lose her own nationality under the laws of her national State, but might not acquire her husband's nationality under the laws of his national State, leaving her stateless. Alternatively, if she loses her own nationality and acquires her husband's, she may be rendered stateless if the husband subsequently changes nationality to that of a third State, or if her married status ceases to exist by virtue of death of the husband or divorce. The effects of dependent nationality on statelessness are ameliorated by the *Convention on the Nationality of Married Women* (1957), which currently binds seventy-four States.[42]

---

41 Clarisa Bencomo, 'Kuwait: Promises Betrayed: Denial of Rights of Bidun, Women, and Freedom of Expression' (Human Rights Watch, 2000) ch. 4.

42 *Convention on the Nationality of Married Women*, opened for signature 29 January 1957, 309 UNTS 65 (entered into force 11 August 1958).

Under the Convention, neither the celebration nor dissolution of a marriage between a national and a non-national, nor a change of nationality by the husband during marriage, automatically affects the nationality of the wife (art. 1). A wife is also entitled to retain her husband's nationality notwithstanding that the husband renounces that nationality or voluntarily acquires a new nationality (art. 2).

CASE STUDY 4.2 Statelessness and the Bihari people of Bangladesh

The Bihari comprise several hundred thousand Muslims who have been stranded in Bangladesh as stateless persons as a result of the redrawing of geopolitical boundaries in the Indian subcontinent. Some of them have lived in 'refugee' camps in abject squalor for over forty years while waiting for the governments of Pakistan and Bangladesh to resolve their national status. Their circumstances provide valuable lessons about the legal challenges of statelessness.

When the British Indian Empire was dissolved in 1947, its territory was partitioned into two States, largely on religious lines. India was created with a predominantly Hindu population and Pakistan was created with a predominantly Muslim population. The territory of Pakistan was divided – it comprised West Pakistan (present-day Pakistan) and East Pakistan (present-day Bangladesh), separated by thousands of kilometres. Because Hindus and Muslims had often lived in mixed communities, the partition led to inter-religious violence that sparked one of the largest population movements in modern history. Eight million Hindus and Sikhs fled Pakistan for India, and 6 or 7 million Muslims fled India for Pakistan; among the latter were the Bihari people, who had lived in the Indian province of Bihar, but fled to East Pakistan following a massacre in 1947. However, the high hopes that many held for their relocation to East Pakistan were not realised, and they 'felt alienated in the new society in terms of language, customs, traditions and culture'.[43]

In the years following partition, the Bihari supported the ruling elite in West Pakistan, with whom they shared both a common religion (Islam) and a common language (Urdu). As discontent grew in East Pakistan over the concentration of political and economic power in West Pakistan, the Bihari found themselves increasingly isolated, and when East Pakistan won a liberation war against West Pakistan and proclaimed the new State of Bangladesh in 1971, the Bihari found themselves stranded in a newly independent State and ostracised from that community.

Several events occurred after Bangladesh's independence that had a direct impact on the nationality of the Bihari. In 1971 Bangladesh offered nationality to the Bihari people in its territory. Some 600,000 Bihari accepted this offer, but many hundreds of thousands declined. In 1973 Pakistan denationalised the Bihari who were resident in Bangladesh, rendering many of them stateless. In the 1970s and 1980s, a number of attempts were made to

43 Kazi Farzana, 'The Neglected Stateless Bihari Community in Bangladesh: Victims of Political and Diplomatic Onslaught' (2008) 2(1) *Journal of Humanities and Social Sciences* 1, 2.

resettle the Bihari in Pakistan, under the auspices of UNHCR and other agencies, but none resulted in any large-scale repatriation. The situation has since been one of governmental procrastination and indecision. Some progress was made in this intractable situation in 2008, when the Bangladesh High Court ruled that the Bihari who were permanently resident in Bangladesh in 1971, or had resided there since, are entitled to Bangladeshi nationality and have the right to vote.[44] Nevertheless, approximately 150,000 stateless persons remain in the camps.

This situation raises complex legal questions, particularly when one takes into account the progressive development of international law over the relevant period. (1) What was the legal effect of the secession of Bangladesh from Pakistan on the nationality of the people who were habitually resident in East Pakistan before independence, including the Bihari? (2) Was the mass denationalisation of the Bihari by Pakistan lawful under international law? (3) Do the Bihari have the right to enter Pakistan as 'their own country' in light of the fact that many have never lived there? (4) What legal obligations are owed under treaty or customary law to the Bihari who remain stateless? (5) Were the Bihari entitled to international protection as refugees when they first migrated to East Pakistan, and do they still enjoy that status in Bangladesh today?

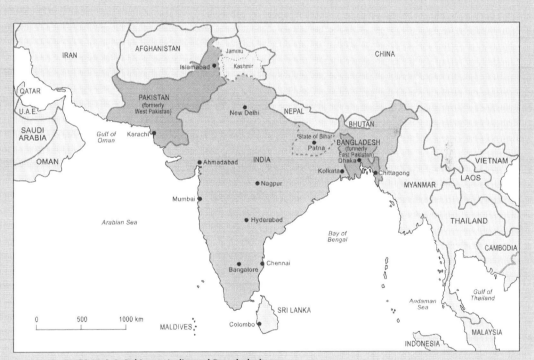

Map 4.1 Pakistan, India and Bangladesh

44 Katherine Southwick, 'The Urdu-Speakers of Bangladesh: An Unfinished Story of Enforcing Citizenship Rights' in Brad Blitz and Maureen Lynch (eds.), *Statelessness and Citizenship: A Comparative Study on the Benefits of Nationality* (Edward Elgar, 2011) 115.

4.2.3. Human rights of stateless persons

Stateless persons are some of the most vulnerable and oppressed people in the world, facing daily obstacles and hardships that do not affect a State's nationals or even foreign nationals residing within a State. Examples of oppressed stateless peoples can be found all over the world, including the Bihari in Bangladesh (see Case Study 4.2), the Bidun in the Middle East, the Rohingya in Myanmar, the Roma in Europe and the Karen in Thailand. In many States with weak human rights records, stateless persons live on the margins of society and are subjected to discrimination at the hands of the State, its agents or private persons. Even in States with generally sound human rights records, stateless persons must deal with the fact that 'nationality is a practical prerequisite for accessing political and judicial processes and for obtaining economic, social, and cultural rights'.[45] Without status or documentation, stateless persons may be unable to obtain healthcare, employment or education; acquire property; or travel. Some may be caught in a limbo of indefinite migration detention if they have entered a State unlawfully and no other State is willing to accept their return.[46]

The legal frameworks that have been developed to address these human rights concerns include both specialised and generalised treaties. UNHCR is also developing 'soft law' guidelines on statelessness to help States and practitioners to better identify, prevent or reduce statelessness, and to protect the rights of stateless persons.

The 1954 Convention

The first major international attempt to address the human rights of stateless persons came with the conclusion of the *Convention relating to the Status of Stateless Persons* (1954) ('1954 Convention').[47] In the aftermath of the Second World War, the international community faced the unprecedented challenge of establishing legal protection for millions of people displaced by war, famine and the redrawing of geopolitical boundaries in Europe. The *Convention relating to the Status of Refugees* (1951) ('Refugee Convention') addressed an important dimension of the problem by establishing an international protection regime for those who feared persecution and were outside the State of their nationality or, if stateless, were outside the country of their habitual residence (see Chapter 7).[48] However, many stateless persons did not qualify for refugee status because they

---

45 David Weissbrodt, *The Human Rights of Non-Citizens* (Oxford University Press, 2008) 97.
46 Christopher Richter, 'Statelessness in Australian Refugee Law: The (Renewed) Case for Complementary Protection' (2005) 24(2) *University of Queensland Law Journal* 545, 554–6.
47 *Convention relating to the Status of Stateless Persons*, opened for signature 28 September 1954, 360 UNTS 117 (entered into force 6 June 1960).
48 *Convention relating to the Status of Refugees*, opened for signature 28 July 1951, 189 UNTS 150 (entered into force 22 April 1954).

had not crossed international borders or their mistreatment did not amount to persecution within the terms of the Refugee Convention.

The 1954 Convention addressed these concerns by creating a new international status – the 'stateless person' – and according a suite of rights to persons holding that status. The 1954 Convention does not require States parties to confer their nationality on stateless persons, which is a matter addressed by a later convention, as discussed below. The 1954 Convention can thus be seen as a temporary response while avenues for the acquisition of nationality are explored.[49]

The 1954 Convention embodies a *de jure* conception of statelessness, namely, persons who are not considered to be a national by any State (art. 1(1)). The drafters expressly rejected a broader coverage that would include *de facto* statelessness.[50] Stateless persons also fall outside the 1954 Convention if they are receiving protection or assistance from a United Nations agency other than UNHCR; if they enjoy nationality-type rights in their country of residence; or if they are not deserving of protection because they have committed a war crime or other serious non-political crime (art. 1(2)). Like the Refugee Convention, the 1954 Convention does not mandate any particular procedure for determining the status of persons who claim to be stateless – this is a matter for each State, subject to the usual international criterion of procedural fairness.

The rights enjoyed by stateless persons depend on a number of factors, which include the subject matter of the right, the standard adopted (a national standard or an 'alien' standard) and the lawfulness of the person's presence in the territory of the State. These layers of rights share a similar architecture to the Refugee Convention and create a nuanced approach that seeks to accommodate the competing interests of the individual and the State. With respect to some rights, stateless persons within the territory of a State must be treated no less favourably than *nationals* of that State. This is the case with freedom of religion (art. 4), access to courts (art. 16), terms and conditions of employment (art. 24) and access to social security (art. 24). With respect to other rights, stateless persons must be treated no less favourably than aliens (i.e., non-nationals) within that State. This is the case for the acquisition of property (art. 13) and the right to work (arts. 17–19). In a few cases, stateless persons must be treated no less favourably than aliens, but only where the stateless person is *lawfully* in the territory of the State. This is the case for freedom of association (art. 15), access to housing (art. 21) and freedom of internal movement (art. 26). The restricted nature of the last-mentioned right allows States to detain stateless persons who have entered their territory irregularly.

The 1954 Convention contains additional provisions that are of special impor-tance to stateless persons. Contracting States are prohibited from expelling a

---

49 United Nations High Commissioner for Refugees, 'Protecting the Rights of Stateless Persons' (UNHCR, 2010) 9.
50 Carol Batchelor, 'Stateless Persons: Some Gaps in International Protection' (1995) 7(2) *International Journal of Refugee Law* 232, 247–8.

stateless person lawfully in their territory, save on grounds of national security or public order (art. 31). Contracting States are required to issue identity papers to stateless persons in their territory (art. 27). If those persons are lawfully in their territory, States are also required to issue travel documents for travel outside the territory, unless there are compelling reasons of national security or public order (art. 28). A Schedule to the Convention sets out the minimum requirements for the travel document of a stateless person, including regulation of fees and the period of validity.

The 1954 Convention binds a significant but still modest proportion of the international community – seventy-four States were party to it in mid-2012. In light of the large number of stateless persons, their global geographic reach and the privations they suffer, this level of international commitment is inadequate. This is certainly so in comparison with the Refugee Convention and its 1967 Protocol,[51] which bind 145 States and 146 States, respectively. In recent years, calls have come from a number of United Nations organs and agencies – the General Assembly, the Human Rights Council and the UNHCR Executive Committee among them – for greater State accession to the 1954 Convention.

Universal human rights norms

Stateless persons are entitled to enjoy the rights set out in the 1954 Convention when in the territory of States parties. However, with the growth of international human rights law, the human rights of stateless persons have been complemented by a raft of universal norms that overshadow many of the earlier developments (see Chapter 6).

International human rights norms are usually expressed in universal terms. In the words of the Preamble to the *Universal Declaration of Human Rights* (1948), they constitute 'a common standard of achievement for all peoples and all nations'. The two international Covenants on human rights thus speak of the rights of 'all peoples', 'every human being' and 'everyone'.[52] It goes without saying that state-less persons are people too, and they are entitled to enjoy the universal benefits of civil, political, economic, social and cultural rights. International human rights treaties have several advantages over the 1954 Convention. They have been ratified by a larger number of States; many of their principles form part of customary international law and bind States irrespective of specific treaty commitments; they protect a broader scope of rights; and there are charter-based and treaty-based mechanisms for monitoring and enforcing compliance. Nevertheless, as discussed

51 *Protocol relating to the Status of Refugees*, opened for accession 31 January 1967, 606 UNTS 267 (entered into force 4 October 1967).
52 *International Covenant on Civil and Political Rights*, opened for signature 16 December 1966, 999 UNTS 171 (entered into force 23 March 1976); *International Covenant on Economic, Social and Cultural Rights*, opened for signature 16 December 1966, 993 UNTS 3 (entered into force 3 January 1976).

below, there are circumstances in which the human rights of stateless persons remain narrower than those of nationals.

A related question is whether the failure of a State to respect the international human rights of its own nationals can amount to a practical denial of the benefits of nationality such as to render those persons *de facto* stateless. This typically arises where there are systemic violations of human rights associated with State repression. Some commentators have found it useful to treat the loss of effective national protection as a matter of *de facto* statelessness.[53] Others argue that there is no need for a special regime for *de facto* statelessness because the denial of the human rights attached to nationality is already covered by other regimes, namely, the refugee regime for persons who are outside the country of their nationality, and the international human rights regime in other cases.[54]

4.2.4. Measures to reduce statelessness

The right to belong to a community has been poignantly described by Hannah Arendt as 'a right to have rights'[55] and underpins the importance of practical measures to reduce statelessness. The idea of 'access to citizenship' – especially for long-term or permanent residents – is increasingly finding expression in international jurisprudence and is reflected in the views of the United Nations human rights treaty bodies.[56] States have long promoted a range of measures to reduce statelessness and its attendant ills, while still recognising the competence of each State to determine its membership through nationality laws. Measures to reduce statelessness have been channelled through provisions in both general human rights treaties and specialised treaties addressing questions of nationality and statelessness.

General treaties

International human rights instruments have confronted the issue of statelessness in three ways – by expressly recognising the right of individuals to have a nationality; by facilitating the acquisition of nationality; and by limiting the capacity of States to revoke nationality. All elements can be seen in the *Universal Declaration of Human Rights* (1948), which states in art. 15 that (1) everyone has the right to a nationality, and (2) no one shall be arbitrarily deprived

53 Carol Batchelor, 'Statelessness and the Problem of Resolving Nationality Status' (1998) 10(1–2) *International Journal of Refugee Law* 156; David Weissbrodt and Clay Collins, 'The Human Rights of Stateless Persons' (2006) 28(1) *Human Rights Quarterly* 245, 251–2.
54 Hugh Massey, 'UNHCR and *de facto* Statelessness: Legal and Protection Policy Research Series' (UNHCR, 2010) 36–40.
55 Hannah Arendt, *The Origins of Totalitarianism* (Allen and Unwin, 2nd edn, 1958) 296.
56 See, e.g., Committee on the Elimination of Racial Discrimination, 'General Recommendation No 30, Discrimination against Non-Citizens' (UN Doc CERD/C/64/Misc.11/rev.3, 2004).

of his or her nationality nor denied the right to change his or her nationality. The international human rights treaties express these ideas in different ways.

The ICCPR promotes the acquisition of nationality at birth by providing that 'every child shall be registered immediately after birth' and 'every child has the right to acquire a nationality' (art. 24). The *Convention on the Rights of the Child* (1989) reiterates these rights, but with the qualification that implementation shall be in accordance with national law (art. 7).[57] This makes explicit that, while children have a right to a nationality, they do not have a right to a *particular* nationality – that is a matter for national laws, informed by any relevant international obligations. The *International Convention on the Protection of the Rights of All Migrant Workers and Members of their Families* (1990) similarly provides that 'Each child of a migrant worker shall have the right to a name, to registration of birth and to a nationality' (art. 29).[58] CEDAW focusses on gender equality in the acquisition and loss of nationality, since the absence of equality can lead to problems of statelessness. It requires States to grant women equal rights with men in acquiring, changing or retaining their nationality, and to grant women equal rights with men with respect to the nationality of their children (art. 9).

Specialised treaties

The international community recognised the need for a universal instrument that prevents and reduces statelessness well before general human rights treaties began to include measures directed to that end. Since *de jure* statelessness results from the absence of a formal bond of nationality between an individual and any State, it is States themselves that must take action to ensure everyone has a nationality. The *Convention on the Reduction of Statelessness* (1961) ('1961 Convention') does this by requiring States parties to provide a safety net for persons who would otherwise fall through the cracks – beyond that, the 1961 Convention does not regulate the terms on which a State confers or withdraws its nationality.[59] Its ratification is presently meagre (forty-five parties in mid-2012), but its provisions have had wider influence in informing the development of regional treaties (discussed below) and national legislation.

The first tranche of provisions deals with the grant of nationality. States parties must grant their nationality to a person who would otherwise be stateless if that person was born in its territory (art. 1) or born outside its territory to parents one of whom was a national of the State at the time of the birth (art. 4). These provisions recognise both *jus soli* and *jus sanguinis* as a basis for attributing responsibility for providing the safety net. The grant of nationality may be made at birth by operation

---

57 *Convention on the Rights of the Child*, opened for signature 20 November 1989, 1577 UNTS 3 (entered into force 2 September 1990).

58 *International Convention on the Protection of the Rights of All Migrant Workers and Members of their Families*, opened for signature 18 December 1990, 2220 UNTS 3 (entered into force 1 July 2003).

59 *Convention on the Reduction of Statelessness*, opened for signature 30 August 1961, 989 UNTS 175 (entered into force 13 December 1975).

of law or at a later time upon application. Children are deemed to be born in the territory of a State if they are found there or are born on a ship or aircraft registered to that State (arts. 2–3).

The second tranche of provisions deals with the loss or deprivation of nationality. States parties cannot withdraw their nationality from a person as a result of voluntary renunciation (art. 7) or a change in personal status (art. 5) unless the person has or acquires another nationality. More generally, the 1961 Convention prohibits a State from depriving a person of his or her nationality if this would render the person stateless (art. 8). To this general principle there are only limited exceptions, including where the nationality was obtained by misrepresentation or fraud; where the person has acted inconsistently with his or her duty of loyalty to the State; or where the person has made a declaration of allegiance to another State. The latter two exceptions are available only to States parties that reserved their right to apply such laws when they ratified the 1961 Convention (art. 8(3)) – of the forty-five States parties, only six have done so.

The third tranche deals with nationality in the context of State succession. Where territory is transferred between States parties, they must include treaty provisions designed to ensure that no person becomes stateless as a result of the transfer. In the absence of such provisions, the relevant States must confer their nationality on persons who would otherwise become stateless as a result of the transfer (art. 10).

The 1961 Convention has had an impact on regional treaties that seek to mitigate statelessness by regulating the acquisition and loss of nationality, such as the *American Convention on Human Rights* (1969) (art. 20); the *African Charter on the Rights and Welfare of the Child* (1990) (art. 6); and the *European Convention on Nationality* (1997) (art. 6).[60] Each is significant for including the right of every person to the nationality of the State in whose territory he or she was born, if he or she does not have the right to any other nationality. This requires States parties to adopt the principle of *jus soli* for any person who would otherwise be stateless.

Article 20 of the *American Convention on Human Rights* was considered by the Inter-American Court of Human Rights in a landmark decision in 2005, *Case of Yean and Bosico Children* v. *Dominican Republic*.[61] The case concerned the nationality of two children who were born in the Dominican Republic to mothers of Dominican nationality and fathers of Haitian nationality. At that time, the Dominican Constitution granted Dominican nationality to children born in the territory unless they were the children of foreign diplomats or foreigners in transit. The Dominican authorities refused to issue the children with birth certificates, as part of a deliberate State policy, because their fathers had been Haitian migrant

---

60 *American Convention on Human Rights*, opened for signature 22 November 1969, 1144 UNTS 123 (entered into force 18 July 1978); *African Charter on the Rights and Welfare of the Child*, opened for signature 11 July 1990, OAU Doc CAB/LEG/24.9/49 (entered into force 29 November 1999); and *European Convention on Nationality*, opened for signature 6 November 1997, ETS No 166 (entered into force 1 March 2000).

61 *Case of Yean and Bosico Children* v. *Dominican Republic*, Inter-Am Ct HR (8 September 2005).

workers. Without these identity documents, the children were unable to apply for nationality or attend school.

The Court upheld the complaint, stating that the Dominican Republic had breached the right to nationality (art. 20) and the right to equal protection of the law without discrimination (art. 24). In reference to art. 20, the Dominican Republic was not authorised to qualify the children's right to nationality by the migration status of their fathers: the *American Convention on Human Rights* provides that Dominican nationality is acquired whenever a person is born in the territory and would otherwise be stateless. The Court ordered the State to compensate the victims, publicise the decision, organise a public act of apology and amend its legislation. Compensation was ultimately paid, but in other respects the decision was a Pyrrhic victory. In 2010 a new constitution entrenched the marginal status of Haitian workers and their off-spring by withholding Dominican nationality from those born in the Republic to 'illegal residents' (art. 18). This outcome contradicts the obligation of States under art. 68 of the *American Convention on Human Rights* to comply with judgments of the Court and guarantee implementation of its rulings at the national level. Although the Court monitors compliance with its judgments, the Inter-American system lacks a formal mechanism for enforcing its orders.

4.3. PARTICULAR ISSUES

4.3.1. Multiple nationality

Multiple nationality occurs where an individual possesses the nationality of more than one State. Multiple nationality can occur as a result of birth of a child in a State that accords nationality on the basis of *jus soli* to foreign parents who are nationals of States that recognise nationality by descent (*jus sanguinis*). It can also occur where individuals become naturalised or married in one State without relinquishing their original nationalities.

In past eras, and to some extent in the present, multiple nationality was disfavoured by States, even though the status is permitted by international law. As late as 1974 the German Federal Constitutional Court regarded dual or multiple nationality as 'an evil that should be avoided or eliminated in the interests of States as well as the interests of the affected citizens'[62] because it was thought that a person should owe only one allegiance and thus have only one nationality. In a past age when the treatment by a State of its own nationals lay behind the walls of exclusive 'domestic jurisdiction' and was not subject to international law, the

---

62 *Opinion of the German Federal Constitutional Court*, 21 May 1974, cited in Alexander Aleinikoff and Douglas Klusmeyer, 'Plural Nationality: Facing the Future in a Migratory World' in Alexander Aleinikoff and Douglas Klusmeyer (eds.), *Citizenship Today: Global Perspectives and Practices* (Carnegie Endowment for International Peace, 2001) 63, 70.

invocation of another nationality was regarded as an unwelcome complication and as subversive of exclusive national sovereignty.

Negative attitudes towards multiple nationality have substantially lessened in recent years. The Preamble to the *European Convention on Nationality* (1997) notes 'the varied approach of States to the question of multiple nationality' and adopts a neutral position on the question, except for its prohibition on depriving children born with a foreign nationality, or married women, of multiple nationality (arts. 14–17). The trend of States towards acceptance of multiple nationality has been informed by several forces. For migrant-sending countries, it has been prompted by their desire to maintain links with their diasporas and also to sustain the inward flow of remittances from migrants working abroad. For migrant-receiving countries, it has been prompted by the desire to encourage the integration of migrant communities by incorporating them into the political and social community of the State, without forcing them to sever all ties of sentiment with their countries of origin. More generally, the incidence of multiple nationality has increased as a result of the greater mobility of individuals through migration and asylum in a globalised world.

Some problems remain, even in States that recognise multiple nationality in principle and accord human rights in their territories to all persons present there, without discrimination. The first of these problems concerns compulsory military service. There are a number of bilateral treaties on this subject, as well as the multilateral *Protocol relating to Military Obligations in Certain Cases of Double Nationality* (1935).[63] This Protocol, which binds only thirteen States, provides that military service must be fulfilled only in the State where the dual national is ordinarily resident. This would seem to be a sensible solution even for States not party to a relevant treaty, but some States persist in their attitude of compulsory service for nationals, leading to diplomatic friction with another State of which the individual is also a national and in which he or she is normally resident. The problem is of diminishing significance as the number of States imposing compulsory military service declines.[64]

The second problem concerns the right of diplomatic protection, including the espousal of an international claim. Article 4 of the *Convention on Certain Questions relating to the Conflict of Nationality Law* (1930) lays down the rule that 'A State may not afford diplomatic protection to one of its nationals against a State whose nationality such person also possesses.' This rule is said to reflect the principle of equality. It has already been noted in connection with the *Nottebohm Case* that the International Court of Justice, by implication, even extended this notion to rule out

---

63 *Protocol relating to Military Obligations in Certain Cases of Double Nationality*, opened for signature 12 April 1935, 178 UNTS 227 (entered into force 25 May 1937).

64 Nevertheless, it has been estimated that 2.49 million people globally provide forced labour at the behest of the state, including through military service: International Labour Office, 'A Global Alliance Against Forced Labour' (ILO, 2005) 10–12.

a right of protection by the national State against a State of permanent residence, albeit falling short of formal nationality (see Case Study 4.1). However, doubts about the binding nature of this rule in customary international law had been voiced even before 1930, and were deepened with the *Merge Claim Case* of 1955.[65] The ILC – a subsidiary organ of the United Nations General Assembly – significantly modified the 1930 formulation in its *Draft Articles on Diplomatic Protection* (2006), as follows (art. 7):

> A State of nationality may not exercise diplomatic protection in respect of a person against a State of which that person is also a national unless the nationality of the former State is predominant, both at the date of injury and at the date of the official presentation of the claim.

A further issue with respect to the right of diplomatic protection arises where a State asserts the right of protection over a person possessing more than one nationality against a third State of which he or she is not a national. The 1930 Convention (art. 5) laid down an 'effective nationality' test, but this has also been rejected by the ILC's *Draft Articles on Diplomatic Protection*, which have adopted a clear-cut approach allowing an unrestricted right by any State to protect its nationals (art. 6):

1 Any State of which a dual or multiple national is a national may exercise diplomatic protection against a State of which that person is not a national.
2 Two or more States of nationality may jointly exercise diplomatic protection in respect of a dual or multiple national.

4.3.2. State succession

A succession of States occurs when one State replaces another in sovereignty over a particular territory. The succession may be complete or partial in relation to the territory. It may involve the extinction of the former State, or the former State may continue to exist in relation to its other territories. Succession may also arise from the unification of two or more States to form a new State. Historically, the most common form of State succession was the result of conquest or annexation. In recent times the emergence of new States by way of independence from former colonial powers is a more common example. So too is the break-up of a State into separate States (e.g., the former Yugoslavia) or the secession of one part of a composite State (e.g., South Sudan).

State succession is to be distinguished from mere governmental succession where, despite even a fundamental change in the nature of the government, the State remains (whether or not under the same name). Examples of governmental succession include Russia after the revolution of 1917, China after the revolution of

---

65 *Merge Claim Case* (1955) 22 ILR 443.

1949 and Iran after the revolution of 1979. Questions of nationality arise under all forms of State succession, but not with respect to governmental succession.

Normally, the inhabitants of a territory that has undergone a State succession will automatically acquire the nationality of the new State and lose that of the former State. Whether this is an established rule of customary law is open to some doubt, since in many cases specific treaty provisions have regulated the position.[66] However, State practice, which may support a general principle of customary international law, may be found in the constitutions of States that acquired independence from former colonial powers: typically these declared to be nationals of the new State only those persons who were born in the territory of the new State.

The ILC has produced *Draft Articles on Nationality of Natural Persons in relation to the Succession of States* (1999) to address some of the difficulties encountered with respect to nationality upon State succession.[67] Although special rules have been developed for particular types of State succession, the general rules applicable to all types of State succession affirm the fundamental human rights of persons affected by the succession. These protections include:

- the right of persons to the nationality of at least one of the States concerned (i.e., the predecessor State or the successor State) (art. 1);
- the obligation of these States to prevent a person becoming stateless as a result of succession (art. 4);
- the obligation of these States to enact legislation on nationality without undue delay (art. 6);
- a presumption that persons having habitual residence in the affected territory shall acquire the nationality of the successor State (to address the time-lag between the act of succession and the adoption of legislation) (art. 5);
- measures to promote family unity (art. 12); and
- prohibitions on discrimination and arbitrariness in decisions with respect to nationality (arts. 15–16).

These approaches are also reflected in the *Council of Europe Convention on the Avoidance of Statelessness in Relation to State Succession* (2006). Particular problems have been encountered by ethnic Russians in seeking the nationality of Estonia, Latvia and Lithuania, where they have been permanent residents, after those States seceded from the Soviet Union.[68]

Significantly, where a person is qualified to acquire the nationality of two or more of the States concerned, the States are obliged to give consideration to the will of that person (art. 11). The idea of an option, exercisable by each individual,

---

66 For example, special provisions on nationality were contained in the *Versailles Peace Treaty* (1919), the *Treaty of Saint-Germain* (1919) and *Treaty of Trianon* (1920) following the First World War.

67 International Law Commission, *Draft Articles on Nationality of Natural Persons in relation to the Succession of States* (Yearbook of the International Law Commission, United Nations, 1999).

68 John Quigley, 'Baltic Russians: Entitled Inhabitants or Unlawful Settlers?' in Roger Clark, Ferdinand Feldbrugge and Stanislaw Pomorski (eds.), *International and National Law in Russia and Eastern Europe* (Kluwer, 2001) 319.

to reject the nationality of the successor State and to retain that of the predecessor State appears to be a dominant trend in practice in cases of State succession. The ILC's *Draft Articles on Nationality of Natural Persons in relation to the Succession of States* do not raise this as high as a *right* of option in all cases (States are obliged only to 'give consideration' to the principle of free choice of nationality), but in some categories of State succession a right of option is recognised, such as where a State dissolves completely and is replaced by two or more successor States (art. 23).

4.3.3. Evidence of nationality

While the vast majority of people have a single nationality that is rarely called into question, there are many others whose nationality is uncertain – perhaps because they did not acquire a nationality at birth, or lost it, or because they have more than one nationality (e.g., acquired through distant lineage). In situations of uncertainty, how is nationality or its absence – statelessness – to be proved? The establishment of nationality through documentary and other sources is an important practical matter, but it is one that should be distinguished from evidence of a person's identity and from the documentation required to facilitate international travel. The modern-day passport serves all three functions.

Proof of nationality can arise under domestic law and international law. Because nationality is a legal bond between a State and an individual, the means by which that status can be evidenced is primarily a matter for the law of each State. Laws differ widely in this regard, but it is common for legislation to authorise the executive to issue certificates of nationality or naturalisation. A certificate is usually *prima facie* evidence that the person named therein is a national of the State. It is not conclusive because the person's status may be called into question if the certificate was obtained by misstatement or fraud, or if the nationality was subsequently lost.

A State may require proof of nationality for many purposes, including voting in elections and accessing healthcare or social security. While a certificate of nationality will satisfy that requirement, other documents may suffice. In States that confer nationality on the basis of *jus soli*, it may be sufficient for a person to produce a birth certificate indicating that he or she was born in the State. The birth certificate is not direct proof of nationality, but proof of a fact that is constitutive of nationality. In States that confer nationality on the basis of *jus sanguinis*, it may be sufficient to prove descent from nationals, although the problem then becomes one of proving the nationality of the parents.[69]

Nationality may also have to be proved for the purposes of international law, but the question will not necessarily receive the same answer here as in domestic law. The manner in which nationality is ascertained is sometimes governed by the terms

---

69 Weiss, above n. 34, 217.

of a treaty, but where there is no relevant treaty provision the matter will fall to be determined in national or international tribunals, where different approaches can be taken.

An example of a class of treaty that often addresses evidence of nationality is that of bilateral readmission agreements, which provide for the rapid and effective return of irregular migrants from one State to another with a minimum of formality (see Chapter 5). The parties typically agree to accept the return of their own nationals, as well as non-nationals who have transited through their territory. To this end, readmission agreements list a wide range of documents that are accepted as *proof* of nationality without further investigation. These documents (whether current or expired) might include passports, civilian or military identity cards, certificates of nationality, official documents that mention nationality and seaman's registration books. The agreements may go further to include a list of documents that are accepted as *prima facie* evidence of nationality, including driving licences, birth certificates, company identity cards and statements by witnesses.[70] When the objective is rapid and effective return, what constitutes 'evidence' can be inappropriately fluid.

By contrast, multilateral treaties rarely address the issue of evidence of nationality directly. The Refugee Convention requires a person to be outside the country of his or her nationality to be considered a refugee, but proof of alienage is left to the determination of States parties (see Chapter 7). The 1954 Convention similarly leaves the determination of statelessness to States parties; and the issuance of international travel documents to a stateless person does not affect his or her national status (art. 28 and Schedule). In the context of these conventions, questions of nationality are decided in domestic tribunals. However, evidence of nationality can also arise in international tribunals – for example, where one State espouses a claim of diplomatic protection on behalf of its national, proof of nationality is a precondition for success. Passports are important evidence. The modern passport is a document issued by a State to its own nationals with intended extraterritorial effect. While it serves mainly as an identity and travel document, it is usually taken as *prima facie* evidence of nationality as well.[71]

4.4. RELEVANCE OF STATUS TO INTERNATIONAL MIGRATION

It will be apparent from the foregoing discussion that whether a person is a national of one or more States, or is stateless, is of great significance to many aspects of

---

70 See, e.g., *Agreement between the European Community and the Democratic Socialist Republic of Sri Lanka on the Readmission of Persons Residing without Authorisation*, opened for signature 4 June 2004, OJ L124 (entered into force 1 May 2005) Annexes 1 and 2.

71 Weis, above n. 34, 222–30; Adam Muchmore, 'Passports and Nationality in International Law' (2004) 10(2) *University of California Davis Journal of International Law and Policy* 301, 317–28.

international migration. These will be explored in detail in later chapters: this section seeks only to summarise the main contexts in which nationality impacts on freedom of international movement or the treatment of migrants.

First, nationality is relevant to whether a person has a right to enter a State. The ICCPR proclaims that 'No one shall be arbitrarily deprived of the right to enter his own country' (art. 12(4)). The Covenant's *travaux préparatoires* indicate that this right was intended to inure to the benefit of nationals and permanent residents who, by reason of their connection with a State, were justified in calling it their own. In the case of other individuals (and with the exception of refugees), States are entitled to deny entry, and they do so regularly on the basis of qualitative and quantitative selection criteria. The right of nationals to enter their own State is discussed further in Chapter 5.

Second, since the State of nationality has the general obligation to admit its nationals, another State wishing to deport a person of that nationality – for criminality, overstaying or other reasons – is entitled to expect that the deportee will be allowed to re-enter the State of nationality. For practical reasons, deportation cannot be effected otherwise than to a particular destination. However, where the deportee is threatened by persecution in his or her national State, the deportee may be protected by human rights principles analogous to *non-refoulement* and thus enter into a period of uncertain status in the deporting State until a third State is found willing to accept the deportee.

Third, the failure to possess any nationality, or the possession of a nationality that is regarded with disfavour by other States, has a practical bearing on the ability of individuals to cross international borders. This is not only because of the difficulty they face in obtaining international travel documents. It is also because stateless persons, and nationals of certain States, are unlikely to fare well in the discretionary admission policies of third States. Conversely, some nationalities have been highly prized because they provide entrée to third States – such as Canadian nationality for access to the United States, and United Kingdom nationality for access to Europe.[72] In time, as the economies of China and India grow in global importance, they too may become highly desired nationalities for future migrants.

Fourth, nationality is relevant to one dimension of departure from a State. Everyone enjoys the freedom to leave any country, including his or her own (see ICCPR art. 12(2)), but the capacity of a State to *require* a person to depart depends on national status. A State can lawfully remove non-nationals from its territory, provided certain procedural safeguards are met (art. 13), and this power has been used throughout history 'to relieve the soil of an obnoxious guest'.[73] However, it is an

---

72 Of the 776,000 persons granted citizenship in the twenty-seven member States of the European Union in 2009, the United Kingdom accounted for the largest share (203,600 persons, or 26 per cent). Of the new United Kingdom citizens, more than one-third were from four developing States: India, Pakistan, Bangladesh and the Philippines: Fabio Sartori, 'Acquisitions of Citizenship on the Rise in 2009' (Statistics in Focus 24/2011, Eurostat, 2011).

73 Gustave Rolin-Jacquemyns, 'Right of Expulsion of Foreigners' (1888) 20 *Revue de Droit International* 498.

established principle of international law that a State cannot deport its own nationals, as a corollary of the right of nationals to re-enter the State of their nationality. One exception to this principle is that States can extradite their own nationals to face criminal charges in another State, with all the protections that the extradition process affords. Yet the strength of the underlying principle is evident in the reluctance of States following the civil law tradition to extradite their own nationals – preferring instead to prosecute them at home for crimes committed abroad. As a legal and symbolic manifestation of a person's 'belonging' to a community, nationality restrains the capacity of States to require persons to leave their territory. The right of States to expel non-nationals is discussed further in Chapter 5.

Fifth, national status can be important in defining the human rights of migrants, despite the fact that many rights enumerated in the ICCPR are generally to be enjoyed in the territory of States parties 'without distinction of any kind, such as . . . national or social origin . . . or other status' (art. 2). The universal enjoyment of human rights is subject to qualifications. Some rights need only be conferred on nationals, such as the right to vote (art. 25); some rights may be derogated from during times of public emergency, including by making distinctions based on national origin (art. 4); and some rights are subject to permissible limitations if prescribed by law and necessary to protect national security, public order, public health or morals, or the rights and freedoms of others (art. 12). The margin of appreciation given to States in implementing treaty obligations grants them latitude in drawing lawful distinctions between persons on the basis of their status – including their nationality, foreign nationality or statelessness – but the degree of latitude is itself controlled by international law.

One consequence of this latitude is that States often confer graduated entitlements to social goods depending on whether a person's connection with the State is transient (e.g., tourists), temporary (e.g., seasonal workers or international students), permanent (e.g., permanent residents) or unbounded, as in the case of nationals. To the extent that liberal democracies have conferred an increasing array of entitlements on persons who are not their nationals, the incentives for migrants to be naturalised in their new homes are diminished. Nevertheless, some settler societies have actively encouraged long-term permanent residents to apply for citizenship, and thus acquire the full rights and responsibilities of nationality.

Finally, nationality is relevant to the mechanisms available for redressing violations of rights at the hands of a foreign State, inflicted through physical injury, denial of justice or expropriation of property without adequate compensation. A State may espouse an international claim against another State for mistreatment of individuals, but only in respect of persons with whom the claimant State has a legal bond of nationality. This right of diplomatic protection is discussed further in Chapter 6.

KEY REFERENCES

Bhabha, Jacqueline (ed.), *Children without a State: A Global Human Rights Challenge* (Massachusetts Institute of Technology, 2011)

Blitz, Brad and Lynch, Maureen (eds.), *Statelessness and Citizenship: A Comparative Study on the Benefits of Nationality* (Edward Elgar, 2011)

Boll, Alfred, *Multiple Nationality and International Law* (Martinus Nijhoff, 2007)

Donner, Ruth, *The Regulation of Nationality in International Law* (Transnational, 2nd edn, 1994)

International Law Commission, *Draft Articles on Diplomatic Protection* (United Nations, 2006)

International Law Commission, *Draft Articles on Nationality of Natural Persons in Relation to the Succession of States* (Yearbook of the International Law Commission, United Nations, 1999)

Spiro, Peter, *Beyond Citizenship: American Identity after Globalization* (Oxford University Press, 2008)

Torpey, John, *The Invention of the Passport: Surveillance, Citizenship and the State* (Cambridge University Press, 2000)

United Nations High Commissioner for Refugees, 'UNHCR Action to Address Statelessness: A Strategy Note' (2010) 22(2) *International Journal of Refugee Law* 297

Van Waas, Laura, *Nationality Matters: Statelessness under International Law* (Intersentia, 2008)

Weis, Paul, *Nationality and Statelessness in International Law* (Sijthoff and Noordhoff, 2nd edn, 1979)

Weissbrodt, David and Collins, Clay, 'The Human Rights of Stateless Persons' (2006) 28(1) *Human Rights Quarterly* 245

KEY RESOURCES

Council of Europe, Treaty Office: http://conventions.coe.int

Inter-American Court of Human Rights: www.corteidh.or.cr

International Law Commission: www.un.org/law/ilc

International Organization for Migration, Migration Law Database: www.imldb.iom.int

Refugees International: www.refugeesinternational.org

United Nations High Commissioner for Human Rights: www2.ohchr.org/english/bodies/treaty

United Nations High Commissioner for Refugees: www.unhcr.org

State sovereignty and freedom of movement

RICHARD PERRUCHOUD[1]

Sovereignty allows States to regulate the movement of persons within and across their borders. It is a power that should not be exercised to the detriment of individual human rights. While the liberty to move freely and in a lawful manner is by no means absolute, limitations imposed by a State should be justified, necessary and proportionate to the state interest. This chapter outlines the concept of sovereignty under international law, the right of States to admit and expel persons, and the regulation and facilitation of migratory movements. By providing an overview of the international legal framework, it analyses whether any significant advancement has been made since the end of the nineteenth century, particularly on the right to leave and the right to return.

5.1. STATE SOVEREIGNTY AND CONTROL OF EXTERNAL BORDERS

The concept of sovereignty, first understood as the supreme and absolute autonomy over a particular territory, evolved from being an 'omnipotent authority' to a totality of legal powers and competences regulated by contemporary international law.[2] As a concept of international law, it comprises three major aspects – external, internal and territorial – each being exercised in accordance with the rules of international law. The *external* aspect of sovereignty concerns the relationship between States: it is the right of a State to determine freely its relations with other States or entities without the restraint or control of another State. This aspect of sovereignty is also known as independence. The *internal* aspect of sovereignty is the State's right or competence to determine the character of its own institutions, to enact laws of its own choice, and to ensure respect for and adherence to national laws. The *territorial* aspect of sovereignty is the authority that a State exercises over all persons and things found within its territory, as well as over its nationals abroad.

---

1 The author is grateful to Anna Lillicrap for research assistance, and to Ruzayda Martens for editorial assistance.
2 James Crawford, *The Creation of States in International Law* (Oxford University Press, 2nd edn, 2006) 103.

Sovereignty therefore encompasses the power to exercise authority over individuals living within the territory of the State and to act on behalf of those individuals. This power authorises the State to prevent other States, and the inhabitants of other States, from interfering with the 'territorial integrity of the State', as stated in art. 2(4) of the *Charter of the United Nations* (1945).

International law allocates competence to States over events inside their boundaries and, with specific limitations, outside their boundaries. A State needs to protect the safety and security of its inhabitants and to administer law and order within its boundaries. To this end, it controls the movement and behaviour of individuals and corporations, and the inflow and outflow of goods, capital and services. Hence the State's interest in, and control of, the movement of individuals is one important element of its broader authority.

At the international level, the principles of State sovereignty and territorial integrity have led to the logical conclusion that international migration – that is, the movement of people across international borders – is subject to State control. At the national level, regulation of international migration is often considered to be the last bastion of State sovereignty, as States are confronted with the flow of non-nationals wishing to enter their territory by lawful or unlawful means. This perception is also due to the close relationship that exists between migration law and national identity, especially in countries where the reality, or mythology, of the State's creation is linked to immigration.

Sovereignty is not only related to control over territory, but also, and foremost, to control over people. Migration law, including laws on nationality, is essential to the creation of States: for a State to exist, it must have both inhabitants (nationals) and borders. Migration and nationality laws establish the dividing line between nationals and non-nationals, and make the border meaningful for people attempting to cross it either way. It is often said that migration law is about borders: geopolitical borders between States, and borders between nationals.

The evolution of the concept of sovereignty in the face of globalisation has not changed the basic relationship between sovereignty and migration – control over territory and people remains essential – but control over a State's population and its borders has taken on increased importance. The border, however, is no longer limited to a State's geographical or territorial boundary; it may also be 'exported' to another State, where immigration officers are posted at airports to grant or refuse the right to enter a given country before boarding a plane (see Chapter 10). In addition, technology and communications have made borders permeable.

While the border remains the (usually imaginary) line that distinguishes one sovereign entity from another, it sometimes takes more subtle forms. A border is not only a line drawn on the ground to separate nationals and other residents from foreigners, but also 'a complex assemblage of various "bordering" mechanisms which make the borderline a social – rather than merely legal – entity'.[3] To this end, a distinction is made between the 'literal' border and the 'metaphorical' one.[4] In the field of migration, the term 'externalisation' defines the action whereby a State transfers responsibility to protect its borders to a third State: in so doing, the third State becomes the guard of another State's border.[5]

In the context of sovereignty, the role of the border is to mark the physical territory over which a State's sovereignty is exercised. A core prerogative of a State is its sovereignty over admission and exclusion of non-nationals. Admission or rejection may take place at the physical border, but also outside the territory of the State. For example, immigration rules may apply extraterritorially – that is, when States decide to move the actual borders beyond the borderline and apply their laws outside the marked territory, transporting the actual borders beyond the borderline by establishing offshore processing centres or resorting to interdictions at sea. In some cases, extraterritoriality may be achieved not only by externalising the borders, but also by contracting them, as when the border 'is withdrawn from its physical limit such that the border is located at different points for different purposes'.[6]

Traditionally, the justification for the power of a State to admit and expel persons lies in the State's sovereign and inherent power to decide on all activities within its territorial jurisdiction, and its authority over all persons and things within its territory. This power flows from the concept of an international society composed of States possessing primary responsibility and authority over their territory and population. This right falls 'essentially within the domestic jurisdiction' of States as referred to in art. 2(7) of the *Charter of the United Nations*.

Nowadays the concept of exclusive domestic jurisdiction is invoked to assert the right of States to admit and exclude migrants, particularly in the wake of terrorism and the increase in irregular movements. However, international law defines what the concept of domestic jurisdiction covers and, over time, restrictions have been imposed by international law on the power of States to admit and expel. It is no longer accurate to assert that States have absolute discretion over admission and expulsion. While they still have a wide margin of discretion, limits are imposed by international legal obligations derived from customary and treaty law, as well as from universally accepted human rights and fundamental freedoms. Thus Sohn and Buergenthal have stated the first governing rule to be that:

---

3   Laura Griffin, 'When Borders Fail: "Illegal", Invisible Labour Migration and Basotho Domestic Workers in South Africa' in Elspeth Guild and Sandra Mantu (eds.), *Constructing and Imagining Labour Migration: Perspectives of Control from Five Continents* (Ashgate, 2011) 15. These control mechanisms include State and non-State actors such as private companies, employers and transport operators, and may take place at a range of sites throughout the State's territory or even beyond.

4   Coined by Lord Bingham in *R* v. *Immigration Officer at Prague Airport; Ex parte European Roma Rights Centre* [2004] UKHL 55 (9 December 2004).

5   Alison Kesby, 'The Shifting and Multiple Border and International Law' (2007) 27(1) *Oxford Journal of Legal Studies* 101.

6   Ibid. 115–16.

A State has the competence to control and regulate the movement of persons across its borders. This competence is not absolute. It is limited by the right of individuals to move across borders and by the obligations of the State that arise from generally accepted principles of international law and applicable international agreements.[7]

5.2. FREEDOM OF MOVEMENT AS A HUMAN RIGHT?

The domestic jurisdiction of States has been interpreted with flexibility and has evolved over the years: human rights are no longer seen as falling exclusively within a State's internal affairs; they now transcend borders.

Provisions on human rights and fundamental freedoms are clearly embedded in the *Charter of the United Nations*.[8] As stated by the International Court of Justice in the *Namibia Case*: 'to establish instead, and to enforce, distinctions, exclusions, restrictions, and limitations exclusively based on grounds of race, colour, descent or national or ethnic origin which constitute a denial of fundamental human rights is a flagrant violation of the purposes and principles of the Charter'.[9]

The foundation document of human rights, the *Universal Declaration of Human Rights* (1948) ('UDHR'), gives full effect to fundamental and inalienable human rights and freedoms.[10] The UDHR forms the basis of human rights treaties and resolutions; in addition, its wide range of protections have acquired force under customary international law by virtue of the near universal State acceptance of the rights and principles enshrined therein.

There are myriad quotes celebrating freedom of movement as the first and most fundamental of human liberties, stating that the world order depends on freedom of movement, or asserting that liberty of movement is an indispensable condition for the free development of a person. Every contemporary writer on public international law deems it necessary to revert to the long list of famous publicists having allegedly supported the principle of free movement as deriving from international morality and being consistent with sovereignty: Bodin, Grotius, Vattel, Pufendorf, Vitoria, Locke and Rousseau are cited as examples.

The UDHR is indeed the cornerstone for recognising and respecting individual liberties and freedoms. Article 13 affirms that:

---

7 Louis Sohn and Thomas Buergenthal, 'The Movement of Persons Across Borders' (1992) 23 *Studies in Transnational Legal Policy* 1.

8 In particular, art. 1(3) includes the purpose of promoting and encouraging respect for human rights and fundamental freedoms; art. 13(1) states that the General Assembly shall undertake initiatives to assist in the realisation of human rights and fundamental freedoms; art. 55 states that the United Nations shall promote universal respect for, and observance of, human rights and fundamental freedoms for all; and art. 56 provides that all members of the United Nations pledge to take joint and separate action for the achievement of the purposes set forth in art. 55.

9 *Legal Consequences for States of the Continued Presence of South Africa in Namibia (South West Africa) notwithstanding Security Council Resolution 276 (1970) (Advisory Opinion)* [1971] ICJ Rep 16, [131].

10 *Universal Declaration of Human Rights*, GA Res 217A (III), UN Doc A/810 (10 December 1948).

Everyone has the right to freedom of movement and residence within the border of each State. Everyone has the right to leave any country, including his own, and to return to his country.

When looking at human rights instruments adopted after the Second World War, it is clear that all of them, at the universal and regional levels, recognise the free movement of persons along the same lines as the UDHR. The *International Covenant on Civil and Political Rights* (1966) ('ICCPR') gives freedom of movement a firm and broad conventional basis, and has been widely ratified.[11] According to art. 12:

2 Everyone shall be free to leave any country, including his own.

3 The above-mentioned rights shall not be subject to any restrictions except those which are provided by law, are necessary to protect national security, public order (*ordre public*), public health or morals or the rights and freedoms of others, and are consistent with the other rights recognized in the present Covenant.

4 No one shall be arbitrarily deprived of the right to enter his own country.

Other universal instruments adopted under the auspices of the United Nations reaffirm the provisions of the ICCPR. Article 5 of the *International Convention on the Elimination of All Forms of Racial Discrimination* (1965) imposes on States parties the obligation to guarantee 'the enjoyment of the ... right to leave any country, including one's own, and to return to one's country'.[12] Moreover, the *International Convention on the Suppression and Punishment of the Crime of Apartheid* (1973),[13] the *Convention on the Rights of the Child* (1989)[14] and the *International Convention on the Protection of the Rights of All Migrant Workers and Members of their Families* (1990) ('ICRMW')[15] confirm the right to leave and the right to return. The latter convention aims to protect migrant workers and their families and imposes sanctions on organisers who facilitate irregular movements of undocumented workers.

At the universal level, the United Nations, through its Human Rights Commission, has conducted in-depth studies on the right to freedom of movement. In 1963, the Special Rapporteur, Judge José Inglés, produced a comprehensive report and a list of draft principles on freedom of movement and non-discrimination in this context.[16] This study was updated in 1988 by Special Rapporteur C. L. C. Mubanga-Chipoya to

---

11 *International Covenant on Civil and Political Rights*, opened for signature 16 December 1966, 999 UNTS 171 (entered into force 23 March 1976). There were 167 States parties in late 2011.

12 *International Convention on the Elimination of All Forms of Racial Discrimination*, opened for signature 21 December 1965, 660 UNTS 195 (entered into force 4 January 1969).

13 *International Convention on the Suppression and Punishment of the Crime of Apartheid*, opened for signature 30 November 1973, 1015 UNTS 243 (entered into force 18 July 1976).

14 *Convention on the Rights of the Child*, opened for signature 20 November 1989, 1577 UNTS 3 (entered into force 2 September 1990).

15 *International Convention on the Protection of the Rights of All Migrant Workers and Members of their Families*, opened for signature 18 December 1990, 2220 UNTS 3 (entered into force 1 July 2003).

16 José Inglés, 'Study of Discrimination in Respect of the Right of Everyone to Leave Any Country, Including His Own, and to Return to His Country' (UN Doc E/CN.4/Sub.2/229/Rev.1, United Nations, 1963).

include an analysis of trends and developments,[17] and again in 1997 by Special Rapporteur Volodymyr Boutkevitch.[18] The studies illustrate that the fundamental rights to leave any country and return to one's own country are equally applicable to migrants.

At the regional level, freedom of movement has found its legal expression in all relevant human rights instruments. In Europe, art. 2 of *Protocol 4 to the European Convention for the Protection of Human Rights and Fundamental Freedoms* (1963) states that:

2 Everyone shall be free to leave any country, including his own.
3 No restrictions shall be placed on the exercise of these rights other than such as are in accordance with law and are necessary in a democratic society in the interests of national security or public safety, for the maintenance of *ordre public*, for the prevention of crime, for the protection of health or morals, or for the protection of the rights and freedoms of others.[19]

Moreover, art. 3(2) adds that: 'No one shall be deprived of the right to enter the territory of the State of which he is a national.' The right to leave and the right to return have been recalled in other treaties, such as the *European Social Charter* (1961)[20] and the *European Convention on the Legal Status of Migrant Workers* (1977).[21]

In the Americas, the principles of the *American Declaration of the Rights and Duties of Man* (1948)[22] and art. 22 of the *American Convention on Human Rights* (1969)[23] include the right to leave and the right to return in similar terms to *Protocol 4 to the European Convention for the Protection of Human Rights and Fundamental Freedoms*.

In Africa, the *African Charter on Human and Peoples' Rights* (1981) has a similar provision.[24] Article 12(2) states that: 'Every individual shall have the right to leave any country including his own, and to return to his country. This right may only be subject to restrictions, provided for by law for the protection of national security, law and order, public health or morality.' In the Middle East and North Africa, the right to leave and the right to return have been reiterated in the *Arab Charter on Human Rights* (1994), as revised in 2004.[25]

17 C. Mubanga-Chipoya, 'Analysis of the Current Trends and Developments Regarding the Right to Leave any Country including One's Own, and to Return to One's Own Country, and Some Other Rights or Considerations Arising Therefrom: Final Report' (UN Doc, E/CN.4/Sub.2/1988/35, United Nations, 1988).
18 Commission on Human Rights, 'Working Paper on the Right to Freedom of Movement and Related Issues' (UN Doc E/CN.4/Sub.2/1997/22, 1997), prepared by Volodymyr Boutkevitch.
19 *Protocol 4 to the European Convention for the Protection of Human Rights and Fundamental Freedoms*, opened for signature 16 September 1963, ETS 46 (entered into force 2 May 1968).
20 *European Social Charter*, opened for signature 18 October 1961, CETS No 35 (entered into force 26 February 1965).
21 *European Convention on the Legal Status of Migrant Workers*, opened for signature 24 November 1977, ETS No 93 (entered into force 1 May 1983).
22 *American Declaration of the Rights and Duties of Man*, OAS Res XXX, OAS Treaty Series No 36, Adopted by the Ninth International Conference of American States (1948), 297.
23 *American Convention on Human Rights*, opened for signature 22 November 1969, 1144 UNTS 123 (entered into force 18 July 1978).
24 *African Charter on Human and Peoples' Rights*, opened for signature 27 June 1981, 1520 UNTS 217 (entered into force 21 October 1986).
25 *Arab Charter on Human Rights*, opened for signature 15 September 1994, 12 International Human Rights Reports 893 (entered into force 15 March 2008).

From the above overview of human rights instruments, it appears that freedom of movement should be understood as a principle of high political importance,[26] not just as a monolithic right. This principle is composed of three elements and each needs a separate analysis to understand its true significance. These elements are: first, the right to leave any country, including his or her own country; second, the right to enter or return to his or her own country; and third, the right of everyone who is found lawfully within the territory of a State to enjoy liberty of movement and freedom to choose his or her residence within that territory. Although the right of movement within a territory is not covered by this chapter, it is worth noting that the three elements are closely intertwined: the right to leave and the right to return 'flow inexorably from the right of freedom of movement and residence within the border of a State'.[27]

To argue that freedom of movement is a right leads to the conclusion that there is no effective or full implementation of such a right in practice. Notwithstanding this point, the fact remains that the situation in the twentieth and twenty-first centuries represents a departure from what had been the social norm in past centuries. Previously, the norm was not to place limitations on free movement, but rather to create avenues for its expansion. When there were no States in the modern sense of the term, free movement could easily flourish: when modern States were created and their geographical borders delineated, nationalism led States to impose restrictions on freedom of movement, especially on the movement of non-nationals.

5.3. REGULATING ENTRY

5.3.1. The entry of nationals

From a conceptual viewpoint, concomitant to the right to leave is the guarantee to be admitted into another country after the departure from one's own country. However, in international law, nationals of one country do not have the right of entry into another country; the right to leave and the right to enter are not symmetrical. The right to leave is incomplete because the effective exercise of the right is contingent upon the right to enter another country.

The right of return to one's own country was originally considered as the only realistic means to strengthen the right to leave, hence the emphasis on right to

---

26 See, e.g., art. 2 of the Constitution of the International Organization for Migration, stating that membership is open to States 'with a demonstrated interest in the principle of free movement of persons'.

27 Rosalyn Higgins, 'The Right in International Law of an Individual to Enter, Stay in and Leave a Country' (1973) 49(3) *International Affairs* 341, 342. The right to move freely within the territory of a State and to choose one's place of residence applies to both nationals and migrants; however, the latter may benefit from this right only if they are lawfully within the territory of the State. States imposing restrictions on migrants to move freely and choose residence have to ensure that such restrictions are consistent with the grounds listed in art. 12(3) of the ICCPR.

return instead of right to enter. However, nowadays the question remains open – what link must exist between an individual and a State for a right to return to apply? Some regional conventions expressly restrict the right of return to nationals of a State. On the other hand, the African Charter makes reference to 'his country' or 'his own country' without stating that a nationality link must exist. This applies equally to the UDHR and the ICCPR. It is commonly accepted that this broad and somewhat ambiguous expression of the right to return applies to both nationals and permanent residents found in the territory of States.[28] According to General Comment No 27 of the UN Human Rights Committee:

> The right of a person to enter his or her own country recognises the special relationship of a person to that country. The right has various facets. It implies the right to remain in one's own country. It includes not only the right to return after having left one's own country; it may also entitle a person to come to the country for the first time if he or she was born outside the country (e.g. if that country is the person's state of nationality) ... The wording of [art. 12(4)] does not distinguish between nationals and aliens ('no one'). Thus, the persons entitled to exercise this right can be identified only by interpreting the meaning of the phrase 'his own country'. The scope of 'his own country' is broader than the concept of 'country of nationality'. It is not limited to nationality in a formal sense, that is, nationality acquired at birth or by conferral; it embraces, at the very least, an individual who, because of his or her special ties to or claims in relation to a given country cannot be considered to be a mere alien. ... The language of [art. 12(4)] more-over, permits a broader interpretation that might embrace other categories of long-term residents, including but not limited to stateless persons arbitrarily deprived of the right to acquire the nationality of the country of such residence. In no case may a person be arbitrarily deprived of the right to enter his or her own country.[29]

Hence the right to return applies to both nationals of the State and stateless persons. According to para 13 of the Schedule to the *Convention relating to the Status of Stateless Persons* (1954),[30] a stateless person is entitled to be a recipient of a travel document and has the right to re-enter the territory of the issuing State at any time during the period of validity of the document (see Chapter 4).

The corollary of the right of a national to enter his or her own State is the obligation of a State to admit or readmit its nationals. This is now considered a norm of customary international law, deriving from a State's sovereignty, and States are thus obliged to admit their own nationals expelled from abroad. Whether this customary rule applies also to the readmission of non-nationals who have resided in the receiving State for a long period is debatable, but State practice tends to give a positive response.

---

28 See Hurst Hannum, *The Right to Leave and Return in International Law and Practice* (Martinus Nijhoff, 1987) 56–7, and art. 7 of the *Strasbourg Declaration* (1986), reproduced in Appendix F, 154–8.

29 Human Rights Committee, *General Comment No 27: Freedom of Movement* (Article 12), 67th sess, UN Doc CCPR/C/21/Rev.1/Add.9 (2 November 1999). See also Sohn and Buergenthal, above n. 7, 7.

30 *Convention relating to the Status of Stateless Persons*, opened for signature 28 September 1954, 360 UNTS 117 (entered into force 6 June 1960). The term 'stateless person' means a person who is not considered as a national by any State under the operation of its law: art. 1(1).

5.3.2. The admission of migrants

States exercise authority to decide on the admission of non-nationals, defining classes of admissible migrants and establishing grounds for refusing admission. In exercising this authority, States must act in accordance with the principle of non-discrimination; they should refrain from adopting laws or policies that are intrinsically discriminatory and make sure that administrative decisions taken by immigration officers in individual cases do not result in discrimination. Entry is governed by the laws and regulations of each State, but 'the conditions and procedures for entry shall conform to generally accepted principles of international law and applicable international agreements'.[31]

States, therefore, have wide discretion to decide on the admission of migrants. Conditions include the number or quota permitted each year, qualifications needed, length of stay, and rights and obligations once granted admission. As a standard, permanent residents and temporary residents are seen as separate categories. Temporary residents include international students, tourists, visitors and temporary workers. Permanent residents are subject to stricter conditions and preference for certain categories of people – for example, family members and relatives; employment-based categories (skilled workers, investors, entrepreneurs); and refugees and others considered on humanitarian grounds. To be eligible for admission, a potential immigrant must, first, fit into one of the migration streams recognised by the receiving State, and, second, not be inadmissible – that is, exclusionary grounds, such as disease or ill health, security-related concerns, lack of economic means or criminal history, should not apply to the particular individual. The categories of exclusion and the requirements to be met to enter another country reflect a number of concerns, ranging from national security to the economic and cultural impact of new arrivals.

The arguments supporting some of these exclusions include the potential for migrants to make excessive demands on health and social services. However, waivers may be granted to some categories of migrants who are visiting for shorter periods. It has been argued that tourists pose a limited risk to public health, while applicants for temporary or permanent status may be denied admission if they test positive for HIV. In this context, refugees are generally subject to the same entry conditions as other immigrants, but very often benefit from a waiver if they suffer from contagious diseases. This is due to the forced nature of their movements and each State's obligation of *non-refoulement*, which is discussed further below.

Exclusionary grounds, as well as their interpretation and implementation, have evolved over time and vary from country to country. Exclusion on the basis of health provides a good illustration. The main criterion for exclusion has been dangerous contagious diseases, usually associated with social stigmatisation,

---

31 Sohn and Buergenthal, above n. 7, 49–64. See also International Migrants Bill of Rights (draft), (2010) 24(3) *Georgetown Immigration Law Journal* 423.

such as tuberculosis, leprosy and venereal diseases. More recently, AIDS and HIV infection have been added to the list, although this remains the subject of heated debate. Research seems to indicate that health-related entry restrictions, in particular HIV-related grounds, serve no useful public health purpose. For instance, international organisations have concluded that HIV travel restrictions are ineffective and counterproductive, and such exclusionary measures are sometimes linked to what is referred to as an 'isolation ritual' (see Box 5.1). The exclusion may seek to bind together the persons carrying out the isolation, or may even be explained by the influence of nativism.[32] In 2010, the United States lifted its restrictions on HIV-positive people entering the country, admitting that the twenty-two-year ban, which affected both visitors and persons wishing to reside in the country, was premised on fear rather than fact.

Some well-defined categories of persons are entitled to enter and stay in a country of which they are not nationals on the basis of international conventions and customary law. The first group comprises diplomats and consuls accredited to a given State: once accredited, these officials have the right to enter the receiving State's territory without having to fulfil any of the requirements to be met by ordinary migrants. The second group comprises representatives of member States to the United Nations system, other international organisations and regional organisations. These benefits also apply to officials of organisations as defined in relevant conventions or bilateral agreements concluded between the State and the organisation. A third group comprises members of armed forces, to the extent foreseen in the constitutive instrument of a military organisation, or in a bilateral agreement concluded between the States concerned.

A last exception, based on customary international law, comprises persons faced with a situation of *force majeure*, such as shipwrecked vessels and aircraft in distress. Where individuals are obliged to seek safe haven in a foreign State, the State has a duty to admit such persons on humanitarian grounds and not to impose penalties for infringement of immigration rules. This duty is without prejudice to the State's right to return the individuals to their country of origin.

5.3.3.   The admission and non-rejection of persons at risk

Specific categories of persons enjoy special protection under international law, particularly when the national protection of his or her country is deficient. The main group that falls into this category is refugees under international law (see Chapter 7). Under the *Convention relating to the Status of Refugees* (1951) ('Refugee

---

32 Margaret Somerville and Sarah Wilson, 'Crossing Boundaries: Travel, Immigration, Human Rights and AIDS' (1997) 43 *McGill Law Journal* 781.

BOX 5.1 UNAIDS/IOM recommendations regarding HIV/AIDS-related travel restrictions (2004)[33]

1 HIV/AIDS should not be considered to be a condition that poses a threat to public health in relation to travel because, although it is infectious, the human immunodeficiency virus cannot be transmitted by the mere presence of a person with HIV in a country or by casual contact ... Restrictive measures can in fact run counter to public health interests, since exclusion of HIV-infected non-nationals adds to the climate of stigma and discrimination against people living with HIV and AIDS, and may thus deter nationals and non-nationals alike from coming forward to utilize HIV prevention and care services ...

2 Any HIV testing related to entry and stay should be done voluntarily, on the basis of informed consent ...

3 Restrictions against entry or stay that are based on health conditions, including HIV/AIDS, should be implemented in such a way that human rights obligations are met, including the principle of non-discrimination, *non-refoulement* of refugees, the right to privacy, protection of the family, protection of the rights of migrants, and protection of the best interests of the child. Compelling humanitarian needs should also be given due weight ...

6 Exclusion on the basis of possible costs to healthcare and social assistance related to a health condition should only be considered where it is shown, through individual assessment, that the person requires such health and social assistance; is likely in fact to use it in the relatively near future; and has no other means of meeting such costs ... and that these costs will not be offset through benefits that exceed them ...

7 If a person living with HIV/AIDS is subject to expulsion (deportation), such expulsion (deportation) should be consistent with international legal obligations including entitlement to due process of law and access to the appropriate means to challenge the expulsion. Consideration should be given to compelling reasons of a humanitarian nature justifying authorisation for the person to remain ...

Convention')[34] and its 1967 Protocol,[35] States have accepted an important limitation to their right to admit and expel. According to art. 33 of the Refugee Convention, when a person arrives at the border of a State and seeks refuge, the State is obliged not to return the asylum seeker to the frontier of a territory where his or her life or freedom would be threatened on account of persecution. This is the internationally accepted obligation of *non-refoulement*. It applies regardless of lawful or unlawful entry into the territory of the State. States have the obligation not to expel refugees, except on grounds of national security or public order. *Non-refoulement* therefore covers the case of non-rejection at the border, as well as refugees who entered the territory legally, irregularly or without documentation. A similar protection is extended to persons benefitting from complementary or subsidiary protection.

There is a divergence of opinion on the legal nature of the 'principle' of *non-refoulement* – that is, whether it has become a rule of customary law or remains a mere treaty obligation binding only those States that are party to the treaty. The difference

---

33 See also International Labour Organization, 'Recommendation concerning HIV and AIDS and the World of Work' (No 200, 17 June 2010).

34 *Convention relating to the Status of Refugees*, opened for signature 28 July 1951, 189 UNTS 150 (entered into force 22 April 1954).

35 *Protocol relating to the Status of Refugees*, opened for accession 31 January 1967, 606 UNTS 267 (entered into force 4 October 1967).

of opinion on this point has obfuscated the fact that, under both the Refugee Convention and relevant human rights instruments, the primary objective is to safeguard the physical integrity of the individual, and to protect the right to life and the right not to be tortured or suffer inhuman and degrading treatment. These are the rights or principles to be protected, and *non-refoulement* is simply a means for achieving it.

The national security motive is increasingly used as an exclusionary ground. Although this seems to be equated with the increase in terrorist activities, terrorism may cover a broader range of conduct that does not necessarily represent a threat to national security. The 'war on terrorism' may also lead to migrants being sent back to a country where there is a credible risk of torture or threat to life. In addition, the practice of rendition or extraordinary rendition may be used by officials to detain and interrogate non-nationals without the standard safeguards of criminal law: this constitutes a violation of international human rights. Extraordinary rendition 'is a policy which involves the secret detention and subsequent extrajudicial transfer or removal of individuals suspected of links to terrorist activity to countries with poor prison conditions and where interrogation under torture is routine, for the purpose of arrest, detention, and/or interrogation by the receiving State'.[36]

The prohibition of torture and cruel, inhuman or degrading treatment or punishment is enshrined in many international instruments at the universal and regional levels, most notably in the *Convention against Torture and Other Cruel, Inhuman or Degrading Treatment or Punishment* (1984) ('Convention against Torture').[37] This limitation on the State's power to expel derives from art. 3, stating that 'no State shall expel, return or extradite a person to another State where there are substantial grounds for believing that he or she would be in danger of being subjected to torture'. A similar limitation derives from art. 7 of the ICCPR, prohibiting torture or cruel, inhuman or degrading treatment or punishment. States are not only prohibited from inflicting torture or other inhuman or degrading treatment, they are also under an obligation not to place a migrant under their jurisdiction in a situation in which that individual could be subjected to such treatment. This implicit obligation derives from the nature of the right, and the indirect protection extended to such persons is referred to as protection by 'ricochet'. The obligation imposed on States not to expel a migrant who may be subjected to torture in a transit country or country of destination is absolute: no derogation is possible, even in times of war, other public emergency or compelling situations of national security. The prohibition of torture is a customary norm and applies both in peacetime and in armed conflict situations. It is a positive and negative right: States have an obligation to prohibit torture and to prevent its occurrence by taking all measures necessary to pre-empt the perpetration

36 Carla Ferstman, 'The Human Security Framework and Counter-Terrorism: Examining the Rhetoric relating to "Extraordinary Renditions"' in Alice Edwards and Carla Ferstman (eds.), *Human Security and Non-Citizens: Law, Policy and International Affairs* (Cambridge University Press, 2010) 532.
37 *Convention against Torture and Other Cruel, Inhuman or Degrading Treatment or Punishment*, opened for signature 10 December 1984, 1465 UNTS 85 (entered into force 26 June 1987).

of torture. However, the question remains open: does the obligation not to return or expel also exist when torture or inhuman treatment would be inflicted not by State organs, but by non-State actors or individuals acting in their private capacity?[38]

5.3.4. State security and terrorism

A central feature of sovereignty is the power of a State to defend its own borders and protect its national security. Not all rights are absolute; international human rights law permits the derogation from certain human rights on limited grounds. In times of public emergency or threat to national security, derogation from a number of rights is permitted. As seen in the context of expulsions, States sometimes display little hesitation in making broad use of their sovereign power and ignoring human rights obligations, particularly in the name of national security. States often overlook the proviso that the derogation should be justified, necessary and proportionate. The non-admission, exclusion or expulsion of migrants suspected of posing a threat to national security is firmly established in State practice. National security, as a ground for non-admission, usually focusses on support for terrorist activities or participation in genocide, torture, extrajudicial killing, espionage, sabotage or other unlawful activities.[39]

National security has always been an issue of concern to States, and the tension between allowing new arrivals and safeguarding the interests of the existing population has long existed. However, since the terrorist attacks on the United States on 11 September 2001, national security has been brought sharply into focus, heightening the concern that foreigners can pose a real threat to the security and safety of a country and its nationals. After the attacks, the United Nations Security Council adopted a resolution asking States to prevent the movement of terrorists or terrorist groups by 'effective border controls and controls on issuance of identity papers and travel documents'.[40]

As a result, migrants are regarded with more suspicion than before – whether they be asylum seekers, refugees, trafficked persons or economically motivated, many are seen, unjustifiably, as potential enemies. The threat of terrorism is being used increasingly to justify actions against migrants. This has the potential to discriminate against them, or to place limitations on the enjoyment of their rights. Migration law and procedures are becoming tools to combat terrorism because international terrorism is very often seen as a migration issue. This is a highly questionable assertion, as the fight against terrorism remains principally a matter of law enforcement. Migration is thus seen through the law enforcement lens, often without due regard for human rights. Migrant profiling at border points has also become widespread.

---

38 Maurice Kamto, 'Fifth Report on the Expulsions of Aliens' (UN Doc A/CN.4/611, International Law Commission, 27 March 2009) 27–41.

39 Elizabeth Bruch, 'Open or Closed: Balancing Border Policy with Human Rights' (2007–8) 96 *Kentucky Law Journal* 197.

40 *UN Security Council Resolution 1373*, UN Doc S/RES/1373 (28 September 2001).

A number of States have taken action to tighten immigration systems through measures such as the use of biometric systems (e.g., fingerprints, facial recognition and iris patterns) for identification, verification and screening of specific categories of non-nationals in their territory. Other measures include increased data exchange, border controls, tighter entry controls such as passenger pre-clearance, and posting of immigration or airline liaison officers.[41] Conservative voices and anti-immigrant feelings have encouraged the adoption of strict immigration policies, even though it is now admitted that immigration control can only be a 'needle in a haystack' measure to counter terrorism. While the arguments put forward for strengthening or closing borders are closely linked to the concept of sovereignty and national security, they also reflect anxieties about the economic, social and cultural impact of potential immigrants in the country. There is a growing tendency to view migration law as a political issue, without acknowledging the human rights dimension or the positive aspects of regulated migration.

Finding the appropriate balance between facilitating migration, protecting human rights, and border control is a key challenge for all countries attempting to secure their territories and keep their nationals safe. It is understandable that States are concerned about the risks posed by terrorism and the capacity of terrorist groups to exploit weaknesses in border control and migration management. Where such weaknesses exist, there is certainly a need for improved security. However, security measures must be justified by, and proportionate to, the level of threat faced by States, particularly if increased security results in potential restrictions on privacy and other human rights. Any such measures should recognise that migration control is not the primary tool in the fight against terrorism.

The Supreme Court of the United States once stated that:

> to preserve its independence, and give security against foreign . . . encroachment, is the highest duty of every nation . . . It matters not in what form such . . . encroachment come[s], whether from the foreign nation acting in its national character, or from vast hordes of its people crowding in upon us . . . If, therefore, the government . . . considers the presence of foreigners of a different race in this country, who will not assimilate with us, to be dangerous to its peace and security, their exclusion is not to be stayed.[42]

This judgment is somewhat outdated. However, on closer consideration, a judgment issued today by some national courts would differ in language but not in substance from the Supreme Court's view in 1889 – the balance between human rights considerations and national security imperatives would still tilt in favour of the latter.

---

41 See Rey Koslowski, 'The Evolution of Border Controls as a Mechanism to Prevent Illegal Immigration' (Migration Policy Institute, 2011), where it is noted that illegal immigration is probably more a function of demand for irregular migrant labour than a function of fencing.
42 *Chan Chae Ping* v. *United States ('Chinese Exclusion Case')*, 130 US 581 (1889), 606.

5.4. REGULATING EXIT

5.4.1. The right to leave

Article 12(2) of the ICCPR states that 'everyone shall be free to leave any country, including his own'. The legal content of this right may be summarised in five points:

- The right makes no distinction between nationals and non-nationals (migrants), and, among the latter category, makes no distinction between non-nationals who are documented or in an irregular situation.
- The right covers any form of travel, irrespective of the duration of the intended stay in the foreign country; it covers the temporary stay of a tourist as well as the permanent stay of an immigrant. The motivation for the travel is irrelevant, as is the intended destination.
- The right to leave imposes on the State of residency a duty of abstention, namely, a duty not to impose arbitrary restrictions on the wishes of an individual to leave the country.
- The right to leave confers no automatic right on the individual to be admitted into the territory of another State, except his or her own country of nationality. Similarly, seen from the State's perspective, the right to leave does not impose an obligation on any State to admit the individual exercising his or her right to leave, except if this individual is its own national.
- The right is not absolute and may be subject to restrictions.

Article 12(3) of the ICCPR provides for exceptional circumstances in which the right to leave may be subject to limitations. This provision authorises the State to impose restrictions only to protect national security, public order (*ordre public*), public health or morals, and the rights and freedoms of others. Furthermore, any restriction must be: provided by law, necessary in a democratic society for the protection of the stated purposes and consistent with all other rights recognised in the ICCPR.

National security is a standard ground on which to deny permission to leave a country. It is an argument frequently criticised because of its vagueness. National security can be interpreted broadly, and may even deprive a person of the right to leave his or her country of nationality. A general prohibition on leaving on the basis of national security would be permissible only in times of armed conflict or public emergency; beyond these cases, the refusal is acceptable only if a particular person is seriously suspected of being willing to engage abroad in activities prejudicial to the security of his or her own State.

In times of international armed conflict, art. 35 of the *Geneva Convention relative to the Protection of Civilian Persons in Time of War* (1949) ('Fourth Geneva Convention') entitles all protected persons who may desire to leave the territory at the outset of, or during, a conflict to do so, unless their departure is contrary to the national interests of the State.[43]

As stated earlier, public order, health or morals also constitute grounds for limiting the right to leave. Some cases are evident – for instance, criminals such as human traffickers and smugglers who are prevented from leaving the country pending criminal proceedings. The same applies to persons evading justice, execution of a sentence, outstanding military service obligations, payment of taxes or maintenance of family members. Other cases are less obvious – for example, the restrictions placed on the movement of nationals in order to prevent brain drain.[44] However, the justification of any such limitation, and its duration, has to be assessed on a case-by-case basis.

The law itself has to establish the modalities under which rights may be restricted; otherwise it leaves unfettered discretion to those responsible for implementing and enforcing the law. Restrictions on the right to leave, therefore, should be firmly embedded in the provisions of the law. Restrictions that are not defined in the law on legitimate and necessary grounds or that are contrary to the requirements of art. 12(3) would violate the rights guaranteed in the ICCPR. In authorising restrictions on the right to leave, States should bear in mind that the restriction must not impair the essence of the right and that the exceptions must not be expanded to the point where they subsume the underlying right; in addition, any restriction is strictly and narrowly construed.[45] Principally, the laws authorising restrictions must use precise criteria and should not confer unfettered discretion on those implementing them.

Article 12(3) of the ICCPR further indicates that it is not sufficient that the limitations serve a legitimate purpose; they must, in addition, be necessary to protect the stated purpose. Restrictions must be consistent with the principles of proportionality and necessity; they must be appropriate to fulfil their protection role and proportionate to the interest they seek to protect. Any restriction must also be the least intrusive means among those that could achieve the desired result. It is, therefore, evident that the application of restrictions in individual cases must be based on clear legal grounds and must respond to the requirements of necessity and proportionality.[46]

The UN Human Rights Committee has highlighted many of the questionable barriers to exit imposed by States, which it has described in *General Comment No 27* in the following terms, and which are further illustrated in Case Study 5.1:

---

43 *Geneva Convention relative to the Protection of Civilian Persons in Time of War*, opened for signature 12 August 1949, 75 UNTS 287 (entered into force 21 October 1950).

44 Hannum, above n. 28, 34–41; Sohn and Buergenthal, above n. 7, 78.   45 Hannum, above n. 28, 21–4.

46 Vincent Chetail, 'Freedom of Movement and Transnational Migrations: A Human Rights Perspective' in Alexander Aleinikoff and Vincent Chetail (eds.), *Migration and International Legal Norms* (TMC Asser Press, 2003) 47–57. For examples of the application of restrictions, see Colin Harvey and Robert Barnidge, 'Human Rights, Free Movement and the Right to Leave in International Law' (2007) 19 *International Journal of Refugee Law* 1.

A major source of concern is the manifold legal and bureaucratic barriers unnecessarily affecting the full enjoyment of the rights of the individuals to move freely, to leave a country, including their own, and to take up residence. Regarding the right to movement within a country, the Committee has criticized provisions requiring individuals to apply for permission to change their residence or to seek the approval of the local authorities of the place of destination, as well as delays in processing such written applications. States' practice presents an even richer array of obstacles making it more difficult to leave the country, in particular for their own nationals. These rules and practices include, *inter alia*, lack of access for applicants to the competent authorities and lack of information regarding requirements; the requirement to apply for special forms through which the proper application documents for the issuance of a passport can be obtained; the need for supportive statements from employers or family members; exact description of the travel route; issuance of passports only on payment of high fees substantially exceeding the cost of the service rendered by the administration; unreasonable delays in the issuance of travel documents; restrictions on family members travelling together; requirement of a repatriation deposit or a return ticket; requirement of an invitation from the State of destination or from people living there; harassment of applicants, for example by physical intimidation, arrest, loss of employment or expulsion of their children from school or university; refusal to issue a passport because the applicant is said to harm the good name of the country.[47]

Another restriction on the right to leave derives from the *Protocol against the Smuggling of Migrants by Land, Sea and Air, Supplementing the United Nations Convention against Transnational Organized Crime* (2000) ('Smuggling Protocol'),[48] which is discussed further in Chapter 9. The Smuggling Protocol requires States to prevent migrants from leaving their territory by unauthorised or irregular means. It imposes on States specific obligations with regard to border measures, control and security, as well as validity of travel and identity documents. While criminal liability of smuggled migrants is excluded, this does not authorise migrants to leave their country by irregular means. To reconcile the right to leave as protected in the ICCPR and the fight against smuggling of migrants, the provisions of the Smuggling Protocol should be interpreted in light of the ICCPR, and any restriction imposed on the right of smuggled migrants to leave should be consistent with the restrictions provided in art. 12(3) of the ICCPR. Specifically, the restriction must fall under one of the listed grounds. It is yet to be determined whether implementation of the Smuggling Protocol will lead to a broad interpretation of the restrictions permitted by the ICCPR, and hence a further limitation of the right to leave, in the fight against irregular migration.

While the right to leave is entrenched in international conventional and customary law, its application shows differences of treatment between nationals and migrants. Foreign nationals or migrants are generally free to leave their State of residence without obstacle, unless there are reasons linked to the grounds in art. 12(3) of the ICCPR. Nationals are sometimes subject to more stringent conditions or restrictions when wishing to leave their country, especially in countries where democratic values, including respect for human rights, are not yet firmly established (see Case Study 5.2).

47 Human Rights Committee, above n. 29, [17].
48 *Protocol against the Smuggling of Migrants by Land, Sea and Air, Supplementing the United Nations Convention against Transnational Organized Crime*, opened for signature 15 November 2000, 2241 UNTS 507 (entered into force 28 January 2004).

CASE STUDY 5.1 The right to a passport

Loubna El Ghar v. *Libyan Arab Jamahiriya*, UN Human Rights Committee (2004)[49]

This claim was deemed by the Committee to fall under art. 12 of the *International Covenant on Civil and Political Rights* (ICCPR) as it involved the claimant's inability to obtain a passport without adequate justification by her government. The facts, as found by the Committee, were as follows.

Born in Morocco in 1981, Loubna El Ghar was 21 years old at the time she made her submission to the Committee. El Ghar lived in Morocco with her mother and had a Moroccan residence permit, though her nationality was of the Socialist People's Libyan Arab Jamahiriya, as this was her father's nationality and place of residence.

In September 1999, El Ghar submitted a passport application to the Passport and Nationality Department of the Socialist People's Libyan Arab Jamahiriya. The claimant stated that she was a student and required a passport to continue her legal studies abroad in France. El Ghar's passport application was refused and the Libyan Consul informed her that it was not possible to issue her a passport, but provided no reasons for this decision. Instead, they told her that they could issue her a *laissez-passer* which would allow her to return from Morocco to the Socialist People's Libyan Arab Jamahiriya. The Human Rights Committee stated (at para 7.2) that 'this laissez-passer cannot be considered a satisfactory substitute for a valid Libyan passport that would enable the author to travel abroad'.

In spite of an official communiqué from the Passport Department to the Libyan Consul in Morocco stating that the claimant should be issued a passport, a passport was never produced for her. At the time of the Committee meeting on 29 March 2004, the claimant had still not been issued a passport and had not received an explanation or justification as to why her requests were refused.

The Committee stated (at para 7.3):

> that a passport provides a national with the means 'to leave any country, including his own', as stipulated in [art. 12(2)] of the Covenant, and that owing to the very nature of the right in question, in the case of a national residing abroad [art. 12(2)] of the Covenant imposes obligations both on the individual's State of residence and on the State of nationality, and that [art. 12(1)] of the Covenant cannot be interpreted as limiting Libya's obligations under [art. 12(2)] to nationals living in its territory. The right recognized by [art. 12(2)] may, by virtue of paragraph 3 of that article, be subject to restrictions 'which are provided by law [and] are necessary to protect national security, public order (*ordre public*), public health or morals or the rights and freedoms of others, and are consistent with the other rights recognized in the present Covenant'. Thus there are circumstances in which a State may, if the law so provides, refuse to issue a passport to one of its nationals. In the present case, however, the State party has not put forward any such argument in the information it has submitted to the Committee but has actually assured the Committee that it issued instructions to ensure that the author's passport application was successful, a statement that was not in fact followed up.

El Ghar's inability to obtain a passport and the lack of justification provided by her government was therefore found by the Committee to be a violation of art. 12(2) of the ICCPR.

49 *Loubna El Ghar* v. *Libyan Arab Jamahiriya*, UN Human Rights Committee, UN Doc CCPR/C/82/D/1107/2002 (15 November 2004).

CASE STUDY 5.2 The right to leave China and North Korea

Chinese legislation imposes an obligation on its nationals to obtain exit documents.[50] The law was formulated in 1985 as part of the first legal recognition of the right of Chinese nationals to leave the country. Also relevant are the *Regulations of the People's Republic of China on Exit and Entry Frontier Inspection*, adopted in 1995.[51] Under the law, Chinese nationals are not required to apply for visas to exit the country, but are required to apply to the proper bureaucratic institution for permission to leave the country, granted as an exit certificate or exit registration form (arts. 2, 5–7). Nationals applying to exit under art. 5 – for private purposes – shall be granted approval unless they fall under the categories of exclusion listed in art. 8. This provision states that approval to exit China shall not be granted to persons falling within listed categories, including those involved in civil or criminal litigation, persons undergoing rehabilitation through labour, and persons whose exit from the country will, in the opinion of the competent department of China's State Council, be harmful to State security or cause a major loss to national interests. Nationals applying under arts. 6 or 7 require the involvement of their work units, which must also approve their exit.

Since reforms in 2001, which have spread through at least 80 per cent of large and medium-sized cities in China, the process for getting a passport has been simplified for private nationals by abolishing the requirement that the applicants provide written permission from their work units and invitation letters from abroad. These reforms, however, do not extend to individuals working in public affairs, who must still provide proof of permission from their work units when applying for a passport.

The broad wording of some exclusion grounds leaves it to the discretion of the State authorities as to whether an individual is granted approval, though they may otherwise be eligible to travel. While on its face the law requiring Chinese nationals to seek approval and an exit certificate prior to leaving the country seems to be an assertion of the right to leave, in practice this process still gives State authorities wide discretionary power in recognising or denying this right to Chinese nationals.

Nationals of the Democratic People's Republic of Korea ('DPRK') have the right under national law to 'reside in or travel to any place'; however, DPRK nationals are prohibited by art. 62 of the DPRK Criminal Code from travelling outside the DPRK without first obtaining the permission of the State in the form of an exit document. In practice, exit visas are generally only granted to small numbers of government officials, business persons, artists, athletes, academics and religious figures, in violation of the freedom of movement obligations of a State party to the ICCPR, to which the DPRK acceded in 1981.

50 *Law of the People's Republic of China on the Control of the Exit and Entry of Citizens* (1 February 1986).
51 *Regulations of the People's Republic of China on Exit and Entry Frontier Inspection* (1 September 1995).

Internal migration is similarly controlled, with limited access for most nationals to Pyongyang.

Emigration is not permitted by the DPRK, and due to recent heightened security along its borders, the number of nationals who have been able to cross into neighbouring countries without an exit visa has dropped significantly since 2008. It is estimated that the number of DPRK nationals living in China without an exit visa ranges from tens of thousands to hundreds of thousands, though the Chinese government puts this number only in the hundreds. Defection is a crime under the DPRK Penal Code, and nationals who are convicted of defection or attempted defection are sentenced to a minimum of five years of 'labour correction', and can be sentenced to indefinite terms of imprisonment and forced labour, confiscation of property or death. Nationals who attempt to access foreign soil for the purposes of claiming asylum are considered defectors under DPRK law. The Special Rapporteur on the Situation of Human Rights in the DPRK has emphasised that presently the DPRK is not meeting its international obligations with regard to freedom of movement. The Special Rapporteur has also stressed that States in which DPRK nationals seek asylum must respect the international principle of *non-refoulement*, so as not to return the asylum seekers when their lives or freedoms may be threatened by such return.[52]

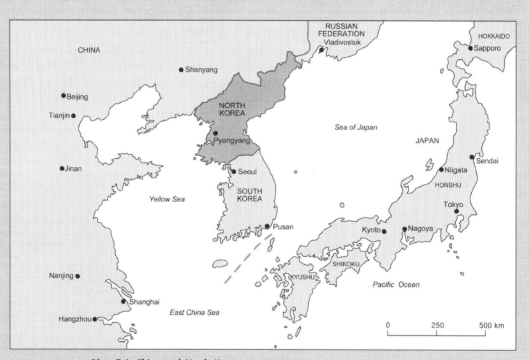

Map 5.1 China and North Korea

52 Human Rights Council, 'Report of the Special Rapporteur on the Situation of Human Rights in the Democratic People's Republic of Korea' (UN Doc A/HRC/16/58, 21 February 2011) [67], [71].

5.4.2. The obligation to leave

The right of a State to admit non-nationals into its territory, for a stated purpose and limited duration, implies the corollary right to request these non-nationals to leave the country at the end of the authorised stay. If the non-national has not left the country upon expiration of the authorised stay, or has otherwise breached the conditions of the stay, States may resort to expulsion and deportation procedures. International law places certain restraints on the manner in which States may expel non-nationals from its territory. The burden of proof is shifted to the individual to prove wrongful expulsion in contravention of the State's obligations under international law.

An expulsion order is the legal order given by a State to a non-national to leave the territory within a given period of time, specifically notifying him or her that failure to comply will lead to deportation or forced removal. Expulsion is, therefore, the prohibition to remain in the territory of the State, while deportation is the factual execution of the expulsion order.[53]

The right of States to expel is not disputed and is usually regarded as an attribute of sovereignty, but a balance must be struck between this sovereign right and the limits imposed by international law. Any person subject to expulsion is entitled to have his or her human rights respected, in particular the inviolable rights deriving from international law instruments. These include the right to life, the right to dignity, the right to integrity of the person, the right to non-discrimination, the right not to be subjected to torture or to inhuman or degrading treatment or punishment, and the right to family life. Procedurally, expulsion orders must be carried out in a dignified and safe manner.

A further limitation to the State's right to remove persons from its territory derives from the obligation to protect children and the unity of the family. As outlined in the *Convention on the Rights of the Child* (1989), the best interests of the child should be a primary consideration in all actions concerning the child (art. 3). The right of the child is paramount; all children should be afforded the same protection as national children. Before deciding to expel a migrant family member, the State must consider whether this separation from the family is proportionate to the public interest it purports to protect. The criterion is one of proportionality between maintenance of public order and security of the State on the one hand, and the need to maintain the unity of the family on the other. In addition, a risk assessment should be conducted prior to the deportation proceedings to ensure that the best interests of the child and the principle of *non-refoulement* are upheld.

---

53 On expulsion, see the reports of Mr Kamto to the International Law Commission: Maurice Kamto, 'Preliminary Report on the Expulsion of Aliens' (UN Doc A/CN.4/554, International Law Commission, 2 June 2005); Maurice Kamto, 'Second Report on the Expulsion of Aliens' (UN Doc A/CN.4/573 and Corr.1, International Law Commission, 20 July 2006); Maurice Kamto, 'Third Report on the Expulsion of Aliens' (UN Doc A/CN.4/581, International Law Commission, 19 April 2007); Maurice Kamto, 'Fourth Report on the Expulsion of Aliens' (UN Doc A/CN.4/594, International Law Commission, 24 March 2008); Kamto, above n. 38; Maurice Kamto, 'Sixth Report on the Expulsion of Aliens' (UN Doc A/CN.4/625 and Add.1, International Law Commission, 19 March 2010).

In addition to prohibiting *refoulement* of persons facing well-founded fear of persecution, the Refugee Convention and the Convention against Torture, as well as some regional instruments, prohibit States from deporting or extraditing persons in such circumstances. However, under art. 32 of the Refugee Convention, refugees may be expelled for reasons of national security and public order, and such expulsions may be ordered without a hearing if 'compelling reasons of national security' so require. In such cases, however, the refugee should be given a reasonable period within which to seek admission to another country. Under the Convention against Torture, no one may be sent to any country where they would be subject to torture, and there is no exception for national security.[54]

In all circumstances, the grounds for expulsion must be clearly stated in the national law. The usual grounds for expulsion appear to be limited to public order and national security, but State practice has revealed other grounds, such as conviction for a serious offence, irregular entry or stay, violation of national legislation, participation in undesirable political activities, and public health considerations. When assessing the legitimacy of the listed grounds and their conformity with international law, a further distinction ought to be made between migrants lawfully present and those who are undocumented or in an irregular situation. It is generally accepted that the irregular presence of a migrant in the territory of a State constitutes a sufficient ground for expulsion.

A migrant facing expulsion is entitled to the benefit of the procedural guarantees contained in human rights instruments. Even though international human rights law and humanitarian principles impose procedural requirements on expulsion, States retain a wide margin of discretion, as illustrated in art. 13 of the ICCPR, which provides:

An alien lawfully in the territory . . . may be expelled therefrom only in pursuance of a decision reached in accordance with law and shall, except where compelling reasons of national security otherwise require, be allowed to submit the reasons against his expulsion and to have his case reviewed by, and be represented for the purpose before, the competent authority or a person or persons especially designated by the competent authority.

These procedural guarantees apply only to those lawfully in the territory and do not cover undocumented migrants or migrants in an irregular situation. Article 13 merely requires a procedure established by law and the opportunity to 'submit the reasons against expulsion', with a requirement for review by and representation before the competent authority. The burden of proof rests with the person subject to the expulsion order. Even these limited guarantees may be waived if there are 'compelling reasons of national security'. These procedural protections are more limited than those that apply under art. 14 of the ICCPR to persons charged with a criminal offence.[55]

---

54 Vesselina Vandova, 'Protection of Non-Citizens against Removal under International Human Rights Law' in Alice Edwards and Carla Ferstman (eds.), *Human Security and Non-Citizens: Law, Policy and International Affairs* (Cambridge University Press, 2010) 495.

55 Human Rights Committee, *General Comment No 15: The Position of Aliens under the Covenant*, 27th sess, UN Doc HRI/GEN/1/Rev.1 at 18 (11 April 1986).

There is no consensus on the scope of application of such guarantees, namely, whether they should apply to all migrants or whether different treatment should be given to migrants depending on the legality of their entry or stay.[56] The usual procedural guarantees include: the right to receive notice of the expulsion decision, the right to challenge the expulsion decision, the right to a fair hearing, the right to consular protection, the right to counsel, the right to legal aid, and the right to interpretation and translation in a language the migrant understands.[57] The best interests of the child and the principle of *non-refoulement* may also be invoked as important considerations in the review of the case.

Article 22 of the ICRMW contains a comprehensive list of expulsion guarantees to be provided to all migrant workers, irrespective of their legal status. These include: the prohibition of collective expulsions; the principle that an individual expulsion can be ordered only in pursuance of a decision taken by the competent authority in accordance with law; that the expulsion decision must be communicated in a language the migrant understands, preferably in writing, and, save in exceptional circumstances on account of national security, the reasons for the decision must be stated; the right of the migrant to submit reasons why he or she should not be expelled and to have his or her case reviewed by the competent authority, unless compelling reasons of national security require otherwise; and the right to have a reasonable opportunity before or after departure to settle any claims for wages and other entitlements due to him or her.

States have no right to expel their own nationals: this is a firmly established rule of international law.[58] It follows that States have no right to use denationalisation as a means to circumvent the principle of non-expulsion of nationals. Notwithstanding this, some States do consider denationalisation as a possibility provided it does not lead to statelessness (see Chapter 4). In the event that migrants have more than one nationality, States may be inclined to invoke the criterion of effective or dominant nationality to counter the principle of non-expulsion of nationals.

Disguised expulsion – also referred to as 'constructive expulsion' – is the forcible departure of a migrant from a State as a result of actions or omissions of the State, or from situations where the State supports or tolerates acts committed by private individuals with a view to provoking the departure of the migrant from its territory. Disguised expulsion violates the human rights of the individuals concerned as it gives them no opportunity to defend their rights. However, such acts of constructive expulsion, even without use of force, are distinct from cases in which States provide incentives for migrants to leave, such as assisted voluntary departures, which do not amount to constructive expulsions.

While the power of States to expel individual migrants is subject to few limitations as defined in law, the expulsion of groups of migrants is not allowed. This

---

56 *Report of the International Law Commission*, UN GAOR, 65th sess, Supp No 10 (A/65/10), 284.
57 International Migrants Bill of Rights, above n. 31, 433.
58 Sohn and Buergenthal, above n. 7, 85. This prohibition is a corollary of the right of nationals to return to the State of their nationality.

so-called 'collective expulsion' is no longer permitted under international law, as is made clear in all regional human rights treaties (see Chapter 14). The concept of collective expulsion implies that the measure adopted targets a specific category of migrants – for instance, members of an ethnic or racial group. This clearly contravenes the principle of non-discrimination – a non-derogable right recognised in the UDHR, which also has force under customary law. Since collective expulsions are now considered a violation of international law, the burden of proving an exception rests with the expelling State. For instance, if a State claims that its very existence or vital interests are at stake, it has to prove this. Prohibition of collective expulsion is a customary norm that is also evident in international conventions. For example, according to art. 22(1) of the ICRMW, 'migrant workers and members of their families shall not be subject to measures of collective expulsion. Each case of expulsion shall be examined individually.'

During an armed conflict, international humanitarian law authorises, under exceptional circumstances, the forced transfer of civilian population. According to art. 49 of the Fourth Geneva Convention, 'individual or mass forcible transfers, as well as deportations of protected persons from occupied territory are prohibited, regardless of their motive. However, the Occupying Power may undertake total or partial evacuation if the security of the population or imperative military reasons so demand.' Similarly, art. 17 of the *Protocol Additional to the Geneva Conventions of 12 August 1949, and relating to the Protection of Victims of Non-International Armed Conflicts* ('Protocol II') states that the displacement of the civilian population shall not be ordered for reasons related to the conflict 'unless the security of the civilians involved or imperative military reasons so demand'.[59]

It is accepted that irregular migration cannot be combated if irregular migrants cannot be removed and returned. Even if an irregular migrant is identified and arrested, and an expulsion decision taken after due process, removal may not be certain. This can be attributed to a number of factors, including *inter alia* the unwillingness or inability of a State to readmit the person. Practical difficulties may arise when a State wants to forcibly return a migrant. The State requested to readmit its national may refuse to cooperate, arguing that the individual does not possess its nationality; it may also refuse to issue travel documents; these objections are even stronger when applied to third-country nationals. Establishing or strengthening cooperation with countries of origin, transit or destination is therefore important.

A readmission agreement is a means to give effect to the expulsion of irregular migrants.[60] It is defined as an international agreement that addresses procedures,

---

59 *Protocol Additional to the Geneva Conventions of 12 August 1949, and relating to the Protection of Victims of Non-International Armed Conflicts*, opened for signature 8 June 1977, 1125 UNTS 609 (entered into force 7 December 1978).

60 Tineke Strik, 'Readmission Agreements: A Mechanism for Returning Irregular Migrants' (Doc 12168, Council of Europe, Parliamentary Assembly, 16 March 2010).

on a reciprocal basis, for one State to return non-nationals in an irregular situation to their home State or to a State through which they have transited.[61] The purpose of a readmission agreement is to establish rapid and effective procedures for the identification and return of persons no longer fulfilling the criteria for residence in the host country: these persons include nationals of the other party, third-country nationals and stateless persons. Readmission agreements constitute a useful instrument to facilitate implementation of a State's duty to admit its nationals. The duty of the State must be distinguished from the individual's right to return, as the obligation to readmit is not dependent on the willingness of the migrant to return. Moreover, the right to return does not include a right of the individual to elect not to return to his or her country if the stay in another country comes to an end.

Notwithstanding their positive aspects, readmission agreements also present some challenging characteristics, in particular the failure to take into account the interests of countries of origin or transit. The type of documents that are accepted as evidence of nationality also raises some concerns. In the absence of a passport, 'proof' of nationality may rest merely on an identity card, a driving licence or a written statement by another migrant certifying that this person is a national of a given country. However, in light of the legal concept of nationality as expressed by the International Court of Justice in the *Nottebohm Case*, namely, 'a legal bond having as its basis a social fact of attachment, a genuine connection of existence, interests and sentiments',[62] proof of nationality in the context of readmission agreements fails to meet the threshold generally applied in international law.

As stated above, States enjoy a wide margin of discretion when resorting to expulsion of migrants. Common grounds for expulsion are the entry in breach of the law; the breach of the conditions attached to the permission to enter and stay, with regard to both the duration of the stay and its purpose; and the involvement in criminal activities and other offences against public order. Readmission agreements are a practical tool aimed at facilitating removal based on listed grounds in the national law: they should in no way diminish the rule of customary international law imposing on States the duty to readmit their own nationals.

5.5.   FACILITATING IMPLEMENTATION OF FREE MOVEMENT

Travel documents are a prerequisite to exercise the right to leave and the right to return: A passport is the usual, indispensable prerequisite for exercising these rights. While possession of a passport is not always required for tourists or other

---

61 Madjid Benchikh, 'Les accords de réadmission' in Vincent Chetail (ed.), *Mondialisation, migration et droits de l'homme: le droit international en question, Volume II* (Bruylant, 2007) 665.
62 *Nottebohm Case (Liechtenstein v. Guatemala) (Second Phase)* [1955] ICJ Rep 4.

short-term visitors as a result of bilateral or multilateral agreements, some form of identification document is nevertheless needed to cross borders. Such documentation includes identity cards, tourist cards, travel documents issued to refugees and stateless persons, and *laissez-passer* for international officials. In addition to having a passport to leave his or her country, a national may have to obtain an entry and exit visa that is granted only if the candidate does not fall within any of the grounds justifying a refusal to leave the country, as recognised by international law. The requirement of an entry and exit visa may also apply to non-nationals.

The free movement of persons may be subject to restrictions when the practicality of obtaining travel documents is made difficult through dubious administrative measures. These restrictions may be applied in a differentiated manner depending on the length of the intended stay abroad. Most of the obstacles to the granting of travel documents affect the right of a national to leave his or her country. So far as the right to return is concerned, problems arise only when there are doubts as to the nationality of the person wishing to return.

The 1963 study carried out by Mr Inglés contained conclusions and recommendations that, to a large extent, are still relevant today.[63] In particular, no one should be arbitrarily denied travel documents that may be required to leave or to return to his or her country, and documents should not be subject to unreasonable costs or taxes. In addition, the formalities for issuing travel documents, including the conditions for denying or cancelling them, should be provided by laws or regulations, which should be made public. In 1986, a meeting of experts on the right to leave and return adopted a Declaration on the right to leave and return, which contained more detailed procedural safeguards concerning travel documents.[64]

A passport is *prima facie* proof of identity and nationality, and it signifies the right of the holder to return to the issuing State. A passport also indicates the destination country to which a State may remove a non-national. The requirement of a passport, therefore, responds to two factors: first, it is a form of authentic identification needed by the receiving State, and second, it is a guarantee to the receiving State that there is a country to which a migrant can return.[65] The country of nationality therefore has an obligation vis-à-vis the country in which its passport holder resides, and it must accept that passport holder in the event of return or expulsion from the country of residence.

A passport may be difficult to obtain when a State asks the person to provide documents that he or she cannot acquire. An exorbitant passport fee may be charged, or financial security may have to be given to ensure return. As stated by Inglés, 'because a passport or other travel document is a legal and a practical

---

63 Inglés, above n. 16, 66–8.   64 Reproduced in Hannum, above n. 28, 154–8.
65 Friedrich Loehr, 'Passports' in Rudolf Bernhardt (ed.), *Encyclopedia of Public International Law* (North-Holland 1985) vol. 8, 428.

necessity, the long accepted discretionary power over its issuance is a matter of increasing concern to the international community'.[66]

Although passports have demonstrated their relevance as travel and identification documents, the travel function has been taken over by visas. A further trend is the adoption of standards for machine-readable passports: an increasing number of States have now issued electronic machine-readable travel documents that conform to International Civil Aviation Organization standards. These standards, and other similar developments, aim at facilitating travel of 'legitimate' migrants by improving processing times through automation in border controls, while increasing security.[67] Critics and privacy advocates, however, consider these developments to pose a risk to the enjoyment of personal privacy and argue that they do not facilitate free movement of people. It is not disputed that visa requirements and other measures are on the increase in response to irregular movements and threats to national security. However, developments to facilitate verification, identification of document fraud and migration management can coexist alongside individual human rights and fundamental freedoms if the use of advanced technology is driven by laws and policies.[68]

Within regional frameworks, the abolition of visas and other obstacles to free movement can be observed at the normative level. For instance, the *Treaty of the Economic Community of West African States* (1975) ('ECOWAS') and its *Protocol relating to Free Movement of Persons, Residence and Establishment* (1979)[69] seek to ensure free movement and labour opportunities between ECOWAS member States without restrictions of visa requirements and residence permits. Similarly, the Caribbean Community ('CARICOM') established a framework in 1989 for the free movement of skilled workers. In Latin America, the Common Market of the South ('MERCOSUR') and the Andean Community of Nations ('CAN') adopted measures aimed at easing requirements for nationals and migrants residing in its member States to travel within the respective regions. The European Union is of course the most advanced project on integration of people within a specific region, having created an area of freedom of movement for nationals of member States of the European Union. Although these examples illustrate the abolition of visa requirements (some of them barely implemented in practice), it should be noted that movement is facilitated within the internal boundaries of a limited group of States that are bound by common interests: external borders and controls, including visa processes, do not disappear.

---

66 Inglés, above n. 16, 62.   67 Koslowski, above n. 41, 21.

68 Jillyanne Redpath, *Biometrics and International Migration*, International Migration Law No 5 (IOM, 2005).

69 *Treaty of the Economic Community of West African States*, opened for signature 28 May 1975, 1010 UNTS 18 (entered into force 1 August 1995); *Protocol relating to Free Movement of Persons, Residence and Establishment*, Official Journal of the ECOWAS Vol 1, Doc A/P 1/5/79 (29 May 1979).

5.6. CONCLUSION

The authority of States to control their borders and to regulate entry and exit is not disputed in legal theory and practice. The exceptions to the discretionary power of States are well defined, if not always respected, and only minor divergences on the scope and legal nature of these exceptions are noted.

What is not often discussed is the political environment that prevailed when the principle of freedom of movement was formulated some sixty years ago, when the emphasis was largely on restrictions on the right to leave. Nowadays, more attention should be paid to the right to remain and the right to enjoy the full exercise of economic, social and cultural rights. This right to stay is very often illusory, and forced migration constitutes the only escape: economic disparities, rising unemployment and demographic growth compel inhabitants of developing countries to look for better opportunities abroad. Consequently, the right to leave is transformed into a necessity to leave. In turn, developed States exercise with utmost severity their right to control their borders and to decide on limited groups who are allowed admission and exit under set conditions. Undocumented migrants or migrants in an irregular situation are sent back to their countries of origin or transit, thereby transforming the right to return into an obligation to depart from the host country and return to a country of origin or transit.

Today, a redrafting of the clauses relating to the right to leave and the right to return would certainly lead to results that may appear surprising at first sight: a stronger emphasis would be placed on national security and the fight against terrorism; the absence of a corresponding right to immigrate would be explicitly stated; and the need for cooperation among States to ensure orderly and humane migration would be added. These new formulations would not affect the basic tenet of international law that States have the authority to regulate the movement of persons within and across their borders.

Such redrafting could then be compared with what was proposed in 1888 by the International Law Institute at a session held in Lausanne. At the time, the Institute adopted a draft 'International Declaration relating to the Right to Expel Foreigners', and 'International Rules on the Admission and Expulsion of Foreigners'.[70] The six articles of the draft Declaration and the forty-one International Rules are surprisingly modern in their substance and would still be largely relevant in any codification or progressive development of the law pertaining to those matters. Even if partly written as what the law ought to be (*de lege ferenda*), they also illustrate the limited progress made by the international community since the end of the nineteenth century.

---

70 Hans Wehberg, *Institut de Droit International: Tableau général des résolutions, 1873–1956* (Éditions juridiques et sociologiques, 1957) 49–58.

KEY REFERENCES

Alegrett, Andrea et al., 'International Migrants Bill of Rights (draft in progress)' (2010) 24(3) Georgetown Immigration Law Journal 423

Chetail, Vincent, 'Freedom of Movement and Transnational Migrations: A Human Rights Perspective' in Alexander Aleinikoff and Vincent Chetail (eds.), Migration and International Legal Norms (TMC Asser Press, 2003) 47

Goodwin-Gill, Guy, 'Migration: International Law and Human Rights' in Bimal Ghosh (ed.), Managing Migration: Time for a New International Regime? (Oxford University Press, 2000) 160

Hannum, Hurst, The Right to Leave and Return in International Law and Practice (Martinus Nijhoff, 1987)

Harvey, Colin and Barnidge, Robert, 'Human Rights, Free Movement and the Right to Leave in International Law' (2007) 19 International Journal of Refugee Law 1

Jagerskiold, Stig, 'The Freedom of Movement' in Louis Henkin (ed.), The International Bill of Rights: The Covenant on Civil and Political Rights (CCPR Commentary) (Kehl, 1993), 197

Juss, Satvinder, 'Free Movement and the World Order' (2004) 16(3) International Journal of Refugee Law 289

Kesby, Alison, 'The Shifting and Multiple Border and International Law' (2007) 27(1) Oxford Journal of Legal Studies 101

Perruchoud, Richard, 'Le droit de quitter tous pays, y compris le sien et de revenir dans son pays' in Migrations de populations et droit de l'homme (Bruylant, 2011), 59

Plender, Richard, International Migration Law (Martinus Nijhoff, 2nd edn, 1988)

Sohn, Louis and Buergenthal, Thomas, 'The Movement of Persons Across Borders' (1992) 23 Studies in Transnational Legal Policy 1

6

International human rights of migrants

DAVID WEISSBRODT AND MICHAEL DIVINE[1]

6.1. INTRODUCTION

As human beings, migrants deserve to be treated with respect. Nonetheless, in many States migrants have not been welcomed. They are exploited and subjected to discrimination. Their security and liberty of movement are infringed. They are denied minority rights, freedom of expression and privacy. Migrants are also placed at risk by arbitrary expulsion and refusal to allow them to acquire the nationality of the host State. They are not accorded economic rights. Despite these problems, there are increasing numbers of migrants – that is, people residing in a State other than the one in which they were born; they comprise over 3 per cent of the world's population (see Chapter 2).

This chapter will address, first, the evolution of human rights norms and their relevance to migrants, and second, some of the specific rights enjoyed by migrants.

6.2. EVOLUTION OF HUMAN RIGHTS NORMS AND THEIR RELEVANCE TO MIGRANTS

From ancient times to the present, there has been a growing but still fragmentary international legal consensus concerning the human rights of non-nationals. The international law of state responsibility originated from issues concerning the treatment of non-nationals, and the rights of non-nationals developed as a precursor to the present-day international human rights regime.[2] What follows is an

---

1 The authors thank Professors Francesco Parisi and Giovanna Dell'Orto for their assistance in excerpting and translating a decision of the Italian Constitutional Court. The authors also thank Mary Rumsey for her help researching this chapter, portions of which draw on David Weissbrodt's earlier work, *The Human Rights of Non-Citizens* (Oxford University Press, 2008).

2 Richard Lillich, *The Human Rights of Aliens in Contemporary International Law* (Manchester University Press, 1984); Richard Baxter, 'Reflections on Codification in Light of the International Law of State Responsibility for Injuries to Aliens' (1965) 16 *Syracuse Law Review* 745, 756–7.

overview of the development of the rights of 'outsiders'. This overview highlights the major themes and developments of these rights from ancient to contemporary times.

6.2.1. Historical context

Wariness towards 'strangers' predates any formal system for granting or denying nationality.[3] In pre-modern times, prejudice against foreigners seems to have been justified by cultural dichotomies distinguishing between 'non-believers' and 'believers', or 'barbarians' and 'civilised people'. The early Greeks, for example, 'sharply distinguished "citizens" from "barbarians", and later distinguished among citizens, naturalized aliens, public guests, domiciled aliens, non-domiciled aliens, and strangers'.[4] Additionally, in ancient Greek, Roman and Hindu societies, non-believers generally had no rights before the law, since the law, influenced by religion, specified that a citizen was 'one who took part in the religion of the city'.[5]

Despite such prejudices, notions of hospitality have long existed in many cultures, and hospitality towards foreigners was generally practised by ancient peoples. It has been suggested that such kindness was due in large part to the lack of official public protection: since society as a whole offered no legal protection, principles of simple kindness and sympathy motivated individuals to welcome strangers. Additionally, many ancient religious ideologies extolled the virtues of extending hospitality to foreigners. As evidenced by the poems of Homer and Hesiod, Buddhist scriptures and the Bible, it was a common belief among the ancients that a 'stranger is sacred and the gods desire that he should be protected'.[6]

The need for trade eventually led to the increased recognition of rights. In the city-states of Ancient Greece, lack of legal personality meant that travellers could be robbed and murdered without any legal consequence – a powerful disincentive for visiting tradesmen. As industry developed and trade with the outside world became increasingly necessary, rulers saw the benefit in providing protections for non-citizens. Such protections took the form of specific grants to certain trades-people, as well as *isopolities*, early treaties between city-states intended to secure rights and privileges to each other's citizens.[7]

During the Middle Ages, the rights of non-citizens improved with the emergence of collective bargaining and letters of reprisal. As the economy of Europe developed, foreigners and persons outside the prevailing feudal order became organised, enabling extraction of privileges,[8] such as the concessions of the Byzantine Empire

3 Lillich, above n. 2, 5.
4 James Nafziger, 'The General Admission of Aliens under International Law' (1983) **77**(4) *American Journal of International Law* 804, 809.
5 Carmen Tiburcio, *The Human Rights of Aliens under International and Comparative Law* (Kluwer, 2001) 23.
6 Giorgio Del Vecchio, 'The Evolution of Hospitality: A Note on the History of the Treatment of Foreigners' (1963) 4(2) *Sydney Law Review* 205–7.
7 Lillich, above n. 2, 5–6.   8 'The Alien in Legal History' (1927) 163 *The Law Times* 497.

to Genoese merchants.[9] Alternatively, if a subject could satisfactorily show that a wrong had been committed, he may have been entitled to seek a 'letter of reprisal' from his sovereign; a document granting the party permission to exact property from any subject of the offending feudal State.

The Renaissance marked the widespread emergence of principles of Natural Law, which heavily influenced both the French and American Revolutions. Essential to this philosophy were the writings of Jean-Jacques Rousseau, who posited that sovereign authority rightly arises from the people, whose collective entrance into society enables the creation of its rules.[10] Concurrently, Natural Law philosophers believed that the sovereign power, having root in the people, must act in conformity with the wellbeing of the people. John Locke's seventeenth-century theory of natural rights stated that the purpose of government is to protect the natural rights of life, liberty and property. According to Locke, governments that failed to protect these rights did not act with the acquiescence of the people, and were thus justly overthrown.

The influence of the Natural Law philosophers can be seen today in the founding documents, constitutions and legal systems of many States. The United States *Declaration of Independence* (1776), for example, put the ideas of natural rights philosophers into practice by proclaiming the principle of equality and by guaranteeing 'as self-evident' the 'unalienable rights' of all men to 'life, liberty and the pursuit of happiness'. These principles were incorporated into the articles of the *Constitution of the United States* and are binding there as the fundamental law of the land. Similarly, the French *Declaration of the Rights of Man and of the Citizen* (1789) affirmed that '[a]ll citizens ... are equally eligible to all public dignities, places and employments, according to their capacities, and without other distinction than that of their virtues and talents'. A number of other nations, such as Belgium, Denmark, Liberia, the Netherlands, Norway, the Russian Federation and Sweden use similar language in their constitutions.

While the United States and French Declarations offer broad protections, they are still flawed in that they connect the concept of *human being* with that of *citizenship*. Indeed, although natural rights theories granted rights at birth to every individual, these rights could only be recognised and enforced in a practical way through membership of a State, which alone could prescribe the criteria for membership. Accordingly, the system of modern nationality – arising from the French and American Revolutions of the late 1700s – protected minority rights from the excesses of majority rule, but only for individuals it labelled 'citizens' and to the exclusion of populations perceived as foreign or non-national.

---

9 Lillich, above n. 2, 6.   10 Jean Rousseau, *Du Contract Social: Ou Principes du Droit Politique* (MM Rey, 1762).

By the eighteenth century, under international law a breach of the rights of an alien by a host State was considered to be an indirect injury to the State of his or her nationality. This breach could only be addressed at the international level if the State of nationality decided to take up the case of its subject injured abroad. In doing so, the State of nationality was asserting its own right to ensure, in the person of its subjects, respect for the rules of international law.[11] It was not until after the events of the Second World War that the international community recognised the human rights of the individual, which could be enforced by that individual directly against a State.

6.2.2. The United Nations

In response to the gross human rights violations of the Second World War period, world leaders acknowledged the need to protect human rights on a global scale. In 1944, leaders from the United Kingdom and the United States met with leaders from the Soviet Union (and later with China) in Washington DC to formulate a 'proposal for the establishment of a general international organization',[12] envisioning, among other things, the means to protect and ensure human rights. The eventual product of these meetings was the adoption of the *Charter of the United Nations* ('Charter') in 1945.

Articles 55 and 56 of the Charter require all members to take joint and separate action in cooperation with the United Nations for the achievement of 'universal respect for, and observance of, human rights and fundamental freedoms for all without distinction as to race, sex, language, or religion'. The *Universal Declaration of Human Rights* (1948) ('UDHR')[13] defines the rights guaranteed by the Charter and reiterates the importance of their adherence. Additionally, the *International Covenant on Civil and Political Rights* ('ICCPR')[14] and the *International Covenant on Economic, Social and Cultural Rights* ('ICESCR')[15] expand upon the protections of the UDHR. Together, the UDHR, ICCPR and ICESCR constitute the International Bill of Human Rights and are the fundamental instruments of the United Nations concerning human rights.

In addition to the International Bill of Human Rights, the United Nations has drafted, promulgated and now helps to implement more than eighty human rights treaties, declarations and other instruments dealing with topics that include: genocide, racial discrimination, discrimination against women, religious intolerance, the rights of persons with disabilities, the right to development, the rights of

11 *Mavrommatis Palestine Concessions (Greece v. UK)* [1924] PCIJ (ser A) No 2, 12.
12 Bruno Simma (ed.), *Charter of the United Nations: A Commentary* (Oxford University Press, 1994) 8.
13 *Universal Declaration of Human Rights*, GA Res 217A (III), UN Doc A/810 (10 December 1948).
14 *International Covenant on Civil and Political Rights*, opened for signature 16 December 1966, 999 UNTS 171 (entered into force 23 March 1976).
15 *International Covenant on Economic, Social and Cultural Rights*, opened for signature 16 December 1966, 993 UNTS 3 (entered into force 3 January 1976).

| BOX 6.1   Principal international treaties on human rights |

Year	Instrument
1965	*International Convention on the Elimination of All Forms of Racial Discrimination,* opened for signature 21 December 1965, 660 UNTS 195 (entered into force 4 January 1969)
1966	*International Covenant on Civil and Political Rights,* opened for signature 16 December 1966, 999 UNTS 171 (entered into force 23 March 1976)
1966	*International Covenant on Economic, Social and Cultural Rights,* opened for signature 16 December 1966, 993 UNTS 3 (entered into force 3 January 1976)
1979	*Convention on the Elimination of All Forms of Discrimination against Women,* opened for signature 18 December 1979, 1249 UNTS 13 (entered into force 3 September 1981)
1984	*Convention against Torture and Other Cruel, Inhuman or Degrading Treatment or Punishment,* opened for signature 10 December 1984, 1465 UNTS 85 (entered into force 26 June 1987)
1989	*Convention on the Rights of the Child,* opened for signature 20 November 1989, 1577 UNTS 3 (entered into force 2 September 1990)
1990	*International Convention on the Protection of the Rights of All Migrant Workers and Members of their Families,* opened for signature 18 December 1990, 2220 UNTS 3 (entered into force 1 July 2003)
2006	*International Convention for the Protection of All Persons from Enforced Disappearance,* opened for signature 20 December 2006, UN Doc A/RES/61/177 (entered into force 23 December 2010)
2007	*Convention on the Rights of Persons with Disabilities,* opened for signature 30 March 2007, UN Doc A/61/611 (entered into force 3 May 2008)

children and the rights of migrant workers. The nine core international human rights treaties are listed in Box 6.1. Many of the specific rights protected by these instruments apply to all people regardless of their nationality. Along with migrant-specific provisions, these generally applicable provisions reflect the core class of rights that are the focus of this chapter.

6.3.   CONTEMPORARY RIGHTS AND THEIR PROTECTION

This section discusses contemporary rights of migrants as provided by international law. It is not exhaustive and many States provide rights in excess of what is mandated by international law. In reviewing the various problems migrants encounter, it should be considered that migrants, particularly those in an irregular situation, are often hesitant to bring claims locally for fear of deportation. Consequently, the paucity of complaints received by international and regional bodies may not reflect a lack of human rights violations, but rather the fear of repercussions against complainants and their families.

6.3.1. General principles of equality and non-discrimination

The architecture of international human rights law is built on the premise that all persons, by virtue of their essential humanity, should equally enjoy all human rights. As such, international human rights law generally requires the equal treatment of nationals and non-nationals. In recognition of this principle, art. 2 of the UDHR states that '[e]veryone is entitled to all the rights and freedoms set forth in this Declaration, without distinction of *any* kind, such as race, colour, sex, language, religion, political or other opinion, *national or social origin*, property, birth or other status' (emphasis added). Similarly, art. 26 of the ICCPR states:

All persons are equal before the law and are entitled without any discrimination to the equal protection of the law. In this respect, the law shall prohibit any discrimination and guarantee to all persons equal and effective protection against discrimination on any ground such as race, colour sex, language, religion, political or other opinion, national or social origin, property, birth or other status.

With regard to civil and political rights, the Human Rights Committee, which is responsible for monitoring the implementation of the ICCPR, explained in its *General Comment No 15* that almost all rights protected by the ICCPR must be guaranteed without discrimination between nationals and non-nationals. Among these rights are freedom from arbitrary killing; freedom from arbitrary detention; freedom from torture or cruel, inhuman or degrading treatment or punishment; equality before courts and tribunals; and freedom of thought, conscience and religion. Furthermore, non-nationals should have the right to marry; to receive protection as minors; and the right to peaceful association and assembly.[16]

General Comment No 15 further states that rights of non-nationals may be qualified only by such limitations as may be lawfully imposed under the ICCPR. Specifically, the ICCPR permits States to draw distinctions between nationals and non-nationals with respect to two categories of rights: political rights explicitly guaranteed to nationals, and freedom of movement. With regard to political rights, art. 25 establishes that 'every citizen' shall have the right to participate in public affairs, to vote and hold office, and to have access to public service. With regard to freedom of movement, art. 12(1) grants 'the right to liberty of movement and freedom to choose [one's] residence' only to those who are 'lawfully within the territory of a State' – thus apparently permitting restrictions on irregular migrants. At the same time, some distinctions made by a State's law that are not specifically permitted under the ICCPR may be consistent with art. 26 of that Covenant if they are justified on reasonable and objective grounds.[17]

16 Human Rights Committee, *General Comment No 15: The Position of Aliens under the Covenant*, 27th sess, UN Doc HRI/GEN/1/Rev.1 at 18 (11 April 1986) [2]–[7].
17 Human Rights Committee, *Views: Communication No 964/2000*, 74th sess, UN Doc CCPR/C/74/D/965/2000 (4 April 2002) ('*Karakurt* v. *Austria*') [8.4].

Likewise, the ICESCR establishes that States shall, in general, protect the rights of all individuals – regardless of national or social origin – to work; to have just and favourable working conditions; to have an adequate standard of living, including adequate food, clothing, housing and the continuous improvement of living conditions; to the highest attainable standard of health; to education; and to other economic, social and cultural rights. Article 2(3), however, allows developing countries 'with due regard to human rights and their national economy' to 'determine to what extent they would guarantee the economic rights recognized in the [ICESCR] to non-nationals'. This exception may be made only with respect to economic rights, and not to social and cultural rights. Further, like all exceptions, those provisos must be narrowly construed so as to maintain the overall thrust of the human rights protections.

The *International Convention on the Elimination of All Forms of Racial Discrimination* (1965) ('ICERD') indicates in art. 1(2) that States may make distinctions between 'citizens and non-citizens'.[18] The Committee on the Elimination of All Forms of Racial Discrimination ('CERD Committee'), however, has stated in its *General Recommendation No 30* that States may draw distinctions between nationals and non-nationals only if such distinctions do not have the effect of limiting the enjoyment by non-nationals of rights enshrined in other instruments, such as the UDHR, ICCPR and ICESCR. The CERD Committee also explained that differential treatment based on nationality or immigration status will constitute discrimination unless the criteria for such differentiation are applied to a legitimate aim under the Convention and are proportional to achieving that aim.[19]

One of the most common problems encountered by human rights treaty bodies in reviewing States' periodic reports is that some national constitutions guarantee rights only to nationals, whereas international human rights law would (with the exceptions of rights of public participation and movement, and economic rights in developing countries) provide rights to all persons – nationals and non-nationals alike. Other constitutions inappropriately distinguish between rights granted to persons who obtained their nationality by birth and those who did not. It must also be noted that the mere recitation of the general principle of non-discrimination in a constitution is not a sufficient response to the equality requirements of human rights law. States are obliged to have in place effective legislation to fight all forms of discrimination, as well as effective remedies to obtain compensation for violations of such legislation. An illustration of the operation of human rights norms in the context of national laws and constitutions is given in Case Study 6.1.

---

18 *International Convention on the Elimination of All Forms of Racial Discrimination*, opened for signature 21 December 1965, 660 UNTS 195 (entered into force 4 January 1969).
19 Committee on the Elimination of Racial Discrimination, *General Recommendation No 30: Discrimination against Non-Citizens*, 64th sess, UN Doc CERD/C/64/Misc.11/rev.3 (1 October 2004) [2]–[4].

CASE STUDY 6.1 Discrimination against non-nationals in Italian criminal law

The United Nations Human Rights Committee has recognised that the principle of equality must necessarily extend to the position of non-nationals before courts and tribunals.[20] However, equality before the courts cannot be realised when national laws require heightened sanctions for criminal offences committed by non-nationals. In 2010, the Italian Constitutional Court had to consider a provision of the *Italian Criminal Code*, introduced in 2008, which treated non-nationality as an aggravating factor in a criminal offence committed by a person illegally in Italian territory. The question was whether this provision violated the *Constitution of the Italian Republic*. The Court held that it was an impermissible violation of the principle of equality.[21]

Presidente Amirante

The Tribunals of Livorno and Ferrara . . . raise the question of the constitutional legitimacy of art. 61, no. 11-bis, of the *Penal Code*, which provides for an aggravating circumstance when deeds are committed by the guilty party 'while illegally present in the national territory'. . . .

The question raised by the Tribunal in Ferrara is valid. . . . This Court, regarding inviolable rights, has said, in general, that those rights belong to people as 'individuals rather than as participants in a certain political community, but as human beings'. The juridical condition of the foreigner should not therefore be considered – as far as the preservation of those rights is concerned – as an admissible cause for different and worse treatment, particularly within the *Penal Code*, which is more directly connected to a person's fundamental freedoms, which are safeguarded by the Constitution with the protections contained in arts. 24 *et seq.*, which regulate the position of individuals vis-à-vis the punitive power of the State.

The rigorous respect of inviolable rights implies the illegitimacy of more severe penal treatment founded on a subject's personal qualities deriving from previous commission of deeds 'entirely extraneous to the charge', introducing therefore a penal responsibility of the actor 'in open violation of the principle of the inherent characteristics of the offence' . . . . In addition, 'the constitutional principle of equality in general does not permit discrimination between the status of the citizen and that of the foreigner'. Any limitation of fundamental rights ought to begin with the assumption that, in the presence of an inviolable right, 'its inherent value cannot be restricted or limited by any one of the powers that be, if not because of the non-derogable satisfaction of a public interest that is primary and constitutionally relevant' . . .

In consideration of all the indicated reasons, the norm complained of ought to be declared constitutionally illegitimate for violation of art. 3(1) and art. 25(2) of the Constitution.

20 Human Rights Committee, *General Comment No 15*, above n. 16, 7.
21 *Judgment No 249*, Italian Constitutional Court (8 July 2010), www.cortecostituzionale.it/actionPronuncia.do.

In addition to universal human rights instruments and domestic legal decisions, regional human rights courts have directed States to refrain from discrimination based upon nationality. In 2003, the Inter-American Court of Human Rights held that non-discrimination and the right to equality are norms of *jus cogens* and are thus applicable to all residents regardless of immigration status.[22] Accordingly, the Court held that governments cannot use immigration status as a justification for restricting the employment rights of unauthorised workers, or their rights to social security. The Court found that governments have the right to deport individuals and refuse to offer jobs to people who do not possess employment documents, but it held that once an employment relationship has been initiated, even unauthorised workers become entitled to all the employment and labour rights that are available to authorised workers.[23]

The European Court of Human Rights and the Inter-American Court of Human Rights have determined that making distinctions between non-nationals of different nationalities may be permissible in certain circumstances. The European Court of Human Rights has found permissible a distinction between European 'citizens' and individuals of non-European nationality in regard to deportation because 'member States of the European Union form a special legal order, which has . . . established its own citizenship'.[24] Similarly, the Inter-American Court of Human Rights found non-discriminatory a proposed amendment to the naturalisation provisions of the Costa Rican constitution that established preferential naturalisation rules for 'nationals of the other Central American countries, Spaniards and Ibero-Americans', because they 'share much closer historical, cultural and spiritual bonds with the people of Costa Rica' and are 'more easily and more rapidly assimilated within the national community'. The Court explained that 'no discrimination exists if the difference in treatment has a legitimate purpose and if it does not lead to situations which are contrary to justice, to reason or to the nature of things'.[25]

6.3.2. Life and liberty, arbitrary detention, diplomatic and consular protection

In nearly every State, non-nationals have been apprehended and detained for failure to obtain or maintain proper immigration status. States are obliged to respect the human rights of detainees, including their legal protection, irrespective of whether they are in the territory of the State in question.[26] Detained non-nationals have the right to contact consular officials, and the receiving State

---

22 *Jus cogens* are peremptory norms of international law from which no derogation is permitted. See Chapter 3.
23 *Juridical Condition and Rights of the Undocumented Migrants (Advisory Opinion)* OC-18/03, Inter-Am Ct HR (Ser A) No 18 (17 September 2003).
24 *C v. Belgium* (European Court of Human Rights, Chamber, Application No 35/1995/541/627, 26 May 1996).
25 *Proposed Amendments to the Naturalization Provisions of the Constitution of Costa Rica (Advisory Opinion)* OC-4/84, Inter-Am Ct HR (Ser A) No 4 (19 January 1984) [57], [60].
26 *Detainees in Guantánamo Bay, Cuba (Request for Precautionary Measures)* Inter-Am Ct HR (13 March 2002).

must notify non-national detainees of this right (see Chapter 3).[27] Where persons find themselves within the authority and control of a State, and where armed conflict may be involved, their rights may be determined in part by reference to international humanitarian law as well as international human rights law.

Article 3 of the UDHR guarantees that '[e]veryone has the right to life, liberty and the security of person'. The right to life is reiterated in art. 6 of the ICCPR, which provides that the right is 'inherent' to human beings and shall be 'protected by law'. Article 4 of the ICCPR forbids derogation from the right to life in times of public emergency. The right is further reflected in the major regional human rights treaties, such as art. 2 of the *European Convention for the Protection of Human Rights and Fundamental Freedoms* (1950) ('European Convention on Human Rights'),[28] art. 4 of the *American Convention on Human Rights* (1969)[29] and art. 4 of the *African Charter on Human and Peoples' Rights* (1981) ('African Charter on Human Rights').[30]

Article 9(1) of the ICCPR provides that '[e]veryone has the right to liberty and security of person. No one shall be subjected to arbitrary arrest or detention. No one shall be deprived of his liberty except on such grounds and in accordance with such procedure as are established by law'. Additionally, art. 9 records the right of the arrested person to be informed of the reasons for his or her arrest; the right to a prompt trial; the right of all detained persons to take proceedings to determine the lawfulness of such detention; and the right to compensation when he or she has been wrongfully arrested or detained. While detained, all persons must be treated 'with humanity and with respect for the inherent dignity of the human person' (art. 10).

Article 16 of the *International Convention on the Protection of the Rights of All Migrant Workers and Members of their Families* (1990) ('ICRMW')[31] reiterates the rights recorded in art. 9 of the ICCPR and clarifies that, for the rights to be adequately realised, detained migrant workers and members of their families must be 'informed at the time of arrest as far as possible in a language they understand of the reasons for their arrest and . . . promptly informed in a language they understand of any charges against them' (art. 16(5)). When a migrant does not understand the language used in court, the assistance of an interpreter must be provided at no cost (art. 16(8)). Article 16(7) further requires that when a migrant worker or member of his or her family is detained: (i) the detainee shall be made aware of the right to contact consular or diplomatic authorities of his or her State of origin, or of any other rights provided by

---

27 *Vienna Convention on Consular Relations*, opened for signature 24 April 1963, 596 UNTS 261 (entered into force 19 March 1967) art. 36.

28 *European Convention for the Protection of Human Rights and Fundamental Freedoms*, opened for signature 4 November 1950, ETS No 005 (entered into force 3 September 1953).

29 *American Convention on Human Rights*, opened for signature 22 November 1969, 1144 UNTS 123 (entered into force 18 July 1978).

30 *African Charter on Human and Peoples' Rights*, opened for signature 27 June 1981, 1520 UNTS 217 (entered into force 21 October 1986).

31 *International Convention on the Protection of the Rights of All Migrant Workers and Members of their Families*, opened for signature 18 December 1990, 2220 UNTS 3 (entered into force 1 July 2003).

treaty; (ii) the proper consular or diplomatic authorities shall be informed of the detention and reasons for it, if the detainee so requests; and (iii) the detainee shall be permitted to communicate with these authorities, and any such communications shall be transmitted without delay.

Regional human rights law is largely consistent with the protection provided by universal standards (to the extent universal standards are defined), but reveals several important elaborations on those standards, as well as particular exceptions to the general principle of equality. Article 5(1) of the European Convention on Human Rights, for example, reiterates the universal principle of the right to liberty and security of the person, but elaborates by providing that '[n]o one shall be deprived of his liberty' except in certain specified cases and only 'in accordance with a procedure prescribed by law'.[32] The list of exceptions to the right to liberty is an exhaustive one and only a narrow interpretation of those exceptions is consistent with the aim of art. 5, namely, to protect the individual from arbitrary detention.[33]

The Working Group on Arbitrary Detention (established in 1991 by the Commission on Human Rights, now the Human Rights Council), and the Special Rapporteur on the Human Rights of Migrants, have clearly stated their opinion that infractions of immigration rules do not make a person a criminal.[34] Administrative detention of irregular migrants (despite the fact that they have not committed an accepted criminal offence) often has far fewer procedural safeguards than criminal detention, which has judicial oversight and review. Furthermore, immigration detention can often be in severely substandard conditions, and in some cases is prolonged or even indefinite.

In the case of *Vélez Loor* v. *Panama*,[35] the Inter-American Court of Human Rights held that Panama was liable for a breach of the *American Convention on Human Rights* for the deprivation of an Ecuadorian migrant's liberty. At the time of the plaintiff's arrest, Panama had legislation in place that mandated detention for those who violated immigration laws. The Court found that while States have a legitimate interest in preventive custody 'to ensure that the individual appears before the immigration proceeding or, in addition, to guarantee the application of an order for deportation',[36] detention could not be used as a punitive measure. Accordingly, the Court stated that States should 'seek alternatives to detention whenever possible'. Since Panama's mandatory detention law did not require authorities to verify the possibility of using less restrictive measures through an individualised evaluation in each case, the Court held that the detention was arbitrary and thus incompatible with the *American Convention on Human Rights*.[37]

---

32 See also *American Convention on Human Rights*, art. 5 (right to humane treatment) and art. 7 (right to personal liberty); African Charter on Human Rights, art. 4 (right to life), art. 5 (right to dignity regardless of legal status), art. 6 (right to liberty) and art. 7 (right to a trial).

33 *Conka* v. *Belgium* (2002) 34 EHRR 54.

34 Human Rights Council, *Report of the Working Group on Arbitrary Detention*, 7th sess, UN Doc A/HRC/7/4 (10 January 2008) [53].

35 *Vélez Loor* v. *Panama*, Inter-Am Ct HR (Ser C) No 218 (23 November 2010).   36 Ibid. [169].   37 Ibid. [171].

6.3.3. Liberty of movement, the right to enter one's own country

The ICCPR provides that everyone lawfully in a territory has the right to 'liberty of movement and freedom to choose his residence' (art. 12(1)); that '[e]veryone shall be free to leave any country, including his own' (art. 12(2)); and that '[n]o one shall be arbitrarily deprived of the right to enter his own country' (art. 12(4)). The Human Rights Committee has interpreted the latter provision broadly to give rights to stateless persons who are resident in a particular State, and to others with a long-term relationship with the State but who are not its nationals.[38] Furthermore, States have been urged to ensure that the residence permits of non-nationals who are long-term residents are withdrawn only under exceptional and clearly defined circumstances, and that adequate recourse to appeal against such decisions is made available.[39]

It is important to note, however, that art. 12(3) allows limitations of these rights in certain circumstances. States are permitted to enact laws restricting the right to liberty of movement when it poses a risk to national security, public order, public health or morals, or the human rights of others. The Human Rights Committee notes that such restrictions must be necessary and proportionate to the risk, and not otherwise impair the essence of the right.[40] Under art. 4 of the ICCPR, States may also derogate further in times of national emergency threatening the life of the nation. Derogations, though, must be tailored strictly to the exigencies of the situation and may not discriminate 'solely on the ground of race, colour, sex, language, religion or social origin'. Article 5 of the ICERD, read in conjunction with art. 1(1) of that Convention, further requires that States parties not discriminate on the grounds of 'national or ethnic origin'.

The major regional human rights treaties also recognise these rights. The African Charter on Human Rights provides '[e]very individual shall have the right to freedom of movement and residence within the borders of a State provided he abides by the law' (art. 12). The right is also found in the *American Convention on Human Rights* (art. 22). Furthermore, the right is reflected in art. 2 of *Protocol 4 to the European Convention for the Protection of Human Rights and Fundamental Freedoms* (1963), which accords with the language of the ICCPR and provides similar restrictions.[41] The right to freedom of movement is discussed more comprehensively in Chapter 5.

---

38 Human Rights Committee, *Concluding Observations: New Zealand*, 75th sess, UN Doc CCPR/CO/75/NZL (7 August 2002) [12].

39 European Commission Against Racism and Intolerance, 'Second Report on Switzerland' (Council of Europe, 2000).

40 Human Rights Committee, *General Comment No 27: Freedom of Movement* (Article 12), 67th sess, UN Doc CCPR/C/21/Rev.1/Add.9 (2 November 1999) [13]–[14].

41 *Protocol 4 to the European Convention for the Protection of Human Rights and Fundamental Freedoms*, opened for signature 16 September 1963, ETS 46 (entered into force 2 May 1968).

6.3.4.   Non-nationals as members of minorities: culture, religion and language

Historically, groups in power have perceived minorities as a potential threat to the political unity of the State. David Wippman has observed that when governing elites have enacted policies addressing that threat, they have tended to do so in one of two ways. The first response has been to eliminate the differences of minority and majority groups through programmes of assimilation or, in more extreme examples, through forced population exchanges, ethnic cleansing or genocide. The second approach has been to promote the rights of minorities, under the theory that to do so may decrease the incentives of minorities to mobilise in a manner capable of jeopardising the unity of the State.[42]

Immediately following the First World War, the League of Nations responded to the demands of national minorities by employing strategies largely resembling the second approach, although there were also examples of the first approach, such as population exchanges. Following the Second World War, the United Nations retained the League's goal of inducing internal stability through promotion of equality, but sought to do so by protecting the rights of all individuals rather than protecting only the rights of discrete minorities within certain selected States. Advocates of this approach 'argued that a broad system of individual rights, including rights to freedom of association, speech and religion, would by itself protect the legitimate interests of members of national minorities, if supported by a strong prohibition against discrimination based on race, ethnicity, language or religion'.[43]

Today, examples of the rights that migrants enjoy as members of minorities can be found in several instruments and in the jurisprudence of their monitoring bodies. Article 27 of the ICCPR provides: '[i]n those States in which ethnic, religious or linguistic minorities exist, persons belonging to such minorities shall not be denied the right, in community with the other members of their group, to enjoy their own culture, to profess and practise their own religion, or to use their own language'. In accordance with the universal recognition of rights envisioned by the United Nations system, the Human Rights Committee has expressly stated that art. 27 applies to non-nationals whenever they constitute a minority within the meaning of that provision.[44] The rights of national and racial minorities to enjoy such rights, therefore, cannot be restricted to nationals. Even where non-nationals do not constitute a national minority within the meaning of art. 27, the Human Rights Committee has observed that they still enjoy the right to freedom of religion.

In addition to the ICCPR, the right to profess and practise one's religion and language is echoed in numerous other human rights instruments. Article 2 of the United Nations' *Declaration on the Rights of Persons Belonging to National or*

---

42 David Wippman, 'The Evolution and Implementation of Minority Rights' (1997) 66 *Fordham Law Review* 597, 598.

43 Ibid. 603–4.   44 Human Rights Committee, *General Comment No 15*, above n. 16.

Ethnic, Religious and Linguistic Minorities (1992) records that all persons belonging to minorities have the right 'to profess and practise their own religion, and to use their own language in private and in public, freely and without interference or any form of discrimination'.[45] The European Convention on Human Rights (art. 9) and the *American Convention on Human Rights* (art. 12) similarly guarantee minorities these rights, although with the caveat that the rights may be limited by legal prescription in certain instances to protect public safety, health or morals. The Council of Europe's *Framework Convention for the Protection of National Minorities* (1995) takes the right a step further by imposing an affirmative duty on States to 'undertake to promote the conditions necessary for persons belonging to national minorities to maintain and develop their culture, and to preserve the essential elements of their identity, namely their religion, language, traditions and cultural heritage'.[46]

On the issue of language rights, the Council of Europe's *European Charter for Regional or Minority Languages* (1992),[47] however, clearly differentiates between 'minorities' and 'non-nationals' in its definition of 'regional or minority languages'. Article 1 states that the phrase 'regional or minority languages … does not include … the languages of migrants'. The Council of Europe nonetheless considers 'community relations' to include 'all aspects of the relations between migrants or ethnic groups of immigrant origin and the host society'.[48]

Article 15 of the ICESCR obliges States to take steps to ensure that everyone, regardless of nationality, enjoys the right to take part in cultural life. States have also been urged to take measures necessary to prevent practices that deny non-nationals their cultural and ethnic identity, such as requirements that non-nationals change their name in order to be naturalised.[49] Article 45 of the ICRMW similarly requires States to 'endeavour to facilitate for the children of migrant workers the teaching of their mother tongue and culture'.

6.3.5. Freedoms of expression, assembly and association; protection of privacy

Non-nationals have the right to freedom of thought and conscience, as well as the right to hold and express opinions. Non-nationals also receive the benefit of the essential right to peaceful assembly and of freedom of association. Freedom of

---

45   *Declaration on the Rights of Persons Belonging to National or Ethnic, Religious or Linguistic Minorities*, GA Res 47/135, UN GAOR 47th sess, 92nd plen mtg, UN Doc A/47/49 (18 December 1992).

46   *Framework Convention for the Protection of National Minorities*, opened for signature 1 February 1995, ETS No 157 (entered into force 1 February 1998) art. 5(1).

47   *European Charter for Regional or Minority Languages*, opened for signature 5 November 1992, ETS No 148 (entered into force 1 March 1998).

48   Council of Europe, 'Tackling Racism and Xenophobia: Practical Action at the Local Level' (Council of Europe, 1995) 5.

49   Committee on the Elimination of Racial Discrimination, *Concluding Observations: Japan*, 58th sess, UN Doc CERD/C/304/Add.114 (27 April 2001) [18].

thought and freedom of conscience are protected by art. 18 of the ICCPR and art. 12 of the ICRMW. These rights are intimately tied to freedom of religion and forbid subjecting anyone to such coercion as might impair a person's ability to adopt or maintain a religion. These provisions reflect the right to raise one's children with the morals and religion that one sees fit. Accordingly, art. 18(4) of the ICCPR and art. 12(4) of the ICRMW recognise an affirmative obligation of States parties to ensure parents' or guardians' 'religious and moral education of their children is in conformity with their own convictions'. The ICCPR reflects that 'everyone' is permitted these rights, and hence they are to be respected for nationals and non-nationals alike.

The rights to freedom of thought and conscience, however, are not without boundaries. The ICCPR (art. 18(3)) and ICRMW (art. 12(3)) permit States parties to limit the manifestation of religion or belief when such limitations are otherwise prescribed by law and are necessary 'to protect public safety, order, health or morals or the fundamental rights and freedom of others'. Accordingly, it is permissible for States parties to prohibit harmful expressions, providing such prohibitions are not imposed retroactively.

Freedom of assembly and freedom of association have long been held to be essential tools for realising other fundamental rights and therefore have not customarily been limited to nationals. The right of peaceful assembly is recorded in art. 20 of the UDHR, as well as in art. 21 of the ICCPR. Further, the right is recognised by all the major regional human rights treaties: the African Charter on Human Rights (art. 11), the *American Convention on Human Rights* (art. 15), the European Convention on Human Rights (art. 11) and the *Charter of Fundamental Rights of the European Union* (2010) (art. 12).[50] The ICESCR (art. 8) also provides that States parties must undertake to ensure 'the right of everyone ... to join the trade union of his choice' and that such unions must be permitted to function freely – a right more forcefully recognised in the ICCPR (art. 22). The same limitations, however, are placed upon these rights as upon the freedom of religion and belief.

Non-nationals may not be subjected to arbitrary or unlawful interference with their privacy, family, home or correspondence. This right is guaranteed by art. 17 of the ICCPR and art. 14 of the ICRMW. It is also reflected in art. 12 of the UDHR, art. 11 of the *American Convention on Human Rights* and art. 8 of the European Convention on Human Rights.

Privacy is a broad term and therefore the scope of the right is not easily defined. Unlike many other rights provisions, there is no limitation clause found in either the ICCPR or the *American Convention on Human Rights*. The Human Rights Committee, in its *General Comment No 16*, has stated that 'the competent public authorities should only be able to call for such information relating to an

---

50 *Charter of Fundamental Rights of the European Union* (2010) OJ C 83/389.

individual's private life the knowledge of which is essential in the interests of society as understood under the Covenant'.[51] Hence, measures encroaching upon the right to privacy should be construed in a limited manner. The Human Rights Committee also stated that, in accordance with art. 17:

> Surveillance, whether electronic or otherwise, interceptions of telephonic, telegraphic and other forms of communication, wire-tapping and recording of conversations should be prohibited. Searches of a person's home should be restricted to a search for necessary evidence and should not be allowed to amount to harassment. So far as personal and body search is concerned, effective measures should ensure that such searches are carried out in a manner consistent with the dignity of the person who is being searched. Persons being subjected to body search by State officials, or medical personnel acting at the request of the State, should only be examined by persons of the same sex.[52]

6.3.6.   Protection from *refoulement* and arbitrary expulsion

Instruments, such as the United Nations *Declaration on the Human Rights of Individuals Who are Not Nationals of the Country in which They Live* (1985),[53] and art. 4 of *Protocol 4 to the European Convention for the Protection of Human Rights and Fundamental Freedoms*, provide that the collective expulsion of non-nationals is prohibited. Based on repetition of this principle in the *American Convention on Human Rights* (art. 22(9)) and the ICRMW (art. 22(1)), the prohibition can be said to bind all States as a matter of customary international law. Any measure that compels non-nationals, as a group, to leave a State is prohibited, except where the measure is taken on the basis of a reasonable and objective examination of the particular case of each individual non-national in the group. The procedure for the expulsion of a group of non-nationals must afford sufficient guarantees demonstrating that the personal circumstances of each of those persons concerned has been genuinely and individually taken into account.[54] Hence, if one member of a group of non-nationals is found not to qualify for refugee status because there is a safe country of origin, and is ordered to be deported, the other members of the group cannot be deported unless they too are individually assessed not to qualify for refugee status.

As individuals, non-nationals are protected from arbitrary expulsion by art. 13 of the ICCPR. Non-nationals may only be expelled 'in pursuance of a decision reached in accordance with law', and are entitled to the right to contest such expulsion 'except where compelling reasons of national security otherwise require'.

---

51 Human Rights Committee, *General Comment No 16: The Right to Respect of Privacy, Family, Home and Correspondence and Protection of Honour and Reputation (Art 17)*, 32nd sess (8 April 1988) [7].
52 Ibid. [8].
53 *Declaration on the Human Rights of Individuals Who Are Not Nationals of the Country in which They Live*, GA Res 40/144, UN GAOR, 40th sess, 116th plen mtg, Supp No 53, UN Doc. A/RES/40/144 (13 December 1985).
54 *Conka* v. *Belgium* (2002) 34 EHRR 54, [21], [46]–[57]; European Commission Against Racism and Intolerance, 'Second Report on Finland' (Council of Europe, 2002).

The Human Rights Committee, though, has stated that even non-nationals sus-pected of terrorism should be provided these rights.[55]

The ICRMW (art. 22) also guarantees a high standard of procedural protection for individual expulsion, and provides an extremely useful checklist of measures to be instituted to ensure migrants have access to effective and individual determination of their defence against expulsion.

The Human Rights Committee has stated that, under the ICCPR, a non-national who is expelled must normally be allowed to leave for any State that agrees to take him or her.[56] Non-nationals enjoy the right to be protected from *refoulement*, or deportation to a State in which they may be subjected to persecution. The principle of *non-refoulement* exists in a number of international instruments with slightly varying coverage, and is considered by many to constitute a principle of customary international law.[57] The expulsion of non-nationals should not be carried out without taking into account possible risks to their lives and physical integrity in the States of destination.[58]

Regarding refugees, the *Convention relating to the Status of Refugees* (1951) ('Refugee Convention') codifies the prohibition against *refoulement*.[59] The United Nations High Commissioner for Refugees ('UNHCR') has noted that the Refugee Convention's *non-refoulement* provision applies 'wherever a State exercises jurisdiction, including at the frontier, on the high seas or on the territory of another State'.[60] The Refugee Convention, however, permits an exception for any refugee 'whom there are reasonable grounds for regarding as a danger to the security of the country in which he is, or who, having been convicted by a final judgment of a particularly serious crime, constitutes a danger to the community of that country'. In addition, art. 1F withholds the protections of the Refugee Convention from any person with respect to whom there are serious reasons for considering that:

(a) he has committed a crime against peace, a war crime, or a crime against humanity …; (b) he has committed a serious non-political crime outside the country of refuge prior to his admission to that country as a refugee; (c) he has been guilty of acts contrary to the purposes and principles of the United Nations.

55 Human Rights Committee, *Concluding Observations: Syrian Arab Republic*, 71st sess, UN Doc CCPR/CO/71/SYR (24 April 2001) [22].
56 Human Rights Committee, *General Comment No 15*, above n. 16, [9].
57 David Weissbrodt and Isabel Hortreiter, 'Principle of Non-Refoulement: Article 3 of the Convention against Torture and Other Cruel, Inhuman or Degrading Treatment or Punishment in Comparison with the Non-Refoulement Provisions of Other International Human Rights Treaties' (1999) 5 *Buffalo Human Rights Law Review* 1.
58 Human Rights Committee, *Concluding Observations: Yemen*, 75th sess, UN Doc CCPR/CO/75/YEM (12 August 2002) [18]; *Ahmed* v. *Austria* (1997) 24 EHRR 423, [54]; Human Rights Committee, *Views: Communication No 586/1994*, 57th sess, UN Doc CCPR/C/57/D/586/1994 (23 July 1996) ('*Adam* v. *Czech Republic*') [12].
59 *Convention relating to the Status of Refugees*, opened for signature 28 July 1951, 189 UNTS 150 (entered into force 22 April 1954) art. 33.
60 United Nations High Commissioner for Refugees, 'Advisory Opinion on the Extraterritorial Application of *non-refoulement* Obligations under the 1951 Convention relating to the Status of Refugees and its 1967 Protocol' (UNHCR, 2007) [24].

UNHCR states that when applying the general exclusion, States parties should balance the degree of persecution feared by the applicant against the severity of his or her crime.[61] The Refugee Convention does not affect States parties' other obligations under international law. Accordingly, 'the host state would be barred from removing a refugee if this would result in exposing him or her, for example, to a substantial risk of torture'.[62] The rights of refugees are covered more extensively in Chapter 7.

In contrast, the *non-refoulement* provision in the *Convention against Torture and Other Cruel, Inhuman or Degrading Treatment or Punishment* (1984) ('Convention against Torture') tolerates no such exception.[63] Article 2(2) stipulates that '[n]o exceptional circumstances whatsoever, whether a state of war or a threat of war, internal political instability or any other public emergency, may be invoked as a justification for torture'. Article 2(2) applies to the entirety of the Convention against Torture, including the *non-refoulement* provision, because the latter provision is intended to prevent torture in the State to which an individual would be returned.

General Comment No 6 of the Committee on the Rights of the Child notes that family reunification in the State of origin is not necessarily in the best interests of an unaccompanied or separated child, and therefore should not be pursued where there is a 'reasonable risk' that such a return would lead to the violation of fundamental human rights of the child.[64] The Committee asks that States balance the best interests of the child, even in situations where the risk is lower than the standard provided in the Refugee Convention ('life or freedom would be threatened' on return – art. 33) or the Convention against Torture ('substantial grounds for believing' there is a danger of torture on return – art. 3). Where indications suggest that children should not be returned to their State of origin, States are asked to consider granting entry to the parents or guardians of unaccompanied children.

6.3.7. Right to acquire, maintain and transmit nationality

Article 15 of the UDHR states that '[e]veryone has the right to a nationality' and '[n]o one shall be arbitrarily deprived of his nationality nor denied the right to change his nationality'. However, the UDHR is not a treaty, and a universal treaty-based right to a nationality is generally confined to children – for example, under art. 8 of the *Convention on the Rights of the Child* (1989),[65] art. 24 of the ICCPR and arts.

---

61 United Nations High Commissioner for Refugees, *Handbook on Procedures and Criteria for Determining Refugee Status* (UNHCR, 1992) [38].

62 United Nations High Commissioner for Refugees, above n. 60, [11].

63 *Convention against Torture and Other Cruel, Inhuman or Degrading Treatment or Punishment*, opened for signature 10 December 1984, 1465 UNTS 85 (entered into force 26 June 1987) art. 3.

64 Committee on the Rights of the Child, *General Comment No 6: Treatment of Unaccompanied and Separated Children outside their Country of Origin*, 39th sess, UN Doc CRC/GC/2005/6 (1 September 2005) [82].

65 *Convention on the Rights of the Child*, opened for signature 20 November 1989, 1577 UNTS 3 (entered into force 2 September 1990).

24(3) and 29 of the ICRMW – and stateless persons, for States that are party to the relevant instruments (see Chapter 4).

The granting of nationality is largely within the prerogative of the State. The Committee on the Rights of the Child has noted that persons should be able to transmit their nationality to their children regardless of their own gender and regardless of whether they are married to the other parent.[66]

Regional human rights treaties also provide guidance on the scope of these rights. The *American Convention on Human Rights* states that '[e]very person has the right to the nationality of the State in whose territory he was born if he does not have the right to any other nationality', and that States may not arbitrarily deprive anyone of their nationality or of the right to change their nationality (art. 20). Although neither the acquisition nor loss of nationality is directly regulated by the European Convention on Human Rights, decisions to confer and revoke nationality are subject to the substantive and procedural requirements outlined therein. Accordingly, an arbitrary deprivation of nationality may rise to the level of 'inhuman or degrading treatment' prohibited under art. 3, or may violate the right to respect for private and family life guaranteed under art. 8. For example, in *Berrehab* v. *Netherlands*,[67] the European Court of Human Rights held that where a non-national has substantial family ties to a State from which he or she is ordered to be deported, and such deportation would place those ties in jeopardy, expulsion is only justifiable if it is pursuant to a legitimate objective (such as the maintenance of public safety) and the resulting interference with the non-national's family is proportionate to achieving that objective.

There are at least three other international instruments that relate to the development of the international law of nationality. First, the *European Convention on Nationality* (1997) reflects many of the basic principles discussed above and, in addition, provides a set of general rules and procedures States parties must follow in implementing nationality rights.[68] Second, the International Law Commission has published recommendations in its *Draft Articles on Nationality of Natural Persons in relation to the Succession of States*.[69] Third, the *Council of Europe Convention on the Avoidance of Statelessness in Relation to State Succession* (2006) indicates that States parties must incorporate its provisions through national legislation.[70] These and other matters regarding nationality and statelessness are discussed in Chapter 4.

---

66 Committee on the Rights of the Child, *Concluding Observations: United Kingdom*, 31st sess, UN Doc CRC/C/15/Add.188 (9 October 2002) [23].

67 *Berrehab* v. *Netherlands* (1988) 138 Eur Court HR (ser A).

68 *European Convention on Nationality*, opened for signature 6 November 1997, ETS No 166 (entered into force 1 March 2000).

69 See also International Law Commission, *Draft Articles on Nationality of Natural Persons in relation to the Succession of States* (Yearbook of the International Law Commission, United Nations, 1999).

70 *Council of Europe Convention on the Avoidance of Statelessness in relation to State Succession*, opened for signature 19 May 2006, CETS No 200 (entered into force 1 May 2009).

6.3.8. Right to health, housing, an adequate standard of living, work and education

As discussed in preceding sections, States must avoid different standards of treatment with regard to nationals and non-nationals that might lead to racial segregation and the unequal enjoyment of economic, social and cultural rights. Furthermore, under the ICESCR, governments should take progressive measures to the extent of available resources to protect the rights of everyone, regardless of nationality, to: social security (art. 9); an adequate standard of living including adequate food, clothing, housing and the continuous improvement of living conditions (art. 11); the enjoyment of the highest attainable standard of physical and mental health (art. 12); and education (art. 13).

In addition to the obligation of progressive realisation, it is important to note that under the ICESCR States have a duty to 'take steps', even when constrained by lack of resources, to target programmes to protect the most disadvantaged, vulnerable and marginalised populations – which in many circumstances are migrants.[71] Accordingly, there are certain immediate obligations in regard to the rights recognised under the ICESCR, including the obligation of non-discrimination, the prohibition of retroactive measures, and the immediate satisfaction of essential levels of certain core obligations. The latter duty applies equally to all individuals present in a State and includes, for example, the right of access to employment;[72] basic shelter;[73] water and sanitation;[74] and the provision of universal, free and compulsory education.[75]

Right to health[76]

The Committee on Economic, Social and Cultural Rights has noted in its *General Comment No 14* that all 'illegal immigrants' should have equal access to 'preventive, curative and palliative health services' under the ICESCR.[77] This protection contrasts with the ICRMW (art. 28), which provides migrant workers and their families with the right only to medical care that is 'urgently required for the preservation of their life or the avoidance of irreparable harm to their health on the basis of equality of treatment with nationals of the State concerned'. In view of the apparent disparity, it is suggested that non-nationals ought to be entitled to the most protective human rights provisions in applicable treaties and their

---

71 Committee on Economic, Social and Cultural Rights, *General Comment No 3: The Nature of States Parties' Obligations*, 50th sess, UN Doc E/1991/23 (14 December 1990) annex III, 86.

72 Committee on Economic, Social and Cultural Rights, *General Comment No 18: The Right to Work*, 35th sess, UN Doc E/C.12/GC/18 (6 February 2006) [31].

73 Committee on Economic, Social and Cultural Rights, *General Comment No 3*, above n. 71, 10.

74 Committee on Economic, Social and Cultural Rights, *General Comment No 15: The Right to Water*, 29th sess, UN Doc E/C.12/2002/11 (20 January 2003) [37].

75 Committee on Economic, Social and Cultural Rights, *General Comment No 13: The Right to Education*, 21st sess, UN Doc E/C.12/1999/10 (8 December 1999) [57].

76 International Organization for Migration, 'Migration and the Right to Health: A Review of International Law' (IOM, 2009).

77 Committee on Economic, Social and Cultural Rights, *General Comment No 14: The Right to the Highest Attainable Standard of Health*, 22nd sess, UN Doc E/C.12/2000/4 (11 August 2000) [34].

authoritative interpretations. As noted by the Special Rapporteur on the Human Rights of Migrants, 'mere commitment to emergency care is unjustified not only from a human rights perspective, but also from a public health standpoint, as a failure to receive any type of preventive and primary care can create health risks for both migrants and their host community'.[78]

The World Health Organization ('WHO') has further undertaken to promote the universal realisation of the right to health, in view of the fact that the objective of attaining the highest possible level of health 'by all peoples' was enunciated at the international level by its Constitution as early as 1946.[79] In 2008, the WHO endorsed a Resolution on the Health of Migrants, calling upon States to promote many migrant-specific policies. Some examples of the WHO's recommendations are 'equitable access to health promotion, disease prevention and care for migrants', promotion of 'migrant-sensitive health policies' and promotion of cooperation between States on migrant health issues.[80]

Right to an adequate standard of living, food and housing

The right to an adequate standard of living comprises numerous other rights, including the right to health, the right to food and nutrition, and the right to adequate housing. The UDHR guarantees the rights to housing and an adequate standard of living in art. 25. The rights are reaffirmed in the ICESCR (art. 11) and, additionally, the right to be free from arbitrary interference with one's home is protected by the ICCPR (art. 17) and the ICRMW (art. 14).

The right to food and nutrition is available without regard to nationality. The Committee on Economic, Social and Cultural Rights has stated that '[t]he right to adequate food is realized when every man, woman and child, alone or in community with others, has physical and economic access at all times to adequate food or means for its procurement'.[81] At a minimum, the right obligates States parties to immediately take steps to 'mitigate and alleviate hunger'.[82] Progressive realisation requires that States parties must further work towards ensuring not only proper quantity of food, but also proper composition of food. Foods of proper composition must 'satisfy the dietary needs of individuals, [be] free from adverse substances, and acceptable within a given culture'.[83]

The right to adequate housing is guaranteed in several other international instruments, including the ICRMW (art. 43(d)), the Refugee Convention (art. 21) and the *Convention on the Rights of the Child* (art. 27). The Committee on Economic, Social and Cultural Rights has also noted that the right to housing belongs to 'everyone', and

---

78 Human Rights Council, *Report of the Special Rapporteur on the Human Rights of Migrants, Jorge Bustamante*, 14th sess, UN Doc A/HRC/14/30 (16 April 2010) [28].

79 *Constitution of the World Health Organization*, opened for signature 22 July 1946, 14 UNTS 185 (entered into force 7 April 1948) art. 1.

80 World Health Organization, *Health of Migrants*, 61st assembly, UN Doc WHA61.17 (24 May 2008).

81 Committee on Economic, Social and Cultural Rights, *General Comment No 12: The Right to Adequate Food*, 20th sess, UN Doc E/C.12/1999/5 (12 May 1999) [6].

82 Ibid.   83 Ibid. [8].

'individuals, as well as families, are entitled to adequate housing regardless of age, economic status, group or other affiliation or status and other such factors', and, accordingly, the right may 'not be subject to any form of discrimination'.[84]

The United Nations Special Rapporteur on Adequate Housing has explained that the right to housing is very broad and includes the right of 'every woman, man, youth and child to gain and sustain a safe and secure home and community in which to live in peace and dignity'.[85] Additionally, the Committee on Economic, Social and Cultural Rights has indicated that there are numerous requirements for housing to be 'adequate'. First, adequate housing must provide 'security of tenure', meaning that inhabitants are protected 'against forced eviction, harassment and other threats'. Second, certain 'services, materials, facilities and infrastructure' must be available – for example, there must be sustainable access to drinking water, sanitation facilities and refuse disposal. Third, homes must be 'affordable', meaning that the 'percentage of housing-related costs is, in general, commensurate with income levels'. Fourth, homes must be 'habitable'. Fifth, homes must be 'accessible' and in such a location as allows access to 'employment options, health-care services, schools, child-care centres and other social facilities'. Further, 'the way housing is constructed, the building materials used and the policies supporting these must appropriately enable the expression of cultural identity and diversity of housing'.[86]

In regional instruments, the right to adequate housing is most clearly expressed by the *Charter of the Organization of American States* (1948)[87] and the *European Social Charter* (1961).[88] Additionally, the *European Convention on the Legal Status of Migrant Workers* (1977) requires any State party to 'accord to migrant workers, with regard to access to housing and rents, treatment not less favourable than that accorded to its own nationals'.[89]

Right to work, to be free from forced labour, and to social security

Realisation of many of the rights discussed in this section is intricately tied to the right to work. The UDHR proclaims in art. 23(1) that '[e]veryone has the right to work, to free choice of employment, to just and favourable conditions of work, and to protection against unemployment'. Article 23 further recognises the right of everyone, 'without any discrimination', to 'equal pay for equal work' and to remuneration capable of ensuring 'human dignity'. The ICESCR (art. 6) echoes the UDHR

---

84 Committee on Economic, Social and Cultural Rights, *General Comment No 4: The Right to Adequate Housing*, 60th sess, UN Doc E/1992/23 (13 December 1991) [6].

85 Miloon Kothari, 'Report of the Special Rapporteur on Adequate Housing as a Component of the Right to an Adequate Standard of Living, and on the Right to Non-Discrimination in this Context' (UN Doc A/HRC/7/16, Human Rights Council, 2008) [4].

86 Committee on Economic, Social and Cultural Rights, *General Comment No 4*, above n. 84, [8].

87 *Charter of the Organization of American States*, opened for signature 30 April 1948, 119 UNTS 3 (entered into force 13 December 1951) art. 34(k).

88 *European Social Charter*, opened for signature 18 October 1961, CETS No 35 (entered into force 26 February 1965) art. 31.

89 *European Convention on the Legal Status of Migrant Workers*, opened for signature 24 November 1977, ETS No 93 (entered into force 1 May 1983) art. 13.

and expands the right to include a right to education, obliging States parties to strive towards implementing 'technical and vocational guidance and training programmes'. In addition, the ICRMW requires that migrants specifically shall not be required to perform compulsory labour (art. 11); shall enjoy equal treatment with nationals with respect to remuneration, conditions of work, such as safety and overtime (art. 25); and shall have the right to join trade unions (art. 26).

The ICCPR (art. 8) forbids 'forced or compulsory labour'. The prohibition against coerced labour is also noted in the African Charter on Human Rights (art. 5), the *American Convention on Human Rights* (art. 6(2)) and the European Convention on Human Rights (art. 4). Likewise, the International Labour Organization has promulgated several multilateral treaties on the rights of everyone, including non-nationals, relating to work, among them the *Convention concerning Forced or Compulsory Labour* (1930),[90] the *Convention concerning Migration for Employment (Revised)* (1949),[91] the *Convention concerning Equal Remuneration for Men and Women Workers for Work of Equal Value* (1951)[92] and the *Convention concerning Migrations in Abusive Conditions and the Promotion of Equality of Opportunity and Treatment of Migrant Workers* (1975).[93]

States must ensure that social services provide a minimum standard of living for non-nationals.[94] Accordingly, the CERD Committee encourages States to engage in initiatives to include non-nationals in national health insurance systems.[95] The right to social security is also addressed by the ICESCR (art. 9), which requires its recognition as a 'right of everyone'.

Right to education

Article 26(1) of the UDHR establishes the right of everyone to education. The scope of this right is elaborated in the ICESCR (art. 13), requiring that '[p]rimary education shall be compulsory and available free to all'; '[s]econdary education ... shall be made generally available and accessible to all by every appropriate means, and in particular by the progressive introduction of free education'; and '[h]igher education shall be made equally accessible to all, on the basis of capacity'. The *Convention against Discrimination in Education* (1960) further indicates that non-nationals must be provided the same access to education as nationals.[96] Specifically regarding migrants,

90 *Convention concerning Forced or Compulsory Labour* (ILO Convention No 29), opened for signature 10 June 1930, 39 UNTS 55 (entered into force 1 May 1932).
91 *Convention concerning Migration for Employment (Revised)* (ILO Convention No 97), opened for signature 1 July 1949 (entered into force 22 January 1952).
92 *Convention concerning Equal Remuneration for Men and Women Workers for Work of Equal Value* (ILO Convention No 100), opened for signature 29 June 1951, 165 UNTS 303 (entered into force 23 May 1953).
93 *Convention concerning Migrations in Abusive Conditions and the Promotion of Equality of Opportunity and Treatment of Migrant Workers* (ILO Convention No 143), opened for signature 24 June 1975 (entered into force 9 December 1978).
94 Committee on Economic, Social and Cultural Rights, *Concluding Observations: Ukraine*, 13th sess, UN Doc E/C.12/1995/15 (28 December 1995) [19].
95 Committee on the Elimination of Racial Discrimination, *Concluding Observations: Saudi Arabia*, 62nd sess, UN Doc CERD/C/62/CO/8 (2 June 2003) [6].
96 *Convention against Discrimination in Education*, opened for signature 14 December 1960, 429 UNTS 93 (entered into force 22 May 1962).

the ICRMW reaffirms that the children of migrant workers have the same basic right to education as nationals, providing that access to schools 'shall not be refused or limited by reason of the irregular situation with respect to stay or employment of either parent or by reason of the irregularity of the child's stay in the State of employment' (art. 30).

The Committee on Economic, Social and Cultural Rights has indicated that the principle of non-discrimination 'extends to all persons of school age residing in the territory of a State party, including non-nationals, and irrespective of their legal status'.[97] Further, the prohibition against discrimination enshrined in art. 2(2) of the ICESCR 'is subject to neither progressive realization nor the availability of resources; it applies fully and immediately to all aspects of education and encompasses all internationally prohibited grounds of discrimination'.[98] In the regional treaties, the right to education is found in the African Charter on Human Rights (art. 17(1)), the *Charter of the Organization of American States* (art. 47) and Protocol 1 to the European Convention on Human Rights (art. 2).[99]

6.4. CONCLUSION

In the majority of cases, the human rights norms contained in the core human rights treaties apply to non-nationals in the same way as nationals of the host State. Further, migrants are provided additional protection under several treaties focussed specifically on this group. Hence, it is clear under international human rights law that governments have the duty to promote, protect and fulfil the civil, political, economic, social and cultural rights of migrants within their jurisdiction. However, despite the fact that migrants are bearers of rights, they often suffer discrimination, exploitation and persecution. Indeed, there is a significant gap between their legal rights and the realities of their lives.

There are various ways in which respect for the human rights of migrants can be promoted effectively. This objective may be through seeking remedies under national law, or through the supervision and monitoring regimes established under various core human rights treaties. An additional, often underutilised, mechanism is that of consular protection and assistance. In contrast to the forms of redress listed above, consular protection and assistance are not only responsive to human rights abuses, they may also be used to prevent breaches of human rights before they occur. Further, they implicate the sending State as well as the host State. Finally, international organisations may assist States in giving effect to their protection obligations; the primary responsibility for protection of the human rights of migrants, however, remains with governments.

---

97 Committee on Economic, Social and Cultural Rights, *General Comment No 13*, above n. 75, [34].
98 Ibid. [31].
99 *Protocol 1 to the European Convention for the Protection of Human Rights and Fundamental Freedoms*, opened for signature 20 March 1952, ETS No 9 (entered into force 18 May 1954).

KEY REFERENCES

Committee on the Elimination of Racial Discrimination, 'General Recommendation No 30, Discrimination against Non-Citizens' (UN Doc CERD/C/64/Misc.11/rev.3, 2004)

Human Rights Committee, 'General Comment No 15: The Position of Aliens under the Covenant', 27th sess (UN Doc HRI/GEN/1/Rev.1, 11 April 1986)

Lillich, Richard, *The Human Rights of Aliens in Contemporary International Law* (Manchester University Press, 1984)

Simma, Bruno (ed.), *Charter of the United Nations: A Commentary* (Oxford University Press, 1994)

Tiburcio, Carmen, *The Human Rights of Aliens under International and Comparative Law* (Kluwer, 2001)

Weissbrodt, David, *The Human Rights of Non-Citizens* (Oxford University Press, 2008)

Wippman, David, 'The Evolution and Implementation of Minority Rights' (1997) **66** *Fordham Law Review* 597

KEY RESOURCES

International Labour Organization: www.ilo.org

International Organization for Migration: www.iom.int

United Nations High Commissioner for Human Rights, Committee on Migrant Workers: www2.ohchr.org/english/bodies/cmw

United Nations High Commissioner for Human Rights, Special Rapporteur on the Human Rights of Migrants: www2.ohchr.org/english/issues/migration/rapporteur

United Nations High Commissioner for Refugees: www.unhcr.org

University of Minnesota, Human Rights Library: www1.umn.edu/humanrts

7 Refugees and asylum

JAMES C. HATHAWAY[1]

During the late nineteenth and early twentieth centuries, European governments enacted a series of immigration laws under which international migration was constrained in order to maximise advantage for States. These new, largely self-interested laws clashed with the enormity of a series of major population displacements within Europe, including the flight of more than a million Russians between 1917 and 1922, and the exodus during the early 1920s of hundreds of thousands of Armenians from Turkey. The social crisis brought on by the *de facto* immigration of so many refugees – present without authorisation in countries where they enjoyed no protection and no ability to support themselves legally – convinced European governments that the viability of the overall migration control project depended on building into that regime a needs-based exception for refugees. Providing specifically for refugees would legitimate what was, in any event, an unstoppable phenomenon; it would thus reinforce the viability of the protectionist norm. Equally important, enfranchising those who were unlawfully present would defuse social tensions in States of reception and position refugees to make a positive contribution to their new societies.

7.1. THE EVOLUTION OF INTERNATIONAL REFUGEE LAW

Between 1920 and 1950, the League of Nations and other intergovernmental bodies were given the task of administering refugee protection, commencing with the mandate of Fridtjof Nansen in the 1920s. This was an extraordinarily fluid era, with the refugee definition evolving from an initial focus on groups of *de jure* stateless persons; then refocussing on groups of persons who were *de facto* disfranchised (i.e., deprived of the substantive benefits of nationality) under the National Socialist regime in Germany; and, in the post-war era, embracing individuals in

1 The assistance of Research Scholar Simone Alt is acknowledged with appreciation. Portions of this analysis draw on the author's earlier work, in particular: James Hathaway, *The Law of Refugee Status* (Butterworths, 1991); James Hathaway, *The Rights of Refugees under International Law* (Cambridge University Press, 2005). Cases referred to herein may be accessed on the Refugee Caselaw Site (www.refugeecaselaw.org).

177

search of escape from perceived injustice in their home State.[2] Not only did the definition of a refugee shift from a juridical, to a social, and finally to an individualist perspective, but the actual rights guaranteed to refugees under the succession of refugee treaties also changed over time. Drawing on the normative structures of international law of aliens and the interwar minorities treaties, the duties owed to refugees were sometimes defined in mandatory terms, sometimes as benchmarks to be strived for. The critical duty of *non-refoulement* – not to return refugees to a territory where they may face persecution – first appeared in 1933.[3] But the predominant focus of refugee treaties was on ensuring access to key socio-economic rights – for example, relief from foreign labour restrictions, access to education, and the right to receive medical and welfare benefits. International agencies were not engaged simply in oversight, but were the lead entities entrusted with protecting refugees.

7.1.1.   The 1951 *Convention relating to the Status of Refugees*

The primary standard of refugee protection today is the *Convention relating to the Status of Refugees* (1951) ('Refugee Convention'), to which roughly 80 per cent of the world's States have bound themselves.[4] While the Refugee Convention provides for the continuing protection of all persons deemed to be refugees under any of the earlier accords, its definition is fundamentally individualist and forward-looking ('a well-founded fear of being persecuted'), and limited to persons who have already fled their own country and whose risk derives from civil or political discrimination. When first adopted, States could restrict their commitments to pre-1951 and European refugees, though few in fact chose to do so.

While clearly born of the strategic goals of Western States in the immediate post-Second World War era, an extraordinary judge-led commitment in the years since 1990 has ensured the continuing viability of this definition to meet most modern needs.[5] A real strength of the Refugee Convention is its rights regime,

---

2 James Hathaway, 'The Evolution of Refugee Status in International Law: 1920–1950' (1984) 33(2) *International and Comparative Law Quarterly* 348.

3 Walter Kälin, *Das Prinzip des Non-Refoulement* (Lang, 1982); Gunnel Stenberg, *Non-Expulsion and Non-Refoulement* (Iustus Förlag, 1989).

4 *Convention relating to the Status of Refugees*, opened for signature 28 July 1951, 189 UNTS 150 (entered into force 22 April 1954). The drafting history of the Refugee Convention is collected in Alex Takkenberg and Christopher Tabhaz (eds.), *The Collected Travaux Préparatoires of the 1951 Geneva Convention relating to the Status of Refugees* (Dutch Refugee Council, 1989).

5 Leading national analyses of refugee law have played a critical support role in this process of normative reinvigoration. See Frédéric Tiberghien, *La protection des réfugiés en France* (Économica, 1988); Walter Kälin, *Grundriss des Asylverfahrens* (Helbing & Lichtenhahn, 1990); Geoffrey Coll and Jacqueline Bhabha (eds.), *Asylum Law and Practice in Europe and North America: A Comparative Analysis* (Federal Publications, 1992); Vitit Muntarbhorn, *The Status of Refugees in Asia* (Clarendon Press, 1992); Mary Crock (ed.), *Protection or Punishment: The Detention of Asylum Seekers in Australia* (Federation Press, 1993); Hélène Lambert, *Seeking Asylum: Comparative Law and Practice in Selected European Countries* (Martinus Nijhoff, 1995); Vincent Chetail and Vera Gowlland-Debbas (eds.), *Switzerland and the International Protection of Refugees* (Kluwer Law International, 2002); Nicholas Blake and Raza Husain, *Immigration, Asylum and Human Rights* (Oxford University Press, 2003); Mark Symes and Peter Jorro, *Asylum Law and Practice* (International Specialized Book Service, 2003); Mary Crock, Ben Saul and Azadeh Dastyari, *Future Seekers II: Refugees and Irregular Migration in Australia* (Federation Press, 2006); Mirko Bagaric *et al.*, *Migration and Refugee Law in Australia: Cases and Commentary*

which not only guarantees such critical rights as non-penalisation for illegal entry, non-expulsion and *non-refoulement*, but provides for the most far-reaching guarantees of socio-economic rights granted to any category of non-nationals under international law. Read together with the subsequently enacted norms of international human rights law, the refugee rights regime is an extraordinarily resilient and comprehensive normative structure.

In exchange for these progressive commitments, however, the States that drafted the Refugee Convention insisted that they – not the international oversight agency, now the United Nations High Commissioner for Refugees ('UNHCR') – would control the refugee protection system. While State parties agree to cooperate with UNHCR in its duty to supervise the application of the Refugee Convention – and while UNHCR has leveraged its convention-based and statutory authority (described below, Section 7.1.4) to establish itself as both the leading source of normative guidance and a critical on-the-ground actor in less developed countries – governments nonetheless remain the lead entities for refugee protection under the terms of the Refugee Convention.

7.1.2. The 1967 *Protocol relating to the Status of Refugees*

At the global level, the most critical legal development since the Refugee Convention was the advent of the *Protocol relating to the Status of Refugees* (1967) ('Protocol').[6] This treaty eliminated the option for States to restrict protection efforts to pre-1951 refugees, or European refugees, or both. While the Protocol is sometimes said to have 'universalised' the Refugee Convention, it did not in fact vary the criteria of the Convention (a well-founded fear of being persecuted for reasons of civil or political status) or broaden its rights guarantees (e.g., to include a right to basic physical security). As such, many involuntary migrants in the less developed world remain excluded from the refugee regime where, for example, their flight is prompted solely by natural disaster, war, or broadly based political and economic turmoil, or where migration does not involve crossing an international border. But because most States are parties to both the Refugee Convention and the Protocol,[7] there is a legal duty to read the Convention's protection responsibilities in the geopolitically and temporally inclusive way mandated by the Protocol:

Because the Convention is universal, it does not speak only of the grounds of persecution that have been most familiar to Western countries … [I]n other societies, and in modern times,

(Cambridge University Press, 2007); Martin Jones and Sasha Baglay, *Refugee Law* (Irwin Law, 2007); Osamu Arakaki, *Refugee Law and Practice in Japan* (Ashgate, 2008); Deborah Anker, *The Law of Asylum in the United States* (West Group, 2011).

6 *Protocol relating to the Status of Refugees*, opened for accession 31 January 1967, 606 UNTS 267 (entered into force 4 October 1967).

7 The Protocol incorporates by reference most of the provisions of the Refugee Convention. A small number of countries (including the United States) that are parties to the Protocol but not the Convention are thus bound to respect the Convention's refugee definition and rights regime.

different cultural norms and social imperatives may give rise to different sources of persecution. ... The concept is not a static one. Nor is it fixed by historical appreciation.[8]

7.1.3. Regional developments

In addition to this duty to interpret global norms in an inclusive way, greater geopolitical inclusivity has also been promoted by regional organisations (see Chapter 14). The African Union administers the *Convention Governing the Specific Aspects of Refugee Problems in Africa* (1969) ('OAU Convention').[9] This treaty broke new ground by extending protection to all persons compelled to flee across national borders by reason of any man-made disaster. In contrast to the Refugee Convention, it does not require a link between risk and civil or political status, and extends protection to persons fleeing harm that affects only a portion of their country of origin. In 2009, the African Union also adopted binding norms on the protection of internally displaced persons, although these are not yet in force.[10]

A similar but somewhat more modest step was taken in Latin America via adoption of the *Cartagena Declaration on Refugees* (1984), approved by the Assembly of the Organization of American States ('OAS') in 1985.[11] While acknowledging the refugee status of groups of persons fleeing widespread occurrences, the OAS standard does not extend protection to persons in flight from problems affecting only a part of their country of origin. Nor is it legally binding, though some States (e.g., Bolivia and Brazil) have incorporated it into their domestic law.

The initial focus of activity in Europe was the Council of Europe, which recognised the notion of *de facto* refugees in 1976.[12] The momentum today, however, is with the European Union, which has enacted binding directives commencing in 2004 on the recognition of refugee status and a broader 'subsidiary protection' class,[13] detailing the content of protection and stipulating the procedures by which protection is to be implemented.[14] Expressly framed as 'minimum standards' and as subordinate to Refugee Convention requirements, since 2009 these directives have been interpreted and applied by the European Court of Justice. In contrast to the principled expansion at the root of African and Latin American initiatives, regional asylum activity in the European Union has been prompted by the protection dictates of European human rights law and, in particular, by the determination of

---

8 A v. *Minister for Immigration & Ethnic Affairs* (1997) 190 CLR 225, 293–4.

9 *Convention Governing the Specific Aspects of Refugee Problems in Africa*, opened for signature 10 September 1969, 1001 UNTS 45 (entered into force 20 June 1974).

10 *African Union Convention for the Protection and Assistance of Internally Displaced Persons in Africa*, adopted 23 October 2009 (not yet in force).

11 *Cartagena Declaration on Refugees*, OEA/Ser.L/II.66, doc 10 rev 1 (22 November 1984) 190–3.

12 *Parliamentary Assembly Recommendation 773 on the Situation of De Facto Refugees*, Council of Europe (26 January 1976).

13 Elspeth Guild and Carol Harlow (eds.), *Implementing Amsterdam: Immigration and Asylum Rights in EC Law* (Hart, 2001).

14 Hemme Battjes, *European Asylum Law and International Law* (Martinus Nijhoff, 2006).

States to achieve regional harmonisation in refugee law. This has been required by national courts – especially those of the United Kingdom[15] – as a legal precondition for the allocation of asylum claims on a regional basis in Europe.

7.1.4.   The mandate of the United Nations High Commissioner for Refugees

Beyond these formal legal developments, the institutional protection mandate of UNHCR now encompasses groups and forms of intervention that go significantly beyond its 1950 Statute,[16] as the result of 'good offices' and other mandates approved by the United Nations General Assembly and financed through voluntary contributions. These enhancements of its competence have enabled the agency to respond to mass movements of refugees outside Europe and, more controversially, to assume responsibility for internally displaced persons. UNHCR sees itself as responsible to respond not just to risks of being persecuted, but to any risk giving rise to a protection need in the context of involuntary migration. In pursuit of this extremely broad mandate, UNHCR has transformed itself into an operational agency in which the resources devoted to oversight of legal protection, while still significant, are dwarfed by the commitments made to relief on the ground.

7.1.5.   Complementary developments in human rights and humanitarian law

Refugee-specific treaties and institutions at both the global and regional levels are also complemented in critical ways by broader norms of international human rights and humanitarian law. In particular, art. 3 of the *Convention against Torture and Other Cruel, Inhuman or Degrading Treatment or Punishment* (1984),[17] and the prohibition in art. 7 of the *International Covenant on Civil and Political Rights* (1966) ('ICCPR')[18] of subjection to torture or to inhuman or degrading treatment or punishment, provide the bases for an expanded category of persons entitled to benefit from the duty of *non-refoulement*. So too does art. 3 of the *European Convention for the Protection of Human Rights and Fundamental Freedoms* (1950) at the regional level.[19] The 1949 Geneva Conventions that form the basis of modern international humanitarian law have also been interpreted to preclude the forced return of civilians to ongoing conflict.[20] While claims that there is a comprehensive

---

15 *R* v. *Secretary of State for the Home Department; Ex parte Adan and Aitseguer* [2000] UKHL 67 (19 December 2000).

16 *Statute of the Office of the United Nations High Commissioner for Refugees*, UN Doc A/RES/428(V) (14 December 1950).

17 *Convention against Torture and Other Cruel, Inhuman or Degrading Treatment or Punishment*, opened for signature 10 December 1984, 1465 UNTS 85 (entered into force 26 June 1987).

18 *International Covenant on Civil and Political Rights*, opened for signature 16 December 1966, 999 UNTS 171 (entered into force 23 March 1976).

19 *European Convention for the Protection of Human Rights and Fundamental Freedoms*, opened for signature 4 November 1950, ETS No 005 (entered into force 3 September 1953).

20 *In re Santos*, US Imm. Ct. Dec. No A29–564–781 (24 August 1990); *Orelien* v. *Canada (Minister of Employment and Immigration)* [1992] 1 FC 592.

duty of *non-refoulement* binding all States by force of customary law are over-stated,[21] there is no doubt that many involuntary migrants outside the Refugee Convention definition of a refugee are today entitled to treaty-based protection at the international or regional level. Equally important, many of these treaties can be relied on to expand the scope and quality of protection owed to classically defined refugees, perhaps most importantly in the realm of civil and political rights.

7.2. REFUGEE STATUS

The refugee definition – the central criterion of which is a 'well-founded fear of being persecuted for reasons of race, religion, nationality, political opinion, or membership of a particular social group' – is to be interpreted purposively and in context, rather than literally.[22] To that end, interpretation is to promote an understanding of refugee law as surrogate or substitute national protection,[23] owed to persons who can no longer benefit from the protection of their own country.

As the House of Lords has observed, while each State party interprets the refugee definition independently, 'as in the case of other multilateral treaties, the Refugee Convention must be given an independent meaning ... without taking colour from distinctive features of the legal system of any individual contracting state. In principle therefore there can only be one true interpretation'.[24] To this end, '[c]onsidered decisions of foreign courts, in particular appellate decisions, should be treated as persuasive in order to strive for uniformity of interpretation'.[25] The lively transnational judicial conversation among judges – significantly aided by the International Association of Refugee Law Judges, established in 1997 – has proved to be the critical means by which interpretation of the refugee definition has been continually updated, allowing it to be 'a living instrument in the sense that while its meaning does not change over time its application will'.[26]

While some courts (and UNHCR) persist in recommending what is sometimes referred to as a 'holistic' interpretive method, by which a general sense of conformity to the definition is sought, 'experience shows that adjudicators and tribunals give better reasoned and more lucid decisions if they go step by step'.[27] Indeed, '[a]lthough the definition must be read as a whole, each of the elements must be present'.[28]

---

21 James Hathaway, 'Leveraging Asylum' (2010) 45(3) *Texas International Law Journal* 503.
22 *A v. Minister for Immigration & Ethnic Affairs* (1997) 190 CLR 225.
23 *Canada (Attorney General) v. Ward* [1993] 2 SCR 689; *Horvath v. Secretary of State for the Home Department* [2000] UKHL 37 (6 July 2000).
24 *R v. Secretary of State for the Home Department; Ex parte Adan and Aitseguer* [2000] UKHL 67 (19 December 2000).
25 *NBGM v. Minister for Immigration and Multicultural and Indigenous Affairs* [2006] FCAFC 60 (12 May 2006) [158].
26 *Sepet v. Secretary of State for the Home Department* [2003] UKHL 15 (20 March 2003) [6].
27 *Svazas v. Secretary of State for the Home Department* [2002] EWCA Civ 74 (31 January 2002) [30].
28 *Minister for Immigration and Multicultural Affairs v. Khawar* [2002] HCA 14 (11 April 2002) [147].

There are six criteria that have to be fulfilled for a person to be a refugee:

1 the person has to be outside his or her country;
2 due to a genuine risk;
3 of the infliction of serious harm;
4 resulting from a failure of state protection;
5 which risk is causally connected to a protected form of civil or political status; and
6 the person must be in need of and deserving of protection.

7.2.1. Alienage

The first element of refugee status under the Refugee Convention is that the claimant be outside his or her own country. The purpose of this alienage requirement is to define the scope of refugee law in a realistic and workable way, dictated by the limited reach of international law. Equally important, the restriction of refugee status to persons outside their own country aligns with the treaty's rights regime, which is attuned precisely to the needs of involuntary *aliens* – and is, as such, not relevant to persons who are displaced internally.

Refugee status is acquired as soon as a person *leaves* his or her own country for a relevant reason, though no State is obliged to protect the person until he or she comes under its formal or *de facto* jurisdiction. Protection is owed to a person meeting the definition (whether or not status has been formally assessed) who is under a State party's jurisdiction. It matters not whether the entry or presence is lawful, and immigration penalties may not be imposed for unlawful entry or presence dictated by flight from persecution.

There is also no duty on the part of refugees to seek protection either in their own region or in the first safe country to which they travel. Despite the proliferation of so-called 'country of first arrival rules', which purport to force refugees to seek protection in a single designated State,[29] a transfer of protective responsibility is lawful under the Refugee Convention only where effected in a timely way and without infringing the refugee's acquired rights (see below). If, and only if, these standards are met, protective responsibility may lawfully be transferred to another State party, whether or not the refugee consents to that transfer.

Assuming that no such transfer occurs, all criteria of the refugee definition are assessed in relation to circumstances in the applicant's country of nationality, whatever the person's relationship with other States. A person with more than one nationality must satisfy the refugee definition in relation to each country of

29 *Council Regulation (EC) No 343/2003 of 18 February 2003 Establishing the Criteria and Mechanisms for Determining the Member State Responsible for Examining an Asylum Application Lodged in one of the Member States by a Third-Country National* ('Dublin II Regulation') [2003] OJ L 50/1; *Agreement between the Government of Canada and the Government of the United States of America for Cooperation in the Examination of Refugee Status Claims from Nationals of Third Countries* ('Safe Third Country Agreement'), Canada Gazette Vol 138 No 22 (5 December 2002).

nationality, while a stateless person may qualify for refugee status if he or she can show a relevant fear of being persecuted in the 'country of former habitual residence' – that is, the *de facto* home, where he or she enjoyed an ongoing protective relationship.[30] The goal in all cases is to restrict refugee status to persons deprived by persecution of the effective enjoyment of their most critical national bond.

Finally, because the Refugee Convention is concerned not with past harms but with forward-looking risk, it protects on equal terms refugees *sur place* – that is, persons who, while already abroad, find they cannot return by reason of the risk of being persecuted at home.

7.2.2. Genuine risk

The requirement of a genuine risk follows from the applicant's duty to show that he or she is outside his or her own country 'owing to a well-founded fear'. Common law jurisprudence has taken the view that the 'well-founded fear' requires not only evidence of forward-looking assessment of objective risk, but also demonstration of subjective fear in the sense of trepidation. However, this two-pronged approach is neither historically defensible nor practically meaningful.[31] The concept of well-founded fear is inherently objective, intended to restrict the scope of protection to persons who fear harm in the sense that they anticipate it may occur – that is, who can demonstrate a present or prospective risk of being persecuted, irrespective of the extent or nature of mistreatment, if any, that they have suffered in the past. This interpretation is not only consistent with the Refugee Convention's drafting history, but the understanding of 'fear' as a forward-looking appraisal allows the English language text to conform to the objective focus of the equally authoritative French text, '*craignant avec raison*'.

Leading formulations of the well-founded fear test are 'reasonable possibility',[32] 'reasonable degree of likelihood',[33] 'serious possibility'[34] and 'real chance'[35] – all intended to identify situations of risk that fall significantly below a probability of harm, but which give rise to more than a speculative chance that persecution may ensue.

The test is ordinarily met by some combination of credible testimony and country data.[36] There is no requirement of past persecution, though where such evidence exists it is usually good evidence of forward-looking risk. Nor is there any

---

30 A stateless person who has no well-founded fear of being persecuted is not a refugee, but may be entitled to protection on the grounds of statelessness as such (see Chapter 4).

31 *Yusuf* v. *Canada* [1992] 1 FC 629; *Win* v. *Minister for Immigration and Multicultural Affairs* [2001] FCA 132 (23 February 2001), approved in *Minister for Immigration and Multicultural Affairs* v. *Islam* [2001] FCA 1681 (20 December 2001).

32 *Immigration and Naturalization Service* v. *Cardoza-Fonseca*, 480 US 421 (1987).

33 *R* v. *Secretary of State for the Home Department; Ex parte Sivakumaran* [1988] 1 All ER 193.

34 *Adjei* v. *Canada (Minister of Employment and Immigration)* [1989] 2 FC 680.

35 *Chan* v. *Minister for Immigration and Ethnic Affairs* (1989) 87 ALR 412.

36 See Gregor Noll (ed.), *Proof, Evidentiary Assessment and Credibility Assessment in Asylum Procedures* (Martinus Nijhoff, 2005).

requirement for the applicant to show that he or she has been singled out or targeted; it suffices to show inclusion in a relevant at-risk group.

7.2.3. Serious harm

A person is a refugee only if he or she apprehends a form of harm that amounts to a risk of 'being persecuted'. This use of the passive voice (rather than 'persecution') signals the need to demonstrate a predicament of risk that calls for surrogate international protection. There is therefore strong support for the view that the risk of being persecuted requires evidence of 'sustained or systemic violation of basic human rights demonstrative of a failure of state protection'.[37]

The first element of this test – requiring the demonstration of a risk of 'serious harm' in the sense of a risk to basic human rights – clearly does not restrict refugee status to persons able to show the possibility of consequences of life or death proportions. The Refugee Convention accepts that deprivation of basic civil and political freedoms is sufficient cause for surrogate international protection. In addition, threats to core social and economic rights are increasingly recognised as persecutory:

> Ordinarily, denial of access to food, shelter, medical treatment and, in the case of children, denial of an opportunity to obtain an education, involve such a significant departure from the standards of the civilized world as to constitute persecution. And that is so even if the different treatment involved is undertaken for the purpose of achieving some legitimate national objective.[38]

7.2.4. Failure of State protection

Because of the predicament-oriented nature of the requirement of 'being perse-cuted', there must not only be demonstration of a risk to basic human rights, but also evidence that the individual's own State cannot or will not respond to that risk. If the applicant's own country can and will remedy the risk, the predicament of 'being persecuted' does not exist. In a world in which many, perhaps most, threats emanate not from States but from non-State actors, this recognition is key to the continuing vitality of the refugee definition:

> [T]he discriminatory practice of the state is at least as important as the discriminatory practice of the attackers. . . . If there are thugs about perpetrating serious acts of maltreatment against the population as a whole, but the state offers protection only to some of its citizens, and not to others, in my view those citizens are being persecuted in just the sort of way that merits the surrogate protection of other states under the Convention.[39]

---

37 *Canada (Attorney General)* v. *Ward* [1993] 2 SCR 689; *R* v. *Immigration Appeal Tribunal; Ex parte Shah and Islam* [1999] 2 AC 629; *Horvath* v. *Secretary of State for the Home Department* [2000] UKHL 37 (6 July 2000); *Sepet* v. *Secretary of State for the Home Department* [2003] UKHL 15 (20 March 2003); *R* v. *Special Adjudicator; Ex parte Ullah* [2004] UKHL 26 (17 June 2004); *Do* v. *Secretary of State for the Home Department [2004] UKHL 26 (17 June 2004); HJ (Iran) and HT (Cameroon)* v. *Secretary of State for the Home Department* [2010] UKSC 31 (7 July 2010).
38 *Chen Shi Hai* v. *Minister for Immigration and Multicultural Affairs* [2000] HCA 19 (13 April 2000), [29].
39 *Secretary of State for the Home Department* v. *Horvath* [1999] EWCA Civ 3026 (2 December 1999) [17].

Even in those States that still embrace an understanding of 'being persecuted' focussed on the harm alone, there is increasing recognition that 'persecution consists of two elements, the criminal conduct of private citizens, and the toleration or condonation of such conduct by the state or agents of the state, resulting in the withholding of protection which the victims are entitled to expect'.[40] At the very least, such concerns are taken into account by virtue of the definition's requirement that a refugee is a person who is 'unable or ... unwilling to avail himself of the protection' of his or her country (art. 1(A)(2)), though this approach raises difficulties meeting the definition's nexus requirement, which requires that the risk of 'being persecuted' be causally connected to a Refugee Convention ground.

The standard of a 'failure of State protection' remains disputed. The formalistic view – that the focus is on whether the home State has 'in place a system of domestic protection and machinery for the detection, prosecution and punishment of [rights abuse and] an ability and a readiness to operate that machinery'[41] – does not conform with the Refugee Convention's focus on the realities of risk, which may persist despite the 'ability and readiness' to act. To be preferred therefore is the view that '[w]hatever the law provides and the officials attempt, if the country of nationality is unable, as a matter of fact, to afford protection ... the conclusion may be reached that "protection is unavailable" in the person's country of nationality.'[42]

Also still the subject of some controversy is whether there can be said to be a failure of state protection where the individual – while at risk in his or her home region – could nonetheless move internally rather than seek protection as a refugee abroad. While there is little doubt that the Refugee Convention's focus on risk in 'the country' of nationality requires consideration of internal alternatives to refugee status, the precise formulation of the test is unclear. It is generally agreed that the internal alternative must be accessible, must provide an antidote to the original risk, and must not present a new risk of being persecuted or of indirect return to the place of origin. The dominant view argues that, beyond these criteria, return need only be 'reasonable'.[43] However, the better view recognises that refugee status should not be subject to the whims of a 'reasonableness' test, given the Refugee Convention's requirement that a refugee 'is unable or, owing to such fear, is unwilling to *avail himself of the protection* of that country'.[44] Rather, refugee status is fairly denied only where the home State will in fact provide protection, evidenced by ensuring respect for basic rights, in the proposed site of internal relocation.[45]

40 *Minister for Immigration and Multicultural Affairs* v. *Khawar* [2002] HCA 14 (11 April 2002) [31].
41 *Horvath* v. *Secretary of State for the Home Department* [2000] UKHL 37 (6 July 2000).
42 *Re Minister for Immigration and Multicultural Affairs; Ex parte Miah* [2001] HCA 22 (3 May 2001) [198].
43 *Januzi* v. *Secretary of State for the Home Department* [2006] UKHL 5 (15 February 2006); United Nations High Commissioner for Refugees, 'Guidelines on International Protection: Internal Flight or Relocation Alternative' (UN Doc HCR/GIP/03/04, UNHCR, 23 July 2003).
44 See James Hathaway and Michelle Foster, 'Internal Protection/Relocation/Flight Alternative as an Aspect of Refugee Status Determination' in Erika Feller, Volker Türk and Frances Nicholson (eds.), *Refugee Protection in International Law* (Cambridge University Press, 2003) 357, 381.
45 *Butler* v. *Attorney General* [1999] NZAR 205.

7.2.5. Nexus to civil or political status

If the peril a claimant faces cannot somehow be linked to his or her civil or political status ('race, religion, nationality, membership of a particular social group, or political opinion'), the claim to refugee status fails. Put succinctly, refugee law requires that there be a nexus between who the claimant is or what he or she believes and the risk of being persecuted in his or her home State (see Case Study 7.1).

A Refugee Convention ground need not be the sole, or even predominant, cause of the risk of being persecuted, though it must be a contributing factor to the risk. It also does not matter whether the risk accrues by reason of actual or (even incorrectly) imputed civil or political status, since in either case the non-discrimination logic of the nexus clause is engaged.

But just what must be causally connected to the Refugee Convention ground? In those States that have adopted the bifurcated understanding of 'being persecuted' described above, the nexus can be to either of the two constituent elements – the serious harm or the failure of State protection – since in either case the predicament of 'being persecuted' is by reason of the Refugee Convention ground. But where the more limited notion of 'being persecuted' focussed on serious harm alone prevails, refugee status will not be recognised where the only discrimination is in relation to the duty to protect, rather than in the infliction of the harm as such.[46] This approach fails to do justice to the protective goals of refugee law,[47] and has proved particularly problematic where the home State is unwilling to afford protection to women on the grounds of their sex (see Chapter 8).[48]

The first ground of 'race' includes all forms of identifiable ethnicity. Closely linked is the concept of 'nationality', which encompasses not only formal citizenship, but also linguistic groups and other culturally defined collectivities. A risk is for reasons of 'religion' whether based on holding or refusing to hold any form of theistic, non-theistic or atheistic belief; or on actions (such as worship or proselytisation) within the scope of religion, as adumbrated in international human rights law.

While it is clear that the political 'opinion' ground does not require an individual to have acted on those beliefs, there is a lively debate about the breadth of what opinions (and cognate actions) are to be deemed 'political'. The traditional broad view comprising an opinion 'on any matter in which the machinery of state, government, and policy may be engaged'[49] has been challenged on the grounds that while the Refugee Convention's understanding 'clearly is not limited to party politics ... [i]t is probably narrower than the usage of the word in connection with the science of politics, where it may extend to almost every aspect of society.'[50]

---

46 *Immigration and Naturalization Service* v. *Elias Zacarias*, 502 US 478 (1992).
47 *Sepet* v. *Secretary of State for the Home Department* [2001] EWCA Civ 681 (11 May 2001).
48 The contrary approach has been applied to the benefit of female refugee claimants: *R* v. *Immigration Appeal Tribunal; Ex parte Shah and Islam* [1999] 2 AC 629; *Minister for Immigration and Multicultural Affairs* v. *Khawar* [2002] HCA 14 (11 April 2002). See also Heaven Crawley, *Refugees and Gender: Law and Practice* (Jordan, 2001); Thomas Spijkerboer, *Gender and Refugee Status* (Ashgate, 2000).
49 *Canada (Attorney General)* v. *Ward* [1993] 2 SCR 689, 693.
50 *V* v. *Minister for Immigration and Multicultural Affairs* [1999] FCA 428 (14 April 1999) [33].

CASE STUDY 7.1   Refugees expelled to North Korea

Hundreds of thousands of North Koreans have fled into China since 1995, hoping to escape starvation and political repression (see Map 5.1). Critical food shortages are endemic in North Korea, with national resources distorted to support the country's militarisation and political elite. Even access to basic healthcare and education often depends on demonstrated loyalty to the regime.

Despite being a party to the Refugee Convention, China refuses to assess these protection claims. It instead stigmatises the North Korean arrivals as 'illegal economic migrants', refusing to provide them with even food or other essentials. China prohibits United Nations agencies, including UNHCR, from meeting these needs, and arrests any of its nationals found to be assisting North Koreans to survive.

China, moreover, routinely removes North Koreans found in its territory, relying on a 1986 bilateral repatriation agreement. Fear of forcible return drives many North Koreans underground, making them especially vulnerable to traffickers.

In truth, the Chinese labelling of the North Koreans as 'illegal economic migrants' is legally irrelevant. Persons who face only a generalised risk of starvation are not Refugee Convention refugees because they cannot show that their risk, while grave, stems from one of the five Convention grounds of race, religion, nationality, membership of a particular social group or political opinion. But Convention refugee status is established if the risk derives from actual or implied political opposition to the regime and consequential denial of access to core economic rights. It is 'well-established that persecution can take the form of economic deprivation as well as physical mistreatment'.[51]

More generally, so long as an individual or group faces the risk of being persecuted for a Refugee Convention reason, the fact that their flight to safety is partly motivated by economic destitution does not compromise their refugee status. Refugee status is to be recognised so long as 'the threat of persecution [is] a material reason, among a number of complementary reasons'.[52]

Given that many (perhaps most) North Korean migrants are, therefore, refugees, they are entitled to benefit from arts. 2–34 of the Refugee Convention – for example, access to rationing and other support systems, work and protection against *refoulement*. China cannot plead its own failure to assess the claims, much less its bald assertion of non-refugee status, as grounds for failing to honour these obligations. Much less can it invoke a bilateral treaty with North Korea to justify breach of international responsibilities to refugees.

Indeed, China is duty-bound to assist refugees to access their Refugee Convention rights (art. 25) and to cooperate with UNHCR's oversight of Convention rights (art. 35). But as this case study shows, the absence of any binding system to enforce the Refugee Convention makes it difficult to bring obligations to bear. Given UNHCR's political and fiscal vulnerability (only about 2 per cent of its annual income is guaranteed), there is presently little it can do when a powerful State such as China decides to breach its freely assumed duties.

51 *Chen* v. *Holder*, 604 F 3d 324 (7th Cir, 2010), 334.
52 *HJ and HT* v. *Secretary of State for the Home Department* [2010] UKSC 31 (7 July 2010) [62].

Most controversial of all is interpretation of the notion of 'membership of a particular social group' – an understandable controversy, since this concept was introduced with little explanation as a last-minute amendment to the Refugee Convention, and is not a recognised term of art. Construction based on the principle of *ejusdem generis* (requiring an ambiguous word to be interpreted in consonance with the meaning of words with which it forms a common class) has resulted in a focus on groups defined by an immutable characteristic, aligning this ground with the other four grounds, all of which derive from norms of non-discrimination law. This approach has resulted in the recognition of, for example, sex or gender, sexual orientation and linguistic groups as 'particular social groups'.[53] The alternative 'social perception' test – which focusses on groups seen to be set apart from society, whether or not for a fundamental reason[54] – has gained traction in recent years. UNHCR has advocated an instrumentalist interpretation that requires recognition as a social group if *either* of the two tests is met. The European Union responded to this view by suggesting instead the need to meet *both* tests – meaning that even groups identified by their 'immutable characteristic' are now potentially at risk of non-recognition as 'particular social groups'.

7.2.6. Cessation and exclusion

Because refugee protection is conceived as protection for the duration of the risk, art. 1C of the Refugee Convention recognises several categories of persons deemed no longer to need international protection because they can once more benefit from the protection of their own country. Refugee status ceases in the case of a refugee who voluntarily and with full understanding seeks out diplomatic protection in his or her country of origin; who lost his or her original nationality but voluntarily elects to reacquire it; who re-establishes himself or herself in the country of origin, in the sense of resuming ongoing presence there; or who it is felt can and should return to the State of origin in view of a fundamental and demonstrably durable change of circumstances that restores protection to that person.

Second, because refugee law is designed to afford surrogate international protection to those who need it, an individual who can already access an approved form of alternative surrogate protection is excluded from refugee status – namely, protection by the United Nations Relief and Works Agency for Palestinian Refugees in the Near East ('UNRWA') in the case of Palestinians (art. 1D), or acquisition by any refugee of nationality or *de facto* nationality in a country that will protect that person (art. 1E).

---

53 *Canada (Attorney General) v. Ward* [1993] 2 SCR 689, adopting *Matter of Acosta*, United States Board of Immigration Appeals, A-24159781 (1 March 1985).
54 *A v. Minister for Immigration & Ethnic Affairs* (1997) 190 CLR 225.

Finally, in order to ensure that it is not sullied by the admission of persons understood to be undeserving of the benefits of refugee status, refugee status is denied under art. 1F to persons reasonably suspected of being international criminals; of having acted contrary to the principles and purposes of the United Nations; or of having committed serious common crimes outside the asylum State that remain justiciable or in relation to which lawful punishment has yet to occur. There is regrettable confusion in practice between this last category and the broader authority under art. 33(2) to remove serious criminals on grounds of danger to the host country. Article 1F is designed to ensure the alignment of refugee law with extradition law, thereby ensuring that asylum does not provide a haven to persons escaping the force of legitimate criminal prosecution or punishment. Article 33(2) permits State parties to send truly dangerous refugees away, even to their home country if necessary. But in contrast to the low threshold for exclusion that applies under art. 1F(b) to persons evading legitimate criminal law prosecution or punishment abroad, art. 33(2) allows security-based removal only if there are 'reasonable grounds' for a determination of danger based on 'final' conviction for a crime that is 'particularly' serious – thus striking a balance not possible under the peremptory exclusion provisions of art. 1(F).[55]

7.3. REFUGEE RIGHTS

The universal rights of refugees today derive from two primary sources – the Refugee Convention itself and general standards of international human rights law. Despite the post-1951 development of a broad-ranging system of international human rights law that can ordinarily be invoked by any person under a State's jurisdiction, the Refugee Convention rights remain critical to ensuring meaningful protection.

First, general human rights norms do not address many refugee-specific concerns (such as non-rejection at the frontier, or non-penalisation for illegal entry). Second, the economic rights in the Refugee Convention are both more extensive than those under general human rights law (e.g., binding rights to private property and to benefit from public relief and assistance) and are defined as absolute and immediately binding (in contrast to general human rights norms). Third, even in the realm of civil rights, where general human rights law is of greatest value to refugees, relevant provisions of the Refugee Convention speak to more specific concerns (such as access to the courts) than are assumed under general norms. Fourth, the ability to withhold civil rights during a national emergency is also much

---

55 *Immigration and Naturalization Service* v. *Aguirre-Aguirre*, 526 US 415 (1999); *Attorney-General* v. *Tamil X and Refugee Status Appeals Authority* [2010] NZSC 107 (27 August 2010).

more limited under the Refugee Convention than under general human rights law, as a consequence of which refugees can invoke refugee-specific norms even when general standards are suspended under the ICCPR. Fifth, the Refugee Convention mandates rights that lead to solutions to refugeehood, reflecting an understanding that refugee status is inherently a temporary status – protection for the duration of risk – that must ultimately be brought to an end in the interests of both the refugee and the receiving State.

7.3.1.   Structure of entitlement

Refugee rights inhere in consequence of one's refugee status. Refugee rights are not dependent on formal status recognition, reflected in the fact that State parties are actually under no duty formally to assess status, and many do not:

A person is a refugee within the meaning of the 1951 Convention as soon as he fulfils the criteria contained in the definition. This would necessarily occur prior to the time at which his refugee status is formally determined. Recognition of his refugee status does not therefore make him a refugee but declares him to be one. He does not become a refugee because of recognition, but is recognized because he is a refugee.[56]

But this does not mean that all the rights stipulated in arts. 2–34 of the Refugee Convention are immediately owed to all persons who meet the refugee definition. Under an ingenious system of 'levels of attachment', refugees become entitled to an expanding array of rights as their relationship with the asylum State deepens.[57] At the lowest level of attachment, some rights (e.g., protection against *refoulement* and access to the courts) are owed to any refugee under a State's *jurisdiction*, in the sense of being under its control or authority. A second set of rights inheres when the refugee is *physically present* within a State's territory (e.g., restrictions on freedom of movement must be justified, and religious freedom rights accrue). Once a refugee is deemed to be *lawfully present* in a State, which may occur tacitly as well as by formal decision, a third group of rights applies (e.g., the right to take up self-employment, and freedom of internal movement). Fourth, when a refugee is *lawfully staying*, which may occur by effluxion of time, especially where no formal refugee status determination process exists, he or she becomes entitled to additional rights (e.g., the right to take up employment and to benefit from public housing). A final group of rights inheres in refugees who are *durably resident* in the asylum country (e.g., entitlement to legal aid and to exemption from legislative reciprocity requirements). The structure of the attachment system is incremental: because the levels build on one another (a refugee in a State's territory

---

56 United Nations High Commissioner for Refugees, *Handbook on Procedures and Criteria for Determining Refugee Status* (UNHCR, 1992) [28].

57 The structure of entitlement is explained in detail in Hathaway, *The Rights of Refugees under International Law*, above n. 1, 154 ff.

is also under its jurisdiction; a refugee lawfully present is also present; a refugee lawfully residing is also lawfully present; and a refugee durably residing is also lawfully residing), rights once acquired are retained for the duration of refugee status.

Not only do refugee rights inhere incrementally, but the standard of compliance with such rights is defined as a mix of absolute and contingent rights. At the very least, refugees receive the benefit of all laws and policies that apply to 'aliens generally'. But even rights defined at this lowest level of compliance generally require that refugees receive 'treatment as favourable as possible', requiring State parties to give good faith consideration to the non-application to refugees of any restrictions generally applied to aliens.

Most Refugee Convention rights mandate compliance at a significantly higher level. The rights to engage in non-political freedom of association and to engage in wage-earning employment, for example, must be guaranteed at the level granted to most-favoured foreign nationals – meaning that refugees are automatically entitled to whatever standard any group of foreigners receives, including under bilateral treaties, customs unions, and so on. Refugees must be assimilated to 'nationals' of the host country with regard to a significant range of rights, including education, welfare and social security. And there are some rights simply owed on an absolute basis – for example, administrative assistance (the duty of State parties to facilitate access to refugee rights), protection against expulsion and access to refugee travel documents. Importantly, the Refugee Convention prohibits any discrimination between and among refugees, meaning that an asylum State may not grant preferential treatment to any subset of the refugee population unless shown to be reasonable and objectively justifiable.

The primary responsibility to implement these rights is attributed to State parties, which must both establish mechanisms of administrative assistance to facilitate access to the rights formally guaranteed, and provide refugees with access to their courts. In addition, art. 35 of the Refugee Convention requires States to cooperate with UNHCR in implementing Convention duties, and art. 38 allows referral to the International Court of Justice in the case of any dispute between States on the interpretation or application of the Convention, though this authority has never been exercised. In practice, regional courts exercising jurisdiction under cognate human rights treaties have also relied on Refugee Convention rights to interpret the application to refugees of broader norms.

7.3.2. *Non-refoulement*

The most urgent need of refugees is to secure entry into a territory in which they are sheltered from the risk of being persecuted. Yet this fundamental concern must somehow be reconciled to the fact that nearly all of the earth's territory is controlled or claimed by governments which, to a greater or lesser extent, restrict access by non-nationals. Article 33's duty of *non-refoulement* – 'No Contracting State shall expel or return ("refouler") a refugee in any manner whatsoever to the frontiers of territories where his life or freedom would be threatened' – is the primary response of the international community to this need, though it is less than a full affirmative right to receive asylum in at least two senses.

First, the duty of *non-refoulement* only prohibits measures that cause refugees to 'be pushed back into the arms of their persecutors';[58] it does not establish an affirmative duty to receive refugees. As an obligation 'couched in negative terms',[59] it applies only where there is a real risk that rejection will expose the refugee directly or indirectly to the risk of being persecuted for a Refugee Convention ground. In such circumstances, art. 33 often amounts to a *de facto* duty to admit the refugee, since admission is normally the only means of avoiding the alternative, impermissible consequence of exposure to risk.

Second, because the *de facto* right of entry that flows from the duty of *non-refoulement* is a function of the existence of a risk of being persecuted, a State party need not allow a refugee to remain in its territory if and when that risk ends.[60]

As one of the rights that inheres on a provisional basis even before refugee status has been formally assessed, the duty of *non-refoulement* applies as soon as an individual claiming to be a refugee comes under the jurisdiction of a State party, and continues until he or she has been fairly determined not to be a refugee. It constrains not simply ejection from within a State's territory, but also non-admittance.[61] A critical challenge in recent years is the adoption by many States of '*non-entrée*' policies, pursuant to which an effort is made to divert refugees away from their jurisdiction by indirect means (such as visa requirements), or by taking action outside their jurisdiction (including on the high seas) to force refugees back to their home State. The latter tactic – despite one worrisome precedent from the United States Supreme Court[62] – is proscribed by the Refugee Convention's attribution of art. 33 duties on the basis of jurisdiction (rather than arrival in a State's territory) if the result is direct or indirect *refoulement* (see Case Study 7.2).

58 *Statement of the Chairman Mr. Chance of Canada*, UN Doc E/AC.32.SR.21 (2 February 1950) 7.
59 *Applicant M38/2002 v. Minister for Immigration and Multicultural and Indigenous Affairs* [2003] FCAFC 131 (13 June 2003) [39].
60 *R v. Secretary of State for the Home Department; Ex parte Thangarasa; R v. Secretary of State for the Home Department; Ex parte Yogathas* [2002] UKHL 36 (17 October 2002).
61 Gregor Noll, *Negotiating Asylum: The EU Acquis, Extraterritorial Protection, and the Common Market of Deflection* (Martinus Nijhoff, 2000); Thomas Gammeltoft-Hansen, *Access to Asylum: International Refugee Law and the Globalization of Migration Control* (Cambridge University Press, 2011).
62 *Sale v. Haitian Centers Council*, 509 US 155 (1993).

CASE STUDY 7.2   Extraterritorial deterrence: a way to avoid obligations?

In May 2009, Italy implemented a policy of interdicting refugees and other migrants on board ships headed for its shores. Detection was facilitated by reports from 'Frontex', the European Union's agency charged with patrolling European Union sea borders. In most cases, the Italian Navy stopped ships believed to be destined for Lampedusa or other Italian territory, and forcibly transferred the passengers onto the Italian vessel. Once on board, the detained persons were not interviewed to assess any protection claims, but were summarily returned to North African ports. During the first three months of the programme Italy carried out seven operations, resulting in the return of at least 600 people to Libya and a smaller number to Algeria.

The European Committee for the Prevention of Torture reported in April 2010 that among the migrants summarily repelled by Italy were persons registered as refugees with UNHCR. Many others from Somalia and Eritrea were later interviewed by UNHCR, which confirmed that they had plausible claims to international protection.

Libya has no functioning national asylum system and is not a party to the Refugee Convention, though it is bound by the regional *Convention Governing the Specific Aspects of Refugee Problems in Africa* (1969).[63] Human Rights Watch reports that migrants forcibly returned there are subject to indefinite detention, and are often mistreated.

In one of the few cases by a senior court to consider such a scheme, the United States Supreme Court held that the Refugee Convention is silent on such extraterritorial action.[64] This holding provoked a United States drafter of the Refugee Convention, the late Professor Louis Henkin, to retort that

> [i]t is incredible that states that had agreed not to force any human being back into the hands of his/her oppressors intended to leave themselves – and each other – free to reach out beyond their territory to seize a refugee and to return him/her to the country from which he sought to escape.[65]

Both the Inter-American Commission on Human Rights[66] and the English Court of Appeal[67] determined that the *Sale Case* was wrongly decided. First, the duty of *non-refoulement* in art. 33 is among a handful of critical rights that inhere as soon as a person claiming to be a refugee (or whose circumstances, including flight from a known refugee-producing State, suggest such status) comes under a State's *de facto* jurisdiction, including being on board a ship flying its flag. The protection obligations of Italy (and of Australia when operating its 'Pacific Solution', as well as of the United States

63 *Convention Governing the Specific Aspects of Refugee Problems in Africa*, opened for signature 10 September 1969, 1001 UNTS 45 (entered into force 20 June 1974).
64 *Sale* v. *Haitian Centers Council*, 509 US 155 (1993).
65 Louis Henkin, Notes from the President (1993) 5 *American Society of International Law Newsletter* 1.
66 *Haitian Centre for Human Rights* v. *United States*, Inter-American Commission on Human Rights, OEA/Ser.L/V/II.95 Doc 7 rev at 550 (13 March 1997).
67 *R (European Roma Rights Centre)* v. *Immigration Officer at Prague Airport* [2003] EWCA Civ 666 (20 May 2003) [34]. In the House of Lords, Lord Hope nonetheless expressed some measure of support for the *Sale* decision: *R v. Immigration Officer at Prague Airport; Ex parte European Roma Rights Centre* [2004] UKHL 55 (9 December 2004) [68].

when it forcibly interdicted Haitians fleeing the murderous Cedrás regime) were thereby engaged.

Second, the drafters of the Refugee Convention were committed to ensuring that subterfuge could not be resorted to in order to avoid protection obligations, leading them to amend the draft treaty to set a duty of non-return 'in any manner whatsoever'. This was specifically said to embrace 'various methods by which refugees could be expelled, refused admittance or removed'.[68] Extraterritorial deterrence is therefore as much a breach of the Convention as expulsion from within a State's territory.

Even if refugees are not indirectly returned to their home countries (as in the case of those indefinitely detained in Libya), this does not make the interdiction scheme lawful. When the refugees were forced on board the Italian vessel, they came under the jurisdiction of a State party, thereby acquiring several core refugee rights in addition to protection against *refoulement*. Because Libya is not a party to the Refugee Convention, but only to the African Union's regional refugee convention (which requires member States only to use 'their best endeavors, consistent with their respective legislations to receive refugees': art. 2.1), any forcible removal of a refugee to Libya is an unlawful rights-stripping exercise. In any event, evidence that Libyan authorities detain and mistreat refugees would trump any *prima facie* argument in favour of requiring refugees to accept 'protection' in Libya predicated on that country's assumption of formal obligations.

Map 7.1 Lampedusa and the Mediterranean

68 *Ad Hoc Committee on Statelessness and Related Problems*, First Session, 22nd meeting, UN Doc E/AC.32/SR.22 (14 February 1950) 20 (Mr Cuvelier of Belgium).

Another tactic that raises difficult legal issues is the diversion of refugees to a non-party State conscripted to act as a buffer (such as Australia's 'Pacific Solution', under which refugees were sent to the Pacific Island country of Nauru). Article 33 is not likely infringed if, as in the case of the 'Pacific Solution', the consequence is long-term confinement without risk of being sent away to face the risk of being persecuted. The best argument against such schemes is rather the duty to ensure respect in the destination State for other Refugee Convention rights accrued by the sending country's exercise of jurisdiction (and possibly by presence in its territory, including its territorial sea).[69] In order to avoid the prospect of rights-stripping, any involuntary assignment of protective responsibility must be predicated on 'anxious scrutiny',[70] not only of respect for the duty of *non-refoulement* by the destination country, but also for other refugee rights already acquired.[71] Responsibility can moreover only be shared with another State party to the Refugee Convention, since only in such States will the refugee continue to enjoy the acquired rights to UNHCR supervision under art. 35 and to international judicial oversight by virtue of art. 38. The termination of these means of effecting and enforcing rights following removal to a non-party State would be as much a deprivation of rights as is the denial of the rights themselves.

The use of visa controls, often enforced by carrier sanctions, poses a more vexing dilemma because jurisdiction over the persons intended to be deterred may never be established. While the duty of *non-refoulement* likely does not apply in such cases, reliance on the ICCPR's guarantee to all of the right to leave their own country may, in the view of the UN Human Rights Committee, afford a plausible avenue of redress.[72]

7.3.3. Civil and political rights

In many instances, the civil rights of refugees, and most certainly their political rights, will be more effectively protected under the ICCPR than by reliance on the comparatively constrained list of guarantees in the Refugee Convention itself. There are three main provisos.

First, it is important to recognise that generic civil rights are usually afforded to non-nationals only on the basis of a guarantee of non-discrimination – that is, State parties may still grant refugees and other aliens lesser civil rights than nationals so long as the differentiation is adjudged to be 'reasonable and objective'.

---

69 *Application of the Convention on the Prevention and Punishment of the Crime of Genocide (Bosnia and Herzegovina v. Yugoslavia)* [1996] ICJ Rep 595, 652 (Separate Opinion of Judge Weeramantry).

70 *R* v. *Secretary of State for the Home Department; Ex parte Thangarasa; R* v. *Secretary of State for the Home Department; Ex parte Yogathas* [2002] UKHL 36 (17 October 2002) [58].

71 *Plaintiff M70/2011* v. *Minister for Immigration and Citizenship; Plaintiff M106 of 2011* v. *Minister for Immigration and Citizenship* [2011] HCA 32 (31 August 2011).

72 Human Rights Committee, *General Comment No 27: Freedom of Movement* (Article 12), 67th sess, UN Doc CCPR/C/21/Rev.1/Add.9 (2 November 1999) [10].

Unfortunately, the UN Human Rights Committee has too frequently been prepared to see differentiation on the basis of nationality as presumptively reasonable. It has also paid insufficient attention to substantive differences that make formal equality an inadequate response, and has afforded governments an extraordinarily broad margin of appreciation, rather than engaging in careful analysis of both the logic and extent of the differential treatment.[73] Because the Refugee Convention guarantees its more constrained catalogue of civil rights on an absolute basis rather than simply without discrimination, it remains a critical source of civil rights entitlement.

Second, civil rights in the Refugee Convention are not subject to the sort of broad-ranging derogation for national emergencies that is provided for in the ICCPR. To the contrary, art. 9 of the Refugee Convention allows restrictions on refugee rights in the context of 'war or other grave and exceptional circumstances' only if such measures are 'essential', not just 'strictly required' as under the ICCPR. Such measures must moreover be individuated ('in the case of a particular person') and therefore cannot be collectively imposed on all refugees or even a subset of them. Perhaps most importantly, art. 9 of the Refugee Convention does not authorise general derogation, but only provisional suspension of rights before formal status verification is completed. Once refugee status is confirmed, no further suspension of rights is allowed.

Third, many of the civil rights in the Refugee Convention are framed in ways that respond to refugee-specific concerns not clearly addressed by general human rights norms. For example, there are provisions that explicitly address the right to religious education, a matter of clear concern to the Refugee Convention drafters in relation to Jewish refugees and other refugee groups of the Second World War era. There are also critical provisions on respect for previously acquired forms of personal status; strong rules prohibiting ongoing detention and affirming a full right to freedom of internal movement; and provisions that ensure that identity and travel documents are made available.

7.3.4. Socio-economic rights

The primary goal of the drafters of the Refugee Convention was to ensure:

> that the refugees will lead an independent life in the countries which have given them shelter. With the exception of the 'hard core' cases, the refugees will no longer be maintained by an international organisation as they are at present. They will be integrated in the economic system of the countries of asylum and will themselves provide for their own needs and for those of their families.[74]

---

73 Hathaway, *The Rights of Refugees under International Law*, above n. 1, 129 ff.
74 Ad Hoc Committee on Refugees and Stateless Persons, 'Memorandum by the Secretary-General' (UN Doc E/AC.32/2, United Nations, 3 January 1950) 6–7.

It is therefore not surprising that there are very strong guarantees of socio-economic rights in the Refugee Convention – arguably the most extensive granted to any class of non-national, and in one case (the right to private property) actually providing for a right not yet guaranteed under general norms of international human rights law.

In contrast to general norms of human rights law, the Refugee Convention's socio-economic rights are immediate duties rather than obligations of progressive implementation as under art. 2 of the *International Covenant on Economic, Social and Cultural Rights* ('ICESCR').[75] Most importantly, there is no ability (as there is under art. 2(3) of the ICESCR) for poorer countries to deny economic rights to non-nationals, which is clearly a critical concern as the overwhelming majority of refugees are present in such States.

This is not to say that the Refugee Convention responds to all socio-economic rights concerns. For example, the urgency of flight frequently means that most refugees in the less developed world are not able to meet their own immediate subsistence needs. The drafters of the Refugee Convention paid surprisingly little attention to the importance of meeting such basic needs as access to food, water, healthcare or shelter. On the other hand, the Convention gives detailed attention to a variety of relatively sophisticated socio-economic rights, such as access to social security, fair treatment under tax laws, and even the protection of refugees' intellectual property.

Many of the Refugee Convention's economic rights are nonetheless of real value to modern refugees, in both the developed and less developed worlds. For example, the Convention broke with precedent by making a clear commitment to provide at least the most basic forms of education to refugees and their children immediately upon coming under a State party's authority, and on terms of equality with nationals (see Chapter 8). As soon as a refugee has complied with any requirements set by the State for seeking validation of the refugee claim, the claimant is entitled to engage in self-employment; once recognised as a refugee, rights to undertake both wage-earning and professional work ensue. Refugees also enjoy an immediate right to acquire both real and personal property, and to benefit from rationing systems. Once lawfully staying, refugees are entitled to access public housing, as well as public relief and social security systems.

Because most of these economic rights are framed in contingent terms, they do not require a host State to provide refugees with more than they have already agreed to provide to other aliens, most-favoured non-nationals or their own nationals – thus not imposing an obligation that would amount to a privileging of refugees over the host society. Yet by virtue of the same contingencies, refugees cannot be disfranchised within their new communities, but rather must be allowed

---

75 *International Covenant on Economic, Social and Cultural Rights*, opened for signature 16 December 1966, 993 UNTS 3 (entered into force 3 January 1976).

to participate in the economy in a way that genuinely enables them to meet their own needs.

7.3.5. Rights of solution

There is increasing impatience among States with the duty simply to honour the rights of persons who are Refugee Convention refugees. The focus of much contemporary discourse is instead on the importance of defining and pursuing so-called 'durable solutions' to refugee flight. Indeed, those who focus on achieving durable solutions increasingly regard respect for refugee rights as little more than a second-best option, to be pursued only until a durable solution can be implemented.

In contrast to this emphasis on the pursuit of durable solutions, the Refugee Convention gives priority to allowing refugees to make their own decisions about how best to respond to their predicament. The only circumstance under which a solution to refugee status may lawfully be imposed without the consent of the refugee is where there has been a fundamental and demonstrably durable change of circumstances in the refugee's State of origin, which has eliminated the refugee's need for the surrogate protection at the heart of refugee law. Refugee status comes to an end in such a case, and the former refugee may be mandatorily returned to the country of origin so long as the requirements of international human rights law are met.[76] The label often attached to this option – 'voluntary repatriation' – is thus not appropriate. The solution of requiring a refugee's departure once the need for protection comes to an end is better referred to simply as 'repatriation', thus avoiding confusion with a second solution, 'voluntary re-establishment'.

While repatriation involves the return of a person who is no longer a refugee (and hence need not be voluntary), a person who remains a refugee may voluntarily decide to re-establish himself or herself in the country of origin despite the risk of being persecuted there. A refugee, like any national, is always free in law to opt for return to his or her own country. Return under such circumstances, however, must be the result of the refugee's free choice if the State of asylum is to avoid breach of the duty of *non-refoulement*. Once there is evidence both of a genuinely voluntary return and of the refugee's *de facto* re-establishment in his or her own country, the Refugee Convention deems refugee status to have come to an end. This is so because the refugee's own actions signal that he or she no longer wishes to benefit from the surrogate protection of an asylum country.

Beyond repatriation and voluntary re-establishment, the third solution to refugee status is resettlement. This solution acknowledges the reality that time spent in an asylum State may afford a refugee the opportunity to explore and secure access

---

76 Marjoleine Zieck, *UNHCR and Voluntary Repatriation of Refugees: A Legal Analysis* (Martinus Nijhoff, 1997).

to durable protection options better suited to his or her needs. The Refugee Convention explicitly envisages the possibility of onward movement by way of resettlement from the first country of arrival, and requires the government in the refugee's initial host State to facilitate that process. Once resettlement has occurred, the continuing need for refugee protection is at an end.

Fourth, and as a logical extension of the Refugee Convention's core commitment to affording refugees greater rights as their attachment to the asylum country increases over time, a point may be reached where the refugee and the authorities of that country agree to the refugee's formal naturalisation by the host State. If a refugee opts to accept an offer of nationality there, with entitlement to participate fully in all aspects of that State's public life, the need for the surrogate protection of refugee law ends. There is no further need for surrogate protection because the refugee is able and entitled to benefit from the protection of the new country of nationality.

7.4.   CHALLENGES FACING THE REFUGEE REGIME

Governments of the developed world are now appropriating the language of 'burden sharing' to further a global apartheid regime under which most refugees remain in the less developed world, and do so under conditions that are often rights-abusive, if not life-threatening. These States have distorted the true object and purpose of the Refugee Convention, erroneously suggesting that it sets only protection obligations of 'last resort' – that is, that refugees may be routinely sent away to any other State that will admit them without risk of return to their country of origin. Governments have further stigmatised refugees who arrive without pre-authorisation as 'illegal', despite the fact that the Refugee Convention requires otherwise.[77]

Perhaps most disingenuously, these same governments increasingly justify their harsh treatment of refugees arriving at their territory on the grounds that harshness is the necessary means to a more rational protection end. This end is said to be the reallocation of resources towards meeting the needs of the overwhelming number of refugees located in the less developed world, with resettlement in the developed world being made available only to those with the most acute need.

7.4.1.   The uneven distribution of burdens and responsibilities

There is no doubt that the burdens and responsibilities of offering protection to refugees are unfairly apportioned today. Nearly 90 per cent of refugees remain in

---

77 Catherine Dauvergne, *Making People Illegal: What Globalization Means for Migration and Law* (Cambridge University Press, 2008).

the less developed world, with some States – Chad, Iran, Jordan, Lebanon, Pakistan, Saudi Arabia, Syria – hosting more than one refugee for every hundred nationals. In contrast, Canada's ratio is nearly 1:460; the ratio for the United States and the European Union is roughly 1:1,900; and for Japan, approximately 1:41,000.[78] Not only is the less developed world doing the overwhelming share of refugee hosting, but it does so with a small fraction of the resources presently allocated to processing and assisting the tiny minority of refugees who reach richer States. In approximate terms, less than 50 US cents per day is available to look after each of the refugees under direct UNHCR care in poorer States.[79] Not even that tiny budget is guaranteed, but has to be garnered each year from the voluntary contributions to UNHCR of a small number of wealthier countries (there is no formula-based funding arrangement). Meanwhile, developed States spend on average USD 20,000 just to process the claim of each refugee able to reach them, with additional sums for transitional support.[80] As such, the world now spends more than a hundred times as much on a refugee arriving in the developed world as it does to protect a refugee who remains in the less developed world.

In such circumstances, it should come as no surprise that the situation of refugees in many less developed countries is often dire. In far too many cases, rights abuse is rampant and rationalised on the basis of extreme resource shortages. There is, thus, a very strong basis to consider apportioning resources more fairly relative to needs. To be taken seriously, however, that reallocation needs to be both much more significant than in the past and, most fundamentally, binding (in contrast to current charity-based models). Countries in regions of origin rightly protest that they cannot be expected to admit massive numbers of refugees, to whom they thus become legally obligated, on the basis of discretionary grants that ebb and flow with the political, budgetary and other preferences of wealthier governments.

More fundamentally still, the rights of refugees in the less developed world are not meaningfully vindicated by dollars sent to run UNHCR or other refugee camps, where rights abuse is often rampant and opportunities for self-reliance usually non-existent.[81] If the transfer of resources is to be meaningful, there must be an ability to ensure verifiable respect for refugee law obligations in recipient States.

78 US Committee for Refugees and Immigrants, 'World Refugee Survey 2009' (US Committee for Refugees and Immigrants, 2009) 31.

79 At the end of 2009, 10.4 million refugees were receiving protection or assistance from UNHCR: United Nations High Commissioner for Refugees, '2009 Global Trends' (UNHCR, 15 June 2010) 2. Total programme support expenditures in 2009 were USD 1.78 billion: United Nations High Commissioner for Refugees, 'Biennial Programme Budget 2010–2011' (UN Doc A/AC.96/1068, United Nations, 17 September 2009) 60. This equates to USD 172 per refugee per year, or approximately 47 cents per day.

80 Jenny Bedlington, 'Creating Shared Solutions to Refugee Protection: An Agenda for the International Community' (Speech delivered at the Advanced Study Center of the International Institute, University of Michigan, 14 April 2004).

81 Guglielmo Verdirame and Barbara Harrell-Bond, *Rights in Exile: Janus-Faced Humanitarianism* (Berghahn, 2005).

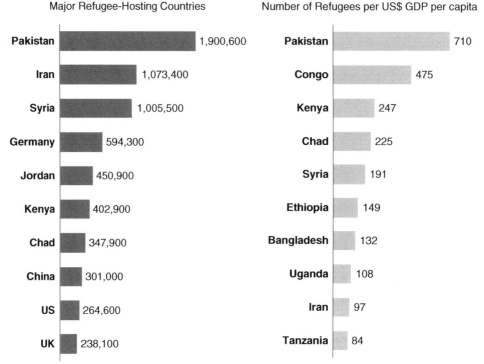

Figure 7.1 Refugee burden sharing, 2010
Source: United Nations High Commissioner for Refugees, Global Trends 2010 (UNHCR, 2011)

7.4.2. The logic of a shift to common but differentiated responsibility

The challenge, then, is to reinvigorate international refugee law in a way that States continue to see as reconcilable to their self-interests, in particular their migration control objectives, yet which does not compromise the right of refugees to access true protection. Given the uneven distribution of resources and protective responsibilities, the critical starting point is to acknowledge the Refugee Convention's flexibility, which allows State parties to allocate burdens and responsibilities among themselves. This process must be a genuine rights-regarding allocation of responsibility, not a simple dumping of refugees abroad on the ground that they will be admitted and protected from expulsion in the destination country. In particular, this operational flexibility may not under any circumstance override the core commitments to protection embodied in the Refugee Convention. This means that governments must allow access to their territory for all persons who wish to claim refugee protection, at least pending an assignment of responsibility, and it means that refugees arriving may not be stigmatised as unlawful entrants. It also means that account must be taken – both at the site of arrival and in any potential State to which protective responsibility is assigned – of the full requirements of refugee law and international human rights law, not just of the ability to secure entry and be protected against *refoulement*. Two cornerstones for a principled and meaningful system to share burdens and responsibilities should be considered.[82]

The first is to move away from a system of unilateral, state-by-state implementation of refugee law towards a system of 'common but differentiated responsibility'. The impetus for States to share refugee protection responsibilities would come from an appreciation that cooperation offers States a form of collective insurance when they, or States with which they have close ties, are faced with a significant refugee influx. It is only by ensuring the broad distribution of the responsibility of physical protection, and the availability of reliable fiscal support, that States will feel able to remain open to the arrival of refugees.

The precise allocation of burdens and responsibilities should be flexible, but should operate against a foundational principle that not even the significant assumption of fiscal burdens can justify withdrawing from human protective responsibilities. Every State would agree to participate in the sharing of both fiscal burdens and human responsibilities, though the precise mix of obligations would vary. Some States might focus on providing immediate protection in the wake of a mass influx; others would provide protection for the duration of risk; others might concentrate on providing an immediate solution for truly difficult cases, or on ensuring access to resettlement opportunities for refugees not able to return home within a reasonable time. As all of these roles are critical to a sound protection regime, there is no reason why every State must take on the same mix of responsibilities.

The second imperative is to establish a meaningful system to oversee the common but differentiated responsibility and resource transfer regimes. The approach on the ground should be based on the central importance of ensuring refugee autonomy and self-reliance, precisely in line with the rights regime established by the Refugee Convention.

In short, the normative structure of refugee law is sound. There is no need to revisit the content of refugee law – thanks to a combination of judicial reinvigoration of the refugee definition, the evolution of powerful general human rights standards to buttress the Refugee Convention's own creative rights regime, and the rise of ancillary regional protection regimes. But the long-term viability of refugee law is under threat from its atomised system of implementation, coupled with the absence of a meaningful mechanism to oversee respect for legal obligations and facilitate the sharing-out of burdens and responsibilities among State parties. The challenge is to update the mechanisms of implementation without undermining the ability of refugee law to continue to play its critical role of ensuring surrogate national protection to those fundamentally disfranchised by their own country.

---

82 A comprehensive model for reform is set out in James Hathaway and Alexander Neve, 'Making International Refugee Law Relevant Again: A Proposal for Collectivized and Solution-Oriented Protection' (1997) 10 *Harvard Human Rights Journal* 115. Relevant social science research is collected in James Hathaway (ed.), *Reconceiving International Refugee Law* (Martinus Nijhoff, 1997).

KEY REFERENCES

Anker, Deborah, *The Law of Asylum in the United States* (West Group, 2011)

Carlier, Jean-Yves *et al.* (eds.), *Who is a Refugee? A Comparative Case Law Study* (Kluwer Law International, 1997)

Foster, Michelle, *International Refugee Law and Socio-Economic Rights: Refuge from Deprivation* (Cambridge University Press, 2007)

Goodwin-Gill, Guy and McAdam, Jane, *The Refugee in International Law* (Oxford University Press, 3rd edn, 2007)

Grahl-Madsen, Atle, *The Status of Refugees in International Law* (Sijthoff, 1966 and 1971)

Grahl-Madsen, Atle, 'A Commentary on the Refugee Convention 1951' (UNHCR, 1963 and 1997)

Hathaway, James, *The Rights of Refugees under International Law* (Cambridge University Press, 2005)

Hathaway, James, *The Law of Refugee Status* (Butterworths, 1991)

Hathaway, James (ed.), *Reconceiving International Refugee Law* (Martinus Nijhoff, 1997)

McAdam, Jane, *Complementary Protection in International Refugee Law* (Oxford University Press, 2007)

Noll, Gregor, *Negotiating Asylum: The EU Acquis, Extraterritorial Protection, and the Common Market of Deflection* (Martinus Nijhoff, 2000)

Robinson, Nehemiah, *Convention relating to the Status of Refugees: Its History, Contents and Interpretation* (Institute of Jewish Affairs, 1953)

United Nations High Commissioner for Refugees, *Handbook on Procedures and Criteria for Determining Refugee Status* (UNHCR, 1992)

Weis, Paul, *The Refugee Convention 1951: The Travaux Préparatoires Analysed* (Cambridge University Press, 1995)

Zieck, Marjoleine, *UNHCR's Worldwide Presence in the Field: A Legal Analysis of UNHCR's Cooperation Agreements* (Wolf Legal, 2006)

Zimmermann, Andreas (ed.), *The 1951 Convention relating to the Status of Refugees and its 1967 Protocol* (Oxford University Press, 2011)

KEY RESOURCES

European Commission, Home Affairs: http://ec.europa.eu/home-affairs/doc_centre/asylum/asylum_intro_en.htm

European Council on Refugees and Exiles: www.ecre.org

Forced Migration Online, Refugee Studies Centre, University of Oxford: www.forcedmigration.org

International Association of Refugee Law Judges: www.iarlj.org

International Journal of Refugee Law: http://ijrl.oxfordjournals.org

Journal of Refugee Studies: http://jrs.oxfordjournals.org

Refugee Caselaw Site, University of Michigan Law School: www.refugeecaselaw.org

Refugee Law Reader: www.refugeelawreader.org

RefWorld, UNHCR: www.refworld.org

8

Women, children and other marginalised migrant groups

JACQUELINE BHABHA[1]

8.1. INTRODUCTION

The paradigmatic migrant has long been considered an able-bodied, adult male who leaves home to seek his fortune or save his life. Some of the principal components of international migration law – attribution of nationality, regulation of border crossing and protection of forced migrants – have been shaped by this perception. In the sphere of nationality, well into the twentieth century, women in many countries lost their nationality of origin on marriage to a foreigner, confirming the prevailing notion that allegiance to a sovereign and rootedness in a State were inherently male attributes.[2] In terms of immigration control, until the mid-1970s and public acknowledgement of the so-called 'feminisation of migration', immigrants were generally assumed to be young, single, male workers, conveniently providing their host States with a discrete unit of labour. It came as something of a shock that workers were attached to families. And in the sphere of forced migration, refugees too were primarily seen as male political activists fleeing state oppression because of aspects of their civic status (such as their race, religion or political opinion). As a result, the foundational *Convention relating to the Status of Refugees* (1951) ('Refugee Convention'), drafted after the Second World War, did not include gender as a possible ground of persecution.[3] There was only one exception to this early masculinist view of migration: nineteenth- and early twentieth-century laws criminalising what we now call trafficking took it as

---

1 I am grateful to Adam Kern for invaluable research assistance.
2 Nancy Cott, *Public Vows: A History of Marriage and the Nation* (Harvard University Press, 2000); Jacqueline Bhabha and Sue Shutter (eds.), *Worlds Apart: Women under Immigration, Nationality, and Refugee Law* (Trentham Books, 1994).
3 *Convention relating to the Status of Refugees*, opened for signature 28 July 1951, 189 UNTS 150 (entered into force 22 April 1954) art. 1.

axiomatic that the victims needing protection were women, especially young women.[4]

Over the past three decades, a more complex and accurate understanding of migration has gradually taken root. Despite some residual gender bias, most notably in United States jurisprudence,[5] nationality law in Western democracies is generally non-discriminatory between men and women. Immigration regulations relating to labour migration now acknowledge the presence of both male and female workers as primary migrants. Refugee law has been substantially reshaped from its narrow early focus on adult males to encompass both gender- and child-based persecution as possible bases for the grant of asylum. International anti-trafficking laws now encompass not only young women, but children, both girls and boys, as well as persons with disabilities.[6]

Other migrant groups are still very much at the margins of migration discussion. The elderly do not yet feature prominently in migration law. Demographic trends such as increasing longevity and declining birth rates are likely to change this. Many countries discriminate by age in their selection of migrant workers, relegating perfectly competent and healthy workers to the end of recruitment queues.[7] Family reunification provisions that limit the ability of children to bring their ageing parents and other relatives are also likely to attract more attention, as family sizes shrink and elderly parents cannot turn to non-migrant offspring for support.[8] Other migrant groups who give rise to issues of equity include permanent resident non-nationals who are excluded from full social and civil benefits despite long residence and contributions to host States.

This gradual transformation in the framework of international migration law accords with current migration realities. Among the 3.1 per cent of today's estimated world population who are international migrants, 49 per cent are women.[9] Children and youth are also very well represented. According to the World Bank, about one-third of migrants from developing countries are aged between 12 and 24 years.[10] And some of the most pressing migration issues arise from the impact of

---

4 See, e.g., *White-Slave Traffic Act*, 18 USC §§ 2421–24 (1910) (also known as the Mann Act); *Convention for the Suppression of the Traffic in Persons and of the Exploitation of the Prostitution of Others*, opened for signature 2 December 1949, 96 UNTS 272 (entered into force 25 July 1951) 282.

5 Linda Kerber, 'The Stateless as the Citizen's Other' in Seyla Benhabib and Judith Resnik (eds.), *Migrations and Mobilities: Citizenship, Borders, and Gender* (New York University Press, 2009) 76.

6 *Victims of Trafficking and Violence Protection Act* 22 USC § 7101 (2000). For discussion of the case that inspired this provision – the 'Deaf Mexican Case' – see Deborah Sontag, 'Poor and Deaf from Mexico Betrayed in Their Dreams', *New York Times* 25 July 1997, A1.

7 Norbert Cyrus and Dita Vogel, 'Briefing Note for the Hearing on Economic Migrant Workers' (Policy Department, European Parliament, 2007).

8 Currently, migration concerns regarding the elderly arise primarily in family reunification cases, where the breadwinning sponsor has to demonstrate that the parent or other elderly relative qualifies for entry on the basis of both age and dependency. See *Council Directive 2003/86/EC of 22 September 2003 on the Right to Family Reunification* [2003] OJ L 251/12.

9 United Nations Department of Economic and Social Affairs, 'Trends in International Migrant Stock: The 2008 Revision' (POP/DB/MIG/Stock/Rev.2008, United Nations, 2009).

10 World Bank, 'World Development Report 2007: Development and the Next Generation' (World Bank, 2006), cited in Hans Van de Glind, 'Migration and Child Labour: Exploring Child Migrant Vulnerabilities and those of Children Left-Behind' (International Labour Office, 2010) 1.

intersections between marginalised statuses – the labour exploitation of disabled children as beggars, or the sexual violation of trafficked young girls. It makes even less sense today than it ever did to view regional or global migration as an adult male activity. Justification for grouping all migrants who are not adult males in a single category of 'marginalised migrant groups' is twofold: the shared tradition of neglect under the law and the shared vulnerabilities suffered by these groups.

8.1.1. Traditionally neglected groups

Women, children and migrants with disabilities share the fact that they were, until recently, neglected because they were thought to be derivative migrants, rather than migrant actors in their own right and deserving of their own status. They featured as appendages of the primary, healthy adult male migrant who had to prove his status to justify their entry. This has had enduring consequences for international migration law: these groups still experience discrimination because of historical misperception. A good example is the impact of nationality on the ability to live at home with one's family. In many countries, adult nationals are entitled to keep their spouses and dependent children with them, even if the latter are non-nationals – having your family with you is part of what it means to be home. Not so for children. A child national is expected to leave home to follow non-national parents or go into foster care – that is, to choose between family and home – if the parents do not have independent permission to stay in the State of the child's nationality. The child's nationality is ineffective where the adult's is effective. This difference in treatment is unjustified.[11] As Lady Hale remarked in a United Kingdom Supreme Court decision in favour of two young British nationals who opposed the deportation of their non-British mother (and therefore their own *de facto* deportation too): 'The intrinsic importance of citizenship [should not] be played down. As citizens, these children have rights which they will not be able to exercise if they move to another country.'[12]

However, discriminatory attitudes do not necessarily lead to worse treatment: different may be better. Stereotypes may lead decision makers to be more generous towards groups they consider vulnerable or defenceless. A case in point is the finding that among asylum applicants in developed States, a higher proportion of women than men were granted refugee status.[13] Though the absence of gender as one of the grounds for 'a well-founded fear of persecution' (the central qualification for establishing a claim to refugee protection) suggests a fundamental disadvantage for female applicants, in practice women who have managed to get

---

11 Jacqueline Bhabha, 'The "Mere Fortuity of Birth"? Children, Mothers, Borders and the Meaning of Citizenship' in Seyla Benhabib and Judith Resnik (eds.), *Migrations and Mobilities: Citizenship, Borders, and Gender* (New York University Press, 2009) 187, 193.

12 *ZH (Tanzania)* v. *Secretary of State for the Home Department* [2011] UKSC 4 (1 February 2011) [32].

13 Jacqueline Bhabha, 'Demography and Rights: Women, Children and Access to Asylum' (2004) 16(2) *International Journal of Refugee Law* 227.

access to a refugee determination system have not fared worse than men. On the contrary, women asylum applicants have had a higher success rate in securing refugee status than men.[14] The qualification about access to a determination system, however, is important. Far more women than men fleeing persecution do *not* manage to access a border where they can claim refugee status – they are much more likely to be trapped in or close to the State they are fleeing, and much less likely to secure the economic, social and legal tools necessary to facilitate long-distance migration, particularly transcontinental migration.

8.1.2. Shared vulnerabilities

This point leads to the second justification often advanced for grouping female, child or disabled migrants together: their supposedly shared vulnerability, including their economic dependence, susceptibility to exploitation and lack of physical or intellectual maturity. This ground is problematic. Feminists have long criticised the hyphenated noun 'women-and-children' because of its infantilising and patronising implications. Whereas young children certainly are vulnerable, economically dependent or lacking in maturity, not all women, and not all women migrants, share those qualities. Millions of women migrants have supported their families as heads of household; millions more have protected their families from the ravages of armed conflict and taken them to safety. In some countries, such as the Philippines, and in some industries, such as healthcare and hotel servicing, migrant women provide the backbone sustaining the edifice as a whole. To categorise them as vulnerable or dependent is at best misleading.

There is another reason why the 'women-and-children' grouping is unsatisfactory: the two groups may have opposing interests. A woman who needs to go abroad to work may deny having children if work permits are only allocated to single women, as has been the case in some host States. This self-interested move may backfire: subsequent applications for family reunification from previously concealed children are much more likely to be refused. The tension may be even more explicit. Mothers may be child abusers, child sellers (in the case of international adoption) or child exploiters. A recent study reveals that women are increasingly involved as the key recruiters of child victims of sex trafficking, both in international and domestic trafficking cases. In a typical case, 'a San Antonio woman and her two daughters were directly responsible for managing the entire operation trafficking Mexican children to the United States for sexual exploitation'.[15] To group 'women-and-children' together in anti-trafficking measures is to simplify the complexity of the regulatory challenge – one cannot assume a unified 'victim' group. Human trafficking is discussed further in Chapter 9.

---

14 Thomas Spijkerboer, *Gender and Refugee Status* (Ashgate, 2000).
15 Alexis Aronowitz, *Human Trafficking, Human Misery: The Global Trade in Human Beings* (Greenwood, 2009) 53.

But there is an even more fundamental issue. Whereas children, particularly young children, need protection and the exercise of 'best interest' judgments by adult decision makers connected to their migration, women need an environment that enables them to act autonomously and independently, and not to be tied to a social and legal role of economically dependent homemaker, nurturer and caregiver. Migrants with disabilities may fit into either set of circumstances, depending on the specificities of their situation. These differences have implications for international migration law, just as they do for other areas of law. They suggest that, in some cases, the disaggregation of the interests of child migrants and women migrants is critical to the furtherance of both groups' human rights. In other cases, however, it is helpful to consider children and gender issues together because there is an intersection between the vulnerabilities – gender and age, or disability and gender, combine to complicate the migrant's situation. Finally, even when no such intersection exists, the fact of historic marginalisation and the growing evidence that women, children or disabled individuals may assume an autonomous role as migrants, justifies consideration of their particular circumstances in relation to migration law. This chapter outlines the international migration law applicable to these groups in turn.

8.2. CHILD MIGRANTS

The composite term 'child migrant' needs some clarification. International law, as set out in the *Convention on the Rights of the Child* (1989) ('CRC'), provides a universally accepted definition of a '*child*' (art. 1): 'every human being below the age of eighteen years unless under the law applicable to the child, majority is attained earlier'.[16] Thus, according to the CRC, national law can lower but not raise the cut-off point for considering a person a child – in some States, thirteen-year-olds are no longer required to enrol in full-time education and are soon after permitted to work.[17] The voluminous flow through the Straits of Gibraltar of North Africans in their early teens in search of work within the European Union provides a case in point.

Other bodies of international law define childhood more expansively. European Union ('EU') law guarantees the freedom of movement within the EU of children of EU nationals (whatever the nationality of the child) up to the age of twenty-one. This does not prevent EU member States from applying the CRC definition, or a lower national law ceiling for childhood, to children of non-EU citizens (so-called 'third-country nationals') seeking family reunification. Thus a German national

16 *Convention on the Rights of the Child*, opened for signature 20 November 1989, 1577 UNTS 3 (entered into force 2 September 1990).

17 The States are Eritrea, Honduras, Morocco and Samoa: Right to Education Project, 'At What Age . . .? Comparative Table' (2010), www.right-to-education.org/node/279.

moving to the United Kingdom for work can bring her twenty-year-old Nigerian son with her thanks to EU law, but a Nigerian permanent resident moving from Germany to the United Kingdom cannot bring a son over eighteen years of age with her as a dependant because of United Kingdom law.

The term 'migrant', by contrast, is not defined in international law. As a matter of fact, child migrants can be divided into three broad categories. First, there are those who migrate for family reasons – whether to travel with relatives and join already migrated family; to stay with family, as in the *de facto* deportation case discussed earlier; or to start a family, as in the case of international adoption. Second, there are those who migrate for exploitation, such as trafficked children. Finally, there are those who migrate for survival – refugees and asylum seekers on the one hand, and economic migrants on the other. The categories are not mutually exclusive – for example, children travelling to join pre-departed immigrant parents may also be escaping armed conflict, and trafficked children may have become ensnared as a result of ill-conceived family reunification plans.

The quantitative picture is less clear. It is generally accepted that a growing proportion of migration consists of children, a trend that is likely to continue given global inequalities, unevenly distributed economic opportunities and shrinking effective distances. Accurate measures of child migration, however, are hard to come by. We do not know exactly what proportion of the estimated 214 million international migrants in the world today are children.[18] More specific quantitative measures, however, are available. We know that family migration is a very significant phenomenon – family reunification constitutes the largest category (66 per cent) of lawful permanent migration into the United States (619,000 persons in 2010).[19] We also know that unaccompanied child migration is widespread. According to the Separated Children in Europe Project, 25,000 unaccompanied child minors entered the EU in 2004.[20] In the United States, according to the Department of Homeland Security, even though the number of irregular child migrants 'apprehended' (i.e., stopped) in the past two years has declined, the number detained has remained constant at over 7,500 per year.[21] Child trafficking has reportedly reached immense proportions, but there is little agreement on the exact figures involved. According to the United Nations Office on Drugs and Crime, 13 per cent of the 2.5 million trafficking victims worldwide are 'girls', which amounts to roughly 325,000. According to the United States Department of State, 800,000 people are trafficked annually across borders; of these, according

18 United Nations Department of Economic and Social Affairs, above n. 9. These data on child migrants are the best available, but better estimates are needed.
19 United States Department of Homeland Security, *2010 Yearbook of Immigration* Statistics (Office of Immigration Statistics, 2010).
20 Data on the annual flow are unavailable, although UNHCR reports that 18,700 filed for asylum in 2009: United Nations High Commissioner for Refugees, 'Statistical Yearbook 2009: Trends in Displacement, Protection and Solutions' (UNHCR, 2010) 10.
21 Jacqueline Bhabha and Susan Schmidt, 'From Kafka to Wilberforce: Is the US Government's Approach to Child Migrants Improving?' (2011) (February) *Immigration Briefings* 1.

to the United States Department of Justice, 50 per cent (or 400,000) are children.[22] A significant but unquantified proportion of the estimated 300,000 child soldiers worldwide are girls, both active combatants and those forcibly enlisted as bush 'wives', cooks or porters. Among refugees, children represent 41 per cent of the total population, amounting to some 4.8 million refugees per year.[23]

8.2.1. General human rights norms

Like all migrants, child migrants are entitled to the protection of general human rights that apply to all people, regardless of nationality, immigration status or age. These rights are set out in the so-called 'International Bill of Rights', which includes the foundational documents of modern human rights – the *Universal Declaration of Human Rights* (1948),[24] and its two implementing covenants, the *International Covenant on Civil and Political Rights* (1966) ('ICCPR')[25] and the *International Covenant on Economic, Social and Cultural Rights* (1966) ('ICESCR').[26] Chapter 6 analyses these human rights in detail. Regional human rights instruments also set out significant standards, some of which impinge directly on the rights and well-being of child migrants.[27] For the purposes of this chapter, it suffices to observe that for child migrants, the most fundamental principle embodied in these documents is that of non-discrimination, according to which all distinctions between people that are arbitrary, disproportionate or unjustifiable are prohibited.[28] As a relatively disenfranchised group, migrant children are likely to be more dependent on state protection and intercession on their behalf than many of their national peers, with long-established families and communities to fall back on. The right not to be discriminated against, a right which is both free-standing and attached to the enjoyment of other child rights, is thus the starting point for child migrants to be treated as children first and foremost, before considerations relating to their immigration status interfere.

---

22 Polaris Project, Human Trafficking Statistics, available from www.polarisproject.org.

23 Right to Education Project, above n. 17, 7, 46.

24 *Universal Declaration of Human Rights*, GA Res 217A (III), UN Doc A/810 (10 December 1948).

25 *International Covenant on Civil and Political Rights*, opened for signature 16 December 1966, 999 UNTS 171 (entered into force 23 March 1976).

26 *International Covenant on Economic, Social and Cultural Rights*, opened for signature 16 December 1966, 993 UNTS 3 (entered into force 3 January 1976). For a more detailed analysis of the ICESCR and ICCPR, see Jacqueline Bhabha, 'Children, Migration and International Norms' in Alexander Aleinikoff and Vincent Chetail (eds.), *Migration and International Legal Norms* (TMC Asser Press, 2003) 203, 206.

27 The European Union 'Return' Directive, which addresses deportation and removal of migrants from EU member States, makes special mention of vulnerable persons (art. 3) and provides for their special needs, including access to emergency healthcare. *Council Directive 2008/115/EC of the European Parliament and of the Council of 16 December 2008 on Common Standards and Procedures in Member States for Returning Illegally Staying Third-Country Nationals* [2008] OJ L 348. Similarly, the *European Social Charter (Revised)*, opened for signature 3 May 1996, CETS No 163 (entered into force 1 July 1999) deals with children's access to healthcare and housing.

28 The ICCPR (art. 24) provides: 'Every child shall have, without any discrimination as to race, colour, sex, language, religion, national or social origin, property or birth, the right to such measures of protection as are required by his status as a minor, on the part of his family, society and the State.'

Child migrants are also guaranteed life, liberty and security; freedom from torture and cruel or degrading treatment or punishment; full access to whichever court system is relevant; equality before the law; protection from arbitrary arrest, detention or exile; full procedural protections in arrest and criminal process; a fair wage; police protection; emergency healthcare; shelter and other social assistance necessary to the preservation of life; recognition as a person before the law; a nationality; and freedom of movement. Some of the guarantees extended to all people are granted to children in even stronger terms. The ICESCR (art. 11) recognises the right of everyone to an adequate standard of living, including adequate housing and the continuous improvement of living conditions. But for children, the CRC (art. 27) imposes an additional obligation on all States parties to assist parents and others responsible for the child's physical, mental, spiritual, moral and social development, and to provide material assistance and support programmes, particularly with regard to nutrition, clothing and housing.

Regarding healthcare, the ICESCR (art. 12) notes that every person has the right to enjoy the highest attainable standard of physical and mental health. But despite the inclusive scope of this provision, the standards for adults and children can differ. The ICESCR obligates States to provide emergency healthcare to all, including adult and child migrants; and many suggest that a State's healthcare responsibilities are more extensive than emergency treatment.[29] Children also benefit from ICESCR provisions aimed at reducing infant mortality and supporting primary child healthcare to secure 'the healthy development of the child'; but adults are not similarly entitled to primary healthcare by virtue of the ICESCR. Many migration destination States have embraced these inclusive provisions by providing emergency, necessary and in some cases comprehensive healthcare to child migrants irrespective of status. Within Europe, for example, there is a broad spectrum of approaches. Spain and Italy provide free healthcare for all within the same comprehensive healthcare system; France, Belgium and the Netherlands administer separate systems for migrants, but envisage free access for some types of healthcare needs; the United Kingdom and Portugal have more restrictive systems; and Hungary and Germany allow free healthcare only in limited cases, but require providers to inform on users with an irregular migration status. In practice, however, even in countries where access to healthcare is permitted, child migrants encounter obstacles to medical treatment arising out of discrimination because they lack health insurance. In the Netherlands, restrictive interpretations of what constitutes 'necessary care' have prevented access for some child migrants. In France, child migrants need a regular address to access emergency medical care if they do not have documents. In the United States, by contrast, undocumented

---

29 The ICESCR (art. 12(d)) requires States parties to take steps necessary for 'the creation of conditions which would assure to all medical service and medical attention in the event of sickness'. Many now interpret this provision to require the performance of health obligations that are more extensive than emergency care.

child migrants must be provided with emergency care, but they are not otherwise eligible for publicly funded health services.

Education is another right of particular significance to children. The ICESCR (art. 13) requires States parties to 'recognize the right of everyone to education', and, in particular, to ensure that primary education is free and available to all; that secondary education, including technical and vocational education, is 'made generally available and accessible to all by every appropriate means'; and that 'higher education is equally accessible to all, on the basis of capacity'. Fortunately, this obligation has been broadly enforced by States. In the United States, for example, primary and secondary education is guaranteed to all children, irrespective of immigration status, and several states permit undocumented children who have graduated from United States high schools to enrol in state universities for the same cost as legal residents. In Europe, the situation varies from State to State. In Italy, undocumented children have the right to attend school, though few migrant children are able to benefit from this entitlement because they are employed in agriculture. In Poland, by contrast, undocumented children must pay to attend schools, which they attend as a matter of compulsion. On the whole, the evidence suggests that undocumented children in Europe encounter significant obstacles to gaining an education. Egregious recent examples include the mandatory finger-printing of Roma children by the Italian government,[30] the attempts to exclude asylum-seeking children from public school in the United Kingdom,[31] and discriminatory document checks on migrant child patients.

8.2.2. Specialised human rights norms

Apart from the rights guaranteed to migrant children under the International Bill of Rights, there is a second cluster of rights guaranteed to them by virtue of their membership of particular identity groups. These rights are embodied in a variety of documents, ranging from the *Convention against Torture and Other Cruel, Inhuman or Degrading Treatment or Punishment* (1984)[32] to the *Convention on the Elimination of All Forms of Discrimination against Women* (1979),[33] but the two most important to migrant children are the CRC (noted above) and the *International Convention on the Protection of the Rights of All Migrant Workers and Members of their Families* (1990).[34] The latter reinforces many rights established in the International Bill of Rights, including the right to fair and public court hearings; protection from collective expulsion; equal treatment regarding employment terms and conditions; and

---

30 Malcolm Moore, 'Italy to Fingerprint all Roma Gipsy Children', *The Telegraph* 26 June 2008.
31 'Croydon Council Ordered to Educate Asylum-Seeking Teenagers', *Croydon Guardian* 24 October 2010.
32 *Convention against Torture and Other Cruel, Inhuman or Degrading Treatment or Punishment*, opened for signature 10 December 1984, 1465 UNTS 85 (entered into force 26 June 1987).
33 *Convention on the Elimination of All Forms of Discrimination against Women*, opened for signature 18 December 1979, 1249 UNTS 13 (entered into force 3 September 1981).
34 *International Convention on the Protection of the Rights of All Migrant Workers and Members of their Families*, opened for signature 18 December 1990, 2220 UNTS 3 (entered into force 1 July 2003).

emergency healthcare. It is therefore comprehensive in its scope, though it is limited in its application: as of late 2011 only forty-five States had ratified the treaty, none of which is a primary receiving State of international migrants.

Child migrants are also entitled to the protection of human rights specific to all children. These rights are set forth in the CRC, the most widely and speedily ratified human rights treaty ever. The CRC consolidates the human rights protections for children previously scattered in different instruments. Some of the specific protections date back to the early twentieth century, when international human rights and migration law were in their infancy. Not surprisingly, these early legal provisions target forced child migrants – a particularly vulnerable subset of migrant children – contradicting the inaccurate but frequently voiced claim that child migrants have always been 'invisible' in international law. The treaties include the first anti-trafficking measures criminalising recruitment 'for immoral purposes' of any woman under the age of twenty-one.[35] They also include measures directly addressing the needs and vulnerabilities of refugee children. In fact, the first international human rights declaration ever adopted, the League of Nations *Declaration of the Rights of the Child* (1924), states: 'The child must be the first to receive relief in times of distress.'[36]

Other provisions in the CRC are of more recent vintage, and derive from the post-Second World War construction of a human rights edifice spanning both civil and political rights on the one hand (the so-called 'negative' or 'first-generation' rights), and economic, social and cultural rights on the other hand (the so-called 'positive' or 'second-generation' rights). Whether out of naïveté, relying on children's apparent lack of legal and political clout, or out of guilt, given the prior lack of attention to child rights issues, member States of the United Nations lost no time in ratifying the CRC. Ratification brought with it the establishment of a treaty-monitoring body, the Committee on the Rights of the Child, charged with overseeing its implementation, receiving periodic reports from States parties, and issuing from time to time detailed guidance on particular issues of relevance to the enforcement of children's rights. In other words, ratification of the CRC did more than simply bring together previously established international law relating to children. It created a new framework of accountability about children, although the most powerful tool for enforcing this – the ability to litigate and force a State to abide by its treaty obligations – is still not available to children. Nevertheless, the

---

35 *International Convention for the Suppression of the 'White Slave Traffic'*, opened for signature 4 May 1910, 98 UNTS 101 (amended by the Protocol of 4 May 1949, entered into force 14 August 1951); *International Convention for the Suppression of the Traffic in Women and Children*, opened for signature 30 September 1921, 53 UNTS 38 (amended by the Protocol of 12 November 1947, entered into force 24 April 1950); and *Supplementary Convention on the Abolition of Slavery, the Slave Trade and Institutions and Practices Similar to Slavery*, opened for signature 7 September 1956, 266 UNTS 3 (entered into force 30 April 1957).

36 *Geneva Declaration of the Rights of the Child*, League of Nations (26 September 1924) art. 3. This mandatory language was subsequently softened to take account of prevailing political realities. A United Nations declaration in 1959 provided that children should be 'among the first' to receive protection and relief: *Declaration of the Rights of the Child*, UN Doc A/4354 (1959) Principle 8.

CRC has spurred new thinking about children, including migrant children, most crucially through the notion that children are to be considered not only as vulnerable and immature adult protégés on whose behalf 'best interests' decisions have to be made, but as progressively evolving individuals. The CRC articulates a new and modern principle of agency – the notion that children as they grow up have a right to have their voices heard and their views taken into account.

This important new entitlement, set out in art. 12, has great relevance to the circumstances of child migrants. It means, first and foremost, that children's opinions – for example, about whether they want to migrate, whether they want to be returned 'home', whether they agree to be *de facto* deported when their parents are – have to be elicited and heard. The children's views are not binding on adult decision makers or on the State, but ignoring those views can be held to vitiate 'best interests' decisions that are made without even considering the child's view. For example, it has become routine to justify the removal of irregular unaccompanied child migrants to their countries of origin by invoking the 'best interests' principle. It is argued that children are best off 'at home', whether 'home' consists of stable accommodation with a caring family or not, and that removal deters future potential child migrants, who are likely to experience hardship in the course of their migration.[37] Under art. 12, this approach is challengeable: children's views of what return would bring must be taken into consideration before a decision is made, given that the impact of return on their identity, private life and future aspirations all form a part of the 'best interests' assessment. As the UN Committee on the Rights of the Child has pointed out in General Comment No 6, unaccompanied migrant children should only be returned to their country of origin if 'secure and concrete arrangements of care and custodial responsibilities, by parents or other carers are available . . . Non-rights based arguments, such as those relating to general migration control, cannot override best interests considerations.'[38]

This chapter turns now to four CRC rights that are of particular significance for migrant children: legal identity, family life, freedom from detention, and freedom from trafficking and smuggling.

Legal identity

The right to a legal identity can be broken down into three constitutive elements identified in CRC art. 7: the right to a name, the right to birth registration and the right to a nationality.[39] Being named is the first step to being a person: it is a necessary condition for securing a birth certificate, itself the key to getting a passport

---

37 Jacqueline Bhabha and Susan Schmidt, 'Seeking Asylum Alone: Unaccompanied and Separated Children and Refugee Protection in the US' (Harvard University, François-Xavier Bagnoud Center for Health and Human Rights, June 2006) 93; Save the Children, 'I minori stranieri in Italia: L'esperienza e le raccomandazioni di Save the Children' (Save the Children, 2010).

38 Committee on the Rights of the Child, *General Comment No 6: Treatment of Unaccompanied and Separated Children outside their Country of Origin*, 39th sess, UN Doc CRC/GC/2005/6 (1 September 2005) [84]–[85].

39 For a fuller discussion, see Jacqueline Bhabha (ed.), *Children without a State: A Global Human Rights Challenge* (Massachusetts Institute of Technology, 2011).

in due course. Having one's birth registered is step two; it links the child to the State in an irrevocable way, and is often critical both for accessing state services such as education and healthcare, and for reducing the risk of gross human rights violations, such as disappearances and extermination. But name and birth registration are not sufficient to guarantee effective legal personhood – a nationality is also necessary. Statelessness is a serious legal impediment because it affects one's ability to make claims on the State for protection, for support and for the right of permanent residence (see Chapter 4). Acquiring the nationality of the State of one's birth is particularly important, unless a clear inherited nationality that links one to one's parents' permanent home is available (e.g., for children born to international students, or short-term migrant workers, or parents who are temporarily self-employed abroad). For a child to acquire nationality at birth is critically important. Nationals are immune from deportation and have full access to civil and political rights denied to non-nationals (e.g., voting and standing for public office). It is not just domestic rights that flow from these fundamental provisions. In an era of increasing globalisation, where geographic mobility may be a key to opportunity and prosperity, the ability to secure legal documents, to 'exist as a person before the law', is fundamental. Children whose births are not registered (around 40 per cent of the world's population)[40] are more likely to be out of school, out of work and excluded from social and other benefits. They are also more likely than their registered counterparts to become undocumented migrants later in life, confronting the perils of insecurity and socio-economic marginalisation associated with irregular immigration status.

Family life

A second right that is particularly significant for migrant children is the right to family life – a right encompassing both the right not to be separated from one's family and the right to family reunification. The CRC (art. 9) mandates that, unless the parents so desire, the child should not be separated unless 'the competent authorities subject to judicial review determine, in accordance with applicable law and procedures, that such separation is necessary for the best interests of the child'. In other words, respect for the integrity of family life is strongly protected in international law. In practice, however, this right is elusive for many migrant children. Several States parties have specifically entered reservations to exempt their immigration control measures from this provision in the CRC (see Chapter 3). As a result, deportable parents of non-deportable children (e.g., irregular migrants with children who are nationals of the host State) are regularly expelled even though this is clearly not in the best interests of their children, who are left without parents or without the home they have always known. National and international courts have challenged some of the States' exclusionary policies. The European Court of Human Rights has elaborated some useful principles for balancing a

---

40 Claire Cody, 'Count Every Child: The Right to Birth Registration' (Plan International, 2009) 27.

State's need to maintain effective immigration control against the personal impact on children and families of divisive or dislocating measures.[41] Factors that the Court has taken into account include the age of the child (young children are considered more easily moveable than older ones); the linguistic, educational and economic environment to which the child would have to accompany the parents (the more unfamiliar, the greater the burden on the State to demonstrate proportionality); and, most relied upon though least logical, the parents' behaviour ('good' parents are more likely to be rewarded, irrespective of how their conduct affects the child's best interests).

Family unity is also violated when children who have been separated from their parents because of the latter's need to seek work abroad are refused the right to join their parents at a later time. The CRC recognises the moral equivalence of these two forms of family separation. Despite the international law principle that involuntary family separation should only be enforced when it is in the child's best interests (e.g., if a parent is abusive or incapable of caring), typical reasons for prohibiting family reunification include the parents' failure to demonstrate adequate ability to support and accommodate their children. This means that children are routinely and permanently separated from their parents, even when the excluded children will have a lower standard of living in the country of origin than they would have in the migration destination country where reunification is sought. These practices violate the CRC's injunction in art. 10 that family reunification applications be dealt with 'in a positive, humane and expeditious manner'. The same is true of widespread administrative practices that make family reunification a lengthy, costly and complicated procedure, fraught with pitfalls such as demands for non-existent or culturally inappropriate documents like formal marriage or birth certificates, or intrusive questioning by immigration officials designed to expose discrepancies between family members' answers and thus demonstrate that the parties are not related as claimed.

A particular issue arises when family reunification cannot take place in the State where one part of the family is located because of the risk of persecution – that is, when there is a need for refugee or other humanitarian protection. Although the Refugee Convention does not guarantee the right to family reunion for refugees, the CRC (art. 22) explicitly guarantees the right to family reunification for refugee and asylum-seeking children, over and above the general family reunification provisions discussed. This right is mutual as between parents and children: 'States Parties shall provide ... co-operation ... to trace the parents or other members of the family of any refugee child in order to obtain information necessary for reunification with his or her family'. In practice, however, States rarely afford refugee or asylum-seeking children the right to secure their parents'

---

41 See, e.g., *Berrehab* v. *Netherlands* (1988) 138 Eur Court HR (ser A); *Moustaquim Case* (1991) 193 Eur Court HR (ser A); *Beldjoudi* v. *France* (1992) 234 Eur Court HR (ser A); *Djeroud Case* (1991) 191 Eur Court HR (ser A); *Bouchelkia* v. *France* (1997) 1 Eur Court HR 47 (ser A); *Boujlifa* v. *France*, App No 24404/94 (1997) 30 Eur HR Rep 419, 437–48.

admission while they are minors. This asymmetry in the enforcement of the right to family reunification as between refugee adults and children mirrors the asymmetry between adults and children who are nationals in the power to preserve family life in the home State. These asymmetries violate both non-discrimination provisions and family unity rights. They illustrate the persistence of adult-centric bias in the implementation of contemporary international and national migration law.

Detention

Turning to the third relevant rights issue, detention presents a particular problem for migrant children. In some countries, notably the United States and Australia, many have experienced prolonged periods of detention with their families while deportation procedures are carried out, experiences that have led to serious documented health problems over the years (see Case Study 8.1). Two family immigration detention facilities – Woomera in Australia[42] and Hutto in the United States[43] – attracted particular attention because of the egregious conditions to which children were subjected over periods of months or years. Unaccompanied and separated child migrants have also experienced prolonged periods of incarceration, some in euphemistically named 'shelters', where immigration authorities, in consultation with subcontracting agencies, placed even very young children; others in more brutal detention facilities, detained alongside convicted juvenile offenders, often in remote locations, far from legal representatives or potentially supportive ethnic communities. Immigration detention is not itself prohibited by law, though it must always be in conformity with national law and of reasonable length (ICCPR art. 9). For children, the provisions governing detention are more stringent: it must be only 'for the shortest appropriate period of time' and 'used only as a measure of last resort' (CRC art. 37). Special rules that establish minimum fair standards for *any* child in detention also apply.[44] According to the United Nations High Commissioner for Refugees, unaccompanied or separated asylum-seeking children should never be detained.[45] Ongoing practices of detaining migrant children have attracted widespread criticism.[46] While improvements have occurred – for example, both Woomera and Hutto have been closed down – the abolition of detention for asylum-seeking children is still a long way off.

---

42 Jacqueline Bhabha and Mary Crock, *Seeking Asylum Alone: Unaccompanied and Separated Children and Refugee Protection in Australia, the UK and the US* (Themis Press, 2007).

43 Nina Bernstein, 'US to Overhaul Detention Policy for Immigrants', *New York Times* 5 August 2009, A1.

44 *United Nations Rules for the Protection of Juveniles Deprived of their Liberty*, UN Doc A/RES/45/113 (14 December 1990) [2].

45 United Nations High Commissioner for Refugees, 'Guidelines on Policies and Procedures in dealing with Unaccompanied Children Seeking Asylum' (UNHCR, 1 February 1997) s 7.6. See also Committee on the Rights of the Child, above n. 38, [61].

46 'Un Bébé Kosovar de 13 Mois en Centre de Rétention à Lyon, Dénonce RESF', *Le Parisien* 2011; *D & E* v. *Australia*, Communication No 1050/2002, UN Doc CCPR/C/87/D/1050/2002 (9 August 2006); *Bakhtiyari* v. *Australia*, Communication No 1069/2002, UN Doc CCPR/C/79/D/1069/2002 (29 October 2003); United Nations High Commissioner for Refugees, 'Submission to the Human Rights and Equal Opportunity Commission Inquiry into Children in Immigration Detention' (UNHCR, 14 May 2002).

CASE STUDY 8.1 Children in immigration detention in Australia[47]

Two Iranian children, ages seven and one, arrived in Australia by boat with their parents in November 2000. Their arduous four-month journey took them through Pakistan, Malaysia and Indonesia. Their life prior to fleeing Iran had not been easy either. D, their mother, had been arrested over the previous years and beaten by the Iranian authorities. They had accused her of involvement in illegal activities, namely, doing the makeup for actresses allegedly making pornographic films, and later for having in her hairdressing salon women wearing clothes and makeup forbidden under Iran's laws. The harsh application of Shari'a law in Iran is well known, and has resulted in the arrest, detention and torture of thousands of civilians since the Islamic Revolution overthrew the monarchy of the Shah. The children's mother was not the only person targeted by the Iranian regime. Their father, E, was also repeatedly arrested, questioned regarding his wife, and prevented from visiting her regularly while she was detained. Eventually, in July 2000, following a visit from one of the prison security guards to the hairdressing salon, the couple decided to flee Iran with their two small children to escape further persecution and harassment by the authorities.

Despite their difficult journey to Australia, D and E and their two small children were immediately detained on arrival. Within days the family claimed asylum, with D as the principal applicant. The family was placed in an immigration detention centre, 1,800 km from the nearest major city. The isolated location was not unusual. Scores of migrant children seeking asylum in Australia have been detained in remote detention facilities, at great distance from family or community contacts and from legal and other sources of assistance. According to the family, no justification for the detention was provided to them. There was no suggestion that they posed a security threat or other specific danger to Australia's national interest. A month after the asylum application was lodged, the Minister for Immigration rejected it; three months later an appeal against the refusal was also rejected, this time by the Refugee Review Tribunal. A request that the Minister for Immigration exercise his discretion to substitute a more favourable decision than that of the tribunal was also rejected. Two years later the primary decision maker rejected the asylum application again, and seven months later an application for a review of that second refusal decision was also turned down. The family's detention lasted for over three years. During this time, one of the children developed a speech impediment.

A complaint was brought to the United Nations Human Rights Committee under the individual complaints procedure of the First Optional Protocol to the ICCPR, to which Australia is a party. In its views on the case, the Committee noted that: 'Whatever justification there may have been for an initial detention, for instance for purposes of ascertaining identity and other issues, [Australia] has not ... demonstrated that their detention was justified for such an extended period'.[48] The Human Rights Committee

---

47 This case study is based on *D & E v. Australia*, Communication No 1050/2002, UN Doc CCPR/C/87/D/1050/2002 (9 August 2006).
48 Ibid. [7.2].

upheld the complaint lodged by the family and found that Australia had violated its obligations under art. 9 of the ICCPR (arbitrary detention) by detaining the children for such an extended period.

This was not the first time Australia was taken to task by an international body for violating international restrictions on the detention of children. At the height of the war in Afghanistan, thousands of young Afghan children, particularly boys, fled enforced recruitment and brutalisation by the Taliban; several hundred arrived in Australia. They were all detained, again in remote sites and often for very long periods. Domestic and international protest eventually secured the children's release.

Trafficking and smuggling

Children who are trafficked or smuggled constitute a particular category of child migrant, explicitly addressed by international migration law. As indicated above, this body of law has a long history and has focussed on two aspects of the issue – criminalising the practice on the one hand and protecting the victims on the other. Both women and children have long been singled out for special protection because of their particular vulnerability to sexual exploitation, which constitutes a huge part of the trafficking business. Reports of the United Nations Special Rapporteur on the Sale of Children, Child Prostitution and Child Pornography have drawn special attention to the egregious harms perpetrated against children.[49] Until recently, the proliferation of international legislative measures generated little clarity for law enforcers, let alone a useful tool for curbing child trafficking – conflicting definitions, disjunctive national regimes and a lack of transborder cooperation militated against effective intervention. Meanwhile, illegal people-transporting networks proliferated, with ever more global and sophisticated organisation, outsmarting official crime prevention agencies in their transnational agility and coordination. State enforcement agencies failed to keep up. However, some progress has been made. After years of discussion, the international community, meeting in Palermo, Sicily, agreed on a new *United Nations Convention against Transnational Organized Crime* (2000).[50] The Convention includes two migration-related protocols, one dealing with smuggling and one with trafficking.

The *Protocol against the Smuggling of Migrants by Land, Sea and Air, Supplementing the United Nations Convention against Transnational Organized Crime* (2000) ('Smuggling Protocol') criminalises smuggling of migrants, but not the smuggled migrants themselves, and encourages States parties to speedily return

---

49 Human Rights Council, 'Report of the Special Rapporteur on the Sale of Children, Child Prostitution and Child Pornography, Najat M'jid Maalla' (UN Doc A/HRC/12/23, 13 July 2009).

50 *United Nations Convention against Transnational Organized Crime*, opened for signature 15 November 2000, 2225 UNTS 209 (entered into force 29 September 2003).

the migrants to their countries of origin.[51] To classify as smuggling, the transport must involve border crossing, unlike trafficking, which also covers purely domestic cases. No specific attention is paid to smuggled children, though their numbers are substantial and their circumstances warrant special care. In particular, speedy return home is generally an inappropriate strategy from a children's rights perspective. This is evident if one considers the main circumstances in which child smuggling occurs. One is family reunification, where parents are not legally entitled to bring their children to join them, or where waiting periods are unacceptably long and, in desperation, families decide to pay an acquaintance or a smuggler to bring the children over. Another situation is where children are fleeing persecution and, like adult refugees, are compelled to resort to the services of smugglers to escape from danger and cross international borders. In both circumstances, the 'best interests of the child' are unlikely to be served by simply returning the child home. Careful inquiries are required into the home circumstances and the likelihood that harm, rather than family care, will ensue from immigration removal. Many States violate these obligations by detaining smuggled children and then returning them home without diligent inquiry.

The second migration-related Protocol concluded in Palermo – the *Protocol to Prevent, Suppress and Punish Trafficking in Persons, Especially Women and Children, Supplementing the United Nations Convention against Transnational Organized Crime* (2000) ('Trafficking Protocol') – addresses trafficking in persons, especially women and children.[52] A significant contribution of the Trafficking Protocol is the establishment of a consensus definition of trafficking, resolving many of the outstanding definitional disputes. For example, trafficking is not restricted to sexual exploitation; nor does it only cover situations where brute force is used to entrap or recruit a victim – deceit, abuse of authority and, in the case of children, even induced consent may also be the mechanisms that lead to establishment of the trafficking relationship.

Unlike the Smuggling Protocol, the Trafficking Protocol explicitly addresses the human rights of the implicated migrants. Several of the protective measures are particularly relevant to trafficked children, including the availability of legal assistance, psychological counselling and housing-welfare assistance. The Trafficking Protocol even includes an option for States parties to allow trafficking victims to stay in the host State permanently. This option has not been widely taken up, but it has relevance for traumatised children because returning home often leads to re-trafficking.

51 *Protocol against the Smuggling of Migrants by Land, Sea and Air, Supplementing the United Nations Convention against Transnational Organized Crime*, opened for signature 15 November 2000, 2241 UNTS 507 (entered into force 28 January 2004).
52 *Protocol to Prevent, Suppress and Punish Trafficking in Persons, Especially Women and Children, Supplementing the United Nations Convention against Transnational Organized Crime*, opened for signature 15 November 2000, 2237 UNTS 319 (entered into force 25 December 2003).

Overall, the Smuggling and Trafficking Protocols represent a step forward for some of the most vulnerable migrant children today, because they clarify that migrants caught up in these situations should not be targeted with criminal or punitive measures. Regrettably, many States fail to abide by these obligations; smuggled and trafficked children are regularly detained, and many face renewed human rights risks and violations because they are returned home. Moreover, from a children's rights perspective, international migration law is at best a partial solution to the fundamental problem in the vast majority of trafficking cases. The lack of opportunities for a stable, rights-respecting life at home – which only consistent long-term development can address – leads impoverished communities to pursue risky and precarious migration and employment strategies that invariably end in gross human rights violations.

8.3.   WOMEN MIGRANTS

Unlike child migrants, women migrants cannot be grouped together as a category that is quintessentially different from the paradigmatic male migrant. Part of the process of challenging the traditional gendered marginalisation of women in migration law has been to interrogate simplistic stereotypes underlying that marginalisation. A familiar example is litigation targeting the discriminatory rules that applied to migrant workers.[53] Because of the uncorroborated assumption that migrant workers were men, domestic immigration law in the United Kingdom allowed migrants with work permits to bring their wives and children to accompany them; when husbands applied as spouses, they were rejected. Immigration officials refused to exercise their discretion in favour of such husbands, suspecting that any husband who followed his wife because of her work was doing so in order to gain an immigration and employment advantage for himself, rather than because of the same desire for enjoyment of family life that presumably motivates migration of the wife of a male migrant worker. Similar challenges have been mounted to assumptions preventing women who are nationals or permanent residents from bringing their foreign husbands to live with them in their own State in circumstances where their male counterparts had no difficulty. Advocates have also targeted obstacles for women heads of households with special entry visas to bring their dependent relatives with them, where male heads of household had no corresponding difficulties.

Over the years, feminist activism and advocacy has succeeded in overturning some of the discriminatory rules driving these exclusions, and produced a measure of formal equality from a gendered perspective in migration law. It has become increasingly clear that the classic pictures of 'third world' migrant women as

---

53 Bhabha and Shutter, above n. 2.

submissive, dependent, vulnerable and economically inactive were produced by decision makers using stereotypes to cut corners and drive policy without careful thought, inquiry or reflection. Confronted by the reality that some migrant women were principal breadwinners or otherwise heads of household, migration law gradually cast off its blinkers as other areas of law, such as employment law and family law, had done before.[54] The final achievement in this long process of emancipation of women migrant workers was the historic adoption on 16 June 2011 of the *Convention concerning Decent Work for Domestic Workers* (2011).[55] This instrument gives household domestic workers, many of whom are migrant workers, fundamental labour rights previously not guaranteed to them because of the informal nature of their employment, an archetypal example of the intersection between several vulnerable statuses. Secure labour rights go hand in hand with secure migration rights to ensure safety and protection from exploitation for these particularly vulnerable workers.

The fact that explicit and lawful discrimination in migration law has been tempered by decades of advocacy and litigation should not be taken to mean that migrant women no longer suffer legal, social or economic disadvantages vis-à-vis their male counterparts. Migrant women still confront the double exclusions of gender and nationality, and the cumulative or multiplier effect that this combination of exclusions produces. On the labour front, they are concentrated in low-pay and low-security jobs, often in the service industry or in informal sector jobs, such as cleaning, home-based piecework or catering (see Case Study 8.2). Access to full-time and permanent employment is increasingly elusive for many demographic groups, but migrant women, for reasons of family responsibility, language and cultural factors, are often at a particular disadvantage.[56] In the domestic sphere, migrant women may be particularly vulnerable to violence and other forms of abuse because of their dependence on familial networks for immigration status, security or financial support. This is especially so if they are relatively new arrivals, because of their unfamiliarity with support structures in the host environment. The assumption that immigrant family networks can be relied upon to provide support and assistance to female migrants is as flawed as the assumption that indigenous nuclear families can be relied on to fulfil that role.[57]

---

54 Thus the *International Convention on the Protection of the Rights of All Migrant Workers and Members of their Families* (1990), discussed below, covers all migrant workers irrespective of gender.

55 *Convention concerning Decent Work for Domestic Workers* (ILO Convention No 189), opened for signature 16 June 2011 (not yet in force).

56 Those in full-time employment in the United States earn 14 per cent less than their native-born counterparts: Jeanne Batalova, 'US in Focus: Immigrant Women' (Migration Policy Institute, December 2009).

57 Margot Mendelson, 'Constructing America: Mythmaking in US Immigration Courts' (2010) 119(5) *Yale Law Journal* 1012.

CASE STUDY 8.2   Domestic worker executed in Saudi Arabia

One week after the ILO's *Convention concerning Decent Work for Domestic Workers* (2011) was signed in Geneva, an Indonesian woman working as a maid in Saudi Arabia was executed for the murder of her employer. Fifty-four-year-old Ruyati binti Sapubi was beheaded with a sword on 18 June 2011, after confessing to killing her employer, whom she accused of abuse and of refusing to allow her to return home. The Saudi authorities proceeded with the execution without informing the Indonesian Government or allowing it to intercede on Sapubi's behalf, in violation of the *Vienna Convention on Consular Relations* (1963), which requires States to inform the consular post of a foreign State of any foreign national who is arrested or committed to prison for an offence.[58]

This incident follows a long line of similar cases: vulnerable migrant workers subjected to exploitation and abuse by their employers eventually snap and retaliate with violence. Sapubi's execution marked the second execution of an Indonesian maid within three years. There are also future challenges. In Saudi Arabia, there are approximately 7 million migrant workers, the majority working in the domestic sphere. At the time of Sapubi's execution, a hundred others were reportedly awaiting execution, including

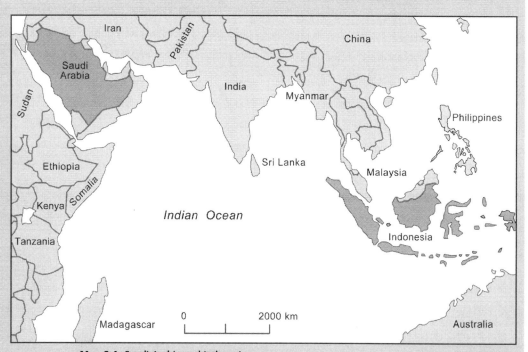

Map 8.1 Saudi Arabia and Indonesia

58 *Vienna Convention on Consular Relations*, opened for signature 24 April 1963, 596 UNTS 261 (entered into force 19 March 1967) art. 36.

twenty-four from Indonesia and twelve from the Philippines. Among them is another Indonesian maid who claims she killed her employer in self-defence as he tried to rape her. Due to the publicity stemming from Sapubi's case, the Indonesian Government is considering paying to secure the maids release.

Many migrant women from South and Southeast Asia travel to the Gulf States to secure work that supports their family back home. Only two days before Sapubis execution, news reports carried the story of a Sri Lankan maid who was rescued after being kept against her will without pay by her Saudi Arabian employers for nearly fourteen years. The forty-five-year-old woman was reportedly found following a tip-off from her neighbour, which led to the arrest of the employer. Family members in Sri Lanka, including her husband, said that they had not heard from the woman for so long that they presumed her dead.

8.3.1. Refugee women

Brief mention has already been made of refugee women – of their under-representation among those seeking asylum because of gendered obstacles to accessing a refugee determination system, but at the same time their relative success in being awarded refugee status once they do manage to claim it, despite the absence of gender as a ground for protection in the Refugee Convention. This point should not be misinterpreted. Thanks to assiduous work on gender-based persecution by advocates and refugee women themselves, progress has been made in expanding the conception of persecution beyond the traditional masculinist boundaries. Rape, domestic violence, child sex abuse, and persecution because of supportive roles in insurgency movements (e.g., cooking or washing rather than fighting) or because of opposition to rigid cultural and religious norms, have all been accepted as bases for the grant of asylum.[59] This represents a welcome transformation of the legal landscape compared to the situation twenty-five years ago.

Yet gender-based asylum claims still present considerable challenges, as demonstrated by the drawn-out and tortuous battle in the United States over a victim of severe domestic violence, Rodi Alvarado.[60] The recipient of excruciatingly brutal abuse from her husband over a long period, Ms Alvarado nevertheless had her asylum case rejected by several decision-making bodies because she failed to demonstrate a qualifying reason for the violence she had endured (being brutalised as a wife was not considered to bring her within the Refugee Convention's grounds). Public pressure and sustained advocacy eventually secured a positive

59 University of California, Center for Gender and Refugee Studies (http://cgrs.uchastings.edu).
60 Shannon McCaffrey, 'Battered Woman's Asylum Plea Could Set Trend', *Miami Herald* 20 February 2004, 8A.

outcome for this case. A similar point about the challenges encountered in securing protection can be made about women who are victims of trafficking. Legislative steps have been taken in many jurisdictions to translate the provisions of the Trafficking Protocol into domestic protections, but in practice the numbers of trafficked women receiving secure immigration status or benefitting from other listed measures, such as housing, welfare support and counselling, remain extremely limited when compared to the huge estimated numbers of trafficking victims. In short, despite the dramatic reduction of explicit discriminatory measures in international migration law, practice remains inconsistent and problematic. The chapter now turns to the relevant legal measures.

Women, including migrant women, benefit from the general rights set out in the International Bill of Rights, described earlier in this chapter. Because of the double exclusion to which they are exposed by virtue of gender and nationality, non-discrimination norms are particularly important. Both the ICCPR (art. 24) and the ICESCR (art. 2) contain powerful anti-discrimination provisions. They impinge on situations of direct discrimination, such as the different rules for admission of spouses of male and female workers, or other gendered family reunification norms. They also affect less immediately apparent, indirect forms of discrimination. An example, already alluded to, arose where women activists supporting liberation movements found themselves excluded from refugee protection because their forms of support were not considered sufficiently 'political', according to a male standard. Non-discrimination measures are important as a means of eliminating arbitrary distinctions between men and women, and between migrant and non-migrant women. The underlying assumption is that of equality, replacing an earlier difference-based model of protection in which specific gender-based provisions were designed to shield all women, irrespective of capability or personal preference, from work considered dangerous or unsuitable (in mines or war). The ICCPR and ICESCR also provide important protections for migrant women in respect to many human rights that are frequently elusive in practice. They include, from the ICCPR, freedom from torture (art. 7) and the right not to be held in slavery (art. 8), which is particularly relevant to migrant domestic workers; and from the ICESCR, the right to work that is freely chosen (art. 6) and in just and favourable conditions (art. 7); and the right to family life and protection of the family (art. 10).

8.3.2. Discrimination against women

The international instrument that consolidates all the non-discrimination provisions relevant to women, including migrant women, is the *Convention on the Elimination of All Forms of Discrimination against Women* (1979) ('CEDAW'),[61] a comprehensive

---

61 *Convention on the Elimination of All Forms of Discrimination against Women*, opened for signature 18 December 1979, 1249 UNTS 13 (entered into force 3 September 1981).

treaty whose equality principle is closely modelled on the *International Convention on the Elimination of All Forms of Racial Discrimination* (1965).[62] The definition of discrimination in art. 2 of CEDAW is broad:

[A]ny distinction, exclusion or restriction made on the basis of sex which has the effect or purpose of impairing or nullifying the recognition, enjoyment or exercise by women, irrespective of their marital status, on a basis of equality of men and women, of human rights and fundamental freedoms in the political, economic, social, cultural, civil or any other field.

This non-discrimination approach has yielded important benefits for migrant women, from gender-neutral family reunification regulations to expanded refugee protection measures. Some CEDAW articles have particular relevance for women in the context of migration, including those that deal with 'all forms of traffic in women and exploitation of prostitution' (art. 6); 'the right to acquire, change or retain their nationality' (art. 9); non-discrimination in employment (art. 11); access to social and financial benefits (art. 13); and the freedom to choose their residence and domicile (as opposed to being compelled to follow the choice of their spouse or parents).

However, CEDAW also has limitations because equality only goes so far in the case of gender. Key differences between men and women, particularly in relation to fertility and physical strength, have to be taken into account if women's human rights are to be fully protected. These differences may be particularly significant for migrant women separated from family, community and other basic support systems that are available in times of crisis or special need. CEDAW does directly address the issue of pregnancy and maternity – prohibiting pregnancy-related dismissal from employment and mandating provision of maternity pay and related benefits (art. 11). Of course, migrant women only benefit from these protections if they are in a position to challenge violations; irregular immigration status or short-term contract work in informal employment situations militate against this.

CEDAW also explicitly obligates States to 'take all appropriate measures, including legislation, to suppress all forms of traffic in women' (art. 6), thus prefiguring the adoption of the Trafficking Protocol. Beyond this specific instance of gender-based oppression, CEDAW does not directly address the question of violence against women, or acknowledge its central role in undermining women's equal standing in the family, the community and society as a whole. It took the widespread evidence of pervasive rape, forced impregnation and sexual violence as forms of ethnic cleansing during the Balkan Wars of the 1990s to propel sexual violence to the centre of the human rights stage and transform the approach to it. The 1993 World Conference on Human Rights in Vienna highlighted the question of sexual violence as one of two central agenda issues. It agreed to create the office of Special Rapporteur on Violence

62 *International Convention on the Elimination of All Forms of Racial Discrimination*, opened for signature 21 December 1965, 660 UNTS 195 (entered into force 4 January 1969).

against Women to strengthen international attention to the issue. Several benefits for migrant women have flowed from this innovation. A substantial body of high-quality research has been conducted and disseminated, putting pressure on stake-holders to focus their attention on the issue more closely.[63] A second positive outcome from the office of the Special Rapporteur is its active voice in women's human rights developments on the international stage. An example relevant to migrant women is the role played by the Special Rapporteur in the human rights lobby that pressured the drafters of the Trafficking Protocol to develop an expansive definition of trafficking, covering women who were tricked or pressured into 'agree-ing' to exploitative trafficking arrangements.

8.3.3. Women as migrant workers

Where CEDAW and the activities of the Special Rapporteur address the particular challenges facing migrant women as women, another international human rights treaty applies to the other element of their vulnerability, their status as non-nationals. This is the *International Convention on the Protection of the Rights of All Migrant Workers and Members of their Families* (1990) ('ICRMW').[64] Just as the CRC codifies the human rights relevant to children and CEDAW does the same for women, so the ICRMW codifies and specifies the rights relevant to migrant workers and their families. This instrument took thirteen years to come into force and, though it is considered a core human rights treaty, it is still not widely ratified, largely because migration destination States wrongly think ratification would limit their ability to regulate migration.[65] Critically, none of the major migrant-receiving States is party to the ICRMW. This means that its measures are not binding where they would count most – a serious constraint that must be taken into consideration in any discussion.

One of the most important aspects of the ICRMW from the perspective of migrant women is that it explicitly affords basic human rights to all, irrespective of legal status. This inclusive approach stems in part from the ICRMW's very broad and simple definition of a migrant worker in art. 1: 'The term "migrant worker" refers to a person who is to be engaged, is engaged or has been engaged in a remunerated activity in a State of which he or she is not a national.' Undocumented migrant women workers, and spouses or partners of workers, therefore have the same rights to protection from sexual abuse and domestic violence as all other women – their irregular migration status is irrelevant.

Another important provision is the ban on collective expulsions – according to the ICRMW, each decision to remove a migrant must be taken individually after all

---

63 International Organization for Migration, 'Working to Prevent and Address Violence against Migrant Workers' (IOM, 2009).
64 *International Convention on the Protection of the Rights of All Migrant Workers and Members of their Families*, opened for signature 18 December 1990, 2220 UNTS 3 (entered into force 1 July 2003).
65 Euan Macdonald and Ryszard Cholewinski, 'The Migrant Workers Convention in Europe: Obstacles to the Ratification of the International Convention on the Protection of the Rights of All Migrant Workers and Members of their Families' (UNESCO, 2007).

the relevant details have been reviewed (art. 22), which is consistent with earlier legal developments on collective expulsion (see Chapter 5). This means that where a group of undocumented migrant women workers are discovered together as a result of a raid on a factory, the whole group cannot legally be removed *en bloc*. States regularly violate this provision, as highly publicised clandestine raids conducted during the final years of the second Bush Administration illustrated.[66] Migrant workers, including women, have the right, along with all foreign nationals, to have their consular officials notified if they or any member of their family are arrested or detained (art. 16(7)).[67] In such circumstances, the state officials are also required to 'pay attention to the problems that may be posed for members of . . . her family, in particular for spouses and minor children' (art. 17(6)). These important measures for migrant women workers are often ignored: where an undocumented woman is arrested from her workplace, this has an immediate and potentially devastating impact on family arrangements for which she is responsible. An example of the problem is that during workplace raids on factories carried out in the past few years in the United States, many single-parent irregular Hispanic women found themselves swept up and placed in detention, sometimes in remote areas far from their residences. United States authorities failed to contact consular officials and, as a result, numerous incidents arose where children had to be taken home by the school bus driver or a neighbour, and where breastfed babies ended up dehydrated in the hospital.

Most important for migrant women workers are the strong family protection provisions included in the ICRMW. Whatever the migrant woman worker's migration status, any child born to her is entitled to birth registration and to a nationality (art. 29). This is an important measure to avoid transmission of statelessness or irregular migration status from one generation to the next. It also facilitates access to schools, including public preschool, which is often obstructed in practice by a school's insistence on identity documents as a prerequisite to enrolment. Not surprisingly, the family unity provisions in the ICRMW apply only to migrant women workers who have a legal status, but in this case they are wide-ranging. States are required to take measures 'they deem appropriate' to promote family reunification, including for relatives beyond the immediate nuclear family of spouse and minor dependent unmarried children where humanitarian considerations apply (art. 44). Given familial ties and needs, the ability to bring in one's parents to help with childcare and simplify filial responsibilities is valuable. Unfortunately, many migrant women workers struggle to enforce their rights to family unity because onerous contractual and immigration restrictions create practical barriers, which often prove insurmountable.

66 Randolph Capps, Rosa Maria Castañeda, Ajay Chaudry and Robert Santos, 'Paying the Price: The Impact of Immigration Raids on America's Children' (Urban Institute, National Council of La Raza, 2007).
67 This provision consolidates a similar one in the *Vienna Convention on Consular Relations*, opened for signature 24 April 1963, 596 UNTS 261 (entered into force 19 March 1967) arts. 36, 53.

8.4. MIGRANTS WITH DISABILITIES

Persons with disabilities have not received as much attention from the human rights community as women and children, but a recent movement has provided them with a comprehensive and codified set of rights. The paradigm document of this effort is the *Convention on the Rights of Persons with Disabilities* (2007) ('CRPD').[68] The CRPD's purpose is 'to promote, protect and ensure the full and equal enjoyment of all human rights and fundamental freedoms by all persons with disabilities, and to promote respect for their inherent dignity' (art. 1). Its principles are respect for dignity, non-discrimination, full inclusion, equality of opportunity, accessibility and equality (art. 3). The CRPD reinforces many of the rights guaranteed in the ICCPR, ICESCR and ICRMW – to individual liberty, to free movement, to public participation, to education, to health, to social security – and mandates non-discriminatory application of all these entitlements. The CRPD as a whole promises to raise the profile of discrimination against all persons with disabilities, including disabled migrant workers, disabled refugees, and disabled women and children who seek protection in a non-discriminatory environment. The intersection between multiple marginal statuses – migrant, disabled person, child, member of a discriminated-against ethnic minority – raises acute protection challenges that fall within the scope of the CRPD. It explicitly addresses the particular challenges facing women and girls with disabilities (art. 6) and children with disabilities (art. 7).

Some CRPD provisions have the potential to be of special relevance to migrants with disabilities, including the right to personal mobility, the right to live independently and to have access to 'information and communications' in appropriate languages and media (arts. 2, 9), and the right to habilitation (the ability to attain and maintain maximum independence) and rehabilitation (art. 26). These protections are relevant to migrants with physical or mental disabilities who are often at a double disadvantage in securing state protection and support. They have implications not only for the migrants themselves, but also for members of their families caring for them or dependent on them. Parents of physically disabled children seeking refugee protection because of persecution in the home State have experienced great difficulties securing permission to stay with their children; dependants of migrant workers with disabilities have been impacted by discriminatory employment and social security policies and practices.[69] The CRPD also protects disabled persons' rights to a legal identity and disabled children's right to registration, a name and a nationality immediately after birth (art. 18). These protections can play a critical role in reducing child statelessness or irregular migration status, which

---

68 *Convention on the Rights of Persons with Disabilities*, opened for signature 30 March 2007, UN Doc A/61/611 (entered into force 3 May 2008).

69 The CRPD (art. 23) notes the importance of providing 'early and comprehensive information, services and support to children with disabilities and their families'.

can have deleterious effects on disabled children who are dependent on state support and services.

None of the CRPD's articles explicitly addresses migrants, but several of its guaranteed rights benefit them. Article 16, concerning freedom from exploitation, violence and abuse, is particularly relevant to victims of trafficking. It reinforces States parties' obligations to punish perpetrators of trafficking: 'States Parties shall put in place effective legislation and policies, including women- and child-focussed legislation and policies, to ensure that instances of exploitation, violence and abuse against persons with disabilities are identified, investigated and, where appropriate, prosecuted.' And it obliges States parties to rehabilitate disabled victims of trafficking: 'States Parties shall take all appropriate measures to promote the physical, cognitive and psychological recovery, rehabilitation and social rein-tegration of persons with disabilities who become victims of any form of exploi-tation, violence or abuse, including through the provision of protection services.'

Several recent cases, including an egregious incident where a group of deaf mutes were trafficked for purposes of labour exploitation,[70] highlight the impor-tance of these measures and the inadequate implementation efforts to date. Article 21(b) also facilitates disabled refugees' search for asylum by compelling the accept-ance of 'sign languages, braille, augmentative and alternative communication, and all other accessible means, modes and formats of communication of their choice by persons with disabilities in official interactions'. Oversight of the CRPD is provided by a Committee (art. 34), State reports (art. 35), guidance through general com-ments (art. 39), and individual communications, monitoring and other procedural guarantees under the Optional Protocol.[71]

8.5. CONCLUSION

International migration law provides a robust framework of rights for traditionally marginalised migrant groups, including children, women and persons with dis-abilities. Through the International Bill of Rights, and specifically tailored consol-idating treaties, core human rights protections as well as targeted measures relevant to particular constituencies have been established. The critical problem facing the relevant communities of migrants is not, therefore, a normative vacuum or a doctrinal impasse. It is a failure of political will to provide the tools necessary for implementation on the ground of the sound policy measures in force primarily on the books. Such tools would include much more generous access to skilled legal representation for migrant children, women and persons with disabilities; and

---

70 See Sontag, above n. 6.
71 *Optional Protocol to the Convention on the Rights of Persons with Disabilities*, opened for signature 30 March 2007, 46 ILM 433 (entered into force 3 May 2008).

much more explicit training on legal entitlements for immigration control officers, asylum adjudicators, border patrol personnel, detention facility staff, judges and school administrators. Given enduring discrimination, entrenched social and economic marginalisation of poor migrant communities and sizeable xenophobic constituencies among electors, change from above through politicians and policy makers is much less likely than change from below through the direct agency of those affected. Migrant children, women and persons with disabilities need to be able, almost literally, to take the laws into their own hands, so they can enforce the reasonable protections international law has long promised them.

KEY REFERENCES

Ayotte, Wendy, *Separated Children Coming to Western Europe: Why They Travel and How They Arrive* (Save the Children, 2000)

Benhabib, Seyla and Resnik, Judith (eds.), *Migrations and Mobilities: Citizenship, Borders, and Gender* (New York University Press, 2009)

Bhabha, Jacqueline, 'Independent Children, Inconsistent Adults: International Child Migration and the Legal Framework', *Innocenti Discussion Papers* No 2008-02 (UNICEF, 2008)

Bhabha, Jacqueline (ed.), *Children without a State: A Global Human Rights Challenge* (Massachusetts Institute of Technology, 2011)

Bhabha, Jacqueline and Crock, Mary, *Seeking Asylum Alone: Unaccompanied and Separated Children and Refugee Protection in Australia, the UK and the US* (Themis Press, 2007)

Bhabha, Jacqueline and Schmidt, Susan, 'From Kafka to Wilberforce: Is the US Government's Approach to Child Migrants Improving?' (2011) February *Immigration Briefings* 1

Crock, Mary, 'Re-thinking the Paradigms of Protection: Children as Convention Refugees in Australia' in Jane McAdam (ed.), *Forced Migration, Human Rights and Security* (Hart, 2008) 155

Crock, Mary, Kenny, Mary Anne and Allison, Fiona, 'Children and Immigration and Citizenship Law' in Geoff Monahan and Lisa Young (eds.), *Children and the Law in Australia* (LexisNexis Butterworths, 2008) 238

European Union Agency for Fundamental Rights, *Separated, Asylum-seeking Children in European Union Member States* (FRA, 2010)

Human Rights Watch, *A Costly Move: Far and Frequent Transfers Impede Hearings for Immigrant Detainees in the United States* (Human Rights Watch, 2011)

International Organization for Migration, *World Migration Report 2010. The Future of Migration: Building Capacities for Change* (IOM, 2010)

Kartashkin, Vladimir, *The Rights of Women Married to Foreigners* (UN Doc E/CN.4/Sub.2/2003/34, Commission on Human Rights, 2003)

Lynch, Maureen, *Futures Denied: Statelessness among Infants, Children and Youth* (Refugees International, 2008)

Platform for International Cooperation on Undocumented Migrants, *PICUM's Main Concerns about the Fundamental Rights of Undocumented Migrants in Europe* (PICUM, 2010)

Ressler, Everett, Boothby, Neil and Steinbock, Daniel, *Unaccompanied Children: Care and Protection in Wars, Natural Disasters, and Refugee Movements* (Oxford University Press, 1988)

United Nations, Committee on the Rights of the Child, *General Comment No 6: Treatment of Unaccompanied and Separated Children outside their Country of Origin*, 39th sess, UN Doc CRC/GC/2005/6 (1 September 2005)

Women's Refugee Commission, *Disabilities among Refugees and Conflict-Affected Populations* (Women's Refugee Commission, 2008)

KEY RESOURCES

Amnesty International, 'Refugees and Migrants':
www.amnesty.org/en/refugees-and-migrants

Center for Gender and Refugee Studies, University of
California: http://cgrs.uchastings.edu

Center for Immigration Studies: www.cis.org

December 18: www.december18.net

Forced Migration Online, Refugee Studies Centre,
University of Oxford: www.forcedmigration.org

International Organization for Migration: www.iom.int

Migration Policy Institute: www.migrationpolicy.org

Platform for International Cooperation on Undocumented
Migrants: http://picum.org

Save the Children: www.savethechildren.org

The People's Movement for Human Rights Education, 'The
Human Rights of Differently-Abled Persons':
www.pdhre.org/rights/disabled.html

UN High Commissioner for Human Rights, Committee on
the Elimination of Discrimination against Women:
www2.ohchr.org/english/bodies/cedaw

UN High Commissioner for Human Rights, Committee on
Migrant Workers: www2.ohchr.org/english/bodies/cmw

UN High Commissioner for Human Rights, Committee on
the Rights of Persons with Disabilities:
www.ohchr.org/EN/HRBodies/CRPD

UN High Commissioner for Refugees:
www.unhcr.org

UNICEF, Innocenti Research Centre: www.unicef-irc.org

Human trafficking and smuggling

RYSZARD PIOTROWICZ AND JILLYANNE REDPATH-CROSS

9.1. INTRODUCTION

Trafficking and smuggling of human beings have increased significantly since the early 1990s, forcing the international community to develop new models to regulate them. Trafficking of human beings has attracted worldwide attention and provoked a considerable response. Smuggling of human beings also poses significant challenges, both to those smuggled and to the States affected.

Trafficking and smuggling may possess common features, which sometimes leads to confusion between them. Whereas smuggling involves the consent of the individual to participation in the process in the belief that he or she will be assisted to enter another State irregularly, trafficking denies the free will and choice of the individual because he or she is forced to move within a State, or between States, for the purpose of exploiting their labour. There is no real consent from the trafficked person. The individual may believe that he or she is being smuggled, when in reality he or she is being trafficked.

This chapter discusses the legal regimes for trafficking and smuggling and addresses salient legal issues, including the protection needs of victims and the tension arising from the fact that trafficking and smuggling are treated primarily as matters of criminal law, yet there is a clear human rights dimension in relation to the treatment of victims.

9.2. TRAFFICKING OF HUMAN BEINGS

Trafficking is commonly, and notoriously, known as a criminal practice that takes place in the context of the sex trade: women and children are taken from one State to another, or within a State, for the purpose of sexual exploitation. A general pattern of trafficking from poorer to wealthier countries is evident.

However, it is misleading to see trafficking as taking place only for the purpose of sexual exploitation. People are trafficked so that their labour can be exploited in sweatshops, for domestic labour, forced marriage, agricultural labour, sport and begging, or for harvesting their organs, body tissue and cells. The victims are often subjected to physical, psychological and sexual abuse (see Case Study 9.1).

Trafficking is a process that usually involves several actors. The victim must first be recruited or brought under the control of the traffickers. This can be by deception (e.g., by recruitment or travel agencies that claim to facilitate jobs and visas), by word of mouth or by force. Transnational trafficking may involve illegal crossing of frontiers: this partly explains why trafficking and smuggling have much in common, and may be confused or difficult to distinguish. The crucial difference is that a smuggled person consents to be smuggled; a trafficked person cannot give real consent to the practice.

Once a victim is under the control of the traffickers, he or she may be transported to the destination State, often through transit countries. This requires the organ-isation of passports and visas, including the falsification of documents, or else being smuggled across borders. Somebody must supply transport and accommo-dation during the journey. The victims may be 'sold' on the way. Eventually, they will reach the destination State, where their passports or identity papers will likely be confiscated, and they are then forced to work for the person who controls them. Each of these actors is criminally responsible for their participation. This is impor-tant in understanding the legal response to trafficking.

Traffickers exploit their victims by gaining control over them, physically or mentally, with the objective of exploiting their labour for profit. Victims are not necessarily physically restrained. They are often subjected to several criminal practices, including forced labour; physical, psychological and sexual abuse; deprivation of liberty; very poor living conditions; and blackmail.

9.2.1. Trafficking under international law

Trafficking is complex: it is a criminal practice, but also involves human rights law. Issues may also arise relating to possible breaches of immigration law and employment law in transit and destination States, as well as laws on prostitution. From the perspective of international law, the core issues are criminal law and human rights.

There has been much debate about whether trafficking is primarily a criminal act or a breach of the human rights of the victims. There may be significant conse-quences for victims of trafficking if States see the practice primarily as a matter of criminal law because they may fail fully to appreciate the ramifications for victims, whether in source, transit or destination States.

CASE STUDY 9.1   Trafficking of domestic workers to the United Kingdom[1]

Ms Mwanamisi Mruke was hired by Ms Saeeda Khan in Tanzania to work at her home in London. Khan organised a domestic service visa for Ms Mruke and agreed to pay 120,000 shillings (£21) monthly into her Tanzanian bank account and £10 monthly pocket money in London.

Ms Mruke suffered severe abuse at the hands of her employer, who confiscated her passport, forced her to sleep on the kitchen floor and gave her meagre amounts of food. She was required to be available to work from 6 a.m. to midnight daily. Her employer would summon Ms Mruke by ringing a bell whenever she was required to assist her or her two adult children. She was sometimes obliged to work at night. She worked for four years without a day off. Ms Mruke was detained in Ms Khan's house and threatened by her, to the extent that she was cowed into submission.

Ms Mruke spoke only Swahili with her employer, who deliberately failed to teach her English, further increasing her isolation. Eventually her employer ceased paying her altogether. She refused to let Ms Mruke return to Tanzania after her parents died, nor was she allowed to travel there for the wedding of her daughter.

At Ms Khan's trial for the crime of trafficking, the prosecutor said: 'From the moment of her arrival in England Mwanamisi was made to sleep, work and live in conditions that fall by any understanding into that of slavery.'

Ms Mruke was released after an interpreter – who went with her to see a doctor – contacted a charity, Kalayaan, which assists people trafficked into domestic servitude. Kalayaan informed the police, who eventually went to Khan's home and removed Ms Mruke to a place of refuge.

Ms Khan was charged with trafficking a person for exploitation. Police found a letter in Swahili, addressed to Ms Mruke and intended to intimidate her. It warned her not to complain about her conditions in London and told her that she had to obey Khan all the time. It said her life could be in danger if she complained, but that she would receive her reward in heaven.

Khan was convicted of trafficking for domestic servitude, given a nine-month prison sentence, suspended for two years, and ordered to pay £25,000 in compensation to Ms Mruke plus £15,000 in costs.

A police spokesman said it was the first time someone had been prosecuted for trafficking a 'slave' for domestic servitude. He said the Metropolitan Police were currently investigating another fifteen cases of trafficking for forced labour, and had worked with other police forces on similar cases. The cases under investigation involved individuals from Saudi Arabia, India, Bangladesh, Tanzania, Uganda and Vietnam.

Concerning Ms Mruke, the spokesman added: 'She may want to go back to Tanzania, because she has a family there. But if she can't go back for fear of reprisals I'm sure that would be looked upon positively by the UK Border Agency.'

1 This case study is based on Chris Summers, A Case of Modern Day Slavery in the Suburbs, BBC News (online) 17 March 2011 (www.bbc.co.uk/news/uk-12687088).

Trafficking is first and foremost a criminal act, like murder, rape and theft. However, it is erroneous to treat it *only* as a criminal act, measurable by the standards of national law. To do so is to risk taking no account of the impact that trafficking has on its victims, as well as the fact that States may have human rights obligations towards victims. The essence of the argument that trafficking is a criminal act is that – in the absence of direct State involvement – it is primarily a private criminal enterprise. There is no doubt that States have sometimes been complicit in trafficking (such as corruption of border officials to facilitate crossing of national frontiers), but in the absence of complicity the State plays no role in trafficking and cannot, on the face of it, be blamed when someone is trafficked. Human rights obligations, on the other hand, are owed by States to all persons (nationals and non-nationals) within their jurisdiction: they require the State to do, or refrain from doing, certain things in its interactions with human beings. Failure to comply gives rise to state responsibility. As noted by the United Nations Human Rights Committee:

> the positive obligations on States Parties to ensure Covenant rights will only be fully discharged if individuals are protected by the State, not just against violations of Covenant rights by its agents, but also against acts committed by private persons or entities that would impair the enjoyment of Covenant rights in so far as they are amenable to application between private persons or entities.[2]

Further, the Committee stressed that the State had a duty 'to take appropriate measures or to exercise due diligence to prevent, punish, investigate or redress the harm caused by such acts by private persons or entities'.[3] Thus, trafficking may give rise to state responsibility for human rights violations, not because the State is directly involved, but because of its failure to prevent trafficking or to protect victims and potential victims. Trafficking is therefore a private criminal enterprise, but with a human rights dimension. The scope and content of that dimension are considered below.

9.2.2.   The Trafficking Protocol

There is a significant body of international law on trafficking. The most important instrument is the *Protocol to Prevent, Suppress and Punish Trafficking in Persons, Especially Women and Children, Supplementing the United Nations Convention against Transnational Organized Crime* (2000) ('Trafficking Protocol'), which entered into force in December 2003.[4] The Trafficking Protocol was negotiated as

---

2 Human Rights Committee, *General Comment No 31: The Nature of the General Legal Obligation Imposed on States Parties to the Covenant*, 80th sess, UN Doc CCPR/C/21/Rev.1/Add.13 (26 May 2004) [8].

3 Ibid.

4 *Protocol to Prevent, Suppress and Punish Trafficking in Persons, Especially Women and Children, Supplementing the United Nations Convention against Transnational Organized Crime*, opened for signature 15 November 2000, 2237 UNTS 319 (entered into force 25 December 2003).

one of three Protocols supplementing the parent Convention, namely, the *United Nations Convention against Transnational Organized Crime* (2000) ('UNCTOC') – the other two deal with people smuggling (discussed later in this chapter) and trafficking in firearms.[5]

The Trafficking Protocol is primarily an instrument of criminal law. While it does contain measures for the protection and rights of victims, some are limited, causing it to be criticised for failing sufficiently to address the interests and needs of victims. However, it should not be forgotten that the Trafficking Protocol was never intended to be primarily a victim-protection measure. Nor does it exist in a vacuum: it does not replace the existing human rights regime, which continues to offer important safeguards for those who have been trafficked or are at risk of it.

Article 3(a) of the Trafficking Protocol defines trafficking thus:

'Trafficking in persons' shall mean the recruitment, transportation, transfer, harbouring or receipt of persons, by means of the threat or use of force or other forms of coercion, of abduction, of fraud, of deception, of the abuse of power or of a position of vulnerability or of the giving or receiving of payments or benefits to achieve the consent of a person having control over another person, for the purpose of exploitation. Exploitation shall include, at a minimum, the exploitation of the prostitution of others or other forms of sexual exploitation, forced labour or services, slavery or practices similar to slavery, servitude or the removal of organs.

There are, therefore, three elements:

- the *act* (recruitment, transportation, transfer, harbouring or receipt of persons);
- the *method* (by means of the threat or use of force or other forms of coercion, of abduction, of fraud, of deception, of the abuse of power or of a position of vulnerability or of the giving or receiving of payments or benefits to achieve the consent of a person having control over another person); and
- the *motivation* (for the purpose of exploitation).

The acts of exploitation listed are only examples. Other forms of exploitation, such as forced begging, are covered so long as the other elements of trafficking are present. The definition shows trafficking to be a process: an individual does not have to perform all of the acts that may constitute the offence to be guilty; one, such as recruitment, is enough. Several actors must be involved to fall within the Trafficking Protocol, and no single individual will necessarily be involved in the whole process from source State to destination State. Were it necessary to demonstrate involvement in all of the qualifying acts, it would probably be impossible to prove that any accused had in fact been trafficking. Moreover, the involvement of the accused must take place knowingly.

---

5 *United Nations Convention against Transnational Organized Crime*, opened for signature 15 November 2000, 2225 UNTS 209 (entered into force 29 September 2003).

Under art. 3(b) of the Trafficking Protocol, any apparent consent by the victim to the intended exploitation 'shall be irrelevant' where any of the means listed have been used. The aim here is to pre-empt a possible defence that there has been no trafficking because the alleged victim was a willing participant. Furthermore, where the victim is a child (i.e., under eighteen years of age), that person will be deemed, under art. 3(c), to have been trafficked if they have been recruited, transported, transferred, harboured or received for the purpose of exploitation, even if none of the methods set out in art. 3(a) has been employed. Establishing that children have been trafficked is thus considerably easier because it is not necessary to show that there has been fraud, force, deception, and so on.

The Trafficking Protocol deals only with transnational trafficking (art. 4);[6] it does not therefore cover trafficking within the geographical limits of one State, although this should be criminalised by the State's national law. This raises a potentially problematic issue where a person has been trafficked from State A to State B, and is subsequently trafficked within State B. The latter might be classified as internal trafficking, but it can also be seen as a continuation of the offence of transnational trafficking. If not, the consequence arguably would be that the Trafficking Protocol ceases to have legal effect the moment that the victim is moved from his or her first place of exploitation in the destination State to another place. Much will depend upon the legislation adopted in each State to address trafficking. It is quite possible for national law to adopt the definition contained in the Trafficking Protocol for all instances of trafficking, minus the transnational dimension.

Article 4 stipulates that the Trafficking Protocol only applies where trafficking involves 'an organized criminal group', which is defined in art. 2 of UNCTOC as 'a structured group of three or more persons, existing for a period of time and acting in concert with the aim of committing one or more serious crimes or offences established in accordance with this Convention, in order to obtain, directly or indirectly, a financial or other material benefit'.

Under art. 5 of the Trafficking Protocol, States parties are obliged to criminalise trafficking – that is, not only the conduct set forth in art. 3, but also attempting to commit the offence, participating as an accomplice in the offence and organising or directing others persons to commit the offence.

Part II of the Trafficking Protocol contains limited measures for the protection of victims. Article 6(3) provides that States parties 'shall consider implementing measures to provide for the physical, psychological and social recovery of victims of trafficking'. This is hardly onerous, although States are obliged to do this in good faith: they cannot simply go through the motions; they must give serious consideration to the adoption of relevant measures.

Particular measures listed are clearly aimed at immediate and, to some extent, longer-term needs: appropriate housing; counselling and information (especially

---

6 See also ibid. art. 3(1).

with regard to legal entitlements); medical, psychological and material assistance; and employment and training opportunities. None of these is stated in mandatory terms; any obligation to assist will have to be founded elsewhere. States parties are also required to try to provide for the physical safety of victims – no small task where the victims have fled from the traffickers (art. 6(5)). As with people who have been smuggled, victims are subject to repatriation. This may be enforced should the victim decline to be returned: art. 8(2) stipulates that repatriation should 'preferably be voluntary'. This is subject to the State's international protection obligations, such as the obligation not to return a person to another State where he or she faces the risk of persecution (see Chapter 7).

Part III (prevention, cooperation and other measures) is more stringent. The language is generally mandatory. Article 9(1) provides that States parties 'shall establish comprehensive policies, programmes and other measures ... to prevent and combat trafficking in persons'. This provision also requires States parties to establish policies, programmes and other measures 'to protect victims of trafficking in persons, especially women and children, from revictimization'. This clearly establishes an obligation of assistance towards those who have been trafficked and may be taken as part of the human rights regime.

The Trafficking Protocol is not the only instrument regulating trafficking. Its significance lies in the fact that it is relatively new and has attracted much support from source, transit and destination States – in late 2011 there were 147 States parties. There exists a plethora of international and regional treaties that address trafficking specifically or are relevant to it (see Box 9.1), including an extensive European Union regime. There are also many non-binding, or 'soft law', measures that relate to trafficking.[7] Some of these instruments focus on the criminal aspect of trafficking. However, many address the human rights dimension, seeking to place the rights of victims at the centre of anti-trafficking activities.

9.2.3.   Trafficking and human rights

The prohibition of trafficking under human rights law

Some human rights instruments expressly outlaw trafficking.[8] Others, while not mentioning trafficking as such, refer to slavery, forced labour and servitude as

---

7 Soft law measures include: United Nations High Commissioner for Human Rights, 'Recommended Principles and Guidelines on Human Rights and Human Trafficking' (UN Doc E/2002/68/Add.1, United Nations Economic and Social Council, 20 May 2002); *Brussels Declaration on Preventing and Combating Trafficking in Human Beings*, Council of Europe, No 14981/02 (29 November 2002); *ASEAN Declaration against Trafficking in Persons Particularly Women and Children* (29 November 2004); United Nations High Commissioner for Refugees, 'Guidelines on International Protection: The Application of Article 1A(2) of the 1951 Convention and/or 1967 Protocol relating to the Status of Refugees to Victims of Trafficking and Persons At Risk of Being Trafficked' (UN Doc HCR/GIP/06/07, UNHCR, 7 April 2006).

8 See, e.g., *American Convention on Human Rights*, opened for signature 22 November 1969, 1144 UNTS 123 (entered into force 18 July 1978) art. 6(1), which refers to trafficking in women (but not men or children); *Convention on the Elimination of All Forms of Discrimination against Women*, opened for signature 18 December 1979, 1249 UNTS 13 (entered into force 3 September 1981) art. 6; *Convention on the Rights of the Child*, opened for signature 20

BOX 9.1 Principal international instruments on human trafficking

Year	Instrument
1926	*Slavery Convention*, opened for signature 25 September 1926, 60 LNTS 254 (entered into force 9 March 1927)
1930	*Convention concerning Forced or Compulsory Labour* (ILO Convention No 29), opened for signature 10 June 1930, 39 UNTS 55 (entered into force 1 May 1932)
1949	*Geneva Convention relative to the Protection of Civilian Persons in Time of War*, opened for signature 12 August 1949, 75 UNTS 287 (entered into force 21 October 1950) plus Additional Protocols I and II (1977)
1949	*Convention for the Suppression of the Traffic in Persons and of the Exploitation of the Prostitution of Others*, opened for signature 2 December 1949, 96 UNTS 272 (entered into force 25 July 1951)
1979	*Convention on the Elimination of All Forms of Discrimination against Women*, opened for signature 18 December 1979, 1249 UNTS 13 (entered into force 3 September 1981)
1989	*Convention on the Rights of the Child*, opened for signature 20 November 1989, 1577 UNTS 3 (entered into force 2 September 1990)
1990	*International Convention on the Protection of the Rights of All Migrant Workers and Members of their Families*, opened for signature 18 December 1990, 2220 UNTS 3 (entered into force 1 July 2003)
1999	*Worst Forms of Child Labour Convention* (No 182), opened for signature 17 June 1999, 38 ILM 1215 (entered into force 19 November 2000)
2000	*Optional Protocol to the Convention on the Rights of the Child on the Sale of Children, Child Prostitution and Child Pornography*, opened for signature 25 May 2000, 2171 UNTS 227 (entered into force 18 January 2002)
2002	*South Asian Association for Regional Cooperation Convention on Preventing and Combating Trafficking in Women and Children for Prostitution* (5 January 2002)
2005	*Council of Europe Convention on Action against Trafficking in Human Beings*, opened for signature 16 May 2005, CETS No 197 (entered into force 1 February 2008)
2007	*Council of Europe Convention on the Protection of Children against Sexual Exploitation and Sexual Abuse*, opened for signature 25 October 2007, CETS No 201 (entered into force 1 July 2010)

violations of human rights.[9] That forced labour, including trafficking, may violate human rights even in the absence of direct State involvement has been confirmed by a number of decisions of human rights tribunals. In 2008, in a case addressing

November 1989, 1577 UNTS 3 (entered into force 2 September 1990) art. 35; *Optional Protocol to the Convention on the Rights of the Child on the Sale of Children, Child Prostitution and Child Pornography*, opened for signature 25 May 2000, 2171 UNTS 227 (entered into force 18 January 2002); *Council of Europe Convention on Action against Trafficking in Human Beings*, opened for signature 16 May 2005, CETS No 197 (entered into force 1 February 2008) Preamble.

9 *Universal Declaration of Human Rights*, GA Res 217A (III), UN Doc A/810 (10 December 1948) art. 4; *European Convention for the Protection of Human Rights and Fundamental Freedoms*, opened for signature 4 November 1950, ETS No 005 (entered into force 3 September 1953) art. 4; *International Covenant on Civil and Political Rights*, opened for signature 16 December 1966, 999 UNTS 171 (entered into force 23 March 1976) art. 8; *African Charter on Human and Peoples' Rights*, opened for signature 27 June 1981, 1520 UNTS 217 (entered into force 21 October 1986) art. 5.

the consequences of holding a person in slavery, the Economic Community of West African States ('ECOWAS') Community Court of Justice held that the failure of Niger to denounce the slave status of one of its nationals amounted to tolerance, possibly even acceptance, of that crime.[10] Furthermore, 'the defendant [Niger] becomes responsible under international law as well as national law for any form of human rights violations of the applicant founded on slavery because of its tolerance, passivity, inaction and abstention with regard to this practice.'[11] In this case, it was the slave owner who forced the applicant into slavery; the State was responsible for allowing this situation to happen and for tolerating it.

The matter has been addressed by the European Court of Human Rights, which in 2010 ruled on an alleged violation of art. 4 of the *European Convention for the Protection of Human Rights and Fundamental Freedoms* (1950) ('European Convention on Human Rights'), which prohibits slavery, forced labour and servitude.[12] In *Rantsev* v. *Cyprus and Russia*, the applicant argued that Cyprus and Russia had failed to protect his daughter from the risk of trafficking and exploitation, contrary to art. 4, although that provision does not refer in specific terms to trafficking.[13] While the Court did not clarify whether it regarded trafficking as 'slavery', 'forced labour' or 'servitude', it stressed that trafficking was certainly covered by art. 4. Furthermore it bore a clear resemblance to slavery:

> trafficking in human beings, by its very nature and aim of exploitation, is based on the exercise of powers attaching to the right of ownership. It treats human beings as commodities to be bought and sold and put to forced labour, often for little or no payment . . . It involves the use of violence and threats against victims, who live and work under poor conditions.[14]

Article 4 therefore required States to prosecute and penalise traffickers effectively. They would also have to put in place measures to regulate businesses often used as a cover for trafficking; and immigration rules would have to address relevant concerns relating to encouragement, facilitation or tolerance of trafficking.

These measures would address trafficking in general: States have an obligation to have appropriate laws in place and to enforce them. However, the *Rantsev Case* is significant also because the Court indicated that art. 4 would sometimes oblige States to go further to meet their obligations. In particular, States might have to take measures beyond legislation to protect a victim or potential victim, where:

> the State authorities were aware, or ought to have been aware, of circumstances giving rise to a credible suspicion that an identified individual had been, or was at real and immediate risk of being, trafficked or exploited . . . In the case of an answer in the affirmative, there will be a

10 *Hadijatou Mani Koraou* v. *Republic of Niger (Economic Community of West African States, Community Court of Justice, Judgment No ECW/CCJ/JUD/06/08, 27 October 2008)*.
11 Ibid. [85].
12 *European Convention for the Protection of Human Rights and Fundamental Freedoms*, opened for signature 4 November 1950, ETS No 005 (entered into force 3 September 1953).
13 *Rantsev* v. *Cyprus and Russia* (European Court of Human Rights, Application No 25965/04, 7 January 2010). See also *Siliadin* v. *France* (European Court of Human Rights, Application No 73316/01, 26 October 2005).
14 *Rantsev* v. *Cyprus and Russia*, ibid. [281].

violation of Article 4 of the Convention where the authorities fail to take appropriate measures within the scope of their powers to remove the individual from that situation or risk.[15]

This means that States might have to take practical steps to assist particular individuals known to be at risk. This goes beyond having good laws. It might, for instance, include provision of safe accommodation and other steps to ensure the physical safety of the person at risk.

The *Rantsev Case* may prove highly persuasive in influencing the legal response to trafficking in other regions. The judgment addressed the violation of a right guaranteed in all the major human rights instruments. There have been few cases anywhere dealing with the prohibition of slavery, forced labour and servitude as a human rights issue. The reasoning of the Court, addressing the obligation to ensure and secure enjoyment of the right, is coherent and consistent with the general understanding of how this should work. The novelty of the decision is twofold. First, it names trafficking as a violation of art. 4, although trafficking is not mentioned in the treaty. There is no reason to see this interpretation as unduly adventurous or flawed. Second, the Court clarified the substance and extent of the obligation in finding that a State's duty goes beyond having appropriate laws that are effectively implemented, and includes the duty to take specific protection measures in particular cases.

It is thus becoming clear that instruments that do not mention 'trafficking' may nevertheless prohibit it because of the common features found in the practices of slavery, forced labour and servitude on the one hand, and trafficking on the other. The link with slavery was recognised by the International Criminal Tribunal for the Former Yugoslavia in the *Kunarac Case*. The Tribunal said:

> indications of enslavement include elements of control and ownership; the restriction or control of a person's autonomy, freedom of choice or freedom of movement; and, often, the accruing of some gain to the perpetrator. The consent or free will of the victim is absent. It is often rendered impossible or irrelevant by, for example, the threat or use of force or other forms of coercion; the fear of violence, deception or false promises; the abuse of power; the victim's position of vulnerability; detention or captivity, psychological oppression or socio-economic conditions. Further indications of enslavement include exploitation; the exaction of forced or compulsory labour or service, often without remuneration and often, though not necessarily, involving physical hardship; sex; prostitution; and human trafficking.[16]

The characterisation of trafficking as slavery is furthermore recognised in the *Rome Statute of the International Criminal Court* (1998).[17] In naming enslavement as a crime against humanity, art. 7 stipulates that enslavement means 'the exercise of any or all of the powers attaching to the right of ownership over a person and

---

15 Ibid. [286].
16 *Prosecutor* v. *Kunarac, Kovac and Vukovic (Trial Judgment)* (International Criminal Tribunal for the Former Yugoslavia, Case No IT-96-23-T and IT-96-223/1-T, 22 February 2001) [542].
17 *Rome Statute of the International Criminal Court*, opened for signature 17 July 1998, 2187 UNTS 3 (entered into force 1 July 2002).

includes the exercise of such power in the course of trafficking in persons, in particular women and children'.

International protection obligations

In addition to the obligation to protect individuals from slavery, forced labour or servitude, any State to which a person has been trafficked may have international protection obligations towards that person: an obligation not to oblige a person to return to his or her home State if there is a real risk either that he or she may be re-trafficked or that his or her physical safety may be jeopardised. This obligation is alluded to in art. 14(1) of the Trafficking Protocol, which states that the Protocol does not exclude the application of the *Convention relating to the Status of Refugees* (1951) ('Refugee Convention').[18] Indirect recognition is also found in the Trafficking Protocol for victims' entitlement, or at least need, to remain in the destination State. Article 7(1) obliges parties to 'consider adopting legislative or other appropriate measures that permit victims of trafficking in persons to remain in [their] territory, temporarily or permanently, in appropriate cases'. Moreover, under art. 9(1)(b), States parties are required '[t]o protect victims of trafficking in persons, especially women and children, from revictimization'. This does not mean that victims have a right to asylum, but it may mean a right to remain in the State (as a form of complementary protection) if it is the only way to prevent revictim-isation. Furthermore, the risk of which States must take account here is wider than re-trafficking: revictimisation could include physical attacks as a means of revenge or punishment, or ostracism by the victim's own community.

An entitlement to international protection is significant because a State is not normally obliged to allow non-nationals to remain in its territory. It is an exception to the rule (see Chapter 5). The fact that someone has already been trafficked will not itself trigger an entitlement to remain in another State – indeed many who have been trafficked transnationally may wish to be repatriated. International protection is granted only because of some future risk or threat to the individual concerned. Accordingly, such protection will be available only where the individual is at risk of being re-trafficked or some other serious infringement of his or her safety. The fact that the person has been trafficked in the past may be significant in assessing the risk facing him or her in future. It is unlikely that an individual who has never been trafficked would be able to demonstrate a real risk of being trafficked in the future if the person were returned to his or her home State.

International protection is granted where the individual is either a refugee in the sense of the Refugee Convention, or else faces some threat to his or her human rights that, while not entitling the person to refugee status, is recognised as triggering an entitlement to complementary, or subsidiary, protection. Victims of

---

18 *Convention relating to the Status of Refugees*, opened for signature 28 July 1951, 189 UNTS 150 (entered into force 22 April 1954).

trafficking have no special right to international protection; the grant of such protection depends upon the individual satisfying the criteria for refugee status or complementary protection.

The Refugee Convention, art. 1A, defines as a refugee any person who:

> owing to a well-founded fear of being persecuted for reasons of race, religion, nationality, membership of a particular social group or political opinion, is outside the country of his nationality and is unable or, owing to such fear, is unwilling to avail himself of the protection of that country.

Most people at risk of being trafficked will not qualify. They may have a well-founded fear of being persecuted and be unwilling to seek protection from their own State. They may also be outside their own country. But the basis for their fear is problematic. If someone fears being trafficked because of their race, religion, nationality, membership of a particular social group or political opinion, there is no difficulty. However, in most cases individuals will not be targeted because they fit into one of these categories; they are trafficked because they are vulnerable to exploitation due to poverty, family breakdown or some other factor. Nevertheless, some may be entitled to refugee status because of their membership of a particular social group. A social group requires that its members be connected by some factor they have in common, additional to the fact that they are being persecuted.[19]

There are cases in which persons at risk of being trafficked have been able to demonstrate that they belonged to a particular social group because they came from a particular country, or part of a country, where there was a real risk of being trafficked.[20] This is difficult to prove. However, it can be argued that where a person has been trafficked in the past and fears being re-trafficked in the future, the fact that he or she has been trafficked is an undeniable feature of their background – one that he or she has in common with other victims of trafficking – which may be sufficient to make them a particular social group and therefore qualify as refugees. It is not the risk of persecution that unites them; they are connected by the historical fact that they have been trafficked, and are at risk of being trafficked in the future because they have been trafficked in the past.[21]

Even if a trafficked person does not qualify as a refugee, other measures may entitle him or her to international protection. It has long been recognised that the scope of the Refugee Convention is rather narrow; there are many who, while not qualifying for refugee status, face real and substantial risks to their human rights in their home State. This dilemma has been addressed by the concept of

---

19 Alexander Aleinikoff, 'Protected Characteristics and Social Perceptions: An Analysis of the Meaning of "Membership of a Particular Social Group"' in Erika Feller, Volker Turk and Frances Nicholson (eds.), *Refugee Protection in International Law* (Cambridge University Press, 2003) 263.

20 See, e.g., *Miss AB* v. *Secretary of State for the Home Department* (Immigration Appellate Authority Decision CC/64057/2002, 2003), where the social group comprised girls trafficked from West Africa.

21 See also United Nations High Commissioner for Refugees, above n. 7.

complementary, or subsidiary, protection:[22] States have an obligation not to return individuals to their home State if there is a real risk that their human rights will be breached there (see Chapter 7).[23]

State practice accepts that a State may not require non-nationals to return to their home States if there is a real risk that they will be exposed to torture or inhuman or degrading treatment or punishment. It is accepted that this threat may come not only from the State itself, but from non-State actors within the State, at least where the State is unable or unwilling to protect against that risk. If one considers the types of harm to which a victim of trafficking might be exposed upon return – for example, through re-trafficking or revenge attacks that could include physical, sexual and psychological abuse – it is evident that the individual may face a risk of being subjected to torture or inhuman or degrading treatment and should therefore qualify for complementary protection.[24]

Finally, it matters what kind of international protection is granted. The Refugee Convention requires States to provide significant benefits and entitlements for refugees. Complementary protection, by contrast, is fundamentally about the right to remain in another country. It does not automatically entitle the beneficiary to the same level of assistance.

9.3. SMUGGLING OF MIGRANTS

Smuggling of migrants involves the facilitated irregular crossing of a border for financial or other material benefit. Stereotypically, trafficking is portrayed as involving women and children for sexual exploitation, and smuggling as involving young men in search of a better life. However men, women and children of all ages are prompted to migrate irregularly with the assistance of smugglers for a variety of reasons, whether to escape human rights abuses, armed conflict or civil unrest, environmental disaster or degradation, or economic want (see Chapter 8).

Smuggling of migrants is a global phenomenon: no country is unaffected, whether as a source, transit or destination State, and possibly as all three. As with irregular migration generally, given the clandestine nature of human smuggling, the numbers involved can only be estimated. Where figures do exist there are often inconsistencies between States, depending on how data are collected, if at all. This is compounded by the fact that those who are smuggled have little incentive to approach authorities, given that they are often considered to be complicit in a

---

22 The former term is favoured by the United Nations High Commissioner for Refugees, the latter by the European Union.

23 Ryszard Piotrowicz and Carina Van Eck, 'Subsidiary Protection and Primary Rights' (2004) 53(1) *International and Comparative Law Quarterly* 107; Hugo Storey, 'EU Refugee Qualification Directive: A Brave New World?' (2008) 20(1) *International Journal of Refugee Law* 1; Guy Goodwin-Gill and Jane McAdam, *The Refugee in International Law* (Oxford University Press, 3rd edn, 2007) 285–354.

24 The risk is especially real if the victim has given evidence against the traffickers.

criminal activity, or are indeed criminals, and are likely to face immediate removal. According to the United Nations Office on Drugs and Crime ('UNODC'), the two largest flows of smuggled persons are from Latin America (in particular, Mexico) to the United States, and from sub-Saharan Africa to Europe. It is estimated that there are approximately 3 million attempted irregular crossings of the southern border of the United States annually, mostly with the help of smugglers. Attempted irregular crossings from Africa to Europe are estimated at approximately 55,000 people annually. The estimated annual gains for the smugglers from these two routes alone are respectively USD 6.6 billion and USD 150 million.[25]

Smuggling of migrants poses a threat to state sovereignty and the rule of law. Failure to control the irregular entry of non-nationals, and to adequately defend the State against the activities of organised crime, undermine the authority of the State and are perceived as threatening the safety of its nationals. The fear of uncontrolled irregular migration in destination States has fuelled governments' increasingly tough responses to the issue. Indeed, in many States, migration management is viewed from a law enforcement perspective. Governments around the world are placing greater emphasis on tighter controls of frontiers and safer travel documents, as well as interdepartmental and cross-border cooperation to combat irregular migration. At the same time, opportunities for regular migration have become more restricted, resulting in people resorting to irregular migration. Thus, as States place greater emphasis on border controls and other migration management tools to protect their frontiers, migrants increasingly resort to smugglers to assist them in circumventing these measures.

Smuggling of migrants is often distinguished from trafficking by the vulnerability and exploitation of the trafficking victim, whereas smuggling is framed as a purely commercial transaction. Similarly, smuggling is generally considered to be a consensual transaction based on the migrant's free choice in purchasing the smuggling services, while the victim of trafficking does not truly consent. In reality, however, the migrant may be vulnerable in all stages of the smuggling process. The circumstances pushing an individual to migrate may leave him or her little real choice but to use a smuggler. Further, the journey is often fraught with danger: images of boats overloaded with desperate migrants being dashed against rocks as they attempt to come ashore, bodies washed up on beaches, people dying of exhaustion as they seek to cross land borders or suffocating in the back of trucks are all too familiar. Given the power disparity between the smuggler and the smuggled, the migrant is vulnerable to exploitation and abuse at the hands of smugglers and corrupt officials during all stages of the process, as illustrated by Case Study 9.2.

---

25 United Nations Office on Drugs and Crime, 'The Globalization of Crime: A Transnational Organized Crime Threat Assessment' (UNODC, 2010) 59, 67.

CASE STUDY 9.2 Smuggling men to South Africa

In 2009, the International Organization for Migration ('IOM') undertook an assessment of the irregular movement of men from East Africa and the Horn to South Africa (the 'Study').[26] The Study estimated that each year 17,000 to 20,000 men paid smugglers to take them south, which had an immediate value to the smugglers of USD 34–40 million. The Study found that all of the men smuggled to South Africa, or part of the way, were motivated by the desire to improve their lives. Few, however, were prepared for or warned of the treatment they would face during the journey, which on average lasted seven to eight weeks for Ethiopians and Somalis, and one week for Kenyans. According to testimonies, some men never reached their final destination, either serving time in various prisons *en route* followed by deportation, or in extreme cases dying during the journey.

A high proportion of the migrants reported that their experiences during the smuggling process were unexpectedly harsh. Many spoke of deprivation of food and water, exposure to the elements, beatings and robberies, extortion or abandonment. Sexual abuse was also reported. The stories highlighted protection dilemmas in relation to those who were abused. Despite their hardships, the smuggled migrants did not want to be rescued, saved or repatriated during their journey: any intervention during their journey could result in personal setbacks that might only increase their hardship, financial burden and exposure to abuse.

The Study found that due to ill-defined and weak legislation in various States in which the smugglers operated, they were operating with almost complete impunity at the time of the Study. If the smugglers were caught and could not bribe their way out of trouble, they faced small fines and possible deportation. The stories told by the migrants highlighted that alleged corruption and complicity of national officials appeared to be one of the forces driving the regional smuggling business. The allegations made by a large portion of those interviewed suggested that many of the complicit officials were not chance opportunists succumbing to occasional bribes. Rather, the extent of their collusion with smugglers implied that they were part of the overall illegal and abusive enterprise.

For some migrants, arrival in South Africa was the start of a long cherished dream; for many more, it was a step in a process that would lead to Europe or North America via similar means. The Study found that exposure to considerable criminal violence and prejudice appeared to be the price many accepted for new lives of opportunity in South Africa or a third country in the West. In this regard, it was found that voluntary smuggled migrants had similar mindsets to victims of trafficking: they were often ignorant of their human rights and, given their alternatives, came to accept violence and abuse as part of their lives.

26 Christopher Horwood, *In Pursuit of the Southern Dream: Victims of Necessity Assessment of the Irregular Movement of Men from East Africa and the Horn to South Africa* (International Organization for Migration, 2009).

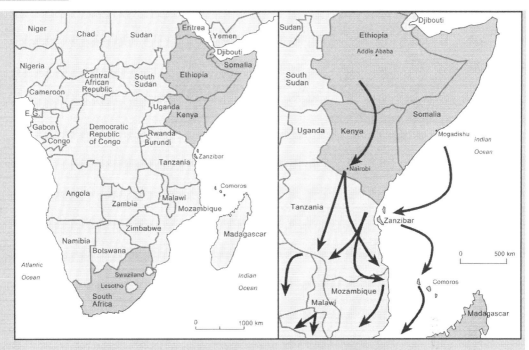

Map 9.1 Smuggling to South Africa

Instances of physical, psychological and sexual abuse, as well as deprivation of food, water and liberty, during the smuggling process are well documented. Once at the destination this may continue, particularly if the migrant is indebted to the smuggler. Thus, notwithstanding the legal distinction between smuggling and trafficking, there may be similarities between the two practices, and categorising a migration experience as smuggling or trafficking may often prove challenging.

9.3.1. The Smuggling Protocol

The key international instrument dealing with smuggling in migrants is the *Protocol against the Smuggling of Migrants by Land, Sea and Air, Supplementing the United Nations Convention against Transnational Organized Crime* (2000) ('Smuggling Protocol').[27] Its purpose is 'to prevent and combat the smuggling of migrants, as well as to promote cooperation among States Parties to that end, while protecting the rights of smuggled migrants' (art. 2). As noted in art. 1, the Smuggling Protocol supplements UNCTOC and is to be interpreted together with it.

As discussed earlier in this chapter, over the past century the international community has adopted a number of instruments responding to the types of

---

27 *Protocol against the Smuggling of Migrants by Land, Sea and Air, Supplementing the United Nations Convention against Transnational Organized Crime*, opened for signature 15 November 2000, 2241 UNTS 507 (entered into force 28 January 2004). In late 2011 there were 129 States parties.

exploitation that can arise from trafficking, such as slavery and labour exploitation. The Trafficking Protocol is a further development addressing such exploitation. In contrast, the Smuggling Protocol represents one of the first times the international community has responded to the smuggling of migrants as a form of organised criminal activity, distinct from legal or illegal activity on the part of migrants themselves. The Smuggling Protocol's response to the criminal exploitation of migration, and profiting therefrom, is a new development.[28] It does so through: (a) providing a definition of smuggling of migrants and mandating its criminalisation; (b) responding to the smuggling of migrants by sea; (c) setting a framework for prevention and cooperation; while (d) protecting the human rights of smuggled migrants. Three of these issues are addressed below; while the smuggling of migrants by sea, on which there is considerable international legal regulation, is discussed in Chapter 10.

Smuggling of migrants and its criminalisation

Under the Smuggling Protocol, 'smuggling of migrants' is defined as 'the procurement, in order to obtain, directly or indirectly, a financial or other material benefit, of the illegal entry of a person into a State Party of which the person is not a national or a permanent resident' (art. 3(a)). 'Illegal entry' is defined as 'crossing borders without complying with the necessary requirements for legal entry into the receiving State' (art. 3(b)).

Several points should be noted. First, unlike trafficking, by definition smuggling of migrants involves crossing an international border – that is, the irregular entry of a non-national into the transit or destination State. Second, smuggling of migrants is characterised by a commercial transaction between the smuggler and the smuggled, involving a financial or other material gain for the former. The smuggled migrant has consented to the transaction and, unlike in trafficking, is considered to be a willing participant. Further, it is this commercial transaction that is the focus of the definition. As noted in the *travaux préparatoires*, the reference to 'financial or other material benefit' was included:

in order to emphasise that the intention was to include the activities of organized criminal groups acting for profit, but to exclude the activities of those who provided support to migrants for humanitarian reasons or on the basis of close family ties. It was not the intention of the protocol to criminalize the activities of family members or support groups such as religious or non-governmental organizations.[29]

Article 6 of the Smuggling Protocol requires the criminalisation of smuggling and related offences. The activities to be criminalised are: smuggling of migrants;

28 United Nations Office on Drugs and Crime, *Legislative Guides for the Implementation of the United Nations Convention against Transnational Organized Crime and the Protocols Thereto* (UNODC, 2004) 339 ('UNODC Legislative Guides').
29 United Nations Office on Drugs and Crime, *Travaux Préparatoires of the Negotiations for the Elaboration of the United Nations Convention against Transnational Organized Crime and the Protocols Thereto* (UNODC, 2006) 489.

producing, procuring or possessing fraudulent travel or identity documents for the purpose of enabling the smuggling of migrants; and enabling a person to remain illegally in the State through illegal means. States parties are required to criminalise attempts to commit an offence, acting as an accomplice, or organising or directing others to commit an offence outlined in the Smuggling Protocol. Finally, it requires that States parties establish as aggravating circumstances those circumstances that endanger, or are likely to endanger, the lives and safety of migrants, or entail inhuman or degrading treatment of migrants.

Under art. 6, only intentional conduct is to be criminalised. Thus, in the context of the offence of smuggling, there must have been an intention to procure illegal entry and an intention of obtaining a financial or other material benefit.[30] However, pursuant to art. 4, as in the case of the Trafficking Protocol, the Smuggling Protocol applies only where the offences are transnational in nature and involve an organised criminal group.

Establishing a framework for the criminalisation of smuggling and related activities is one of the cornerstones of the Smuggling Protocol. The language used in art. 6 is mandatory: States parties must enact legislation that establishes the named offences. However, the article leaves it to States parties to determine the severity of the penalties in the event of breach. A consistent legislative approach among States parties against smuggling is important given the transnational nature of the phenomenon, where smugglers use routes that present the least resistance. Establishing uniform criminal offences at the national level seeks to promote a common response, thereby avoiding the redirection of flows to or through States where the legislative response is weaker. The Smuggling Protocol specifies the criminal offences that must be established through legislative and other measures, thereby setting a minimum standard. Pursuant to art. 34(3) of UNCTOC, States parties are free to take more stringent responses and establish further measures if they so wish.

The focus of the Smuggling Protocol is on the activities of the smuggler – the organised criminal group – not on those of the migrant. Article 5 provides that '[m]igrants shall not become liable to criminal prosecution under this Protocol for the fact of having been the object of conduct set forth in article 6 of this Protocol'. While some commentators believe this to establish protection for the migrant, it must be read in light of art. 6(4), which states that '[n]othing in this Protocol shall prevent a State Party from taking measures against a person whose conduct constitutes an offence under its domestic law'. Thus, the Protocol is neutral on the criminalisation of the migrant for irregular entry: it simply provides that the smuggled migrant shall not be criminalised for irregular entry pursuant to the Protocol. A migrant may, however, be prosecuted for offences relating to irregular entry under national law.

---

30 UNODC Legislative Guides, above n. 28, 342.

Prevention, cooperation and other measures

The drafters of the Smuggling Protocol recognised that, for responses to smuggling of migrants to be effective, they must be based on international cooperation: given the global nature of the phenomenon, unilateral responses would have little impact.[31] The Smuggling Protocol therefore takes a comprehensive view of migration management and recognises that many States lack both the capacity and the resources to respond effectively to the smuggling of migrants. It requires States parties, unilaterally and in cooperation with others, to exchange information (art. 10), strengthen borders (art. 11), take measures to ensure the security and control of travel and identity documents (art. 12), and undertake training and technical cooperation to support these measures (art. 14). In practice, there is now broad recognition of the benefits of international cooperation in responding to this form of irregular migration. Cooperation has developed at the bilateral, regional and international levels on each of the areas outlined in the Smuggling Protocol.

The Smuggling Protocol also recognises the need to address root causes in order to respond effectively to the smuggling of migrants, and focusses on responding to root causes in the country of origin, such as poverty and underdevelopment. It also calls for cooperation in the field of public information concerning the risks of irregular migration and falling victim to organised crime.

Protection

The Smuggling Protocol provides certain minimum protections for smuggled migrants. Article 16 is the main provision on assistance and protection. It calls upon States parties in implementing the Smuggling Protocol to take appropriate measures, consistent with their obligations under international law, to preserve and protect the rights of smuggled migrants, particularly in relation to the right to life and the right not to be subjected to torture or other cruel, inhuman or degrading treatment. It requires parties to take appropriate measures to afford migrants appropriate protection against violence, as well as afford appropriate assistance to those whose lives or safety are endangered by reason of being the object of conduct outlined in art. 6. It specifies that States parties shall take into account the special needs of women and children in applying art. 16. Where the migrant is in detention, he or she must be informed without delay of the right to consular protection and assistance.

In addition, there are various references throughout the text acknowledging that migrants have protection needs. In this context, art. 9 requires that States parties ensure the safety and humane treatment of migrants on board when taking measures outlined in the Protocol against a vessel; art. 14 calls for training for relevant officials

---

31 In this regard, the Smuggling Protocol takes a similar approach to the *International Convention on the Protection of the Rights of All Migrant Workers and Members of their Families*, opened for signature 18 December 1990, 2220 UNTS 3 (entered into force 1 July 2003) ('ICRMW'). Part VI of the ICRMW calls on States parties to collaborate with a view to preventing and eliminating illegal or clandestine movements of migrant workers in an irregular situation.

on the humane treatment of migrants and respect for their rights; art. 15 requires that information campaigns highlight the risks involved for migrants during the smuggling process; and art. 18 requires that measures to return smuggled migrants pay due regard to their safety and dignity, while upholding any rights they may have under the national law of the receiving State. In addition, the Smuggling Protocol must be read in light of UNCTOC, which requires each party to take 'appropriate measures within its means' to provide assistance and protection to victims of offences under the Convention, particularly in the context of retaliation or intimidation (art. 25(1)). It also requires that States parties establish appropriate procedures to provide access to compensation and restitution for victims of offences under the Convention.

When contrasted with the protection and assistance provisions of the Trafficking Protocol (art. 6), the Smuggling Protocol is notably thin in the protection it provides. Article 16 essentially restates the right of smuggled persons to physical survival – the right to life; freedom from torture or other cruel, inhuman or degrading treatment; assistance where lives or safety are endangered; and protection from violence. Unlike the Trafficking Protocol, there is no provision for assistance in legal proceedings, or any reference to the physical, psychological or social recovery of the smuggled migrant. Nor is there provision for the possibility of allowing the migrant to remain on the territory permanently or temporarily, nor any reference to cooperation with non-governmental and other relevant organisations. Consistent with the disparity in protections provided under the two instruments, the Trafficking Protocol refers to those who have been trafficked as 'victims', whereas the Smuggling Protocol refers to those who are smuggled as 'migrants'.

This difference in treatment is based on the perception of the drafters that the two groups can be neatly categorised and contrasted: those who are trafficked are deceived or coerced into the process and are subjected to exploitation for the profit of the traffickers; those who are smuggled undertake the journey voluntarily, personally benefit from the process, and are not necessarily subjected to exploitation. However, this distinction often does not accord with the reality experienced by the migrant where, for example, the process starts off as smuggling, but becomes trafficking during the journey or on arrival in the destination State. Similarly, it does not correspond to the reality that many smuggled migrants suffer exploitation and abuse during or after the smuggling process, at the hands of smugglers or third parties, but do not experience all the stages typical of the trafficking continuum. The effect of this rigid distinction is that while victims of trafficking are viewed through a human rights lens, smuggled migrants are primarily seen as irregular migrants complicit in a criminal activity, or as criminals. As a result, the protection and assistance needs of smuggled 'illegal' migrants may be overlooked, notwithstanding that victims of trafficking and smuggled migrants may have similar needs. This could put the destination State in breach of its international protection obligations towards the smuggled migrant.

To the extent that the Smuggling Protocol provides for protection of the migrant, it is interesting to note the difference in language used in establishing the obligations of the States parties. Article 16, on assistance and protection, requires that the State take 'appropriate' measures or provide 'appropriate' assistance in relation to the action in question. Thus, it is for the State to determine if any action is necessary and what that action will be. In contrast, in the context of the obligations concerning the criminalisation of smuggling and international cooperation, the language is mandatory: States 'shall' implement the specified measures. In the case of art. 16, leaving such discretion to the State raises concerns that the protection and assistance needs of the smuggled migrant may not be adequately met.

The relatively weak protections provided by the Smuggling Protocol are in keeping with the circumstance that it is primarily an instrument of criminal law that focusses on international cooperation to combat organised crime. It is not a human rights instrument. To the extent that human rights are addressed, given the non-prescriptive language in the areas of protection and assistance, it is arguable that the greatest contribution it makes to protecting the rights of smuggled migrants is an indirect one through the development of state obligations to criminalise smuggling. However, while the Smuggling Protocol does not create any new rights for irregular migrants, it does not detract from their established rights under other instruments. Article 19 expressly maintains the rights of migrants under other areas of international law, including international humanitarian law, international human rights law and refugee law. It further states that measures taken under the Protocol shall be consistent with the principle of non-discrimination. Thus, while the instrument itself is neutral on the issue of the rights of the smuggled migrant, the extensive protections from which the migrant benefits under other branches of international law remain binding on States parties.

9.3.2. Smuggling and human rights

As has been highlighted, the smuggling of migrants often involves serious abuse and exploitation, both during the smuggling process and on arrival in the State of destination. Under international human rights law, the State has an obligation to take positive steps to prevent smuggling and to protect those who have been or may be smuggled. Criminalisation of the activities outlined in the Smuggling Protocol contributes to meeting the first of these obligations. The remainder of this section focusses on the second.

There is a common misconception that, due to their irregular status, smuggled migrants have no rights. This is incorrect. As noted in Chapter 5, States have the right to determine which non-nationals enter their territory and the conditions of such entry. This power to manage migration must, however, be exercised with full respect for the human rights and freedoms of non-nationals, which are granted under a wide range of human rights instruments and customary international law, regardless of whether those persons are in a regular or an irregular situation. With few exceptions, the core human rights treaties apply to *all persons* in the territory and subject to the State's jurisdiction, without discrimination: this applies to the civil, political, economic, cultural and social rights outlined therein. For example, art. 2(3) of the *International Covenant on Civil and Political Rights* (1966) ('ICCPR') provides that States parties shall respect and ensure to all individuals within their territory and subject to their jurisdiction the rights recognised in the Covenant, without distinction of any kind, on the basis of, *inter alia*, race, colour, sex, language, religion, political or other opinion, national or social origin, birth or other status.[32] While distinctions between nationals and non-nationals are permitted in certain circumstances, these distinctions must serve a legitimate purpose and measures taken must be proportionate to the purpose in question.

Thus, a State has the obligation to protect all persons subject to its jurisdiction, regardless of their nationality or legal status. The following discussion focusses on those human rights of particular relevance to smuggled migrants when intercepted by state authorities during transit or on arrival in the destination State. It does not deal with the labour rights of smuggled migrants, which are addressed in Chapter 11, or the human rights of irregular migrants more generally, which are dealt with in Chapter 6.

Food, shelter, medical care

Often migrants are discovered by authorities in a state of sheer exhaustion, having been deprived of food, water or shelter for days or even weeks. They may also be in urgent need of medical attention. Regardless of the irregular status of smuggled migrants, the State has an obligation to ensure that their basic needs are met. Under art. 2(1) of the *International Covenant on Economic, Social and Cultural Rights* (1966) ('ICESCR'), each State party must take steps to the 'maximum of its available resources, with a view to achieving progressively' the full realisation of the rights outlined in the ICESCR.[33] In interpreting this phrase, the Committee on Economic, Social and Cultural Rights has noted that, notwithstanding the progressive nature of the obligation:

a minimum core obligation to ensure the satisfaction of, at the very least, minimum essential levels of each of the rights is incumbent upon every State party. Thus, for example, a State party in which any significant number of individuals is deprived of essential foodstuffs, of essential primary health care, of basic shelter and housing, or of the most basic forms of education is, prima facie, failing to discharge its obligations under the Covenant.[34]

---

32 *International Covenant on Civil and Political Rights*, opened for signature 16 December 1966, 999 UNTS 171 (entered into force 23 March 1976).

33 *International Covenant on Economic, Social and Cultural Rights*, opened for signature 16 December 1966, 993 UNTS 3 (entered into force 3 January 1976).

34 Committee on Economic, Social and Cultural Rights, *General Comment No 3: The Nature of States Parties' Obligations*, 50th sess, UN Doc E/1991/23 (14 December 1990) [10].

Bearing in mind the principle of non-discrimination, the right under the ICESCR to adequate food and shelter, as well as urgent healthcare, applies equally to nationals and non-nationals, and must be ensured by the State without delay.[35]

Protection of life and security

In addition to food, shelter and urgent medical attention, the State is also obliged to ensure that smuggled migrants are treated in a humane manner and with dignity. As recognised by the Smuggling Protocol, the civil and political rights of particular relevance to smuggled migrants, both during the migration process and on arrival in the destination State, include: the right to life; freedom from torture or cruel, inhuman or degrading treatment; and the right to be free from slavery and servitude. Under human rights law, these rights are non-derogable: they cannot be derogated from even in times of national emergency. Thus, they must be respected at all times by the State in which the migrant finds himself or herself. This applies to treatment on interception, but must also be considered prior to any removal of the migrant from the territory, as many smuggled migrants may have legitimate claims for international protection. In this context the principle of *non-refoulement* is particularly important because many individuals resort to smuggling to escape persecution in their home State. According to this principle, a State shall not remove someone to a place where his or her life or freedom would be threatened. This principle is enshrined in art. 33 of the Refugee Convention and is widely considered to be a principle of customary international law. Similarly, under the *Convention against Torture and Other Cruel, Inhuman or Degrading Treatment or Punishment* (1984),[36] a State cannot remove someone to another State where there are substantial grounds for belief that he or she would be subjected to torture (art. 3). Thus, not only does a State have an obligation to protect the life and security of the smuggled migrant once that person is subject to its jurisdiction, it has an obligation not to take any enforcement action against the migrant that would threaten his or her life or security on removal.

Detention

Some States detain smuggled migrants on arrival and prior to their removal. While detention is permitted under international human rights law, it must be in accordance with the law and must not be arbitrary. Conditions of detention must be humane and the migrant must be entitled to take proceedings before a court so that it can decide on the lawfulness of the detention without delay. Where the migrant is the victim of unlawful arrest or detention, he or she shall have a right to compensation.[37]

---

35 Article 2(3) of the ICESCR recognises that developing countries may determine to what extent they will guarantee economic rights to non-nationals, but this primarily relates to the right to work.

36 *Convention against Torture and Other Cruel, Inhuman or Degrading Treatment or Punishment*, opened for signature 10 December 1984, 1465 UNTS 85 (entered into force 26 June 1987).

37 *International Covenant on Civil and Political Rights*, above n. 32, arts. 9–10. See also *International Convention on the Protection of the Rights of All Migrant Workers and Members of their Families*, above n. 31, art. 16, which provides additional protections for irregular migrants.

The detention of women and children requires particular attention. Except in the family context, women should be separated from men, and children from adults. The detention of children should be only as a matter of last resort and for the shortest possible time.[38] Access to detention centres for non-governmental organisations to identify vulnerable cases is also important. Finally, access to consular protection and assistance from the country of nationality must be granted.

Removal

Where a migrant is in an irregular situation and does not have a claim to international protection, the State has the right to remove him or her from its territory. Similarly, the State of origin is obliged under international law to accept the return of its nationals (see Chapter 4). Often the most humane, effective and sustainable returns are undertaken voluntarily by the smuggled migrant. However, if he or she does not wish to return voluntarily, forced removal is an option. In the context of expulsion, the procedural protections under ICCPR art. 13, which entitle a migrant to a review of the removal decision by a competent authority, apply only to those lawfully in the territory.[39] When implementing the return, the emphasis must be on respect for the dignity of the individual. In this context, readmission agreements may facilitate the issuance of necessary documentation and the efficiency of the return process. Where the return involves a child, the best interests of the child must be a primary consideration.

There is no shortage of instruments guaranteeing the human rights of smuggled migrants, the majority of which guarantee these rights on an equal footing with nationals of the destination country. The challenge is to give practical expression to these rights and to make them a reality during and after the smuggling process. Regrettably, there is a marked disparity between the principle of universal application of human rights norms to smuggled migrants and the actual practice of States. This is due both to the resistance of States to be seen as giving rights to 'illegals', but also to a lack of understanding of these rights and how they apply to irregular non-nationals at the operational level. This has led to calls for 'soft law' frameworks to be developed at the universal level to respond to the needs of vulnerable migrants, including those who have been smuggled and have suffered abuse and exploitation during the smuggling process.[40]

Whether such a response is necessary and will materialise remains to be seen. One benefit of such an approach is that it may focus the discussion and responses

---

38 *Convention on the Rights of the Child*, opened for signature 20 November 1989, 1577 UNTS 3 (entered into force 2 September 1990) art. 37(b).

39 However, under art. 16 of the ICRMW the right of review applies to all migrants, regardless of their immigration status.

40 Stefanie Grant, 'International Migration and Human Rights' (Global Commission on International Migration, September 2005); Alexander Aleinikoff, 'International Legal Norms on Migration: Substance without Architecture' in Ryszard Cholewinski, Richard Perruchoud and Euan Macdonald (eds.), *International Migration Law* (TMC Asser Press, 2007) 467; Alexander Betts, 'New Issues in Refugee Research, Towards a "Soft Law" Framework for the Protection of Vulnerable Migrants' (United Nations High Commissioner for Refugees, 2008).

on the needs of the individual rather than on whether the individual is a victim of trafficking in need of protection or a smuggled migrant who has breached immigration law. At the same time, it is necessary that more be done to draw to the attention of States their existing human rights obligations towards smuggled people and the duty to give full effect to them in good faith.

9.4. CONCLUSION

The Trafficking and Smuggling Protocols have become the cornerstone of the international community's efforts to combat these forms of criminal activity. They make a significant contribution to standardising national legislation in criminalising the phenomena, and promoting cooperation between States in their efforts to combat the activities of organised crime.

While both instruments state as objectives the protection of the human rights of those affected, the protections provided are limited, particularly for those who have been smuggled. However, as acknowledged in both instruments, the Protocols are not exhaustive in the protections they provide. Human rights law has particular relevance and continues to apply to the affected individuals regardless of whether they have been involved in irregular migration.

Since the adoption of the Trafficking Protocol, a substantial body of hard and soft law relating to the trafficking of human beings has developed. The international community has rallied to raise awareness of the plight of victims and appropriate responses by those officials who come into contact with them. However, longer-term protection for those who have been rescued but are still in an irregular situation remains a challenge in most destination countries.

In contrast, the development at the international level of hard and soft law for the protection of smuggled migrants has been far more circumspect. Smuggling has to some extent been neglected by lawmakers, many of whom still believe that those who have been smuggled are complicit in a criminal offence, and still view them simply as irregular migrants, or criminals, to be removed.

Given the clandestine nature of trafficking and smuggling of human beings, it is difficult to quantify the effectiveness of the Protocols in the fight against these practices, or the progress that has been made in combating organised crime in this regard. Nevertheless, the international framework for the criminalisation of the two phenomena, and international cooperation in prevention, detection and return, are far more robust as a result of their adoption. While their effective implementation at the national level has its challenges, a helpful framework has been established, and there are many international and non-governmental organisations working with governments to implement the Protocols at the national level. Nevertheless, a key challenge remains in ensuring the effective protection of those who have been trafficked or smuggled.

KEY REFERENCES

Bhabha, Jacqueline, *Trafficking, Smuggling, and Human Rights* (Migration Policy Institute, 2005)

Edwards, Alice, 'Trafficking in Human Beings: At the Intersection of Criminal Justice, Human Rights, Asylum/Migration and Labor' (2007) 36(1) *Denver Journal of International Law and Policy* 9

Gallagher, Anne, 'Human Rights and Human Trafficking: Quagmire or Firm Ground? A Response to James Hathaway' (2009) 49(4) *Virginia Journal of International Law* 789

Gallagher, Anne, 'Human Rights and the New UN Protocols on Trafficking and Migrant Smuggling: A Preliminary Analysis' (2001) 23(4) *Human Rights Quarterly* 975

Hathaway, James, 'The Human Rights Quagmire of "Human Trafficking"' (2008) 49(1) *Virginia Journal of International Law* 1

International Council on Human Rights Policy, *Irregular Migration, Migrant Smuggling and Human Rights: Towards Coherence* (International Council on Human Rights Policy, 2010)

Obokata, Tom, 'Smuggling of Human Beings from a Human Rights Perspective: Obligations of Non-State and State Actors under International Human Rights Law' (2005) 17(2) *International Journal of Refugee Law* 394

Piotrowicz, Ryszard, 'The Legal Nature of Trafficking in Human Beings' (2009) 4 *Intercultural Human Rights Law Review* 175

Piotrowicz, Ryszard, 'Victims of People Trafficking and Entitlement to International Protection' (2005) 24 *Australian Year Book of International Law* 159

United Nations Office on Drugs and Crime, *Global Report on Trafficking in Persons* (UNODC, 2009)

United Nations Office on Drugs and Crime, *Legislative Guides for the Implementation of the United Nations Convention against Transnational Organized Crime and the Protocols Thereto* (UNODC, 2004)

KEY RESOURCES

Anti-Slavery: www.antislavery.org

Council of Europe, Action against Trafficking in Human Beings: www.coe.int/t/dghl/monitoring/trafficking/default_en.asp

European Union, Fight against Trafficking in Human Beings: http://ec.europa.eu/anti-trafficking

UNODC, Human Trafficking and Migrant Smuggling: www.unodc.org/unodc/en/human-trafficking/index.html?ref=menuside

US Department of State, Office to Monitor and Combat Trafficking in Persons: www.state.gov/g/tip

10 International migration by sea and air

NATALIE KLEIN[1]

10.1. INTRODUCTION

The plight of migrants travelling by sea was graphically highlighted at the end of 2010 with the destruction of a vessel and attempted rescue of predominantly Middle Eastern asylum seekers in waters off the Australian territory of Christmas Island. Of the men, women, children and babies on board, few knew how to swim and many did not have life jackets. Approximately fifty people died before they could be reached by the Royal Australian Navy. This incident was far from unique. In May 2011, a vessel from Libya carrying 600 Somali asylum seekers, including children, was reported as having sunk before reaching Italy. Many comparable incidents have occurred in Mediterranean crossings in recent years. These tragedies reflect the desperate measures that will be undertaken as migrants journey to resettle in a new State.

When considering the voyages undertaken by migrants across land, air and sea, it is hard to deny the very human factor involved in international migration, as people endure risks, sacrifices and hardships. The role of law is often intimately connected with the difficulties that migrants face. The movement of people by sea and air between States entails an intricate legal framework of rights and duties associated with people leaving and entering States, the conditions of carriage, and responsibilities associated with incidents that may occur during the course of passage. For migrants, the legal processes involved provide an additional complication to the physical and emotional challenges, as States seek to preserve their sovereign right to determine who may enter their territory (see Chapter 5).

The preferred modes for entering a State's territory have shifted over time as developments in technology have improved transportation, as well as the means of surveillance and the tools used for border control. Air travel has increasingly permitted migrants to travel over much greater distances than in the past, although

1 The author gratefully acknowledges the excellent research assistance of Sonali Seneviratne, the helpful suggestions of the editors and other contributors to this volume, and the editorial assistance of Nicholas Lennings and Danielle Selig in the preparation of this chapter.

the financial cost is usually greater than travel by land or sea. Sea travel is no longer marked by significant numbers of international passenger liners; rather people travel predominantly on tourist or cargo vessels. Migration by pleasure craft and other small vessels reflects one of the more poorly monitored modes of transport. Migrants will also voyage across land in trains, trucks and cars; and some still travel by foot. Much migration uses mixed modes of transport, using land, sea and air at different stages of the journey. While some of the legal issues addressed in this chapter apply to all modes of transport, the focus is on departure and arrival by sea and air.

As States attempt to secure their borders, legal barriers to entry are erected through visa requirements, interception measures are put in place at foreign airports, and the physical interdiction of vessels on the high seas is undertaken to prevent unauthorised entry to the State's maritime territory. Attempts to intercept irregular migrants before they reach the territory of a State are consonant with national security concerns and are viewed as 'one of the most effective measures to enforce [a State's] migration laws and policies'.[2] The very concept of a border is no longer static, as States seek to alter their geographic and political boundaries to better control international migration.

Migrants sometimes feel compelled to take great risks in travelling to other States, such as by stowing away or being smuggled, thereby exposing themselves to trafficking, abuse or exploitation, or abandonment at sea in unseaworthy vessels. Even if they reach the borders of another State, they may be immediately returned, detained for varying lengths of time, or find themselves caught in limbo in the event that no State wishes to take responsibility for them. This chapter addresses the journeys of irregular migrants and the legal barriers they encounter in their voyages by sea and air.

From the outset, it should be acknowledged that international migration may encompass different categories of migrants. 'Regular' or 'legal' migrants refer to those moving through recognised legal channels.[3] 'Irregular' or 'illegal' migration does not have a universally accepted definition, but relates to the illegal entry, stay or work in a State without necessary authorisation or documents, or leaving a State without valid documentation or without completing administrative requirements. This chapter focusses on irregular migration, which is used with its broad understanding, but with acknowledgement that separate sets of rules have evolved in relation to particular classes of irregular migrants.

Mixed migration is a term often used to describe the complex and varied reasons that motivate people to leave one State and enter another. It has been suggested that 'while outward movement may be forced, precipitated by persecution, conflict,

---

2 United Nations High Commissioner for Refugees, 'Global Consultations on International Protection: Refugee Protection and Migration Control: Perspectives from UNHCR and IOM' (UNHCR, 31 May 2001) 14; Barbara Miltner, 'Irregular Maritime Migration: Refugee Protection Issues in Rescue and Interception' (2006) 30(1) *Fordham International Law Journal* 75, 83.

3 Richard Perruchoud and Jillyanne Redpath-Cross (eds.), *Glossary on Migration* (IOM, 2nd edn, 2011) 54, 81. See also the Glossary in this book.

war or some other life-threatening circumstance, inward or onward movement, including the choice or determination of the destination, may be shaped by economic, livelihood, betterment, or life-chance considerations'.[4] Ultimately, the reasons for leaving a State may be shared by asylum seekers and other migrants, and both groups may follow the same routes, utilise the same means of transport or even the services of the same smugglers.

The existence of mixed migration has sometimes encouraged States to treat all irregular migrants as 'illegal' entrants, without the proper identification and protection of refugees as a distinct class. A recurring difficulty in State efforts to reduce irregular migration is the risk that asylum seekers may be denied the right to have their claims determined, and thus may be returned to States from which they are fleeing persecution, in violation of the principle of *non-refoulement* (see Chapter 7).

Section 10.2 addresses some of the legal barriers imposed on migrants while they are still outside the State of their intended destination, with the object of preventing irregular migrants from reaching that State's borders. These extraterritorial measures include: visa requirements; posting immigration officials in other States to identify fraudulent documentation; training and posting airline officials abroad to screen documents and migrants prior to boarding aircraft; safe third country and country of first asylum determinations; excising territory for the application of immigration laws; and preferring extraterritorial processing of asylum-seeker claims.[5]

Section 10.3 considers the use of carrier sanctions, which seek to penalise private industry for transporting irregular migrants into the territory of a State. Section 10.4 examines the physical interdiction of irregular migrants on the high seas as a further means of preventing arrivals into the territory of a State. Sections 10.5 and 10.6 then turn to other tactics employed in the context of migration by sea, namely stowing away and smuggling. Section 10.7 explores one of the possible consequences of attempts to migrate by sea and addresses the rescue of people in distress. The final section offers a brief conclusion.

10.2. EXTRATERRITORIAL INTERCEPTION

The use of the term 'interception' in the migration context relates to the measures taken by States to prevent embarkation of passengers on international voyages (principally by air and sea), to prevent further onward international travel, or to assert control of vessels (ships or aircraft) where there are reasonable grounds to believe the vessel is transporting irregular migrants.[6] Interdictions – where ships

4 Nicholas Van Hear, Rebecca Brubaker and Thais Bessa, 'Managing Mobility for Human Development: The Growing Salience of Mixed Migration' (UNDP, 2009) 4.
5 Sam Blay, Jennifer Burn and Patrick Keyzer, 'Interception and Offshore Processing of Asylum Seekers: The International Law Dimensions' (2007) 9 *UTS Law Review* 7, 11.
6 This definition of interception is drawn from UNHCR Executive Committee, 'Conclusion on Protection Safeguards in Interception Measures' (No 97 (LIV), UNHCR, 2003).

are stopped, boarded and possibly arrested at sea – are a subset of interception measures. Interception measures are taken both to prevent entry of irregular migrants and to protect the lives and security of those involved.[7]

10.2.1. Visa restrictions

Visa policies allow States to assess individuals to determine whether or not to grant them entry. The requirement of a visa has been one of the critical tools used by States that are frequently destinations for irregular migrants, including refugees. Morrison and Crosland have noted: 'The imposition of visa restrictions on all countries that generate refugees is the most explicit blocking mechanism for asylum flows and it denies most refugees the opportunity for legal migration.'[8] Refugees who fear persecution from the State are unlikely to seek travel documents from the State. They may also have difficulties reaching an embassy or consulate of the destination State to obtain a visa, or they may be refused a visa precisely because they plan to seek asylum in the State in question.[9] In these circumstances, it becomes increasingly likely that the migrant may seek to enter a foreign State without the necessary documentation or with fraudulent documentation.

10.2.2. Airline screening

Airline representatives, or affiliated private security companies, have taken an increasingly active role in detecting fraudulent or improper passports, visas or other entry documentation to prevent the embarkation of irregular migrants and thereby avoid the imposition of carrier sanctions. In this regard, governments and the International Air Transport Association have run training programmes to assist airline staff in identifying fraudulent documentation. Airline officials thus become a critical element in preventing irregular migration, even though assessment of claims to admission is a responsibility of States.

Immigration control officers have also been deployed by States to act in airports in foreign States that are frequently used by irregular migrants in transit. They provide training and act in an advisory capacity to local officials in assessing documentation, rather than exercising extraterritorial policing powers themselves. Australia, Canada, Denmark, Germany, the Netherlands, the United Kingdom and the United States have all utilised immigration control officers. A key criticism of their use is that they do not have a mandate to examine an individual's motivations for migrating and are thus not in a position to make an assessment of whether a migrant is a refugee. This criticism is borne out by Case Study 10.1, relating to the posting of British officials at Prague airport.

---

7 Ibid.; Miltner, above n. 2, 80.
8 John Morrison and Beth Crosland, 'Working Paper No 39: The Trafficking and Smuggling of Refugees: The End Game in European Asylum Policy?' (UNHCR, 2001) 28.
9 Andrew Brouwer and Judith Kumin, 'Interception and Asylum: When Migration Control and Human Rights Collide' (2003) 21(4) *Refuge* 6, 8–9.

CASE STUDY 10.1 British immigration screening at Prague airport

The United Kingdom's practice of posting immigration officials in overseas airports was tested in *R* v. *Immigration Officer at Prague Airport; Ex parte European Roma Rights Centre*.[10] The United Kingdom and the Czech Republic had entered into a Memorandum of Understanding in 2001, permitting British immigration officials to be stationed at Prague airport in order to give or refuse leave to enter the United Kingdom to passengers prior to embarking on an aircraft. Leave to enter was granted to passengers who satisfied the officials that they were intending to visit for a permitted purpose under British legislation. However, passengers were denied entry to board if they stated they were intending to claim asylum, or if the immigration officials concluded that they were planning to do so. The British officials were not permanently posted at Prague airport, but spent limited time there without advance warning. This approach served to have a deterrent effect. The overall impact of the programme was to drastically reduce the number of asylum claims made by Czech nationals in the United Kingdom.

This programme was challenged before the British courts by Czech nationals of Romani ethnic origin (Roma), who had all been refused permission to board by British immigration officials because of their stated or inferred intention to claim asylum in the United Kingdom. Before the House of Lords, the procedures were challenged as incompatible with the Refugee Convention and customary international law, and as unjustifiable discrimination on racial grounds. In considering this case, Lord Bingham observed that there is neither a right to be admitted to a State nor any right to asylum. He further considered whether there had been a violation of the Refugee Convention, and in this context focussed on the requirement that foreign nationals applying for refugee status must be outside their State of nationality.

A distinction was drawn between this case and the United States decision of *Sale* v. *Haitian Centers Council*.[11] The latter had considered a challenge to the United States practice of interdicting vessels on the high seas to prevent Haitian asylum seekers from reaching United States territory. Lord Bingham noted that the facts differed from the situation of the Roma because the Haitians were outside Haiti, their State of nationality, even though they did not reach the United States. The United States Supreme Court had confirmed the legality of an executive order requiring the United States Coast Guard to drive back or repel Haitian asylum seekers, forcing them to return to their State of origin. *Sale* was not entirely different, however, as the United States was instead facilitating refugee claims by accepting applications at the Embassy of the United States in Haiti. The House of Lords did not accept that the Roma individuals in question were outside their State of nationality and had only presented themselves at the United Kingdom border in 'a highly metaphorical sense'. As such, the obligation of *non-refoulement* was not engaged. The requirements for claiming refugee status had been set out in the *Convention relating to the Status of Refugees* (1951) and there was no basis to consider filling gaps that had been left in the protective scope of the treaty.

10 *R* v. *Immigration Officer at Prague Airport; Ex parte European Roma Rights Centre* [2004] UKHL 55 (9 December 2004).

11 *Sale* v. *Haitian Centers Council*, 509 US 155 (1993).

A further ground of appeal related to allegations that Roma were being targeted for longer and more intrusive questioning, that they were required to provide more proof than non-Roma, and that more Roma than non-Roma were refused leave to enter. Under British law, a public authority may not discriminate on racial grounds in carrying out any of its functions. No exception under a special authorisation applied to the operation at Prague airport. The system established was declared unlawful by the House of Lords on the basis of the inherent and systematic racial discrimination against Roma, contrary to the *Race Relations Act 1976* (UK).

10.2.3. Excising territory

States resisting an influx of irregular migrants have also prevented migrants from arriving by excising particular territory for migration purposes. For example, Australia has created a migration zone in which valid applications for protection visas can be made. The migration zone excludes some Australian territory on Australia's northern borders, the practical effect of which is to deny migrants access to regular migration processes when arriving in the excised areas, usually by sea.[12]

10.3. CARRIER SANCTIONS

The involvement of carriers in the control and regulation of migration through the inspection of migrant documentation is of long standing. While carrier liability most commonly arises in relation to migration by air, carrier liability regimes usually also include migration by sea and land. The imposition of carrier sanctions for transporting irregular migrants increased throughout the 1980s and reflects the diffusion of migration control to private actors.[13]

Carrier sanction regimes typically provide that a carrier that has transported an irregular migrant is financially accountable for the migrant's return and any costs associated with the migrant's stay, as well as being subjected to a monetary penalty. 'Carrier sanctions are ... an enforcement mechanism for visa requirements.'[14] In penalising the carriers, States are able to reduce costs that would otherwise be associated with assessing claims from asylum seekers, their accommodation and possible expulsion.[15] Moreover, if irregular migrants can be stopped before they have

12 *Migration Amendment (Excision from Migration Zone) Act 2001* (Cth). See Penelope Mathew, 'Australian Refugee Protection in the Wake of the Tampa' (2002) 96 *American Journal of International Law* 661, 663–4.
13 Maryellen Fullerton, 'Restricting the Flow of Asylum-Seekers in Belgium, Denmark, the Federal Republic of Germany, and the Netherlands: New Challenges to the Geneva Convention relating to the Status of Refugees and the European Convention on Human Rights' (1988) 29 *Virginia Journal of International Law* 33, 92.
14 Erika Feller, 'Carrier Sanctions and International Law' (1989) 1 *International Journal of Refugee Law* 48, 50.
15 Sophie Scholten and Paul Minderhoud, 'Regulating Immigration Control: Carrier Sanctions in the Netherlands' (2008) 10(2) *European Journal of Migration and Law* 123, 129.

the opportunity to arrive at a State's border, it has been suggested that the State need be less concerned with violating the *non-refoulement* principle.[16] Fullerton, however, has argued that the nature of the carrier sanctions regime itself amounts to a violation of *non-refoulement* due to the procedural deficiencies in the legislative framework.[17]

The relevant international law rule is set out in art. 13 of the *Convention on International Civil Aviation* (1944) ('Chicago Convention'), which provides:

> The laws and regulations of a contracting State as to the admission or departure from the territory of passengers, crew or cargo of aircraft, such as regulations relating to entry, clearance, immigrations, passports, customs and quarantine shall be complied with by or on behalf of such passengers, crew or cargo upon entrance.[18]

Some writers have suggested that while there is a clear obligation on air passengers to fulfil requirements to enter a particular State – which includes complying with visa and other documentary requirements – there is also an implicit responsibility falling elsewhere (arguably on the carrier or on the State bound by the treaty obligation) to ensure that passengers comply with the rules of the State of destination.[19] Others have asserted instead that 'the Chicago Convention requires compliance by passengers with entrance formalities, but does not oblige airlines to enforce this'.[20]

Annex 9 to the Chicago Convention provides that an airline that is carrying a passenger is responsible for his or her custody and care until they are accepted for examination for the purposes of immigration in the receiving State.[21] If a person is found to be inadmissible,[22] the carrier is then responsible for taking him or her back to their State of origin or to another State that will accept them.[23] It is expressly provided that a carrier is not to be fined in the event that a passenger is found to be inadmissible 'unless there is evidence to suggest that the carrier was negligent in taking precautions to the end that passengers complied with the documentary requirements for entry into the receiving State'.[24] Any fines or penalties may be mitigated where the carrier has cooperated with State authorities to the satisfaction of those authorities,[25] which is consistent in any event with the imposition of a due diligence standard.

The *Protocol to Prevent, Suppress and Punish Trafficking in Persons, Especially Women and Children, Supplementing the United Nations Convention against Transnational Organized Crime* (2000) ('Trafficking Protocol') has also endorsed the use of carrier sanctions in relation to trafficking offences. Article 11 provides in part:

---

16 Ibid. 130.   17 Fullerton, above n. 13, 96.

18 *Convention on International Civil Aviation*, opened for signature 7 December 1944, 15 UNTS 295 (entered into force 4 April 1947).

19 R. Abeyratne, 'Air Carrier Liability and State Responsibility for the Carriage of Inadmissible Persons and Refugees' (1998) 10 *International Journal of Refugee Law* 675, 677.

20 Feller, above n. 14, 55.

21 *Convention on International Civil Aviation*, above n. 18, Annex 9, Ch 3, Sec E, Standard 3.38.1.

22 An 'inadmissible person' is defined as one 'who is or will be refused admission to a State by its authorities'. Ibid. Annex 9, Ch 1.

23 Ibid. Annex 9, Ch 3, Sec E, Standard 3.39.   24 Ibid. Standard 3.40.1.   25 Ibid. Standard 3.40.3.

2 Each State Party shall adopt legislative or other appropriate measures to prevent, to the extent possible, means of transport operated by commercial carriers from being used in the commission of [trafficking] offences . . .

3 Where appropriate, and without prejudice to applicable international conventions, such measures shall include establishing the obligation of commercial carriers, including any transportation company or the owner or operator of any means of transport, to ascertain that all passengers are in possession of the travel documents required for entry into the receiving State.

4 Each State Party shall take the necessary measures, in accordance with its domestic law, to provide for sanctions in cases of violation of the obligation set forth in paragraph 3 of this article.[26]

Similar provisions are made, in relation to smuggling, by the allied *Protocol against the Smuggling of Migrants by Land, Sea and Air, Supplementing the United Nations Convention against Transnational Organized Crime* (2000) ('Smuggling Protocol').[27]

Carrier sanctions have been criticised in line with other extraterritorial interception measures because they make no distinction between asylum seekers and other irregular migrants. Moreover, carrier sanctions impose documentary requirements on refugees, who are not otherwise expected to be in possession of full documentation in view of the plight they face in fleeing persecution. Where an airline prevents the passage of an irregular migrant in order to avoid carrier sanctions, airline officials or border security guards are required to make immediate and discretionary decisions on refugee claims, without affording the claimant due process. Some commentators have thus queried whether States, rather than airlines, should take responsibility for issues relating to the security of passports and admission into their States.[28] The importance of national security, as well as the State responsibility that may arise for violations of international legal obligations, should militate in favour of States assuming greater responsibility over entry into their territory rather than relying on private actors.

10.4.   INTERDICTION AT SEA

In light of the difficulties that irregular migrants may face in seeking to enter a State because of extraterritorial interception measures, clandestine migration by sea may be preferred to avoid scrutiny of entry documentation prior to departing. A State's powers to regulate migration by sea depend in part on whether the vessel carrying the migrants is registered or 'flagged' to that State

---

26 *Protocol to Prevent, Suppress and Punish Trafficking in Persons, Especially Women and Children, Supplementing the United Nations Convention against Transnational Organized Crime*, opened for signature 15 November 2000, 2237 UNTS 319 (entered into force 25 December 2003).

27 *Protocol against the Smuggling of Migrants by Land, Sea and Air, Supplementing the United Nations Convention against Transnational Organized Crime*, opened for signature 15 November 2000, 2241 UNTS 507 (entered into force 28 January 2004) art. 11.

28 Abeyratne, above n. 19, 679; Amnesty International, 'No Flights to Safety: Carrier Sanctions, Airline Employees and the Rights of Refugees' (ACT 34/21/97, Amnesty International, 1997) 3.

(the flag State). They also depend on the maritime zone in which the vessel is located and, in particular, whether the State is a coastal State vis-à-vis the location of the vessel. The major maritime zones are illustrated in Figure 10.1 and are discussed below. Any action taken by a State must be consistent with the rights and duties of different States under the international regime of the law of the sea, established by the *United Nations Convention on the Law of the Sea* (1982) ('UNCLOS').[29]

10.4.1. Ports

When a vessel is in port, the general position is that the vessel is subject to the laws of the coastal State, while the flag State is responsible only in relation to matters considered 'internal' to the vessel. Coastal States are entitled to establish the conditions under which vessels may enter their ports, and are allowed to close their ports to particular vessels.[30] An exception to this level of coastal State control applies to vessels in distress, and this may be relevant in the context of rescuing

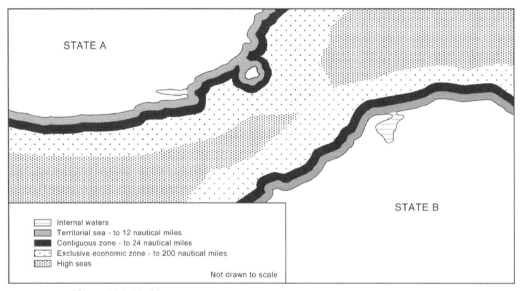

Figure 10.1 Maritime zones

29 *United Nations Convention on the Law of the Sea*, opened for signature 10 December 1982, 1833 UNTS 3 (entered into force 14 November 1994).
30 Louise De La Fayette, 'Access to Ports in International Law' (1996) 11 *International Journal of Marine and Coastal Law* 1, 30; A. Lowe, 'The Right of Entry into Maritime Ports in International Law' (1977) 14 *San Diego Law Review* 597, 607.

migrants at sea. Vessels in distress are entitled to enter a port and are not necessarily bound by the laws of the coastal State in these circumstances.[31]

10.4.2. Territorial sea

The waters immediately adjacent to the coastline are a coastal State's territorial sea.
While the territorial sea is subject to the sovereignty of the coastal State, any vessel
simply traversing these waters has a right of innocent passage. This right is lost if a
vessel undertakes an activity seen as prejudicial to the peace, good order and
security of the coastal State (arts. 18–19). The loading or unloading of a person
contrary to the immigration laws of a coastal State is an activity that renders
passage non-innocent (art. 19(2)), and the coastal State may then take action to
prevent such passage (art. 25). The precise parameters of action have not been fully
articulated under the law of the sea, but may include preventing passage or
requiring the vessel to leave the territorial sea.[32]

A coastal State is able to exercise criminal jurisdiction against a foreign flagged
vessel in its territorial sea if the transport of irregular migrants is a crime the
consequences of which extend to the coastal State, or is a crime that disturbs the
peace of the coastal State or the good order of the territorial sea (art. 27). People
smuggling is likely to fall within these categories because irregular migration has
consequences within the destination State, and trafficked persons, by definition,
are exploited upon arrival in the destination State. It could also be argued that, even
if the vessel is merely transiting the territorial sea, the transport of irregular
migrants may disturb the good order of the territorial sea if the vessel is unseaworthy or if the conditions of transport may precipitate a rescue of those on board.
The coastal State has regulatory and enforcement powers in this regard. The
exercise of enforcement jurisdiction by the coastal State may extend in these
circumstances to arresting the vessel and its crew and pursuing criminal proceedings under the national law of the coastal State.

10.4.3. Contiguous zone

The infringement of immigration laws also provides the coastal State with authority to exercise the necessary control to prevent and punish the infringement of
those laws within the contiguous zone (art. 33). The contiguous zone is a band of
sea that extends beyond the territorial sea, but no more than twenty-four nautical
miles from the maritime baseline of a State, which is normally the low-water mark
along the coast (art. 5). Although a coastal State has rights of control over fiscal,
immigration, sanitary and customs matters within this area, it does not exercise

---

31 De La Fayette, ibid. 1.
32 Robin Churchill and Alan Lowe, *The Law of the Sea* (Manchester University Press, 3rd edn, 1999) 99;
Donald Rothwell and Tim Stephens, *The International Law of the Sea* (Hart Publishing, 2010) 218.

sovereignty over the contiguous zone. Hence, a vessel only arrives in the territory of a State once it enters the territorial sea.

10.4.4.   Exclusive economic zone and high seas

Beyond the contiguous zone, the coastal State has no regulatory or enforcement powers over immigration in its exclusive economic zone (EEZ). Instead, freedom of navigation applies in this maritime zone, as well as on the high seas that lie beyond the EEZ. The lawful bases for a coastal State to interdict a vessel beyond its territorial sea and contiguous zone are much more limited, given the legal recognition of freedom of navigation and associated rights both in the EEZ and on the high seas. In particular, in these zones, no State may exercise authority over a vessel flagged to another State, apart from certain limited situations recognised under treaty (art. 110). For example, States have relied on the principles associated with rescue at sea as a means of interdicting vessels that could not otherwise lawfully be visited outside a State's territorial sea.[33] If the coastal State reasonably suspects a vessel to be engaged in migrant smuggling, then it may have certain rights of interdiction against that vessel pursuant to the Smuggling Protocol. In the absence of such treaty rights, the coastal State must rely on the flag State of the vessel to take appropriate action, or it must secure the consent of the flag State to take steps against the foreign vessel.

In practice, States have sought to intercept vessels suspected of transporting irregular migrants while on the high seas irrespective of the potential violation of flag State rights. The United States Coast Guard has intercepted vessels during mass migrations from Cuba and Haiti on the basis of bilateral agreements with those States or obligations to rescue migrants in distress. It has also confronted irregular migration of Chinese and Dominican migrants.[34] Italy, Spain and Malta, as destination States for irregular migrants, have been engaged in interdictions through the European Union's Frontex operation. Frontex is 'a specialised and independent body tasked to coordinate the operational cooperation between [European Union] Member States in the field of border security'.[35] Interception of vessels carrying irregular migrants on the high seas appears to be incompatible with the *Convention relating to the Status of Refugees* (1951) ('Refugee Convention').[36] Yet it has been observed that the increasing practice among destination States of repelling such vessels, without drawing protest from flag States or other States parties to the treaties, might be leading to the formation of a new rule of international law that allows interdiction on the high seas to prevent irregular migration.[37]

33 See Miltner, above n. 2, 111–12.
34 Douglas Guilfoyle, *Shipping Interdiction and the Law of the Sea* (Cambridge University Press, 2009) 187–97.
35 European Union, Frontex (www.frontex.europa.eu).
36 *Convention relating to the Status of Refugees*, opened for signature 28 July 1951, 189 UNTS 150 (entered into force 22 April 1954).
37 Guilfoyle, above n. 34, 225–6.

10.5. STOWAWAYS

The issue of stowaways is not confined to migration by sea, but also arises in air transport and rail and truck haulage. For air and land transport, issues relating to carrier sanctions for irregular migrants come to the fore, as discussed above. In the maritime context, the issue of stowaways has resulted in a series of legal developments under international law, as well as responses at an operational level by the affected shipping industries. While the number of stowaway incidents, and the number of stowaways, declined between 1999 and 2005, numbers have increased since then, although there is no consistent trend. In 2009, 1,070 stowaways were reported to the International Maritime Organization ('IMO').[38]

The first significant intergovernmental effort to regulate the treatment of stowaways has proven to be one of the least successful. The *International Convention relating to Stowaways* (1957) ('1957 Convention') has failed to enter into force and faces no prospect of doing so.[39] In essence, the 1957 Convention required a stowaway to be delivered to the next port of a contracting State visited by the vessel, and it set out a scheme for determining where a stowaway should then be sent. States have been unwilling to accept this responsibility. The 1957 Convention further established the financial liability of the shipowner for the costs associated with maintaining and returning the stowaway.

The allocation of responsibilities for stowaways was revisited by IMO in its 1997 *Guidelines on the Allocation of Responsibilities to Seek the Successful Resolution of Stowaway Cases* ('IMO 1997 Guidelines').[40] These Guidelines provide greater clarity about the steps to be followed and the duties of the relevant actors – masters; shipowners; the States of embarkation, disembarkation and nationality of the stowaway; and the flag State – and they underline the need for cooperation among them all. Key responsibilities are accorded to port States, although, as with the failed 1957 Convention, the primary financial burden remains with the shipowner.[41] A further feature of the IMO 1997 Guidelines is the acknowledgement of the place of the stowaway within the broader context of international migration law – a stowaway may be considered under national law as any other irregular entrant, and a stowaway who is an asylum seeker should be accorded appropriate treatment consistent with refugee law.[42]

In the allocation of responsibilities under the IMO 1997 Guidelines, the master has initial duties to ascertain information regarding the stowaway (including nationality and place of embarkation), and to notify the shipowner and appropriate

---

38 See International Maritime Organization, 'Reports on Stowaway Incidents: Annual Statistics for the Year 2009' (Doc FAL.2/Circ. 117, IMO, 2010).
39 *International Convention relating to Stowaways*, opened for signature 10 October 1957 (not yet in force).
40 International Maritime Organization, *Guidelines on the Allocation of Responsibilities to Seek the Successful Resolution of Stowaway Cases*, Res A.871(20), (adopted on 27 November 1997).
41 This aspect is less explicit in the IMO 1997 Guidelines than in the 1957 Convention.
42 IMO 1997 Guidelines, above n. 40, Principles 4.1, 4.2.

authorities of the port of embarkation, next port of call and the flag State.[43] Masters are not to alter their journey for the purposes of disembarking the stowaway unless repatriation has been properly arranged or unless there are extenuating security or compassionate reasons.[44]

The port of disembarkation, which should be the State of the first scheduled port of call following the discovery of the stowaway, is to accept the stowaway for examination in accordance with its national laws and to consider allowing disembarkation. The port of disembarkation is to give directions to remove the stowaway to the 'port of embarkation, country of nationality/citizenship or to some other country to which lawful directions may be made, in cooperation with the shipowner and his nominated representative'.[45] The port of embarkation is then to accept any returned stowaway who has nationality or right of residence in that State. Where a stowaway is discovered either before a ship sets sail or before it leaves the territorial sea, the embarkation State may apprehend and detain the stowaway pursuant to its national laws, and neither charges for detention or removal, nor any penalty, are to be imposed on the shipowner.[46] In light of this exception, ships sometimes hire specialised security companies to search the vessel for stowaways prior to their departure.

Financial responsibility otherwise largely rests with the carrier. Under national law, carriers may be held criminally liable for the entry of stowaways.[47] This approach is supported under the Smuggling Protocol (art. 6(c)), which requires States parties to criminalise the harbouring and concealing of irregular migrants. The imposition of carrier liability for stowaways results in the carrier being responsible for the costs of housing, feeding and guarding the stowaway; costs associated with medical treatment; costs of a translator to deal with immigration officials at the port of disembarkation where required; and, most substantially, the costs of transporting the stowaway to a particular destination. These costs are incurred in addition to any fines that may be imposed if a stowaway escapes ashore or if there is a failure to report the unauthorised landing of an irregular migrant. The financial burden imposed in this regard has sometimes resulted in brutal treatment of stowaways, such as throwing them overboard upon discovery or setting them adrift in small rafts.

Although formally non-binding, the IMO 1997 Guidelines have effectively been given a mandatory application through amendments to the *Convention on Facilitation of International Maritime Traffic* (1965) ('Facilitation Convention').[48] The Facilitation Convention contains security measures to prevent stowaways accessing ships, in addition to measures addressing the disembarkation of stowaways. In seeking to prevent stowaways, the amendments

---

43 Ibid. Principles 5.1.4, 5.2.1.   44 Ibid. Principle 5.1.5.   45 Ibid. Principle 5.3.5.   46 Ibid. Principle 5.4.
47 See, e.g., the Australian provisions: *Migration Act 1958* (Cth) s 230.
48 *Convention on Facilitation of International Maritime Traffic*, opened for signature 9 April 1965, 591 UNTS 265 (entered into force 5 March 1967), as amended 10 January 2002 (amendment entered into force 1 May 2003).

establish minimum shipboard security arrangements that must be followed when a vessel is calling at a stowaway-prone port. These measures include thorough searches prior to departure, locking or otherwise securing the means of access, keeping watch and maintaining adequate lighting at night, as well as tallying the boardings and disembarkations of the ship's crew and other authorised entrants.

The allocation of responsibility to the flag State is not significant under the IMO 1997 Guidelines, which is unusual in the law of the sea given the emphasis that is usually placed on the authority of the flag State over its vessels. The flag State's role is a supportive one, such as assisting the master or shipowner and making representations to relevant authorities for the removal of the stowaway.[49] Under the amendments to the Facilitation Convention, flag States are under a duty to require masters of their vessels to take appropriate steps to ensure the wellbeing and safety of any stowaway on board. These responsibilities again reflect the obligations of States towards asylum seekers, in circumstances where migration by sea is typically mediated by private industry.

10.6. HUMAN SMUGGLING AND TRAFFICKING BY SEA[50]

Irregular migrants sometimes seek the services of smugglers as a means of entering a State to allow their claim for asylum to be processed or to live there without authority. While human trafficking has different goals and criminal intent to people smuggling, the risks posed at sea are the same (see Chapter 9). People smuggling has been considered a maritime security threat by the United Nations Secretary-General in light of the frequent use of unseaworthy vessels, the inhumane conditions on board, the risk of the smugglers abandoning their vessel at sea, and the challenges faced by those required to conduct rescues at sea.[51] Security concerns also arise in relation to the identity of those arriving and their possible criminal motives.

An initial response to the increasing problem of migrant smuggling came from IMO in 1998, which adopted interim, non-binding measures for combating unsafe practices associated with the trafficking or transport of migrants by sea.[52] These cover both preventive measures and steps that States should take to suppress people smuggling and trafficking. Among the recommendations are that States ensure compliance with the *International Convention for the Safety of Life at Sea* (1974)

49 IMO 1997 Guidelines, above n. 40, Principle 5.6.
50 This section is based on material in Natalie Klein, *Maritime Security and the Law of the Sea* (Oxford University Press, 2011) 122–7.
51 United Nations General Assembly, 'Oceans and the Law of the Sea, Report of the Secretary-General' (UN Doc A/63/63, 10 March 2008) [89].
52 International Maritime Organization, *Interim Measures for Combating Unsafe Practices Associated with the Trafficking or Transport of Migrants by Sea*, IMO Doc MSC/Circ.896/Rev.1 (adopted 1998, revised 2001). IMO issued revised guidelines in 2001, but the core elements of the 1998 Circular, discussed here, were not altered.

('SOLAS');[53] that States collect and disseminate information on ships believed to be engaged in unsafe practices associated with trafficking or transporting migrants; that appropriate action be taken against those involved on the vessel; and that any such ship be prevented from engaging in unsafe practices and, if in port, from sailing.

In addition to these preventive measures, the IMO recommendations extended to possible measures and procedures for suppression. In this context, States could request, and those States requested should render, assistance in dealing with a ship of that State's nationality (or a stateless vessel) that is reasonably suspected of being engaged in unsafe practices associated with the trafficking or transport of migrants at sea. For foreign flagged vessels, Recommendation 12 allows for States to request authorisation from the flag State 'to take appropriate measures in regard to that ship'.

In 2000, the United Nations adopted a package of measures to combat transnational organised crime, including the Smuggling Protocol, which addresses the question of migrant smuggling at sea. Under the Smuggling Protocol, vessels potentially targeted in relation to migrant smuggling by sea encompass 'any type of water craft' except those subject to immunity, namely, warships or other vessels owned or operated by a government and used on non-commercial service (art. 3(d)). An initial obligation imposed on States parties is to 'cooperate to the fullest extent possible to prevent and suppress the smuggling of migrants by sea, in accordance with the international law of the sea' (art. 7). An important aspect of the Smuggling Protocol is the inclusion of a boarding provision in art. 8, which follows to some extent the recommendations in the IMO 1997 Guidelines.

Under art. 8, a State party that has reasonable grounds to suspect that a foreign flagged ship is engaged in migrant smuggling may request authorisation from the flag State to take appropriate measures, including boarding and searching the vessel, and, if evidence of migrant smuggling is found, may take 'measures with respect to the vessel and persons and cargo on board, as authorized by the flag State'. The flag State is to be promptly informed of the results of any measure taken. These steps may be taken against a vessel 'exercising freedom of navigation', hence in the EEZ or on the high seas.

Requirements imposed on the flag State to facilitate these measures include responding expeditiously to requests regarding information for claims of registration of a vessel and requests for authorisation to board. Consistent with traditional law of the sea principles, another State would not be able to act against a suspect vessel in the absence of authorisation from the flag State. The flag State and the requesting State are to agree to conditions for the authorisation to board the

---

53 *International Convention for the Safety of Life at Sea*, opened for signature 1 November 1974, 1184 UNTS 3 (entered into force 25 May 1980).

suspect vessel, including conditions as to responsibility and the extent of effective measures to be taken. Consistent with art. 110(3) of UNCLOS, if suspicions prove to be unfounded following the boarding of a vessel, then the vessel is to be compensated for any loss or damage that may have been sustained if the vessel did not commit any act justifying the measures taken.

The Smuggling Protocol includes a number of safeguards when measures are taken to board a suspect vessel exercising the freedom of navigation (art. 9). States must ensure the safety and humane treatment of persons on board; ensure that any measure taken is environmentally sound; take due account of the need not to endanger the security of the vessel or its cargo; and not to prejudice the commercial or legal interests of the flag State or any other interested State. The implementation of these principles and safeguards has been undertaken through cooperative political arrangements, such as bilateral agreements[54] and regional migration processes (see Chapter 14).

10.7. RESCUE OF PERSONS IN DISTRESS AT SEA

Irregular migration by sea raises the prospect of rescuing migrants in distress in the event that the vessel being used is unseaworthy or is abandoned at sea as part of the operation of people smugglers. As a result, a Rescue Coordination Centre may request a nearby vessel to undertake a rescue operation or may institute its own rescue operation. Alternatively, a passing ship may encounter the vessel carrying persons in distress and seek to render assistance.

The legal obligations arising in these scenarios are predominantly drawn from UNCLOS, SOLAS and the *International Convention on Maritime Search and Rescue* (1979) ('SAR Convention'),[55] as well as the more recent *Guidelines on the Treatment of Persons Rescued at Sea* adopted by IMO in 2004 ('IMO 2004 Guidelines').[56] Although international obligations associated with rescue at sea may be traced back to the sinking of the *Titanic* in 1912, current concerns relating to rescue at sea are largely associated with irregular migration rather than with accidents or the malfunction of vessels at sea.

The obligation to rescue those in distress at sea is a well-established rule of customary international law and is enshrined in treaty law as well.[57] Although

---

54 Efthymios Papastavridis, 'Interception of Human Beings on the High Seas: A Contemporary Analysis Under International Law' (2009) 36(2) *Syracuse Journal of International Law and Commerce* 145, 178–87.

55 *International Convention on Maritime Search and Rescue*, opened for signature 27 April 1979, 1405 UNTS 119 (entered into force 22 June 1985).

56 International Maritime Organization, *Guidelines on the Treatment of Persons Rescued at Sea*, IMO Doc MSC 78/26/Add.2, Annex 34 (adopted 20 May 2004).

57 *United Nations Convention on the Law of the Sea*, above n. 29, art. 98; *International Convention for the Safety of Life at Sea*, above n. 53, ch V, reg 10(a); *International Convention on Salvage*, opened for signature 28 April 1989, 1953 UNTS 165 (entered into force 23 December 1996). See also Mark Pallis, 'Obligations of States towards Asylum

queries arise as to whether the obligation to render assistance rests on States or shipmasters, a more critical issue is whether States have implemented the obligation to render assistance into their national law so that a binding and enforceable obligation is imposed on shipmasters who sail vessels flagged to or registered in that State.[58] A difficulty here is that the prevalent use of 'flags of convenience' may mean that some flag States have not taken the necessary steps to impose these obligations on the masters of their vessels.[59] Such a lapse is easily conceivable when account is taken of the financial loss that may be incurred by a merchant vessel that deviates from its journey to conduct a rescue, and is thereby delayed in completing its voyage.

At an operational level, States are obligated to establish search and rescue centres. This obligation is set forth in UNCLOS (art. 98), SOLAS (ch V, reg 15) and the SAR Convention (Annex, [2.1.1]).[60] The process is facilitated through use of the Global Maritime Distress and Safety System, which is used to alert search and rescue authorities and shipping in the vicinity of a vessel in distress so that a rescue effort may be coordinated. The adoption of an IMO Regulation on Long Range Identification and Tracking, as part of SOLAS, further provides a tracking service that may be utilised for rescue efforts.[61]

As to what assistance should be afforded, the SAR Convention defines rescue as retrieving persons in distress, seeing to their medical and other needs, and delivering them to a place of safety (Annex, [1.3.2]). No distinction should be made based on the nationality or condition of those who are being rescued. Masters are under an obligation to treat rescued individuals 'with humanity, within the capabilities and limitations of the ship'.[62] Clearly, this obligation, like the general obligation to render assistance, needs to be implemented in the national law of the flag State and enforced accordingly for this stricture to have meaningful application for irregular migrants rescued at sea.

One question that arises for rescues at sea is when the duty to render assistance has been fulfilled: is it enough for the persons to be delivered to a safe vessel, or is the duty complete only once the persons are disembarked? The standard maritime practice is to take those rescued to the next port of call and deliver them to their consular officials or national authorities. However, States have resisted this outcome to avoid the burden of having to assess irregular migrants and potentially return them to their State of nationality or a safe third State.[63] This problem came to

Seekers at Sea: Interactions and Conflicts between Legal Regimes' (2002) 14(2–3) *International Journal of Refugee Law* 329, 331–4; Arthur Severance, 'Duty to Render Assistance in the Satellite Age' (2006) 36(2) *California Western International Law Journal* 377, 379–81.

58 Richard Barnes, 'Refugee Law at Sea' (2004) 53(1) *International and Comparative Law Quarterly* 47, 50–1; Severance, above n. 57, 387.

59 A flag of convenience ship is one that flies the flag of a State other than the State of ownership. Ships are generally registered under flags of convenience to reduce operating costs or avoid the regulations of the owner's State.

60 The language of the SAR Convention is more onerous: States 'shall ensure', not merely 'undertake to ensure' (SOLAS Convention) or 'shall promote' (UNCLOS).

61 Klein, above n. 50, 229–34; Jessica Tauman, 'Rescued at Sea, but Nowhere to Go: The Cloudy Legal Waters of the Tampa Crisis' (2002) 11(2) *Pacific Rim Law and Policy Journal* 461, 471.

62 *International Convention for the Safety of Life at Sea*, above n. 53, reg 33–6.   63 Miltner, above n. 2, 89.

the fore during the 1980s with the increasing numbers of 'boat people' leaving Vietnam. It prompted the development of resettlement guarantee programmes, whereby developed States would agree to resettle refugees once the nearby coastal States had allowed disembarkation and undertaken temporary processing. It has been noted that the recommended approach of the United Nations High Commissioner for Refugees ('UNHCR') is 'for the coastal authorities to disembark the refugees and grant them access to UNHCR officials, but this is not always possible and in certain cases status determination interviews have been carried out on board the vessel'.[64]

States have not yet accepted the notion of a duty of disembarkation, whereby States would be required to allow a vessel carrying persons rescued at sea to disembark within their territory. The SAR Convention provides only that States 'should authorize ... immediate entry' subject to applicable national laws, rules and regulations (Annex, [3.1.2]). This lack of a definitive obligation of disembarkation has enabled States to resist the entry of vessels that have rescued migrants at sea, as was most clearly illustrated by Australia's actions in relation to the *Tampa* incident, described in Case Study 10.2.

In relation to disembarkation under SOLAS, the SAR Convention amendments and the IMO 2004 Guidelines, the primary role is accorded to the State responsible for the search and rescue region in which the vessel is rescued. This State has primary authority for ensuring coordination and cooperation among States parties to these treaties so as to alleviate the burden imposed on shipmasters.[65] Weight is accorded to the decisions of the master in that the owner, charterer or company operating the ship are not to prevent or restrict the decisions of the master in relation to the safety of life at sea.[66] Governments are to ensure that the masters providing assistance are released from their obligations with minimum further deviation from the ships' intended voyage.[67] In terms of timing, 'disembarkation [is] to be effected as soon as reasonably practicable'.[68] In this regard, the IMO 2004 Guidelines further provide that every effort is to be made by governments to minimise the time that survivors remain on board the assisting ship, and that masters should understand that the need to coordinate may result in unavoidable delays.[69] If these Guidelines had been adopted prior to the *Tampa* incident, they would still not have required Australia to accept those rescued, although they would have brought greater clarity to the rights and responsibilities of the various actors.

---

64 Pallis, above n. 57, 361.
65 This responsibility was reinforced in 2009: International Maritime Organization, 'Principles relating to Administrative Procedures for Disembarking Persons Rescued at Sea' (IMO Doc FAL.3/Circ.194 IMO, 22 January 2009) [2.1], [2.3].
66 *International Convention for the Safety of Life at Sea*, above n. 53, Amendments reg 34–1.
67 Ibid. reg 33–1–1; *International Convention on Maritime Search and Rescue*, above n. 55, Amendment [3.1.8].
68 *International Convention for the Safety of Life at Sea*, above n. 53, Amendments reg 33–1–1; *International Convention on Maritime Search and Rescue*, above n. 55, Amendment [3.1.8].
69 International Maritime Organization, above n. 56, [6.8].

CASE STUDY 10.2 The *Tampa* incident

On 26 August 2001, a Norwegian vessel, *MV Tampa*, responded to a request from Australian search and rescue authorities to assist a vessel in distress, the *Palapa 1*, seventy-five miles south of Christmas Island (an external territory of Australia located in the Indian Ocean between Indonesia and mainland Australia).[70] The sinking *Palapa 1* was an Indonesian-flagged vessel carrying 433 asylum seekers. Those on board were successfully transferred to the *MV Tampa* and the Norwegian captain initially diverted course to Indonesia. Following threats from some of the asylum seekers, the *MV Tampa* changed course for Christmas Island. Australia opposed this decision and the Norwegian vessel was threatened with people-smuggling charges if it offloaded rescued asylum seekers in Australia. Australia subsequently closed its territorial sea to the vessel. The *MV Tampa* ultimately entered the territorial sea in distress, in light of the scarcity of food and water on board, and the medical condition of those rescued. Australia's response was to send its Special Armed Services troops to board and take control of the vessel.

As a result of the *Tampa* incident, Australia initiated an array of legislative changes to respond to irregular migration, including the institution of what it referred to as the 'Pacific Solution'. This policy involved offshore processing of asylum seekers by Australian and UNHCR officials in Nauru and Papua New Guinea (Manus Island). The asylum seekers who disembarked from the *MV Tampa* were processed this way and the majority were ultimately determined to be refugees. The Federal Court of Australia ultimately endorsed Australia's actions as consistent with the Refugee Convention.[71] Australia also commenced Operation Relex, a military operation to intercept irregular migrant vessels and return them to Indonesia. Commentators have espoused different views as to whether Australia's legislative changes were violations of the Refugee Convention.[72]

The *Tampa* incident further raised issues under the international law of the sea,[73] particularly in relation to the rescue of those in distress at sea. Australia correctly fulfilled its responsibilities in responding to the distress signal of the *Palapa 1* and requesting a nearby vessel to go to its assistance. Equally, the Master of the *MV Tampa* fulfilled his responsibilities in rescuing those on board the *Palapa 1*. Yet it was unclear whether Australia had continuing responsibilities once those on board the *Palapa 1* were rescued. Although

---

70 For a factual account, see Mathew, above n. 12; Donald Rothwell, 'The Law of the Sea and the *MV Tampa* Incident: Reconciling Maritime Principles with Coastal State Sovereignty' (2002) 13(2) *Public Law Review* 118.

71 *Ruddock* v. *Vadarlis* (2001) 110 FCR 491.

72 Mathew and Crock have been critical: see Mathew, above n. 12; Mary Crock, 'In the Wake of the *Tampa*: Conflicting Visions of International Refugee Law in the Management of Refugee Flows' (2003) 12(1) *Pacific Rim Law and Policy Journal* 49. Heiser considered the measures to be largely consistent with international law: Anthony Heiser, 'Border Protection: UNCLOS and the *MV Tampa* Incident 2001' (2002) 16 *Australian and New Zealand Maritime Law Journal* 84.

73 Other questions concerned whether the *MV Tampa* was in distress and its rights in entering Australian territorial waters, as well as the right of Australia to board the *MV Tampa* forcibly when it entered Australia's territorial sea. See Rothwell, above n. 70; Barnes, above n. 58; Pallis, above n. 57.

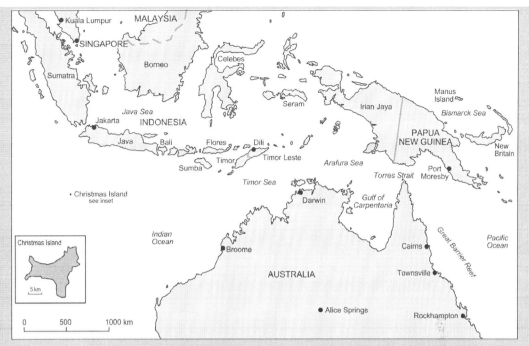

Map 10.1 Indonesia and Australia

Australia asserted that the question of disembarkation was one between Norway and Indonesia, there was no legal certainty about where the rescued migrants had to be, or could be, disembarked.[74]

In light of the legal uncertainties exposed by the *Tampa* incident, amendments to SOLAS and the SAR Convention were adopted in 2004, along with adoption of the IMO 2004 Guidelines.[75] These instruments seek to bring greater clarity to States and shipmasters in the exercise of their duties in rendering assistance or rescuing persons in distress at sea. While the Guidelines are not formally binding, States are still required under the treaty amendments to take them into account when assisting survivors rescued at sea.

74 Rothwell, above n. 70, 1201.
75 The Guidelines are intended to address important issues not covered by the treaty amendments: Miltner, above n. 2, 75 and 110.

The treaty amendments require that rescued persons be 'disembarked from the assisting ship and delivered to a place of safety'. The IMO 2004 Guidelines then indicate that a 'place of safety' is a location where rescue operations are considered terminate; where the survivors' safety of life is no longer threatened and their basic human needs can be met; and is one from which transportation arrangements can be made for their next or final destination.[76] Miltner has observed that the IMO 2004 Guidelines do not preclude the possibility of rescued persons being transferred to another vessel, and potentially remaining at sea for an indefinite period while arrangements for their disembarkation are formulated.[77] The Guidelines do, however, provide that the need to assess the status of the individuals concerned should not be used as a reason to unduly delay disembarkation. The implication from the IMO 2004 Guidelines was that screening should occur in the State of disembarkation.[78] Any ambiguity was removed in 2009 through principles adopted as a circular by IMO's Facilitation Committee.[79] These principles provide that screening and status assessment are to be carried out after disembarkation to a place of safety.

10.8. CONCLUSION

While the journey of regular migrants is relatively straightforward, irregular migrants often encounter a series of barriers put in place to prevent their movement from one State to another. These controls or interception measures may be encountered whether their migration is effected by land, air or sea. However, migration by sea has developed some distinct rules relating to stowaways, rescue at sea and migrant smuggling, in light of the jurisdictional rights that States exercise in different maritime zones.

Several key themes emerge when considering the international laws relating to the mode of migration. The first is the importance of a State's sovereign power to regulate the flow of people across its borders, particularly inwards. The exercise of this power has become increasingly complex as the concept of the border has become more fluid. Most international migrations do not commence literally at the territorial boundary of one State or end literally at the territorial boundary of another. Rather, journeys begin and end somewhere within the land or maritime territory of a State, which enhances the capacity of States to regulate international migration because of their jurisdiction over the territory or the vessel in question, be it ship or aircraft.

A second theme is the need to balance the human rights of migrants with the interests of States when the migration is effected through different modes of transport. The international regulatory regimes governing civil aviation and maritime transportation are primarily focussed on delimiting the rights and obligation of actors in respect of commercial activities that have frequent points of contact with

---

76 Ibid. [6.12].
77 Miltner, above n. 2, 110. Indeed, there is express provision for a 'place of safety' to be another vessel or unit at sea: International Maritime Organization, above n. 56, [6.14].
78 Miltner, above n. 2, 110.
79 International Maritime Organization, above n. 65. See Jasmine Coppens and Eduard Somers, 'Towards New Rules on Disembarkation of Persons Rescued at Sea?' (2010) 25(3) *International Journal of Marine and Coastal Law* 377, 393–8.

different States. In this regulatory environment, the human rights of the migrants who make those journeys are sometimes obscured. Nevertheless, humanitarian concerns do underpin many of the regimes, such as the obligation to rescue persons in distress at sea and to treat humanely persons who are smuggled at sea.

A third theme is the distribution of responsibility in regulating international migration. This diffusion of responsibility arises not only among the States involved in international migration by dint of the very nature of the process, but also between State and non-State actors.[80] The latter is seen in the important role of carriers, in the penalties for carrying stowaways or undocumented migrants, and in the obligations on masters and shipping companies to render assistance to persons in distress at sea. The involvement of private actors is notable given that migration control at its core is concerned with protecting the sovereignty of a State.[81]

A fourth theme is the challenge of fulfilling obligations towards refugees – particularly the obligation not to return them to the frontier of a territory where their life or freedom would be threatened on account of their race, religion, nationality, membership of a particular social group or political opinion – when those seeking asylum are irregular migrants travelling by air or sea. In relation to air travel, problems arise when States station immigration officers in foreign airports to screen out persons who might claim refugee status if they were ever to reach the territory of that State (see Case Study 10.1).

The difficulties are also acute in relation to migration by sea because of the special regimes applicable to stowaways, those rescued at sea, or those subject to smuggling or trafficking. While persons on board a ship are subject to the jurisdiction of the flag State, it has been noted that there is no obligation on the flag State to consider and grant asylum.[82] How the principle of *non-refoulement* is applied becomes intimately linked with the issues surrounding where the individuals on board may be disembarked. States may resist the disembarkation of irregular migrants precisely because they seek to avoid the costs associated with processing asylum claims and accommodating those found to be refugees. Although views are mixed, a refusal to allow entry is not necessarily equivalent to a violation of *non-refoulement*.[83] The critical question is the point at which that obligation applies in the maritime context. If the obligation does not adhere when an asylum seeker is on a vessel flagged to a particular State, does it apply when that vessel enters the territorial sea of another State? It is consistent with human rights principles to confine the application of the Refugee Convention to land territory.[84] Yet a State that refuses to allow disembarkation may argue that denying a vessel

---

80 Scholten and Minderhoud, above n. 15, 125.   81 Ibid. 126.   82 Barnes, above n. 58, 63.

83 See ibid. 64; Pallis, above n. 57, 344–5 and 349 (arguing there is authority for the view that the obligation of *non-refoulement* applies to States in international waters); and Miltner, above n. 2, 93–4 (suggesting States may deny entry unless the person would be exposed to a real risk of return).

84 Barnes, above n. 58, 68; Pallis, above n. 57, 343.

entry is not equivalent to sending a refugee back to the place where he or she faces persecution. Until States can agree on this issue, asylum seekers risk being denied the right to have their claims properly assessed and risk losing much-needed international protection.

As developed States endeavour to secure their borders, increasingly at the expense of humanitarian protection that should be afforded to irregular migrants, it can be expected that international laws regulating migration will evolve in favour of state sovereignty. The flexibility increasingly accorded to the notion of a border, and especially the ability of States to push their borders outward, further underscores efforts to deter irregular migration by sea and by air in favour of protecting national sovereignty (see Chapter 5). In addition, national laws pursued by States to implement international standards or initiate new nationalistic policies will become more complex, thereby entrenching and augmenting the barriers faced by irregular migrants.

KEY REFERENCES

Barnes, Richard, 'Refugee Law at Sea' (2004) 53(1) *International and Comparative Law Quarterly* 47

Blay, Sam, Burn, Jennifer and Keyzer, Patrick, 'Interception and Offshore Processing of Asylum Seekers: The International Law Dimensions' (2007) 9 *UTS Law Review* 7

Brouwer, Andrew and Kumin, Judith, 'Interception and Asylum: When Migration Control and Human Rights Collide' (2003) 21(4) *Refuge* 6

Coppens, Jasmine and Somers, Eduard, 'Towards New Rules on Disembarkation of Persons Rescued at Sea?' (2010) 25(3) *International Journal of Marine and Coastal Law* 377

Feller, Erika, 'Carrier Sanctions and International Law' (1989) 1 *International Journal of Refugee Law* 48

Mathew, Penelope, 'Australian Refugee Protection in the Wake of the *Tampa*' (2002) 96 *American Journal of International Law* 661

Miltner, Barbara, 'Irregular Maritime Migration: Refugee Protection Issues in Rescue and Interception' (2006) 30(1) *Fordham International Law Journal* 75

Papastavridis, Efthymios, 'Interception of Human Beings on the High Seas: A Contemporary Analysis under International Law' (2009) 36(2) *Syracuse Journal of International Law and Commerce* 145

Rothwell, Donald, 'The Law of the Sea and the *MV Tampa* Incident: Reconciling Maritime Principles with Coastal State Sovereignty' (2002) 13(2) *Public Law Review* 118

Schloenhardt, Andreas, *Migrant Smuggling: Illegal Migration and Organised Crime in Australia and the Asia Pacific Region* (Martinus Nijhoff, 2003)

KEY RESOURCES

Frontex: www.frontex.europa.eu

International Civil Aviation Organization: www.icao.int

International Maritime Organization: www.imo.org

Migrants at Sea, Niels W. Frenzen newsblog: http://migrantsatsea.wordpress.com

United Nations High Commissioner for Refugees: www.unhcr.org

United Nations Office on Drugs and Crime, Human Trafficking and Migrant Smuggling: www.unodc.org/unodc/en/human-trafficking/index.html

United States Coast Guard: www.uscg.mil

11 International labour migration

RYSZARD CHOLEWINSKI[1]

11.1. INTRODUCTION

Regulation of labour migration today remains largely a matter for States, which retain the sovereign prerogative to determine which non-nationals may enter and take up employment in their territory, and there is currently no global system for regulating international labour migration. Moreover, demographic projections for the next forty years suggest that international labour migration will become an increasingly important factor in sustaining the productivity of national economies.[2] Unlike free movement of goods and capital, however, the movement of labour across international borders involves human beings, with profound social implications for countries of origin and destination. While international trade law regulates to a certain degree the movement of persons in the context of service provision, for the time being this system is confined to the temporary movement of a limited category of skilled persons, such as managers, business visitors and specialists, and is hardly aligned with national immigration regulations (see Chapter 12).

The human dimension of international labour migration was captured as early as 1919 in the Preamble to the *Constitution of the International Labour Organization*, which considers exploitative labour conditions as a threat to world peace and calls for an improvement in these conditions, including 'protection of the interests of workers when employed in countries other than their own'.[3] The *Declaration concerning the Aims and Purposes of the International Labour Organisation (1944)* ('Declaration of Philadelphia'), annexed to the Constitution, also reaffirms

---

1 The ideas and observations in this chapter are the personal views of the author and do not necessarily reflect those of the ILO. This chapter draws on a number of publications by the author referred to in the key references, as well as a recent paper: Ryszard Cholewinski, 'Migration for Employment' (Paper presented at the Conference on International Migration Law, University of Groningen, 31 March–1 April 2011).

2 International Organization for Migration, 'World Migration 2008: Managing Labour Mobility in the Evolving Economy' (IOM, 2008) 36–8.

3 *Constitution of the International Labour Organization* (1919) (as amended), second recital.

the fundamental principle that 'labour is not a commodity'.[4] The founding documents of the International Labour Organization ('ILO') thus recognise that the protection of migrant workers is an imperative part of the response to international labour migration.

After outlining the importance of migrant workers in migrant stocks and flows in Section 11.2, this chapter considers the constitutional mandate of the ILO to protect migrant workers in advancing social justice, which is articulated in the ILO's Decent Work Agenda.[5] Section 11.3 focusses on the ILO's work in drawing up international minimum labour standards, including conventions and recommendations aimed at safeguarding the rights of migrant workers. The *ILO Multilateral Framework on Labour Migration* ('ILO Multilateral Framework'),[6] containing non-binding principles and guidelines for a rights-based approach to labour migration, is also discussed as an important 'soft law' instrument and policy tool. Section 11.4 considers the response to labour migration in the broader United Nations ('UN') context, most notably through the adoption of a core human rights instrument, the *International Convention on the Protection of the Rights of All Migrant Workers and Members of their Families* (1990) ('ICRMW').[7] Despite shortcomings in ratification and implementation of the instruments protecting migrant workers and their families, discussed in Section 11.5, an international rule of law framework exists for protecting the rights of migrant workers and is even more timely today in the present wave of globalisation and increasingly precarious employment.

Section 11.6 considers legal developments taking place in the regions. Regulation of labour migration at the regional level is evident in moves to establish regimes for the free movement of workers, as well as in common policies to regulate the conditions of admission and residence of non-nationals from outside these regions with regard to their employment. The European Union ('EU') is the most advanced regime in this respect, but significant developments have taken place in other regions characterised by nascent economic integration arrangements, supported in some instances by human rights frameworks.

Section 11.7 considers the role of 'soft law' or non-binding standards and related policy developments concerning international labour migration, of which the ILO Multilateral Framework is one significant manifestation. The admission of foreign nationals, including for the purpose of employment, remains close to the heart of sovereignty in many States, with the result that governments increasingly prefer to discuss the subject in intergovernmental fora on migration outside the ILO and the UN. These discussions, addressed in Section 11.8, are taking place at global and

---

4 *Declaration concerning the Aims and Purposes of the International Labour Organisation* (Declaration of Philadelphia) (1944) XXVI(1) *International Labour Office Official Bulletin* 1 [I(a)].

5 *ILO Declaration on Social Justice for a Fair Globalization*, adopted by the Conference at its 97th sess, Geneva (10 June 2008) Pt I.A, I.B.

6 International Labour Organization, *Multilateral Framework on Labour Migration: Non-Binding Principles and Guidelines for a Rights-Based Approach to Labour Migration* (ILO, 2006).

7 *International Convention on the Protection of the Rights of All Migrant Workers and Members of their Families*, opened for signature 18 December 1990, 2220 UNTS 3 (entered into force 1 July 2003).

regional levels, with a view to exchanging information and 'best practices', with little or no intention of agreeing any normative content.

11.2.   THE IMPORTANCE OF MIGRANT WORKERS IN MIGRANT STOCKS AND FLOWS

The Population Division of the United Nations Department of Economic and Social Affairs estimates that there were 214 million persons (3 per cent of the world's population) living outside their States of birth or nationality in 2010, with women comprising nearly half this population.[8] A great part of this migration is bound up with the world of work. The ILO estimates that 105 million of the 214 million international migrants in 2010 were economically active.[9] This global estimate does not capture all migrant workers because it counts only those persons who have been in the destination country for one year or more, thus excluding temporary forms of employment, such as seasonal work. In some European States, the proportion of the labour force that is foreign-born is even higher: over 12 per cent in the United Kingdom, 16 per cent in Austria, 18 per cent in Spain, 20 per cent in Ireland and 46 per cent in Luxembourg.[10]

International migration for employment is not only driven by demand for labour due to demographic changes, such as ageing populations and declining workforces in many destination countries, but is also an integral part of the globalisation process, which is profoundly reshaping the world of work.[11] Readily available migrant labour is an important response to these transformations:

In the economic realm, migrant labour has become a key feature in meeting economic, labour market and productivity challenges in a globalized economy. Migration today serves as an instrument to adjust the skills, age and sectoral composition of national and regional labour markets. Migration provides responses to fast-changing needs for skills and personnel resulting from technological advances, changes in market conditions and industrial transformations.[12]

These developments should be viewed in the context of increasing migration pressures on the 'supply side' in countries of origin, where employment opportunities are diminishing and economic survival is threatened due to reduced domestic industrial and agricultural production in the face of cheap trade imports. On the

---

8 United Nations Department of Economic and Social Affairs, 'Trends in International Migrant Stock: The 2008 Revision' (POP/DB/MIG/Stock/Rev.2008, United Nations, 2009).

9 International Labour Organization, 'International Labour Migration: A Rights-Based Approach' (ILO, 2010).

10 Organisation for Economic Co-operation and Development, 'International Migration Outlook: SOPEMI 2010' (OECD, 2010) 352 (Table A.2.2).

11 *ILO Declaration on Social Justice for a Fair Globalization*, above n. 5, first recital.

12 Patrick Taran, 'Clashing Worlds: Imperative for a Rights-Based Approach to Labour Migration in the Age of Globalization' in Vincent Chetail (ed.), *Globalization, Migration and Human Rights: International Law under Review, Volume II* (Bruylant, 2007) 403, 405.

'demand side', growing competition for specialists in expanding service sectors in many industrialised States is resulting in more skilled labour migration, while the drive to achieve economic competitiveness through high productivity generates a continuous need for cheap and low-skilled migrant workers to undertake 3-D jobs (dirty, dangerous and demeaning) that are shunned by the native population.[13]

These global forces mean that international labour migration is likely to remain high on national, regional and international political agendas, even in the wake of weaknesses in the global economy. The legal challenges that flow from this are threefold – how best: to regulate migration for employment in a testing economic climate (if regulation is a feasible goal), to mitigate the inherent vulnerabilities of migrant workers and their families in the migration process, and to ensure their equitable and dignified treatment.

11.3. THE ROLE OF THE INTERNATIONAL LABOUR ORGANIZATION

As observed above, the ILO is constitutionally mandated to protect 'the interests of workers when employed in countries other than their own'. In addition to the social justice rationale for this protection,[14] international rules in this area were also needed to counteract any economic and competitive advantages that might result from governments maltreating their workforce.[15] This justification continues to resonate today in light of the economic, employment, social and development challenges raised by globalisation, and the aftermath of the 2008 global financial crisis.

11.3.1. Fundamental rights conventions

The ILO has identified eight conventions as fundamental to the rights of human beings at work, regardless of the level of development of individual member States (see Box 11.1). These rights are considered 'a precondition for all the others in that they provide a necessary framework from which to strive freely for the improvement of individual and collective conditions of work'.[16] The special importance of the fundamental rights conventions is recognised by the ILO's *Declaration on Fundamental Principles and Rights at Work* (1998).[17] The Declaration states that all ILO Members, including those that have not ratified the instruments in question, have an obligation by virtue of their membership in the organisation 'to respect, to promote and to realise in good faith and in accordance with the Constitution, the principles concerning the fundamental rights which are the subject of those conventions'. While the specific instruments relating to

---

13 Ibid. 406–7.   14 Declaration of Philadelphia, above n. 4, [II(a)].
15 Virginia Leary, *International Labour Conventions and National Law: The Effectiveness of the Automatic Incorporation of Treaties in National Legal Systems* (Martinus Nijhoff, 1982) 6.
16 International Labour Office, *The International Labour Organization's Fundamental Conventions* (ILO, 2002) 7.
17 *ILO Declaration on Fundamental Principles and Rights at Work*, adopted by the International Labour Conference, 86th sess (18 June 1998).

BOX 11.1 ILO fundamental rights conventions

Forced labour

- *Forced Labour Convention* (1930) (ILO Convention No 29)
- *Abolition of Forced Labour Convention* (1957) (ILO Convention No 105)

Child labour

- *Minimum Age Convention* (1973) (ILO Convention No 138)
- *Worst Forms of Child Labour Convention* (1999) (ILO Convention No 182)

Trade union rights

- *Freedom of Association and Protection of the Right to Organise Convention* (1948) (ILO Convention No 87)
- *Right to Organise and Collective Bargaining Convention* (1949) (ILO Convention No 98)

Equality and non-discrimination in employment and occupation

- *Equal Remuneration Convention* (1951) (ILO Convention No 100)
- *Discrimination (Employment and Occupation) Convention* (1958) (ILO Convention No 111)

migrant workers are not considered as ILO fundamental rights conventions, the Declaration underscores the need to devote 'special attention to the problems of persons with special social needs, particularly the unemployed and migrant workers'. Moreover, all international labour standards apply to all workers, irrespective of their nationality or immigration status, unless otherwise stated.

11.3.2. Specific conventions protecting migrant workers

The two legally binding ILO instruments specifically protecting migrant workers are the *Migration for Employment Convention (Revised)* (1949) ('ILO Convention No 97') and the *Convention concerning Migrations in Abusive Conditions and the Promotion of Equality of Opportunity and Treatment of Migrant Workers* (1975) ('ILO Convention No 143').[18] Both are supported by non-binding Recommendations.[19] These conventions are concerned not only with the protection of migrant workers while in the country of employment, but with the whole labour migration process from departure to return.

One principal objective of ILO Convention No 97 is to outline the conditions governing the orderly recruitment of migrant workers from States with labour surpluses to States with labour shortages, which is reflected in a number of its provisions (e.g., arts. 2–4) as well as the Annexes. While the State-organised context of fulfilling this objective may no longer be as relevant to labour migration, which is

18 *Convention concerning Migration for Employment (Revised)* (ILO Convention No 97), opened for signature 1 July 1949 (entered into force 22 January 1952); *Convention concerning Migrations in Abusive Conditions and the Promotion of Equality of Opportunity and Treatment of Migrant Workers* (ILO Convention No 143), opened for signature 24 June 1975 (entered into force 9 December 1978).

19 *Migration for Employment Recommendation (Revised)* (ILO No R86) (1 July 1949); *Recommendation concerning Migrant Workers* (ILO No R151) (28 June 1975).

frequently organised by private intermediaries,[20] a number of States seek to retain an element of control by actively managing the flow of migrant workers between them. This is evident in the proliferation of bilateral labour agreements between countries of origin and destination in the 1990s, as borders in Central and Eastern Europe began to open up.[21] This development ensures the continued practical relevance of the standards set out in ILO Convention No 97 and its accompanying Recommendation. The latter contains a 'Model Agreement on Temporary and Permanent Migration for Employment', which has been used by many governments as a blueprint for concluding their own bilateral labour migration agreements (see Case Study 11.1). Another important objective of ILO Convention No 97 is to secure, for lawfully resident migrants, equal treatment with nationals in respect of working conditions, trade union membership and enjoyment of the benefits of collective bargaining, accommodation, social security, employment taxes and legal proceedings relating to matters outlined in the Convention (art. 6).

ILO Convention No 143 is broader in personal and material scope. It was discussed and adopted in the period following the stop on immigration to Western Europe after the oil crisis in the early 1970s. At this time, increasing irregular migration – particularly the smuggling of migrants and trafficking of persons for the purpose of exploitative or forced labour – was attracting the attention of the international community,[22] as it continues to do today. ILO Convention No 143 therefore devotes its first part to the phenomenon of irregular migration for employment and the measures for inter-State cooperation considered necessary to prevent and eliminate the exploitation to which such migration gives rise. In keeping with the ILO's ethical prerogative of social justice and protecting all persons in their working environment, art. 1 imposes an obligation on States parties 'to respect the basic human rights of *all* migrant workers', thus confirming its applicability to migrant workers in an irregular situation. The ILO Committee of Experts on the Application of Conventions and Recommendations ('ILO Committee of Experts') views this provision as applying both to civil and political rights and to economic and social rights.[23] Moreover, art. 9(1) of ILO Convention No 143 explicitly states that migrant workers in an irregular situation are entitled to equal treatment in respect of 'rights arising out of past employment as regards remuneration, social security and other benefits'. On the other hand, Part II of the Convention covers only lawfully resident migrant workers and their families and requires States parties to declare and pursue a national policy to promote and guarantee equality of opportunity and treatment, and thus assisting in their integration in host societies.

---

20 International Labour Conference, *General Survey on the Reports on the Migration for Employment Convention (Revised) (No. 97), and Recommendation (Revised) (No. 86), 1949, and the Migrant Workers (Supplementary Provisions) Convention (No.143), and Recommendation (No. 151), 1975*, International Labour Conference (87th sess, Report III (1b) 1999) ('General Survey 1999'), [657].

21 Organisation for Economic Co-operation and Development, *Migration for Employment: Bilateral Agreements at a Crossroads* (OECD, 2004) 12.

22 Roger Böhning, *A Brief Account of the ILO and Policies on International Migration* (International Institute for Labour Studies, 2008) 20.

23 General Survey 1999, above n. 20, [96].

CASE STUDY 11.1 Bilateral labour migration agreements[24]

A 'bilateral labour migration agreement' is an umbrella term referring to a variety of arrangements that facilitate labour mobility between two States, often in specific employment sectors of the labour market and on a temporary basis. These arrangements may be found in a legally binding treaty, in less formal Memoranda of Understanding ('MOUs'), or in other forms of cooperation between administrations in the States concerned. Examples of formal instruments include the bilateral labour migration agreements concluded by Spain with Colombia, Ecuador and the Dominican Republic, or the agreement on circular migration between France and Mauritius. Examples of MOUs include those that Canada has concluded with Mexico or the Caribbean States, facilitating the movement of workers from those countries into the Canadian Seasonal Agricultural Worker Program. There are also a series of MOUs between the Gulf States and South and Southeast Asian countries.

A comprehensive bilateral labour migration agreement may contain provisions relating to the following elements: identification of the competent government authority; exchange of information; notification of job opportunities; pre-selection and final selection of candidates; medical examination; entry visas; residence and work permits; transportation; employment contracts; conditions of employment; dispute settlement; trade union rights; social security; accommodation; family reunification; activities of social and religious associations; remittances; establishment of a joint commission to monitor the implementation of the agreement; and the applicable law and place of jurisdiction.[25]

In practice, most bilateral agreements do not regulate all of these areas, and some elements – for example, social security – are subject to separate arrangements.

Implementation is central. Some agreements are only framework documents and require further operational measures for their implementation. In its 2004 study, the Organisation for Economic Co-operation and Development observed that many bilateral labour migration agreements had not entered into force, had not commenced or involved only small quotas of migrant workers.[26] This is because the rationale for engaging in bilateral cooperation may have less to do with matching labour demand and supply than with other economic, social or political considerations.

While bilateral agreements can play an important role in ensuring that labour migration between two States takes place in a lawful and regulated manner, they can only afford adequate protection to migrant workers if their provisions (and laws in the States concerned) meet the minimum norms established by international labour standards and human rights law.

24 Some information in this case study is drawn from Sophie Nonnenmacher, 'Achieving Best Outcomes from Global, Regional and Bilateral Cooperation' in International Organization for Migration, *World Migration 2008: Managing Labour Mobility in the Evolving Economy* (IOM, 2008), 372–83.

25 Eduardo Geronimi, 'Acuerdos Bilaterales de Migración de Mano de Obra: Modo de Empleo' (International Migration Paper No 65, International Labour Office, 2004) 23–6.

26 Organisation for Economic Co-operation and Development, above n. 21, 221–46.

Moreover, a number of destination countries prefer unilateral arrangements effected through their national migration laws and policies, which are open to all comers provided the admission criteria are met. Such arrangements, on paper at least, do not necessarily discriminate in favour of foreign nationals from States with which there may be strong historical, cultural, trading or post-colonial ties, or with which readmission agreements have been concluded.

A particularly liberal provision in ILO Convention No 143 is art. 14(a), which provides for the right of geographic mobility and free choice of employment. The provision stipulates that States parties may restrict free choice of employment for lawfully resident migrant workers for no more than two years, or until completion of the first employment contract if this is shorter in duration. The progressive nature of some articles in ILO Convention No 143, in contrast to the ICRMW discussed below, may be explained in part by the unique tripartite structure of the ILO, where governments, worker organisations and employer organisations participate formally in discussing international labour standards adopted by the annual International Labour Conferences and in the decision making of the ILO's executive organ, the Governing Body.

It has been difficult for some States to accept legally binding international obligations for the protection of migrant workers. While fifty States had ratified ILO Convention No 97 by late 2011, ILO Convention No 143 had received only twenty-three ratifications. Since 2000, eight States have ratified the first instrument, and six the second, including significant countries of origin, such as Albania, Armenia, Kyrgyzstan, Philippines and Tajikistan. Clearly, some of the more progressive provisions identified above contrast starkly with the position in national law and practice in a number of States, and thus constitute considerable obstacles to the acceptance of these Conventions.[27] This low rate of ratifications may also be due in part to the inability of States parties to make reservations to particular provisions in ILO Conventions,[28] even though it is possible to ratify parts of ILO instruments selectively, as is the case under art. 16 of ILO Convention No 143.[29]

Nonetheless, it would be incorrect to conclude that the adoption of international labour standards relating specifically to migrant workers has had little or no impact in practice. First, while relatively few States have ratified the applicable instruments, the States that have done so encompass a diverse range of countries in all parts of the world and include a good mix of origin and destination countries (which is not the case with the ICRMW). Second, Conventions No 97 and No 143 provided inspiration for the adoption of the ICRMW, and some of their provisions still represent the highest level of protection afforded migrant workers at the

27 Ibid. [643].
28 International Labour Organization, *Rules of the Game: A Brief Introduction to International Labour Standards* (ILO, 2009) 18.
29 This facility is rarely used. In late 2011, only Albania had declared that it excluded Part II.

international level. Third, ILO standards have made a broad impact on national law in ILO member States, not merely in States that have ratified the two conventions.[30] They are also seen as influencing the development of regional standards – including the equal treatment provisions in EU free movement law, which draw from art. 6 of ILO Convention No 97.[31]

With regard to ratifying States, which are required to report to the ILO supervisory system on the implementation of Conventions No 97 and No 143, the Committee of Experts plays an important role in urging States parties to re-examine their national law and practice in light of the principles in these instruments. For example, in its report to the 2011 International Labour Conference, the Committee expressed its concerns to the French Government about the 'major problems [that] continue to exist with respect to integration of the immigrant population in French society, including a climate of suspicion and negativity, as well as widespread discrimination against migrant workers, having an impact on their general living conditions as well as their educational and employment opportunities'.[32] Such problems bring into focus several provisions of ILO Convention No 97, including art. 6(1)(a)(iii) on equality of treatment between lawfully resident migrant workers and nationals in respect of housing.

11.3.3. Other ILO instruments

Conventions No 97 and No 143 are not the only ILO instruments specifically addressing the protection of migrant workers and their families. Other conventions and recommendations contain specific provisions on migrants, and are complemented by instruments of general application that are also relevant to the protection of migrant workers.

ILO social security instruments are especially relevant in ensuring equal treatment between migrant workers and nationals in respect of access to social security, as well as maintenance of acquired rights (see Box 11.2). In addition to the social security instruments, the *Convention concerning Private Employment Agencies* (1997) ('ILO Convention No 181') aims to regulate the recruitment process in the private sector, where abuse and exploitation of migrant workers often begins.[33] This instrument espouses the important principle that private employment agencies should not charge fees to workers unless there are

---

30 See General Survey 1999, above n. 20, [646]–[647].

31 Kees Groenendijk, 'Equal Treatment of Workers under EU Law and Remedies against Violations by Employers' (2010) 1 *FMW: Online Journal on Free Movement of Workers within the European Union* 16, 17.

32 International Labour Office, 'Report of the Committee of Experts on the Application of Conventions and Recommendations: Report III (Part 1A), International Labour Conference, 100th sess, Geneva' (2011) 757.

33 *Convention concerning Minimum Standards of Social Security* (ILO Convention No 102), opened for signature 28 June 1952 (entered into force 27 April 1955). In late 2011 there were forty-seven States parties.

BOX 11.2 ILO social security standards: equal treatment of migrant workers

Equal treatment in the field of social security between nationals and non-nationals is enshrined in art. 68 of the ILO's flagship convention on social security, the *Convention concerning Minimum Standards of Social Security* (1952).[34]

The *Convention concerning Equality of Treatment of Nationals and Non-Nationals in Social Security* (1962) ('ILO Convention No 118'),[35] adopted ten years later, is designed to treat these issues in more detail. Article 3(1) stipulates that each State party ratifying the Convention is obliged 'to grant within its territory to the nationals of any other Member for which the Convention is in force equality of treatment under its legislation with its own nationals, both as regards coverage and as regards the right to benefits, in respect of every branch of social security for which it has accepted the obligations of the Convention'. Consequently, ILO Convention No 118 affords migrants equal treatment with nationals on the basis of reciprocity, although its provisions also apply to refugees or stateless persons without any condition of reciprocity.

The principle of equality of treatment between migrant workers and nationals in social security is also guaranteed in the specific ILO instruments protecting migrant workers, namely, ILO Convention No 97 (art. 6) and ILO Convention No 143 (Part II), and, importantly, is not made subject to reciprocity.

exceptional circumstances (art. 7).[36] It also imposes an obligation on States parties to consult with 'the most representative organizations of employers and workers' (art. 8) and then to:

adopt all necessary and appropriate measures, both within its jurisdiction and, where appropriate, in collaboration with other Members, to provide adequate protection for and prevent abuses of migrant workers recruited or placed in its territory by private employment agencies. These shall include laws or regulations which provide for penalties, including prohibition of those private employment agencies which engage in fraudulent practices and abuses.

However, in late 2011, ILO Convention No 181 had been ratified by only twenty-three States, sixteen of which were in Europe.

The thorny issue of domestic work, which remains unregulated by many national labour codes, despite the predominance of women migrants, was the subject of discussion by the International Labour Conference in 2010.[37] The Conference resolved to develop a comprehensive standard concerning decent work for domestic workers in the form of a Convention supplemented by a Recommendation. Subsequently, the International Labour Office prepared draft instruments, which

---

34 *Convention concerning Equality of Treatment of Nationals and Non-Nationals in Social Security* (ILO Convention No 118), opened for signature 28 June 1962 (entered into force 25 April 1964). In late 2011 there were thirty-seven States parties.

35 *Convention concerning Private Employment Agencies* (ILO Convention No 181), opened for signature 19 June 1997 (entered into force 10 May 2000).

36 The *Convention concerning Migration for Employment (Revised)*, above n. 18, (art. 7) requires States parties to ensure that services provided by their *public* employment agencies to migrant workers are also rendered free of charge.

37 International Labour Office, 'Decent Work for Domestic Workers, International Labour Conference, 99th sess, Geneva' (2010) [328]–[340]. The report observes, at [21], that migrant women comprise the majority of domestic workers in Europe, the Gulf countries and the Middle East.

were adopted by the 100th International Labour Conference in June 2011. The resulting *Convention concerning Decent Work for Domestic Workers* (2011) ('ILO Convention No 189') stipulates in art. 2(1) that it 'applies to all domestic workers', thus ensuring that migrant domestic workers, including those in an irregular situation, also fall within its scope.[38] The Convention contains a number of provisions concerning labour migration and the protection of migrant domestic workers, including:

- the requirement that they possess, before departure, a written job offer or employment contract that is enforceable in the country of employment (art. 8);
- the obligation on States parties to cooperate with one another to ensure the effective application of the Convention's provisions to migrant domestic workers (art. 8);
- the right of domestic workers to retain their travel and identity documents (art. 9); and
- the obligation on States parties to prevent abusive practices in the recruitment of migrant domestic workers (art. 15).

With regard to ILO instruments of more general application, the Committee of Experts has underlined the importance of labour inspection for the adequate protection of migrant workers. However, the Committee has also advised States parties to the *Convention concerning Labour Inspection in Industry and Commerce* (1947)[39] of the need to distinguish the powers and working methods of labour inspectors from those of officials responsible for addressing unauthorised employment and migration. In essence, labour inspectors should not become the enforcers of national immigration laws.[40]

11.3.4.   ILO Multilateral Framework on Labour Migration

In 1999 the Committee of Experts issued a General Survey on migrant workers based on the law and practice of all ILO member States, whether or not they had ratified Conventions No 97 and No 143. The objectives of the General Survey were to re-examine the possibility of including migrant workers as an item for discussion on the agenda of a forthcoming International Labour Conference and to clarify the possible need for revision of Conventions No 97 and No 143.[41] The Committee of Experts recommended two options for addressing the difficulties posed by the low rate of ratification of the two Conventions. The first was to maintain the status

---

38 *Convention concerning Decent Work for Domestic Workers* (ILO Convention No 189), opened for signature 16 June 2011 (not yet in force). See also *Domestic Workers Recommendation* (ILO No R201) (16 June 2011).

39 *Convention concerning Labour Inspection in Industry and Commerce* (ILO Convention No 81), opened for signature 11 July 1947, 54 UNTS 3 (entered into force 7 April 1950). In late 2011 there were 142 States parties.

40 ILO Committee of Experts on the Application of Conventions and Recommendations, 80th sess, 2009, Labour Inspection Convention (1947) Italy, Observation.

41 General Survey 1999, above n. 20, [2].

quo by recognising the problems member States experience in accepting legally binding international standards on labour migration, accompanied by a vigorous promotion of existing standards, and the possible elaboration of supplementary Protocols to address the gaps and shortcomings in these instruments. The second option was a complete revision of the two instruments, preferably into a single framework Convention.[42]

In response, the Governing Body earmarked a general discussion on migrant workers based on an 'integrated approach' at the 2004 International Labour Conference, recognising that 'the issues raised by migrant workers for economic and social policy on the one hand, and the protection of human rights on the other, cut across practically all spheres of the normative and technical activities of the ILO'.[43]

The International Labour Office submitted a comprehensive preparatory report to the International Labour Conference in 2004, proposing that the Conference adopt a plan of action that would 'engage the ILO and all its constituents in the development of a coherent multilateral framework for the governance of international migration'.[44] The report suggested that the Conference examine how the gaps in protection could be filled, and requested the Conference to consider how the ILO could promote coherent, transparent and comprehensive rights-based labour migration policies and best practices. The 2004 International Labour Conference adopted a plan of action for migrant workers, which was to include the 'development of a non-binding multilateral framework for a rights-based approach to labour migration, which takes account of labour market needs'.[45]

The ILO Multilateral Framework was subsequently adopted by a Tripartite Meeting of Experts in 2005 and approved by the ILO Governing Body in 2006.[46] It sets out a number of principles in the following nine areas:

- decent work;
- means for international cooperation on labour migration;
- global knowledge base (recognising that knowledge and information are critical to formulate, implement and evaluate labour migration policy and practice);
- effective management of labour migration;
- protection of migrant workers;
- prevention of and protection against abusive migration practices;

---

42 Ibid. [666]–[667].
43 International Labour Office, 'Second Item on the Agenda: Date, Place and Agenda of the 92nd sess (2004) of the International Labour Conference' (ILO Doc GB.283/2/1, 2002) [108].
44 International Labour Office, *Towards a Fair Deal for Migrant Workers in the Global Economy* (ILO, 2004) [312].
45 International Labour Conference, 92nd sess, 2004, *Report of the Committee on Migrant Workers: Conclusions on a Fair Deal for Migrant Workers in a Global Economy*, [21], [23].
46 ILO Multilateral Framework, above n. 6.

- migration processes;
- social integration and inclusion; and
- migration and development.

These principles are supported by detailed guidelines and a compendium of 'best practices'. Governments have since taken account of the ILO Multilateral Framework in their national labour migration policies. For example, in 2009 the Government of Sri Lanka adopted a national labour migration policy guided by the ILO Multilateral Framework, on the basis of tripartite discussions and with the ILO's support.[47]

11.4. INTERNATIONAL HUMAN RIGHTS AND THE 1990 CONVENTION ON MIGRANT WORKERS

Given the ILO's historical and constitutional concern for migrant workers, the need for the UN to adopt a legally binding instrument to protect this group was somewhat contentious. The reasons given for the UN's involvement have ranged from the broad human rights mandate of the UN, to the self-interested wishes of a number of States to regulate the content of the final text without the intervention of non-State parties, such as the social partners (i.e., worker and employer organisations), which play a formal role in ILO processes.[48] Given this latter justification, it is paradoxical that few States were prepared to ratify the ICRMW upon its adoption, and that its entry into force on 1 July 2003 was due to the considerable efforts of civil society.[49] To date, the ICRMW has not been widely ratified: by mid 2012, forty-six States were party to it, few of which are major destination countries.

The broader human rights mandate of the UN means that the ICRMW is able to address most of the concerns and interests of migrant workers and members of their families. Its adoption reinforces that migrant workers are more than just a factor of production; they are social entities with families, and accordingly are entitled to protection of their economic, social, cultural and civil rights, elaborated in the International Bill of Rights, namely the *Universal Declaration of Human Rights* (1948) ('Universal Declaration') and the widely ratified *International Covenant on Civil and Political Rights* (1966) ('ICCPR') and the *International Covenant on*

---

47 Ministry for Foreign Employment Promotion and Welfare, 'National Labour Migration Policy for Sri Lanka' (International Labour Office, 2008).

48 Ryszard Cholewinski, *Migrant Workers in International Human Rights Law: Their Protection in Countries of Employment* (Clarendon Press, 1997) 141–2.

49 On the role of civil society in promoting ratification, see International Steering Committee for the Campaign for Ratification of the Migrants Rights Convention, 'Guide on Ratification of the International Convention on the Protection of the Rights of All Migrant Workers and Members of their Families' (International Steering Committee, 2009).

Economic, Social and Cultural Rights (1966) ('ICESCR').[50] As with ILO international labour standards specifically addressing this group of workers, the ICRMW goes beyond the treatment of migrant workers in the country of employment and covers the entirety of the migration process, particularly with a view to the prevention of abuses. As with Part I of ILO Convention No 143, Part VI of the ICRMW calls upon States parties to cooperate to prevent irregular migration and the exploitation of migrant workers, and to impose sanctions on those who facilitate irregular migration (art. 68). Migrant smugglers, traffickers in human beings and unscrupulous recruitment agencies and employers of migrant workers in an irregular situation would be covered under this head. The ICRMW explicitly protects migrants in irregular status as well as those who are lawfully resident, and Part III lists the fundamental civil and political, and economic, social and cultural rights to which all migrant workers are entitled, whether in regular or irregular status.

Moreover, the ICRMW contains broad protections in connection with the whole labour migration process. Comprehensive procedural and substantive safeguards against expulsion are found in art. 22, which is applicable to all migrant workers, irrespective of their immigration status. The scope of this provision is therefore much broader than art. 13 of the ICCPR, which is limited to non-nationals who are lawfully in the territory of a State party. The ICRMW recognises the right of migrant workers to transfer their earnings and savings, and requires States parties to take appropriate measures to facilitate such transfers.[51] These are important provisions given that migrant workers' remittances are considered to bring substantial economic benefits to developing States, especially in some smaller States where remittances of foreign workers constitute a significant share of gross domestic product ('GDP').[52]

Despite the existence of such progressive provisions, others in the ICRMW reflect its more State-centred ethos, in contrast to the tripartite 'tone' of ILO instruments. For example, the so-called 'sovereignty clause' underlines that migrant worker admission policies fall in the remit of States parties (art. 79):

Nothing in the present Convention shall affect the right of each State Party to establish the criteria governing admission of migrant workers and members of their families. Concerning other matters related to their legal situation and treatment as migrant workers and members of their families, States Parties shall be subject to the limitations set forth in the present Convention.

Some of the liberal standards in ILO Convention No 143 have also been diluted considerably in the ICRMW, such as the right to free choice of employment

---

50 *Universal Declaration of Human Rights*, GA Res 217A (III), UN Doc A/810 (10 December 1948); *International Covenant on Civil and Political Rights*, opened for signature 16 December 1966, 999 UNTS 171 (entered into force 23 March 1976); *International Covenant on Economic, Social and Cultural Rights*, opened for signature 16 December 1966, 993 UNTS 3 (entered into force 3 January 1976).

51 ICRMW arts. 32 and 47.

52 E.g., in 2009, in Tajikistan, Tonga, Lesotho and Moldova, remittances constituted 35, 28, 25 and 23 per cent of GDP respectively: World Bank, 'Migration and Remittances Factbook 2011' (World Bank, 2011) 14.

(arts. 52–53), where States parties retain considerably more discretion than in the ILO instruments. Moreover, while the ICRMW contains a wider and more detailed definition of migrant worker than that found in ILO instruments, as well as separate definitions of the different groups of migrant workers (art. 2), the rights of certain categories of temporary migrants, such as seasonal workers, project-tied workers or specified-employment workers, are explicitly curtailed in Part V of the ICRMW, and students and trainees are excluded from its scope (art. 3). The attempt in Part III of the ICRMW to list the fundamental human rights applicable to all migrant workers has also led to some anomalies; in particular, a literal reading of the text suggests that migrant workers in an irregular situation have no right to *form* their own trade unions.[53] Such a reading is contrary to the general protections afforded by the Universal Declaration (art. 23), the ICCPR (art. 22), the ICESCR (art. 8) and ILO's *Convention concerning Freedom of Association and Protection of the Right to Organise* (1948) ('ILO Convention No 87') (art. 2).[54] Box 11.3 gives an example of the application of the latter provision to Spain in 2001.

Fortunately, the Committee on Migrant Workers – the body responsible for monitoring the application of the ICRMW by States parties – has adopted an expansive interpretation of the trade union rights of migrant workers, despite the

---

BOX 11.3 Irregular migrant workers and trade union rights

In March 2001, the General Union of Workers of Spain ('UGT') filed a complaint against the Spanish Government.[55] The complaint related to Law No 8/2000 on the *Rights and Freedoms of Foreigners in Spain and their Social Integration,* which had entered into force two months earlier and contained a provision stipulating that only those persons who are authorised to stay in Spain are entitled to join trade unions. The UGT argued that this clause unlawfully restricted the right to organise, freedom of association and collective bargaining, contrary to ILO Convention No 87.

The ILO supervisory Committee on Freedom of Association concluded that the Spanish law was not in conformity with the broad scope of art. 2 because it made the trade union rights of migrant workers dependent on authorisation of their presence or residence in Spain. The Committee stated that art. 2 covers all workers; exceptions were permissible only for armed forces and police under art. 9.

The Committee invited the ILO Governing Body to approve the recommendation that the Spanish Government 'as concerns the legislation in cause ... take into account the terms of art. 2 of ILO Convention No. 87 according to which workers, without distinction whatsoever, have the right to join organizations of their own choosing'.[56]

In 2007, the Spanish Constitutional Court annulled the provisions of the 'Foreigners' Law' and declared unconstitutional the distinction between regular migrants and migrants in an irregular situation in respect of a number of rights, including the right to freedom of association and the right to organise.

---

53 Compare ICRMW art. 26(1)(b) (the right to *join* a trade union) and art 40(1) (the right to *form* a trade union).
54 *Convention concerning Freedom of Association and Protection of the Right to Organise* (ILO Convention No 87), opened for signature 9 July 1948, 68 UNTS 17 (entered into force 4 July 1950). In mid 2012, there were 151 States parties.
55 *Case No 2121: General Union of Workers of Spain,* ILO, Report No 327, Vol LXXXV, 2002, Series B, No 1 (23 March 2001).
56 Ibid. [562].

narrower wording found in Part III. In its first General Comment on migrant domestic workers, issued in 2011, the Committee observed that: 'The laws of States Parties, particularly countries of employment of migrant domestic workers, should recognize the right of the latter to form and join organizations, regardless of migration status (article 26) and self-organization should be encouraged.'[57]

11.5. THE MYTH OF NON-RATIFICATION

While the three international instruments specifically protecting migrant workers (Conventions No 97 and No 143, and the ICRMW) have not been widely ratified in comparison to the fundamental international labour standards and core human rights instruments, taken together they comprise an international charter on labour migration, providing a comprehensive framework covering most issues of treatment of migrant workers and members of their families. Moreover, they are not just instruments on rights alone, but contain provisions to encourage and guide intergovernmental consultation, information sharing and cooperation on most aspects of international labour migration.[58]

To contend that these instruments are irrelevant because they have not been widely ratified is somewhat of a myth, especially when they are considered together. Of the approximately 130 States for which international labour migration is an important feature, nearly two-thirds (eighty-six States) have ratified at least one of the three conventions, thus demonstrating that they accept the application of the rule of law to the governance of labour migration. Eleven member States of the EU and the European Economic Area have ratified one or both of the ILO conventions on migrant workers, including many large destination countries for migrant workers in the EU.[59] On the southern shores of the Mediterranean, Algeria, Egypt, Libya and Morocco have ratified the ICRMW, and Algeria and Israel have also ratified ILO Convention No 97.

Nevertheless, the continued reluctance of many States to agree to legally binding multilateral instruments regulating international labour migration and protecting the rights of migrant workers remains a concern. In its General Survey of ILO instruments on migrant workers, the Committee of Experts identified the following obstacles to the ratification of Conventions No 97 and No 143, in addition to difficulties arising from their progressive provisions:

---

57 Committee on Migrant Workers, *General Comment No 1: Migrant Domestic Workers*, UN Doc CMW/C/GC/1 (23 February 2011) [46].

58 Ryszard Cholewinski and Patrick Taran, 'Migration, Governance and Human Rights: Contemporary Dilemmas in the Era of Globalization' (2009) 28(4) *Refugee Survey Quarterly* 1, 20.

59 The States are Belgium, France, Germany, Italy, the Netherlands, Norway, Portugal, Slovenia, Spain, Sweden and the United Kingdom.

- the non-conformity of national legislation with the instruments' provisions in many origin and destination countries;
- the financial cost of implementing the instruments and the additional workload for national labour administrations that ratification would entail;
- the existence of a difficult economic situation and high unemployment rates in some States resulting in preference being given to national over foreign labour;
- the relative novelty of large-scale international labour migration for a number of States and the need to develop appropriate national measures;
- the specificity of labour markets in certain States (e.g., the high proportion of foreigners in the labour force in Bahrain and Luxembourg); and
- the views of some significant countries of origin (e.g., Mexico and Pakistan) that the instruments are primarily concerned with addressing labour shortages in countries of employment rather than the needs of countries of origin.[60]

Some of these obstacles also apply to ratification of the ICRMW, such as the technical challenges posed for domestic administrations by the size and complexity of the instrument, and its non-conformity with national legislation in a number of countries. On the other hand, studies conducted in selected EU member States have found that national legislation in these States is already largely or entirely in conformity with the ICRMW,[61] while other studies have concluded that resistance to ratification is primarily for political rather than legal reasons.[62]

In addition to a lack of political will, other obstacles relate to the general lack of awareness and knowledge of the ICRMW, and the absence of adequate promotional activity.[63] In an empirical study undertaken in 2003 on obstacles to the ratification of the ICRMW in seven countries in the Asia-Pacific region, researchers identified two major hurdles applicable to origin and destination countries respectively.[64] First, some countries of origin fear that ratification will result in a loss of labour markets in destination countries to their non-ratifying competitors. The authors argued that this hurdle could be offset by better collaboration among countries of origin in the

---

60 General Survey 1999, above n. 20, [629]–[635].

61 Dirk Vanheule, Marie-Claire Foblets, Sander Loones and Steven Bouckaert, 'The Significance of the UN Migrant Workers' Convention of 18 December 1990 in the Event of Ratification by Belgium' (2004) 6(4) *European Journal of Migration and Law* 285.

62 René Plaetevoet and Marika Sidoti, 'Ratification of the UN Migrant Workers Convention in the European Union Survey on the Positions of Governments and Civil Society Actors' (18 December 2010); Euan Macdonald and Ryszard Cholewinski, 'The Migrant Workers Convention in Europe: Obstacles to the Ratification of the International Convention on the Protection of the Rights of All Migrant Workers and Members of their Families' (UNESCO, 2007).

63 Antoine Pécoud and Paul De Guchteneire, 'Global Migration Perspectives No 3: Migration, Human Rights and the United Nations: An Investigation into the Low Ratification Record of the UN Migrant Workers Convention' (Global Commission on International Migration, 2004).

64 Nicola Piper and Robyn Iredale, 'Identification of the Obstacles to the Signing and Ratification of the UN Convention on the Protection of the Rights of All Migrant Workers, the Asia-Pacific Perspective' (UNESCO, 2003).

region[65] and the encouragement of regional leadership by States, such as the Philippines (which is widely regarded as a model country of origin in the Asia-Pacific region in terms of acceptance of international instruments on migrant workers and innovative policies to protect its nationals employed abroad). Second, destination countries face sensitive political challenges because of the protections afforded by the ICRMW to migrants in an irregular situation, as well as the incorrect perception that the ICRMW obliges States parties to admit family members of migrant workers.

Despite these obstacles, ratification of the ICRMW is being supported through activities in the UN Human Rights Council. Universal Periodic Review is an important new mechanism, which ensures that the human rights obligations of all 193 UN member States, including the obligations applicable to migrant workers and their families, are subject to scrutiny.[66] By the end of 2011, all UN member States had been subjected to their first Universal Periodic Review, which has revealed interesting information relating to the human rights of migrants, as well as the position of States vis-à-vis ratification of the ICRMW. The UN Special Rapporteur on the Human Rights of Migrants – a special procedures thematic mandate of the Human Rights Council – promotes respect for the human rights of all migrants, including migrant workers, by raising specific concerns in his annual reports, undertaking country visits, and recommending that States accept and apply relevant human rights standards, including ratification and implementation of the ICRMW.[67]

11.6. REGIONAL INSTRUMENTS ON LABOUR MIGRATION

In addition to the role of international human rights law and international labour standards in the field of labour migration, normative developments in the legal protection of migrant workers and their families at the regional level are contributing to raising political awareness of their precarious plight and opening doors to their improved treatment.

Within the African and inter-American systems for the protection of human rights, there are no legally binding instruments specifically protecting migrant workers and their families. However, these individuals do enjoy general human rights protections in Africa under the *African Charter on Human and Peoples' Rights* (1981) ('African Charter on Human Rights'),[68] and in the Americas under the *American Declaration on the Rights and Duties of Man* (1948)

---

65 Collaboration among Asian countries of origin is already taking place under the 'Colombo Process': see Chapter 14.
66 Office of the High Commissioner for Human Rights, *Universal Periodic Review* (OHCHR, 2011).
67 Office of the High Commissioner for Human Rights, *Special Rapporteur on the Human Rights of Migrants* (OHCHR, 2011) (www2.ohchr.org/english/issues/migration/rapporteur/index.htm).
68 *African Charter on Human and Peoples' Rights*, opened for signature 27 June 1981, 1520 UNTS 217 (entered into force 21 October 1986). The African Charter has been ratified by fifty-three States.

('American Declaration') and the *American Convention on Human Rights* (1969) ('American Convention').[69] These instruments guarantee equal protection before the law and freedom from discrimination on a number of grounds, which are not exhaustive.[70] Certain principles applicable to migrant workers and their families have also been developed on the basis of the work of the Inter-American Commission on Human Rights and the case law of the Inter-American Court of Human Rights.

The Inter-American Court significantly advanced the human rights of migrant workers in an irregular situation in its Advisory Opinion concerning the legal status and rights of undocumented migrants in 2003.[71] At the request of Mexico, the Court held that such migrants are entitled to all international human rights, including rights as workers. This Advisory Opinion, which drew inspiration from a broad range of international and regional human rights norms and labour standards, has implications beyond the Americas. In light of the importance that labour migration has acquired in the region, the Inter-American Commission on Human Rights has also devoted special attention to the situation of migrant workers and their families. The General Assembly of the Organization of American States has adopted a series of resolutions on this topic and organised Summits of Heads of State. In 1997, the Inter-American Commission appointed a Special Rapporteurship on Migrant Workers and their Families, with a view to promoting their human rights in the region.[72] This mechanism complements the UN Special Rapporteur on the Human Rights of Migrants, referred to above. To date, the Inter-American Special Rapporteur has visited and reported on the situation of migrant workers and their families in Canada, Costa Rica, Guatemala, Mexico and the United States.[73]

The Council of Europe, which comprises forty-seven member States spanning the whole European continent, represents a region with a broad range of legally binding instruments for protecting human rights. The best known is the *European Convention for the Protection of Human Rights and Fundamental Freedoms* (1950) ('European Convention on Human Rights'),[74] which applies to 'everyone' within the jurisdiction of a State party (art. 1), and thus does not generally make distinctions on the basis of

69   *American Declaration of the Rights and Duties of Man*, OAS Res XXX, OAS Treaty Series No 36, Adopted by the Ninth International Conference of American States (1948); *American Convention on Human Rights*, opened for signature 22 November 1969, 1144 UNTS 123 (entered into force 18 July 1978). The American Convention has been ratified by twenty-four States.

70   African Charter on Human Rights, arts. 2, 3; American Declaration, art. II; American Convention, arts. 1(1), 24.

71   *Juridical Condition and Rights of the Undocumented Migrants (Advisory Opinion)* OC-18/03, Inter-Am Ct HR (Ser A) No 18 (17 September 2003).

72   Inter-American Commission on Human Rights, *Special Rapporteurship on Migrant Workers and their Families* (2011) (www.cidh.org/Migrantes/defaultmigrants.htm).

73   Special Rapporteurship on Migrant Workers and their Families, *Country Visit Reports* (2011) (www.cidh.org/Migrantes/migrants.countryreports.htm).

74   *European Convention for the Protection of Human Rights and Fundamental Freedoms*, opened for signature 4 November 1950, ETS No 5 (entered into force 3 September 1953). The European Convention on Human Rights has been ratified by all Council of Europe member States.

nationality or immigration status.[75] The judicial body authorised by the European Convention on Human Rights to give legally binding rulings – the European Court of Human Rights – has issued a series of judgments relating to the human rights of migrants, including protection against *refoulement* in cases where the person concerned is subject to a real risk of serious harm in the country to which he or she is being returned;[76] conditions of detention of asylum seekers;[77] the protection of family life in the context of expulsion from and admission to the territory;[78] safeguards against collective expulsion;[79] and protection from discrimination on the grounds of nationality in the field of social security.[80] Much of this case law is also applicable to migrant workers and their families in comparable situations.

The complementary social rights instrument of the Council of Europe, the *European Social Charter* (1961), as well as its revised version (1996),[81] are on their face considerably more restrictive in scope than the European Convention on Human Rights, because they apply only to nationals from other contracting parties who are 'lawfully resident or working regularly' within the territory of the contracting party. Nonetheless, the European Committee of Social Rights, charged with monitoring the Social Charter's application, has sought to give it an expansive interpretation to protect vulnerable groups of migrants. In complaints against France and the Netherlands,[82] the Committee adopted a liberal interpretation of the Charter to underscore that migrant children in an irregular situation should be afforded effective access to rights to healthcare and housing.[83] The Committee also underlined the need to interpret the Charter in light of other international human rights instruments:

---

75 However, some rights are restricted to nationals, such as the right to free movement within a State: *Protocol 4 to the European Convention for the Protection of Human Rights and Fundamental Freedoms*, opened for signature 16 September 1963, ETS 46 (entered into force 2 May 1968) art. 2; and procedural safeguards in expulsion are limited to non-nationals lawfully resident in the territory: *Protocol 7 to the Convention for the Protection of Human Rights and Fundamental Freedoms*, opened for signature 22 November 1984, ETS No 117 (entered into force 1 November 1988) art. 1. Compare ICRMW art. 22.

76 European Convention on Human Rights art. 3: *Chahal* v. *United Kingdom* (15 November 1996) 1996-V, No 22, App No 22414/93.

77 European Convention on Human Rights art. 3: *S.D.* v. *Greece* (2009) App No 53541/07, Eur Court HR; *M.S.S.* v. *Belgium and Greece* (2011) App No 30696/09, Eur Court HR.

78 European Convention on Human Rights art. 8: *Boultif* v. *Switzerland* (European Court of Human Rights, Chamber, Application No 54273/00, 2 November 2001); *Sen* v. *Netherlands* (2001) App No 31465/96, Eur Court HR.

79 Protocol No 4 to the European Convention on Human Rights art. 4: *Conka* v. *Belgium* (2002) 34 EHRR 54.

80 European Convention on Human Rights art. 14 and *Protocol 1 to the European Convention for the Protection of Human Rights and Fundamental Freedoms*, opened for signature 20 March 1952, ETS No 9 (entered into force 18 May 1954) art. 1: *Gaygusuz* v. *Austria* (1996), App No 17371/90, Eur Court HR; *Poirrez* v. *France* (2003) App No 40892/98, Eur Court HR; *Andrejeva* v. *Latvia* (2009), App No 55707/00, Eur Court HR. For an overview, see Paul Minderhoud, 'Social Security Rights of Third Country Nationals in EU Legislation and in the Case Law of the European Court of Human Rights' (2010) 17(4) *Journal of Social Security Law* 227, 234–8.

81 *European Social Charter*, opened for signature 18 October 1961, CETS No 35 (entered into force 26 February 1965); *European Social Charter (Revised)*, opened for signature 3 May 1996, CETS No 163 (entered into force 1 July 1999).

82 The complaints were made under the *Additional Protocol to the European Social Charter Providing for a System of Collective Complaints*, opened for signature 9 November 1995, ETS No 158 (entered into force 1 July 1998). In late 2011, twelve Council of Europe member States had ratified it.

83 *International Federation of Human Rights Leagues (FIDH)* v. *France* (2005) Complaint No 14/2003, European Committee of Social Rights; *Defence of Children International* v. *Netherlands* (2009) Complaint No 47/2008, European Committee of Social Rights.

[T]he Charter cannot be interpreted in a vacuum. The Charter should so far as possible be interpreted in harmony with other rules of international law of which it forms a part, including in the instant case [against the Netherlands] those relating to the provision of adequate shelter to any person in need, regardless whether s/he is on the State's territory legally or not.[84]

It is conceivable that this case law may be applied beyond children to other vulnerable migrant groups, such as migrant workers in an irregular situation.

The Council of Europe also has its own instrument that specifically aims to protect migrant workers, namely, the *European Convention on the Legal Status of Migrant Workers* (1977).[85] The relevance of this instrument has been questioned because, for a long period, it had been ratified by a limited number of States, and it applies only on the basis of reciprocity to lawfully resident migrant workers who are nationals of other States parties. However, the ratifications since 2006 by Moldova, Albania and Ukraine are breathing new life into this instrument, because a significant number of their nationals are working lawfully in EU member States that have ratified the Convention, such as Italy and Portugal.

In the European Union, efforts to develop a common normative approach to labour migration from outside the EU have encountered numerous sensitivities on the part of member States and the results to date have been somewhat mixed (see Case Study 11.2). While this economic and political system of regional integration is widely regarded as affording a best practice model of social rights protection for those nationals and their family members who move from one EU member State to another to take up work,[86] the legal situation of third-country (i.e., non-EU) nationals employed in the EU differs from one member State to another.

There are signs that considerably more importance is now being attached to addressing the 'rights deficit' in the EU. First, the entry into force of the Lisbon Treaty on 1 December 2009[87] has given legally binding force to the *Charter of Fundamental Rights of the European Union* (2000),[88] which applies to member States when they are implementing EU law (art. 51), and which generally does not distinguish between persons on the grounds of nationality or immigration status. However, there are exceptions in relation to migrant workers in an irregular situation, which are difficult to justify in light of international human rights and labour standards. For example, the entitlement to 'working conditions equivalent to those of citizens of the Union' is afforded only to 'nationals of third countries who are authorized to work in the territories of the Member States' (art. 15). Similarly, only those persons 'residing and moving legally' within the EU are 'entitled to social benefits and social advantages in accordance with Union law and national laws and practices' (art. 34).

84 *Defence of Children International* v. *Netherlands*, ibid. [35].
85 *European Convention on the Legal Status of Migrant Workers*, opened for signature 24 November 1977, ETS No 93 (entered into force 1 May 1983).
86 Nonnenmacher, above n. 24, 355, 362–8.
87 *Treaty of Lisbon amending the Treaty on European Union and the Treaty establishing the European Community* (2007) OJ 2007 C 306/1.
88 *Charter of Fundamental Rights of the European Union* (2010) OJ C 83/389.

CASE STUDY 11.2 EU law and policy on labour migration from third countries

The European Union gained greater competence over migration from third countries in May 1999 when the Treaty of Amsterdam came into force. Before then, asylum and immigration matters were the subjects of intergovernmental cooperation, but the Treaty of Amsterdam transferred these issues to what was then the 'first pillar' of the European Community, giving the Council of Ministers the mandate to adopt legally binding measures. However, not all EU member States participated fully in this endeavour,[89] and member States retained the competence to determine the number of nationals coming to their territory from third countries for the purpose of seeking employment.[90]

To date, the substantive measures adopted have focussed on steps towards the creation of a common European asylum system and prevention of irregular migration. Formulation of coherent and robust EU rules on legal or labour migration from outside the EU has faced stiff opposition from some member States, exacerbated by the global financial and economic crisis. The intention of a proposed Directive in 2001 was to adopt clear and workable rules on the conditions governing lawful entry and residence of third-country nationals for the purpose of employment[91] (i.e., by way of a 'horizontal' approach applicable to most forms of labour migration), thus mirroring the approach taken by international instruments protecting migrant workers. However, the draft Directive did not meet with consensus in the Council of Ministers. After consultation with member States and other stakeholders, in 2005 the European Commission issued a 'Policy Plan on Legal Migration', proposing a sectoral approach, which focussed on legal measures to address conditions of entry and residence for specific categories of migrant workers.[92] Thus, a Directive on the conditions of entry and residence of highly qualified third-country nationals ('Blue Card' Directive) was adopted in 2009,[93] and a Directive that provides for a single permit for work and residence, and safeguards a minimum level of rights for lower-skilled third-country nationals, was adopted in 2011.[94] However, proposed Directives on seasonal migrant workers[95] and intra-corporate transferees[96] are still undergoing difficult negotiations in the Council of Ministers and the European Parliament.

89 Denmark, Ireland and the United Kingdom secured 'opt-outs' at the time the Treaty of Amsterdam entered into force.
90 *Consolidated Versions of the Treaty on European Union and the Treaty on the Functioning of the European Union* (2010) OJ C 83/01 art. 79(5).
91 European Commission, 'Proposal for a Council Directive on the Conditions of Entry and Residence of Third-Country Nationals for the Purpose of Paid Employment and Self-Employed Economic Activities' (COM(2001) 386 final, 11 July 2001).
92 Commission of the European Communities, 'Policy Plan on Legal Migration' (COM(2005) 669 final, 21 December 2005) 58.
93 *Council Directive 2009/50/EC of 25 May 2009 on the Conditions of Entry and Residence of Third-Country Nationals for the Purposes of Highly Qualified Employment* [2009] OJ L 155/17.
94 Directive 2011/98/EU of the European Parliament and of the Council of 13 December 2011 on a single application procedure for a single permit for third-country nationals to reside and work in the territory of a Member State and on a common set of rights for third-country workers legally residing in a Member State [2011] OJ L 343/1.
95 European Commission, 'Proposal for a Directive on the Conditions of Entry and Residence of Third-Country Nationals for the Purposes of Seasonal Employment' (COM(2010) 379 final, 13 July 2010).
96 European Commission, 'Proposal for a Directive of the European Parliament and of the Council on Conditions of Entry and Residence of Third-country Nationals in the Framework of an Intra-Corporate Transfer' (COM(2010) 378 final, 13 July 2010).

The proposed texts reveal a lower level of protection for these groups of third-country nationals, reflecting the approach taken at the national level in many member States. In particular, the fragmentation of the equal treatment principle between workers from third countries and nationals, as well as between different categories of third-country nationals, in such areas as working conditions and social security, is a concern. International human rights and labour standards, if adopted and properly applied, would guarantee them a higher level of protection.

None of these adopted or proposed measures is applicable to migrant workers who are third-country nationals in an irregular situation, although some safeguards in the expulsion or return process are provided in the *Directive on Common Standards and Procedures in Member States for Returning Illegally Staying Third-Country Nationals* ('Returns Directive').[97] Migrant workers in an irregular situation may also bring complaints against employers for unpaid wages, with the assistance of trade unions or other associations, under the Directive on employer sanctions.[98]

Map 11.1 Member States of the European Union

97 *Council Directive 2008/115/EC of the European Parliament and of the Council of 16 December 2008 on Common Standards and Procedures in Member States for Returning Illegally Staying Third-Country Nationals* [2008] OJ L 348 arts. 12–17.
98 *Directive 2009/52/EC of the European Parliament and of the Council of 18 June 2009 Providing for Minimum Standards on Sanctions and Measures against Employers of Illegally Staying Third-Country Nationals* [2009] OJ L 168/24 arts. 6, 13.

Second, as a result of the Lisbon Treaty's entry into force, the EU has committed itself to ratifying the European Convention on Human Rights.[99] Third, with regard to asylum and immigration matters, the legislative role of the European Parliament in the decision-making process, including in the field of legal labour migration, is now complete.[100] Finally, the competence to refer cases in this field to the European Court of Justice, which oversees the uniform application of EU law, has been extended to all courts in member States and not just to final courts of appeal.[101]

11.7. THE ROLE OF 'SOFT LAW' AND RELATED POLICY DEVELOPMENTS

Outside the Americas and Europe, there have been fewer legal developments at the regional level relating to labour migration and the protection of the human rights of migrant workers and their families, but it is worth drawing attention to a number of 'soft law' and related policy activities that have taken place under the auspices of burgeoning regional integration processes (on 'soft law', see Chapter 3). The human rights architecture of the African Union has been complemented by a holistic policy document on migration, *The Migration Policy Framework for Africa*, which attaches particular importance to labour migration and the protection of the human rights of migrants.[102]

While there is no legally binding instrument in Asia protecting human rights generally, there is some prospect that a convention protecting the rights of migrant workers in Southeast Asia may be adopted in the near future. In 2007, the Association of Southeast Asian Nations ('ASEAN') adopted a *Declaration on the Protection and Promotion of the Rights of Migrant Workers*, which includes a political commitment to finalise a legally binding instrument in this field.[103] A committee to oversee the implementa-

---

99 *Consolidated Versions of the Treaty on European Union and the Treaty on the Functioning of the European Union* (2010) OJ C 83/01 art. 6(2).

100 The ordinary EU legislative process (i.e., co-decision of the Council and European Parliament) has been incrementally applied to asylum and migration matters. Before the Lisbon Treaty, the European Parliament had only a consultative role in the adoption of measures on legal migration.

101 The positive role of the European Court of Justice in protecting the rights of third-country nationals has been highlighted in two cases concerning the detention of migrants in an irregular situation: *Kadzoev* v. *Direktsia* (C–357/09) [2009] ECJ; and *El Dridi* (C–61/11 PPU) [2011] ECJ.

102 African Union, *The Migration Policy Framework for Africa*, Executive Council, 9th Ordinary sess, AU Doc EX.CL/ 276 (IX) (2006).

103 *ASEAN Declaration on the Protection and Promotion of the Rights of Migrant Workers* (13 January 2007) [22].

tion of the Declaration, including realisation of the commitment to develop a legally binding instrument, has been established.[104] Although this may not be surprising in a region where labour migration features prominently on the economic and social landscape (see Chapter 2), it is a notable development given the absence of an Asian human rights instrument, and the fact that international human rights and labour standards have not been extensively ratified by States in this region.[105]

The Council of Europe is also becoming an important source of 'soft law' standards on the human rights of migrants, including migrant workers, due in part to national parliamentarians who participate in its Parliamentary Assembly. This body has recently adopted recommendations and resolutions on such politically sensitive topics as the human rights of migrants in irregular status,[106] and the detention of asylum seekers and irregular migrants.[107]

The conclusions of high-level international conferences may also have a 'soft law' value or play an important role in influencing policy developments at the regional and national level. In this regard, the UN World Conference Against Racism, Racial Discrimination, Xenophobia and Related Intolerance, held in Durban, South Africa in 2001, was particularly relevant to advancing equality of treatment for migrant workers and their protection from discrimination. The Conference's Declaration and Programme of Action included forty-five paragraphs on migrants,[108] with a number of specific references to migrant workers, such as the reaffirmation of the need to eliminate racial discrimination against migrant workers with respect to employment, social services and access to justice.[109] The Programme of Action calls upon States to 'design or reinforce, promote and implement effective legislative and administrative policies, as well as other preventive measures, against the serious situation experienced by certain groups of workers, *including migrant workers,*

---

104 Association of Southeast Asian Nations, 'Committee on the Implementation of the ASEAN Declaration on the Protection and Promotion of the Rights of Migrant Workers, Work Plan' (ASEAN, 2008). The ACMW's work plan identifies three tracks along the lines of the Declaration, namely: (i) protection of migrant workers against exploitation, discrimination and violence; (ii) labour migration governance; and (iii) the fight against trafficking in persons – as well as an additional track concerned with the development of a legally binding instrument.

105 On the evolving role of the ASEAN Intergovernmental Commission on Human Rights, see Association of Southeast Asian Nations, 'ASEAN Intergovernmental Commission on Human Rights' (ASEAN, October 2009) [1.1], [1.6].

106 *Human Rights of Irregular Migrants*, Parliamentary Assembly, Council of Europe, res 1509 (27 June 2006) and Parliamentary Assembly, 'Human Rights of Irregular Migrants' (Recommendation 1755, Council of Europe, 2006).

107 *Detention of Asylum Seekers and Irregular Migrants in Europe*, Parliamentary Assembly, Council of Europe, res 1707 (28 January 2010) and Parliamentary Assembly, 'Detention of Asylum Seekers and Irregular Migrants in Europe' (Recommendation 1900, Council of Europe, 2010).

108 Office of the High Commissioner for Human Rights, 'Report of the World Conference Against Racism, Racial Discrimination, Xenophobia and Related Intolerance' (UN Doc A/CONF 189/12 UNHCHR, 31 August–8 September 2001).

109 Ibid. [51].

who are victims of racism, racial discrimination, xenophobia and related intolerance'.[110] Moreover, with a view to emphasising the difficult situation of
migrant women in certain employment sectors, the Programme of Action
notes that special attention should be given to protecting trafficked persons
and people engaged in domestic work, and urges States to consider signing and
ratifying ILO Conventions No 97 and No 143, and the ICRMW.[111]

The developments discussed above are largely intergovernmental initiatives, but other actors in international labour migration can also play a key
role in developing non-binding standards or related policies. The ILO
Multilateral Framework, discussed above, was drawn up by the ILO's tripartite constituents of governments, and employer and worker organisations, as
are all ILO Conventions and Recommendations. In principle, such documents
should best reflect labour migration and workplace realities, since they have
been drawn up with the participation of the principal stakeholders. However,
this very participation is seen by some as challenging state sovereignty and
questioning the role played by government ministries or state agencies in
regulating labour migration.

11.8. INTERGOVERNMENTAL PROCESSES ON LABOUR MIGRATION

Labour migration and the rights of migrant workers, and the human rights of
migrants generally, are increasingly topics of discussion in global and regional
intergovernmental processes. While these processes are regarded as informal and
non-binding,[112] the binding standards protecting migrant workers, discussed
above, also contain obligations on States parties to cooperate with one another,
particularly in preventing abuses in labour migration and ensuring it occurs under
sound, equitable, humane and lawful conditions.[113]

International and regional migration processes are discussed in more detail in
Chapters 13 and 14, but international labour migration is particularly relevant to
some of these processes and warrants a mention here. The Global Forum on
Migration and Development ('GFMD') is a States-owned process conducted
outside the UN system, which came into being following the UN General
Assembly's High-Level Dialogue on International Migration and Development

110 Ibid. [67] (emphasis added).   111 Ibid. [78].
112 Michele Klein Solomon, 'International Migration Management Through Inter-State Consultation
   Mechanisms' (United Nations Expert Group Meeting on International Migration and Development,
   2005) 14.
113 *Convention concerning Migrations in Abusive Conditions and the Promotion of Equality of Opportunity and
   Treatment of Migrant Workers*, above n. 18, Pt I; ICRMW, Pt VI.

in September 2006.[114] The GFMD retains links to the UN via the Secretary-General's Special Representative on Migration, and has held annual meetings in Belgium (2007), the Philippines (2008), Greece (2009), Mexico (2010) and Switzerland (2011). Given that a large part of international migration today is for the purpose of employment, the migration and development discourse is inextricably bound up with the world of work, and this is evident from the themes that have been discussed in GFMD meetings.

Finally, two intergovernmental regional consultative processes – both facilitated by the International Organization for Migration ('IOM') – the Colombo Process and the related Abu Dhabi Dialogue, exclusively address labour migration in Asia and the Gulf States, devoting specific attention to the protection, welfare and wellbeing of migrant workers.

11.9. CONCLUSION

The tendency among migration policy makers today is to downplay the role of international law in the sphere of migration governance.[115] This chapter demonstrates, however, that the governance of international labour migration is underpinned by the rule of law, which manifests itself in a broad range of human rights and labour standards applicable to all human beings, irrespective of their nationality and immigration status. To argue otherwise is to deny the legacy of lawmaking in this area, as well as the success of the free movement components of regional integration systems, particularly in the EU, which have been and continue to be built on a foundation of legal principles. The international community has also seen fit to formulate specific standards – both legally binding and of a 'soft law' nature – to protect migrant workers and their families, precisely because these groups are at particular risk of exploitation in the migration process and the world of work. Given the reshaping of the world of work in the current wave of globalisation – characterised by unemployment and underemployment, increasing temporary and precarious employment, the growth of the informal economy and an absence of social protection – these standards are all the more important today. The key challenges lie in their acceptance by States and in their adequate implementation.

---

114 United Nations General Assembly, 'High-Level Dialogue on International Migration and Development' (United Nations, 14–15 September 2006). For a summary, see United Nations General Assembly, 'Summary of the High-Level Dialogue on International Migration and Development' (UN Doc A/61/515, 13 October 2006).
115 This trend is also evident in academic and policy literature: see Alexander Betts (ed.), *Global Migration Governance* (Oxford University Press, 2011); International Organization for Migration, *World Migration Report 2010: The Future of Migration: Building Capacities for Change* (IOM, 2010) ch 8.

KEY REFERENCES

Böhning, Roger, *A Brief Account of the ILO and Policies on International Migration* (International Institute for Labour Studies, 2008)

Cholewinski, Ryszard, 'The Human and Labor Rights of Migrants: Visions of Equality' (2008) 22(2) *Georgetown Immigration Law Journal* 177

Cholewinski, Ryszard, 'The Rights of Migrant Workers' in Ryszard Cholewinski, Richard Perruchoud and Euan Macdonald (eds.), *International Migration Law: Developing Paradigms and Key Challenges* (TMC Asser Press, 2007) 255

Cholewinski, Ryszard, 'International Labour Law and the Protection of Migrant Workers: Revitalizing the Agenda in the Era of Globalization' in John Craig and Michael Lynk (eds.), *Globalization and the Future of Labour Law* (Cambridge University Press, 2006) 409

Cholewinski, Ryszard, *Migrant Workers in International Human Rights Law: Their Protection in Countries of Employment* (Clarendon Press, 1997)

Cholewinski, Ryszard and Taran, Patrick, 'Migration, Governance and Human Rights: Contemporary Dilemmas in the Era of Globalization' (2009) 28(4) *Refugee Survey Quarterly* 1

De Guchteneire, Paul, Pécoud, Antoine and Cholewinski, Ryszard (eds.), *Migration and Human Rights: The United Nations Convention on Migrant Workers' Rights* (UNESCO, 2009)

International Labour Conference, *General Survey on the Reports on the Migration for Employment Convention (Revised) (No. 97), and Recommendation (Revised) (No. 86), 1949, and the Migrant Workers (Supplementary Provisions) Convention (No. 143), and Recommendation (No. 151), 1975* (87th sess, Report III (1b), 1999)

International Labour Organization, *International Labour Migration: A Rights-Based Approach* (ILO, 2010)

International Labour Organization, *Multilateral Framework on Labour Migration: Non-Binding Principles and Guidelines for a Rights-Based Approach to Labour Migration* (ILO, 2006)

International Organization for Migration, *World Migration 2008: Managing Labour Mobility in the Evolving Economy* (IOM, 2008)

Leary, Virginia, 'Labor Migration' in Alexander Aleinikoff and Vincent Chetail (eds.), *Migration and International Legal Norms* (TMC Asser Press, 2003) 227

Macdonald, Euan and Cholewinski, Ryszard, 'The Migrant Workers Convention in Europe: Obstacles to the Ratification of the International Convention on the Protection of the Rights of All Migrant Workers and Members of their Families' (UNESCO, 2007)

Organization for Security and Cooperation in Europe et al., *Handbook on Establishing Effective Labour Migration Policies in Countries of Origin and Destination* (OSCE, IOM and ILO, 2006)

Plaetevoet, René and Sidoti, Marika, 'Ratification of the UN Migrant Workers Convention in the European Union: Survey on the Positions of Governments and Civil Society Actors' (18 December 2010)

Taran, Patrick, 'Clashing Worlds: Imperative for a Rights-Based Approach to Labour Migration in the Age of Globalization' in Vincent Chetail (ed.), *Globalization, Migration and Human Rights: International Law under Review, Volume II* (Bruylant, 2007) 403

KEY RESOURCES

Amnesty International: www.amnesty.org/en/refugees-and-migrants

December 18: www.december18.net

European Commission, Justice and Citizens' Rights: http://ec.europa.eu/policies/justice_citizens_rights_en.htm

Global Campaign for Ratification of the Convention on Rights of Migrants: www.migrantsrights.org/committee.htm

Global Forum on Migration and Development: www.gfmd.org

Human Rights Watch: www.hrw.org/en/topic/migrants

International Catholic Migration Commission: www.icmc.net

International Labour Organization, NORMLEX Information System on International Labour Standards: www.ilo.org/dyn/normlex/en

International Labour Organization, International Migration Branch: www.ilo.org/public/english/protection/migrant

International Organization for Migration, International Migration Law Database www.imldb.iom.int/section.do

International Trade Union Confederation: www.ituc-csi.org

Office of the United Nations High Commissioner for Human Rights, Committee on Migrant Workers: www2.ohchr.org/english/bodies/cmw

Platform for International Cooperation on Undocumented Migrants: www.picum.org

United Nations Educational, Scientific and Cultural Organization, Project on the International Migrants' Rights Convention: www.unesco.org/new/en/social-and-human-sciences/themes/international-migration/projects

United Nations Office of the High Commissioner for Human Rights, Special Rapporteur on the Human Rights of Migrants: www.ohchr.org/EN/Issues/Migration/SRMigrants

International trade law and labour mobility

SOPHIE NONNENMACHER[1]

12.1. INTRODUCTION

This chapter considers the role of international trade law in facilitating international migration. Although it is discussed only infrequently within the mainstream of international migration law, the topic is important because it is the only multilateral legal framework that seeks to liberalise the international movement of persons. At present, the stream of international migration that occurs under the framework of 'international trade in services' is modest in volume and limited in scope, since it applies only to the temporary movement of specific categories of labour. However, it has substantial potential for growth if States demonstrate their willingness to liberalise trade in services in future rounds of trade negotiations.

Globalisation has resulted in new ways of connecting workers, producers and consumers, and of performing trade. Freer flows of capital and goods are in part the consequence of international trade negotiations in goods and capital that have taken place since the Second World War. Initially, these negotiations occurred under the auspices of the General Agreement on Tariffs and Trade ('GATT'). In 1994 those arrangements were superseded by a new treaty framework, and a multilateral trade organisation – the World Trade Organization ('WTO') – was established. Today, the *Marrakesh Agreement Establishing the World Trade Organization* (1994) ('Marrakesh Agreement') forms the foundation of a complex system of international trade law.[2]

The liberalisation of the remaining factor of production – labour – has lagged behind, with only 3 per cent of the world population residing in a State other than their own. The movement of persons has been introduced into the trade agenda comparatively recently. Attention was first given to the movement of persons

---

1 I would like to thank Antonia Carzinaga (World Trade Organization) and Marion Panizzon (World Trade Institute) for their comments on a draft of this chapter.

2 *Marrakesh Agreement Establishing the World Trade Organization*, opened for signature 15 April 1994, 1867 UNTS 3 (entered into force 1 January 1995).

during the Uruguay Round negotiations (1986–94), leading up to the Marrakesh Agreement, when the rapid expansion of trade in international services led to a focus on reducing barriers to trade for intangible products (services), as a natural counterpart to GATT's focus on goods.

The negotiation of the *General Agreement on Trade in Services* (1994) ('GATS') as an annex to the Marrakesh Agreement, and its entry into force in 1995, marked a new stage in the history of the multilateral trading system, as well as in the global regulatory framework on human mobility.[3] GATS is the only legal instrument facilitating international mobility at the global level.[4] It is in the highly specific context of trade that States have agreed to do what they are often reluctant to do elsewhere, namely, make formal multilateral commitments that limit their sovereign right to determine whether non-nationals may enter their territory and provide labour there (see Chapter 5).

The movement of persons is included in GATS due to the particular nature of the trading of services. Services very often require contact between the service client and the service supplier. In contrast to GATT, which only covers the product (i.e., the goods), GATS applies both to the product (i.e., the service) and to the providers of that service. GATS aims to progressively reduce barriers to trade in services through rounds of negotiations to encourage economic growth and development. The services sector is the fastest-growing part of the global economy, and accounts for 60 per cent of global output, 30 per cent of employment and nearly 20 per cent of global trade – with global exports of commercial services estimated at US$3,350 billion in 2009.[5]

Reducing barriers to the mobility of service providers is an important dimension for a more efficient trade in services. While transport and communications facilitate the movements of persons, and globalisation of production and investment creates a need for foreign expertise and the movement of labour, immigration policies in most States today are rather restrictive. These restrictions on mobility reflect economic, social and cultural issues – concerns that can be based as much on perceptions about the impact of foreign workers on the economies of destination countries as on the realities.

When the WTO was established in 1995, it took under its umbrella the three multilateral trade agreements that had previously been negotiated – goods (GATT), services (GATS) and intellectual property.[6] While GATS is likely to remain the only global treaty to liberalise international mobility, its coverage is limited to particular types of international movement: it does not apply to permanent migration, nor to all types of temporary migration. It excludes migration for 'employment', and

---

3 *Marrakesh Agreement Establishing the World Trade Organization*, opened for signature 15 April 1994, 1867 UNTS 3 (entered into force 1 January 1995) annex 1B ('*General Agreement on Trade in Services*').
4 Alexander Betts (ed.), *Global Migration Governance* (Oxford University Press, 2011).
5 World Trade Organization, *International Trade Statistics 2010* (WTO, 2010) 123, Table III.1.
6 *Marrakesh Agreement Establishing the World Trade Organization*, opened for signature 15 April 1994, 1867 UNTS 3 (entered into force 1 January 1995) annex 1C ('*Agreement on Trade-Related Aspects of Intellectual Property Rights*'). The TRIPS Agreement, as it is known, was negotiated in the Uruguay Round (1986–94) and introduced intellectual property rules into the multilateral trading system for the first time.

instead regulates only the temporary provision of a service by a service supplier of one State in the territory of another. Nonetheless, progress on the movement of persons under GATS is said to yield important gains for the world economy, which will be shared between developing and developed States alike.

This chapter discusses how international trade law addresses labour mobility. Section 12.2 reviews the scope of GATS and the rules that relate to the movement of natural persons. It describes the different categories of service providers and the type of mobility covered by the agreement. Section 12.3 discusses the migration management and labour issues raised by GATS. Section 12.4 examines the progress achieved during successive rounds of trade negotiations since the Uruguay Round and reviews the state of play under the current Doha Round.

12.2. GATS AND THE RULES RELATING TO THE MOVEMENT OF NATURAL PERSONS

12.2.1. GATS and trading rules

GATS is a multilateral legal framework that applies to all 153 WTO member States. The agreement applies to all services provided on a commercial basis. However, it excludes most air transport and 'services supplied in the exercise of governmental authority', which is defined in art. I(3) to mean 'any service which is supplied neither on a commercial basis, nor in competition with one or more service suppliers'. GATS applies to government measures that affect trade; individuals have no immediate rights or obligations under the treaty.[7]

In contrast to GATT (which imposed tariff reductions), GATS does not impose a specified level of trade liberalisation, but instead provides for flexibility by allowing each WTO member to make commitments on the opening of their markets according to their situation. Thus it is up to each WTO member to decide which categories of service providers (e.g., managers, specialists) and for which sectors (e.g., tourism, construction) they will provide market access. These commitments are made through successive rounds of trade negotiations, which aim to promote the interests of all WTO members and achieve an overall balance of rights and obligations.

GATS comprises two main parts – 'general obligations and disciplines' and specific commitments. The first part consists of obligations of general application. Among them is the 'most favoured nation' ('MFN') clause, a pillar of the trading system whereby members are required to provide to all WTO members any concession they are offering to a specific WTO member. In the language of art. II(1), 'each Member shall accord immediately and unconditionally to services and service

---

7 Steve Charnovitz, 'Trade Law Norms on International Migration' in Alexander Aleinikoff and Vincent Chetail (eds.), *Migration and International Legal Norms* (TMC Asser Press, 2003) 241, 242.

suppliers of any other Member treatment no less favourable than that it accords to like services and service suppliers of any other country'. Another general obligation is the transparency requirement, which obliges WTO members to make publicly available at the national level all relevant measures of general application that pertain to GATS (art. III).

Other general obligations relate to domestic regulation, which comprises several components. In sectors where specific commitments are undertaken, measures of general application affecting trade in services should be administered in a 'reasonable, objective and impartial manner' (art. VI(1)). There should be domestic procedures to review administrative decisions affecting trade in services (art. VI(2)). All measures relating to qualifications and procedures, technical standards and licensing requirements should 'not constitute unnecessary barriers to trade in services' (art. VI(4)). Furthermore, in sectors where specific commitments are made regarding professional services, WTO members shall provide for adequate procedures to verify the competence of professionals of any other member (art. VI(6)).

The second part of GATS lays down the framework under which WTO members decide to authorise foreign suppliers to provide services in their States and for which sectors – the so-called specific commitments.[8] Twelve service sectors and around 160 subsectors have been identified for the purpose of assisting WTO members in drafting their specific commitments. The twelve service sectors are: business; communication; construction and engineering; distribution; education; environment; financial; health; tourism and travel; recreation, culture and sporting; transport; and other.[9]

GATS distinguishes between four possible 'modes' for trading services between WTO members (art. I(2)). Mode 1 is known as 'cross-border supply', where the service itself crosses a border (e.g., banking via the internet). Mode 2 is known as 'consumption abroad', where a service consumer of one State goes to another State and consumes (i.e., receives) the service in the territory of the service supplier (e.g., a person going to another State to receive medical treatment or education). Mode 3 is about 'commercial presence', where the service supplier establishes a commercial presence in the territory of another WTO member in order to provide the service there (e.g., a bank or other service firm that opens a branch in a foreign State). Lastly, Mode 4 is when an individual service supplier moves to another State to supply a service (e.g., an architect providing his or her services in a foreign State). Two of the four modes have human mobility implications, namely, Mode 2, where consumers cross an international border to receive a service, and Mode 4, where labour crosses an international border to provide a service. This chapter focusses on Mode 4, since it discusses the interplay between trade in services and labour mobility.

---

8 Commitments made by WTO members are contained in individual schedules, which are annexed to GATS. The schedules are available on the WTO website (www.wto.org).

9 For a full list, see *Services Sectoral Classification List*, WTO Doc MTN.GNS/W/120 (10 July 1991) (Note by the Secretariat).

WTO members can make specific commitments by sector or subsector, and by mode of supply (*sectoral commitments*). For example, under 'legal services' (a subsector of business services), commitments can be made for 'foreign legal consultants', with access given under Mode 3 and Mode 4.[10] Such a commitment would allow a law firm in State A to establish an office in the territory of State B and to provide services there (Mode 3), or for a lawyer from the firm in State A to temporarily migrate to State B for the purpose of providing legal services in State B (Mode 4). WTO members can also opt for *horizontal commitments*. Horizontal commitments cover a single mode of supply and apply to all sectors listed in the schedule. Most commitments made for Mode 4 are horizontal rather than sectoral.

For each commitment, for each sector or subsector, and for each mode of supply, WTO members must specify limitations on *market access* and limitations on *national treatment*. Regarding market access, a WTO member can offer full market access for a particular mode, which is indicated in the schedule by 'none' (i.e., no limitations); it can make no commitment, which is indicated in the schedule by 'unbound'; or it can offer partial commitments by indicating the nature of the limitations. WTO members are authorised to inscribe only six different types of limitation on their schedules (art. XVI(2)):

a limitations on the number of service suppliers;
b limitations on the total value of service transactions or assets;
c limitations on the total number of service operations or the total quantity of service outputs;
d limitations on the total number of natural persons who may be employed in a particular service sector or that a service supplier may employ;
e limitations on or requirements for certain types of legal entity or joint venture through which the service may be supplied; and
f limitations on the participation of foreign capital in terms of a maximum percentage limit on foreign shareholding or the total value of individual or aggregate foreign investment.

National treatment refers to a situation where foreign services and service suppliers are granted treatment no less favourable than that accorded to like national services and service providers. In contrast to the restrictions imposed on WTO members in identifying their market access limitations with regard to national treatment, it is for each State to judge what measures it considers appropriate and to inscribe them on the schedule (e.g., restriction on ownership of land by foreigners, or nationality requirements for professionals). Despite their apparent similarity, national treatment differs from the MFN principle. MFN is concerned with abolishing differences in treatment between foreign service providers by treating foreign

---

10 Julia Nielson and Daria Taglioni, 'A Quick Guide to the GATS and Mode 4' (Paper presented at the OECD, World Bank, IOM Seminar on Trade and Migration, Geneva, 12–14 November 2003) 10.

providers equally, regardless of their WTO member State of origin. National treatment is concerned with abolishing differences in treatment between foreign service providers and national service providers by treating the former the same as national service providers that provide the same type of services.

In summary, WTO members are free to decide whether or not they wish to make a commitment to liberalise trade in services for a specific sector or a mode of supply. If they do, they are also free to determine the extent of the commitment, as well as whether they wish to discriminate between foreigners and nationals.

12.2.2. Who is covered under Mode 4?

The movement of labour across borders may take various forms: it can be undertaken by a self-employed professional, an employee of a company that provides services across borders, an employee who is transferred from company headquarters to a branch in the country of destination, or an individual seeking employment in another country. GATS covers the movement of people, but only to the extent that such movement has the provision of a service as its objective. In the examples given above, all but the last could qualify as GATS movement if exercised for the purpose of providing a service. The last example covers the situation of cross-border mobility for the purpose of employment. The GATS *Annex on Movement of Natural Persons Supplying Services under the Agreement* ('Annex on Movement of Natural Persons') specifies that GATS does not apply 'to measures affecting natural persons seeking access to the employment market of a Member'.[11] GATS is thus concerned with facilitating the provision of services by foreign entities, not with facilitating access to employment in the local labour market.

Nonetheless, GATS is somewhat imprecise in its definition of the type of service provider covered by the agreement. Mode 4 is defined in art. I(2)(d) as the supply of a service 'by a service supplier of one Member, through presence of natural persons of a member in the territory of another Member' – a natural person being an individual rather than a legal or juridical entity, such as a corporation. Article XXVIII defines a 'service supplier' as 'any person that supplies a service'. A service supplier can be either a natural or a juridical person. Thus, the service supplier and the natural person supplying the service can be but are not necessarily the same.[12]

GATS obligations are owed towards *foreign* service suppliers from another WTO member. It would make little sense to have a multilateral trade agreement focussing on local market access for national service suppliers, which can be dealt with at the national level. Some provisions in GATS assist in determining the rule of origin.

---

11 *Marrakesh Agreement Establishing the World Trade Organization*, opened for signature 15 April 1994, 1867 UNTS 3 (entered into force 1 January 1995) annex 1B ('*General Agreement on Trade in Services: Annex on Movement of Natural Persons Supplying Services under the Agreement*'). See also WTO Council for Trade in Services, *Presence of Natural Persons (Mode 4)*, WTO Doc S/C/W/301 (15 September 2009) (Background Note by the Secretariat) 6.

12 For example, they are distinct in the case of foreign individuals who are employed by foreign service suppliers and sent by their companies to deliver the service abroad.

Article XXVIII(k) stipulates that 'a natural person of another member' is a natural person who resides in the territory of that other WTO member and who is a national or, in certain circumstances, a permanent resident of that other member. Article XXVIII(m) stipulates that a 'juridical person of another Member' is a juridical person constituted or organised under the law of that other member and engaging in substantive business operations in the territory of that other member.

Further guidance on Mode 4 is provided in the Annex on Movement of Natural Persons, which distinguishes between two types of natural persons. The first type concerns natural persons who are service suppliers – for example, a physician who supplies medical services through a foreign medical institution established in the host State or a concert pianist giving a concert in the host State. The second type covers 'natural persons of a Member who are employed by a service supplier of a Member'. Article I(2) specifies that the natural persons must be 'natural persons *of* a Member' in the territory of another member, and the service supplier must be 'a service supplier *of* one Member'; therefore they must *both* be of foreign origin. This implies that foreign nationals employed by nationally owned companies are not covered by GATS.[13] However, this possibility seems to be included in the specific commitments of some WTO members, who refer to 'short-term employment', or to foreign workers as employees in order to subject their conditions of work and pay to domestic labour law.[14] There is also some legal uncertainty about whether the scope of Mode 4 is defined only by the framework provisions of GATS or also by specific commitments made by WTO members, casting further doubt on the exact coverage of the agreement.

It is sometimes difficult to distinguish between an employee and a self-employed person. Although this distinction is crucial to identifying whether a service provider falls under GATS, the agreement does not provide further guidance. A good deal of national legislation distinguishes between them by reference to their entitlement to social security benefits and fiscal treatment. In the absence of a common set of definitions for categories of service providers, a number of general categories can be found in WTO members' schedule of commitments (see Box 12.1).

One significant qualification to Mode 4 labour mobility relates to the notion of temporary presence. The Annex on Movement of Natural Persons states that GATS does not apply to 'measures regarding citizenship, residence or employment on a permanent basis'. If such measures are excluded, it implies that Mode 4 is about temporary movement. However, the Agreement does not determine what constitutes a temporary presence only. The WTO's scheduling guidelines invite WTO members to specify in their schedule of specific commitments the authorised duration of stay for the different categories of natural persons included.[15]

---

13 However, nationally owned companies are authorised to use foreign service suppliers on a contractual basis (e.g., a self-employed person).
14 Nielson and Taglioni, above n. 10, 8.
15 WTO Council for Trade in Services, *Guidelines for the Scheduling of Specific Commitments under the General Agreement on Trade in Services (GATS)*, WTO Doc S/L/92 (28 March 2001).

A final difficulty in identifying the scope of Mode 4 arises from the challenges of identifying what constitutes a service in the context of increased outsourcing in a globalised economy. The production of a steel chair by a corporation would generally be classified as manufacturing, but could the same activity subcontracted to another corporation be categorised as a service? The same difficulty arises in agriculture: should the temporary resort to foreign workers for harvesting crops be categorised as agriculture or as a service incidental to agriculture?[16]

BOX 12.1 Categories of GATS service providers

During the Uruguay Round of trade negotiations (1986–94), States failed to agree on a common set of definitions for categories of service providers according to their skill levels and occupations. The only common tool made available by the Secretariat was the *Services Sectoral Classification List*, which includes cross-references to the United Nations Central Product Classification.[17] This list describes different types of services in broad categories. In the absence of common definitions, it is difficult to assess which service providers are covered in each WTO member's schedule of commitments.

To remedy this situation, some WTO members advocated the adoption of the International Labour Organization's *International Standard Classification of Occupations* ('ISCO-88', revised in 2008 as 'ISCO-08') as a means of classifying service providers.[18] A group of developing States, led by India, issued a request that defined a new common classification for categories of natural persons under Mode 4.[19] The European Commission collaborated with Canada, Bulgaria and Romania on a similar communication that called for a 'common approach to scheduling'.[20] These efforts were blocked by labour-receiving States.

The argument in favour of applying ISCO-88 was that it would expand the potential scope of GATS visa holders because the ISCO-88 criteria are more accommodating of low-skilled services than the WTO's *Services Sectoral Classification List*. For example, in the area of computing and related services, the adoption of ISCO-88 would extend this category to less-skilled service providers, such as technical support personnel.

In practice, WTO member schedules frequently use four categories of natural persons based on the purpose of a presence:

(a) *Independent professionals*: self-employed persons providing a service on the basis of a service contract.
(b) *Contractual service suppliers*: employees of a foreign service supplier without a commercial presence in the State where the service is delivered. They operate on the basis of a service contract between their employer and the client, and receive their remuneration from the employer.
(c) *Intra-corporate transferees*: employees of a foreign service supplier that has a commercial presence in the State where the service is provided. The provider is transferred to the local branch in the context of the supply of a service.
(d) *Business visitors*: employees of a foreign service supplier who seek entry to a State to set up a commercial presence or negotiate the sale of a service. They do not receive remuneration in the State where they operate.

Many WTO members also opt for a hierarchical arrangement of their scheduled commitments based on functional criteria, using categories such as 'executives', 'managers' and 'specialists'.[21]

---

16 See Nielson and Taglioni, above n. 10.   17 *Services Sectoral Classification List*, above n. 9.
18 ISCO is a tool for arranging jobs into clearly defined groups according to the duties undertaken.
19 WTO Council for Trade in Services, *Categories of Natural Persons for Commitments under Mode 4 of GATS*, WTO Doc TN/S/W/31 (18 February 2005) (Communication from Argentina, Bolivia, Brazil, Chile, Colombia, India, Mexico, Pakistan, Peru, Philippines, Thailand and Uruguay).
20 WTO Council for Trade in Services, *Mode 4: A Common Approach to Scheduling*, WTO Doc TN/S/W/32 (18 February 2005) (Communication from Bulgaria, Canada, the European Communities and Romania).
21 Hamid Mamdouh, 'Mode 4: Definition, Commitments, State of Play in the Negotiations' (Paper presented at the WTO Symposium: Mode 4 of the GATS – Taking Stock and Moving Forward, 22–23 September 2008).

The uncertainty that arises from the generality of the GATS provisions, and the lack of definition of essential terms makes the scope of GATS somewhat nebulous. This has important consequences because, if the scope of Mode 4 labour mobility is not clarified in the context of GATS negotiations, the degree of effective trade liberalisation in services will depend on broad or narrow interpretations adopted at the national level at the discretion of WTO members. At present, there is no WTO jurisprudence on Mode 4 that would help to clarify these uncertainties.

12.3.   THE IMMIGRATION AND LABOUR DIMENSIONS OF GATS MODE 4

GATS is a trade agreement and therefore covers the movement of persons in an ancillary way. Mobility is only encompassed in so far as it is a manner of providing services. The agreement therefore facilitates the movement of service providers, but does not touch upon the social and economic rights of workers, nor on migration management policy. In these two areas, from a WTO perspective, WTO members retain the right to design and implement the policies they choose. This is emphasised in art. 4 of the Annex on Movement of Natural Persons, which states that '[t]he Agreement shall not prevent a member from applying measures to regulate the entry of natural persons into, or their temporary stay in, its territory, including those measures necessary to protect the integrity of, and to ensure the orderly movement of natural persons across its borders'.

12.3.1.   The immigration dimension

Trade policy makers do not regard Mode 4 as a type of labour migration because service providers are not 'seeking access to the employment market' to seek jobs,[22] but rather to perform specified tasks under a service contract. Nevertheless, Mode 4 mobility generates migration issues and can be seen as a subset of temporary migration.

The trade and migration agendas have so far followed two different paths because they are based on different rationales. Multilateral trade agreements are about predictability and guaranteed access to foreign markets on an equal footing for all players. Economic migration policy is about flexibility and regulating the entry of labour according to the economic situation (availability of employment and labour shortages) and political issues, such as the reaction of the population to inflows of migrants. Some of these economic considerations have also been introduced into the trade agenda – for example, through the imposition of an economic needs test, which conditions the entry of foreign workers according to the circumstances of the domestic labour market and the availability of national

---

22 Annex on Movement of Natural Persons, above n. 11, art. 2.

workers to fill labour shortages. However, such limitations have been criticised by some labour source countries on the ground that they are contrary to the spirit of trade liberalisation.[23]

Migration regulators have other concerns, such as the impact of labour movements on public health and welfare systems and national security. They are also concerned that Mode 4, albeit limited to temporary movement, may open the door to longer stay through overstaying an authorised permit or switching to another visa category that provides for more permanent residence status. For some developing States, an additional issue is the emigration of skilled workers, which can lead to a 'brain drain' and result in local skills shortages, with the associated costs of training new workers or replacing them by hiring expensive expatriates.

However, as a trade agreement, GATS has been shaped by its focus on trade liberalisation and increasing market access, with no consideration for migration management issues, such as preventing the potential negative effects of migration (e.g., irregular migration) or maximising the potential positive outcomes (e.g., remittances).

Mode 4 movements need to be managed like other movements of foreign workers in terms of entry and stay. One of the difficulties of distinguishing between GATS Mode 4 movement and other temporary labour migration lies in the absence of a definition of duration of presence, as well as the more general difficulty of distinguishing a job performed as a service provider from one performed as a migrant worker. A salient example is the difference, if any, between picking apples as a contract worker or as an agricultural foreign employee. This has implications for ensuring that Mode 4 commitments are fully implemented but not abused by utilising an ambiguous distinction to expand entry to cover all kinds of temporary migrant workers.

The translation of GATS outcomes into national migration regimes remains problematic. Most States do not have specific streamlined procedures for service providers; rather they treat Mode 4 movements within their general migration framework, applying to them existing visa categories for temporary or permanent labour migration or business visits. Each State determines its own admission criteria. The only limitation on a WTO member's competence to regulate the entry and temporary stay of natural persons within its borders is the obligation to ensure that such measures are not applied in such a manner as 'to nullify or impair the benefits accruing to any Member under the terms of a specific commitment'.[24] Visa requirements, work permits and other regulatory measures can discriminate between nationals of different States without being inconsistent with the MFN principle. These migration management tools are recognised as remaining within

---

23 In principle, WTO members can negotiate emergency safeguard measures whereby States can temporarily close their markets to foreign services: GATS art. X.
24 Annex on Movement of Natural Persons, above n. 11, art. 4.

the realm of domestic competence and not of themselves against the spirit of the trade agreement.[25]

There exist nearly as many visa regimes and requirements as there are States. The difficulty of finding out which visa classes implement a State's Mode 4 commitments does not create an easy environment in which service providers can tap into the advantages of GATS. Some WTO members would therefore like to see the scope of GATS expanded, with the adoption of multilateral rules in the area of admission.[26] India has suggested introducing a special 'GATS visa' to avoid lengthy procedures in many States, especially where the immigration framework does not distinguish between persons seeking temporary or permanent stay.[27] The visa would be delivered rapidly and be time-limited.[28] Other commentators have taken this idea a step further and would like the WTO to monitor or participate in the allocation of visas regarding the movement of natural persons.[29] India's suggestion of additional commitments to ensure transparency and better-harmonised immigration procedures was supported by a request submitted by a number of developing States in 2003.[30] Among the suggestions for greater transparency is the idea of a one-stop shop for information on all relevant procedures and requirements via a dedicated website.[31]

GATS does not have a regulatory mandate to manage the possible negative effects of economic migration. However, some WTO members and trade specialists have given thought to introducing a few migration management elements in the GATS framework. The rationale is to address the concerns of migration regulators regarding security and overstay, which are seen as playing a major role in the limited commitments made by WTO members to date and the lack of coverage of lower skills.

Some commentators have suggested that a GATS visa could embody elements to prevent irregular migration, such as a bond. This would support the *bona fide* nature of the candidates and provide sanctions for abuses.[32] Others suggest inscribing a 'regulatory' source country obligation into the 'additional commitments' section of a

---

25 A footnote to art. 4 of the Annex on Movement of Natural Persons states that '[t]he sole fact of requiring a visa for natural persons of certain Members and not for those of others shall not be regarded as nullifying or impairing benefits under a specific commitment'.

26 Alan Winters, 'Developing Country Proposals for the Liberalization of Movements of Natural Service Suppliers' (Development Research Centre on Migration, Globalisation and Poverty, 2005).

27 WTO Council for Trade in Services, *Proposed Liberalisation of Movement of Professionals under General Agreement on Trade in Services (GATS)*, WTO Doc S/CSS/W/12 (24 November 2000) (Communication from India).

28 GATS visas exist in the Netherlands, but are not utilised because they are less generous than some other visa classes: Simon Tans, 'The Unwanted Service Provider: Implementation of WTO and EU Liberalisation of Service Mobility in the Dutch Legal Order' (2011) 30(2) *Refugee Survey Quarterly* 67.

29 Eric Ng and John Whalley, 'Visas and Work Permits: Possible Global Negotiating Initiatives' (2008) 3(3) *Review of International Organizations* 259.

30 WTO Council for Trade in Services, *Proposed Liberalization of Mode 4 Under GATS Negotiations*, WTO Doc TN/S/W/14 (3 July 2003) (Communication from Argentina, Bolivia, Chile, the People's Republic of China, Colombia, Dominican Republic, Egypt, Guatemala, India, Mexico, Pakistan, Peru, Philippines and Thailand).

31 Nielson and Taglioni, above n. 10, 15.

32 World Bank, Organisation for Economic Co-operation and Development and International Organization for Migration, 'Trade and Migration: Building Bridges for Global Labour Mobility' (OECD, 2004).

State's schedule of commitments (art. XVIII).[33] Labour source countries would commit to taking appropriate measures to ensure the timely return of their service providers to their country of origin, thus discouraging irregular migration. This approach would require a change of mindset for trade negotiators because the current scheduling structure of GATS commitments does not provide for obligations other than to 'liberalise', and is therefore not well adapted to a regulatory approach.[34]

The proposed inclusion of migration management issues within WTO competences is highly controversial and probably unlikely to secure the support of all WTO members, as is required for an amendment of its mandate. On the other hand, the need to bring the migration and trade communities together has been increasingly recognised. Since the early 2000s many workshops have been convened to help the stakeholders understand their respective regulatory concerns and consider ways to facilitate the implementation of Mode 4.

12.3.2. The labour dimension

A further contentious aspect of GATS is that Mode 4 does not refer to social and labour standards, such as the quality of working conditions for service providers. The argument usually advanced in this context is that WTO is a trade body and therefore not the appropriate forum to set social or labour standards for the protection of workers worldwide.[35] However, this issue is present in trade negotiations in an oblique fashion through limitations to market access in each State's schedule of commitments. Indeed, over fifty WTO members stipulate in their commitments that they require wage parity between nationals and foreigners. In addition, twenty-two WTO members have reserved the right to suspend Mode 4 commitments in the event of labour–management disputes, with a view to precluding local employers from hiring foreigners as 'strike-breakers' to replace national workers.[36]

The difficulty of addressing protection concerns in the context of trade agreements can be seen at the bilateral and regional levels as well. A number of recent bilateral and regional trade agreements contain explicit references to social issues or core labour standards, either in the text of the agreement or indirectly through side agreements on labour cooperation.[37] These provisions do not secure any

---

33 Mohammad Amin and Aaditya Mattoo, 'Does Temporary Migration Have to Be Permanent?' (World Bank, 2005); Rupa Chanda, 'Low-Skilled Workers and Bilateral, Regional and Unilateral Initiatives: Lessons for the GATS Mode 4 Negotiations and other Agreements' (United Nations Development Programme, 2008).

34 Marion Panizzon, 'Trade and Labor Migration: GATS Mode 4 and Migration Agreements' (Friedrich-Ebert-Stiftung, 2010) 24–5.

35 The importance of labour standards was, however, recognised in arts. 7, 93–5 of the *Havana Charter of the International Trade Organization* (1947), which never came into force.

36 Caroline Dommen, 'Migrants' Human Rights: Could GATS Help?' (Migration Policy Institute, 2005).

37 For example, the *United States–Central America–Dominican Republic Free Trade Agreement* (2004) and the *United States–Chile Free Trade Agreement* (2004) include commitments to core labour standards. Similarly, a labour cooperation agreement was concluded in parallel with the *Canada–Costa Rica Free Trade Agreement* (2001). It obliges the States parties to embody in their labour legislation the principles enshrined in the *ILO Declaration on Fundamental Principles and Rights at Work* (1998).

particular labour protections for migrant workers or service providers, but such individuals can benefit from broader requirements, such as the obligation to enforce domestic labour standards in a non-discriminatory manner. From a legal point of view, these provisions and their enforcement mechanisms remain generally weak.

The question arises whether it would be possible to include a social clause in GATS to ensure respect for core labour standards – such as non-discrimination in wages – at the multilateral level. Those in favour of such a clause argue that it will protect local workers from 'social dumping', whereas those against express the view that it will reduce the advantages for States in recruiting workers or sending them abroad. To date, it seems that there are no strong voices to advance this issue, apart from those of trade unions and some non-government organisations.[38]

12.4.   CURRENT STATE OF AFFAIRS

Commitments on Mode 4 remain more restrictive than for the other modes of supply, for both developed and developing States. Most of the current commitments made under Mode 4 reflect actual migration policy or are even more restrictive than current policy on the admission of service providers. Mode 4 is therefore seen as a trade area with the greatest scope for further liberalisation.

Most specific commitments under Mode 4 are horizontal, that is, they apply the same conditions to all service sectors inscribed in a WTO member's schedule. However, some subsectors – like professional services, or information and communication technology – are particularly relevant for Mode 4 and would benefit from deeper liberalisation. The fact that WTO members have adopted a horizontal approach has resulted in the application of the 'lowest common denominator' to the admission of all service providers.[39]

The degree of Mode 4 access specified in current WTO members' schedules is quite limited. Most WTO members have scheduled an initial 'unbound' response (meaning that the State makes no commitment to liberalisation), and then specified greater levels of access for particular categories of service providers.

According to the WTO Council for Trade in Services,[40] the bulk of commitments target 'Intra Corporate Transferee' ('ICT') (42 per cent), followed by 'Business

---

38 Global Union Research Network, *Global Union Research Network* (2011) www.gurn.info. Service providers are protected from certain abusive conditions under some conventions: *International Convention on the Protection of the Rights of All Migrant Workers and Members of their Families*, opened for signature 18 December 1990, 2220 UNTS 3 (entered into force 1 July 2003); *Convention concerning Migrations in Abusive Conditions and the Promotion of Equality of Opportunity and Treatment of Migrant Workers* (ILO Convention No 143), opened for signature 24 June 1975 (entered into force 9 December 1978) Part I. For discussion, see International Organization for Migration, 'World Migration 2008: Managing Labour Mobility in the Evolving Economy' (IOM, 2008) 45–6.

39 WTO Council for Trade in Services, *Presence of Natural Persons (Mode 4)*, WTO Doc S/C/W/301 (15 September 2009) (Background Note by the Secretariat) [73].

40 Ibid.

Visitors' ('BV') (24 per cent)[41] and 'Executives, Managers and Specialists' ('EMS') (22 per cent).[42] The remaining commitments cover 'Contractual Service Suppliers' ('CSS') (4 per cent),[43] 'other categories' (4 per cent) and 'Independent Professionals' (1 per cent). The 'other' category encompasses a heterogeneous set of service providers who do not fall easily into the main groups, ranging from low-skilled workers (e.g., installers) to trainees or persons with specific abilities (e.g., sports-persons, artists). In principle, Mode 4 applies to all skills levels, but in practice commitments have generally focussed on higher-skilled individuals with high levels of education and expertise. When the wording of commitments potentially allows room for lower-skilled workers, this is limited to the categories of business visitors, contractual service suppliers and 'other'.

Because the majority of commitments on Mode 4 relate to intra-corporate trans-ferees, the movement of natural persons under GATS remains substantially linked to commercial presence (Mode 3). Behind this approach lies the idea that any costs associated with the temporary movement of labour (on the welfare system or from competition with the local workforce) are compensated by the inflow of foreign direct investment to destination States. Yet most developing and least developed States lack capital. These States import foreign capital from abroad rather than export their own, which hinders them in establishing a commercial presence in other States. Few corporations from these States have a significant global presence. Accordingly, Mode 4 commitments that are conditioned on the establishment of a commercial presence are of minimal benefit to developing States.

In addition to restrictions relating to the categories of service providers, other limitations are frequently included in schedules: application of an economic needs test to specialists, highly qualified personnel, managers and executives; limitations on numbers of foreign service suppliers through imposition of quotas or a ceiling on the proportion of foreigners in the workforce; pre-employment requirements (thus excluding the self-employed); and obligations to train local staff, especially in developing States. Some countries have scheduled conditions relating to con-ditions of work, domestic wage legislation, working hours and social security, and have reserved the right to suspend the commitment in case of a labour dispute. Finally, some WTO members impose nationality and residence requirements.

Exemptions from MFN treatment are also applied. They are difficult to assess for Mode 4 movement because the exemptions are not expressed in modal terms and often relate to regional trade agreements. Around forty exemptions concern the movement of natural persons (see Box 12.2).[44]

---

41 All developed States bar one have inscribed 'Business Visitors' in their horizontal commitments.

42 Most of the forty-three WTO members that use a functional classification with commitments on 'Executives, Managers and Specialists' are developing countries. Eighty per cent of these commitments are restricted by quota or an economic needs test.

43 'Contractual Service Suppliers' commitments have been made mainly by European Union members and new WTO members.

44 World Trade Organization, *Movement of Natural Persons* (2011) www.wto.org/english/tratop_e/serv_e/mouvement_persons_e/mouvement_persons_e.htm.

BOX 12.2 Most favoured nation and its exemptions

The MFN obligation to grant to all WTO members any concession made to a particular member (art. II) is 'unconditional', meaning that it applies irrespective of whether a member has listed a market access commitment in its schedule. The MFN obligation applies only to 'services' and 'service suppliers', and therefore natural persons who are not service suppliers do not have to be accorded MFN treatment. Preferential recruitment of foreign employees of certain nationalities would not be inconsistent with the MFN requirement unless this leads to discrimination against the service suppliers who employ them or the services they supply.

States can depart from the MFN obligation in certain circumstances. Each WTO member had a one-off opportunity at the time GATS entered into force in 1995, or upon later accession, to seek an exemption from the MFN obligation for up to ten years. GATS also allows for limited departures from MFN treatment that are not subject to time constraints. MFN treatment does not have to be applied if the preferential treatment given to some WTO members is provided under the framework of an economic integration agreement within the meaning of art. V. An economic integration agreement can be between two or more States, and to qualify it must have substantial coverage in all services sectors and modes, not just Mode 4 (see Case Study 12.1).

A regional trade agreement that is limited to labour mobility will be inconsistent with GATS unless it qualifies as a 'labour market integration agreement' as defined in art. V bis. This provision requires that the agreement exempt citizens of States parties to the agreement from requirements concerning residence and work permits. Such agreements normally apply national treatment for pay and other conditions of employment and social benefits. The willingness of States to achieve such a deep level of labour market integration is quite rare, and it is unlikely that this article will be often invoked. An example of such an agreement is provided by the European Union.

Departure from MFN treatment is also permitted when WTO members agree to recognise 'the education or experience obtained, requirements met, or licenses or certifications granted in a particular country' (art. VII). However, this concession is available only where WTO members afford adequate opportunity to other interested States to negotiate similar recognition agreements.

Other trade barriers relate to the capacity of States to implement their commitments and the ability of WTO members to actually benefit from the market access provided. As previously mentioned, the difficulty relates to the vague definition of categories of service providers used in WTO members' schedules. Many commitments do not indicate a length of stay. Thus, while the most frequently specified periods are for business visitors (three months), contractual service suppliers (three months) and intra-corporate transferees (two to five years), only twelve commitments on executives, managers and specialists specify a duration (ranging from one to four years).

While immigration procedures may clarify the way in which a State accommodates its Mode 4 commitments, in most instances WTO members do not create special visas or work permits to match their commitments. It can therefore be difficult for service providers to obtain a clear understanding of their actual market access. Moreover, immigration regulations may be cumbersome, lengthy and expensive, and not adapted to the need for quick deployment of service providers to perform a service.

Difficulties in having skills and qualifications recognised may seriously affect Mode 4 trade. They can impede individuals from practising their professions in a foreign country. In an attempt to overcome such impediments, mutual recognition agreements have been concluded between WTO members with a view to facilitating the assessment of skills. GATS encourages members to enter into such agreements (art. VII), but thus far they have been concluded mainly between developed States or between States that share geographical proximity and historical or linguistic ties.

12.4.1. Measurement and impact of GATS Mode 4

GATS does not create universal criteria for the admission of defined categories of service providers and their access to labour markets. Indeed, it does not provide a definition of service providers, nor does it prescribe the range, depth or sectoral coverage of country commitments, which would have created a common understanding of GATS Mode 4. Instead, GATS is multiform and there are as many GATS Mode 4 formulae as country schedules. Attempting to measure the current value of GATS Mode 4 would require a summation of very diverse patterns of movement and varied national experiences. It is all too easy to forget the highly diverse approaches to GATS Mode 4 at a State level when using generic terms such as 'Mode 4' or 'service providers'.

No comprehensive estimates on Mode 4 trade exist today. It has been stated that Mode 4 accounts for less than 5 per cent of the total value of international supply of services,[45] but it is not known how many individual cross-border movements this represents. The 'measurement' of Mode 4 means different things to different stakeholders. From a trade perspective, what is important is the value that accrues from liberalising Mode 4, that is, its economic benefit to the economy. The number of persons involved in Mode 4 movement is a useful proxy of value because it is difficult to isolate the trade value of such movement. From a migration perspective, on the contrary, the priority is establishing the number of persons crossing international borders and residing in one State or another.

The measurement of Mode 4 trade poses several challenges as no statistical framework is currently in place to capture the value of trade in services occurring under Mode 4. Some work has been undertaken at the international level and a United Nations *Manual on Statistics of International Trade in Services* has been drafted to improve data collection and analysis.[46] In order to assess the value of Mode 4 trade, information on both the value of the services provided by service providers covered by GATS and the flows and stocks of service providers need to be captured. The Balance of Payment items 'compensation of employees' and 'workers' remittances' are often used as statistical indicators. However, they capture labour income from international movement, but not Mode 4 trade specifically. They cannot

---

45 Joscelyn Magdeleine and Andreas Maurer, 'Measuring GATS Mode 4 Trade Flows' (WTO, 2008).
46 Department of Economic and Social Affairs, 'Manual on Statistics of International Trade in Services, Statistical Papers, Series M No 86, UN Doc ST/ESA/STAT/SER.M/86' (United Nations, 2002).

substitute for indicators that measure the value of trade flows (by capturing the value of services transactions), even though it is difficult to break down by mode because services are often traded using several modes at the same time.

Tourism and migration statistical frameworks provide some information on the flows and stocks of persons abroad, but they need to be adapted to permit the collection of more reliable information on categories of services providers covered by Mode 4.[47]

One of the difficulties in assessing the impact of Mode 4 is that, while it concerns cross-border trade, it deals with people. Conventional trade theory describes the benefits of liberalising trade in goods by eliminating inefficiencies, stimulating innovation through competition, and so on. Although this theory remains relevant to trade in services under Mode 4, it does not capture other elements at stake with service providers, similar to those of any migration, in that it temporarily changes a State's labour supply. An adequate conceptual framework that captures the full economic implications of Mode 4 labour mobility is yet to be developed.

Nonetheless, several studies have attempted to measure the potential economic impact of liberalising the international movement of service providers. Given the difficulties in identifying Mode 4 movement, these studies seek to estimate the gains from freeing up the temporary movement of workers rather than liberalising the movement of service providers as defined by GATS. Walmsley and Winters estimated that if developed States were to raise their intake of labour from developing States to 3 per cent of their labour force, an overall annual gain of US$150 billion would be realised and shared equally between developed and developing States.[48] Rodrik comes up with the figure of US$200 billion in gains per year.[49]

It is generally considered that the costs and benefits of the temporary movement of labour depend on the situation of the labour market, the economy, the skills level and the regulatory framework in source and destination States. For source States, temporary labour migration can alleviate labour surpluses, provide family livelihoods through remittances, and create technology and skills transfer. These must be weighed against the costs of family disruption, dependency on remittances over employment creation and skills shortages due to emigration. For destination States, the temporary movement of labour can decrease labour shortages and release pressure on wages, but it can also generate social tension and lead to irregular migration. Since Mode 4 is seen as the service trade area that could generate the greatest benefits for developing States, several attempts have been made to release this potential for development (see Box 12.3).

---

47 Different statistical sources are reviewed in Magdeleine and Maurer, above n. 45; and in WTO Council for Trade in Services, *A Review of Statistics on Trade Flows in Services: Data Compilation and Availability*, WTO Doc S/C/W/329 (22 December 2010) (Note by the Secretariat).

48 Terrie Walmsley and Alan Winters, 'Relaxing the Restrictions on the Temporary Movements of Natural Persons: A Simulation Analysis: Discussion Paper No 3719' (Centre for Economic Policy Research, 2003). This gain results mainly from the difference in productivity between low-skilled workers in developing and developed States.

49 Dani Rodrik, 'Feasible Globalizations: NBER Working Paper No 9129' (National Bureau of Economic Research, 2002) 20.

BOX 12.3 GATS and developing States

From its inception during the Uruguay Round of trade negotiations, GATS was intended to facilitate the participation of developing States. Article IV calls for increasing the participation of developing States, with special priority to be given to WTO members that are the least developed. Specific safeguards were included in other provisions to recognise the disparities between developed, developing and least developed countries ('LDCs') in the WTO. Examples include differences in the permitted restrictions on trade in services in the event of serious balance-of-payments and external financial difficulties (art. XII) and differential obligations for progressive liberalisation having regard to a country's level of development (art. XIX). Supporting the participation of developing States, and acknowledging their particular needs within the negotiations, were key objectives of GATS drafters.

Nonetheless, developed States have made limited commitments in sectors of greatest interest to developing States, particularly under Mode 4. Moreover, commitments made under Mode 4 have generally been linked to commercial presence (Mode 3). Developing States have benefitted little from this type of liberalisation because they have limited capacity to pursue foreign investment and have limited commercial presence in other WTO member States. Most of the commitments made have been directed to the higher end of the skills spectrum, where developed States have a comparative advantage, rather than to low- or middle-skilled labour, where developing States would benefit most.

The lack of progress on issues that developing States had identified as priorities at the end of the Uruguay Round was a motive to include GATS under the Doha Development Agenda. The Doha Round was created on the premise of establishing a fair market-oriented trading system. Special and differential treatment for developing States was as an integral feature of the Doha Round.

In 2003, guidelines were finalised for LDCs, highlighting that 'LDCs have identified ... GATS Mode 4 as important to them and [stating] that members shall to the extent possible consider undertaking commitments to provide access'.[50] Furthermore, 'the July 2004 package' led to a set of new recommendations reaffirming the importance of 'ensuring a high quality of offers, in particular in sectors and modes of export of interest to developing countries, with special attention being given to least developed countries'. In 2005, the Hong Kong Ministerial Declaration[51] indicated that LDCs would not be expected to make new commitments in the Doha Round, and it created 'Modalities for the Special Treatment of Least-Developed Country Members'.[52]

However, despite the foundation of the Doha Round as development-friendly and the establishment of modalities directed to this end, few concrete offers have been made under Mode 4. Commitments under Mode 4 remain limited, and those that are in place target the movement of highly skilled workers. In practice, Mode 4 has been the counterpart offered to developing States for their agreement to include commitments on Mode 3 (services provided through commercial presence). However, increased market access under Mode 3 can only benefit States that are able to export capital, which is primarily the developed States.[53]

The disconnection between market access under Mode 3 and labour mobility under Mode 4 is considered by some to 'reflect a basic imbalance in negotiating positions and lobbying power between the two sides'.[54] Conflict between the goals of developed and developing States has been a major point of contention as negotiations have progressed and has contributed to the delay in finalising the Doha Round. Though few concessions have been made so far to the demands of developing States, special consideration of their demands on Mode 4 may be a key to finalising GATS negotiations in the Doha Round.

50 Nielson and Taglioni, above n. 10, 14.
51 *DOHA Work Programme*, Ministerial Conference, Sixth Session, Hong Kong, 13–18 December 2005, WTO Doc WT/MIN(05)/DEC (22 December 2005) (Ministerial Declaration).
52 World Trade Organization, above n. 44.
53 Antonia Carzaniga, 'The GATS Mode 4, and Patterns of Commitments' in Aaditya Mattoo and Antonia Carzaniga (eds.), *Moving People to Deliver Services* (World Bank and Oxford University Press, 2003) 21.
54 Chanda, above n. 33, 13.

12.4.2.   State of negotiations

WTO members remain reluctant to liberalise Mode 4. In the Uruguay Round (1986–94), commitments scheduled under Mode 4 were largely limited to two categories – intra-company transferees regarded as 'essential personnel', such as managers and technical staff linked to a commercial presence in the host State; and business visitors, that is, short-term visitors not generally remunerated in the host State. Some progress was made after GATS came into force, with further commitments by some member States on additional categories of service suppliers (mainly independent professionals) and extension of duration of stay.[55]

Under the current Doha Round of negotiations that started in 2001, progress on Mode 4 has remained unsatisfactory. In comparison to the other three modes of supply, Mode 4 commitments are the least liberal, due to the requirement of positive listing (trade is not liberalised unless a State voluntarily agrees to list a commitment) and a proliferation of limitations. Although about thirty of around seventy offers on Mode 4 propose some improvements to horizontal commitments (half from developed, half from developing States), Mamdouh recalls that the value of horizontal commitments in Mode 4 depends on the number of sectors included in the schedule.[56] The main progress relates to the inclusion of new categories of service suppliers (e.g., installers and maintainers by Switzerland; graduate trainees by the European Union);[57] an expanded list of sectors to which the commitments apply; extended periods of stay; possibility of renewal; clarification of the scope of economic needs tests; reduction of discriminatory measures; and some improvements in transparency.

The services negotiations in the Doha Round are being conducted essentially on two tracks. First, bilateral negotiations (between two WTO members) and plurilateral negotiations (between several but not all WTO members) are directed towards improving specific commitments on market access and national treatment, and promoting MFN treatment. Second, multilateral negotiations among all WTO members are directed towards establishing the necessary rules and disciplines that will apply to the whole WTO membership on issues such as domestic regulation, emergency safeguard measures, government procurement and subsidies.[58] The Doha Round was supposed to be completed by January 2005, but negotiations came to a standstill at the WTO ministerial meeting in Cancun in September 2003, casting doubt on the timely completion of the rounds. Despite the attempt of several WTO members, particularly developing States, to secure better commitments and de-link Mode 4 from commercial presence, the quality of the changes proposed on Mode 4 remained disappointing compared to other service areas.

---

55 *Third Protocol to the General Agreement on Trade in Services*, opened for signature 6 October 1995, 2061 UNTS 193 (entered into force 26 July 1996).

56 Mamdouh, above n. 21.

57 WTO Council for Trade in Services, '*Temporary Admission of Installers and Maintainers under the GATS: A Case for Mode 4 Commitments*, WTO Doc TN/S/W/61 (2 April 2007) (Communication from Switzerland)' (2007); WTO Council for Trade in Services, *Report by the Chairman to the Trade Negotiations Committee*, WTO Doc TN/S/23 (28 November 2005).

58 World Trade Organization, *Negotiating Mandates* (2011) www.wto.org/english/tratop_e/serv_e/nego_mandates_e.htm.

Some commentators blame the 'July 2004 Package' and the Doha Work Programme for the lack of progress. These instruments reinforced the special and differential treatment provisions of GATS under arts. IV and XIX, according to which developing States are not required to reciprocate offers by making commitments in sectors of interest to developed States. The 'July 2004 package' led to a new set of recommendations reaffirming the importance of 'ensuring a high quality of offers, in particular in sectors and modes of export of interest to developing countries, with special attention being given to least-developed countries'.[59] Given the lack of reciprocity, few developed States felt an incentive to oblige. Offers remained limited and the worthy intention of making Doha's agenda development-friendly contributed further to the bottleneck in Mode 4 negotiations.[60]

Nonetheless, a new momentum to services negotiations occurred with the Hong Kong Ministerial Declaration of 2005.[61] The Declaration called for new or improved commitments on categories linked to or de-linked from commercial presence, the removal or substantial reduction of economic needs tests, and an indication of the duration of stay and renewal. The Declaration also established modalities for plurilateral negotiations, and such a process was launched in 2006 through a collective request made by fifteen developing States to nine developed States. Commitments were called for in a number of sectors (including business, construction, tourism, and environmental and recreational services) and removal of the economic needs tests was also requested.[62] Least developed countries have also submitted a Mode 4 request on similar lines.[63]

However, the entire Doha round of negotiations stalled between mid-2006 and early 2007. To assess how much the state of play may have changed in the meantime, a services signalling conference was held in 2008 to gauge the extent to which governments were willing to incorporate requests they had received. Indications were exchanged on new and improved commitments as well as on the contributions expected from others.[64] Generally, positive indications were given about market access commitments across all major services sectors and modes of supply. Yet, although the signals were better than expected, progress has tapered since July 2008.[65] Little progress has been made on market access, although there has been some progress on domestic regulations and on the preferential treatment of LDC members.[66]

---

59 World Trade Organization, *Key Stages in the Negotiations* (2011) www.wto.org/english/tratop_e/serv_e/key_stages_e.htm.

60 Panizzon, above n. 34, 18.

61 *DOHA Work Programme*, Ministerial Conference, Sixth Session, Hong Kong, 13–18 December 2005, WTO Doc WT/MIN(05)/DEC (22 December 2005) (Ministerial Declaration).

62 WTO Council for Trade in Services, *Report of the Meeting Held on 7 April 2006*, WTO Doc TN/S/M/19 (18 May 2006) (Note by the Secretariat).

63 Mamdouh, above n. 21.

64 Some WTO members have expressed their readiness to open specific services sectors, such as tourism and travel, private hospitals, and services incidental to mining and agriculture: *Report by the Chairman of the TNC*, Services Signalling Conference, WTO Doc JOB(08)/93 (30 July 2008).

65 Trade in Services Division, 'Services Negotiation under the GATS: Background and Current State of Play' (WTO, 2009) 7.

66 WTO Council for Trade in Services, *Negotiations on Trade in Services*, WTO Doc TN/S/35 (22 March 2010) (Report by the Chairman).

CASE STUDY 12.1   Free movement under the regional trade agreement in the Caribbean

The Caribbean Community ('CARICOM') offers a good example of an attempt to strengthen regional labour mobility in parallel with efforts to create a single market economy. Established in 1973 as a Common Market by the Treaty of Chaguaramas, CARICOM promotes economic integration and collaboration among its members, while also cooperating on foreign policy. CARICOM comprises fifteen States – the thirteen original signatories (all former British colonies),[67] together with Suriname and Haiti. In 2001, the Heads of Government concluded a Revised Treaty with nine Protocols to facilitate the transition of CARICOM's Common Market into a Caribbean Single Market Economy ('CSME').[68] Twelve States have now ratified the Revised Treaty; two States (the Bahamas and Montserrat) have indicated their intention not to participate; and one (Haiti) has ratified the Revised Treaty but remains under a temporary trade concession agreement.[69] Through the CSME, freedom of movement was designated as a priority issue in the Caribbean integration agenda. The concept of free movement is embodied in three elements of the Single Market – the movement of skills, the movement of services and rights of establishment.[70]

Free movement of skills grants CARICOM nationals the right to pursue employment in any member State without the need for a work permit; however, before implementing universal labour mobility, CARICOM members opted to liberalise movement though a phased approach.[71] The Revised Treaty initially prioritised five categories of CARICOM nationals for free movement university graduates, media workers, artists, musicians and sportspersons. By 2006, tertiary-trained nurses and teachers were added to the mobility framework. Between 2007 and 2009, three additional skill categories artisans, associate degree recipients and certified domestic workers also became eligible for free movement.[72]

Although almost all States participating in the CSME have adopted legislation to permit movement of skilled labour, few qualifying nationals have taken advantage of the opportunity to move. By the end of 2008, a two-year total of 6,210 Certificates of Skills Recognition had been issued (representing 0.1 per cent of the CSME population), but no statistics are available to show the number used during that period.[73] By 2010 the

---

67 Antigua and Barbuda, the Bahamas, Barbados, Belize, Dominica, Grenada, Guyana, Jamaica, Saint Kitts and Nevis, Saint Lucia, Saint Vincent and Grenadines, Trinidad and Tobago, and Montserrat.

68 Sophie Nonnenmacher, 'Free Movement of Persons in the Caribbean Community' in Ryszard Cholewinski, Richard Perruchoud and Euan Macdonald (eds.), *International Migration Law: Developing Paradigms and Key Challenges* (TMC Asser Press, 2007) 3879.

69 Caribbean Community Secretariat, *Press Release NF01/2011: News Feature: Five Years On The CARICOM Single Market and Economy* (2011) www.caricom.org/jsp/pressreleases/presnf01.11.jsp.

70 Nonnenmacher, above n. 68, 390.

71 Alicia Brcena, Antonio Prado, Osvaldo Rosales and Susana Malchik, Latin America and the Caribbean in the World Economy: A Crisis Generated in the Centre and a Recovery Driven by the Emerging Economies (UNECLAC, 2010) 130.

72 Caribbean Community Secretariat, *Press Release 159/2010: Free Movement Working in the CSME: CARICOM Secretary-General* (14 April 2010) www.caricom.org/jsp/pressreleases/pres159.10.jsp.

73 Norman Girvan, Caribbean Community: The Elusive Quest for Economic Integration (Caribbean Community, 2010) 3.

cumulative total of Skills Certificates recipients had increased to about 9,000 persons. Women constituted the majority of migrants and most Skills Certificate recipients were university graduates.[74] However, most labour movement in CARICOM continues to come from unskilled labour, which is neither regulated nor statistically recorded.[75] This trend in labour mobility exemplifies the problems endemic to CARICOMs freedom of movement scheme.

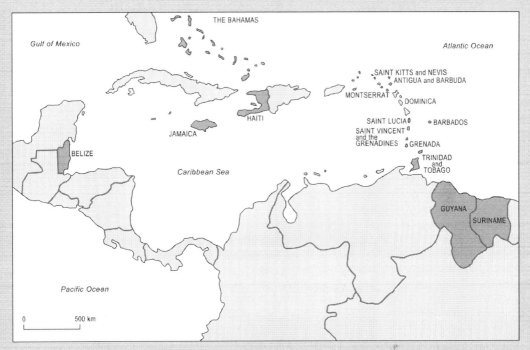

Map 12.1 Member States of CARICOM

74 Caribbean Community Secretariat, above n. 71.   75 Nonnenmacher, above n. 70, 397.

The state of play of services negotiations cannot be understood in isolation from difficulties in negotiations on agricultural and non-agricultural market access. In the absence of agreement on these areas, not much progress is expected to be achieved in the field of services. With the Doha Round 4 negotiations still continuing after more than a decade, tensions remain high. According to the WTO Director-General, the cost of failure could be a debilitating blow to a multilateral trading system that has been established for seventy years.[76]

76 World Trade Organization, *Think of Cost of Doha Round Failure, Lamy Urges Members as Deadline Looms* (2011) www.wto.org/english/news_e/news11_e/tnc_dg_infstat_29mar11_e.htm.

12.5. CONCLUSION

In conclusion, the negotiation of new commitments under GATS is the only initiative at the global level to liberalise labour mobility. The GATS Mode 4 agenda covers only a subset of temporary labour mobility, but the possibility of ensuring a degree of market openness for foreign service providers makes GATS a unique playing field where nationals from WTO member States are generally treated alike. This is important because trade in services comprises a growing share of the global economy. Irrespective of the success or failure of the Doha Round, Mode 4 movements are likely to increase, given the growth in demand for services worldwide. In the absence of a supporting global framework, these movements will be accommodated through national legislation or bilateral and regional agreements.

The multilateral framework of GATS is not the only context to favour the movement of individuals to economies with a high demand for labour. Regional trade agreements between two or more States, including labour mobility provisions, are flourishing (see Case Study 12.1).[77] Regional trade agreements are thought to offer a facilitating environment for liberalising trade in services through the movement of natural persons. Regional frameworks are seen as more effective because of the smaller number of States involved and the greater likelihood of identifying shared interests. At the same time, they are often criticised as a diversion from the effort required to secure a global agreement that would benefit all WTO members.

Objectives and achievements at the regional level have been diverse. Some regional trade agreements are largely supportive arrangements for the recognition of qualifications; others provide market access to specified groups, such as professionals and investors (e.g., the North American Free Trade Agreement) or for specified skills (e.g., the Japan–Philippines Economic Partnership Agreement, targeting nurses and care workers). Much rarer are regional trade agreements that provide for free movement of labour – where they exist, they are generally between highly integrated economies, such as States within the European Union or the Trans-Tasman Travel Arrangement between Australia and New Zealand.

Regardless of the format – multilateral, regional or bilateral – the inclusion of labour mobility in the international trade agenda remains relatively new. With the anticipated increase in human mobility, new ways will have to be found to close the gap between the legal regimes regulating migration and trade, and thereby synthesise the human and economic dimensions of international migration.

---

77 The WTO maintains a list of regional trade agreements of which it has been notified (www.wto.org/english/ tratop_e/region_e/region_e.htm).

KEY REFERENCES

Amin, Mohammad and Mattoo, Aaditya, 'Does Temporary Migration Have to Be Permanent?' (World Bank, 2005)

Bast, Jürgen, 'Annex on the Movement of Natural Persons Supplying Services under the Agreement' in Rüdiger Wolfrum, Peter-Tobias Stoll and Clemens Feinäugle (eds.), *WTO Trade in Services: Max-Planck Commentaries on World Trade Law* (Martinus Nijhoff, 2008) 573

Betts, Alexander (ed.), *Global Migration Governance* (Oxford University Press, 2011)

Carzaniga, Antonia, 'The GATS Mode 4 and Patterns of Commitments' in Aaditya Mattoo and Antonia Carzaniga (eds.), *Moving People to Deliver Services* (World Bank and Oxford University Press, 2003) 21

Chanda, Rupa, 'Mobility of Less-Skilled Workers under Bilateral Agreements: Lessons for the GATS' (2009) 43(3) *Journal of World Trade* 479

Jackson, John, Sykes, Alan and Davey, William, *Legal Problems of International Economic Relations: Cases, Materials and Text on the National and International Regulation of Transnational Economic Relations* (Thomson West, 2008)

Lucas, Robert, 'International Labor Migration in a Globalizing Economy' Carnegie Paper No 92 (Carnegie Endowment for International Peace, 2008)

Magdeleine, Joscelyn and Maurer, Andreas, 'Measuring GATS Mode 4 Trade Flows' (World Trade Organization, 2008)

Nielson, Julia, 'Labor Mobility in Regional Trade Agreements' in Aaditya Mattoo and Antonia Carzaniga (eds.), *Moving People to Deliver Services* (World Bank and Oxford University Press, 2003) 93

Panizzon, Marion, 'Trade and Labor Migration: GATS Mode 4 and Migration Agreements' (Friedrich-Ebert-Stiftung, 2010)

Puri, Lakshmi, 'Assuring Development Gains and Poverty Reduction from Trade: The Labor Mobility and Skills Trade Dimension' (UNCTAD, DITC and TNCD, 2007)

Tans, Simon, 'The Unwanted Service Provider: Implementation of WTO and EU Liberalisation of Service Mobility in the Dutch Legal Order' (2011) 30(2) *Refugee Survey Quarterly* 67

Varma, Sabrina, 'Facilitating Temporary Labor Mobility in African Least-Developed Countries' (International Centre for Trade and Sustainable Development, 2009)

Winters, Alan, 'The Temporary Movement of Workers to Provide Services (GATS Mode 4)' in Aaditya Mattoo, Robert Stern and Gianni Zanini (eds.), *A Handbook of International Trade in Services* (Oxford University Press, 2008) 480

WTO Council for Trade in Services, *A Review of Statistics on Trade Flows in Services: Data Compilation and Availability*, WTO Doc S/C/W/329 (22 December 2010) (Note by the Secretariat)

KEY RESOURCES

International Centre for Trade and Sustainable Development: www.ictsd.org

South Centre: An Intergovernmental Policy Think Tank of Developing Countries: www.southcentre.org

United Nations Conference on Trade and Development: www.unctad.org

World Trade Organization: www.wto.org

World Trade Organization, Documents Online: http://docsonline.wto.org

World Trade Organization, Services Database: http://tsdb.wto.org

13 Global migration institutions and processes

IRENA OMELANIUK

13.1. INTRODUCTION

A complex array of international institutions and processes has emerged around migration in recent decades. This is partly a function of the increasingly globalised and interlinked nature of human mobility, and partly a response to the level of attention devoted by governments to international migration. Sending States are concerned about the rights of their nationals abroad, and receiving States are concerned about meeting their labour market needs. Despite growing awareness of the interdependence of migration experiences across regions and countries, little progress has been made towards an effective, coherent system of global migration governance. There continues to be an absence of shared vision, leadership and political will for migration policy making at the international level, which makes it difficult to develop appropriate structures and laws to regulate and coordinate international responses to global human mobility.[1]

Attention to migration differs dramatically among governments, in terms of institutions and policies. Even within a single government, there can be a wide range of policies and practices across temporary and permanent categories of migration. The autonomy of governments to deal with their own migration challenges, combined with the lack of a single body of international law on migration or a global entity to cohere their practice, has left a governance vacuum. In contrast to trade, labour, environment and health, there are no regular global fora in which ministers responsible for migration meet to discuss issues of common concern, although this does occur in some regions.[2]

---

1 On the lack of a global migration organisation or global migration regime, see Alexander Betts (ed.), *Global Migration Governance* (Oxford University Press, 2011); Jagdish Bhagwati, 'Borders Beyond Control' (2003) 82(1) *Foreign Affairs* 98; Bimal Ghosh (ed.), *Managing Migration: Time for a New International Regime?* (Oxford University Press, 2000).

2 For example, the Regional Conference on Migration in Central and North America (the Puebla Process), regularly engages Ministers or senior officials.

But government practices are converging and there is increasing awareness of the need for coordinated international efforts to manage migration. More sophisticated arguments are being advanced by the international community in support of a formalised 'global governance' of international migration.[3] International migration continues to grow, diversify and involve more players at public and private levels. It can no longer be managed effectively by national migration policies alone. Growing numbers of migrants around the world are vulnerable, exploited and insufficiently protected by either States or international institutions. Global governance of migration is clearly linked to the international politics of migration, and both directly affect States and migrants. But both need to be better understood and researched.

Most multilateral agencies – within the United Nations and outside it – were created by States since the mid-twentieth century specifically to foster better global governance. While this may have worked in public policy areas, such as trade and economics, it has not worked in the field of migration. Indeed, today there may be more cooperation on migration among governments at bilateral and regional levels than in multilateral institutions.

Bilateral, regional and inter-regional forms of cooperation have mushroomed in recent decades in a natural response to the globalisation of migration. The reasons for this range from cost sharing to better linking the interests and needs of sending and receiving States, in an effort to address the causes of migration, not just its symptoms. Bilateral and regional consultative processes have reached common understandings and approaches on migration that have not yet been possible at the global level. For example, the Philippines is able to build its statute-based minimum wage for domestic workers into bilateral agreements with labour-receiving partner States; and member States of the Caribbean Community ('CARICOM') are able to negotiate reciprocal social security arrangements with partner States under the *CARICOM Agreement on Social Security* (1996).[4] How effective these agreements are varies from scenario to scenario, and is often more influenced by resources, finances and institutional capacities than by legislative frameworks.

Yet new forms of multilateral collaboration on migration are also emerging. From regional and inter-regional consultative processes, to the Global Forum on Migration and Development ('GFMD'), new mechanisms are contributing in different ways to the global governance of migration. These government-led developments are challenging the traditional roles and behaviour of international organisations in the field of migration. They have created an imperative for a stronger international system, based on greater coordination among the institutions. This can help governments manage the sheer scale of global migration,

---

3 Commission on Global Governance, 'Our Global Neighborhood: The Report of the Commission on Global Governance' (Oxford University Press, 1995). The Commission defined 'global governance' as a broad, dynamic, complex process of interactive decision making that evolves according to changing circumstances.

4 *CARICOM Agreement on Social Security*, opened for signature 1 March 1996 (entered into force 1 April 1997).

maintain transparency, and avoid relinquishing both the management and perception of migration to ideology and public opinion.

Many questions remain. Is there real movement towards more coherent global governance of migration? What role should the existing international institutions and processes play in this? Is a global regime emerging from the bottom up among governments and other major stakeholders, or should it be imposed on governments by the multilateral system? Is there a need for different structures and approaches, or just better utilisation of existing ones? Is a body of common principles and practices developing organically akin to customary international law, or should States just continue their dialogue without real institutional change?

13.2.   WHAT IS THE GLOBAL GOVERNANCE OF MIGRATION?

There has been increased talk of 'international migration governance' since the turn of the century. This is partly due to the realisation that traditional unilateral approaches to migration have proven inadequate in managing migration in the context of globalised economies and labour markets. Greater equality and efficiency are often cited as the rationales for considering a global regime of migration management.

Global migration governance can mean many things to many people. For Ghosh, it has meant a global integrated migration regime of inter-State cooperation based on an awareness of the interrelationship between different areas of migration management and a commonality and reciprocity of interests of sending and receiving States. This would make movement of people more orderly, predictable, productive and humane. For some, it signifies any institutional effort to manage migration – at national, bilateral, regional or global levels – including the legislative, policy and operational underpinnings of such efforts. For others, the global governance of migration encompasses the set of international laws and principles related to migration management.[5] The International Organization for Migration ('IOM') has captured these ideas in its definition of 'governance of migration' as a:

system of institutions, legal frameworks, mechanisms and practices aimed at regulating migration and protecting migrants. Used almost synonymously with the term 'migration management', although migration management is also sometimes used to refer to the narrow act of regulating cross-border movement at the state level.[6]

---

5 Compare: Migration Working Group, 'Report to the Secretary-General on Migration (Doyle Report)' (2002); Bimal Ghosh, 'New International Regime for Orderly Movements of People' in Bimal Ghosh (ed.), *Managing Migration: Time for a New International Regime?* (Oxford University Press, 2004) 220; Bimal Ghosh and Sergio Marchi, *Migration Governance: Towards a Global Integrated Migration Regime* (2010) www.eurasylum.org; Betts, above n. 1.

6 Richard Perruchoud and Jillyanne Redpath-Cross (eds.), *Glossary on Migration* (IOM, 2nd edn, 2011) 43.

Some pundits believe it would make sense to have a 'world migration organisation' to help reduce barriers to migration, in ways similar to the role of the World Trade Organization ('WTO') in reducing barriers to international trade in goods and services. Others counter that trade and migration cannot be compared because migration involves people, not goods, and individuals cannot be regulated on the basis of economic efficiencies.[7]

In 2004, the Global Commission on International Migration ('GCIM') dedicated one of its reports to the issue of global migration governance.[8] In 2008, a workshop on this theme was held at Oxford University. In 2009, the International Labour Organization ('ILO') and the Organization for Security and Co-operation in Europe ('OSCE') undertook a study on how OSCE member States across the region were strengthening their governance of migration.[9] In the same year, the International Catholic Migration Commission ('ICMC') commenced its 'Conversations on the Global Governance of Migration' to consider the value of global governance and any practical actions that could improve the management of global migration in the short to medium term.[10] The 'Conversations' concluded that 'it is not a question of *whether* a discussion of global governance of migration goes forward, but rather *when* and *how*'.[11] In 2010, Newland published a helpful overview of how the global governance of migration has evolved as a policy issue over the past decade.[12] And by 2011, a book on global migration governance had been published under the Oxford Global Migration Governance Project, examining the reasons for, and consequences of, the current fragmented system of governance and how to work towards more inclusive multilateral governance.[13]

The European Union is expanding its global approach to migration management beyond Europe through circular migration agreements and 'mobility partnerships' between European Union member States and sending States in Africa and elsewhere.[14] Similarly, the Swiss Agency for Development and Cooperation has included migration – alongside climate change, food security and water – as a key plank in its Global Programmes to develop innovative solutions for global

---

7 World Bank, 'Global Economic Prospects 2006: Economic Implications of Remittances and Migration' (World Bank, 2006).

8 Rey Koslowski, 'Global Migration Perspectives No. 8: Possible Steps towards an International Regime for Mobility and Security' (Global Commission on International Migration, 2004).

9 August Gachter, 'Strengthening Migration Governance: Implementation of OSCE Commitments related to Migration by OSCE Participating States' (ILO, OSCE, 2009). The report concluded with recommendations for new policies and specific activities. More particularly, it called for immediate measures to mitigate the impact of the 2008 global economic crisis on migrant workers.

10 International Catholic Migration Commission, 'Conversations on the Global Governance of Migration' (ICMC, 2009).

11 International Catholic Migration Commission, 'Connecting the Dots: A Fresh Look at Managing International Migration' (ICMC, 2009) 1.

12 Kathleen Newland, 'The Governance of International Migration: Mechanisms, Processes and Institutions' (2010) 16(3) *Global Governance* 331.

13 See Betts, above n. 1. The Global Migration Governance Project is part of the Global Economic Governance Programme, Department of Politics and International Relations, University of Oxford.

14 Commission of the European Communities, 'Circular Migration and Mobility Partnerships between the European Union and Third Countries' (COM(2007) 248 final, Commission of the European Communities, 2007).

poverty reduction. This is part of a new approach by Switzerland to deal with migration at the level of global governance as well as at the level of national migration policy making.[15]

The ICMC has described international migration governance as characterised by five pillars, namely, (a) national policies and programmes; (b) bilateral, regional and global dialogues and exchange of practices; (c) formal regional structures and forms of cooperation, exemplified by the various economic communities; (d) the multilateral system, including international agencies that deal directly with migration; and (e) the international legal framework, especially human rights law and refugee law.[16] This chapter focusses on the second and fourth pillars, giving special attention to the newer instruments of regional and global cooperation. The chapter does not speculate about a global migration agency or world migration organisation, while other pillars are addressed elsewhere in this book.

13.3. INTERGOVERNMENTAL ORGANISATIONS

Many intergovernmental organisations have become indispensable to governments. Through their global reach and network of offices they bring a multilateral perspective to policy making, often covering more ground than individual or regional groupings of governments. Arguably, the United Nations enjoys the political legitimacy and broad representation to make changes where individual governments may not. However, migration is spread thinly across the various United Nations agencies, and their mandate to play a normative, standard-setting role to protect individuals before the sovereign interests of governments can be a limiting factor in their work with governments. This mandate is weakened, in turn, by the limited enforcement authority of these organisations.

Outside the United Nations system, IOM is the only intergovernmental organisation with an exclusive migration mandate. It has laid some foundations for global governance through its global technical cooperation on migration management, international dialogue on migration and international migration law activities, but it has not explicitly advocated for global migration governance. In recent years, other international entities, such as the World Bank and the Organisation for Economic Co-operation and Development ('OECD'), as well as a host of academic institutions and knowledge centres, have begun to advocate for greater global governance. Few, however, have the mandate or capacity to make international goals, such as the Millennium Development Goals, operational on the ground.

Multilateral organisations can establish common practices across States and regions that begin to resemble global approaches to managing migration, and are

---

15 See Swiss Agency for Development and Cooperation: www.sdc.admin.ch, Activities.
16 International Catholic Migration Commission, above n. 11, 7.

not always anchored in international treaties. The ILO, IOM and the United Nations High Commissioner for Refugees ('UNHCR') work to strengthen common approaches to migration – increasingly in the context of development – in cooperation with the OECD, OSCE, World Bank and the United Nations Department of Economic and Social Affairs ('UNDESA'). As the guardians of universal principles, they can make the wider connections that governments often cannot make, although their enforcement powers remain limited.

By combining their facilities across borders and across the disparate interests and resources of sending and receiving States, they can help achieve economies of scale through joint or linked actions. In this, they often partner strategically with umbrella government entities, such as the European Union, the Organization of American States and the African Union. Many have multiple programmes across regions, from which lessons can be drawn for other regions and governments.

There is currently little appetite for establishing new international agencies. The preference among States continues to be to reform the existing ones. The development of new legal instruments may be a more pressing concern, as the ILO has demonstrated with the conclusion of the *Convention concerning Decent Work for Domestic Workers* (2011) at the International Labour Conference in June 2011.[17] The following sections examine select examples of major intergovernmental players, their contributions towards a global approach to managing migration, and areas in which their efforts may be converging.

13.3.1.   International Organization for Migration

Established in 1951 for the specific purpose of resettling millions of Europeans displaced by the Second World War, and assisting migrants wishing to emigrate, IOM is today the only global, intergovernmental organisation exclusively mandated to deal with migration. In late 2011, it had a membership of 146 States and 97 observers. It operates outside the United Nations system, but ties much of its work to other United Nations partners and programmes. It has a far-reaching migration mandate, ranging from the organised transfer of migrants, refugees and displaced persons to States offering resettlement opportunities, to capacity building for governments and other agencies in the management of migration.

IOM assists governments and migrants in the areas of migrant labour recruitment, selection, processing, language training, orientation activities, medical examination, placement, facilitating reception and integration, advisory services on migration issues, and assisted voluntary return services for migrants needing or wishing to return home. IOM also does considerable work with returnees and

---

17 *Convention concerning Decent Work for Domestic Workers* (ILO Convention No 189), opened for signature 16 June 2011 (not yet in force).

communities in situations of post-conflict rehabilitation and reparation. A key aim is to better regulate migration and establish enabling conditions that benefit migrants, governments and communities.

In 2007, the IOM Council adopted a landmark resolution on IOM strategy,[18] stating that the primary goal of IOM is to facilitate the orderly and humane management of international migration, and that IOM should continue its role as a leading global organisation focussing on migration management, addressing the phenomenon of migration from an integral and holistic perspective, including links to development. This resolution, confirmed in 2010, further asked IOM to focus on twelve activities, which included:

- enhancing the humane and orderly management of migration and effective respect for the human rights of migrants in accordance with international law;
- offering expert advice to States and other stakeholders to build national capacities and facilitate international, regional and bilateral cooperation on migration matters;
- contributing to the economic and social development of States through migration-related programmes;
- being a primary reference point for migration information, research, best practices and data collection;
- promoting and supporting regional and global debate and dialogue on migration so as to identify comprehensive approaches and measures for advancing international cooperation; and
- providing migration assistance in emergency and post-crisis situations, thereby contributing to the protection of affected individuals.

In particular, IOM has accumulated unique expertise in areas such as migrant health[19] and assistance to victims of human trafficking, and has established a database on counter-trafficking based on its experience with 20,000 assisted cases. IOM has also worked directly with governments, such as Canada, Colombia, Guatemala, Mauritius, Portugal, Spain, Ukraine and United Arab Emirates, to establish and manage programmes for temporary and circular labour exchange. The outcomes of these efforts are of interest to global processes in Latin America and in other continents.

IOM has tied its migration activities more closely to economic and community development in sending countries, including capacity building through the assisted return of qualified individuals and experts in diaspora populations. IOM has also strengthened global cooperation by helping governments to estab-lish regional and inter-regional consultative processes, and providing secretariat support to them (see Chapter 14).

---

18 International Organization for Migration, Council Resolution No 1150, 'IOM Strategy' (7 June 2007).
19 IOM's Migration Health Department deals with migration health assessments, travel health assistance, and health promotion and assistance for migrants and crisis-affected populations.

CASE STUDY 13.1 Child migration in the Caribbean

Much like the rest of the world, child migration is a topic that the Caribbean is only beginning to explore, despite the region's strong intra-regional and extra-regional migration flows (see Map 12.1). IOM implemented the Child Migration in the Caribbean project between 2008 and 2010, to increase understanding and improve the protection of child migrants.[20] The United Nations Children's Fund's ('UNICEF') office for the Eastern Caribbean, the CARICOM Secretariat and IOM formed a partnership to implement the project. IOM collected information on the negative and positive effects of migration on children in the region, facilitated cooperation among partners, and enhanced regional and national capacity to better understand and establish policies.

An inter-agency working group comprising nine Caribbean countries, CARICOM, UNICEF and IOM was formed to exchange information about national contexts and to develop a framework and recommendations for action on children affected by migration. The working group identified three general categories of children who stay behind, migrate (whether accompanied or unaccompanied) or return.

(a) Children who stay behind when their legal guardians migrate often lack proper adult supervision, care and basic necessities, such as food, shelter and clothing. They can feel abandoned or rejected and become violent and delinquent, at great risk to their wellbeing and development.

(b) Children who migrate may not be able to access identity documents or basic services, such as education, healthcare or social services, due to language barriers, lack of knowledge about available services or fear of deportation.

(c) Children who return to their State of birth or origin (e.g., in the Caribbean) can encounter similar challenges, with a largely unfamiliar culture and social support system.

In this complex situation, the rights of the child, as prescribed by the *Convention on the Rights of the Child* (1989), can often be violated. Since many children never enter formal State systems (educational, medical or legal, to name a few), there are not enough data to track numbers or inform policy decisions. Consequently, policy makers, humanitarian agencies and even academics rarely consider children as independent actors in the migration context.

The IOM project helped to situate the issue of child migration on the agendas of multilateral fora. For example, children affected by migration in the region were discussed at CARICOM's Council for Human and Social Development. As a result, CARICOM member States were urged to implement the framework and use it as a tracking instrument to assess progress in the region of the 'Education For All Children' programme – a non-governmental, non-profit scholarship and education programme for the poor.

---

20 International Organization for Migration, *Child Migration in the Caribbean* (2011) www.iom.int/unitedstates/ CAR%20PMV/ChildMigrationCaribbean.htm.

IOM is also a facilitator of international cooperation on migration through its Council and the International Dialogue on Migration. Launched in 2001, the International Dialogue on Migration provides a forum for governments, inter-governmental and non-governmental organisations ('NGOs') and other stakeholders to discuss migration policy, explore and study policy issues of common interest, and cooperate in addressing them.[21] The dialogue takes place at IOM's annual Council sessions and at inter-sessional workshops that explore the multidisciplinary aspects of migration and foster linkages with related policy fields, such as trade, health and development.

IOM is one of the founding members of the Global Migration Group ('GMG'). This group – endorsed by the United Nations – is an effort by the Geneva community of international organisations dealing with migration to understand each other better and work together coherently. IOM has also strongly supported the GFMD since its inception in 2007.

The question has often been asked whether IOM could function as a world migration organisation. In some senses it already does, but it continues to be constrained by its not-yet-universal membership, a predominantly operational mandate from member States, and the lack of an underpinning international treaty on migration, such as UNHCR enjoys with the *Convention relating to the Status of Refugees* (1951) ('Refugee Convention').[22]

13.3.2. World Trade Organization

The WTO is the international body that deals with rules of trade between States and provides fora for States to negotiate trade agreements and settle trade disputes. Its main function is to ensure that trade flows as smoothly, predictably and freely as possible. Accounting for 97 per cent of world trade, WTO has 150 members, of which three-quarters are developing countries.[23] There is a Ministerial Conference that meets every two years and a General Council that convenes throughout the year. The 2001 Ministerial Conference in Doha, Qatar, has acquired the moniker 'the Doha Development Round' because the conference established tasks on a range of issues specifically for the benefit of developing States. Developing States enjoy special provisions in some WTO agreements to allow them more time to implement the agreements and to provide opportunities to increase their trading capacities, infrastructure for handling disputes and ability to implement technical standards.

The WTO has explored the migration and development issue from the narrow angle of temporary labour migration under Mode 4 of the *General Agreement on*

---

21 International Organization for Migration, *International Dialogue on Migration* (2011) www.iom.int/jahia/Jahia/international-dialogue-migration.
22 *Convention relating to the Status of Refugees*, opened for signature 28 July 1951, 189 UNTS 150 (entered into force 22 April 1954).
23 World Trade Organization: www.wto.org.

Trade in Services (1994) ('GATS').[24] As discussed in Chapter 12, this involves the supply of a service by a service supplier of one State through the temporary presence of 'natural persons' in the territory of another State. This has not progressed very far in GATS negotiations, despite the fact that services constitute a large and growing share of overall economic activity of developing countries, and liberalising rich markets could bring more gains for both developing and developed countries. The major obstacle remains the concern of many labour-receiving States to retain their sovereign right to determine who enters their territory and under what conditions, rather than have these determined by a multilateral mechanism of commitments and obligations such as GATS Mode 4.[25]

13.3.3. Organisation for Economic Co-operation and Development

The OECD dates back to 1960, when eighteen European States, together with Canada and the United States, joined forces to create an organisation dedicated to global development.[26] Although its membership is still limited to mostly advanced States (by mid-2011 it had thirty-four members), and migration forms only part of its overall mandate, it has produced valuable data and analysis on migration, particularly in the development context. The OECD's continuous reporting system, 'SOPEMI', has compelled a number of member States to produce annual updates on migration trends, policy, legislative changes and outlooks.[27] The OECD summary report of its members' inputs, *International Migration Outlook*, provides useful comparative overviews of migration trends and prospects, including by age, gender and visa category. It nevertheless remains difficult to make comparisons across disparate legal structures, policies, programmes, definitions and data sets.

The OECD's 2007 report, *Gaining from Migration*, produced in partnership with the European Commission, provides broad policy guidance on how the emerging global system of labour mobility could be managed to better meet the needs of sending States, receiving States and migrants.[28] Some key recommendations have been carried forward in the international migration and development debates since then. Examples include the European Union's expansion of circular migration arrangements with third States, and the GFMD's efforts to foster greater integration

---

24 *Marrakesh Agreement Establishing the World Trade Organization*, opened for signature 15 April 1994, 1867 UNTS 3 (entered into force 1 January 1995) annex 1B ('*General Agreement on Trade in Services*'). Another important step towards better understanding the relationship between trade and migration was the joint seminar held in 2004: International Organization for Migration, World Bank and World Trade Organization, 'Trade and Migration Seminar: Background Paper' (IOM, World Bank, WTO, 4–5 October 2004).

25 Under Mode 4, migrant workers are not granted access to the local labour market; they must be employed by a foreign firm with commercial presence in the host State or work under a contract for provision of a service.

26 *Convention on the Organisation for Economic Co-operation and Development*, opened for signature 14 December 1960, 888 UNTS 179, (entered into force 30 September 1961).

27 SOPEMI (Système d'Observation Permanente sur les Migrations) was established in 1973 to furnish European members of the OECD with data that could be shared and compared across countries.

28 Jeff Dayton-Johnson, Louka T. Katseli, Gregory Maniatis, Rainer Münz and Demetrios Papdemetriou , 'Gaining from Migration: Towards a New Mobility System' (OECD, 2007).

of migration in national development planning and general coherence of policy making within and between governments.

In addition to IOM, the WTO and the OECD, there are myriad reputable international organisations, academic institutions and knowledge centres dealing with migration in some form or another. These include the OSCE, the International Centre for Migration Policy Development (an international organisation with a European focus), the Migration Policy Institute (an independent think tank based in Washington DC) and the Center for Global Development (another independent think tank based in Washington DC).

13.4. UNITED NATIONS AND ITS AGENCIES

Many agencies in the United Nations deal with migration in some form or another. Current and former Secretaries-General, and the United Nations Secretariat itself, have raised the profile of migration and sought to cohere these efforts in recent years. The United Nations has laid tracks for a more sustained global, multilateral debate on migration and development among governments, culminating in the establishment of the GFMD in 2007. In addition, the GMG – formed in 2008 from sixteen United Nations agencies and IOM – is the first serious attempt at improving coordination of migration matters within the United Nations system. The impetus for these initiatives came from the International Conference on Population and Development in 1994, which is described further below.

This section examines the key United Nations players in the migration field, both principal and specialised agencies, starting with UNHCR and the ILO, which are the largest and possibly most political actors, with treaty-based mandates that are clearly linked to some aspects of migration. The remaining United Nations also have a significant influence on the migration debate, and all are members of the inter-agency group, the GMG. This selection is not exhaustive and does not attempt to rank the agencies.

13.4.1. United Nations High Commissioner for Refugees

UNHCR emerged in 1950 as a post-Second World War effort by the United Nations to help Europeans displaced by the war. The following year, the Refugee Convention was adopted, setting the legal foundation for UNHCR's continuing work. As with IOM, UNHCR marked its sixtieth anniversary in 2011. Today, it has operations in more than 120 States around the world. Its eighty-five-member Executive Committee approves its annual programme and budget.[29]

---

29 United Nations High Commissioner for Refugees: www.unhcr.org.

In the wider field of migration, UNHCR has a relatively narrow portfolio, but with a sharp focus on international protection of refugees mandated by the Refugee Convention and its 1967 Protocol.[30] UNHCR strives to ensure that everyone can exercise their right to seek asylum. It safeguards the rights of refugees, and most especially their right to be protected from return (*refoulement*) to frontiers of territories where their life or freedom would be threatened on account of race, religion, nationality, membership of a particular social group or political opinion. It offers refugees durable solutions through voluntary repatriation, local integration in the State where asylum was sought, or resettlement to another (third) country. UNHCR also fosters extensive intergovernmental dialogue on refugee and asylum issues.

UNHCR's main activities include: protecting stateless and displaced persons by ensuring respect for their human rights in States of residence; emergency response in the form of non-food aid items; assistance in the form of water, sanitation, healthcare, and provision of necessities such as clothing, blankets and household goods; arrangement of transportation for returnees; and integration and reintegration programmes for income generation, restoration of infrastructure and education. Over the years, the responsibilities of UNHCR have expanded to include returnees, stateless persons and internally displaced persons in some situations.

The mandate to protect refugees and find durable solutions for them is of necessity linked to a broader range of migration issues and activities. While legal distinctions are made between 'migrants' and 'refugees', in reality the root causes of human mobility are mixed. In recognition of the fact that this can confuse policy and operational responses, and place vulnerable persons at risk of *refoulement*, UNHCR has increasingly concerned itself with assisting in the management of mixed migration flows. These often consist of asylum seekers, refugees, trafficked persons, unaccompanied or separated children, and migrants in irregular situations, all of whom may be migrating for different reasons but using the same routes and means of transportation.

In 2007 UNHCR developed a '10-Point Plan of Action' on refugee protection and mixed migration, to provide guidance to governments on how to manage mixed migration flows in ways that address the sovereignty and security concerns of States, but also consider the needs and rights of individuals involved in mixed movements.[31] The plan is systematically being implemented in the major regions of the world where mixed flows occur.

UNHCR and IOM have a long-standing partnership in assisting refugees in camps and with resettlement. More recently, IOM and UNHCR have joined forces to explore the nexus between human trafficking and refugee protection, since some

---

30 *Protocol relating to the Status of Refugees*, opened for accession 31 January 1967, 606 UNTS 267 (entered into force 4 October 1967).

31 United Nations High Commissioner for Refugees, 'Refugee Protection and Mixed Migration: A 10-Point Plan of Action' (UNHCR, January 2007).

trafficked persons may have a well-founded fear of persecution or be at risk of serious human rights violations and therefore be in need of asylum. At the same time, asylum seekers and refugees who are in vulnerable situations (e.g., those who live in camps, lack a livelihood or travel through irregular means) are often targeted by recruiters in the trafficking network. IOM and UNHCR have addressed this nexus by developing standard operating procedures to refer cases between the two agencies and enhance protection measures. In Asia, UNHCR and IOM are working with States, in the context of the Bali Process (discussed below) on a model regional cooperation strategy in this regard.

UNHCR is one of the founding members of the GMG. Refugees remains one area where there is a well-defined, monitored and documented 'global regime', based on coherent international law. Refugee law and the role of UNHCR are discussed further in Chapter 7.

13.4.2. International Labour Organization

As a specialised agency of the United Nations, the ILO has been dealing with labour migration issues since 1919, longer than any other international organisation.[32] Migration may not appear prominently in the structure and core responsibilities of the ILO, but all key sectors of the organisation – standards, employment, social protection and social dialogue – work on labour migration.

The ILO is the global standard bearer for 'decent work for all', and within that ambit deals with labour migration issues from a tripartite perspective that encompasses governments, employers and workers. Until the adoption of the *International Convention on the Protection of the Rights of All Migrant Workers and Members of their Families* (1990) ('ICRMW'),[33] it was the only United Nations agency with a mandate to protect migrant workers.[34] It does so largely by pioneering and promoting with governments a range of rights-based international conventions, regulations and standards relating to migration. To ensure that these treaties and principles guide migration and labour policy, the ILO offers training and technical cooperation to government officials, often at its international training centre in Turin, Italy.

The ILO sets minimum standards of basic labour rights: freedom of association, the right to organise, collective bargaining, abolition of forced labour, equality of opportunity and treatment, and other standards that regulate conditions across the

---

32 The ILO was established in 1919 as part of the Treaty of Versailles and became the United Nations' first specialised agency in 1946. It has 183 member States, and its tripartite Governing Body comprises twenty-eight government members, fourteen employer members and fourteen worker members.

33 *International Convention on the Protection of the Rights of All Migrant Workers and Members of their Families*, opened for signature 18 December 1990, 2220 UNTS 3 (entered into force 1 July 2003). Article 72 establishes the Committee on Migrant Workers.

34 *Declaration concerning the Aims and Purposes of the International Labour Organisation* ('Declaration of Philadelphia') (1944) XXVI(1) *International Labour Office Official Bulletin* 1; *ILO Declaration on Fundamental Principles and Rights at Work*, adopted by the International Labour Conference, 86th session (18 June 1998).

entire spectrum of work-related issues. It promotes the development of independent employers' and workers' organisations and provides training and advisory services to those organisations.

The ILO produces credible research and information about labour and employment through its unique global labour surveys, which in turn strengthen the knowledge base both for its own recommendations about good practices and policies and for governments' policy choices.[35] These surveys have provided important data on trends, conditions of migrant workers, the state of law and practice, and the impact of migration – all critical to the development of the ILO's 2004 'Plan of Action for Migrant Workers'.[36] The centrepiece of this Plan of Action is the non-binding ILO *Multilateral Framework on Labour Migration* (2006), which guides governments in developing their national laws and practices on labour migration.[37] The ILO acts as a focal point both for international debate on labour migration and for labour statistics and databases worldwide. It is indisputably the world's resource centre for information, analysis and guidance about labour and employment.

Within its *Multilateral Framework on Labour Migration*, the ILO offers practical guidelines and models to maximise the benefits and contributions of labour migration to employment, economic growth and poverty alleviation. For example, the ILO's technical assistance and input into a system of skills recognition can help avoid a mismatch of skills between sending and receiving States, which often leads to exploitation of migrant workers, irregular migration and reduced developmental outcomes.

The ILO works with other organisations on labour migration tools. For example, in 2006, the OSCE, IOM and the ILO produced a handbook on labour migration policies for the GFMD.[38] It has been used as a tool to assist governments to manage labour migration in the Mediterranean region and elsewhere. Similarly, in 2009, the OSCE and the ILO launched a new study on 'Strengthening Migration Governance', which reviewed implementation of OSCE commitments on migration and serves as a reference document for officials of governments and stakeholder organisations throughout the OSCE regions to strengthen migration governance.[39]

The ILO's constitutional mandate on labour migration equips it to develop rights-based standards and build the capacities of its constituencies to deliver

---

35 International Labour Organization, *Database on International Labour Migration Statistics* (2009) www.ilo.org/public/english/protection/migrant/info/ilm_dbase.htm; International Labour Organization, *Database on Anti-Discrimination Actions Profiles* (2009) www.ilo.org/public/english/protection/migrant/info/dbase_practices.htm; International Labour Organization, *Good Practices Database: Labour Migration Policies and Programmes* (2010) www.ilo.org/dyn/migpractice/migmain.home.

36 International Labour Office, 'Towards a Fair Deal for Migrant Workers in the Global Economy' (ILO, 2004).

37 International Labour Organization, 'Multilateral Framework on Labour Migration: Non-Binding Principles and Guidelines for a Rights-Based Approach to Labour Migration' (ILO, 2006).

38 Organization for Security and Co-operation in Europe, 'Handbook on Establishing Effective Labour Migration Policies in Countries of Origin and Destination' (OSCE, IOM and ILO, 2006).

39 Gachter, above n. 9.

such an agenda. It has models that enable governments to regulate labour migration in a way that allows all stakeholders to benefit, while minimising negative impacts. The ILO's tripartite structure and orientation is both a strength and a weakness. It can create greater multilateral context around an issue, which can bolster cooperation with some partners. On the other hand, the need for tripartite consensus is an additional challenge that other agencies do not face in their efforts to foster adherence to international labour standards and migrants' rights.[40]

13.4.3. Office of the High Commissioner for Human Rights

The Office of the High Commissioner for Human Rights ('OHCHR') was established by the United Nations General Assembly in 1993, following the World Conference on Human Rights, to promote and coordinate human rights activities throughout the United Nations system. OHCHR also supports the thematic mandates of the Human Rights Council, two of which have special significance for migration. The first of these, established in 1999, is the Special Rapporteur on the Human Rights of Migrants, who reports to the Human Rights Council on the state of protection of migrants' rights around the world;[41] the second, established in 2004, is the Special Rapporteur on Trafficking in Persons, Especially in Women and Children.[42] OHCHR also services the Committee on Migrant Workers, which monitors compliance with the ICRMW. The Committee on Migrant Workers reviews reports submitted by States parties to the Convention to assist them in improving implementation of Convention standards.

OHCHR advocates for a human rights-based approach to migration and migration management by offering practical guidance to policy makers and practitioners on the obligations and benefits of applying international human rights principles when dealing with migrants. As a practical aid, OHCHR makes available through the internet a series of papers on how to translate international norms and standards into workable practices on the ground. OHCHR draws its information from the actual situations reported by the Human Rights Council, and from the conclusions and jurisprudence of the human rights treaty bodies. The papers explain the legal context of protection applicable in specific cases, such as administrative detention of migrants (particularly children and victims of trafficking), family reunification and the right of migrant children to education. OHCHR is an active member of the GMG and has consistently supported and participated in the debates of the GFMD.

---

40 Philip Martin, Manolo Abella and Christiane Kuptsch, *Managing Labor Migration in the Twenty-First Century* (Vail-Ballou Press, 2006).

41 Office of the High Commissioner for Human Rights, *Special Rapporteur on the Human Rights of Migrants* (2011) www.ohchr.org/EN/Issues/Migration/SRMigrants.

42 Office of the High Commissioner for Human Rights, *Special Rapporteur on Trafficking in Persons, Especially in Women and Children* (2011) www.ohchr.org/EN/Issues/Trafficking.

Issues of migration, development and human rights are further addressed and analysed (including at regional and national levels) through a variety of other mandates and programmes, such as that of national human rights institutions.

13.4.4.   United Nations Office on Drugs and Crime

Among the remaining United Nations agencies dealing indirectly with migration is the United Nations Office on Drugs and Crime ('UNODC'), whose focus is on enforcement and compliance with the *United Nations Convention against Transnational Organized Crime* (2000)[43] and its two cognate instruments, the *Protocol to Prevent, Suppress and Punish Trafficking in Persons, Especially Women and Children, Supplementing the United Nations Convention against Transnational Organized Crime* ('Trafficking Protocol')[44] and the *Protocol against the Smuggling of Migrants by Land, Sea and Air, Supplementing the United Nations Convention against Transnational Organized Crime* ('Smuggling Protocol').[45] UNODC provides secretariat support to the Conference of the Parties to the Convention and Protocols, and facilitates coordination with the secretariats of relevant international and regional organisations on implementation of these instruments. Under its Global Programme to Combat Trafficking in Persons, UNODC compiles data, assesses progress in combating trafficking and smuggling, and provides technical cooperation to governments.

From the outset, compliance with the international law set out in the Convention and Protocols has been problematic in the absence of an international mechanism to enforce the law. In the case of trafficking, UNODC set up the multi-stakeholder United Nations Global Initiative to Fight Human Trafficking in 2007, to provide funding, information and technical assistance for States to legislate and implement the Trafficking Protocol. It has managed this programme in cooperation with a steering committee comprising the ILO, IOM, UNICEF, OHCHR, the OSCE and the donor, the Emirate of Abu Dhabi. An evaluation of the Initiative in 2011 showed mixed results, but with some important benefits at the level of inter-agency and inter-State cooperation.[46]

UNODC is an important illustration of the relative lack of power and authority of multilateral agencies to enforce standards and principles set by international treaties, even where they are ratified. This is particularly relevant in view of the

---

43   *United Nations Convention against Transnational Organized Crime*, opened for signature 15 November 2000, 2225 UNTS 209 (entered into force 29 September 2003).

44   *Protocol to Prevent, Suppress and Punish Trafficking in Persons, Especially Women and Children, Supplementing the United Nations Convention against Transnational Organized Crime*, opened for signature 15 November 2000, 2237 UNTS 319 (entered into force 25 December 2003).

45   *Protocol against the Smuggling of Migrants by Land, Sea and Air, Supplementing the United Nations Convention against Transnational Organized Crime*, opened for signature 15 November 2000, 2241 UNTS 507 (entered into force 28 January 2004).

46   United Nations Office on Drugs and Crime, 'Evaluation of the United Nations Global Initiative to Fight Human Trafficking' (UNODC, 2011).

fact that the Trafficking Protocol and Smuggling Protocol are among the few examples of international treaties directly related to migration. They are discussed further in Chapter 9.

13.4.5.   United Nations Educational, Scientific and Cultural Organization

Since its inception in 1945, the United Nations Educational, Scientific and Cultural Organization ('UNESCO') has dealt peripherally with migration issues. It has contributed to 'the building of a culture of peace, the eradication of poverty, sustainable development and intercultural dialogue through education, the sciences, culture, communication and information'.[47] UNESCO's mission and activities also aim to promote human rights, mutual respect and poverty alleviation. Its strategies are guided by internationally agreed development goals, including the Millennium Development Goals.[48] UNESCO links migration to gender, youth empowerment and urbanisation, and it addresses these interlinked issues through its Management of Societal Transformation ('MOST') programme. Recent global priorities set by UNESCO include Africa and gender equality. Within its strategic programme objectives for 2008–13, UNESCO incorporates migration into its third objective (leveraging scientific knowledge for the benefit of the environment and the management of natural resources) and its seventh objective (enhancing research–policy linkages on social transformations).[49] Many of UNESCO's programmes are implemented in developing and least developed countries, and small island developing States, which are often also major migrant-sending States.

13.4.6.   United Nations Department of Economic and Social Affairs

The United Nations Secretariat has a small migration unit – UNDESA – that compiles and disseminates comprehensive statistics on world population, principally for the use of the General Assembly, its committees, the Economic and Social Council and its functional commissions. UNDESA's remit is narrow; nevertheless its data inform much of the analytical work on migration by other leading agencies, including the World Bank, IOM and academia around the world (see Chapter 2). UNDESA also routinely coordinates international debates on migration within the United Nations Secretariat in New York.

UNDESA analyses global development prospects and supports the policy debate on the causes and consequences of migration and efforts to maximise its benefits for development. UNDESA is preeminent in multilateral fora and commissions, along with the World Bank and other agencies that deal with statistics. In

---

47 United Nations Educational, Scientific and Cultural Organization: www.unesco.org.
48 United Nations Educational, Scientific and Cultural Organization, *Strategic Planning* (2011) www.unesco.org/en/strategic-planning.
49 United Nations Educational, Scientific and Cultural Organization, '2008–2013 Medium-Term Strategy' (UNESCO, 2008) 20, 24.

collaboration with the regional commissions, UNDESA monitors national and regional policies on international migration. Its work has helped to improve the availability and comparability of global migration data.

13.4.7.   United Nations Development Programme

The United Nations Development Programme ('UNDP') is the main United Nations body responsible for coordinating policy advice and technical assistance to governments on development issues globally. It includes migration in its focus on good governance as a key development strategy. It works on a number of different migration-related fronts, including support to persons displaced by conflict, post-conflict relief and rehabilitation, mobilising skilled persons from abroad to contribute to development projects back home, and 'South–South' migration dynamics (i.e., migration between developing States).

UNDP's *Human Development Report 2009: Overcoming Barriers: Human Mobility and Development*, specifically features internal and international migration as themes of increasing prominence in national and international debates about development.[50] The report examines how migration can foster human development; who moves where, when and why; how migrants fare; the impact in sending and receiving States; and policies to enhance human development outcomes. The report argues that 'migrants boost economic output, at little or no cost to locals', and proposes that '[l]arge gains to human development can be achieved by lowering the barriers to movement and improving the treatment of movers.'[51]

The report has changed the global discourse on migration and development. In October 2009, noting UNDP's 2009 Report, the Commonwealth Secretariat declared it would establish a Commission to bring a Commonwealth perspective to international migration, including compiling the wide-ranging work on migration that has already been undertaken by the Commonwealth and other bodies.[52]

The report has helped shift the migration–development discourse away from purely financial and economic benefits of migration, such as remittances and diaspora bonds. Within the GFMD, governments moved to a broader focus on human and social development, as demonstrated by the roundtables dealing with integration (Athens 2009), gender and family (Mexico 2010), and social security and health schemes for temporary migrants (Mexico 2010, Switzerland 2011).

---

50 United Nations Development Programme, *Human Development Report 2009: Overcoming Barriers: Human Mobility and Development* (UNDP, 2009).
51 Ibid. 3.
52 Commonwealth Secretariat, *Secretary-General Briefed on Migration Commission* (2009) www.thecommonwealth. org/news/190676/163079/216130/171109migrationcommission.htm.

13.4.8. The World Bank

Among the United Nations specialised agencies, the World Bank has become an important and increasingly visible player in linking economic and financial development with migration.[53] However, migration occupies only a small space within the institution, mostly in connection with the economic gains that remittances and other assets can bring to migrants, their families, and their home and host economies.

The World Bank member institutions are predisposed to address migration as a global governance issue, and seek to foster greater coherence across financial, economic and trade reform in low-income States. However, this coherence is still lacking, in part due to an endemic lack of institutional cohesion in such large institutions, and in part due to a chronic lack of empirical data and the inadequacy of economic and trade-based formulae in producing irrefutable policy solutions to the challenges of global migration.

It is still easier to combat poverty through economic and trade-related solutions than through better migration governance and its development effects. The links between migration and development are still being explored and measured. Yet the World Bank has made considerable strides in offering the international migration and development community empirical evidence of the positive impact of migration and remittances on poverty and the wellbeing of families, particularly the health and education of women and children.[54]

13.4.9. United Nations Institute for Training and Research

The United Nations Institute for Training and Research ('UNITAR') is the technical cooperation and training arm of the United Nations. Established in 1963, in recent years it has sought to increase its capacity to contribute to the emerging training and capacity development needs of governments. Relevantly, it has helped to promote the United Nations' effectiveness with governments by training and informing diplomats and civil servants on legal, policy and procedural matters of migration, and international dialogue on migration. It has consistently supported the international dialogue processes of the GFMD and the United Nations General Assembly's debates on international migration and development. In 2011, it co-organised with IOM a series of seminars on migration and development in support

---

53 See, generally: www.worldbank.org. The World Bank is not composed of member States directly, but of other international organisations whose members are States. The organisations that make up the World Bank Group are: the International Bank for Reconstruction and Development; the International Development Association; the International Finance Corporation; the Multilateral Investment Guarantee Agency; and the International Centre for Settlement of Investment Disputes.

54 See, e.g., Dilip Ratha, Sanket Mohaptra, Çağlar Özden, Sonia Plaza, William Shaw and Abebe Shimeles, 'Leveraging Migration for Africa: Remittances, Skills and Investments' (World Bank, 2011), which presents data from surveys in Africa.

of the GFMD's efforts to promote understanding and use of 'Migration Profiles', pioneered by IOM and the European Commission.[55]

13.4.10. United Nations Children's Fund

The work of UNICEF in helping 'children survive and thrive from early childhood through adolescence' is shaped by the *Convention on the Rights of the Child* (1989).[56] According to UNICEF, there are approximately 35 million international migrants between the ages of ten and twenty-four years, which represents about 17 per cent of the total migrant population.[57] Children migrating internationally, whether accompanied or unaccompanied, and whether travelling through regular or irregular mechanisms, are particularly vulnerable to abuse, exploitation, violence and homelessness. They are also often excluded from accessing the receiving State's social services and education system, due to their immigration status as well as social, cultural and language barriers. Consequently, the rights of child migrants are violated, leaving them even more at risk and vulnerable to abuse. In response, UNICEF partners with governments, international organisations and civil society organisations to incorporate the protection needs of child migrants in the broader discussion of migration and development. The legal framework for protecting child migrants is discussed in Chapter 8.

13.4.11. UN Women

UN Women was created by the United Nations General Assembly in 2010 by merging several existing agencies dealing with gender equality and the empowerment of women. Since 2011, it has sharpened its interest in migration by building on earlier coordination work between governments, non-governmental organisations and the private sector (e.g., standard contracts for migrant domestic workers in Asia), and by taking the lead on gender issues in the GFMD. In partnership with governments in several regions of the world, and other agencies, UN Women has organised focal meetings on global care workers as part of the GFMD 2011 thematic agenda.

55 Migration Profiles, first proposed by the European Commission in 2005, were intended to gather information on migration-related issues, including the labour market situation, unemployment rates, labour demand and supply, skill shortages by sector and occupation, skills available in the diaspora, migration flows, incoming and outgoing financial flows linked with migration, gender and minors: Commission of the European Communities, 'Migration and Development: Some Concrete Orientations' (COM(2005) 390 final, Commission of the European Communities, 1 September 2005), 37. Today, expanded versions of Migration Profiles are being discussed within the GFMD: Global Forum on Migration and Development, 'Roundtable 3: Policy and Institutional Coherence to Address the Relationship between Migration and Development' (GFMD, 2009).
56 *Convention on the Rights of the Child*, opened for signature 20 November 1989, 1577 UNTS 3 (entered into force 2 September 1990).
57 United Nations Children's Fund, 'Adolescents, Youth and International Migration: Figures and Facts' (UNICEF, 2011).

13.4.12. United Nations Conference on Trade and Development

The United Nations Conference on Trade and Development ('UNCTAD') emerged in 1964 as the principal organ of the United Nations General Assembly to deal with trade, investment and development issues. UNCTAD was essentially intended to offer developing States a forum to share information, ideas and policies against a backdrop of globalising markets and growing disparities between developed and developing worlds. It was established because there were concerns that existing institutions, such as the General Agreement on Tariffs and Trade (since replaced by the WTO), the International Monetary Fund and the World Bank, were not able to deal with the particular challenges of developing States.

Traditionally, UNCTAD has dealt mostly with policies on trade, aid, transport, finance and technology, but today it also routinely includes migration in its forum and research activities. Like UNITAR in New York, the Geneva-based UNCTAD offers a series of short courses on international economic issues, including migration and development, for government delegates and staff of Permanent Missions in Geneva who deal with trade and development issues.

13.4.13. Global Migration Group

In response to the disparate and often piecemeal treatment of migration in the United Nations, the GMG is an attempt to increase coordination among international organisations that work on migration. Established in 2006 at the behest of the United Nations Secretary-General to support the efforts of the GFMD, it brings together fifteen mostly Geneva-based international organisations. The current members are the ILO, IOM, OHCHR, the Regional Commissions, UNCTAD, UNDESA, UNDP, UNESCO, the United Nations Population Fund ('UNFPA'), UNHCR, UNICEF, UNITAR, UNODC, UN Women and the World Bank. It grew out of an earlier grouping, the 'Geneva Migration Group', established in 2003 by the heads of three of these agencies.[58] Since then, the GMG has striven to achieve its objectives of promoting the wider application of international instruments and norms relevant to migration and encouraging the adoption of more coherent, comprehensive and better-coordinated approaches to international migration.

However, the GMG has been variously described, mostly in the GFMD context, as ineffective, paralysed by competition and territorialism, and insufficiently cohesive in its support for the GFMD. Some believe it lacks shared vision and leadership, and that it continues to reflect contradictions.[59] This could be ascribed to mandate- and resource-related constraints, real or perceived, but also to a certain leadership vacuum in the field of international migration. Despite the criticisms and evident growing

---

58 These were the ILO, IOM and UNHCR, later joined by OHCHR, UNCTAD and UNODC.   59 Newland, above n. 12.

pains, most observers consider that the concept of bringing together the leading agencies engaged with migration policy is a worthy one and should be continued.

The GMG remains the only group of United Nations and intergovernmental agencies that meets regularly on migration and development issues. Individual member agencies have given invaluable input to the GFMD – through studies, best practices, models, background papers and expert participation in roundtables – but the GMG as a collective entity is also increasing its output. The question has been asked: 'Could the GMG become more than simply a forum for exchange; perhaps a group for joint advocacy?'[60] The first GMG practitioners' symposium on migration and youth, which was held in New York in May 2011, did not indicate any major shift in this direction.

Nonetheless, the GMG has produced some useful work, including an assessment of the legal framework for protecting the human rights of migrants in 2009.[61] Moreover, at the impetus of the GFMD, with its practical, bottom-up approach, the GMG agencies jointly published a handbook for policy makers and practitioners on 'Mainstreaming Migration into Development Planning'.[62] By 2011, some of the GMG members had begun piloting this as part of the GFMD thematic programme.

13.5. GLOBAL AND REGIONAL FORA ON MIGRATION

There has been a proliferation of government-led fora and conferences on migration in recent decades. Regional and inter-regional consultative processes have been established, mostly since the 1990s, to better deal with migration in cooperative ways, first among neighbours, but increasingly between migrant-sending and -receiving regions. The features that have helped these processes to succeed include the informality and the non-binding nature of their interactions and outcomes.

13.5.1. Regional and inter-regional consultative processes on migration

Regional consultative processes ('RCPs') are relatively recent phenomena, but they are increasingly important in fostering international cooperation on migration. An interesting question is whether and how these regional processes can provide the elements for an enhanced form of global migration governance.[63] Most RCPs are not

---

60 International Catholic Migration Commission, above n. 11, 8.
61 Global Migration Group, 'International Migration and Human Rights: Challenges and Opportunities on the Threshold of the 60th Anniversary of the Universal Declaration of Human Rights' (Global Migration Group, 2008) 98–100.
62 Global Migration Group, 'Mainstreaming Migration into Development Planning' (International Organization for Migration, 2010).
63 International Organization for Migration, 'Regional Consultative Processes and Development: Advancing Cooperation: Background Paper for Roundtable 3' (Paper presented at the Global Forum on Migration and Development, Brussels, Belgium, 9–11 July 2007).

formally associated with larger regional trade or economic integration processes, but they have helped to bring migration into the agendas of such processes in recent years. Examples of this include the Asia-Pacific Economic Cooperation ('APEC') Business Travel Card scheme;[64] the social security agreements under CARICOM and the Common Market of the South ('MERCOSUR');[65] and the common regional passport under the Economic Community of West African States ('ECOWAS'). These often entail legislative reform that can remove barriers to the protection of migrants.

Some processes today straddle geographical regions and hence have become known as inter-regional processes ('IRPs'). Notable examples include the 'Abu Dhabi Dialogue' (derived from the Colombo Process); '5+5' (involving five European and five Maghreb States); and the Ibero-American Forum on Migration and Development. The Abu Dhabi Dialogue has generated ground-breaking work, through partnership between sending States in South and Southeast Asia and receiving States in the Gulf region, to better protect overseas contract workers and leverage the development benefits of their mobility.[66]

While most of these processes continue to serve an exploratory and consultative purpose, they have also developed practical models of cooperation, many of which remain to be proven in the implementation. Reports on RCPs and IRPs show that the most significant achievement of these processes has been to remove impediments to national and international cooperation, and hence to migration governance. These impediments include a lack of trust between States (and even between parts of government within States), fears of political or financial costs, adversarial international relationships, and lack of understanding of the perspectives and concerns of others.[67]

At the global level, there is sustained interest in the regional processes, in particular in the lessons to be learned about effective bilateral and regional cooperation, and whether regional models could lay the foundations for better global governance. If RCPs and IRPs are to become the foundations for global migration governance, they still have a long way to go. In the meantime, they offer some of the best models of practical, workable cross-border cooperation on migration management (see Chapter 14).

13.5.2.   The Berne Initiative

The Berne Initiative was one of the first efforts to engage States from every region of the world in developing a common orientation to migration management, based on notions of cooperation, balance and predictability. Conceived as a State-owned

---

64 The scheme helps to expedite business movements between APEC States and further APEC's goal of free and open trade in the Asia-Pacific region.

65 Wouter Van Ginneken, 'Making Social Security Accessible to Migrants' (International Social Security Association, 2010).

66 Global Forum on Migration and Development, 'Roundtable Session 2.1: Reducing the Costs of Migration and Maximizing Human Development' (GFMD, 2010).

67 Randall Hansen, 'An Assessment of Principal Regional Consultative Processes on Migration' (IOM, 2010) 43–6.

consultative process, the initiative was launched by the Government of Switzerland at the International Symposium on Migration in Berne in 2001, with IOM serving at its secretariat. There were two major Berne conferences – in 2001 and 2004 – engaging a wide spread of governments, international organisations, NGOs and academia; a testimony of the considerable interest in cooperative approaches to migration.

The most important outcome of the Berne Initiative was a broad intergovernmental policy framework to facilitate cooperation between States in planning and managing the movement of people in a humane and orderly way.[68] As one of the first platforms for international cooperation and dialogue among countries of migration, it complemented the International Dialogue on Migration held in the IOM's governing Council. Some see the Berne Initiative as the precursor of the United Nations High Level Dialogue and the GFMD, and indeed most policies and practices highlighted by the Berne Initiative have been taken up in the GFMD.

13.5.3. United Nations initiatives – from the International Conference on Population and Development to the High Level Dialogue

The United Nations has been instrumental in establishing a longer-term government-led forum on migration and development, which systematically looks at governance issues. The Programme of Action resulting from the International Conference on Population and Development (1994) ('ICPD') is probably the first document calling for global action on migration in the context of development.[69] Chapter X, on international migration, exhorts governments to address the causes and consequences of migration, and the situation of documented and undocumented migrants, refugees, asylum seekers and displaced persons. This includes gathering sound data on migration; promoting integration and reintegration of the displaced; sanctioning international trafficking, especially exploitation, prostitution and coercive adoption; enhancing mechanisms for cross-border responsibility; and respecting the principle of *non-refoulement* where a person's return to another territory would threaten their life or freedom.

Little action was taken following the ICPD, and in 2003 a survey of United Nations member States indicated little interest in expanding the international normative framework for migration policies.[70] However, the tide began to turn when former United Nations Secretary-General, Kofi Annan, commissioned the Doyle Report in 2003.[71] Many events followed: the creation of the GCIM in 2003;

---

68 Berne Initiative, 'International Agenda for Migration Management' (International Organization for Migration, Swiss Federal Office for Migration, 2005).

69 United Nations Population Information Network, 'Programme of Action' (International Conference on Population and Development, 1994). The document presents a twenty-year plan to promote sustainable, human-centred development and a stable population.

70 The questionnaire resulted in only 47 member States favouring a global conference on migration, 26 opposing it, and 111 not responding. See Koslowski, above n. 8.

71 Migration Working Group, above n. 5.

> ## BOX 13.1 International Conference on Population and Development (1994)
>
> The International Conference on Population and Development ('ICPD'), which was held in Cairo, Egypt, in 1994, adopted the first global Programme of Action on population and development.[72]
>
> Chapter X of the Programme of Action, which focusses on international migration, recommends that action be designed to: reduce undocumented migration by addressing its root causes; encourage more cooperation between sending and receiving countries; ensure the wellbeing and social integration of documented migrants; protect both the documented and undocumented from racism and xenophobia; seek to resolve conflicts; and find durable solutions to the plight of refugees and displaced persons. The action in Chapter X is proposed specifically for migrant-sending and -receiving States, as relevant.
>
> The *Cairo Declaration on Population and Development* (1994) ('Cairo Declaration') made a call to all parliamentarians to channel their personal commitment into political action to implement the Programme of Action.[73] The Cairo Declaration also advocated for updating and strengthening the recommendations originally laid out in the 1974 'World Population Plan of Action'. Updates were necessary because there had been dramatic changes between 1974 and 1994 in global demographic, social, economic and political conditions, as well as in the relevant legal framework of Conventions and Protocols. Reinforcing the Programme of Action, the recommendations in the Cairo Declaration addressed population and sustainable development, reproductive health and family planning, gender equality and the empowerment of women, health and mortality, and resource mobilisation.

the convening of the first United Nations General Assembly High Level Dialogue on Migration and Development in 2006 to discuss the report; the appointment of a United Nations Special Representative on Migration; the establishment of the GFMD; and the creation of the inter-agency GMG in 2007. All these initiatives have represented a serious effort to address migration from a global perspective in the broader context of development.

Building on the global momentum on migration and development, in 2006 the United Nations dedicated a General Assembly plenary session to migration issues in a 'High Level Dialogue on International Migration and Development'. This ground-breaking international event offered a unique opportunity for sending, transit and receiving States to move towards a concerted approach to migration and development. This will be followed by a second High Level Dialogue in 2013, to take stock of initiatives in this field, including the GFMD.

13.5.4. Global Forum on Migration and Development

The GFMD was born in 2007 of a strong belief and agreement among the majority of United Nations member States that an independent, informal and State-led international forum for migration discussion and exchange of experience would enhance international cooperation on migration. It may also have been seen by some key United Nations members as a more acceptable alternative to a world

---

72 See above n. 69.
73 *Cairo Declaration on Population and Development*, International Conference of Parliamentarians on Population and Development (4 September 1994).

migration organisation. After only five years, the GFMD has matured into the largest, relatively coherent global forum on migration and development. From the outset, its informal, State-led nature was strongly supported and jealously guarded by the governments involved. The majority of GFMD member States have reaffirmed this every year. The GFMD has no rules or legal or constitutional anchors. It is not part of the United Nations, but is linked to it through the United Nations Secretary-General's Special Representative for International Migration, who presents an annual progress report to the Secretary-General.

In 2008, the Manila GFMD dealt with fundamental human rights of migrants, both in society and in the workplace, where many temporary migrants suffer from discrimination and xenophobia. In 2009, the Athens GFMD took the rights discussion a little deeper by focussing on integration of immigrants in host States and the possible impacts of successful integration on development. In 2010, the focus of the Mexico GFMD was on the partnerships needed to underpin these efforts (partnerships between States, public and private sectors, migrants and communities) to optimise the human development of migrants through education, social welfare, healthcare, gender- and family-oriented policies, and through comprehensive approaches to facilitate regular migration and minimise irregular forms of migration. In 2011, the Switzerland GFMD took the forum 'into the field' to learn from the practical experiences of governments on the ground, and to bring those back to a concluding debate.

After five years of operation, many questions can be posed about the GFMD. Is it making a difference to migration governance? Is it institutionalising itself in ways similar to those of the United Nations? And, most especially, what changes has it wrought? The High Level Dialogue that is scheduled for 2013 will report on progress and on the outcomes of an evaluation being undertaken by a small group of GFMD governments. In the meantime, it is worthwhile speculating about its contribution.

The GFMD has changed the way governments deal multilaterally with migration. By approaching migration governance through the development lens, it has been possible to discuss controversial issues that have led to rancour and stalemate in other multilateral fora. It has done this partly by pursuing a rights-based approach to managing migration through practical examples that prove the efficacy of the principle.

An informal survey undertaken by the GFMD shows that attitudes and policies are changing, in part as a consequence of the GFMD. Some European governments (e.g., Spain, Italy, Portugal, France, Sweden and the Netherlands) have new or pending circular migration programmes aimed at benefitting partner States. New pilot circular migration programmes – such as between Mauritius and France, Ukraine and Portugal, and Costa Rica and Nicaragua – are testing circulation schemes and keeping the GFMD informed about their progress. Through the circular migration examples, the GFMD has learned that developing States can come to the negotiating table with high-income States as equals rather than inferior business partners, and agree on labour exchanges that meet mutual labour market needs. While not all these initiatives have grown directly from the GFMD, it has provided an important backdrop for them.

Key recommendations from earlier GFMD meetings have also been implemented, further reinforcing the thematic coherence between annual meetings. Governments are exploring comprehensive packages to better protect the social and financial integrity of foreign contract workers. This follows work begun by Bangladesh in 2007 on the recruitment industry, and GFMD studies since then on the feasibility of low-cost loans for labour migrants from Bangladesh, social security benefits for temporary labour migrants, and migrant resource centres as facilities for better informing migrants.[74] United Arab Emirates is making strides to reform its labour migration laws to better protect its foreign contract workers.[75]

Governments have agreed to continue pursuing policy and institutional coherence on migration and development, and research and data to underpin these efforts. States are increasingly considering the use of Migration Profiles as a standard tool for collecting data, fostering analysis and incorporating migration into development planning.

The GFMD still has a lot of unfinished business. For example, some governments and civil society representatives continue to call for a stronger development focus in the migration and development equation, including the right to stay home. Developing States that receive official development assistance need to locate migration in their development and foreign policies, while developed States must do the same. More progress is still needed in ensuring migrants' economic rights and adopting positive approaches to migrants' short-term and long-term integration. The GFMD has tried to move this forward by addressing ways of regulating and improving the conduct of the recruitment industry. However, in the absence of cooperative government efforts to ensure that regulations are reasonable and that voluntary compliance is beneficial, a call on the industry to self-regulate may have few positive impacts.

Informal, non-binding agreement has been reached at GFMD meetings on principles that can help to protect and support migrants working abroad. These principles include access to and transparency of information for migrants, employers, recruiters and governments at both ends of the migration corridor; skills–job matching; standardised contracts; working conditions; accountability and enforcement; and regulation of recruiters.

---

74 See John Willoughby and Heath Henderson, 'Preparing Contract Workers for Return and Reintegration: Relevant for Development?' (Global Forum on Migration and Development, 2009); Philip Martin, 'Reducing the Cost Burden for Migrant Workers: A Market-Based Approach' (Global Forum on Migration and Development, 2009); International Organization for Migration, 'Migrant Resource Centres: Examining Global Good Practices in Providing Services to Empower Migrants for Development and Protection' (IOM, 12 October 2009).

75 In January 2011, United Arab Emirates established new regulations for recruiting agencies, including higher value bonds for agencies engaged in overseas recruitment. It also developed a set of principles to guide sending and receiving States in better managing the recruitment industry: Global Forum on Migration and Development, 'Workshop on Recruitment of Workers for Overseas Employment' (GFMD, 18–19 January 2011).

The question remains: is the GFMD an embryo for the formation of an eventual global migration regime? Too little is known about the effects of the GFMD on migration governance to provide an answer. A key lesson is that migration governance is not just about human mobility; it is also about combating poverty, improving development strategies and outcomes, better labour market planning within and between States, and smarter employment creation in low- and high-income States. Yet the connections between these issues are still not fully understood. In the meantime, speculation continues about the value and viability of the GFMD, especially since it is self-funding, has no coherent mandate based in law, and is relatively free-floating.

13.6. CONCLUSION

One glaring problem in the discussion of migration governance is that most States still do not have comprehensive national migration laws, policies or unified governance structures to manage migration. Even in traditional countries of immigration it is rare to find migration policies that incorporate all the critical, interrelated disciplines, such as human rights, economic, trade, security, demographic, environmental, integration and developmental considerations. Without a critical mass of national migration policies, a commitment to global policies and approaches is even more difficult to envision, and a concerted global effort will continue to be elusive.

Similarly, many States simply do not see the value of a multilateral or global governance regime in this field. There remain too many unequal needs and capacities among sending and receiving States. For decades it was said that closer cooperation between sending and receiving States was economically efficient, and that an enhanced global regime of cooperation might help to improve the access of poorer migrant source countries to wealthy migrant destination markets, and thus reduce global inequalities. Yet we have also heard the flipside of this argument, namely, that for many high-income receiving States the economic benefits of globalised migration management are negligible compared with the social and political costs.

These positions may be softening, but this does not necessarily warrant a formal global migration governance regime, or new institutional approaches or frameworks. Many governments prefer to sharpen and improve existing tools and processes, and they see the GFMD as meeting some of these needs, without the formalities. The GFMD can spotlight and disseminate the best practices among the range of governance options, and help tease out the common features among them as agreed foundations for global governance.

The number of intergovernmental and international agencies dealing with migration today is dizzying, but many of them clearly have a significant part to play in the overall comprehension and management of the phenomenon.

International law is clear and wide-ranging in its protection of individual human rights, but less clear on how to achieve this in practice and on the powers of multilateral agencies to enforce it. A single coordinating agency – a global migration organisation – may be an option, but there seems to be less serious discussion about it now than some years ago, which possibly reflects the growing competitiveness among lead agencies in this field. The most obvious contender, IOM, does not yet have universal membership, United Nations context or the confidence to assume these responsibilities.

A useful role for the GFMD or the GMG might be for its members to affirm a set of international principles to assist and guide the development of international approaches to migration governance – law, policies and practices. The GCIM made precisely this suggestion in its report in 2005.[76]

The newer institutions of regional and global cooperation on migration, namely, the GMG, the GFMD and regional and inter-regional consultative processes, may be the best hope for the immediate future. In striving to maintain a balance among all parties, institutions of global cooperation are unlikely to advocate for stronger global governance of migration. In any case, they still need to overcome the hurdle of coherence and coordination among their own parts before reaching the second, and more important, goal of widening the application of regional and international instruments and norms.

Governance issues of this kind will no doubt be debated at the United Nations High Level Dialogue in 2013. One question it is unlikely to ask, or answer, is: 'Will we ever progress beyond dialogues, or are they a convenient way of avoiding real institutional change?'

KEY REFERENCES

Global Migration Group, 'Briefing Paper: Enhancing Development through International Cooperation on Migration' (GMG, 2011)

Global Migration Group: Acting Together in a World on the Move (GMG, 2011)

International Organization for Migration, 'An Assessment of Principal Regional Consultative Processes on Migration', Migration Research Series No 38 (IOM, 2010)

Kahler, Miles and Lake, David, 'Globalization and Governance: Definition, Variation, and Explanation' (Asrudian Center, 2008)

Koslowski, Rey, 'Possible Steps towards an International Regime for Mobility and Security' Global Migration Perspectives No. 8 (Global Commission on International Migration, 2004)

Marchi, Sergio, 'Global Governance: Migration's Next Frontier' (2010) 16(3) Global Governance 323

Martin, Susan, 'Making the UN Work: Forced Migration and Institutional Reform' (2004) 17(3) Journal of Refugee Studies 301

Migration Working Group, 'Background Report on Migration Prepared for the Senior Management Group' (United Nations, 2003)

76 Global Commission on International Migration, 'Migration in an Interconnected World: New Directions for Action' (GCIM, 2005) Annex I.

KEY RESOURCES

Global Forum on Migration and Development: www.gfmd.org

Global Migration Group: www.globalmigrationgroup.org

International Catholic Migration Commission: www.icmc.net/conversations-global-governance-migration

International Labour Organization, International Migration Branch: www.ilo.org/migrant

International Organization for Migration: www.iom.int

Organisation for Economic Co-operation and Development: www.oecd.org

Organization for Security and Co-operation in Europe: www.osce.org

UN Women: www.unwomen.org

United Nations Children's Fund: www.unicef.org

United Nations Conference on Trade and Development: www.unctad.org

United Nations Department of Economic and Social Affairs: www.un.org/en/development/desa

United Nations Development Programme: www.undp.org

United Nations Educational, Scientific and Cultural Organization: www.unesco.org

United Nations Office of the High Commissioner for Human Rights: www.ohchr.org

United Nations High Commissioner for Refugees: www.unhcr.org

United Nations Institute for Training and Research: www.unitar.org

World Trade Organization: www.wto.org

Regional processes, law and institutional developments on migration

KAROLINE POPP[1]

14.1. INTRODUCTION

The preceding chapters have examined various facets of international migration law at the universal level, as well as developments in the governance of migration in the global context. In parallel, legal frameworks and 'softer' governance arrangements and policy processes on migration gained prominence at the regional level in many parts of the world. Globalisation and regionalisation trends have been proceeding hand in hand for decades and are particularly evident in regional economic and political integration processes, which build on geographical proximity and historical affinity. Furthermore, there is a strong regional rationale for migration governance: driven by historical, linguistic, cultural and economic ties, most international migration takes place at a regional level among neighbouring States. For instance, approximately two-thirds of migrants from sub-Saharan Africa have moved within the region, and the same is true for 43 per cent of Asian migrants. Likewise, most European Union nationals who live outside the State of their birth are in another State of the European Union, and the vast majority of migration in the Americas is intra-regional. The picture is very similar in other regions of the world (see Chapter 2).[2]

These migration realities, as well as broader geopolitical shifts towards greater regional and global cooperation on a range of issues, have created a natural impetus for developments in migration law and governance at the regional level, which will be examined in this chapter. Section 14.2 explores the growing role of regional institutions – principally political and economic associations and integration processes – in migration governance. Section 14.3 reviews developments in regional consultative processes on migration, which are non-binding collaborative

---

1 Portions of Section 14.3 of this chapter are drawn from an earlier draft prepared by Colleen Thouez. Kristina Touzenis and colleagues from IOM's International Migration Law Unit contributed to Section 14.4.
2 International Organization for Migration, *World Migration Report 2010: The Future of Migration: Building Capacities for Change* (IOM, 2010).

arrangements among States, dedicated solely to migration issues. They emerged in the 1980s and now exist in all major regions of the world. This section also examines a relatively new form of collaboration known as inter-regional fora. Section 14.4 focusses on elements of regional law of particular relevance to migrants, taking as examples nationality and statelessness, the entry and exit of non-nationals, and some aspects of forced migration, to illustrate the potential inherent in regional legal instruments and their contribution to international migration law. The chapter concludes with observations about the future impact and interaction of these processes in the complex global fabric of migration law and governance.

14.2.   REGIONAL INSTITUTIONS AND THEIR ROLE IN MIGRATION LAW AND GOVERNANCE

Nowhere has the trend towards regionalisation been more evident than in the multiplication and growing importance of regional institutions. There is hardly a State in the world that is not part of one or more such arrangements. Regional institutions were created to advance peace, cooperation, trade and prosperity among their members through economic or political integration, or both. While in some cases migration was part of the institution's original scope, others adopted the issue only later on, once institutional set-ups, trust and cooperation mechanisms had become sufficiently firm to broach a topic traditionally considered to be one of exclusive national concern. As it stands today, most regional institutions address the question of migration in some way within their legal framework, and in many instances regional rules or guidelines seek to harmonise national frameworks.

Regional institutions have moved at varying speeds, and the level of institutionalised cooperation on migration continues to differ significantly between regions. Differences are also evident with respect to the regional outlook on migration: some institutions focus on migration coming to, or emanating from, the region; for others the primary concern is the management of intra-regional migration; and yet others cover both aspects or have added different dimensions of migration relevant to the region over time. With regard to intra-regional mobility arrangements, three distinctive approaches can be identified: a right to full mobility; mobility agreements based on the model of Mode 4 of the *General Agreement on Trade in Services* (1994) ('GATS') (see Chapter 12);[3] and facilitated entry and stay with no market access. Given the large number of regional institutions and vast array of migration laws and policies covered by them, this

---

3 *Marrakesh Agreement Establishing the World Trade Organization*, opened for signature 15 April 1994, 1867 UNTS 3 (entered into force 1 January 1995) annex 1B ('*General Agreement on Trade in Services*').

section sketches a descriptive overview of a few of the major regional institutions and their migration arrangements.[4]

14.2.1. Africa

The African Union ('AU') was established in 2002 as the successor to the Organisation of African Unity and has developed a number of policies oriented towards a vision of how migration can support development efforts.[5] The 2001 'Strategic Framework for a Policy on Migration' contained two broad focus areas: first, stemming brain drain through the creation of employment opportunities, and second, mobilising the African diaspora for the development of their home States. The development dimension of migration has remained a priority for the AU throughout the years. In 2004, the AU further strengthened its strategic framework to ensure integration of migration and related issues into national and regional agendas for security, development and cooperation, and in 2006 it developed the 'Migration Policy Framework for Africa' and the 'African Common Position on Migration and Development'.[6] In the same vein, the AU Commission also created the African Citizens Directorate to connect diasporas and home State governments.

At the sub-regional level, economic associations have left their mark on migration policy since the 1970s, long before the birth of the AU. West Africa is the region within Africa that has the most developed institutional arrangements governing mobility. The Economic Community of West African States ('ECOWAS') was set up in 1975 to foster economic and political cooperation in the region (see Chapter 2, Map 2.1), and the removal of obstacles to the free movement of persons between ECOWAS member States is enumerated as one objective in its founding treaty.[7] A 1979 Protocol grants ECOWAS nationals the right to visa-free entry, residency and employment in the whole region.[8] This aim was reaffirmed in the revised ECOWAS Treaty of 1993. In practice, the implementation of this Protocol has been halting, particularly with regard to the issuance of ECOWAS travel certificates and ECOWAS passports, compounded by the fact that access to national passports is often limited.[9]

---

4 This section draws on International Organization for Migration, 'Free Movement of Persons in Regional Integration Processes' (IOM, 2010) and Global Forum on Migration and Development, 'Roundtable Session 3.3, Regional Consultative Processes (RCPs), Inter-Regional Consultative Fora and Regional Organizations and Economic Integration Processes at the Interface of Migration and Development' (GFMD, 2008). See also Ryszard Cholewinski, Richard Perruchoud and Euan Macdonald (eds.), *International Migration Law: Developing Paradigms and Key Challenges* (TMC Asser Press, 2007).

5 Aderanti Adepoju, 'The Future of Migration Policies in Africa' (International Organization for Migration, 2010) 5.

6 African Union, *The Migration Policy Framework for Africa*, Executive Council, 9th Ordinary Session, AU Doc EX.CL/276 (IX) (2006); African Union, *African Common Position on Migration and Development*, Executive Council, 9th Ordinary Session, AU Doc EX.CL/277 (IX) (25–29 June 2006).

7 *Treaty of the Economic Community of West African States*, opened for signature 28 May 1975, 1010 UNTS 18 (entered into force 1 August 1995) art. 27(1).

8 *Protocol relating to Free Movement of Persons, Residence and Establishment*, Official Journal of the ECOWAS Vol 1, Doc A/P 1/5/79 (29 May 1979).

9 International Organization for Migration, 'World Migration 2008: Managing Labour Mobility in the Evolving Economy' (IOM, 2008) 363.

Likewise, progress on the abolition of border checks and mass expulsions has been slow, and restrictive national laws vis-à-vis 'foreigners' from within the ECOWAS region remain in place in many member States.[10] The institution is also increasingly looking to address the external dimension of migration, as reflected in its 'Common Approach on Migration' (2008), which aims to address the challenges relating to the movement of persons within the ECOWAS region and to third States.

14.2.2.   Americas

The Common Market of the South ('MERCOSUR') is a classic example of an institution that commenced (in 1991) as a common market with a focus on economic integration and gradually added migration to its agenda. In 1998, the principles of non-discrimination and equal rights for migrant workers and national workers were laid down in the *Social and Labour Declaration*. Further, the 2002 Agreement on Residency for Nationals of MERCOSUR States, Bolivia and Chile,[11] and a 2003 agreement on a common visa for the MERCOSUR area,[12] consolidated the mobility provisions and effectively gave rise to a free movement zone for nationals of the southern cone. Created in the same year, the MERCOSUR Specialized Forum on Migration brings together relevant policy makers from the institution's member States, plus the associated States of Bolivia, Chile, Colombia, Ecuador, Peru and Venezuela. It serves as a platform for capacity building, consultation and information sharing with regard to the movement of persons in the region. Protecting the human rights of migrants has emerged as a key concern for MERCOSUR, reflected in the *Declaration of Santiago on Migration Principles* (2004) and in the body's advocacy for regularising irregular migrants. The establishment of the Union of South American Nations, with effect from 2011, is likely to further advance regional integration efforts in the realm of migration. Bridging MERCOSUR and the Andean Community, plus Chile, Guyana and Surinam, its objectives specifically include 'Cooperation on issues of migration with a holistic approach, based on an unrestricted respect for human and labour rights, for migratory regularisation and harmonisation of policies'.[13]

In Central America and the Caribbean, migration is addressed through the Central American Integration System ('SICA') and through the Caribbean

---

10 Jonathan Martens, 'Moving Freely on the African Continent: The Experiences of ECOWAS and SADC with Free Movement Protocols' in Ryszard Cholewinski, Richard Perruchoud and Euan Macdonald (eds.), *International Migration Law: Developing Paradigms and Key Challenges* (TMC Asser Press, 2007) 349.

11 *Agreement on Residence Status for Nationals of the MERCOSUR States Parties and Associated States*, opened for signature 2002. This agreement grants migrants the right to equal treatment, transfer remittances, family reunification and access to education for children regardless of their parents' migration status.

12 *Agreement for the Creation of the MERCOSUR Visa*, Common Market Council Decision 16/03 (2003).

13 *Constitutive Treaty of the Union of South American Nations*, opened for signature 23 May 2008 (entered into force 11 March 2011) art. 3.

Community ('CARICOM'), respectively. While there is no reference to migration issues in SICA's institutional framework, the body has hosted the Central American Commission of Migration Directors since its beginnings in the early 1990s. Supported by a technical secretariat run by the International Organization for Migration ('IOM'), the Commission serves as a forum for consultation and coordination among migration authorities, with a view to managing the movement of people in Central America. In the CARICOM region, the establishment of the Caribbean Single Market Economy in 1989 also set in motion a gradual move towards intra-regional freedom of movement, reinforced by an agreement on the portability of social security benefits in 1997 (see Chapter 12, Map 12.1). Nonetheless, the implementation of provisions and their uptake by the region's nationals have remained low.[14]

14.2.3. Asia

The Association of Southeast Asian Nations ('ASEAN') was established in 1967 to maintain and enhance peace, security, and economic and socio-cultural development in the region. Migration is absent from the founding declaration and has appeared on the institution's agenda only very recently; long perceived as too sensitive an issue to be discussed in a formal multilateral context. As a result, 'regional governance of migration remains weak and is in its early stages'.[15] The *ASEAN Framework Agreement on Services* (1995) contains relevant provisions,[16] while an agreement was reached in 2006 to grant a two-week visa-free entry to ASEAN nationals travelling in the region. There are plans to move towards an ASEAN Economic Community by 2015; however, incorporation of migration dimensions continues to be limited. Significantly, ASEAN adopted a *Declaration on the Protection and Promotion of the Rights of Migrant Workers* (2007), which commits States to recognise the rights of migrant workers, ensure dignified and decent working conditions, and protect migrant workers from exploitation and all forms of human rights violations.

14.2.4. Europe

The European Union ('EU') is considered to have gone furthest and deepest in its legislation on the movement of persons within its region, some elements of which are discussed further in Case Study 14.1. The scope of its internal arrangements has

---

14 Sophie Nonnenmacher, 'Free Movement of Persons in the Caribbean Community' in Ryszard Cholewinski, Richard Perruchoud and Euan Macdonald (eds.), *International Migration Law: Developing Paradigms and Key Challenges* (TMC Asser Press, 2007) 387.

15 Graeme Hugo, 'The Future of Migration Policies in the Asia-Pacific Region' (IOM, 2010) 14.

16 *ASEAN Framework Agreement on Services*, opened for signature 15 December 1995 (entered into force 30 December 1998) art. 1.

had repercussions for the EU's migration policy vis-à-vis the rest of the world, and migration has thus also entered into the EU's external policies. With regard to its internal policies, the EU was originally a free market project characterised by the 'four freedoms': the free movement of goods, the free movement of capital, the freedom to provide services and the free movement of persons. The free movement of persons, however, was not fully implemented until the adoption of secondary legislation in 1968.[17] The concept of EU citizenship was established in the *Treaty on European Union* (1992) ('Treaty of Maastricht'),[18] and today EU citizens enjoy equal treatment irrespective of their nationality and have full mobility rights within the EU, covering entry, residency and employment (with certain limitations on a temporary basis for nationals of EU member States admitted in 2004 and 2007). Any EU citizen is therefore entitled to take up employment in any EU member State, under the same conditions as nationals of that State, including the right to family reunification.[19]

In moving towards the free movement of persons, one of the most important steps was the creation of the borderless Schengen zone in 1985, its subsequent consolidation in EU law and its expansion to twenty-six States. Agreeing on a common external migration policy, by contrast, has proved more difficult. Traditionally, the main areas of focus have included visa policy, border control and irregular and return migration, but demographic and labour market trends in Europe have also led to a growing interest in mobility of the highly skilled.[20] The EU's Stockholm Programme – a five-year plan (2010–14) in the areas of freedom, justice and security – represents the overlap between internal and external dimensions of EU migration policy, encompassing provisions in the realm of border controls, readmission agreements, labour migration and integration.[21] It also recognises the increasingly important place of migration in the EU's external policies, principally through the 2005 Global Approach to Migration (renamed the Global Approach to Migration and Mobility in 2011), which integrates external relations, migration and development policy. The EU's external migration policy is also manifest in two other initiatives – the growing number of bi-regional dialogues on migration between the EU and selected priority regions of origin; and mobility partnerships, which are collaborative efforts between the EU and third States to combat irregular migration and enhance labour mobility.

17 *Regulation (EEC) No 1612/68 of the Council of 15 October 1968 on Freedom of Movement for Workers within the Community* [1968] OJ L 257/2.
18 *Treaty on European Union*, opened for signature 7 February 1992, 1757 UNTS 3 (entered into force 1 November 1993) art. 8.
19 International Organization for Migration, above n. 9, 364.   20 Ibid. 367.
21 European Council, 'The Stockholm Programme: An Open and Secure Europe Serving and Protecting Citizens, OJ 2010/C 115/01' (2010).

CASE STUDY 14.1 Free movement in the European Union

In 1985, Belgium, France, Germany, Luxembourg and the Netherlands signed the Schengen agreement, which aimed to eliminate all passport and other checks between participating States, and to establish a single external border. This concept of free movement was later expanded to include free travel of nationals of third countries within the Schengen area, as it was not feasible to maintain border checks for third-country nationals while eliminating such checks for the nationals of participating States.

In 1990, the same five States signed the *Convention Implementing the Schengen Agreement.*[22] The Convention harmonised rules on short-term visas of less than ninety days, while the regulation of longer visas remained under State control. It also covered asylum provisions, as well as police and judicial cooperation, particularly in fighting organised crime. Internal border controls were abolished and external borders remained under the purview of States, but were subject to uniform procedures. The Schengen framework also established the Schengen information system, to allow for the exchange of information between the authorities of Schengen members.

Other States gradually joined the Schengen area, which today encompasses twenty-six States, including most EU members as well as some non-EU members, such as Norway, Iceland and Switzerland.[23] Bulgaria, Cyprus and Romania, though part of the EU, are not yet fully part of Schengen, while Denmark, unlike other Schengen States, can choose whether or not to apply any new decisions made under the Schengen agreements. Under Schengen, States may re-establish their national border checks for a short period of time if it is necessary for national security.

Schengen became part of EU legislation through the *Treaty of Amsterdam* in 1997, as the Schengen *acquis.*[24] When the *Treaty of Amsterdam* came into force in 1999, decision-making power for Schengen was given to the EU Council of Ministers. Although Schengen had officially become part of the EU, the United Kingdom and Ireland opted out, preferring to maintain their own national borders and joint Common Travel Area. The United Kingdom and Ireland do, however, participate in some aspects of Schengen, including the Schengen information system. Meanwhile, Iceland and Norway signed an agreement with the EU in 1999 to continue their participation in the Schengen area.

Under art. 2 of the Schengen *acquis*, internal borders may be crossed at any point without any checks on persons being carried out. Without prejudice to the provisions on travel documents applicable to national border controls, all EU citizens with a valid identity card or passport (plus family members who are not nationals of a member State and who hold a valid passport) have the right to leave the territory of a member State to travel to another member State. No exit visa or equivalent formality may be imposed on such persons.

[22] Europa: Summaries of EU legislation, *The Schengen Area and Cooperation* (2009) http://europa.eu/ legislation.summaries/justice.freedom.security/free.movement.of.persons.asylum.immigration/l33020.fn.htm.

[23] Norway and Iceland had formed a Nordic passport union together with Finland, Sweden and Denmark, in effect since the 1950s. Norway and Iceland are not members of the EU, but both joined Schengen to preserve this union. See Julia Gelatt, Schengen and the Free Movement of People Across Europe (Migration Policy Institute, 2005).

[24] *The Schengen Acquis Convention Implementing the Schengen Agreement of 14 June 1985 between the Governments of the States of the Benelux Economic Union, the Federal Republic of Germany and the French Republic on the Gradual Abolition of Checks at their Common Borders* [2000] OJ L 239/19.

14.3. REGIONAL PROCESSES FOR MIGRATION COOPERATION

Just as regional institutions have increasingly taken up migration and related issues, the growing importance of migration at the regional level is also reflected in the expansion of other regional processes for cooperation on migration. As with formal regional institutions, virtually all States in nearly every part of the world participate in at least one such process.

Regional consultative processes on migration ('RCPs') are repeated, regional meetings of States dedicated to the topic of migration.[25] RCPs are characteristically informal, where informality refers to the relatively depoliticised nature of the setting and the discussions rather than an absence of rules and procedures that guide the way in which the RCP operates. They are also non-binding, since they do not produce legally binding outcomes in and of themselves. Among the other hallmarks of RCPs is the fact that they were designed to focus exclusively on migration, thus setting them apart from the regional institutions discussed in Section 14.2, which were created for broader economic and political purposes and later added migration to their agendas. Traditionally, RCPs were considered to be independent of the formal regional institutions described above, but this is neither true for all RCPs (particularly those in developing regions) nor necessarily desirable, given the expanding role of regional institutions in migration governance. While RCPs are State-led, they often receive support from international organisations, principally IOM as the main international migration organisation, as well as smaller, regionally based organisations.

The regional element of RCPs is somewhat ambiguous and serves mainly to denote what RCPs are not, namely, global. Geographic regions are not precisely defined and a number of RCPs span two or more regions or sub-regions, especially the larger RCPs. Other RCPs – the Inter-governmental Consultations on Migration, Asylum and Refugees being the main example – are regional not in the sense of being geographically contiguous, but in terms of their migration geography: as 'coalitions of the like-minded', the constituent States define themselves primarily as States of destination for migration, and they come together on the basis of this shared feature. As a result, it has become common to mention RCPs in the same breath as inter-regional fora ('IRF'), which typically bridge two geographically distinct regions.[26] In large measure, IRFs are testimony to the importance of migration corridors that connect two or more regions – for example, between North Africa and Europe (across the Mediterranean) or between South Asia and the Gulf States. An important distinction between RCPs and IRFs, however, lies in

---

25 Randall Hansen, *An Assessment of Principal Regional Consultative Processes on Migration* (IOM, 2010) 12.
26 See Global Forum on Migration and Development, 'Roundtable Session 3.3, How Can Regional Consultative Processes (RCPs) and Inter-Regional Fora (IRF) Best Include the Migration and Development Nexus?' (GFMD, 2010) 2: 'It is increasingly difficult to distinguish clearly between RCPs and IRFs, not least because some RCPs … also involve countries from different regions.'

the fact that the latter often grew out of regional institutions and more formal, pre-existing, inter-regional processes that cover broader agendas, with migration being just one item on the list. IRFs also tend to bring together political counterparts at higher levels, often through ministerial meetings.

Furthermore, a clear distinction can be drawn between States' motivations in joining an RCP and their motivation in collaborating in an IRF. Within many RCPs, the incentive is to build a regional understanding of priorities and potentially to harmonise accordingly. Within an IRF, the incentives of States may also be better governance, but the goals or 'hierarchies of interests' are likely to be quite different. IRFs are about finding different areas on which to agree where there is a mutual incentive to cooperate. The process is as much about defining mutually acceptable trade-offs in order to fulfil each regional bloc's migration-related objectives as it is to maintain a spirit of collaboration.

14.3.1. Principal regional consultative processes on migration and inter-regional fora[27]

Founded in 1985, the Inter-governmental Consultations on Migration, Asylum and Refugees ('IGC') is generally considered to be the ancestor of all RCPs, spawning similar processes in other parts of the world, which eventually gave rise to RCPs as a recognised category. Based on like-mindedness rather than geographical contiguity, the IGC encompasses fifteen States in Europe and North America, in addition to Australia and New Zealand. The IGC has broadened its original focus on asylum regimes to also cover questions of admission, control, enforcement, immigration and integration.

The IGC model was borrowed in the establishment of the second RCP in 1991, the Budapest Process, whose first objective was to support the accession of Central and Eastern European States to the EU by assisting in the development of their migration management capacities. Over the years, its geographical spotlight has moved to the Commonwealth of Independent States, the Black Sea region, South Eastern Europe and the 'Silk Routes' region, while the thematic scope has expanded beyond irregular movements to include migration and development, labour migration and integration.

Also in Europe, the Söderköping Process was initiated in 2001 to build capacities in the areas of migration, refugee protection and border management. Following the 2004 wave of accessions to the EU, the process served to transfer lessons learned from new EU member States to Belarus, Moldova and Ukraine. It has undergone significant reform in recent years, reflected in stronger government leadership and growing membership (Sweden joined the process in 2010, and Armenia, Azerbaijan and Georgia in 2011).

27 The RCPs and IRFs described here are not exhaustive. See International Organization for Migration, *Regional Consultative Processes* (2011) www.iom.int/rcps.

On the other side of the Atlantic, in the Americas, the Regional Conference on Migration ('Puebla Process') initiated in 1996 for Central America, Mexico, the United States and Canada, focusses its regular technical and ministerial-level meetings on migration policy and management, human rights, and migration and development. One distinctive feature of this RCP is the systematic participation of civil society representatives via the Regional Network for Civil Society Organizations on Migration.

Meanwhile, the South American Conference on Migration ('SACM') has been in existence since 1999 and addresses, as its main priorities, the economic, cultural and development contributions of migrants to home and host countries; information and statistics on migration; integration; trafficking and smuggling; and migrants' human rights. SACM, too, has developed mechanisms to enhance the involvement of civil society in its work.

As yet, there is no dedicated RCP for the Caribbean region, although regional meetings were initiated in 2000 and 2001 with a view to establishing one.[28] Discussions have been ongoing ever since; at the 2011 gathering of IOM member States, the representative of the Latin American and Caribbean Group of States and the Director-General of IOM made reference to the imminent creation of a Caribbean RCP.

In Africa, RCPs tend to be closely aligned with pre-existing regional mechanisms for cooperation, due in no small measure to the greater availability of resources within the regional institutions. The Migration Dialogue for Southern Africa ('MIDSA') was founded in 2000 and facilitates migration policy dialogue in the Southern African Development Community, with emphasis on regional capacity development in information gathering and exchange; border management; the fight against human trafficking and people smuggling; the human rights of migrants; and the promotion of development aspects of migration. MIDSA received fresh political impetus in 2010 when it held its first ministerial meeting since its inception.

In 2001, the Migration Dialogue for West Africa ('MIDWA') was set up in close cooperation with ECOWAS to address topics ranging from border management and irregular migration, to migrant rights and migration and development. Weak political and financial backing has left MIDWA largely dormant in recent years. Nonetheless, a MIDWA programme of action adopted in 2010 aims to revitalise the process in the run-up to the second United Nations High Level Dialogue on International Migration and Development in 2013.

A third African RCP, the Intergovernmental Authority on Development – Regional Consultative Process on Migration ('IGAD-RCP'), was established in 2008 for the IGAD States of East Africa. Its objectives are to foster greater understanding and policy coherence; strengthen regional institutional and technical capacities to implement the AU Migration Policy Framework for Africa; and improve inter-State and intra-regional cooperation. In order to close the remaining gap in the RCP map of the

---

28 Colleen Thouez and Frédérique Channac, *Regional Consultative Processes for Migration: An Evaluation Based on IMP's Work* (UNFPA, 2005).

continent, efforts have been directed towards creating a process for central Africa in conjunction with the Economic Community of Central African States and with support from IOM. This new RCP is expected to come into being in 2012.[29]

RCPs have a strong presence in Asia and Oceania, which may be explained in part by the relative weakness or absence of comprehensive regional institutions compared to other parts of the world (see Section 14.2 above). Since 1996, the Intergovernmental Asia-Pacific Consultations on Refugees, Displaced Persons and Migrants ('APC') has been dedicated to discussion of migration issues and regional cooperation on the movement of refugees, trafficked persons and migrants. The Bali Ministerial Conference on People Smuggling, Trafficking in Persons and Related Transnational Crime ('Bali Process'), established in 2002, concentrates on strengthening regional policy and law enforcement cooperation to combat human trafficking and migrant smuggling, and on developing regional responses to irregular migration, while improving comprehensive and sustainable solutions for refugee flows. The 2003 Ministerial Consultations on Overseas Employment and Contractual Labour for Countries of Origin in Asia ('Colombo Process') provides a forum for Asian origin States to share experiences in order to ensure the welfare and protection of migrant workers; optimise the benefits of labour mobility; and enhance capacity building, data collection and inter-State cooperation. Linked to the Colombo Process, the similarly titled Ministerial Consultations on Overseas Employment and Contractual Labour for Countries of Origin and Destination in Asia ('Abu Dhabi Dialogue') was established in 2008 to connect the Colombo Process States with nine destination countries in Southeast Asia and the Gulf (see Case Study 14.2).

Among IRFs, prominent examples include the Euro-African Conferences on Migration and Development and its Three-Year Cooperation Programme adopted in Paris in November 2008; the EU–Africa Partnership on Migration, Mobility and Employment ('Tripoli Process'); the Ibero-American Forum on Migration and Development; the Regional Ministerial Conference on Migration in the Western Mediterranean ('5+5 Dialogue'); the Mediterranean Transit Migration Dialogue; the Asia–Europe Meetings, including its Meetings for Directors-General on Management of Migratory Flows between Asia and Europe; the ASEAN–EU Summit; and the European Union–Latin America and the Caribbean Summits ('EU-LAC').

As is evident from the list, the EU is a strong force behind a number of IRFs, with an emphasis on dialogue between Europe and Africa. Cooperation between the AU and the EU is based on the framework of the *Joint EU–Africa Declaration on Migration and Development* (2006) ('Tripoli Declaration'); the Continental Policy Framework on Migration; and the Ouagadougou Action Plan to Combat Trafficking in Human Beings. At the end of the first phase of the above-mentioned Tripoli Process (2008–10), the second action plan was launched in 2010 to last until 2013.[30]

---

29 Global Forum on Migration and Development, above n. 26, Annex 4.

30 Africa and Europe in Partnership, *More on Migration, Mobility and Employment* (2012) www.africa-eu-partnership.org/more-on-migration-mobility-and-employment; Africa and Europe in Partnership, *Africa–EU*

CASE STUDY 14.2 The Abu Dhabi Dialogue

The Abu Dhabi Dialogue was created in 2008 as an offspring of the Colombo Process, with the Government of United Arab Emirates ('UAE') as a driving force. The initiative was prompted by the need for enhanced dialogue between Asian countries of origin for labour migration and States of the Gulf Co-operation Council.

Its goals are to improve the management of temporary contractual labour mobility; enhance knowledge of labour market trends, skill profiles, temporary contractual workers, remittances policies/flows and their interplay with regional development; build capacity for effective management of labour demand and supply; and prevent illegal recruitment practices and promote the welfare and protection of contractual workers.

The Abu Dhabi Dialogue has put in place a pilot project that seeks to improve the outcomes of migration through the entire migration cycle for temporary contractual workers in the sectors of healthcare, hospitality and construction. The pilot project covers UAE, India and the Philippines, and is looking into issues such as recruitment practices, standards for contracts, health and safety on the job, and other services for migrants. Implemented by the Government of UAE, the project will inform subsequent actions that UAE takes with a view to better managing temporary labour migration flows. Other Gulf States are also using this pilot project to inform actions that they might eventually undertake.

In the context of the 2011 Global Forum on Migration and Development, the Abu Dhabi Dialogue has been identified as a testing ground for 'lowering the costs of migration for higher development gains' through a three-pronged approach: (a) better regulating the labour recruitment industry; (b) granting low-cost up-front loans to migrants; and (c) social security and income protection for mobile workers.

14.3.2. What value do RCPs and IRFs add to international migration law and governance?

In the past, expectations about the concrete outcomes that can be achieved by RCPs and IRFs were rather modest: the mere fact that States were prepared to come together in a multilateral setting was celebrated as an achievement in itself. As has been acknowledged elsewhere,[31] the reticence of States to submit to multilateralism on migration is as striking as it is real, especially when compared to other issues of international importance. Thus, RCPs and IRFs cannot be assessed solely in terms of their outputs for migration governance, but must be evaluated also for their role in creating a culture of cooperation on migration. Globally, the multiplication of this

Meeting Sets Out Priorities (2010) www.africa-eu-partnership.org/news/africa-%E2%80%93-eu-meeting-sets-out-priorities.

31 Hansen, above n. 25, 22.

cooperation model, recently described as 'informal network based governance',[32] mirrors the recognition by States that they can benefit from cooperation on migration issues.

An assessment commissioned by IOM in 2010 gauges the way in which the principal RCPs contribute to migration governance in three distinct areas, namely, by (a) building trust between States and increasing understanding of migration issues; (b) breaking down divisions between States, and between government departments within States, creating networks and facilitating a harmonisation of positions across regions; and (c) building capacity and effecting changes in specific laws, policies and practices that govern how migration is managed at national and regional levels.[33]

With respect to the last point, it should not be forgotten that RCPs and IRFs were not primarily designed to create national legislation or regional policies, or to further the ratification or implementation of international instruments. Quite simply, had this been the intention, many processes may never have got off the ground. This is not to say that there is no interaction between regional processes and international migration law and governance, as regional processes can potentially serve as platforms to encourage ratification of and adherence to international treaties. In a few cases, the actions of RCPs in this regard may amount to no more than lip service, but this should not discredit many other instances in which RCPs have contributed to concrete changes in laws, policies and practices for the benefit of migrants.

With regard to international standards, the protection of the human rights of migrants is explicit in the work plan or objectives of a number of RCPs and IRFs, such as MIDWA, IGAD-RCP, the Colombo Process, SACM, the Puebla Process, the EU-LAC dialogue, and the Ibero-American Forum on Migration and Development, among others. SACM, for instance, adopted the South American Plan on Human Development for Migration in 2010, which focusses on human development and the rights of migrants, and compiles the various principles that have emerged during the course of the process's ten years of deliberations. It sets out guidelines and detailed action plans to achieve SACM's vision for regional migration governance. Similarly, the Abu Dhabi Dialogue is credited with introducing the human rights of migrant workers (in particular, labour rights) into the discussions between origin and destination States, in a region in which the issue of rights was virtually absent from the discourse.

Combating human trafficking has been high on the agendas of many RCPs and IRFs: the Budapest Process, for instance, has promoted among its membership the

---

32 Alexander Betts, 'Global Migration Governance: The Emergence of a New Debate' (Oxford University, 2010) 3. See also Randall Hansen and Jobst Koehler, *The Future of Migration Governance and Regional Consultative Processes: Background Paper WMR 2010* (IOM, 2010).

33 Hansen, above n. 25, 9.

ratification of the *United Nations Convention against Transnational Organized Crime* (2000) and its two Protocols on Trafficking in Human Beings (*Protocol to Prevent, Suppress and Punish Trafficking in Persons, Especially Women and Children, Supplementing the United Nations Convention against Transnational Organized Crime* ('Trafficking Protocol')) and on Smuggling of Migrants (*Protocol against the Smuggling of Migrants by Land, Sea and Air, Supplementing the United Nations Convention against Transnational Organized Crime* ('Smuggling Protocol')).[34] The Bali Process is another example of the way in which RCPs build capacities and effect changes in national laws and policies, as well as in the implementation of certain international obligations, in this instance the Trafficking Protocol and the Smuggling Protocol. The Bali Process has also issued model legislation on people smuggling to ensure common standards within the region. RCPs also influence regional practices and strengthen cooperative mechanisms, as in the case of the Puebla Process, which adopted two regional guidelines regarding the return of migrant children.[35]

Refugee matters also feature in many RCPs: discussions within the Söderköping Process prompted Belarus to introduce complementary protection provisions for persons fleeing civil conflict, while Ukraine adopted a cabinet resolution in favour of refugee integration.

The flexibility of RCPs vis-à-vis more formal and sluggish processes gives them a comparative advantage in responding to rapidly changing situations. One such example is the Colombo Process, which decided to include an item on the impact of humanitarian emergencies on migrant workers in its 2011 Ministerial Conference in Dhaka, Bangladesh, in light of the situation of migrant workers during the uprisings in North Africa. The Puebla Process proved to be similarly responsive in taking up the migration-related impacts of Hurricane Mitch in 1998, and providing a forum for discussing the consequences of the terrorist attacks in New York in 2001 for migration management.

RCPs and IRFs have in the past also been subject to criticism on account of a perceived bias towards migration 'control', their lack of transparency – operating behind 'closed doors' in order to encourage candid discussions among States – and the lack of civil society participation. While it is true that certain RCPs initially set out on an enforcement path, they have broadened their agendas without exception. With regard to transparency and the representation of civil society, important differences remain between the various processes in terms of the extent to which

---

34 *United Nations Convention against Transnational Organized Crime*, opened for signature 15 November 2000, 2225 UNTS 209 (entered into force 29 September 2003); *Protocol against the Smuggling of Migrants by Land, Sea and Air, Supplementing the United Nations Convention against Transnational Organized Crime*, opened for signature 15 November 2000, 2241 UNTS 507 (entered into force 28 January 2004); *Protocol to Prevent, Suppress and Punish Trafficking in Persons, Especially Women and Children, Supplementing the United Nations Convention against Transnational Organized Crime*, opened for signature 15 November 2000, 2237 UNTS 319 (entered into force 25 December 2003).

35 *Regional Guidelines for Special Protection in Cases of Repatriation of Child Victims of Trafficking* (2007); *Regional Guidelines for the Assistance to Unaccompanied Minors in Cases of Repatriation* (2009).

meetings or their conclusions are made public. Some RCPs operate on a strictly 'members only' basis, whereas others systematically dialogue with non-governmental organisations and publish their working documents and resolutions online. It should be recalled, however, that RCPs do not generally produce binding outcomes, and, in fact, few policy processes (e.g., Cabinet meetings) are entirely open even at the national level.[36] Moreover, the exclusivity of RCPs is generally deemed necessary to generate the depoliticised atmosphere that constitutes the raison d'être and added value of RCPs, particularly during the early stages of inter-State cooperation on migration issues.

In short, RCPs have enhanced policy making and contributed to legislative developments at the national level through building trust, creating networks, and cross-fertilising experiences, approaches and information among neighbouring States. In addition, many have contributed to reinforcing commitments to international or regional instruments relating to the movement of people – for instance, by facilitating their practical implementation – and have increasingly accorded central importance to the human rights of migrants. In the complex, multi-level system of law and policy making on migration – involving local, national, regional and international actors – RCPs play a complementary role. As Hansen concludes, 'rather than determining policy in any direct and uni-causal way ... [they] are facilitators not generators'.[37] Nonetheless, these actions have led to tangible changes at the national level and, on occasion, to a *de facto* convergence of positions within a region.

14.3.3. Regional processes, global players?

Regional processes on migration cooperation are experiencing a push to leave their closets of informality and make a more concerted collective appearance on the global stage. This push comes from three different directions. First, RCPs and IRFs themselves have realised the value of exchange and have, to date, met on three separate occasions. The first meeting took place in 2005 in the framework of the Global Commission on International Migration. This was followed by a global meeting of chairs and secretariats of RCPs in Bangkok, Thailand, in 2009, which allowed RCPs to share experiences, activities and achievements, and to increase interaction and cross-fertilisation between them. The third meeting, in Gaborone, Botswana, in 2011 brought together ten RCPs and focussed on common challenges, possible contributions of RCPs to the global debate on migration and available tools to enhance the capacities of RCPs.[38] In addition, there are more and more instances of 'bilateral' exchanges among RCPs and IRFs: the Ibero-American Forum on Migration and Development, SACM and the Puebla Process, for example,

36 See Colleen Thouez, 'The Role of Civil Society in the Migration Policy Debate' (Global Commission on International Migration, 2004).
37 Hansen, above n. 25, 43.   38 For more on the global meetings of RCPs organised by IOM, see www.iom.int/rcps.

participate in each other's conferences as observers; and a joint meeting was held between APC and IGC in 2001 to engage the two regions in discussions on common asylum, refugee and migration issues.

A second push comes from parallel regional developments, since formal regional institutions for economic and political cooperation have become key actors in governing migration, including through relevant regional standards binding on member States. This issue, too, was raised at the Gaborone global meeting, as RCPs increasingly find themselves coexisting, cooperating or competing with other regional institutions. In fact, many RCPs are already closely linked to corresponding regional bodies, in particular in Africa, but also in South America, where SACM is seeking closer integration with MERCOSUR and the newly founded Union of South American Nations. This is even more common with respect to IRFs, which in many cases are umbilically tied to existing regional institutions. According to Hansen and Koehler, the relevance of formal regional institutions for RCPs is that they can provide RCPs with greater direction, for example, as implementation mechanisms for regional agreements and strategies.[39] Conversely, by offering an open and informal platform for discussion, RCPs can also be envisaged as drawing boards for joint actions and policies, which can then be formally implemented through regional institutions.

A third push arises from the interaction between RCPs, IRFs and global mechanisms; the foremost being the Global Forum on Migration and Development ('GFMD') and the United Nations High Level Dialogue on International Migration and Development. The arrival of these fora has left its mark on the agendas of individual RCPs and their global meetings. The GFMD, in its various iterations, has consistently looked to RCPs for best practices, featured RCPs and IRFs in various roundtables, and come to rely on them as testing grounds for migration policies, particularly as part of the GFMD's regional approach in 2011. Nonetheless, RCP representatives present in Gaborone conceded that joint action between RCPs and the GFMD remained *ad hoc* and sporadic.

The possibility, necessity and desirability of elevating regional processes for migration cooperation to the status of global actors continue to be contested. To simplify the question: Should RCPs and IRFs serve a greater global purpose – as yet ill-defined – or should they concentrate on their original mission – as yet incomplete – to improve migration governance at national and regional levels? The attitudes of RCPs towards this question vary markedly: while some have a deliberately global outlook and speak with one voice at the GFMD (e.g., the Puebla Process, MIDSA and SACM), others insist on the value of informal information sharing and dialogue within the group. Many would be inclined to argue that the diversity among RCPs and IRFs – in terms of historical development, size, political backing, resources, purpose and priority areas – is such that

39 Hansen and Koehler, above n. 32.

unified collective action is unlikely. Nonetheless, the multiplication of multi-lateral initiatives of varying shapes and sizes at regional and international levels will, at a minimum, compel RCPs and IRFs to seek synergies and reduce unnecessary overlaps among themselves, and with other regional and global processes and institutions.

14.4. REGIONAL INSTRUMENTS RELATING TO MIGRATION

While the previous sections have focussed on the *processes* through which regional migration law and governance has evolved, this section turns to some of the *substantive* areas where developments at the regional level have had a significant impact. In most regions of the world, regional legal frameworks have arisen based on norms existing at the international level. This is particularly true in the human rights context, but also in other areas of international migration law. Regional treaties relevant to migration, *inter alia*, provide an opportunity to address regional issues, allow for the development of standards responding to gaps at the international level, and may give rise to more relevant and effective oversight bodies.

Given the proliferation of regional treaties, and related case law, that have impacted on migration over the past five decades, it is not possible to review here all of the relevant developments. Instead, this section examines three issues that have been highlighted in other chapters in this volume – nationality and statelessness; the entry and exit of non-nationals; and some aspects of forced migration – in order to provide a point of comparison and to draw attention to the role that regional frameworks can play in developing specific aspects of migration law and strengthening the protection of migrants. The primary focus is on hard law developments, although it should be noted that significant 'soft law' developments have also taken place at the regional level (see Chapter 3).

14.4.1. Nationality and statelessness

As discussed in Chapter 4, there are a number of international instruments that contain provisions on nationality. However, these instruments only regulate specific aspects of nationality, mainly due to the fact that the regulation of nationality has traditionally been considered one of the most important expressions of sovereignty, falling within the exclusive jurisdiction of the State. Nonetheless, treaties and case law at the regional level are contributing to the development of a more robust framework for the regulation of nationality. This is particularly true in relation to the prevention of statelessness and the arbitrary deprivation of nationality, the conditions for naturalisation and the regulation of multiple nationality.

The *European Convention on Nationality* (1997) consolidates new ideas emerging from developments in national and international law in a single document.[40] In comparison to other international treaties, it reflects new paradigms of international law, giving more importance to the position of the individual.[41] This approach is reflected in its Preamble, which states that: 'in matters concerning nationality, account should be taken of both the legitimate interests of States and those of individuals'. The attention paid to individuals' rights is clearly visible in the provisions of the Convention that are relevant to the protection of migrants. Notably, art. 6(3) provides for the naturalisation of persons lawfully and habitually resident in the territory of the State within a period that should not exceed ten years, and art. 6(4) requires States to facilitate the acquisition of nationality for other categories of persons having a link to the State, such as spouses or children of nationals. In addition, art. 5(2) lays down the principle of non-discrimination between nationals by birth and by naturalisation – the first such provision in a treaty.[42] A contemporary approach to multiple nationality is also reflected in Chapter V of the Convention. Previous international[43] and regional[44] instruments have aimed to prevent or reduce the incidence of multiple nationality in order to protect States' prerogatives, particularly with regard to military obligations. The *European Convention on Nationality*, however, encourages a consensus at the regional level on new rules regarding multiple nationality in order to strike a fair balance between the interests of States to determine whether their nationals can possess another nationality, and the rights of certain categories of individuals to retain their previous nationality.[45]

The *European Convention on Nationality* is a pertinent example of the progressive role that regional instruments can play in the development of international law. Unfortunately, however, the low number of ratifications demonstrates the difficulty in reaching a consensus in this domain, even in a regional context.[46]

---

40 *European Convention on Nationality*, opened for signature 6 November 1997, ETS No 166 (entered into force 1 March 2000); Council of Europe, 'Explanatory Report to the European Convention on Nationality' (1997) [11].

41 Lisa Pilgram, 'International Law and European Nationality Laws' (European University Institute, 2011) 6.

42 Ibid. 7.

43 See, e.g., *Protocol relating to Military Obligations in Certain Cases of Double Nationality*, opened for signature 12 April 1930, 178 LNTS 227 (entered into force 25 May 1937).

44 In Europe, see, e.g., *Convention on the Reduction of Cases of Multiple Nationality and on Military Obligations in Cases of Multiple Nationality*, opened for signature 6 May 1963, CETS No 043 (entered into force 28 March 1968). Two Protocols were concluded to alleviate the most drastic consequences of the Convention: *Protocol amending the Convention on the Reduction of Cases of Multiple Nationality and Military Obligations in Cases of Multiple Nationality*, opened for signature 24 November 1977, CETS No 095 (entered into force 8 September 1978); *Second Protocol amending the Convention on the Reduction of Cases of Multiple Nationality and Military Obligations in Cases of Multiple Nationality*, opened for signature 2 February 1993, CETS No 149 (entered into force 24 March 1995).

45 Article 14 identifies two categories of individuals who can retain their other nationality: children having different nationalities acquired automatically at birth, and nationals having acquired another nationality automatically by marriage.

46 In late 2011, only twenty States were party to the *European Convention on Nationality*. On possible obstacles to ratification, see Pilgram, above n. 41, 15.

The earliest conventions on nationality in the Americas date back to the 1930s.[47] More recently, a provision relating to nationality was included in the *American Convention on Human Rights* (1969) (art. 20)[48] in terms identical to the right enshrined in art. 15 of the *Universal Declaration of Human Rights* (1948).[49] This provides that 'Everyone shall have the right to a nationality' and that 'No one shall be arbitrarily deprived of his nationality nor denied the right to change his nationality'. In addition, art. 20(2) contains a specific provision aimed at preventing statelessness. One of the advantages of the regional context in which the *American Convention on Human Rights* was adopted lies in the enforcement capacity of the Inter-American Court of Human Rights. Through its interpretation of art. 20 in its advisory opinions[50] and case law,[51] the Inter-American Court is contributing to the standardisation of national legislation of member States in the field of nationality, and promoting increased protection of the rights of individuals. As with Europe, this is an example of an advantage of regional human rights frameworks, especially in regions with well-developed systems for monitoring and enforcement.

14.4.2. Human rights instruments with provisions on entry and exit

States enjoy wide discretion when deciding on the standards for the admission and removal of non-nationals from their territory (see Chapter 5). Consequently, the criteria for entry or exit vary among States and the restrictions set forth in international instruments are rather limited. Nevertheless, regional institutions, economic communities and treaties increasingly establish common standards on these matters, although their scope and focus vary. The competences of States with respect to the entry and exit of persons are limited by human rights treaties, and, in some respects, regional human rights instruments set higher standards than their universal counterparts. In many cases the enforcement mechanisms established under regional treaties are binding, and are thereby able to promote respect for the treaty provisions by States parties.

One example of the contribution of regional instruments to the rights that migrants should enjoy in the context of removal is the prohibition of collective or mass expulsion. The principle is recognised in all regional human rights

---

47 See, e.g., *Inter-American Convention on the Nationality of Women*, opened for signature 26 December 1933, 49 Stat 2957 (entered into force 29 August 1934).

48 *American Convention on Human Rights*, opened for signature 22 November 1969, 1144 UNTS 123 (entered into force 18 July 1978).

49 *Universal Declaration of Human Rights*, GA Res 217A (III), UN Doc A/810 (10 December 1948).

50 *Proposed Amendments to the Naturalization Provisions of the Constitution of Costa Rica (Advisory Opinion)* OC-4/84, Inter-Am Ct HR (Ser A) No 4 (19 January 1984).

51 See, e.g., *Case of Yean and Bosico Children* v. *Dominican Republic*, Inter-Am Ct HR (8 September 2005); *Case of Ivcher-Bronstein* v. *Peru*, Inter-Am Ct HR (Ser C) No 74 (6 February 2001); *Serrano Saenz* v. *Ecuador*, Inter-American Commission on Human Rights, Report No 84/09, OEA/Ser.L/V/II, Doc 51 (6 August 2009).

instruments,[52] and prohibits measures compelling a group of individuals to leave a country in the absence of 'a reasonable and objective examination of the particular case of each individual alien in the group'.[53] The interpretation of this principle is most developed in the European context.[54]

The principle of *non-refoulement* provides a further limitation on the State's power of removal (see Chapter 7). The scope of this principle, initially applicable only to refugees, has been expanded through the interpretation given by human rights bodies to the prohibition of torture and inhumane and degrading treatment. The case law of the European Court of Human Rights is particularly broad and encompasses expulsion or *refoulement* in the following type of cases, namely, where there is indiscriminate violence in the State to which the person is to be returned;[55] the individual is a member of a group systematically exposed to a practice of ill-treatment; the living and detention conditions in the State to which the person is to be returned would amount to degrading treatment; or the individual suffers from a serious health condition that requires specialised medical treatment that is not available or accessible in the applicant's State of origin.

Finally, an individual's rights regarding admission to and removal from the host State have also been considered within the concept of family reunification, which has been addressed by the European Court of Human Rights, with regard to both admission of non-nationals and limits to expulsion.[56] In EU law, the right to family reunification is expressly recognised in Council Directive 2003/86/EC, and the European Court of Justice has developed a rich jurisprudence clarifying the conditions of application of this right in practice.[57] In contrast, the right to family reunification is conspicuous by its absence at the universal level.[58]

14.4.3. Refugees and internally displaced persons

In the context of forced migration, hard and soft law developments at the regional level have made a significant contribution to the protection of refugees and

---

52 *American Convention on Human Rights*, opened for signature 22 November 1969, 1144 UNTS 123 (entered into force 18 July 1978) art. 22(9); *Protocol 4 to the European Convention for the Protection of Human Rights and Fundamental Freedoms*, opened for signature 16 September 1963, ETS 46 (entered into force 2 May 1968) art. 4; *Arab Charter on Human Rights*, opened for signature 15 September 1994, 12 International Human Rights Reports 893 (entered into force 15 March 2008) art. 26(2); *African Charter on Human and Peoples' Rights*, opened for signature 27 June 1981, 1520 UNTS 217 (entered into force 21 October 1986) art. 12(5).

53 The definition is taken from the case law of the European Court of Human Rights: see, e.g., *Sultani v. France* (European Court of Human Rights, Chamber judgment, Application No 45223/05, 20 January 2007) [81].

54 *Conka* v. *Belgium* (2002) 34 EHRR 54.

55 *Sufi and Elmi* v. *United Kingdom* (European Court of Human Rights, Chamber, Application Nos 8319/07 and 11449/07, 28 June 2011).

56 Betty De Hart, 'Love Thy Neighbour: Family Reunification and the Rights of Insiders' (2009) 11 *European Journal of Migration and Law* 235.

57 See, e.g., *Pehlivan* v. *Staatssecretaris van Justitie* (C-484/07) [2011] ECJ; *Land Baden-Württemberg* v. *Bozkurt* (C-303/08) [2010] ECJ; *Chakroun* v. *Minister van Buitenlandse Zaken* (C-578/08) [2010] ECJ.

58 *International Convention on the Protection of the Rights of All Migrant Workers and Members of their Families*, opened for signature 18 December 1990, 2220 UNTS 3 (entered into force 1 July 2003). Article 44 merely encourages States parties to facilitate family reunification. See also art. 50.

internally displaced persons (see Chapter 7). They have gone beyond the protection provided in their universal counterparts and have acted as a catalyst for subsequent developments in other regions, as well as at the international level.

In the African context, the *Convention Governing the Specific Aspects of Refugee Problems in Africa* (1969) ('OAU Convention')[59] is a regional complement to the *Convention relating to the Status of Refugees* (1951) ('Refugee Convention'),[60] and provides a refugee definition that is broader than that at the international level. The OAU Convention includes as a refugee:

> every person who, owing to external aggression, occupation, foreign domination or events seriously disturbing public order in either part or the whole of his country of origin or nationality is compelled to leave his place of habitual residence in order to seek refuge in another place outside his country of origin or nationality.

The OAU Convention's definition addresses the issue of armed conflict in the African continent by including people who flee from war or disturbance and seek refuge outside their State. A refugee under the OAU Convention is not required to prove 'well-founded fear of persecution' and needs only to prove that his or her State is subjected to foreign aggression, occupation or domination or that other events result in serious public disorder.[61]

In practice, the interpretation of the OAU Convention has been more accommodating of large-scale refugee situations than the Refugee Convention. The OAU Convention has thus assisted millions of people in need of protection in Africa and in other parts of the world where it has inspired similar legal developments or applications of refugee law.[62]

One such example is the *Cartagena Declaration on Refugees* (1984) ('Cartagena Declaration'), which also recognises a broader definition of refugee than the Refugee Convention. In addition to the elements of the Refugee Convention definition, the concept of refugee encompasses 'persons who have fled their country because their lives, safety or freedom have been threatened by generalized violence, foreign aggression, internal conflicts, massive violation of human rights or other circumstances which have seriously disturbed public order'. Although the Cartagena Declaration is not legally binding, its principles have been incorporated into the law and policies of a number of States in Latin America. Thus, in response to what some would say is an inadequate definition of 'refugee' in the Refugee Convention, Africa and Latin America have adopted a definition based on the tenets of humanitarianism, as well as the dictates of pragmatism, in responding to the reality of regional conflicts.[63]

---

59 *Convention Governing the Specific Aspects of Refugee Problems in Africa*, opened for signature 10 September 1969, 1001 UNTS 45 (entered into force 20 June 1974).

60 *Convention relating to the Status of Refugees*, opened for signature 28 July 1951, 189 UNTS 150 (entered into force 22 April 1954).

61 Gaim Kibreab, *Refugees and Development in Africa: The Case of Eritrea* (Red Sea Press, 1987).

62 United Nations High Commissioner for Refugees, *OAU Convention Remains a Key Plank of Refugee Protection in Africa after 40 Years* (2009) www.unhcr.org/4aa7b80c6.html.

63 Eduardo Arboleda, 'Refugee Definition in Africa and Latin America: The Lessons of Pragmatism' (1991) 3(2) *International Journal of Refugee Law* 185.

In the context of internally displaced persons ('IDPs'), a remarkable development took place with the adoption of the *African Union Convention for the Protection and Assistance of Internally Displaced Persons in Africa* (2009) ('Kampala Convention'). The Kampala Convention builds on international humanitarian law and international human rights law, as well as the 'Guiding Principles on Internal Displacement' (1998) (see Chapter 15).[64] The definition of an IDP in the Kampala Convention is consistent with that provided in the 'Guiding Principles on Internal Displacement', and affords equal treatment to all IDPs, whether displaced by armed conflict, generalised violence, human rights violations, disasters or development projects. The definition is not restricted to nationals, but includes non-nationals who are displaced within their State of habitual residence. The Kampala Convention's objectives include promoting and strengthening regional and national measures to prevent, mitigate, prohibit and eliminate the root causes of internal displacement. It also sets out the responsibilities of armed groups and non-State actors with respect to both preventing internal displacement and protecting and assisting IDPs. In general, the Kampala Convention addresses the prevention of internal displacement, protection and assistance during displacement, as well as durable solutions. The Kampala Convention incorporates mechanisms to monitor compliance with its provisions (art. 14), including a regular conference of States parties and regular reporting under the *African Charter on Human and Peoples' Rights* and the African Peer Review Mechanism.

Once the Kampala Convention enters into force it will provide a comprehensive regional framework governing the protection and assistance of IDPs before, during and after displacement. It will be the first legally binding instrument in the world (regional or universal) to impose on States the obligation to protect and assist IDPs. It provides another example of the impact of regional developments on the protection of individuals, as well as the development of international law.

14.5. CONCLUSION

The trend towards economic and political regionalisation is one of the most striking developments of the past few decades, notwithstanding the much discussed processes of globalisation. Whether this trend has promoted greater global coordination and joint decision making, or reflects resistance towards globalised policy making, remains a matter of debate. In the arena of international migration, which is marked by the strong desire of States to maintain national authority over migration governance, the regional trend is expressed through a tension between different, but potentially complementary, processes. On the one hand are the informal and non-binding arrangements and processes, such as soft law instruments and RCPs; on the other hand are the formal and binding ones, including regional treaties and regional

---

64 Office for the Coordination of Humanitarian Affairs, 'Guiding Principles on Internal Displacement' (OCHA, 2004).

institutions for economic and political integration, which have incorporated migration issues into their legal and policy frameworks.

It is possible to identify both risks and opportunities in regard to the effect of regional arrangements and processes for international migration law and governance. With respect to the risks, the first pertains to inefficiencies, duplication and competition as regional processes of various kinds multiply: RCPs overlap with each other, RCPs overlap with regional institutions, and regional legal instruments overlap with international ones. Given that government resources and capacities are typically overstretched, engagement in too many processes may risk engaging properly in none. The second risk may be termed the 'regional fortress' effect,[65] whereby greater levels of intra-regional mobility are achieved only, or mainly, at the expense of inter-regional migration. In sum, regional processes and arrangements may turn out to be stumbling blocks for global cooperation, in part because of isolationist effects and 'bloc mentalities' that are already evident in some inter-regional dialogue efforts, but also because of the emergence of a wide range of differing regimes and standards, which could prove difficult to harmonise.

With respect to the opportunities, regional approaches allow smaller groups of actors to make greater and faster progress, due to the higher probability of finding common ground. In some cases, this argument may prove to be a circular one, as proximity in terms of geography, history and interests is one of the main reasons why regional arrangements arise in the first place. This is not a general rule, however, as some regional arrangements, and more so the inter-regional ones, bridge States with very different migration experiences. The limited number of parties helps to reduce the 'lowest-common-denominator' effect afflicting larger or global processes. This aspect is well illustrated by some of the binding regional legal instruments described in this chapter, which go significantly further and deeper in their protections than their international counterparts. Again, somewhat tautologically, regional approaches also allow for more tailored approaches to regional issues. This advantage should not be underestimated in view of the diversity and complexity of migration patterns around the world. Finally, the 'copycat' effect that is evident with RCPs shows that cooperation mechanisms have a tendency to spread, especially if early examples are demonstrably successful and advantageous for participants. Moreover, parallel regional processes and arrangements can expand what is imaginable in the field of migration: approaches that may be unthinkable in one region can find resonance among governments in another. As regional groupings learn from each other, and as States are socialised into multilateral cooperation on migration in regional settings, regional cooperation on migration may serve as a stepping stone not just for more, but also for improved, global cooperation and migration governance.

65 Hansen and Koehler, above n. 32, 14.

KEY REFERENCES

Global Forum on Migration and Development, 'Roundtable Session 3.3, How Can Regional Consultative Processes (RCPs) and Inter-Regional Fora (IRF) Best Include the Migration and Development Nexus?' (GFMD, 2010)

Global Forum on Migration and Development, 'Roundtable 3.2 Regional and Inter-Regional Processes and Fora' (GFMD, 2009)

Global Forum on Migration and Development, 'Roundtable Session 3.3, Regional Consultative Processes (RCPs), Inter-Regional Consultative Fora and Regional Organizations and Economic Integration Processes at the Interface of Migration and Development' (GFMD, 2008)

Hansen, Randall, *An Assessment of Principal Regional Consultative Processes on Migration*, Migration Research Series No 38 (IOM, 2010)

Hansen, Randall and Koehler, Jobst, *The Future of Migration Governance and Regional Consultative Processes: Background Paper WMR 2010* (IOM, 2010)

International Organization for Migration, 'Free Movement of Persons in Regional Integration Processes', International Dialogue on Migration No 13 (IOM, 2010)

International Organization for Migration, *World Migration Report 2010: The Future of Migration: Building Capacities for Change* (IOM, 2010)

Thouez, Colleen and Channac, Frédérique, *Regional Consultative Processes for Migration: An Evaluation Based on IMP's Work* (UNFPA, 2005)

KEY RESOURCES

Asia-Pacific Consultations on Refugees, Displaced Persons and Migrants: www.apcprocess.net

Bali Process: www.baliprocess.net

Budapest Process: www.icmpd.org/Budapest-Process.1528.0.html

Colombo Process: www.colomboprocess.org

Intergovernmental Consultations on Migration, Asylum and Refugees: www.igc.ch

International Organization for Migration, Migration Law Database: www.imldb.iom.int/section.do

International Organization for Migration, Regional Consultative Process: www.iom.int/rcps

Migration Dialogue for Southern Africa: www.queensu.ca/samp/midsa

Puebla Process: www.rcmvs.org

Söderköping Process: http://soderkoping.org.ua

South American Conference on Migration: www.iom.int/jahia/Jahia/policy-research/sacm

15 Emerging legal issues in international migration

GERVAIS APPAVE[1]

15.1. INTRODUCTION

It is clear that there is no comprehensive universal legal framework governing the mobility of human beings.[2] Nonetheless, it is generally agreed that there are numerous, albeit somewhat scattered, elements of a legal and normative framework, derived from binding global and regional instruments and accompanied by informal and non-binding understandings among States.[3]

The exact nature and status of this assemblage is subject to debate, but the research literature leaves readers in no doubt that they are in the presence of work in progress. The body of dispersed, disparate, rather unevenly joined items has been characterised variously as an emergent regime or 'substance without architecture'.[4] Lillich's early observation that the topic of the rights of aliens in international law was like a 'giant unassembled jigsaw'[5] may appropriately be applied today to the more comprehensive framework now thought needed, or at least desirable, to ensure effective governance of human mobility in all of its manifestations. Construction sites abound. Some have a bilateral regulatory focus, as in the case of the management of labour migration flows; some have a rights-based orientation and dwell on the definition and protection of those rights; still others address mobility from the point of view of the necessity to balance facilitation of movement with entry control.[6] Some boast robust and finished structures, such as the *International Convention on the Protection of the Rights of All Migrant Workers and Members of*

---

1 The author wishes to acknowledge research assistance from Karoline Popp in the preparation of this chapter.
2 Ryszard Cholewinski, Richard Perruchoud and Euan Macdonald (eds.), *International Migration Law: Developing Paradigms and Key Challenges* (TMC Asser Press, 2007) xl.
3 Global Commission on International Migration, 'Migration in an Interconnected World: New Directions for Action' (GCIM, 2005).
4 Alexander Aleinikoff, 'International Legal Norms on Migration: Substance without Architecture' in Ryszard Cholewinski, Richard Perruchoud and Euan Macdonald (eds.), *International Migration Law* (TMC Asser Press, 2007) 467.
5 Richard Lillich, *The Human Rights of Aliens in Contemporary International Law* (Manchester University Press, 1984) 4.
6 Aleinikoff, above n. 4.

their Families (1990);[7] others are best conceptualised simply as passageways to major adjoining policy areas, such as trade.

While some thematic areas (e.g., consular protection and assistance) have a relatively long history, others, such as migration and development, or the norms governing the use of biometrics and DNA testing, are of more recent origin. New topics can and do emerge at regular intervals, although they tend to evolve at different speeds depending on factors as diverse as their public salience at a point in time, their political sensitivity, or the energy deployed by key stakeholders and advocates.[8]

Not infrequently these advances attend to the specific needs of a migrant constituency identified as being of concern to the international community. The term 'migrant' covers a very large number of categories of people on the move, and one matter of perennial interest is how their particular needs, aspirations or vulnerabilities might be brought within the ambit of international law. 'Migrant workers', 'refugees', 'asylum seekers', 'unaccompanied minors', 'irregular migrants', 'victims of trafficking' and 'highly qualified professionals' are just a few examples of the migrant configurations that have attracted attention in recent times.

This chapter traces and analyses the emergence of three clusters of issues having specific groups of migrants at their heart – first, the internally displaced; second, those affected by climate or environmental change; and third, the recently identified group of stranded migrants. The chapter defines the broad migratory situation of each group and the features shared by its members; discusses the reasons for the emergence of the group as a focus of international interest; and delineates the manner and extent to which they have been brought within the purview of international legal norms and standards. The chapter concludes by linking these observations to evolving discussions about global governance of migration.

A brief explanation is needed to justify the inclusion of internal displacement in this set of issues. While it is unlikely that anyone would dispute the characterisation of environmental or stranded migrants as 'emerging' groups of interest, some might argue, on the grounds of the existence and wide acceptance of the United Nations' 'Guiding Principles on Internal Displacement' (1998) alone, that the internally displaced now benefit from a level of juridical recognition that is of a very different, and more substantial, character. This is true. Nevertheless, the process by which the principles on internal displacement are being given practical effect, at both regional and national levels, is ongoing and instructive. It serves as a helpful gauge against which to assess and discuss progress in the two other domains.

---

7 *International Convention on the Protection of the Rights of All Migrant Workers and Members of their Families*, opened for signature 18 December 1990, 2220 UNTS 3 (entered into force 1 July 2003).

8 A spurt of growth in interest or activity can be followed by a period of relative stagnation, if not dormancy, as in the case of the movement of natural persons under Mode 4 of the *Marrakesh Agreement Establishing the World Trade Organization*, opened for signature 15 April 1994, 1867 UNTS 3 (entered into force 1 January 1995) annex 1B ('*General Agreement on Trade in Services*'). See Chapter 12.

15.2. INTERNAL DISPLACEMENT

During the late 1980s and early 1990s, the international community was strongly engaged in three separate consultative processes to identify multilateral solutions to long-standing population displacements in Africa, Southeast Asia and Central America. In due course, these efforts led to the development and implementation of programmes of intervention now better known by the acronyms SARRED (International Conference on the Plight of Refugees, Returnees and Displaced Persons in Southern Africa), CPA (Comprehensive Plan of Action for Indochinese Refugees) and CIREFCA (from the Spanish title for the International Conference on Central American Refugees).[9] In each situation, large populations were set adrift in the wake of armed conflict, and exposed to a wide range of humanitarian, social or economic vulnerabilities. In the cases of SARRED and CIREFCA there was the added complication that very large numbers of those affected had been displaced within their own States rather than across borders.

There were equally large contingents of internally displaced persons (often known as 'IDPs') elsewhere in the world – for instance, in the African Great Lakes and Horn of Africa regions, in the Middle East, and in many republics of the former Soviet Union. Some of these persons were clearly victims of persecution. There was, therefore, an early inclination to see them as quasi-refugees,[10] in other words, persons likely to have been recognised as refugees but for the fact that they had not crossed an international border.[11] It quickly became apparent, however, that many displaced persons had left their homes not because of individually targeted persecution or fear of persecution, but on account of armed conflict, civil unrest, human rights violations or generalised violence.[12] The displacement of others was a response to acute economic distress. Yet others had moved on account of natural or human disasters, environmental degradation linked to climate change, or large-scale development projects. Not infrequently the cause of displacement could not be reduced to a single event or group of events, but was a combination of many circumstances.

What all of those affected did share, however, was a common profile of vulnerability. Internally displaced persons suffer from being uprooted from their established places of residence and cut adrift from their community of origin. They

---

9 Alexander Betts, 'Comprehensive Plans of Action: Insights from CIREFCA and the Indochinese CPA' (Working Paper No 120, UNHCR, January 2006); Courtland Robinson, 'The Comprehensive Plan of Action for Indochinese Refugees 1989–1997: Sharing the Burden and Passing the Buck' (2004) 17(3) *Journal of Refugee Studies* 319.

10 Catherine Phuong, *The International Protection of Internally Displaced Persons* (Cambridge University Press, 2004).

11 Some of the internally displaced would have been recognised as refugees under the terms of the *Convention Governing the Specific Aspects of Refugee Problems in Africa*, opened for signature 10 September 1969, 1001 UNTS 45 (entered into force 20 June 1974) or the *Cartagena Declaration on Refugees*, OEA/Ser.L/II.66, doc 10 rev 1 (22 November 1984), both of which provide broader coverage than the *Convention relating to the Status of Refugees* (1951).

12 Roberta Cohen and Francis Deng, *Masses in Flight: The Global Crisis of Internal Displacement* (Brookings Institution, 1998).

experience loss of property and livelihood. They suffer from exposure to human rights abuses, acts of violence, harassment and discrimination. They are frequently separated from family members. They are unable to exercise freely their civil and political rights. They also have difficulty in accessing essential services, such as health and education, and are sometimes deprived of them altogether.

Cohen and Deng offer several reasons why the plight of these persons came to be a subject of priority interest for the international community.[13] The steady increase of internally displaced persons over time clearly had an impact. According to estimates of the Internal Displacement Monitoring Centre, there were some 16.5 million internally displaced persons around the world in 1989.[14] By 1992 this figure had risen to 25 million and was still climbing. Statistical visibility was paralleled by media visibility. Beginning with reportage on the famines in Ethiopia and Sudan in the mid-1980s, the electronic media sensitised public opinion to the existence of humanitarian disasters that would otherwise have gone unnoticed. Following the outbreak of war in the Gulf in 1990, daily televised accounts of the displacement of Kurds in northern Iraq added a sense of urgency to the need for effective solutions to internal displacement. Political visibility was then unavoidable. This was the case in developing countries, where the presence of internally displaced persons was seen as contributing to economic stress and social instability. It was equally so in developed countries, where in-country displacement was viewed with similar if not greater concern. At a time when the so-called 'countries of refugee resettlement' (primarily the United States, Canada and Australia, but also a number of European countries) were struggling to find durable solutions for 'long-stayer' refugee caseloads in Southeast Asia and Central America, internal displacement was seen as a prelude to large cross-border out-flows. One additional element was the growing readiness among governments to canvass and define terms for broad international responses to in-country humanitarian emergencies, as demonstrated by the adoption of a United Nations Security Council Resolution in 1991 requesting that humanitarian organisations be given access to all parts of Iraq.[15]

These contextual factors cannot be construed as an integral part of the process that led to the development of a formal United Nations response to internal displacement, but they did contribute in an important way to a climate of readiness for that exercise.

---

13 Ibid.
14 Internal Displacement Monitoring Centre, *Countries, Statistics: Global IDP Estimates (1990–2010)* (2011) www. internal-displacement.org. These statistics cover internal displacement caused by armed conflict, situations of generalised violence or violations of human rights. They do not include people internally displaced by natural or human disasters, or by development projects.
15 SC Res 688, UN SCOR, 2982nd mtg, UN Doc S/RES/0688 (5 April 1991). Cohen notes: 'It was not until the end of the Cold War that there was some evolution in thinking about the concept of sovereignty. UN resolutions, for example, began to demand access for the delivery of relief and to authorize the establishment of relief corridors and cross-border operations to reach people in need'. Roberta Cohen, 'Key Policy Debates in the Internal Displacement Field' (2008) 32 *Refugee Watch* 84.

15.2.1.   'Guiding Principles on Internal Displacement'

The challenge for those who wished to mobilise international energies and resources towards the search for an effective instrument to protect the internally displaced was the identification of an appropriate methodology. The approach chosen was innovative, one that bypassed the traditional intergovernmental negotiating apparatus and focussed on extensive research and consultation with stakeholders.[16] The process consisted of several steps. The first was the appointment, in 1992, of a Representative of the Secretary-General on Internally Displaced Persons, whose task was 'to seek views and information from all Governments on the human rights issues related to internally displaced persons, including an examination of existing international rights, humanitarian and refugee law and standards and their applicability to the protection of and relief assistance to internally displaced persons'.[17]

His consultations were to extend beyond governments to include 'specialised agencies, relevant United Nations organs, regional intergovernmental and non-governmental organisations and experts in all regions on these issues'.[18] In addition, the Representative of the Secretary-General was requested to produce a comprehensive study identifying existing laws and mechanisms for the protection of internally displaced persons and signalling additional or alternative measures deemed necessary.

The second key step was the compilation and analysis of existing legal norms. This required an exhaustive survey of the situations and needs of internally displaced persons and a detailed mapping of international law – especially human rights, humanitarian and refugee law – applicable to them. Even though the initial focus was on the norms and standards applicable to situations of displacement and return, the scope was extended to address the right to be protected from arbitrary displacement.[19] In other words, the study brought out the need to address the phenomenon of displacement in the most comprehensive way possible – from prevention, to protection and assistance during phases of displacement, to eventual return and reintegration.

The next step was the development of the 'Guiding Principles on Internal Displacement' (1998) ('Guiding Principles') by a team of international experts working under the direction of the Representative of the Secretary-General on Internally Displaced Persons.[20] This work was completed in January 1998 and the Guiding Principles were presented to the United Nations Commission on Human Rights in the same year.[21] With the establishment of the Human Rights Council in 2004 to replace

---

16 Simon Bagshaw, 'Responding to the Challenge of Internal Forced Migration: The Guiding Principles on Internal Displacement' in Ryszard Cholewinski, Richard Perruchoud and Euan Macdonald (eds.), *International Migration Law: Developing Paradigms and Key Challenges* (TMC Asser Press, 2007) 189.

17 UN Commission on Human Rights, Res 1992/73, 48th sess, UN Doc E/CN.4/RES/1992/73 (5 March 1992).

18 Ibid.   19 Bagshaw, above n. 16.

20 Commission on Human Rights, 'Report of the Representative of the Secretary-General, Mr Francis Deng, submitted pursuant to Commission Resolution 1997/39. Addendum: Guiding Principles on Internal Displacement' (UN Doc E/CN.4/1998/53/Add.2, United Nations, 11 February 1998).

21 Office for the Coordination of Humanitarian Affairs, 'Guiding Principles on Internal Displacement' (OCHA, 2004).

the Commission on Human Rights, greater focus was brought on the human rights of internally displaced persons, and the office was renamed as the Representative of the Secretary-General on the Human Rights of Internally Displaced Persons.

15.2.2. Essential features of the Guiding Principles

Several features of the Guiding Principles distinguish them from other major international human rights instruments, chief among which is the fact that they are informal in nature and therefore not binding on States. The reasons for that choice were largely circumstantial – in the 1990s, States were wary (as they still are today) of surrendering their sovereign prerogatives, and were thus unwilling to enter into a legally binding treaty stipulating what they could or could not do within their own territories. There was also a desire to avoid lengthy negotiations over the format of an instrument at a time when international norms in this field were urgently needed. Finally, there was a prevailing view that there was a broad, if rather dispersed, set of existing legal norms to meet the general needs of internally displaced persons.[22]

Flowing from this is a second distinguishing feature of the Guiding Principles. They do not set out to create new law. In the main they are a restatement, consolidation and exposition of many existing norms and principles, shedding light on the vulnerabilities of the internally displaced and pointing to appropriate safeguards and remedies already available within the framework of human rights and humanitarian law. However, they do seek to clarify some grey areas and bridge perceived gaps.

Another important characteristic lies in the fact that the Guiding Principles are premised on the State's prime responsibility for protecting internally displaced persons. A comparison with the *Convention relating to the Status of Refugees* (1951) ('Refugee Convention') is instructive.[23] In both cases there is displacement and a need for protection. In the latter instance, however, the State is viewed as being delinquent in its relationship to the national concerned, who is then entitled to seek international protection. In the former, the locus of responsibility lies unequivocally with the State, so that protection becomes an integral part of the exercise of sovereignty.[24]

One additional distinguishing feature is that the Guiding Principles, in keeping with their informal nature, do not envisage the grant of a special legal status to persons who fall within its scope. A descriptive approach is preferred, encompassing a collectivity of individuals and drawing attention to their shared vulnerabilities, rather than prescribing a status determination procedure that would assign a special status to each individual. Internally displaced persons are defined as:

---

22 Cohen, above n. 15.

23 *Convention relating to the Status of Refugees*, opened for signature 28 July 1951, 189 UNTS 150 (entered into force 22 April 1954).

24 Francis M. Deng, Sadikiel Kimaro, Terrence Lyons, Donald Rothchild and I. William Zartman, *Sovereignty as Responsibility: Conflict Management in Africa* (Brookings Institution, 1996).

persons or groups of persons who have been forced or obliged to flee or to leave their homes or places of habitual residence, in particular as a result of or in order to avoid the effects of armed conflict, situations of generalized violence, violations of human rights or natural or human-made disasters, and who have not crossed an internationally recognized State border.[25]

The specific provisions of the Guiding Principles are laid out in four distinct clusters. The first section sets out a number of general framing principles, including the right of internally displaced persons to enjoy the same rights and freedoms as other persons in their country; the primary responsibility of national authorities in the provision of protection and humanitarian assistance to internally displaced persons; and non-discrimination in the application of the Guiding Principles. The second section, while acknowledging implicitly that not all displacement is unjustified, provides for a right of protection from displacement in diverse circumstances (such as ethnic cleansing or armed conflict), as well as minimisation of the impact on populations of unavoidable and government-sanctioned displacement. The third and most substantial section covers the principles relating to protection during displace-ment, including the rights to life, liberty and personal security, and principles relating to provision of an adequate standard of living and access to essential services. The fourth and final section outlines the conditions that have to be met to allow the safe and dignified return of internally displaced persons to their places of origin, and the measures necessary to their social and economic reintegration.

To sum up, the Guiding Principles are an innovative instrument of international protection. They provide practical guidance to a wide range of stakeholders, including the United Nations Secretary-General, States, international organisa-tions and non-governmental organisations, in relation to 'rights and guarantees relevant to the protection of persons from forced displacement and to their pro-tection and assistance during displacement as well as during return or resettlement and reintegration'.[26] They have immediate pedagogical value, for consciousness raising and educational purposes as well as for policy formulation, but beyond that they are constructed so as to leave room for further efforts towards the develop-ment of binding instruments.[27] Developments since the submission of the Guiding Principles to the Commission on Human Rights in 1998 have demonstrated that there is indeed potential for the international community to make use of their 'soft' substance to fashion instruments with a harder and sharper legal edge.

15.2.3.   Application and impact of the Guiding Principles

In his introduction to the first version of the Guiding Principles, Francis Deng, then Representative of the Secretary-General on Internally Displaced Persons, observed cautiously that 'although they do not constitute a binding instrument, these Principles reflect and are consistent with international human rights and

---

25 Office for the Coordination of Humanitarian Affairs, above n. 21, 1.   26 Ibid.   27 Bagshaw, above n. 16.

humanitarian law and analogous refugee law'. He went on to express the modest hope that they would be 'widely circulated and given practical application in the field'.[28] The international reaction over the past decade has largely exceeded this expectation, whether at the global, regional or national levels, although specific responses have varied significantly in scope and nature.

Global impact

At the global level, the Guiding Principles have received wide endorsement, notably by the 2005 World Summit,[29] the United Nations General Assembly[30] and the United Nations Human Rights Council.[31] These statements variously establish the Guiding Principles as an important framework for the protection of internally displaced persons; they call for international support to enable States to build capacity towards their implementation; they promote solidarity in action among States in dealing with situations of displacement; and they note with satisfaction that an increasing number of States, United Nations organisations and regional and non-governmental organisations are applying them as a standard. Progress in this area has been substantial enough for the Representative of the Secretary-General on the Human Rights of Internally Displaced Persons to express the view that 'there are some indications that the Guiding Principles are emerging as customary law, providing a binding interpretation of the international legal norms upon which they are based'.[32]

Another line of development at the international level is the extent to which the Guiding Principles have been adopted, individually or jointly, by international organisations as an authoritative guide to their interventions in situations of internal displacement. United Nations agencies, such as the United Nations High Commissioner for Refugees ('UNHCR'), the United Nations Development Programme ('UNDP'), the Office of the High Commissioner for Human Rights ('OHCHR') and the United Nations Children's Fund ('UNICEF'), have incorporated the Guiding Principles into their internal displacement policies or operating procedures. The Inter-Agency Standing Committee Working Group on Internal Displacement has placed the Guiding Principles at the centre of its Framework on Durable Solutions for Internally Displaced Persons.[33] The Representative of the Secretary-General on the Human Rights of Internally Displaced Persons has also played a very important part in promoting and disseminating the Guiding

---

28 Office for the Coordination of Humanitarian Affairs, above n. 21, 1.

29 United Nations General Assembly, '2005 World Summit Outcome' (UN Doc A/60/L.1, United Nations, 15 September 2005).

30 See, e.g., United Nations General Assembly, 'Protection of and Assistance to Internally Displaced Persons' (UN Doc A/RES/62/153, United Nations, 6 March 2008).

31 See, e.g., Human Rights Council, 'Mandate of the Representative of the Secretary-General on the Human Rights of Internally Displaced Persons' (Resolution 6/32, 14 December 2007).

32 Human Rights Council, 'Report of the Representative of the Secretary-General on the Human Rights of Internally Displaced Persons, Walter Kälin' (UN Doc A/HRC/13/21, 5 January 2010).

33 Inter-Agency Standing Committee, 'IASC Framework on Durable Solutions for Internally Displaced Persons' (Brookings Institution and University of Bern, 2010).

Principles, and in mobilising public opinion through consultation with governments and the development of pedagogical resources.

National impact

At the national level, a steadily growing number of States have begun to bring the Guiding Principles within the ambit of their legislative or policy frameworks. Peru adopted a law in 2004, based on the Guiding Principles, establishing material benefits for internally displaced persons. In Colombia, the Constitutional Court has cited the Guiding Principles to support its judgments in favour of internally displaced persons. Burundi, Colombia, the Philippines, Sri Lanka and Uganda are all reported as having incorporated elements of the Guiding Principles into their national policies on internal displacement.[34]

Regional impact

It is at the regional level that the Guiding Principles are exercising greatest influence across several continents. In 2006, the Council of Europe's Committee of Ministers adopted thirteen recommendations on internally displaced persons that do not simply restate the substance of the Guiding Principles, but underline binding obligations undertaken by the Council of Europe member States.[35] Quite separately, the members of the Organization for Security and Co-operation in Europe have acknowledged the usefulness of the Guiding Principles as a framework for the work of the Organization.[36] In the Americas, the General Assembly of the Organization of American States has urged its member States to consider the Guiding Principles in designing public policy.[37]

The most significant advances have been achieved in Africa, which remains the only region that has developed and adopted binding instruments to protect internally displaced persons.[38] It is appropriate that it should be in the Great Lakes region – a vast area that has been affected by massive flows of internally displaced persons in recent decades – that a group of States should commit not only to adopting the Guiding Principles, but also enshrining them in law. The International Conference on the Great Lakes Region was launched in 1999 under the joint auspices of the United Nations and the African Union, to create a climate of trust and cooperation against a history of conflict, political volatility and economic instability. Its major outcome was the signing, by eleven participating States, of a *Pact on Security, Stability and Development in the Great Lakes Region* (2006)

---

34 Roberta Cohen, 'The Guiding Principles on Internal Displacement: An Innovation in International Standard Setting' (2004) 10(4) *Global Governance* 459.
35 Corien Jonker, 'Protecting IDPs in Europe' (2008) Special Issue (December) *Forced Migration Review* 15.
36 Cohen, above n. 34.
37 United Nations General Assembly, 'Internally Displaced Persons' (UN Doc AG/RES. 2055 (XXXIV-0/04), United Nations, 8 June 2004).
38 Human Rights Council, above n. 32.

('Pact').[39] The Pact entered into force in June 2008, after ratification by the requisite eight States.

The *Protocol on the Protection and Assistance to Internally Displaced Persons* (2006) is an integral part of the Pact.[40] It takes note of the level of international recognition enjoyed by the Guiding Principles; provides a definition of internally displaced persons; sets down, as one of its central objectives, the establishment of a legal framework in the Great Lakes region for ensuring adoption and implementation of the Guiding Principles by member States; lays prime responsibility on member States for the physical and material safety of internally displaced persons; and requires member States to enact legislation to incorporate the Guiding Principles into national law.

The continent-wide *African Union Convention for the Protection and Assistance of Internally Displaced Persons in Africa* (2009) ('Kampala Convention') took much of its inspiration from the Great Lakes Protocol, but is broader in scope (see Chapter 14).[41] Here also there is acknowledgement of the Guiding Principles as an important international framework for protecting internally displaced persons. Upon the foundation of the Guiding Principles, the Kampala Convention builds a binding instrument specifying both rights and responsibilities.

The Kampala Convention deals with the cycle of displacement in a comprehensive manner, prescribing a panoply of measures to prevent the occurrence of displacement, ensure appropriate protection and assistance during phases of displacement, and provide durable solutions to those affected. The overarching goal is the establishment of an African Union legal framework to address all aspects of internal displacement with emphasis on state responsibility, on the one hand, and mutual support and solidarity among member States, on the other. It is noteworthy that the notion of responsibility for preventing displacement and protecting the internally displaced is extended to armed groups and non-State actors. The role of humanitarian organisations is also underlined, as is their duty to respect principles of 'humanity, neutrality, impartiality and independence'.

From an administrative point of view, States parties commit to three broad lines of action: (a) promulgating national legislation incorporating their Convention obligations; (b) allocating budgetary resources for purposes of protection and assistance; and (c) designating an appropriate authority to coordinate national responses. To ensure compliance and accountability on the part of States parties, the Kampala Convention provides for the establishment of a monitoring mechanism in the form of a Conference of States parties, to be convened regularly and

---

39 International Conference on the Great Lakes Region, *Pact on Security, Stability and Development in the Great Lakes Region* (14 and 15 December 2006).

40 *Protocol on the Protection and Assistance to Internally Displaced Persons to the Pact on Security, Stability and Development in the Great Lakes Region* (30 November 2006).

41 *African Union Convention for the Protection and Assistance of Internally Displaced Persons in Africa*, opened for signature 22 October 2009 (not yet in force). See Prisca Kamungi, 'Beyond Good Intentions: Implementing the Kampala Convention' (2010) 34 *Forced Migration Review* 53.

facilitated by the African Union. By mid-2011, the Kampala Convention had been signed by thirty-one member States of the African Union and ratified by four. Fifteen ratifications are required for its entry into force.

By any reasonable measure of progress, the Guiding Principles have had considerable impact on international thinking and action towards the protection of internally displaced persons. They have been given practical application in a variety of ways across the world, and have also anchored the development of regional legal instruments. There is no reason to believe that further developments will not occur. One of the interesting possible lines of evolution may be towards the shaping of international legal thinking on other aspects of the broader migration landscape.

15.3. MIGRATION, CLIMATE CHANGE AND THE ENVIRONMENT

It is difficult to pinpoint the precise moment when the international community first took notice of the link between environmental and climate change and human mobility. Yet there is little doubt that one of the first alerts to have global resonance was that of the Intergovernmental Panel on Climate Change when its first assessment report on climate change posited, in 1990, that impacts on human settlement would rank among the 'most significant' possible effects of climate change.[42]

Since then the international community has struggled to address the issue in a considered and systematic way. Boncour and Burson advance three reasons for this.[43] First, there is the difficulty of establishing simple, direct, causal relationships between environmental events and processes (e.g., cyclones, floods, desertification, soil erosion and changing coastlines), climate change and migration flows. Besides, environmental drivers of migration often interact with economic, social and developmental factors that can accelerate or mask the effects of climate change. Second, migration related to climate change straddles many policy domains, including migration proper, development, the environment and humanitarian assistance. Issues of policy or administrative ownership have to be resolved, and effective lines of communication between policy makers and researchers working in each of these fields need to be established, before serious work can commence. Third, there is an inclination among migration policy makers and programme managers to give priority of attention to security-related objectives. From this standpoint, climate change-related migration movements are likely to be addressed from a defensive perspective – that is, as threats to national security needing to be countered – rather than as potentially adaptive responses to climate change.

---

42 Intergovernmental Panel on Climate Change, 'Climate Change: The IPCC Scientific Assessment' (World Meteorological Organization, United Nations Environment Programme, 1990) 5.
43 Philippe Boncour and Bruce Burson, 'Climate Change and Migration in the South Pacific Region: Policy Perspectives' in Bruce Burson (ed.), *Climate Change and Migration: South Pacific Perspectives* (Institute of Policy Studies, 2010) 5.

Despite these difficulties, in recent years there has been a surge of consultation and research on the issue. There is broad consensus that, while climate change on its own does not necessarily lead to population displacements, it can produce environmental effects that will make it difficult and, in time, perhaps impossible for people to stay where they are. These environmental effects include phenomena such as droughts, floods and storms that may dictate sudden movement, but also slow-onset changes such as coastal erosion and desertification, which may ultimately affect a larger number of people over longer periods of time (see Case Study 15.1).[44]

One matter that makes the issue even more complex as a topic of research and policy debate is the uncertainty about numbers. Very large numbers of persons have been said to be at risk, on the basis of rather limited evidence. The emphasis seems to have been less on accuracy than on the felt need to arouse public consciousness to the huge potential for social and economic disruption that might accompany potentially massive population displacements. Many authors are persuaded that very large numbers will be affected,[45] but both Black and Castles have queried the assumptions underlying the large-scale scenarios.[46] More recently, Tacoli has cautioned that 'alarmist predictions will backfire and result in policies that marginalise the poorest and most vulnerable groups'.[47]

Much will depend on which climate change scenarios come to pass, and that may, in turn, be influenced by the action taken by the international community. The international community is far from attaining the levels of purposefulness or consultation, let alone action, that it has reached in the field of internal displacement. However, the topic does feature increasingly in intergovernmental deliberations. Three themes dominate the agenda: (a) the nature of the relationship between climate change, environmental change and migration; (b) the definition of those who move as a result of climate change; and (c) the case for an appropriate legal framework to address the protection and assistance needs of these persons.

15.3.1.   Climate change, environmental change and mobility

Drawing upon Docherty and Giannini, the relationship between climate change, environmental change and human mobility may be explored along a series of dyadic dimensions (see Case Study 15.1):[48]

---

44 International Organization for Migration, 'Migration, Climate Change and the Environment' (IOM, May 2009).

45 Frank Biermann and Ingrid Boas, 'Protecting Climate Refugees: The Case for a Global Protocol' (2008) (November–December) *Environment* 8; David Hodgkinson, Tess Burton, Heather Anderson and Lucy Young, 'The Hour when the Ship Comes in: A Convention for Persons Displaced by Climate Change' (Hodgkinson Group, 2010).

46 Richard Black, 'Environmental Refugees: Myth or Reality?' (UNHCR, March 2001); Stephen Castles, 'Environmental Change and Forced Migration: Making Sense of the Debate' (UNHCR, October 2002).

47 Cecilia Tacoli, 'Not Only Climate Change: Mobility, Vulnerability and Socio-Economic Transformations in Environmentally Fragile Areas of Bolivia, Senegal and Tanzania' (International Institute for Environment and Development, 2011) v.

48 Bonnie Docherty and Tyler Giannini, 'Confronting a Rising Tide: A Proposal for a Convention on Climate Change Refugees' (2009) 33(2) *Harvard Environmental Law Review* 349.

- *Slow-onset versus sudden or catastrophic change*: Slow-onset change includes rises or falls in temperature, rises or falls in sea level, desertification, coastal erosion and changes in amounts of precipitation. Sudden-onset change includes cyclones and tornadoes, floods, landslides and avalanches. Earthquakes and tsunamis are also environmental events, but they are of tectonic origin and, as a general rule, not climate-related.[49] In the short term, disasters capture attention, but it is slow-onset change that is likely to have a major impact in the longer term.

- *Forced versus voluntary movement*: There can be clear cases of unavoidable and therefore forced movement, as well as clear cases of planned and voluntary movement. However, most current and anticipated movement may lie in the grey zones in between, where it is difficult to determine precisely the point at which movement is no longer optional.

- *Permanent versus temporary movement*: Historically, human beings have often moved in response to seasonal changes, more so in certain parts of the world where particularly sharp and generally expected variations in rainfall and temperature determine the nomadic behaviour of traditional pastoralists. Alterations in habitat due to climate change, such as desertification, may require longer-term residential change, but here again it is difficult to establish precisely why and when the option of return is no longer available and the stay away from home turns into permanent relocation.

- *Survival versus adaptation strategy*: Most people think about migration as a survival gesture, especially in the event of impending or acute natural disasters when people have no choice but to leave their homes – that is, a case of genuine displacement. However, migration can also be an adaptation strategy developed over a longer period of time. It helps people to cope with gradual environmental changes that have an impact on their way of life. In this case, migration is not so much an accident that is best avoided as a positive adaptation strategy.

- *Internal versus international mobility*: Most climate change-related migration to date has been from one location to another within the borders of a State. This is expected to continue. However, flows can also spill across a border into another State, and one of the policy challenges of the future may lie in the management of population movements that have both internal and international manifestations, either simultaneously or sequentially.

---

49 There is some scientific evidence that tectonic movements might be related to global warming because of the impact it has on the volume and weight of the water column. See Agence France-Presse, 'Climate Change Affects Tectonic Plate Movement, Causing Earthquakes: Study', *The Raw Story* 13 April 2011 (www.rawstory.com/rs/2011/04/13/climate-can-drive-seismic-shifts-study).

CASE STUDY 15.1 Environmental change and migration in Bangladesh

When Cyclone Aila swept over Bangladesh in May 2009, it breached 1,742 kilometres of embankments and affected 3.9 million people. One year later, large areas remained flooded and 100,000 displaced people were still living on embankments, roads and other available patches of high ground. Cyclones, however, are just one of the many displacement-inducing environmental threats to which the country is vulnerable.

The spectrum of threats is very wide. It includes not only sudden-onset or extreme events, such as cyclones and floods, but also slow-onset processes of environmental change and degradation. Both gradual environmental change and extreme environmental events influence population migration patterns, but in different ways. Extreme environmental events may cause affected populations to leave their homes at least temporarily – leading to sudden, large-scale movements – but return is often feasible in the long run. However, a larger number of people are expected to migrate due to gradual deterioration of environmental conditions, and migration of this sort may have longer-term impacts owing to the long-lasting and in some cases irreversible effects of these processes.

Sudden-onset events

- Large areas of Bangladesh are and will continue to be highly vulnerable to the threat of floods for the foreseeable future, and climate change may aggravate the situation over the course of the twenty-first century. More than 50 million people still live in poverty in Bangladesh and many of them occupy remote and ecologically fragile parts of the country, such as flood plains and river islands. These people are the most vulnerable to displacement and destitution as a result of floods.
- The coastal zone in Bangladesh will always be vulnerable to the threat of cyclones and associated storm surges, but climate change may bring about an increase in the severity of these phenomena. In these circumstances temporary migration may act as a 'safety net' for many households, by providing alternative livelihoods for one or more family members, resulting in additional sources of income during a period of considerable stress.
- The effects of climate change on river erosion are unclear at present, and, consequently, relatively little attention has been directed towards those whose life patterns may be affected by it. Nonetheless, the potential for torrential monsoon rainfall to exacerbate erosion and drive vulnerable populations away from their villages is considered to be very real.

Slow-onset processes

- The coastal zones of Bangladesh are changeable, fragile and under constant threat from sea erosion. While mitigation through early intervention is possible, there may be locations where this is technically challenging or economically unfeasible. In these cases, contingency planning is necessary to assist affected households and, in the most severe cases, to provide for whole communities that may need to move *en masse*.

- Over recent decades, rising sea levels have been slowly but steadily adding to many of Bangladesh's environmental vulnerabilities in the coastal zones – for instance, the waterlogging or swamping of agricultural lands. However, given the timescales involved and the relatively small changes expected over the next fifty years, timely adaptation and community-strengthening measures may stave off mass population displacements.

- Even without the projected impacts of climate change, the evidence suggests that, in the south and west of the country, salt-water intrusion combined with population pressure will tend to increase emigration pressures in these regions over the coming years. Attempting to identify specific outflows of 'environmental migrants' is a difficult task given the complex and multi-causal nature of migration decisions in areas of gradual environmental degradation. However, what can be predicted is that the impacts will be felt most severely by marginal and rural landless farmers who rely on agricultural labour opportunities for their livelihood. Existing data support the notion that people who choose to undertake long-term or permanent migration will mostly make their way to urban centres in their region. Given the proximity of southwest Bangladesh to India, it also seems reasonable to conclude that some individuals and households will choose to cross the border, although it is too early to draw conclusions about the possible magnitude of these movements.

- Bangladesh's variable climate already presents significant challenges to its farmers, who have developed various strategies to cope with unpredictable weather patterns. Rising temperatures, changing rainfall distribution and drought will make it even more difficult to maintain or improve its agricultural productivity. With or without these changes, urban areas are expected to continue to have a strong pull effect on rural populations. Identifying 'environmental migrants' within this flow, and mapping increases in volume over time, will be a difficult research assignment.

15.3.2. Defining those who move

As a matter of common linguistic usage, persons who leave their homes in situations of distress to seek residence elsewhere, whether temporarily or permanently, are often referred to as 'refugees'. Terms such as 'climate change refugee' or 'environmental refugee' are therefore commonly found in the media, but there is a lively debate in the scholarly literature about the terminology that ought to be used to describe those who move as a consequence of climate or environmental change.

An early proposal by El-Hinnawi envisages three categories of environmentally displaced 'refugees': a first group consists of those whose displacement is of a purely temporary nature, and who return home once their habitat is restored to its original state following a natural or human-made disaster;[50] a second group includes those whose relocation is of a permanent nature following permanent degradation of their original living environment, including as a consequence of a major development project; a third group comprises those who have made the choice to move in search of better life prospects as a consequence of deteriorating environmental circumstances.[51]

Those who continue to favour the use of the term 'climate change refugee', 'environmental refugee' or some variant, argue by analogy that those who flee for reasons of climate or environmental change do so in circumstances of such overwhelming distress as to be tantamount to persecution. Biermann and Boas cannot see any reason why inhabitants of the Maldives, threatened as they are by a rise in sea levels, should receive less protection than those who fear political persecution.[52] Other scholars, and UNHCR itself – the custodian of the Refugee Convention – are much less inclined to accept that equation outright.[53] They point out that the term 'refugee' has acquired precise legal meanings and political values which, at best, will have to be uncomfortably stretched if they are to cover those who move as a consequence of environmental or climate change. At worst, there may be a risk of disturbing status determination procedures and seriously undermining the refugee protection regime. They see no reason to hope that the international community will agree to renegotiate the Refugee Convention to make it more inclusive. They note, in any case, that most climate change mobility will occur within the territorial borders of States rather than across those borders. In addition, from a conceptual viewpoint, they argue that the term 'environmental refugee' is misleading because it implies a notion of mono-causality that is rarely obtainable in reality.[54]

In the absence of academic consensus on a fully defensible definition, the International Organization for Migration ('IOM') has proposed a working definition that is inclusive enough to enable broad discussion of human mobility related to environmental factors. According to this definition:

---

50 This important reference to the time dimension is somewhat lost to sight in subsequent research.

51 Essam El-Hinnawi, 'Environmental Refugees' (United Nations Environment Programme, 1985).

52 Biermann and Boas, above n. 45.

53 Jane McAdam and Ben Saul, 'Displacement with Dignity: International Law and Policy Responses to Climate Change, Migration and Security in Bangladesh' (Sydney Law School, November 2010); Angela Williams, 'Turning the Tide: Recognizing Climate Change Refugees in International Law' (2008) 30(4) *Law & Policy* 502; Bruce Burson, 'Protecting the Rights of People Displaced by Climate Change: Global Issues and Regional Perspectives' in Bruce Burson (ed.), *Climate Change and Migration: South Pacific Perspectives* (Institute of Policy Studies, 2010) 159; António Guterres, 'Climate Change, Natural Disasters and Human Displacement: A UNHCR Perspective' (UNHCR, 2009).

54 Castles, above n. 46.

Environmental migrants are persons or groups of persons who, predominantly for reasons of sudden or progressive changes in the environment that adversely affect their lives or living conditions, are obliged to leave their habitual homes, or choose to do so, either temporarily or permanently, and who move within their country or abroad.[55]

The intention behind this wording is to attempt comprehensive coverage of all forms of environmentally induced movement, whether temporary or permanent, internal or international, voluntary or forced, or triggered by sudden or incremental change. No legal status is intended to flow from IOM's working definition.

15.3.3. Which responses?

The terminological debate will be a busy worksite for academics and policy makers for some time to come. Greater attention, however, will have to be devoted to the nature and purpose of any overarching international framework that might be needed to respond to present and future challenges.

National-level responses will necessarily form part of that framework. Some countries have already introduced provisions in law or policy to respond to the protection or residence needs of victims of environmental disturbances, especially sudden, unforeseen and generally unpredictable events, such as earthquakes, tsunamis or volcanic eruptions. The range of solutions offered is limited, with a heavy focus on the provision of temporary stay, fast-tracking of family reunion applications, and the suspension of return for irregular migrants or overstayers. In Finland and Sweden, someone who left his or her State and is unable to return due to environmental disaster qualifies as a person in need of protection. The United States may authorise the grant of a 'Temporary Protection Status' to persons already in the United States and unable to return home as a result of environmental disaster; this was applied, for example, after Hurricane Mitch in Honduras and Nicaragua in 1998. The designation of Temporary Protection Status is discretionary and applies only to persons already within the territory of the United States at the time the disaster strikes. In the European Union, the 'Temporary Protection Directive' allows for temporary protection under certain circumstances, when people are suddenly displaced in large numbers and it is not feasible to deal with their cases on an individual basis. After the Indian Ocean tsunami in 2004, Canada, Switzerland and the United Kingdom temporarily suspended the removal of nationals of affected States. However, there is no indication at this stage that these efforts will lead to the development of a larger, coordinated international framework; on the contrary, efforts tend to

---

55 Richard Perruchoud and Jillyanne Redpath-Cross (eds.), *Glossary on Migration* (IOM, 2nd edn, 2011) 33. For a discussion of the usefulness of the concept 'environmental migrant', see Howard Chang, 'The Environment and Climate Change: Is International Migration Part of the Solution or Part of the Problem?' (Paper presented at the 16th Symposium of the Fordham Environmental Law Review, 2009).

be *ad hoc* and reactive. None of these measures is mandatory or grants rights to individuals; neither do they provide a basis for admission to the territory of the host State.

At the global level, there has been much discussion, exchange and debate in recent years, driven in large part by speculation about the imminence and magnitude of environmental outflows, and hence the perceived urgency to act. It is not possible within the limits of this chapter to give a full account of all proposals that have been advanced, but the following discussion identifies a number of models that have been discussed extensively in the literature.

Amending the Refugee Convention?

One option that has been canvassed is bringing persons who move for environmental or climate change reasons within the ambit of the Refugee Convention, possibly through the introduction of an amendment. Biermann and Boas observe that such a proposal was put forward by the Maldives delegation at a 2006 conference convened by the Maldives government itself.[56] The authors express doubt about the political feasibility of the idea. They point out that industrialised countries are most unlikely to take on additional protection commitments, given their claim that their capacity to meet current refugee protection needs is vastly overstretched. Developing countries may also view mass population inflows into their territory from neighbouring countries with alarm. An additional argument against the proposal is that it might give rise to questions of priority of treatment between persons currently within the scope of the Refugee Convention and a new category of 'climate refugees'. For these and similar reasons, scholarly opinion is generally of the view that the disadvantages of recourse to the Refugee Convention would outweigh any possible advantages.[57]

A new international convention?

Several authors have proposed alternatives to the Refugee Convention, although it features almost always as a benchmark or an important point of reference. Proposals by Biermann and Boas, Docherty and Giannini, and Hodgkinson *et al.*, all opt for a Convention model.[58] Each one has particularities of design and content that are expounded in detail and vigorously defended. For instance, there are noteworthy differences in the definitions of climate or environmental refugees. Biermann and Boas propose a protocol directly linked to the *United Nations*

---

56 Biermann and Boas, above n. 45.

57 For a contrary view, see Tiffany Duong, 'When Islands Drown: The Plight of "Climate Change Refugees" and Recourse to International Human Rights Law' (2010) 31(4) *University of Pennsylvania Journal of International Law* 1239.

58 Biermann and Boas, above n. 45; Docherty and Giannini, above n. 48; Hodgkinson *et al.*, above n. 45. The strong references to tidal or nautical imagery in the literature are noteworthy for their allusion to impending disaster and the need for rescue.

Framework Convention on Climate Change (1992) ('UNFCCC').[59] Docherty and Giannini acknowledge that it would be theoretically possible for their instrument to be developed as a protocol to the UNFCCC, but have doubts about the suitability of such a construction. They would, on balance, favour a stand-alone version, as would Hodgkinson *et al*. Biermann and Boas and Hodgkinson *et al*. find scope in their models for both internally and internationally displaced persons, and seek to attend to the specific needs of small islands threatened by climate change. By contrast, Docherty and Giannini cater exclusively for those who cross international borders. In relation to status determination, Docherty and Giannini allow for both group and individual determination, while the others prescribe only group determination.

The three models also differ substantially in their legal and administrative machinery. Biermann and Boas envisage an emanation of the States parties operating as an executive committee, which would have overall responsibility for issues of recognition, protection and resettlement. A funding mechanism would complement this set-up, while implementation of the protocol would be effected through existing United Nations agencies. Docherty and Giannini's core structure rests on three essential components: a global fund, an independent coordinating agency broadly resembling UNHCR in its mode of functioning; and a body of scientific experts that would identify at-risk populations. Hodgkinson *et al*. propose an administrative establishment that is, by several lengths, the most complex, with a new Climate Change Displacement Organization at its peak, under which there would be an Assembly, a Council, a Climate Change Displacement Fund, and a Climate Change Displacement Environment and Science Organization. Climate Change Implementation Groups and a Permanent Secretariat complete the set-up.

Those differences will continue to fuel controversies about the respective strengths of the proposals, but, despite the differences, they all share several fundamental features. They all draw upon and seek to be consistent with existing human rights and humanitarian law. One way or another, they invoke the notion of shared responsibility between origin and destination countries on the one hand, and between developed and developing countries on the other. They provide for both humanitarian assistance and protection, including strong emphasis on resettlement options; and they imply the formation of complex administrative structures and bureaucracies. Yet their most striking common trait is their adherence to what McAdam refers to as the 'protection paradigm',[60] emulating, on the basis of international law, the grant of asylum to people fleeing from harm. McAdam acknowledges advocacy of international responses by the governments of certain

---

59 *United Nations Framework Convention on Climate Change*, opened for signature 9 May 1992, 1771 UNTS 107 (entered into force 21 March 1994).

60 Jane McAdam, 'Swimming against the Tide: Why a Climate Change Displacement Treaty is Not the Answer' (2011) 23(1) *International Journal of Refugee Law* 2.

developing countries, but queries whether global treaties will provide the answer. She observes that movement due to climate change is difficult to establish in isolation from other causal factors, and that exclusive emphasis on forced or flight-related movement is unwarranted when there is likely to be a range of migration patterns. The problem is thus more likely to require adaptive migratory answers rather than remedial refugee solutions.

Non-binding principles?

McAdam and Saul are also concerned that a refugee-oriented climate change treaty might prove damaging to the cause of refugee protection and give rise to abusive claims and even people smuggling.[61] The alternative foreseen is, first, recourse to existing international legal principles that are sufficiently adaptable to respond to a variety of scenarios, and, second, development of an array of policies to address various aspects of human mobility related to climate change. On the basis of fieldwork conducted in Bangladesh and the South Pacific, McAdam and Saul find considerable virtue in the 'Guiding Principles on Internal Displacement' as a broad-based tool capable of framing protection and assistance endeavours throughout the mobility continuum, from the pre-displacement phase, to displacement, to return and resettlement. This proposition has certain points in common with Williams' suggestion of regional approaches built around the Guiding Principles, albeit with linkages to the UNFCCC.[62]

Clearly, a vast programme of research and consultation has already been broached in the field of migration and climate and environmental change, although it will be some time before choices are resolved. One development that could contribute to the resolution of the ongoing debates is the further evolution of the Guiding Principles as instruments of protection.

15.4.   STRANDED MIGRANTS

Although the term 'stranded migrants' is not new,[63] it does not yet have a clear and unambiguous meaning. In the literature, the term has been applied to, or used as a synonym for, groups as diverse as irregular migrants, undocumented migrants, trafficked migrants, smuggled migrants, migrant over-stayers, migrants 'in orbit', and even migrants in need of consular assistance.

The reasons behind the phenomenon of stranded migrants are similar to those shaping other forms of contemporary mobility: steep economic gradients between

---

61 McAdam and Saul, above n. 53.   62 Williams, above n. 53.

63 Rebecca Dowd, 'Trapped in Transit: The Plight and Human Rights of Stranded Migrants' (UNHCR, June 2008) found reference to it in an unidentified 1981 publication, while Stefanie Grant, 'The Legal Protection of Stranded Migrants' in Ryszard Cholewinski, Richard Perruchoud and Euan Macdonald (eds.), *International Migration Law* (TMC Asser Press, 2007) 29, records an even earlier use by the United States Supreme Court in 1953.

developed and developing States; equally sharp demographic disparities between the two groups of States; ease of networking and communication that facilitates exchange of information about opportunities for work abroad; ready means of transport; and affordability of travel, even when a high premium is paid for clandestine conveyance.

Media reports on stranded migrants are common, but they rest on scattered understandings of what it means to be stranded. Stranded migrant fishermen are found in Southeast Asia after having been press-ganged into service, sometimes bought and sold into slavery, made to work long hours for little or no pay and then disembarked at an unknown foreign port. Stranded migrants are found in detention centres around the world, caught somewhere in the intricate web of rules and regulations surrounding entry, stay or employment in their State of destination. When the State of destination is unwilling to pay for the costs of their removal and their State of origin cannot afford to do so, is indifferent to their plight or does not recognise them as nationals, they are sometimes known as 'forgotten migrants'.

During 2011, there was much focus on yet another group characterised as stranded migrants: hapless migrant workers (often referred to incorrectly as 'third-country nationals'), such as those caught in the midst of the civil conflict in Libya. As many as 700,000 of those in Libya fled to neighbouring countries; 200,000 of these were helped by IOM to return home to forty-six different countries. Nor was this a new phenomenon: following the outbreak of the Gulf War in 1990, IOM helped more than 165,000 migrant workers to return to their homes in Asia and Africa. But if there is an archetypical stranded migrant it is probably the irregular migrant, whose journey towards an intended destination has been brought to a halt, without the means to either continue or return home. Migrants from South Asia have been found stranded in the Mauritanian desert after passage to South Africa and a long, slow and ultimately unsuccessful obstacle course northwards towards Europe (see Case Study 15.2). Irregular migrants are also found along other migration corridors, between zones of high economic prosperity and zones with high densities of young people seeking to enter the labour market, as in Central America and Central and Southeast Europe.

In the absence of an agreed meaning, Grant suggests that 'in practice, migrants become legally stranded when they are caught between removal from the State in which they are physically present, inability to return to their State of nationality or former residence, and refusal by any other State to grant entry'.[64] She adds that they could also be stranded because of practical or humanitarian reasons preventing their return home; that many of the stranded enter the State in which they find themselves in an irregular manner; and that some of them are stateless.

---

64 Grant, ibid. 30.

CASE STUDY 15.2 The plight of stranded migrants from Africa

The conflicts and humanitarian crises that have plagued the African continent since the 1990s have induced profound changes in traditional migration patterns. In particular, they have encouraged the emergence and development of smuggling networks and over-taxed the countries' resources to respond to this rising problem.

In the absence of reliable and precise data, the number of irregular migrants on the move across Africa towards Europe is estimated at roughly 2 million. Many of them transit northwards through the upper part of the continent *en route* to Europe and further afield, in search of economic opportunities and a better life for themselves and their families left at home. There are indications that the proportion of non-African migrants (many from South Asia) among this migrant population has increased substantially in recent years.

The criminal networks supporting such irregular flows excel at taking advantage of the poor security situation and the difficulty of effective movement control across extensive land borders. They have the resources and capability to recruit clients both within and outside the African continent, with tempting promises of a fail-proof package of travel services, covering air and ground transport, passports and related travel documentation, and accommodation on the way.

What is delivered almost always falls short of expectations. The chances of making it across the Mediterranean to Europe are very slim and the prospects of being left stranded very high.

In recent years, IOM has been called upon repeatedly to assist groups of South Asian stranded migrants originating from India, Bangladesh and Pakistan. Typically, they have been flown into Bamako (Mali) via Dubai and Casablanca, and then transported by land to the vicinity of the Mauritanian border, in the belief that other smugglers would meet them and provide them with onward assistance. The long coastline from Senegal to Morocco, and then east to Algeria, Tunisia and Libya, is traversed by numerous smuggling routes, but as often as not they can lead to 'unfinished migration' traps. Those who are left stranded on the shores on the Mediterranean have very few choices. Some will simply try to stretch out their meagre financial resources or plead for more money from relatives or friends while they wait for an opportunity to cross over. Large numbers will look for casual employment on the informal labour market. Others still may seek international protection through asylum procedures. Some have been found disoriented and helpless in the desert. There is no way of knowing how many have lost their lives.

Some will eventually come to the conclusion that returning home is the preferable option, but given the substantial investment of time, effort and money, the acknowledgement of failure is hard to take. Opportunities for assistance towards return and reintegration remain very limited.

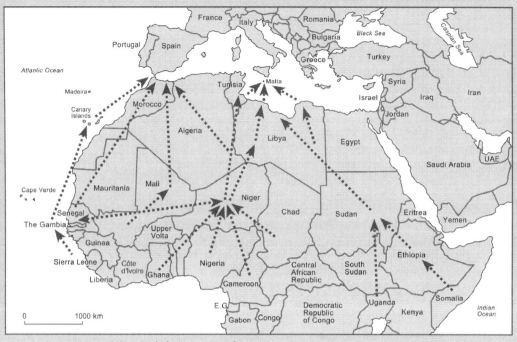

Map 15.1 Stranded migrants in Africa

A more recent definition, presented to the Global Migration Group, gives a descriptive rather than a legal rendition, portraying them as:

> people who leave their own country for reasons unrelated to refugee status, but who become subject to human rights abuses in the course of their journey, at least part of which is usually undertaken in an irregular manner. Such people are "stranded" in the sense that they are unable or unwilling to return to their country of origin, cannot regularize their status in the country where they reside, and do not have access to legal migration opportunities that would enable them to move on to another state.[65]

The exemption of refugee concerns from the definition is significant, implying that those who claim refugee protection, or have had those claims recognised, fall within the refugee protection framework, but those who are outside that framework are in danger of being caught in a legal or administrative no-man's-land. The distinction is not necessarily followed in research work and this makes it almost impossible to advance a set of comparable statistics. Fargues' detailed study of irregular migration in Southern and Eastern Mediterranean States counts three categories of irregular migrants as stranded: those who do not have a work permit but are gainfully employed in the informal labour market (about 2 million); *de facto* refugees (i.e., those without official recognition) awaiting a durable solution (about

65 United Nations High Commissioner for Refugees and Global Migration Group, 'Background Paper: Building Partnerships for Identifying, Protecting, Assisting and Resolving the Situation of Stranded and Vulnerable Migrants' (Global Migration Group, May 2010) 1.

1.5 million); and the somewhat fewer than 200,000 migrants who were initially bound for Europe but are unable to get there without appropriate authorisation.[66] On the basis of case studies in Morocco, Collyer divides his stranded migrants into three somewhat different groups: those waiting to be recognised as refugees, those already recognised as refugees, and those with other protection needs – or, in the words of the author, 'terminally stranded' migrants.[67]

15.4.1. Vulnerabilities of stranded migrants

Setting aside the problem of whether stranded migrants should be defined as a smaller or larger category, it is useful to review the vulnerabilities that generally pertain to their situation, although not all of them are applicable all the time. The non-exhaustive list, drawn from several sources,[68] includes:

- physical abuse and harassment by traffickers, smugglers and law enforcement officials;
- risk of arbitrary detention;
- risk of statelessness;
- forced labour or exploitation in employment, including sex work and hence exposure to sexually transmissible infections, such as HIV/AIDS;
- deprivation or lack of access to basic services;
- absence of, or inability to recover, personal and travel documentation;
- susceptibility to xenophobia and discrimination;
- interception and abandonment at sea;
- lack of resources or means of support; and
- criminalisation of their situation.

The tableau is inescapably grim, but the question that arises is whether it makes legal or practical sense in the longer term to formally define this putative category of migrant. A related question is whether one can point to a locus of vulnerability that differs from other groups already identified – for example, trafficked migrants, smuggled migrants, asylum seekers and migrant workers – who fall within the scope of existing international legal instruments.

15.4.2. Questions for further reflection and research

It is probably much too early to reach a conclusion, but while the answer is being worked out a number of considerations should be borne in mind. First, a great deal

---

66 Philippe Fargues, 'Work, Refuge, Transit: An Emerging Pattern of Irregular Immigration South and East of the Mediterranean' (2009) 43(3) *International Migration Review* 544.

67 Michael Collyer, 'Stranded Migrants and the Fragmented Journey' (2010) 23(3) *Journal of Refugee Studies* 273.

68 Dowd, above n. 63; Grant, above n. 63; United Nations High Commissioner for Refugees and Global Migration Group, above n. 65.

more research is needed before it can be confidently asserted that the category of stranded migrants has sufficient empirical coherence and validity to justify the development of a new framework of law and policy.[69] Currently the term is too easily used as a catch-all for many types of migrants in circumstances of distress. Second, given that stranded migrants so often end up in a state of unwanted 'suspension' between their State of origin and destination (and unwelcome residence in a State of transit), there is good reason to encourage consultation and cooperation among these three parties, relevant regional bodies and concerned international organisations. The topic could be usefully placed on the agendas of regional consultative processes. Third, as Grant insists, it is important for States to recognise that they are already under a responsibility in light of existing international law 'to respect and protect the migrants' rights while they remain within national territory, and to facilitate their safe return to a home State or State of former residence in safety and dignity.[70]

15.5. CONSULTATION, COOPERATION AND GOVERNANCE

The exploration of emerging legal and policy issues in international migration is inseparable from growing interest in the concept of global migration governance. The notion is still in its infancy, since States have traditionally been closely protective of their sovereign right to determine who can and cannot enter their territory. Nonetheless, a world that is increasingly reliant on the flow and exchange of capital, goods and services is also a world where greater mobility becomes desirable and necessary for a range of economic, social, cultural and recreational reasons. Along with that realisation has come acceptance that international consultation and cooperation are necessary complements to national-level initiatives (see Chapters 13 and 14).

This does not mean that multilateral undertakings are easily set in motion: there are many obstacles to effective international consultation and cooperation in the field of migration.

The first of these is simply the issue of sovereignty (see Chapter 5). The right to determine who may or may not enter its territory remains a defining prerogative of the State. This can act as a powerful brake on the willingness or ability of a State to share information or discuss its policy concerns and priorities with other States, let alone to explore avenues of cooperation.

A second obstacle is differences in priorities among participating States. While all States are affected by international migration, they are not necessarily affected by the same type of flows, or to the same extent, or in a similar way. It follows that policy priorities can differ widely. Consider, for instance, the emphasis often placed

---

69 For IOM, the stranded migrant category has programmatic value. For example, after the 1990–1 Gulf War, IOM's Executive Committee authorised IOM to assist migrants who were stranded as a result of that conflict. IOM's focus is on assisting voluntary return, and the concept of 'strandedness' is very loosely defined.

70 Grant, above n. 63, 35.

by countries of destination on orderliness of movement, on selection as the basis for successful integration, and on return as a mechanism for the deterrence of irregular migration. Countries of origin, for their part, are more likely to focus on issues such as the protection of the rights of their nationals working abroad, or how to achieve sustainable development through the use of worker remittances. These differences do not mean that States cannot engage in meaningful conversation, but they do highlight the need for laying down common understandings and expectations to ensure that engagement is productive.

Another difficulty lies in the complexity of the international migration field and the interdisciplinary policy and administrative linkages it brings into play: human rights, asylum, employment, development, trade, the environment, health, and social assistance, to name a few. Discourse among partners becomes easily confused if the different strands of policy interest are not clearly defined and their relationship to international migration is not properly established.

A wide range of agencies and other stakeholders are involved at domestic and international level (e.g., ministries, other government bodies, international organisations, academic institutions, the business sector, trade unions, nongovernmental organisations), and effective coordination at the national level is required before consultation can be undertaken successfully at the international level. The ministry responsible for migration in developing States is typically one that deals with social welfare or employment issues; the ministry that deals with migration in developed States is typically the ministry of interior or home affairs.

Finally, mention must be made of the relative paucity of data and documentation: in no other field of international affairs is there as much heated debate on the basis of such fragmented data. It comes as no surprise, then, that international consultation and cooperation in the field of migration has lagged far behind what has been achieved in other fields of multilateral endeavour, such as human rights, trade or the environment.

It was in 1994, in Cairo, at the International Conference on Migration and Development, that the international community sought for the first time to develop a comprehensive blueprint to address international migration. The main outcome of the conference was the Programme of Action, of which an entire chapter focussed on international migration, both documented and undocumented.[71] It mapped out a series of policy orientations covering the rights of migrants; developing orderly migration programmes; preventing the trafficking of migrants; reducing the causes of unwanted migration; promoting the development potential of migration; and cooperating between States for the successful management of migration.

It was the last of these policies that attracted the most attention at the General Assembly at the end of that year, duly giving rise to a resolution that called for an

---

71 United Nations International Conference on Population and Development, Cairo, 5–13 September 1994, Programme of Action, chapter X.

international conference on international migration and development.[72] In the years that followed, however, United Nations member States were unable to reach consensus on whether it should be convened or what agenda it should address. In 1995, 1997 and 1999, the Population Division of the United Nations Secretariat wrote to United Nations member States seeking their opinions about objectives and modalities for convening such a conference. Seventy-eight member States eventually provided a reply, but they remained deeply divided in their views.

What happened instead was spontaneous rather than planned: the emergence at the regional or sub-regional level of exploratory discussions about the changing nature of migration behaviour and attendant policy issues and challenges, in the form of what are commonly referred to as regional consultative processes on migration.[73] States had come to the realisation that while global initiatives would undoubtedly be needed at some point, it was at the regional level that initial progress could be made towards the development of a common policy language on migration management. This made all the more sense since the majority of migration flows are intra-regional rather than inter-regional (see Chapter 2). To give a few examples, outflows from the Balkans tend to have a disproportionate impact on Europe; labour migrants to Japan and Korea originate for the most part from Southeast Asia; Pacific Islanders view Australia and New Zealand as a preferred destination. Another impetus was the realisation that within a regional grouping there can be historical, economic and cultural linkages that facilitate discussion and debate.

These informal, open-ended and non-binding consultations would eventually prepare the ground for the launching by Switzerland, with the support of IOM, of the Berne Initiative, which produced in 2005 a comprehensive International Agenda for Migration Management.[74] Soon after, in 2006, the International Labour Organization adopted its Multilateral Framework on Labour Migration, a similarly non-binding set of guidelines and principles for a rights-based approach to labour migration (see Chapter 11).

With this change in orientation towards a more global outlook, the climate was appropriate for the launch of the Global Commission on International Migration, whose recommendations paved the way for the United Nations High Level Dialogue held in 2006 in New York.[75] The High Level Dialogue would in turn set the stage for the Global Forum on Migration and Development, which has become the broadest platform for the discussion of matters of pertinence to the governance of migration.

---

72 United Nations General Assembly, 'International Migration and Development' (UN Doc A/RES/49/127, United Nations, 19 December 1994).

73 The result has been described as 'a complex and fragmented tapestry of overlapping, parallel, and nested institutions': Alexander Betts, 'Introduction: Global Migration Governance' in Alexander Betts (ed.), *Global Migration Governance* (Oxford University Press, 2011) 1, 2.

74 Berne Initiative, 'International Agenda for Migration Management' (International Organization for Migration, Swiss Federal Office for Migration, 2005).

75 United Nations General Assembly, 'High-Level Dialogue on International Migration and Development' (United Nations, 14–15 September 2006).

The consultation processes are still largely about building confidence and developing a common language among protagonists with widely differing agendas. At least three distinct, if overlapping, approaches to migration governance can be detected among these strands of interest. The first concerns the elaboration of a rights-based approach to protecting migrants and particularly migrant workers. Proponents of this line of action focus on the human beings who engage in migration, on their fundamental rights, and on protecting them against the commodification of their labour. Their ultimate hope is to develop a comprehensive international framework linking mobility, protection and security.[76] The second approach gives priority to the need for an institutional infrastructure for migration governance, with the objective of allocating prime responsibility to an appropriate organisation. There are complex issues of mandate, administrative architecture and funding that will have to be processed. The third approach sets out to lay a platform for the management, at global level, of supply and demand for migrant labour, in much the same way that the international trading system facilitates the increasingly free flow of capital, goods and services. Various experiments conducted at the bilateral and multilateral levels may yield some useful building blocks, but ultimately the need may be felt for a global system of exchange of human resources.

15.6. CONCLUSION

A cliché that is frequently quoted in international conferences depicts migration as the 'unfinished business of globalisation'. The image is hackneyed, but nonetheless true. Compared to most other large socio-political issues of interest to the international community, migration is a young and growing topic.

This chapter has described developments of legal interest pertaining to three constituencies of migrants: the internally displaced, those who move as a consequence of environmental and climate change, and stranded migrants. It has sought to describe the broad migration situation of each group, their essential features, and the principal reasons why each group has attracted international attention.

The analysis has pointed out that each group has received a noticeably different measure of legal attention. The 'Guiding Principles on Internal Displacement', although developed as 'soft' law, have more than validated Kälin's early prediction that they 'might actually turn out to be much harder than many well-known soft law instruments'.[77] There is a considerable amount of work going on regarding migration and the environment, with issues of definition and appropriate

---

76 Johan Ketelers, *'Pooling' Sovereignty into New Definitions of International Responsibility* (2011) www.icmc.net/article/pooling-sovereignty-new-definitions-international-responsibility.

77 Walter Kälin, 'How Hard is Soft Law? The Guiding Principles on Internal Displacement and the Need for a Normative Framework' (Ralph Bunche Institute for International Studies, 19 December 2001).

instruments of protection receiving ongoing attention without agreed outcomes. Stranded migrants are a category still in need of basic study and research.

The future exploration and development of these issues will be inseparable from the evolution of international consultation and cooperation, and the development of a governance model that is most appropriate to the field of migration. One tempting, albeit tentative, conclusion to be drawn is that, without prejudice to the more travelled road of negotiated and binding instruments, there is virtue in exploring opportunities for instruments that can 'begin soft and grow hard', and that establish responsibility as the proper manifestation of sovereignty.

KEY REFERENCES

African Union, 'Explanatory Note on the African Union Convention for the Protection and Assistance of Internally Displaced Persons in Africa (Kampala Convention)', adopted October 2009 (not yet in force) (www.internal-displacement.org/kampala-convention)

Betts, Alexander, 'Towards a "Soft Law" Framework for the Protection of Vulnerable Irregular Migrants' (2010) 22(2) *International Journal of Refugee Law* 209

Black, Richard, *Refugees, Environment and Development* (Longman, 1998)

Brookings Institution, 'Protecting Internally Displaced Persons: A Manual for Law and Policymakers' (University of Bern, 2008)

Brookings Institution–University of Bern, 'Addressing Internal Displacement: A Framework for National Responsibility' (Brookings Institution–University of Bern, 2005)

Commission on Human Rights, 'Comprehensive Study Prepared by Mr. Francis M. Deng, Representative of the Secretary-General on Internally Displaced Persons, pursuant to Commission on Human Rights Resolution 1992/73' (UN Doc E/CN.4/1993/35, 21 January 1993)

Cooper, Jessica, 'Environmental Refugees: Meeting the Requirements of the Refugee Definition' (1998) 6(2) *New York University Environmental Law Journal* 480

De Haas, Hein, 'The Myth of Invasion: Irregular Migration from West Africa to the Maghreb and the European Union' (International Migration Institute, 2007)

Gemenne, François, 'Climate Change and Forced Displacements: Towards a Global Environmental Responsibility?' (Paper presented at the 47th Annual Convention of the International Studies Association, San Diego, 2006)

Guzmán, José Miguel, Martine, George, McGranahan, Gordon, Schensul, Daniel and Tacoli, Cecilia (eds.), *Population Dynamics and Climate Change* (UNFPA and IIED, 2009)

Internal Displacement Monitoring Centre, 'The Great Lakes Pact and the Rights of Displaced People, A Guide for Civil Society' (IDMC, 2008)

Kälin, Walter, 'Guiding Principles on Internal Displacement: Annotations' *Studies in Transnational Legal Policy No 38* (American Society of International Law and The Brookings Institution, 2008)

Keane, David, 'Environmental Causes and Consequences of Migration: A Search for the Meaning of Environmental Refugees' (2004) 16(2) *Georgetown International Law Review* 209

Kolmannskog, Vikram and Myrstad, Finn, 'Environmental Displacement in European Asylum Law' (2009) 11(4) *European Journal of Migration and Law* 313

McAdam, Jane, 'Climate Change Displacement and International Law: Complementary Protection Standards' (UNHCR, May 2011)

McAdam, Jane (ed.), *Climate Change and Displacement: Multidisciplinary Perspectives* (Hart Publishing, 2010)

Myers, Norman and Kent, Jennifer, *Environmental Exodus: An Emergent Crisis in the Global Arena* (Climate Institute, 1995)

Weiss, Thomas and Korn, David, *Internal Displacement: Conceptualization and its Consequences* (Routledge, 2006)

White, James and Marsella, Anthony (eds.), *Fear of Persecution: Global Human Rights, International Law, and Human Well-Being* (Lexington Books, 2007)

APPENDIX 1

Cases

A v. *Minister for Immigration & Ethnic Affairs* (1997) 190 CLR 225 180, 182, 189

Adjei v. *Canada (Minister of Employment and Immigration)* [1989] 2 FC 680 184

Aegean Sea Continental Shelf (Greece v. *Turkey) (Judgment)* [1978] ICJ Rep 3 58

Ahmed v. *Austria* (1997) 24 EHRR 423 168

Al-Adsani v. *United Kingdom* (2002) 34 Eur Court HR 273 80

Andrejeva v. *Latvia* (2009), App No 55707/00, Eur Court HR 302

Applicability of the Obligation to Arbitrate under Section 21 of the United Nations Headquarters Agreement of 26 June 1947 (Advisory Opinion) [1988] ICJ Rep 12 66

Applicant M38/2002 v. *Minister for Immigration and Multicultural and Indigenous Affairs* [2003] FCAFC 131 (13 June 2003) 193

Application of the Convention on the Prevention and Punishment of the Crime of Genocide (Bosnia and Herzegovina v. *Yugoslavia)* [1996] ICJ Rep 595 196

Asylum Case (Colombia v. *Peru) (Judgment)* [1950] ICJ Rep 266 74

Attorney-General v. *Tamil X and Refugee Status Appeals Authority* [2010] NZSC 107 (27 August 2010) 190

Avena and Other Mexican Nationals (Mexico v. *United States)* [2004] ICJ Rep 12 83, 84

Bakhtiyari v. *Australia*, Communication No 1069/2002, UN Doc CCPR/C/79/D/1069/2002 (29 October 2003) 218

Barcelona Traction, Light and Power Company Limited (Belgium v. *Spain), (Second Phase)* [1970] ICJ Rep 3 80, 83

Beldjoudi v. *France* (1992) 234 Eur Court HR (ser A) 217

Berrehab v. *Netherlands* (1988) 138 Eur Court HR (ser A) 170, 217

Borzov v. *Estonia*, Human Rights Committee, UN Doc CCPR/C/81/D/1136/2002 (25 August 2004) 100

Bouchelkia v. *France* (1997) 1 Eur Court HR 47 (ser A) 217

Boujlifa v. *France*, App No 24404/94 (1997) 30 Eur HR Rep 419 217

APPENDIX 2

Treaties and other international instruments

1907 *Hague Convention (IV) respecting the Laws and Customs of War on Land and its Annex: Regulations concerning the Laws and Customs of War on Land*, opened for signature 18 October 1907 (entered into force 26 January 1910) 100

1910 *International Convention for the Suppression of the 'White Slave Traffic'*, opened for signature 4 May 1910, 98 UNTS 101 (amended by the Protocol of 4 May 1949, entered into force 14 August 1951) 214

1919 *Peace Treaty of Versailles* 117, 348

1919 *Treaty of Saint-Germain* 117

1920 *Treaty of Trianon* 117

1921 *International Convention for the Suppression of the Traffic in Women and Children*, opened for signature 30 September 1921, 53 UNTS 38 (amended by the Protocol of 12 November 1947, entered into force 24 April 1950) 214

1924 *Geneva Declaration of the Rights of the Child*, League of Nations (26 September 1924) 214

1926 *Slavery Convention*, opened for signature 25 September 1926, 60 LNTS 254 (entered into force 9 March 1927) 3, 214

1930 *Convention concerning Forced or Compulsory Labour* (ILO Convention No 29), opened for signature 10 June 1930, 39 UNTS 55 (entered into force 1 May 1932) 3, 62, 174, 241, 287

1930 *Convention on Certain Questions relating to the Conflict of Nationality Laws*, opened for signature 13 April 1930, 179 LNTS 89 (entered into force 1 July 1937) 2, 64, 77, 96, 99, 101, 115

1930 *Protocol relating to Military Obligations in Certain Cases of Double Nationality*, opened for signature 12 April 1930, 178 LNTS 227 (entered into force 25 May 1937) 383

1933   *Convention relating to the International Status of Refugees,* opened for signature 28 October 1933, 159 LNTS 3663 (entered into force 13 June 1935) 3

1933   *Inter-American Convention on the Nationality of Women,* opened for signature 26 December 1933, 49 Stat 2957 (entered into force 29 August 1934) 384

1935   *Protocol relating to Military Obligations in Certain Cases of Double Nationality,* opened for signature 12 April 1935, 178 UNTS 227 (entered into force 25 May 1937) 2, 64, 115

1938   *Convention concerning the Status of Refugees coming from Germany,* opened for signature 10 February 1938, 192 LNTS 4461 (entered into force 25 October 1938) 3

1944   *Convention on International Civil Aviation,* opened for signature 7 December 1944, 15 UNTS 295 (entered into force 4 April 1947) 63, 266

1944   *Declaration concerning the Aims and Purposes of the International Labour Organisation (Declaration of Philadelphia)* (1944) XXVI(1) International Labour Office Official Bulletin 1 283, 284, 286, 348

1946   *Constitution of the World Health Organization,* opened for signature 22 July 1946, 14 UNTS 185 (entered into force 7 April 1948) 172

1947   *Convention concerning Labour Inspection in Industry and Commerce* (ILO Convention No 81), opened for signature 11 July 1947, 54 UNTS 3 (entered into force 7 April 1950) 293

1948   *American Declaration of the Rights and Duties of Man,* OAS Res XXX, OAS Treaty Series No 36, Adopted by the Ninth International Conference of American States (1948) 128, 300, 301

1948   *Charter of the Organization of American States,* opened for signature 30 April 1948, 119 UNTS 3 (entered into force 13 December 1951) 173, 175

1948   *Convention concerning Freedom of Association and Protection of the Right to Organise* (ILO Convention No 87), opened for signature 9 July 1948, 68 UNTS 17 (entered into force 4 July 1950) 62, 287, 297

1948   *Universal Declaration of Human Rights,* GA Res 217A (III), UN Doc A/810 (10 December 1948) 3, 4, 72, 76, 98, 101, 110, 111, 126, 155, 211, 241, 295–297, 357, 384

1949   *Convention concerning Migration for Employment (Revised)* (ILO Convention No 97), opened for signature 1 July 1949 (entered into force 22 January 1952) 62, 86, 174, 287, 288, 290–292, 298

1949   *Convention for the Suppression of the Traffic in Persons and of the Exploitation of the Prostitution of Others,* opened for signature 2 December 1949, 96 UNTS 272 (entered into force 25 July 1951) 62, 206, 241

1949   *Geneva Convention relative to the Protection of Civilian Persons in Time of War,* opened for signature 12 August 1949, 75 UNTS 287 (entered into force 21 October 1950) 137, 138, 141

1949   *Migration for Employment Recommendation (Revised)* (ILO No R86), (1 July 1949) 87, 287

1963 *Convention on the Reduction of Cases of Multiple Nationality and on Military Obligations in Cases of Multiple Nationality*, opened for signature 6 May 1963, CETS No 043 (entered into force 28 March 1968) 383

1963 *Optional Protocol concerning Acquisition of Nationality to the Vienna Convention on Consular Relations*, opened for signature 24 April 1963, 596 UNTS 469 (entered into force 19 March 1967) 63, 77, 83, 99, 161, 224, 229

1963 *Protocol 4 to the European Convention for the Protection of Human Rights and Fundamental Freedoms*, opened for signature 16 September 1963, ETS 46 (entered into force 2 May 1968) 96, 128, 163, 302, 385

1963 *Vienna Convention on Consular Relations*, opened for signature 24 April 1963, 596 UNTS 261 (entered into force 19 March 1967) 77, 83, 161, 224, 229

1965 *Convention on Facilitation of International Maritime Traffic*, opened for signature 9 April 1965, 591 UNTS 265 (entered into force 5 March 1967), as amended 10 January 2002 (amendment entered into force 1 May 2003) 272

1965 *International Convention on the Elimination of All Forms of Racial Discrimination*, opened for signature 21 December 1965, 660 UNTS 195 (entered into force 4 January 1969) 60, 102, 127, 156, 158, 227

1966 *International Covenant on Civil and Political Rights*, opened for signature 16 December 1966, 999 UNTS 171 (entered into force 23 March 1976) 4, 60, 102, 110, 127, 155, 156, 181, 211, 241, 255, 296

1966 *International Covenant on Economic, Social and Cultural Rights*, opened for signature 16 December 1966, 993 UNTS 3 (entered into force 3 January 1976) 4, 60, 110, 155, 156, 198, 211, 255, 296

1967 *Declaration on Territorial Asylum*, GA Res 2312, UN GAOR 22nd sess, 1631st plen mtg, Supp No 16, UN Doc A/RES/2312(XXII) (14 December 1967) 85

1967 *Protocol relating to the Status of Refugees*, opened for accession 31 January 1967, 606 UNTS 267 (entered into force 4 October 1967) 4, 59, 110, 133, 179, 347

1969 *American Convention on Human Rights*, opened for signature 22 November 1969, 1144 UNTS 123 (entered into force 18 July 1978) 113, 128, 161, 240, 301, 384, 385

1969 *Convention Governing the Specific Aspects of Refugee Problems in Africa*, opened for signature 10 September 1969, 1001 UNTS 45 (entered into force 20 June 1974) 180, 194, 386, 392

1969 *Vienna Convention on the Law of Treaties*, opened for signature 23 May 1969, 1155 UNTS 331 (entered into force 27 January 1980) 57

1973 *International Convention on the Suppression and Punishment of the Crime of Apartheid*, opened for signature 30 November 1973, 1015 UNTS 243 (entered into force 18 July 1976) 127

1974 *International Convention for the Safety of Life at Sea*, opened for signature 1 November 1974, 1184 UNTS 3 (entered into force 25 May 1980) 86, 274

1975 *Convention concerning Migrations in Abusive Conditions and the Promotion of Equality of Opportunity and Treatment of Migrant Workers* (ILO Convention No 143), opened for signature 24 June 1975 (entered into force 9 December 1978) 63, 86, 87, 174, 287, 288, 290–293, 296, 298, 308, 324

1975 *Recommendation concerning Migrant Workers* (ILO No R151), (28 June 1975) 87, 287

1975 *Treaty of the Economic Community of West African States*, opened for signature 28 May 1975, 1010 UNTS 18 (entered into force 1 August 1995) 149, 368

1976 *Parliamentary Assembly Recommendation 773 on the Situation of De Facto Refugees*, Council of Europe (26 January 1976) 180

1977 *European Convention on the Legal Status of Migrant Workers*, opened for signature 24 November 1977, ETS No 93 (entered into force 1 May 1983) 128, 173, 303

1977 *Protocol Additional to the Geneva Conventions of 12 August 1949, and relating to the Protection of Victims of Non-International Armed Conflicts*, opened for signature 8 June 1977, 1125 UNTS 609 (entered into force 7 December 1978) 146

1977 *Protocol amending the Convention on the Reduction of Cases of Multiple Nationality and Military Obligations in Cases of Multiple Nationality*, opened for signature 24 November 1977, CETS No 095 (entered into force 8 September 1978) 383

1979 *Convention on the Elimination of All Forms of Discrimination against Women*, opened for signature 18 December 1979, 1249 UNTS 13 (entered into force 3 September 1981) 99, 156, 213, 226, 240, 241

1979 *International Convention on Maritime Search and Rescue*, opened for signature 27 April 1979, 1405 UNTS 119 (entered into force 22 June 1985) 86, 275

1979 *Protocol relating to Free Movement of Persons, Residence and Establishment*, Official Journal of the ECOWAS Vol 1, Doc A/P 1/5/79 (29 May 1979) 149, 368

1981 *African Charter on Human and Peoples' Rights*, opened for signature 27 June 1981, 1520 UNTS 217 (entered into force 21 October 1986) 84, 128, 161, 241, 300, 385

1982 *United Nations Convention on the Law of the Sea*, opened for signature 10 December 1982, 1833 UNTS 3 (entered into force 14 November 1994) 77, 86, 268

1984 *Cartagena Declaration on Refugees*, OEA/Ser.L/II.66, doc 10 rev 1 (22 November 1984) 180, 386, 392

1984 *Convention against Torture and Other Cruel, Inhuman or Degrading Treatment or Punishment*, opened for signature 10 December 1984, 1465 UNTS 85 (entered into force 26 June 1987) 60, 134, 156, 169, 181, 213, 256

1984 *Protocol 7 to the Convention for the Protection of Human Rights and Fundamental Freedoms*, opened for signature 22 November 1984, ETS No 117 (entered into force 1 November 1988) 302

1985 *Declaration on the Human Rights of Individuals Who Are Not Nationals of the Country in which They Live*, GA Res 40/144, UN GAOR, 40th sess, 116th plen mtg, Supp No 53, UN Doc. A/RES/40/144 (13 December 1985) 85, 167

1986 *Vienna Convention on the Law of Treaties between States and International Organizations or between International Organizations*, opened for signature 21 March 1986, UN Doc A/CONF.129/15 (not yet in force) 57

1989 *Convention on the Rights of the Child,* opened for signature 20 November 1989, 1577 UNTS 3 (entered into force 2 September 1990) 4, 60, 112, 127, 156, 169, 209, 240, 241, 257, 355

1989 *International Convention on Salvage,* opened for signature 28 April 1989, 1953 UNTS 165 (entered into force 23 December 1996) 63, 275

1990 *African Charter on the Rights and Welfare of the Child,* opened for signature 11 July 1990, OAU Doc CAB/LEG/24.9/49 (entered into force 29 November 1999) 113

1990 *International Convention on the Protection of the Rights of All Migrant Workers and Members of their Families,* opened for signature 18 December 1990, 2220 UNTS 3 (entered into force 1 July 2003) 4, 59, 112, 127, 156, 161, 213, 228, 241, 252, 284, 324, 348, 385, 391

1992 *Declaration on the Rights of Persons Belonging to National or Ethnic, Religious or Linguistic Minorities,* GA Res 47/135, UN GAOR 47th sess, 92nd plen mtg, UN Doc A/47/49 (18 December 1992) 165

1992 *European Charter for Regional or Minority Languages,* opened for signature 5 November 1992, ETS No 148 (entered into force 1 March 1998) 165

1992 *Treaty on European Union,* opened for signature 7 February 1992, 1757 UNTS 3 (entered into force 1 November 1993) 96, 371

1992 *United Nations Framework Convention on Climate Change,* opened for signature 9 May 1992, 1771 UNTS 107 (entered into force 21 March 1994) 408

1993 *Convention on Protection of Children and Cooperation in respect of Intercountry Adoption,* opened for signature 29 May 1993, 1870 UNTS 167 (entered into force 1 May 1995) 101

1993 *Second Protocol amending the Convention on the Reduction of Cases of Multiple Nationality and Military Obligations in Cases of Multiple Nationality,* opened for signature 2 February 1993, CETS No 149 (entered into force 24 March 1995) 383

1994 *Arab Charter on Human Rights,* opened for signature 15 September 1994, 12 International Human Rights Reports 893 (entered into force 15 March 2008) 128, 385

1994 *Cairo Declaration on Population and Development,* International Conference of Parliamentarians on Population and Development (4 September 1994) 88, 360

1994 *Marrakesh Agreement Establishing the World Trade Organization,* opened for signature 15 April 1994, 1867 UNTS 3 (entered into force 1 January 1995) 61, 312, 313, 317, 345, 367, 391

1995 *Additional Protocol to the European Social Charter Providing for a System of Collective Complaints,* opened for signature 9 November 1995, ETS No 158 (entered into force 1 July 1998) 302

1995 *ASEAN Framework Agreement on Services,* opened for signature 15 December 1995 (entered into force 30 December 1998) 370

1995 *Framework Convention for the Protection of National Minorities,* opened for signature 1 February 1995, ETS No 157 (entered into force 1 February 1998) 165

GLOSSARY

The following terms are extracted in substance from Richard Perruchoud and Jillyanne Redpath-Cross (eds.), *Glossary on Migration* (IOM, 2nd edn, 2011)

accession '"Ratification", "acceptance", "approval", and "accession" mean in each case the international act so named whereby a State establishes on the international plane its consent to be bound by a treaty' (art. 2(1)(b), *Vienna Convention on the Law of Treaties* (1969)).

acquisition of nationality Obtaining the nationality of a State by a person who is a non-national by birth, whether on the person's application, following from a change in personal status, or as the result of the ceding of territory from one State to another.

administrative detention A measure to deprive a person of his or her liberty taken by the competent administrative authority of a State. Legislation in many countries foresees the placement in administrative detention of migrants in an irregular situation, either on their arrival in the territory or with a view to their expulsion.

admission The granting of entry into a State. A non-national has been 'admitted' if he or she passed through a checkpoint (air, land or sea) and is permitted to enter by border officials. A non-national who has entered clandestinely is not considered to have been admitted.

alien A person who is not a national of a given State.

asylum A form of protection given by a State on its territory based on the principle of *non-refoulement* and internationally or nationally recognised refugee rights. It is granted to a person who is unable to seek protection in his or her country of nationality and/or residence, in particular for fear of being persecuted for reasons of race, religion, nationality, membership of a particular social group or political opinion.

asylum seeker A person who seeks safety from persecution or serious harm in a country other than his or her own and awaits a decision on the application for refugee status under relevant international and national instruments. In case of a negative decision, the person must leave the country and may be expelled, as may any non-national in an irregular or unlawful situation, unless permission to stay is provided on humanitarian or other related grounds.

bilateral Involving two parties or two States.

bilateral labour migration agreements Formal mechanisms concluded between States, which are essentially legally binding commitments concerned with inter-State cooperation on labour migration. The term is also used to describe less formal arrangements regulating the movement of workers between countries entered into by States as well as a range of other actors, including individual ministries, employer organisations, and so on.

birth certificate An original document, usually issued under governmental or religious authority, stating, *inter alia*, when and where an individual was born.

bonded labour Service rendered by a worker under condition of bondage arising from economic considerations, notably indebtedness through a loan or an advance. Where debt is the root cause of bondage, the implication is that the worker (or dependants or heirs) is tied to a particular creditor for a specified or unspecified period until the loan is repaid.

border A line separating land territory or maritime zones of two States or subparts of States. It can also refer to a region that is found at the margin of settled and developed territory.

border control A State's regulation of the entry and departure of persons to and from its territory, in exercise of its sovereignty, whether this is conducted at the physical border or outside of the territory in an embassy or consulate.

border management Facilitation of authorised flows of persons, including business people, tourists, migrants and refugees, across a border and the detection and prevention of irregular entry of non-nationals into a given country. Measures to manage borders include the imposition by States of visa requirements, carrier sanctions against transportation companies bringing irregular migrants to the territory, and interdiction at sea. International standards require a balancing between facilitating the entry of legitimate travellers and preventing that of travellers entering for inappropriate reasons or with invalid documentation.

carrier 'Carrier' in relation to conveyance means the owner or charterer of the conveyance. A carrier usually refers to an airline, bus or rail company, or cruise line. Under the laws of some States, the term includes any owner of a means of conveyance, which carries a person onto its territory.

carrier liability law In the migration context, a law imposing a series of administrative or penal sanctions, including fines or other penalties, upon carriers who bring into the territory of a State persons who do not have valid entry documents.

cessation clauses Legal provisions in an instrument that set out the conditions under which refugee status comes to an end because it is no longer needed, such as in art. 1 (c) of the *Convention relating to the Status of Refugees* (1951) ('Refugee Convention').

child An individual being below the age of eighteen years unless, under the law applicable to the child, majority is attained earlier (art. 1, *Convention on the Rights of the Child* (1989)).

child labour Any work performed by a child that deprives him or her of his or her childhood, potential and dignity, is detrimental to his or her health, education, physical, mental, spiritual, moral or social development.

circular migration The fluid movement of people between countries, including temporary or long-term movement that may be beneficial to all involved, if occurring voluntarily and linked to the labour needs of countries of origin and destination.

citizen *See national.*

citizenship *See nationality.*

clandestine migration Secret or concealed migration in breach of immigration requirements. It can occur when a non-national breaches the entry regulations of a country; or having entered a country legally overstays in breach of immigration regulations. The generic term 'irregular migration' should be used in preference.

complementary protection Formal permission, under national law or practice, to reside in a country, extended by that country to persons who are in need of international protection even though they do not qualify for Refugee Convention status.

consular protection Consular functions aiming at helping nationals abroad, including assisting in the protection of their rights and interests before local courts. In particular, protection extended to migrants arrested or committed to prison or custody pending trial or detained in any other manner; such migrants must be informed without delay of the right to communicate with consular authorities.

contiguous zone A maritime area adjoining the territorial sea of a coastal State. In its contiguous zone, a State may exercise the necessary control to (a) prevent infringement of its customs, fiscal, immigration or sanitary laws and regulations within its territory or territorial sea, and (b) punish infringement of the above laws and regulations committed within its territory or territorial sea (art. 33, *United Nations Convention on the Law of the Sea* (1982) ('UNCLOS')).

country of destination The country that is a destination for migratory flows (regular or irregular).

country of origin The country that is a source of migratory flows (regular or irregular).

country of transit The country through which migratory flows (regular or irregular) move.

customary international law A source of international law. The two criteria for a norm to be recognised as 'customary law' are State practice and *opinio juris* (the concept that the practice is required by or consistent with the prevailing law).

***de facto* statelessness** Situation of individuals who possess the nationality of a State but, having left the State, enjoy no protection from it, either because they decline to claim such protection or because the State refuses to protect them. *De facto* statelessness is a term often connected with asylum seekers and recognised refugees.

denationalisation *See loss of nationality.*

deportation The act of a State in the exercise of its sovereignty in removing a non-national from its territory to his or her country of origin or third State after refusal of admission or termination of permission to remain.

derogation Restriction or suspension of rights in certain defined situations. For example, the *International Covenant on Civil and Political Rights* (1966) ('ICCPR') permits a State to derogate from certain obligations under the Covenant 'in time of public emergency which threatens the life of the nation and the existence of which is officially proclaimed'. States parties to the Covenant 'may take measures derogating from their obligations under the present Covenant to the extent strictly required by the exigencies of the situation, provided that such measures are not inconsistent with their other obligations under international law and do not involve discrimination solely on the ground of race, colour, sex, language, religion or social origin'.

detention Restriction on freedom of movement through confinement that is ordered by an administrative or judicial authority. There are two types of detention: criminal detention, having as a purpose punishment for the committed crime; and administrative detention, guaranteeing that another administrative measure (such as deportation or expulsion) can be implemented. In the majority of countries, irregular migrants are subject to administrative detention, as they have violated immigration laws and regulations that are not considered to be crimes. In many States, a non-national may also be administratively detained pending a decision on refugee status or on admission to or removal from the State.

diasporas Diasporas are broadly defined as individuals and members or networks, associations and communities, who have left their country of origin, but maintain links with their homelands. This concept covers more settled expatriate communities, migrant workers based abroad temporarily, expatriates with the nationality of the host country, dual nationals, and second-/third-generation migrants.

diplomatic protection 'It is an elementary principle of international law that a State is entitled to protect its subjects, when injured by acts contrary to international law committed by another State, from whom they have been unable to obtain satisfaction through the ordinary channels. By taking up the case of one of its subjects and by resorting to diplomatic action or international judicial proceedings on his behalf, a State is in reality asserting its own rights – its right to ensure, in the person of its subjects, respect for the rules of international law' (*Mavrommatis Palestine Concessions (Greece* v. *UK)* [1924] PCIJ (ser A) No 2, 12).

displacement A forced removal of a person from his or her home or country, often due to armed conflict or natural disasters.

documented migrant A migrant who entered a country lawfully and remains in the country in accordance with his or her admission criteria.

dual/multiple nationality Simultaneous possession of the nationality of two or more countries by the same person.

durable solution Any means by which the situation of refugees can be satisfactorily and permanently resolved to enable them to lead normal lives. Traditionally this involves voluntary repatriation, local integration or resettlement.

economic migrant A person leaving his or her habitual place of residence to settle outside his or her country of origin in order to improve his or her quality of life. This term is often used loosely to distinguish from refugees fleeing persecution, and is also used similarly to refer to persons attempting to enter a country without legal permission and/or by using asylum procedures without *bona fide* cause. It may be applied equally to persons leaving their country of origin for the purpose of employment.

emigration The act of departing or exiting from one State with a view to settling in another.

entry Any entrance of a non-national into a foreign country, whether voluntary or involuntary, authorised or unauthorised.

entry into force The moment at which all provisions of a treaty are legally binding on its parties. According to art. 24 of the *Vienna Convention on the Law of Treaties* (1969), the entry into force of a treaty takes place in such a manner and on such date as the treaty may provide or the negotiating States agree, or, failing any such provision or agreement, as soon as all the negotiating States have consented to be bound. Where a State joins the circle of parties after a treaty has already come into force, unless the treaty otherwise provides, it enters into force for that State on that date.

environmental migrant Environmental migrants are persons or groups of persons who, predominantly for reasons of sudden or progressive changes in the environment that adversely affect their lives or living conditions, are obliged to leave their habitual homes, or choose to do so, either temporarily or permanently, and who move within their country or abroad.

environmentally displaced person Persons who are displaced within their country of habitual residence or who have crossed an international border and for whom environmental degradation, deterioration or destruction is a major cause of their displacement, although not necessarily the sole one. This term is used as a less controversial alternative to environmental refugee or climate refugee, which have no legal basis or raison d'être in international law, to refer to a category of environmental migrants whose movement is of a clearly forced nature.

exclusion The formal denial of a non-national's admission into a State. In some States, border officials or other authorities have the power to exclude non-nationals; in other States, exclusion is ordered by an immigration judge after a hearing.

exit visa Visa issued for individuals with expired visas who need to extend them before leaving the country. Some countries also refer to this as a 'bridging visa'.

expatriate A person who voluntarily withdraws (him/herself) from residence in or allegiance to his or her native country; who leaves his or her home country to live elsewhere. If done with the intention to change allegiance from one country to another, an absolute termination is effected of all civil and political rights as of the date of such act.

expulsion An act by an authority of the State with the intention and the effect of securing the removal of a person or persons (non-nationals or stateless persons) against their will from the territory of that State.

expulsion order The judicial or administrative order of a State obliging a non-national to leave its national territory.

extradition The formal surrender by one State to another of an individual accused or convicted of an offence outside its territory and within the jurisdiction of the other, for the purpose of trial and punishment. The process of extradition is usually based on a combination of national legislation, bilateral treaties, and in some cases multilateral conventions (e.g., *European Convention on Extradition* (1957)).

family reunification/reunion Process whereby family members separated through forced or voluntary migration regroup in a country other than the one of their origin.

first country of asylum First country in which a refugee or a displaced person outside of his or her country benefits or could benefit from protection. The notion of first country of asylum is frequently used as a condition of access to the asylum determination procedure.

flag State The flag State is the State of nationality of a vessel. The flag State is responsible for ensuring that the vessels under its flag respect relevant obligations under customary and conventional international law.

forced/compulsory labour All work or service that is exacted from any person under the menace of any penalty and for which the said person has not offered him/herself voluntarily (art. 2(1), *Convention concerning Forced or Compulsory Labour* (ILO Convention No 29) (1930)).

forced migration A migratory movement in which an element of coercion exists, including threats to life and livelihood, whether arising from natural or man-made causes (e.g., movements of refugees and internally displaced persons, as well as people displaced by natural or environmental disasters, chemical or nuclear disasters, famine or development projects).

forced return The compulsory return of an individual to the country of origin, transit or third country, on the basis of an administrative or judicial act.

fraudulent document Any travel or identity document that has been falsely made or altered in some material way by anyone other than a person or agency lawfully authorised to make or issue the travel or identity document on behalf of a State; or that has been improperly issued or obtained through misrepresentation, corruption or duress or in any other unlawful manner; or that is being used by a person other than the rightful holder (art. 3(c), *Protocol against the Smuggling of Migrants by Land, Sea and Air, Supplementing the United Nations Convention against Transnational Organized Crime* (2000) ('Smuggling Protocol'). In a broader migration context, such documents may also include false education certificates in connection with the recognition of diplomas and qualifications as well as fraudulent documents relating to employment such as curricula vitae (CVs) and reference letters from employers.

freedom of movement A human right comprising three basic elements: freedom of movement within the territory of a country (art. 13(1), *Universal Declaration of Human Rights* (1948): 'Everyone has the right to freedom of movement and residence within the borders of each state'); the right to leave any country; and the right to return to his or her own country (art. 13(2), *Universal Declaration of Human Rights* (1948): 'Everyone has the right to leave any country, including his own, and to return to his country'). See also art. 12 of the ICCPR. Freedom of movement is also referred to in the context of freedom of movement arrangements between States at the regional level (e.g., European Union).

frontier See *border.*

frontier worker A migrant worker who retains his or her habitual residence in a neighbouring State to which he or she normally returns every day or at least once a week (art. 2(2)(a), *International Convention on the Protection of the Rights of All Migrant Workers and Members of their Families* (1990) ('ICRMW')).

governance of migration System of institutions, legal frameworks, mechanisms and practices aimed at regulating migration and protecting migrants. Used almost synonymously with the term 'migration management', although migration management is also sometimes used to refer to the narrow act of regulating cross-border movement at the State level.

guest worker Generally considered to be an economic migrant recruited for a restricted time of settlement and employment. This term is more or less restricted to migration flows in the 1950s and 1960s and is no longer used.

high seas All parts of the sea that are not included in the exclusive economic zone, the contiguous zone, the territorial sea or internal waters of a State, or in the archipelagic waters of an archipelagic State. The ocean spaces considered by the concept of the high seas are not under the territorial sovereignty of any State. Controls envisioned on the high seas are those exerted on a ship by the flag State or those exerted in the fight against activities prohibited on the high seas (e.g., slave transporting, trafficking in persons, piracy, illicit traffic in narcotic drugs or psychotropic substances and smuggling).

holding centre A facility lodging asylum seekers or migrants in an irregular situation on arrival in a receiving country, while their status is determined; in practice, such a facility is very often a detention centre. Also known as a reception centre.

humanitarian assistance Aid that addresses the needs of individuals affected by crises. It is primarily the responsibility of the State, but is also supported by international organisations, non-governmental organisations (NGOs) and the Red Cross/Red Crescent Movement. This assistance is provided in accordance with the humanitarian principles, particularly the principles of humanity (human suffering must be addressed wherever it is found, with particular attention to the most vulnerable in the population, such as children, women and the elderly; the dignity and rights of all victims must be respected and protected), neutrality (humanitarian assistance must be provided without engaging in hostilities or taking sides in controversies of a political, religious or ideological nature) and impartiality (humanitarian assistance must be provided without discriminating as to ethnic origin, gender, nationality, political opinions, race or religion. Relief of the suffering must be guided solely by needs and priority must be given to the most urgent cases of distress).

identity document A piece of documentation issued by the competent authority of a State designed to prove the identity of the person carrying it.

illegal entry 'Act of crossing borders without complying with the necessary requirements for legal entry into the receiving State' (art. 3(b), Smuggling Protocol).

immigration A process by which non-nationals move into a country for the purpose of settlement.

immigration quota A quota established by a country for the entry of immigrants, normally for the purposes of labour migration.

immigration status Status of a migrant under the immigration law of the host country.

interception Any measure applied by a State outside its national territory to prevent, interrupt or stop the movement of persons without required documentation from crossing borders by land, air or sea, and making their way to the territory of that State.

internal migration A movement of people from one area of a country to another area of the same country for the purpose or with the effect of establishing a new residence. This migration may be temporary or permanent. Internal migrants move, but remain within their country of origin (e.g., rural to urban migration).

internally displaced persons (IDPs) Persons or groups of persons who have been forced or obliged to flee or to leave their homes or places of habitual residence, in particular as a result of or in order to avoid the effects of armed conflict, situations of generalised violence, violations of human rights or natural or human-made disasters, and who have not crossed an internationally recognised State border ('Guiding Principles on Internal Displacement' (1998)).

international migration Movement of persons who leave their country of origin, or the country of habitual residence, to establish themselves either permanently or temporarily in another country. An international frontier is therefore crossed.

international migration law International norms and principles relating to migration deriving from State sovereignty – such as the right to admit, detain and expel migrants, to combat trafficking and smuggling, to protect borders, to confer nationality – and from human rights instruments. These two elements constitute the main pillars of international migration law. Instruments of international migration law are spread across various branches of law, such as human rights law, humanitarian law, labour law, refugee law, consular law, trade law and maritime law.

irregular migration Movement that takes place outside the regulatory norms of the sending, transit and receiving countries. There is no clear or universally accepted definition of irregular migration. From the perspective of destination countries it is entry, stay or work in a country without the necessary authorisation or documents required under immigration regulations. From the perspective of the sending country, the irregularity is seen, for example, in cases in which a person crosses an international boundary without a valid passport or travel document, or does not fulfil the administrative requirements for leaving the country. There is, however, a tendency to restrict the use of the term 'illegal migration' to cases of smuggling of migrants and trafficking in persons.

itinerant worker A migrant worker who, having his or her habitual residence in one State, has to travel to another State or States for short periods, owing to the nature of his or her occupation (art. 2(2)(e), ICRMW).

jus cogens Rule of law that is peremptory in the sense that it is binding irrespective of the will of individual parties. A peremptory norm of general international law (*jus cogens*) is a norm accepted and recognised by the international community of States as a whole, as a norm from which no derogation is permitted and which can be modified only by a subsequent norm of general international law having the same character (art. 53, *Vienna Convention on the Law of Treaties* (1969)) – for example, the prohibition of torture.

jus sanguinis The rule that a child's nationality is determined by its parents' nationality, irrespective of the place of its birth.

jus soli The rule that a child's nationality is determined by its place of birth (although nationality can also be conveyed by the parents).

labour migration Movement of persons from one State to another, or within their own country of residence, for the purpose of employment. Labour migration is addressed by most States in their migration laws. In addition, some States take an active role in regulating outward labour migration and seeking opportunities for their nationals abroad.

laissez-passer A travel document issued in exceptional circumstances by the consular officials of a country to nationals of a country of origin (e.g., in the case of loss or theft of their passport) or to strangers to whom the State has assured protection (e.g., the nationals of States that are under the protection of a given State in the absence of diplomatic representation or consular officials, in the case of loss or theft of their passport). It may also refer to a travel document issued by an international organisation to its agents. In the terms of art. VII(24) of the *Convention on the Privileges and Immunities of the United Nations* (1946), 'The United Nations can issue the *laissez-passer* for its civil servants. These *laissez-passer* shall be recognised and accepted by the authorities of the Member States.'

loss of nationality Loss of nationality may follow an act of the individual (expatriation, deliberate renunciation of nationality by an individual, or automatic loss of nationality upon acquisition of another nationality) or of the State (denationalisation). Denationalisation is a unilateral act of a State, whether by decision of administrative authorities or by the operation of law, which deprives an individual of his or her nationality. Although there are no uniform provisions for denationalisation, some States have developed a number of statutory grounds for it, including: entry into foreign civil or military service, acceptance of foreign distinctions, conviction for certain crimes. Although acquisition and loss of nationality are in principle considered as falling within the domain of domestic jurisdiction, the States must comply with norms of international law when regulating questions of nationality, such as art. 15(2) of the *Universal Declaration of Human Rights* (1948): 'No one shall be arbitrarily deprived of his nationality nor denied the right to change his nationality.'

migrant At the international level, no universally accepted definition for 'migrant' exists. The term migrant was usually understood to cover all cases where the decision to migrate was taken freely by the individual concerned for reasons of 'personal convenience' and without intervention of an external compelling factor; it therefore applied to persons, and family members, moving to another country or region to better their material or social conditions and improve the prospect for themselves or their family. The United Nations defines 'migrant' as an individual who has resided in a foreign country for more than one year, irrespective of the causes, voluntary or involuntary, and the means, regular or irregular, used to migrate. Under such a definition, those travelling for shorter periods as tourists and business persons would not be considered migrants. However, common usage includes certain kinds of shorter-term migrants, such as seasonal farm-workers who travel for short periods to work planting or harvesting farm products.

migrant flow The number of migrants counted as moving, or being authorised to move, to or from a given location in a defined period of time.

migrant stock The number of migrants residing in a country at a particular point in time.

migrant worker 'A person who is to be engaged, is engaged or has been engaged in a remunerated activity in a State of which he or she is not a national' (art. 2(1), ICRMW).

migration The movement of a person or a group of persons, either across an international border or within a State. It is a population movement, encompassing any kind of movement of people, whatever its length, composition and causes; it includes migration of refugees, displaced persons, economic migrants and persons moving for other purposes, including family reunification.

migration management A term used to encompass numerous governmental functions within a national system for the orderly and humane management of cross-border migration, particularly managing the entry and presence of foreigners within the borders of the State, and the protection of refugees and others in need of protection. It refers to a planned approach to the development of policy, legislative and administrative responses to key migration issues.

mixed flows Complex migratory population movements that include refugees, asylum seekers, economic migrants and other migrants, as opposed to migratory population movements that consist entirely of one category of migrants.

national A person, who, either by birth or naturalisation, is a member of a political community, owing allegiance to the community and being entitled to enjoy all its civil and political rights and protection; a member of the State, entitled to all its privileges. A person enjoying the nationality of a given State.

nationality Legal bond between an individual and a State. The International Court of Justice defined nationality in the *Nottebohm Case* (1955) as 'a legal bond having as its basis a social fact of attachment, a genuine connection of existence, interests and sentiments, together with the existence of reciprocal rights and duties ... the individual upon whom it is conferred, either directly by law or as a result of the act of the authorities, is in fact more closely connected with the population of the State conferring the nationality than with any other State'. According to art. 1 of the *Convention on Certain Questions relating to the Conflict of Nationality Law* (1930), 'it is for each State to determine under its own laws who are its nationals. This law shall be recognised by other States in so far as it is consistent with international conventions, international custom, and the principles of law generally recognised with regard to nationality'. The tie of nationality confers individual rights and imposes obligations that a State reserves for its population. Founded on the principle of personal jurisdiction of a State, nationality carries with it certain consequences as regards migration, such as the right of a State to protect its nationals against violations of their individual rights committed by foreign authorities (particularly by means of diplomatic protection), the duty to accept its nationals onto its territory, and the prohibition to expel them.

naturalisation Granting by a State of its nationality to a non-national through a formal act on the application of the individual concerned. International law does not provide detailed rules for naturalisation, but it recognises the competence of every State to naturalise those who are not its nationals and who apply to become its nationals.

net migration Difference between the number of persons entering the territory of a State and the number of persons who leave the territory in the same period. Also called 'migratory balance'. This balance is called net immigration when arrivals exceed departures, and net emigration when departures exceed arrivals.

non-derogable human rights Human rights of an absolute character that must be recognised and respected at all times. The ICCPR establishes the following rights as non-derogable: the right to life, freedom from torture, inhuman or degrading treatment or punishment, freedom from slavery, the prohibition of imprisonment for inability to fulfil a contractual obligation, the non-retroactivity of criminal law, right to recognition as a person before the law, right to freedom of thought, conscience and religion. The listing of non-derogable human rights notwithstanding, the tendency in the international community is to consider all human rights as universal, indivisible, interdependent and to be treated equally.

non-national A person who is not a national or citizen of a given State.

non-refoulement Principle of international refugee law that prohibits States from returning refugees in any manner whatsoever to countries or territories in which their lives or freedom may be threatened. The principle of *non-refoulement* is considered by many authors as part of customary international law, while for others the two requirements for the existence of a customary norm are not met.

orderly migration The movement of a person from his or her usual place of residence to a new place of residence, in keeping with the laws and regulations governing exit of the country of origin, and travel, transit and entry into the destination or host country.

overstay To remain in a country beyond the period for which entry was granted. Also sometimes used as a noun (e.g., 'the undocumented migrant population is evenly divided between overstays and those who entered irregularly').

passport A document issued by the competent authority in a State identifying a person as a national of the issuing State, which is evidence of the holder's right to return to that State. In Western traditions, passports have been used for foreign travel purposes, not as domestic identity documents. The passport is the accepted international certificate or evidence of nationality, although its evidentiary value is *prima facie* only.

permanent resident A non-national benefitting from the right of permanent residence in a host State.

persecution In the refugee context, a threat to life or freedom on account of race, religion, nationality, political opinion or membership of a particular social group. Persecution comprises human rights abuses or other serious harm often, but not always, perpetrated in a systematic or repetitive way. Discrimination does not always amount to persecution, although it may do so if it affects a fundamental right of the person concerned, or if the effect of several discriminatory measures cumulatively causes serious harm.

protection 'The concept of protection encompasses all activities aimed at ensuring full respect for the rights of the individual in accordance with the letter and the spirit of the relevant bodies of law, i.e. human rights law, international humanitarian law and refugee law. Human rights and humanitarian organisations must conduct these activities in an impartial manner (not on the basis of race, national or ethnic origin, language or gender)' (Inter-Agency Standing Committee). Protection given to a person or a group by an organisation, in keeping with a mandate conferred either by international instruments, in application of customary international law, or by the activities of the organisation. Such protection has as its aim to ensure respect for rights identified in such instruments as the Refugee Convention, the 1949 Geneva Conventions and 1977 Protocols, right of initiative of the International Committee of the Red Cross, *de facto* protection by the International Organization for Migration, International Labour Organization Conventions and human rights instruments.

push–pull factors Migration is often analysed in terms of the 'push–pull model', which looks at the push factors that drive people to leave their country (such as economic, social or political problems) and the pull factors attracting them to the country of destination.

ratification Ratification refers to the 'acceptance' or 'approval' of a treaty. In an international context, ratification 'is the international act so named whereby a State establishes on the international plane its consent to be bound by a treaty' (art. 2(1)(b), *Vienna Convention on the Law of Treaties* (1969)). Instruments of ratification establishing the consent of a State take effect when exchanged between the contracting States, deposited with a depositary or notified to the contracting States or to the depositary, if so agreed (art. 16). In a domestic context, it denotes the process whereby a State puts itself in a position to indicate its acceptance of the obligations contained in a treaty. A number of States have in their Constitutions procedures that have to be followed before the government can accept a treaty as binding.

readmission Act by a State accepting the re-entry of an individual (own national, third-country national or stateless person).

readmission agreement International agreement that addresses procedures, on a reciprocal basis, for one State to return non-nationals in an irregular situation to their home State or a State through which they have transited.

refugee A person who, 'owing to a well-founded fear of persecution for reasons of race, religion, nationality, membership of a particular social group or political opinions, is outside the country of his nationality and is unable or, owing to such fear, is unwilling to avail himself of the protection of that country' (art. 1(A)(2), Refugee Convention). In addition to this definition, art. 1(2) of the Organization of African Unity *Convention Governing the Specific Aspects of Refugee Problems in Africa* (1969) defines a refugee as any person compelled to leave his or her country 'owing to external aggression, occupation, foreign domination or events seriously disturbing public order in either part or the whole of his country of origin or nationality'. Similarly, the *Cartagena Declaration on Refugees* (1984) states that refugees also include persons who flee their country 'because their lives, security or freedom have been threatened by generalised violence, foreign aggression, internal conflicts, massive violations of human rights or other circumstances which have seriously disturbed public order'.

refugee (mandate) A person who meets the criteria of the United Nations High Commissioner for Refugees ('UNHCR') Statute and qualifies for the protection of the United Nations provided by the High Commissioner, regardless of whether or not he or she is in a country that is a party to the Refugee Convention or the *Protocol relating to the Status of Refugees* (1967), or whether or not he or she has been recognised by the host country as a refugee under either of these instruments.

refugee status determination A process (conducted by States and/or UNHCR) to determine whether an individual should be recognised as a refugee in accordance with applicable national and international law.

refugees *sur place* Persons who are not refugees when they leave their country of origin, but who become refugees (that is, acquire a well-founded fear of persecution) at a later date. Refugees *sur place* may owe their fear of persecution to a coup d'état in their home country, or to the introduction or intensification of repression or persecutory policies after their departure. A claim in this category may also be based on *bona fide* political activities, undertaken in the country of residence or refuge.

regional consultative processes Non-binding, consultative fora, bringing representatives of States, civil society (NGOs) and international organisations together at the regional level to discuss migration issues in a cooperative manner. Some regional consultative processes ('RCPs') also allow participation of other stakeholders (e.g., NGOs or other civil society representatives).

regularisation Any process or programme by which the authorities in a State allow non-nationals in an irregular or undocumented situation to stay lawfully in the country. Typical practices include the granting of an amnesty (also known as 'legalisation') to non-nationals who have resided in the country in an irregular situation for a given length of time and are not otherwise found inadmissible.

remittances Monies earned or acquired by non-nationals that are transferred back to their country of origin.

removal Enforcement of the obligation to return; physical transportation out of the country.

rescue at sea Situation in which a vessel renders assistance to a person or ship in distress at sea. The duty to rescue those in distress at sea is firmly established by both treaty and customary international law. The State responsible for the coordination of the rescue effort will negotiate disembarkation to a place of safety. The State providing assistance can refuse the unloading of the ship and may require that the crew leave its territory. It may also place conditions on the disembarkation that must be met by the flag State, a third State or an international organisation, such as resettlement, an interview, return, and so on.

resettlement The relocation and integration of people (refugees, internally displaced persons, etc.) into another geographical area and environment, usually in a third country. In the refugee context, it is the transfer of refugees from the country in which they have sought refuge to another State that has agreed to admit them. The refugees will usually be granted asylum or some other form of long-term resident rights, and, in many cases, will have the opportunity to become naturalised.

return migration The movement of a person returning to his or her country of origin or habitual residence, usually after spending at least one year in another country. This return may or may not be voluntary. Return migration includes voluntary repatriation.

safe third country A country in which an asylum seeker could have had access to an effective asylum regime, and in which he or she has been physically present prior to arriving in the country in which he or she is applying for asylum.

seasonal migrant worker/migration A migrant worker whose work, or migration for employment, is by its character dependent on seasonal conditions and is performed only during part of the year (art. 2(2)(b), ICRMW).

slavery The status or condition of a person over whom any or all of the powers attaching to the right of ownership are exercised (art. 1, *Slavery Convention* (1926), as amended by the 1953 Protocol). Slavery is identified by an element of ownership or control over another's life, coercion and the restriction of movement, and by the fact that someone is not free to leave or to change employer (e.g., traditional chattel slavery, bonded labour, serfdom, forced labour and slavery for ritual or religious purposes).

smuggling 'The procurement, in order to obtain, directly or indirectly, a financial or other material benefit, of the illegal entry of a person into a State Party of which the person is not a national or a permanent resident' (art. 3(a), Smuggling Protocol). Smuggling, contrary to trafficking, does not require an element of exploitation, coercion or violation of human rights.

soft law Standards that are not legally binding.

stateless person 'A person who is not considered as a national by any State under the operation of its law' (art. 1, *Convention relating to the Status of Stateless Persons* (1954)). As such, a stateless person lacks those rights attributable to nationality: the diplomatic protection of a State, the inherent right of sojourn in the State of residence and the right of return in case he or she travels.

step migration Where a person moves to one or more locations within the country before emigration to another country, or from one country to another before moving to his or her ultimate or final country of destination.

temporary migrant workers Skilled, semi-skilled or untrained workers who remain in the destination country for definite periods as determined in a work contract with an individual worker or a service contract concluded with an enterprise. Also called contract migrant workers.

temporary protection An arrangement developed by States to offer protection of a temporary nature to persons arriving *en masse* from situations of conflict or generalised violence, without prior individual status determination.

territorial sea The adjacent belt of sea over which the sovereignty of the coastal State extends. The territorial sea may not extend beyond twelve nautical miles.

tourism Movement of one person or a group of people, whether internationally or within one country, for purposes of leisure, sport or discovery. Tourism does not imply a change of habitual residence for those participating, and it is not a form of migration in the strict sense, even though the term 'tourism migration' is occasionally used.

trafficking in persons 'The recruitment, transportation, transfer, harbouring or receipt of persons, by means of the threat or use of force or other forms of coercion, of abduction, of fraud, of deception, of the abuse of power or of a position of vulnerability or of the giving or receiving of payments or benefits to achieve the consent of a person having control over another person, for the purpose of exploitation' (art. 3(a), *Protocol to Prevent, Suppress and Punish Trafficking in Persons, Especially Women and Children, Supplementing the United Nations Convention against Transnational Organized Crime* (2000) ('Trafficking Protocol')). Trafficking in persons can take place within the borders of one State or may have a transnational character.

travel documents Generic term used to encompass all documents issued by a competent authority that are acceptable proof of identity for the purpose of entering another country. Passports and visas are the most widely used forms of travel documents. Some States also accept certain identity cards or other documents, such as residence permits.

treaty 'An international agreement concluded between States in written form and governed by international law, whether embodied in a single instrument or in two or more related instruments and whatever its particular designation' (art. 2.1(a), *Vienna Convention on the Law of Treaties* (1969)).

unaccompanied children Persons under the age of majority in a country other than that of their nationality who are not accompanied by a parent, guardian or other adult who by law or custom is responsible for them. Unaccompanied children present special challenges for border control officials, because detention and other practices applied to undocumented adult non-nationals may not be appropriate for children.

undocumented migrant A non-national who enters or stays in a country without the appropriate documentation. This includes, among others: a person (a) who has no legal documentation to enter a country but manages to enter clandestinely, (b) who enters or stays using fraudulent documentation, (c) who, after entering using legal documentation, has stayed beyond the time authorised or otherwise violated the terms of entry and remained without authorisation.

visa An endorsement by the competent authorities of a State in a passport or a certificate of identity of a non-national who wishes to enter, leave or transit the territory of the State that indicates that the authority, at the time of issuance, believes the holder to fall within a category of non-nationals who can enter, leave or transit the State under the State's laws. A visa establishes the criteria of admission into a State. International practice is moving towards issuance of machine-readable visas that comply with International Civil Aviation Organization ('ICAO') standards, printed on labels with security features.

voluntary repatriation Return of eligible persons to the country of origin on the basis of freely expressed willingness to so return. Most often used in the context of refugees, prisoners of war and civil detainees. It is also one of the three durable solutions to address the plight of refugees.

voluntary return The assisted or independent return to the country of origin, transit or another third country based on the free will of the returnee.

INDEX